WHO IS THE DOCTOR

THE UNOFFICIAL GUIDE TO DOCTOR WHO
THE NEW SERIES

GRAEME BURK & ROBERT SMITH?

ECW PRESS

Published by ECW Press
2120 Queen Street East, Suite 200, Toronto, Ontario, Canada M4E 1E2
416-694-3348 / info@ecwpress.com

Library and Archives Canada Cataloguing in Publication

Burk, Graeme, 1969-
Who is the doctor : the unofficial guide to Doctor Who — the
new series / Graeme Burk and Robert Smith.

ISBN 978-1-55022-984-4
Also issued as: 978-1-77090-238-1 (PDF); 978-1-77090-239-8 (ePUB)

1. Doctor Who (Television program : 2005-). I. Smith,
Robert, 1972 Oct. 28- II. Title.

PN1992.77.D63B87 2012   791.45'72   C2011-906952-0

Editor for the press: Jennifer Hale
Cover design: Natalie Racz
Cover illustration: M. Racz
Text design: Tania Craan
Typesetting: Troy Cunningham
Printing: Webcom   1   2   3   4   5

ECW Press acknowledges the financial support of the Government of Canada through the Canada Book Fund for our publishing activities, and the contribution of the Government of Ontario through the Ontario Book Publishing Tax Credit. The marketing of this book was made possible with the support of the Ontario Media Development Corporation.

 Canada Council Conseil des Arts
for the Arts   du Canada    Canadä   ONTARIO ARTS COUNCIL
CONSEIL DES ARTS DE L'ONTARIO

Printed and bound in Canada

MIX
Paper from
responsible sources
FSC   FSC® C004071
www.fsc.org

. . . .

For Scott Clarke, for all the adventures in time and space and friendship
— GB

For Anthony Wilson, for friendship across the continents
— RS?

Contents

Introduction

We are here today because *Doctor Who* is the greatest show on television. We really mean this, by the way. That's not hyperbole.

Doctor Who was already the world's longest-running science-fiction series (26 seasons, from 1963 to 1989) before its relaunch in 2005. What took everyone by surprise was how big of a runaway hit *Doctor Who* became upon its return. It immediately became a top-rated series and made stars out of Billie Piper and David Tennant, and now Matt Smith and Karen Gillan. It's the hot new science-fiction series internationally, with its popularity ever increasing, especially in North America. It has spun off two series, *Torchwood* and *The Sarah Jane Adventures.*

What sets *Doctor Who* above every other show on television is that, unlike any series before or since, it can do anything. The titular character, the Doctor, is the last of the Time Lords from the planet Gallifrey. He travels through time and space in a time machine that's bigger on the inside than the outside. Along the way, he fights monsters wherever — and whenever — they may be. *Doctor Who* can not only go anywhere, it can tell any kind of story as a result — in any genre, in any location, in any period.

How We Got Here

This book is a co-authored affair, written by two people with very different experiences. Here's how we came to the world of *Doctor Who*.

Graeme Burk (GB): I'll never forget the first time I watched *Doctor Who*. It was May 1984. I was 14 years old, growing up in Oakville, Ontario, Canada, and I was sick. I was lying on the couch in our family room, wrapped in a blanket. My then eight-year-old sister was watching something — probably *Vegetable Soup* — on the Buffalo PBS station, WNED. She left the room partway through to do something else. Six o'clock came, and with it *Doctor Who*. My best friend had been trying to get me to watch it for ages. I'd like to say it was his interest that kept me from changing the channel; unfortunately, it was more likely down to a lack of energy from the flu. What I can say is that, 23 minutes and 53 seconds later, as the inevitable cliffhanger occurred, I desperately wanted to see what happened next as a set of robots dressed like giant Egyptian mummies advanced on the Doctor and his companion Sarah.

Over the years, my interest turned to mania as I collected, read and watched anything to do with *Doctor Who*. It continued during the roughly 15-year gap when it was off the air, during which time I authored a few *Who* short stories in BBC-published anthologies, helped organize *Doctor Who* conventions and wrote for and edited the *Doctor Who* fanzine *Enlightenment* for over a decade. The arrival of the New Series was one of the biggest things in my life: I proposed to Julie, who's now my wife, in 2005, but I still think of that year first and foremost as when *Doctor Who* came back.

Suffice it to say, I love *Doctor Who*. It has all the right ingredients for a great TV show. There's a compelling central character who draws upon the best elements of the British: he's an eccentric, an amateur, a scientist, a wit, a bon vivant. Then there's the universe the show is set in: a dark sinister place where wit, brains and a bit of action can change things for the better. And best of all there's the approach of the program: everything is treated with utter seriousness and yet nothing is taken truly seriously. Throw in some of the funniest dialogue, some of the broadest and boldest acting, some of the most absurd ideas of any TV program ever, and add a dash of playing willy-nilly with other genres and stories and you've got something delicious that serves and satisfies millions.

Robert Smith? (RS?): I was six years old and my TV viewing schedule was already overbooked. My father had been a fan of actor William Hartnell and had watched *Doctor Who* back in the day. He'd tuned in to a rerun of the final episode of "The Green Death" for old times' sake and I caught a glimpse of it. I knew I should go back to my bedroom, telling myself that I already had too many TV shows to watch and I couldn't possibly add another . . . but something kept drawing me back.

Hello. My name's Robert and I'm a *Doctor Who* fan.

I've loved *Doctor Who* ever since. Growing up in Australia, an episode was shown on the national broadcaster every weeknight, so at times it was the most talked-about show in the playground. Later, I connected with Australian fandom and made friends I still keep in touch with today. When I moved across the world to Canada to embark on my Ph.D., I knew nobody, but *Doctor Who* was the best icebreaker you could possibly imagine. I connected with North American fans at monthly meetings and travelled to conventions, where I've made some of the best friends I've ever had.

My academic career forced me to move again and again. Each time, I had to start over in a new city where I knew almost no one. *Doctor Who* became the one constant in my life, a way to connect to like-minded people and a show that I found endlessly analyzable and enjoyable, even when it was off the air.

Especially when it was off the air, because then it was ours. No one else cared, so we had to.

In 2005, the New Series appeared, and I was terribly afraid. What if it sucked? Or worse, what if it was a hit, but it wasn't for me? I anticipated a new audience for a new show: it might be for kids or supremely populist or it might be for the hardcore fan. Miraculously, the New Series was all of those things. And when I watched the opening minutes of the first episode, "Rose," I fell in love all over again.

But that's another story. One that we're about to tell you . . .

About the Book
Who Is The Doctor is a celebration of the New Series of *Doctor Who*. Every episode in the New Series' first six seasons is examined, analyzed and discussed in detail. We look at the great moments, the connections to *Doctor Who* lore, the story arcs, the relationships, the goofs, the accumulated trivia and much, much more.

We have tried to write a book for every type of fan. We hope there's something for fans who think they know everything about *Doctor Who* and for newbies who are just learning what it's all about.

The Episode Guide
The 74 stories (including mini-episodes and the two animated episodes) that make up the first six seasons of the new *Doctor Who* each have a guide entry, which include the following categories:

The Big Idea A short plot synopsis.

Roots and References These are the sources that either influenced a story or are directly cited in a particular episode, whether literary, film, TV, music or pop culture references. We track them here.

Adventures in Time and Space Connections to the past episodes of *Doctor Who*, particularly the Classic Series.

The Story Arc Effect Each season has a story arc. Sometimes it's explicitly sign-posted by an ongoing meme, like the words "Bad Wolf"; other times it involves character and plot details that resonate across the entire season. We track each season's particular story arc, while including information about past or future ones as well, showing how a particular episode fits into the ongoing story.

Who is the Doctor? New information about the Doctor, including insight into his character.

The Doctor and the Companion A statement on the progress of the relationship of the central pair of characters, as it develops.

Monster of the Week Time to wave a tentacle out to the crowd.

Stand Up and Cheer The great moment in this story . . .

Roll Your Eyes . . . and the one that made you cringe.

You're Not Making Any Sense Really gaping plot holes.

Interesting Trivia Intriguing facts about the story, the *Doctor Who* universe and what was going on behind the scenes.

The TARDIS Chronometer Where and when the story takes place.

Fantastic?/Brilliant?/Cool? The bottom-line critique by one of the authors.

Second Opinion The co-author also gets his say. Sometimes the two authors agree. Sometimes we don't. Sometimes we *really* don't. And then the fun begins . . .

The Psychic Papers

Also included in the book are chronicles of the history of various elements of the series' mythos, monsters and production. These entries give complete histories, and therefore contain spoilers of the Classic Series and New Series in some instances. If you're reading the episode guide in this book while watching the New Series for the first time, read these sections at your own risk.

And Now, the Unbelievably Geeky Part

If you're not a hardcore fan, you can skip to the end of this introduction. If you are, stick around, we need to talk about the stuff we know you're dying to argue over. Many *Doctor Who* fans love talking about the intricacies of episode selection, titles and numbering. But for the purpose of consistency, we had to choose one style within which to write this book.

We take the stance in *Who Is The Doctor* that the version of *Doctor Who* that began in 2005 is effectively a new TV series, albeit one linked by continuity and heritage with the original, or what we call the Classic Series of *Doctor Who*. That's how most fans see it, how the press sees it, how the Internet Movie Database sees it. More importantly, that's how the BBC sees it, as demonstrated by the nomenclature used in their publications and DVD releases. Thus, we follow that convention and we refer to the 13 episodes from 2005 as Series One, not Series 27. (We also follow the British convention of calling a season a "series" in this context.)

Our approach has been to include anything *Doctor Who* that aired on BBC1 in some form. Thus, we have not only included all the episodes and Christmas specials, but the mini-episodes made for the Children in Need and Comic Relief charity shows (two of which directly lead into full episodes). We've even included the animated cartoon episodes in an appendix. We have avoided material that didn't air on BBC1, such as the interactive game "Attack of the Graske," the BBC Proms video "Music of the Spheres" and the additional content on the official BBC website and the DVD releases.

We tend to follow the convention used by the producers of *Doctor Who* for our numbering, which has the season opener as episode one and the season finale as episode 13. Thus we number the Christmas episodes as "zero." We have deviated from this somewhat with the 2008–2010 specials (which were production-coded as an extension of Series Four) by identifying them with an S. In 2010, the BBC attempted to rebrand the first season of Matt Smith's episodes as "Series One" (with the technical code 11.1). We have decided, like everyone other than *Doctor Who Magazine* (including the BBC's own DVD boxset) to call it Series Five.

Lastly . . .

Hey, welcome back if you skipped the geeky part. (And if you didn't, good for you!)

Doctor Who, probably more than any other television series, has long been an "open-source" fandom, in that it encourages fans to go beyond what's happening onscreen and to appreciate the inner workings and dramatic techniques used to create it. It's this open-source quality that brought fans like Russell T Davies and Steven Moffat to write for television. Our approach in *Who Is The Doctor* has been informed by our open-source fandom. While we talk about the relationships, the adventures, the story arc and the monsters onscreen, we also talk about the writing, the characterization, the acting and the direction. In short, we talk about what's both inside and outside the *Doctor Who* universe that makes it so great.

If there's one thing we want this book to be, it's fun. At the end of the day, *Doctor Who* is a TV show about a man who travels through time and space in a police box that's bigger on the inside than the outside. It's meant to be fun. We hope that *Who Is The Doctor* expands your understanding of *Doctor Who*, that it gives you something to laugh at, think about and argue with. (And we want you to argue with us. As *Doctor Who* writer Paul Cornell used to say, back in the days when he wrote episode guides like this, "Dissent is good.")

Because, when it comes down to it, it's the fact that this series is so fun, has so much to discover and so much to argue about that makes *Doctor Who* the greatest show on television.

Geronimo!

Previously, on *Doctor Who*...

It's the longest running science-fiction series on television, and yet *Doctor Who* owes its life not to an individual creator but to the organic workings of the bureaucracy that ran the British Broadcasting Corporation.

By 1963, the BBC television service identified that it needed programming to fill its early evening teatime slot on Saturdays. This slot transitioned between the Saturday afternoon sports programs and the Saturday evening programs, which were family-oriented light entertainment. The key demographic for this timeslot was children. At the same time, the BBC's drama department had launched a commission to discuss the production of more science-fiction series.

These factors were bubbling under the surface when a Canadian named Sydney Newman became the head of drama at the BBC. Newman had cut his teeth setting up the fledgling Canadian Broadcasting Corporation's television service and had been headhunted to Britain in the late 1950s to work for the new independent network, ITV, which was then just starting. Under Newman's watch at ITV, programs like *Coronation Street* and Newman's own creation *The Avengers* became unqualified hits. The BBC hired Newman in the hopes that he could have similar success there.

Newman wanted to create a series to primarily appeal to children and young adults that would teach them about history and science. His basic idea involved an older, crotchety scientist, some school teachers and a child winding up in a time machine. They would travel back in time to see history unfold and forward to witness Wellsian parables of present-day society. With the help of a group of staff writers, the series eventually came to be known as *Doctor Who*. Newman hired his personal assistant at ITV, Verity Lambert, to produce the show. (As a woman in the men's club that was the BBC in 1963, Lambert's hiring was quite radical for the time.) One of the first things Lambert did was hire veteran actor William Hartnell to play the title character.

A pilot was shot in September 1963. In that pilot, two schoolteachers, Barbara Wright and Ian Chesterton, are puzzled by a new student of theirs, Susan Foreman. They follow her to a junkyard where they find a police telephone box and an old man. They stumble inside the police box and discover it's a spaceship called the TARDIS (an acronym standing for Time And Relative Dimension In Space). Fearing the teachers will alert others, the old man, who is

Susan's grandfather (later to be known as the Doctor), sends the time machine back to the Stone Age.

After some adjustments — mostly to soften the anti-heroical nature of the central character — a second version of the first episode was made and was transmitted on BBC1 24 hours after the assassination of President Kennedy, at 5:25 p.m. on November 23, 1963.

The original intention was to hew closely to Sydney Newman's format, with trips to the days of Marco Polo and the Aztecs alternating with adventures in the future and a planned story where the travellers became an inch tall. But the series' second story changed things radically. The Daleks were robotic tanks that housed aliens who threatened to exterminate anyone not like them. Newman hated them — he did not want the series going into "bug eyed monster" territory — but Lambert rebuffed Newman's request to kill the script, saying nothing else was ready. The Daleks caught on with the British public, however, and by the time this story concluded in early 1964, *Doctor Who* was a hit. Newman famously told Lambert, "You clearly know this better than I do," and scaled back his involvement with the series.

The Daleks changed *Doctor Who* from a pseudo-educational children's drama to a show featuring monsters and high adventure watched by the whole family. It was a winning format that continued through the 1960s, surviving the departure of several of the original actors (it became a feature that the Doctor travelled with different companions) and its original producer Verity Lambert. It even survived William Hartnell's departure from the title role in 1966. At that point, the drastic decision was made to recast the Doctor with a slightly younger actor, played by Patrick Troughton. To account for the change, it was revealed that the Doctor could physically alter his form, a process later named regeneration.

Sydney Newman suggested that this new Doctor be more of a "cosmic hobo" and Patrick Troughton's Doctor was quieter, more thoughtful and more comedic than his predecessor. During Troughton's tenure, the purely historical adventures were abandoned and *Doctor Who* became even more about the monsters, with several of the Daleks' greatest rivals either being introduced or coming to dominance, including the Cybermen, the Ice Warriors and the Yeti. It was an era when the *Doctor Who* production team often fought budgetary woes by pooling the money into one large set and putting the characters on a base under siege.

In 1969, Patrick Troughton wanted to depart, and the show was having a serious dip in the ratings. The producers decided to make a radical change in format. The Doctor finally encountered his own people, revealed to be the

Time Lords, beings of great power who used their ability to travel through time and space to observe, never to interfere. The Doctor, it turned out, was bored living with his own race, so he stole a TARDIS — a research vessel used by the Time Lords to observe events in time and space — and left to become involved and have adventures. In the last episode of the 1960s, the nature of his travels changed. Captured by the Time Lords, the Doctor had his form altered once more and was exiled to Earth in the 20th century.

This new format started in 1970 (when the series was first broadcast in colour) with Jon Pertwee playing the Doctor. Pertwee was well known as a comedian in Britain, but surprised everyone when he played the role totally straight. His Doctor dressed in dandified formal wear and was a Renaissance action man who practised martial arts, drove vintage cars and enjoyed the finer things in life. During his exile, the Doctor became the scientific advisor to the top-secret military organization UNIT, the United Nations Intelligence Taskforce, investigating alien invasions and mad scientists. The series changed its look and feel too, moving at a faster pace and using advances like chromakey, where actors could be electronically composited with models and special effects, to allow greater scope and scale to the adventures (though *Doctor Who* would always be budgetarily challenged). The series gained a regular villain in the rival Time Lord known as the Master. The show soared in popularity.

After the series' tenth anniversary, which brought back Patrick Troughton and William Hartnell to reprise their roles in an adventure featuring all three Doctors together, the third Doctor's exile was lifted, allowing him to travel through space and time once more. A year later, in 1974, Jon Pertwee departed. An unknown actor named Tom Baker replaced him. Baker, in many ways, defined the role of the Doctor. With his curly hair, enormous smile and iconic, multicoloured scarf, Baker played the Doctor as a larger-than-life eccentric, and for seven years the series experienced ever-increasing ratings and new-found popularity in North America, thanks to the increased presence of British dramas on PBS during the 1970s. The series expanded its repertoire into more sophisticated suspense and atmospheric, gothic horror (although its increased violence landed *Doctor Who* at the centre of controversy), then into science fiction with a comedic bent, with scripts penned by *The Hitchhiker's Guide to the Galaxy* writer Douglas Adams. *Doctor Who* was part of what was considered a golden age for BBC programming with an unbeatable Saturday lineup.

Tom Baker left in 1981, just as the series took a shift toward more serious science fiction. His replacement, Peter Davison, was only 29 when he was cast; a youthful Doctor was considered quite revolutionary, given that his predecessors had all been at least 40. Already a popular and acclaimed actor, Davison played the Doctor as a sweet, gentle figure who seemed to be somewhat uncomfortable in a younger body.

But the times were changing in the 1980s. During Davison's tenure, *Doctor Who* was moved from Saturday at teatime to a mid-week slot. Davison-era stories pushed the boundaries of the *Doctor Who* format while bringing back many familiar elements. The series celebrated its 20th anniversary with a special adventure in which all five Doctors appeared. Troughton and Pertwee reprised their roles, alongside actor Richard Hurndall, who replaced the late William Hartnell as the first Doctor. (Tom Baker's presence was via previously filmed footage from 1980.)

Davison's replacement, Colin Baker, started playing the Doctor in 1984. The second Baker made his mark on the role instantly: his Doctor was brash, arrogant, egotistical and full of bravado. His era was mired in controversy as BBC management threatened cancellation in 1985. It was ostensibly a cost-cutting exercise, a way for the BBC to find money to produce its new soap *EastEnders*, but the controversy brought into sharp relief ratings that were beginning to decline. The BBC's decision caused a public outcry that resulted in management guaranteeing that the show would be back after an 18-month hiatus. But the series never recovered from the blow, and ratings continued to slide upon its return. Colin Baker was dumped after his second season, the shortest tenure of any actor in the Classic Series proper.

His replacement, Sylvester McCoy, ushered in a creative resurgence as new writers radically retooled the series, drawing on influences from contemporary science fiction and comic books such as *Halo Jones* and *Watchmen*. McCoy, an actor mostly known for clowning on children's television, brought a world-weary pathos to the Doctor while the scripts made the character more mysterious and powerful than previously. Unfortunately, the BBC had scheduled *Doctor Who* opposite ITV's *Coronation Street*, which then, as now, was the most popular drama on British television. While *Doctor Who* held its own in this death slot — and ratings even marginally improved — the series was finally cancelled in 1989. BBC management stated that it was impossible to do science fiction to the high-gloss standards of shows like *Star Trek: The Next Generation* and it would not bring back the series until there was a co-production partner capable of that.

That partner came in the mid-1990s, when a British-born American television executive named Philip Segal decided to bring the series to the U.S. Segal had worked with Columbia, and then with Amblin Entertainment and Steven Spielberg to develop a pilot for an American co-production of *Doctor Who* that would have rebooted the series completely. However, after much negotiating, a deal to produce the series for Fox fell through. Segal did manage to negotiate a deal with the BBC and Universal Television for a TV Movie to air on Fox, which he hoped might serve as a backdoor pilot for the series. The *Doctor Who* TV Movie was broadcast in May 1996 and, unlike the proposed series, was a direct continuation of the original BBC series. Sylvester McCoy's seventh Doctor regenerated into the eighth Doctor (played by Paul McGann) who faced off against his arch enemy the Master in San Francisco on New Year's Eve, 1999. The TV Movie had excellent ratings in the U.K., but disastrous ones in the U.S. The series was not picked up.

After the TV Movie, *Doctor Who* lay fallow for almost a decade, its fans continuing to keep the flame alive with novels and audio adventures on CD. In 2003, BBC controller Lorraine Heggessey decided to bring Saturday night programming on BBC1 back to its glory days of the 1970s. Heggessey also wanted to bring to the BBC writer and producer Russell T Davies, a phenomenally successful creative force in British television who had scored success after success on Channel 4 and ITV with *Queer as Folk*, *Bob and Rose* and *The Second Coming*. Davies only agreed to come to the BBC if he could bring back *Doctor Who*.

On September 25, 2003, Lorraine Heggessey announced that *Doctor Who* would be back on British television in 2005 in a series written and produced by Russell T Davies. We pick up the story from there . . .

SERIES ONE

Starring
Christopher Eccleston as the Doctor
Billie Piper as Rose Tyler

Executive Producers
Russell T Davies, Julie Gardner
and Mal Young

Producer
Phil Collinson

1.01 Rose

Written by Russell T Davies **Directed by** Keith Boak

Supporting cast Camille Coduri (Jackie Tyler); Noel Clarke (Mickey Smith); Mark Benton (Clive); Elli Garnett (Caroline); Alan Ruscoe, Paul Kasey, David Sant, Elizabeth Fost, Helen Otway (Autons); Nicholas Briggs (Nestene voice)

Original airdate March 26, 2005

The Big Idea Ordinary shopgirl Rose Tyler encounters a mysterious man called the Doctor, who is in the midst of foiling an invasion by creatures made of living plastic.

Roots and References *The X-Files* (Clive's website and conspiracy theories). The Doctor flips through Alice Sebold's *The Lovely Bones*. The music from the opening montage was inspired by the Pixies' song "Cecilia Ann."

Adventures in Time and Space The Autons, and the Nestene Consciousness controlling them, appeared in 1970's "Spearhead From Space" and 1971's *Terror of the Autons*. The scene of the shop window dummies breaking out is a recreation of a famous scene from "Spearhead From Space." TARDIS stands for "Time And Relative Dimension In Space," going back to the original derivation of the word from 1963's "An Unearthly Child." (From 1965 to 1996, the D stood for dimensions, plural.)

The Bad Wolf Effect The meme that defines this season, Bad Wolf, doesn't appear in this story (unless you count that Rose is wearing a red hoodie, which brings to mind Little Red Riding Hood). However, this episode does set up another important element of this season's ongoing story arc, as the Doctor tells the Nestene that he fought in a war, which eventually will be called the Time War. The Time War becomes very important as the season develops and influences several key events in episodes to come — as it does here, with the Nestene looking to invade Earth because their homeworld was destroyed in the war.

Who is the Doctor? We're introduced to a brand new Doctor, *in medias res*. Although the history from Clive's website suggests a large backstory to this ninth Doctor, the fact that he looks in a mirror and comments on his ears suggests that he's recently regenerated. The two details aren't incompatible: his adventures at Kennedy's assassination and Krakatoa may well have not yet happened to him (or he simply hasn't had a chance to look in a mirror). While the new Doctor is quite a step away from past Doctors — he's outwardly tougher and he wears a leather jacket rather than the Victorian or Edwardian style of his predecessors — there are also a number of clues that reassure us that this is the same show. He carries a sonic screwdriver, the Nestene Consciousness calls him a Time Lord and his morality is consistent: he can't kill the Nestene Consciousness without first giving it a chance. In among the dizzying array of changes that the New Series brings, it's this last point that's probably the most important: the Doctor's moral centre is unchanged.

The Doctor and Rose Rose is an ordinary girl, working in an ordinary job, with an ordinary life. She's a teenager and, outwardly, there's nothing special about her. Even her climactic decision to get involved in the Doctor's world — via her bronze in gymnastics — actually reveals that she hasn't really excelled at anything. And yet, the Doctor is immediately drawn to her, taking her hand in a way that's incredibly sweet, even if it does occur amid an atttack by plastic aliens. It's Rose's compassion and humanity — two qualities that the Doctor clearly struggles with, thanks to some as-yet-unidentified trauma — that the Doctor's drawn to. For her part, it's clearly love at first sight, as a mysterious and attractive older man turns her world upside down and then invites her to join his thrilling and dangerous lifestyle.

Monster of the Week The Nestene Consciousness is made of living plastic and can control anything plastic. It can make plastic copies of people and uses Autons (which are never named in the episode itself, though they are in the credits) as its invasion force. The Autons resemble shop window dummies, but with guns built into their hands.

Stand Up and Cheer The scene where the Doctor has to explain what a police box is should be a boring scene, but Christopher Eccleston instead proclaims, "It's a disguise!" as though it really were the cleverest disguise in history. This is a plot point for new viewers, a nod to the series' history for long-time viewers, a character point about the Doctor and a really funny joke rolled into one. This is the moment when you realize that — despite the leather jacket, the northern accent and the gruff exterior — Christopher Eccleston truly is the Doctor.

Roll Your Eyes Mickey getting his hands stuck in melted plastic is quite good. His fighting with a poorly rendered CGI wheelie bin is a bit silly. But its final burp after it's swallowed him is downright embarrassing to anyone over the age of 12.

You're Not Making Any Sense Given how observant and curious Rose is in every other respect, it does seem incredible she doesn't notice that, after visiting Clive, her boyfriend has a darker complexion, different hair, a plastic sheen and a tendency to stutter mechanically.

Interesting Trivia Mickey telling Rose not to read his emails is a little bizarre. Is he cheating on her? That seems the obvious conclusion, although he could just be planning a surprise party, for all we know. It's meant to indicate frission in their relationship, so that when she leaves him for the Doctor at the story's conclusion we don't feel that Rose is heartless, but it's an odd way of going about it. Especially as it never gets resolved.

The website Rose uses to look for information on the Doctor is search-wise .net. It isn't a real search engine, but a "prop" search engine used in a variety of films and TV shows. This neatly circumvents using an actual brand name, which public broadcasters like the BBC avoid unless absolutely necessary. Oddly, search-wise.net only turns up one link to the search term "Doctor Blue Box": that of Clive's webpage. It's a little bizarre that there aren't traces of the Doctor all over the internet.

The Doctor uses anti-plastic to kill the Nestene Consciousness. There are two strange things about this: the first is that we're never told anything more about what the substance is, not even given a technobabble explanation. The second is that the Doctor is carrying it at all. Although he claims he wasn't going to use it, the very fact that he's walking around with a substance that can entirely destroy his enemy has to be seen as an act of war. The Doctor is supposed to be the man who doesn't use weapons, so why was he (presumably) spending hours in the TARDIS laboratory brewing up a fiendish bioweapon?

Rose lives on the Powell Estate, a housing complex in Peckham, London. These kinds of estates are operated by local councils in a bid to supply uncrowded housing at reasonable rents for working-class people. While many Classic Series companions were decidedly middle class, Rose's background marks her as an everywoman. It's a subtle way to endear new viewers to a character who has to be likeable and sympathetic from the outset, as we see the Doctor's world through her eyes.

The new TARDIS interior features coral-like pillars, a hexagon pattern on the walls and a metal mesh floor. For the first time in *Doctor Who*, the exterior TARDIS doors directly open onto the interior; we even see the back of the Police (Public Call) Box sign inside the console room. There's a ramp from the door up to the central console, which consists of a central glass pillar with pipes inside and a six-sided console. The organic nature of it, suggesting the TARDIS has been grown rather than built, is a superb touch.

This episode, infamously, was leaked onto the internet a month before its broadcast; on March 6, 2005, an employee at a Toronto dubbing facility contracted out by the CBC decided to make a copy for himself and put it online. (He then got fired. Let that be a lesson to you.) The main change from the viewing copy to the final, transmitted version is that a stereo mix of the original Delia Derbyshire theme music was used.

The TARDIS Chronometer It's established in "Aliens of London" that this story is set mostly on March 6, 2005. The TARDIS is seen throughout London: outside

Henrik's, near the Powell Estate, in the alley of a restaurant and across from the London Eye. Each time, a little more is revealed for new viewers: it first dematerializes offscreen, then the interior is shown, then a materialization from within and finally one from the exterior. This gives viewers new to *Doctor Who* an idea of the TARDIS's capabilities without drowning them in exposition.

Fantastic? (RS?) After 15 long years of waiting, after all the cul de sacs and dead ends, *Doctor Who* finally returns and it's on the BBC on Saturday nights, starring a heavyweight actor as the Doctor and a celebrity as the companion in a continuation of the original series. For fans who'd been waiting, this was everything we could have possibly dreamed of.

But what of the episode itself? How can the story — how can anything — live up to the hype, the promise and the dreams fans have had for 15 years?

"Rose," fortunately, is fantastic.

It's not just okay, or as good as could be hoped for in the circumstances, it's utterly, utterly wonderful. There are so many great things about "Rose," from the Doctor's entrance and Rose's day to Clive's description and the disembodied hand actually attacking from behind the sofa. The first five minutes alone will have you grinning like a fool — and it's a grin that will stay with you for the next 24 hours.

The new show is smart, sassy, witty, scary, laugh-out-loud funny, touching and clever. It has all these things in spades; although for my money, it's the humour that succeeds best of all. Everything from "Give a man a plastic hand" and "Lots of planets have a north!" to Clive's wife being surprised that a girl would be interested in a website about the Doctor makes this an episode that you just can't help loving.

The opening montage gives us Rose's day in 30 seconds and then you hit the ground running. Although it appears light and fluffy, this is actually plotted incredibly carefully so that, without even realizing it, casual viewers are absorbed into the Doctor's world. If you're used to the Classic Series format of a longer story built over several 25-minute episodes, this takes some getting used to: there's a sense we've stepped into episode three of a four-part story in the Classic Series.

What's amazing is the introduction to both the Doctor and the sensibilities of the show. At first, he's a mysterious man who blows up buildings for his own agenda. In a post-9/11 age, this has the potential to be rather unsettling. Rose experiences the TARDIS as you or I would: running out and walking all around it before asking blunt questions. It's through her eyes that new viewers are meeting the Doctor and seeing his world. She gets to ask all the questions that the brand new viewer at home is wondering about and gradually her skepticism breaks down until she's ready to embrace both the Doctor and his universe. Stunt casting a celebrity pop singer sounded like a recipe for disaster, but Piper pulls it off beautifully by creating a character who's completely believable and grounded.

This premiere episode is a character piece, not a plot-driven spectacle. Which is fabulous, because it's the characters we really care about. There's a reason it's called "Rose" and not "Return of Some Extraterrestrials." For a series that needs to appeal to the general public in order to survive, making Rose the focus is crucial. And Russell T Davies is exactly the right man for the job: with extensive experience in kitchen-sink drama, he knows how to get an audience's attention and keep it.

What blows everything out of the water, though, is Christopher Eccleston's Doctor. He's incredible. What's more, he's unlike any Doctor we've ever seen and almost the complete antithesis of what you'd imagine the Doctor should be. He's not the genial old professor of the past, he doesn't wear flowing cloaks or hats and he doesn't speak with Received Pronunciation. But none of this matters, because he's utterly convincing. Right from his first appearance, you're never in doubt that he's the Doctor. What's more, he gets actual acting to do and carries the role with a boyish enthusiasm that's instantly infectious. He had me at "Run!"

I'm amazed at just how great "Rose" is. I honestly never thought they could recreate the series I fell in love with and prepared myself to adapt to whatever new incarnation it appeared in . . . but somehow they have. There are lots of little moments that really set it apart, but the whole thing unfolds like a dream. *Doctor Who* is back, but "Rose" is so good that it's like it never went away.

Second Opinion (GB) When it comes down to it, the new *Doctor Who* is so successful because of the first seven minutes of "Rose." That introduction pretty much distills what is, and what will forever be, great about *Doctor Who*. An ordinary person goes to a basement and not only faces something out of a nightmare but something incredibly daft. She meets a barmy man who is smarter than anyone else but also seems to be charismatically bonkers. There's an exciting chase, and a brilliant speech, followed by the best exchange of dialogue: "I'm the Doctor by the way . . . what's your name?" "Rose." "Nice to meet you, Rose. Run for your life!"

No wonder everyone became hooked. What's even more impressive is that it's these seven minutes that drive the rest of the story.

Like the very first *Doctor Who* story, 1963's "An Unearthly Child," "Rose" is about an ordinary person who gets caught up in a mystery and finds something extraordinary. While the Doctor's very first human companions, Ian and

Barbara, only discovered the TARDIS, Rose gets a primer on everything that *Doctor Who* can be: monsters, danger, death and a scary, mad, eccentric hero. The focus on Rose pushes the whys and wherefores of the Doctor into backstory, which is maddening for those who want to know what the Doctor is all about, but it makes the mythology that much more intriguing. Likewise, there are old monsters in "Rose," but they're used more as shorthand for what an iconic *Doctor Who* monster should be like. And the Doctor is a full-fledged hero from the first second we see him.

A scene in a *Doctor Who* revival like the one where the Doctor has to fend off an Auton arm while Rose blithely makes coffee was beyond even the wildest dreams of many fans. Here, Russell T Davies has remembered something important: *Doctor Who* is, at heart, a comedy where everything is treated with utter seriousness and yet nothing is taken truly seriously. You may wince at Auton Mickey, but you can't deny the power that draws you into the story.

It's a shame that Keith Boak's direction is so lacklustre, not even meeting, much less exceeding, the possibilities of the script. Fortunately, Christopher Eccleston's performance manages to cover any directing flaws. By the time he does the speech about feeling the turn of the Earth . . . well, we would pretty much follow him anywhere. And Piper is wonderful. The episode only works because we believe in Rose Tyler: a person stuck in a dead-end life who has so much potential when finally given the opportunity to show it. Piper makes Rose the best friend we've never had.

With all those masterstrokes, *Doctor Who* has become a force to be reckoned with once more. It's back, baby. Oh yes it is!

. . . .

Christopher Eccleston

Born in the Salford area of Manchester in 1964, Christopher Eccleston achieved critical acclaim for one of his first major roles in *Let Him Have It* (1991), but he became known by the British public for his portrayal of Robbie Coltrane's boss, DCI Bilborough in *Cracker*, particularly when his character was spectacularly killed off by a serial killer. Eccleston continued building his name with edgy roles including David in *Shallow Grave* (1994) and Nicky Hutchinson in the acclaimed BBC series *Our Friends in the North* (1996). Other roles included *Jude* (1996), *Elizabeth* (1998), *eXistenZ* (1999), *Gone in 60 Seconds* (2000), *The Others* (2001) and *28 Days Later* (2002). In 2003, he played a modern day incarnation of the Son of God in Russell T Davies' *The Second Coming*.

Eccleston emailed Davies when he heard about the new *Doctor Who* to express his interest in the role of the Doctor; he wanted to play a part that could be watched by children and he was interested in the approach Davies would take with the series.

He only played the Doctor for a season and has rarely spoken about his time in the role. Subsequently, Eccleston played Claude in *Heroes* (2007), Destro in *G.I. Joe: The Rise of Cobra* (2009) and John Lennon in *Lennon Naked* (2010).

. . . .

1.02 The End of the World

Written by Russell T Davies **Directed by** Euros Lyn

Supporting cast Simon Day (Steward), Yasmin Bannerman (Jabe), Jimmy Vee (Moxx of Balhoon), Zoë Wanamaker (Cassandra), Camille Coduri (Jackie Tyler), Beccy Armory (Raffalo) Sara Stewart (computer voice), Silas Carson (alien voice), Nicholas Briggs (alien voice)

Original airdate April 2, 2005

The Big Idea The Doctor takes Rose to witness the end of the world, where there's flirting, disaster and a *Scooby-Doo*-esque mystery.

Roots and References The Mos Eisley cantina scenes in *Star Wars*; Oompa-Loompas from the 1971 film *Willy Wonka & the Chocolate Factory* (the blue-skinned people); Agatha Christie (the mystery involving monied classes); Michael Jackson (Cassandra's plastic surgery); *The Hitchhiker's Guide to the Galaxy* (observing the end of the world from a viewing platform). Soft Cell's "Tainted Love" and Britney Spears's "Toxic" play on the jukebox "iPod."

Adventures in Time and Space The Doctor admits to Rose that he's a Time Lord, a revelation made in 1969's "The War Games." His home planet (Gallifrey, though it's unnamed in the New Series until "The Runaway Bride") and his people have been destroyed, which is a significant sea change from the Classic Series. The Doctor explains that the TARDIS's telepathic field translates alien languages for the Doctor and his companions, an explanation that harkens back to 1976's "The Masque of Mandragora."

The Bad Wolf Effect As concern rises among the visitors in the Manchester Suite, the Moxx of Balhoon says, "This is the Bad Wolf scenario." Meanwhile, we have the Doctor's admission that his people were all killed in a war against an as-yet-unnamed opponent.

Who is the Doctor? The Doctor is the very last Time Lord. He watched his planet's destruction as it burned like the Earth did in the year five billion. His refusal to save Cassandra — he tells Rose "All things have their time" — is quite probably deflected anger from that experience.

The Doctor and Rose The story plays as a rather intense sort of first date, as Rose goads the Doctor into taking her to the most impressive place he can. She has a moment of regret about going with him, which dissipates when the Doctor fixes her phone, allowing her a connection to her world.

Monster of the Week This episode introduces a plethora of alien races, including the Steward's people, the Trees from the Forest of Cheem, the Moxx of Balhoon and the Face of Boe. But the one to watch out for is Cassandra, the last human, who has taken cosmetic surgery to the extreme and is now just a stretched piece of skin with a face attached to a brain in a jar.

Stand Up and Cheer The scene where Rose meets Raffalo is quietly magnificent. Rose realizes how far out of her depth she is (and how reckless her decision to travel with the Doctor was) in the midst of a conversation about how, even in the far future, people still need plumbers. It's the mixture of the fantastic and the different, aided by a lovely, natural performance by Beccy Armory, that makes this moment special.

Roll Your Eyes We're not sure what the Doctor was getting at with his Deep South remark, either . . .

You're Not Making Any Sense Just because the Doctor points out the ridiculousness of the override switch being at the end of a hallway with giant fans doesn't make it any less silly — or any less contrived.

Interesting Trivia This story marks the first appearance of a number of items the Doctor uses regularly in his travels. The slightly psychic paper shows people whatever the Doctor wants them to see, enabling him to get into practically anywhere. (Curiously, this is the only time it's called "slightly" psychic paper.) It's the first time we see the modified mobile phone that enables the companion to dial home from anywhere, anywhen. (Unlike subsequent phones the Doctor zaps with the sonic screwdriver, here he puts a piece of technology in the battery slot.) It's also the first appearance of the Doctor's watch, which he uses to check for information beyond what hour, minute and second it is, as though he can see something with it others can't. (The eleventh Doctor also looks at his watch in this way; the tenth doesn't wear one.)

By the year five billion, the Earth is restored to its "classic" condition and maintained by the National Trust, which is presumably a far-future version of the National Trust for Places of Historic Interest or Natural Beauty, an organization that owns heritage sites around Britain. How this setup worked before the planet was left to roast is not stated: were there still indigenous lifeforms? Did people come to visit Earth on weekends taking bored children in tow, leaving volunary donations in kiosks scattered across the globe?

Cassandra uses that classic science-fiction trope of showing how things get muddled in the historical record: she possesses an "iPod" (a classic jukebox) and plays Britney Spears's "Toxic," thinking it to be an ancient Earth folk song.

Incidentally, "Toxic" was never released as a 45 RPM single; the record was a mock-up by the art department.

There were more special effects shots created for this episode than any *Doctor Who* story before or since.

The TARDIS Chronometer After taking Rose to the 22nd century and the New Roman Empire in the year 12,055 (though they don't leave the TARDIS on either occasion), the Doctor takes her to Platform One, orbiting the Earth in the year 5.5/apple/26, or what Rose would term the year five billion. When Rose calls her mum, Jackie asks Rose to put some money in the lottery syndicate at work, which would indicate the TARDIS placed the call to Jackie before Henrik's department store blew up in "Rose."

Fantastic? (GB) You have the ability to travel through all of time and space to impress the person you're with. Where do you take her? To the most beautiful, awe-inspiring place imaginable? Or five billion years into the future to watch the destruction of her home planet?

That the Doctor chooses the second option is what makes *Doctor Who* more than just a great adventure series. Had the Doctor chosen the first option, the episode would still have had all the jeopardy, intrigue, laughs and eye-popping effects, but it would have missed all the emotional content, which is at the core of this new *Doctor Who*. The Doctor's destination for the couple's "first date" gives her some insight into his psyche: he wants Rose to see a little of what he's seen. There's something at once haunting and pathetic about the Doctor's need to make an emotional connection to Rose; it's as though he's been carrying his burden forever and has finally met someone with whom he can share it.

It's this perceived connection that makes the final scene so powerful. The immediate reaction of a hardcore *Doctor Who* fan is likely "Ohmigod, Gallifrey is destroyed! Does this contradict Classic Series stories like 'The Invasion of Time'?" Which is a grand exercise in missing the point. The final scene is moving not because of the plot revelations and their impact on the ongoing storyline (or how they affect *Doctor Who* continuity), but because we witness a character revealing his deepest pain to another person for the first time in a very long while. Christopher Eccleston and Billie Piper deliver these lines with such utter conviction and heartfelt emotion to cut to the real point here — the Doctor allows himself to trust someone for the first time in ages.

The Doctor has, for the first time ever, an emotional arc for his character: he goes from telling Rose initially, "This is who I am, right here, right now" to admitting he's the last Time Lord in the final scene. The character who proves to be pivotal to this journey is Jabe. She starts out as someone the Doctor can flirt with, but she manages to get through the emotional armour Rose couldn't.

We see the Doctor well up with tears when Jabe tells him she's sorry for his loss. It's powerful stuff.

But to linger solely on these emotional beats does the story a disservice. "The End of the World" is sheer, unadulterated fun. It's a great adventure story with breathless pacing, ever-increasing jeopardy and some spooky moments (the death of the Steward is delightfully horrific). The mystery of who is behind the menace could have been built up instead of the *Scooby-Doo* affair here, but, come on, it's Cassandra. Cassandra is a delightfully camp, freakish caricature of Cher and Michael Jackson who is constantly requesting to be moisturized while delivering barbed one-liners ("I bet you were the swot in the back of the class who never kissed the girl"). She's such a counter-intuitive choice for a villain that a lot of the success of the story is due to her. It would have been easy to write a more typical science-fictiony sour-faced adversary. To make her a bitchy trampoline, well, that's just plain inspired.

But there's even more to Cassandra. As a character who has extended her life to the point where she's a gross parody of humanity — vain and avaricious — her presence is thematic as well. "The End of the World" is about realizing that everything has its time and cherishing the life we have. That's what the Doctor teaches Rose when he takes her back to present-day Earth. It's not just about showing Rose what it's like to see one's planet blow up; it's about showing her how wonderful something seemingly insignificant — like chips — can be.

While "Rose" establishes the characters and the premise of *Doctor Who* brilliantly, "The End of the World" is Russell T Davies' manifesto on what *Doctor Who* is and should be. This is *Doctor Who* with real emotion, funny dialogue, heartbreaking moments, a couple of earnest preachy bits and a pop soundtrack. I love it.

Second Opinion (RS?) Despite the fact that we see Rose confronted with the destruction of her planet, "The End of the World" is very firmly the Doctor's story and one that allows Christopher Eccleston to shine. From the almost sexual way he operates the TARDIS and his disturbing delight in pushing Rose to go ever further forward to his bopping away to Soft Cell and his righteous fury at the confrontation with Cassandra, we see the Doctor experiencing almost every emotion imaginable. He's someone who survived a massive trauma, is wracked with survivor's guilt, and is now just going through the motions of living, his mental compass all over the map.

In the "This is who I am, right here, right now" scene, he's defensive, angry, stews in silence and then kindly fixes Rose's phone — allowing her to reach her family in a way that he never can — all in the space of about three minutes. And then, when she starts to experience intense loss, he dismisses her feelings with a quip: "Bundle of laughs you are!" This is an enormous range of emotions, suggesting either someone who isn't quite stable or someone who, even among the variety of aliens present, is the most alien of them all. In a story whose theme is that everyone dies — from Jabe and Cassandra to Earth itself — he's the only one who can't. Instead, he coldly stands by and watches Cassandra die immediately after he's angrily claimed that he's bristling with ideas.

But then, at the end, he opens himself up to Rose, just a little. And, through her, he learns that there's an alternative to just carrying on: he can also find joy in the tiniest of things. That chips scene is a stroke of genius: it brings the story down to Earth, showing us that a story about weird aliens in the year five billion has the potential to speak deeply and poignantly to us in the 21st century.

"The End of the World": it's the end of Planet Earth, the end of Rose's comfortable worldview and the end of the Doctor's solitary world. It's perhaps the fastest story ever told on *Doctor Who* — the entire adventure takes place in about an hour — and is an effects showcase featuring an all-alien cast, putting an end to the world of mocking that the show once experienced. In just the second episode of the New Series, we see that this is not just an enjoyable sci-fi adventure show, but something that's going to be quite special indeed.

· ·

Russell T Davies

By the time Russell T Davies became executive producer and head writer of *Doctor Who*, he was already one of the most well-known television writers in Britain. Davies began his career in children's TV, producing and writing *Why Don't You . . . ?* (which was originally a factual program but Davies turned it into a drama!) and then writing the acclaimed series *Dark Season* and *Century Falls*. He turned to adult drama with the 1997 series *The Grand*. A lifelong *Doctor Who* fan who started watching when William Hartnell was the Doctor, Davies wrote the *Doctor Who* New Adventures novel *Damaged Goods* for Virgin Publishing in 1996.

From 2000 to 2001, he wrote (and produced) two seasons of the popular Channel 4 drama *Queer as Folk* (which later had an American remake) and followed that up with the successful series *Bob and Rose* (2001) and *The Second Coming* (2003, starring Christopher Eccleston). He was headhunted by the BBC in 2003; before revamping *Doctor Who*, he wrote and produced the 2005 BBC series *Casanova* (starring David Tennant).

Davies was executive producer and head writer for the first four seasons of the New Series, as well as the 2008–2010 specials. Davies wrote 31 episodes of *Doctor Who* and as showrunner usually wrote an uncredited final draft of most other scripts (the only exceptions included scripts written by Steven Moffat, Stephen Greenhorn or Matthew Graham). Davies was involved in just about every creative decision in the New Series, alongside fellow executive producer Julie Gardner.

After departing in 2010, he continued to executive produce (and occasionally write) episodes of *Torchwood* and *The Sarah Jane Adventures*, the two *Doctor Who* spinoffs he created during his tenure.

. . . .

1.03 The Unquiet Dead

Written by Mark Gatiss **Directed by** Euros Lyn

Supporting cast Alan David (Gabriel Sneed), Eve Myles (Gwyneth), Simon Callow (Charles Dickens), Huw Rhys (Redpath), Jennifer Hill (Mrs. Peace), Zoe Thorne (The Gelth)

Original airdate April 9, 2005

The Big Idea It's Cardiff, 1869, and Charles Dickens' lecture tour is interrupted by gaseous beings inhabiting corpses. Fortunately, Dickens' number one fan, the Doctor, is on hand.

Roots and References Dickens' own work, especially *A Christmas Carol* (1843), but also his ghost story "The Signal Man" (1866), which the Doctor calls the greatest ghost story ever; Simon Callow's one-man show about Dickens, particularly the BBC production *An Audience with Charles Dickens*, influenced the casting process.

Adventures in Time and Space The idea that ghosts (and the accompanying psychic phenomena) are actually an echo caused by a space-time event harkens back to 1977's "Image of the Fendahl." The Doctor's explanation to Rose that the future still can be changed was demonstrated in 1975's "Pyramids of Mars."

The Bad Wolf Effect The Gelth make the first explicit reference to the Time War: "The whole universe convulsed. The Time War raged, invisible to smaller species but devastating to higher forms." Gwyneth, using her second sight, tells Rose, "The things you've seen. The darkness. The big bad wolf!"

Who is the Doctor? The Doctor is a gushing fanboy when it comes to Dickens, behaving like someone on an internet forum, alternately praising and mocking Dickens' work.

The Doctor and Rose Rose and the Doctor seem to be on different pages with their relationship. Rose suggests that the infinite times and places the TARDIS can go to is "better with two" while the Doctor tells Dickens that Rose "is in his care." He also says she's beautiful . . . considering she's a human. This is an awkward attempt to progress the Doctor's interest in Rose while highlighting he's an alien, and to make the Doctor both interested and aloof. Even so, ouch.

Monster of the Week The Gelth are beings whose physical forms were destroyed as collateral damage in the Time War. They now exist as gaseous entities who can inhabit corpses.

Stand Up and Cheer If we had the ability to travel back in time, we too would probably find the first step into the past as awesome an experience as Rose does here. It's a nicely observed moment.

Roll Your Eyes What's up with the Doctor smirking while Rose chastises Sneed for copping a feel while she was chloroformed?

You're Not Making Any Sense Never mind the Classic Series; everything we know about the Doctor from the past two episodes indicates that he would never descend into a cowardly screed when faced with death (in Cardiff) as he is here. It seems incredibly out of character.

Interesting Trivia As we will find with succeeding stories set in historical times (and continuing a tradition begun in the Classic Series), this episode plays fast and loose with the factual record. By 1869, Dickens had suffered a mild stroke; he was barely able to perform his farewell tour of readings between January and March 1870. He was never in Cardiff at Christmas and certainly wouldn't have been gallivanting about. Dickens saying "What the Shakespeare?" — while extremely funny — has no basis in historical fact; the expression "What the Dickens?" is about the Devil. *The Mystery of Edwin Drood* is Dickens' final, unfinished novel, though it seems unlikely the mystery hinged on blue gaseous creatures. A 19th-century hearse would not have had the name of the funeral parlour on it; that's pure dramatic convention.

This story features the first appearance of the rift in time in the city of Cardiff. This rift will help fuel the TARDIS in "Boom Town" and "Utopia." The rift in Cardiff also becomes central to the *Doctor Who* spinoff series *Torchwood* (2006–present). Eve Myles, who plays Gwyneth, went on to play Gwen Cooper in *Torchwood*. The Doctor gives an explanation for the similarities between the two characters in "Journey's End."

The TARDIS Chronometer The Doctor attempts to take Rose to Naples, 1860. Instead, they wind up in the Welsh capital of Cardiff on Christmas Eve, 1869.

Fantastic? (GB) On first viewing, "The Unquiet Dead" is terribly, terribly disappointing. The characterization of the Doctor and Rose drives the plots and themes of "Rose" and "The End of the World." Here we have an ordinary *Doctor Who* episode. And that would be all right if the story didn't play it so safe.

There is an honest-to-goodness compelling moral dilemma: the Gelth need human cadavers to survive. Rose's response to that is coloured by her father's death, mentioned for the first time in this episode. However, all that dramatic potential is squandered the second the Gelth turn red and cackle menacingly. Alien morality? Pshaw. Let's just make them evil; it makes things less messy.

Worse, Rose becomes almost peripheral to the action. Several times while writing notes on this episode, I accidentally called Rose "Ace," the name of the last companion in the Classic Series. And that subconscious slip says a lot about her characterization here: the scene where Rose talks with Gwyneth about boys and school isn't all that different from the sort of thing Ace did back in 1989. After two stories where Rose was so central, this one stands out like a sore thumb.

And yet, I don't want to bury "The Unquiet Dead" as simply a generic *Doctor Who* story. There's a lot that works. The story's setup with an undertaker chasing down the resurrected dead is delightfully ludicrous and worthy of Mark Gatiss's work with *The League of Gentlemen*. The period setting is vividly realized. There are great characters and performances too. Charles Dickens is charmingly brought to life, not just because Simon Callow has played him multiple times on stage and screen, but because the script captures a man who suddenly discovers that life is bigger than he thought. Gatiss's script does a nice job of showing Gwyneth as a person shaped by a particular time and place, and Eve Myles gets that Gwyneth is innocent but not naive. Her performance steals the show.

"The Unquiet Dead" suffers a bit with its climax, with the Doctor whining while the high-profile guest star figures out how to stop the Gelth. Gwyneth's beyond-the-grave sacrifice is also more than a bit predictable. But the denouement with the Doctor, Rose and a restored Dickens almost makes it worth it.

The episode isn't perfect, but it's enjoyable. In many ways, the problem is not the story itself, but rather the slow inexorable triumph of the Classic Series *Doctor Who* format over the innovations made in this reincarnation. This is the first ordinary *Doctor Who* story we've seen in the New Series. It won't be the last.

Second Opinion (RS?) My co-author is dead wrong. "The Unquiet Dead" isn't just ordinary or generic; it's a complete mess. It should be a tight little tale of spooks inside a haunted house, but it decides to go to the theatre. It should pit the Doctor and Rose against each other in a profound moral quandary, but instead they disagree for a bit before the aliens reveal themselves to be villainous, rendering the argument moot. It should take a subtle step forward in the Doctor and Rose's relationship, but instead they flirt like mad at the outset rather than grow subtly closer throughout the course of the story.

Sneed is a case in point. He starts off as villainous, kidnapping and sexually molesting Rose, then the tone shifts entirely and he's suddenly the comic relief whom we're supposed to laugh along with. And, rather than get his comeuppance for his earlier villainy, he's killed by accident and turned into a zombie, simply because he was standing in the wrong spot.

The real problem is that Mark Gatiss hasn't realized the potential of the New Series. He gets some of it right — Rose's first step into the past is lovely — but he's desperately trying to recreate the glories of yesteryear's *Doctor Who*, only it all comes across so half-heartedly. For example, the episode starts with a bog-standard haunting, featuring characters we don't yet know or care about, rather than inside the TARDIS with the Doctor and Rose as the previous two episodes have.

That said, the leads are again excellent. Piper shines as she brings Rose's compassion to life, while Eccleston is sublimely impressive with his forced jollity and his tendency to suddenly appear in the background of scenes, looking ever-so-slightly menacing. Best of all, when Rose is trapped, he doesn't use his sonic screwdriver, but rather kicks down the door with his boot. It's a most un-Doctorish moment, but it suits this Doctor to a tee.

Oddly, given its backward-looking premise, "The Unquiet Dead" turned out to be the basis for much of *Doctor Who*'s future. We'll revisit this location in a few stories' time, which in turn will form the basis of the spinoff series *Torchwood*, as well as other episodes set in Cardiff. All this retroactively gives "The Unquiet Dead" far more weight than it deserves. On its own, it's all over the map.

1.04—1.05 Aliens of London / World War Three

Written by Russell T Davies **Directed by** Keith Boak

Supporting cast Camille Coduri (Jackie Tyler); Noel Clarke (Mickey Smith); Penelope Wilton (Harriet Jones); Annette Badland (Margaret Blaine); Rupert Vansittart (General Asquith); David Verrey (Joseph Green); Navin Chowdhry (Indra Ganesh); Naoko Mori (Dr. Sato); Eric Potts (Oliver Charles); Fiesta Mei Ling (Ru); Basil Chung (Bau); Morgan Hopkins (Sergeant Price); Andrew Marr (himself); Matt Baker (himself); Corey Doabe (spray painter); Ceris Jones (policeman); Jack Tarlton (reporter); Lachele Carl (reporter); Jimmy Vee (space pig); Steve Speirs (Strickland); Elizabeth Fost, Paul Kasey, Alan Ruscoe (Slitheen)

Original airdates April 16 and 23, 2005

The Big Idea The Doctor returns Rose to London a year late, just in time to see Big Ben destroyed in a plot to turn Earth into molten fuel.

Roots and References The 9/11 terrorist attacks (the spaceship crashing into an iconic building, sparking mass panic) and the subsequent Iraq war ("Massive weapons of destruction, capable of being deployed within 45 seconds"); the Girls Aloud video for "Jump," which featured the girl band running around 10 Downing Street; the hacking in *WarGames*.

Adventures in Time and Space Mickey researched the Doctor over the past 12 months and knows of his involvement with UNIT (identified by the Doctor as "United Nations Intelligence Taskforce"). UNIT first appeared in 1968's "The

Invasion" and the Doctor was its scientific advisor throughout the Jon Pertwee episodes of the early 1970s.

The Bad Wolf Effect A young boy spray-paints "Bad Wolf" on the TARDIS.

Who is the Doctor? This is the first time we see the Doctor's past directly come back to haunt him, in the form of his Classic Series allegiance with UNIT. Mere mention of his name sets off alerts in the military and, amusingly, what looks like a government operation to bring him in turns out to be exactly that, only they're bringing him in as an acknowledged expert on aliens. Despite his revelling in the attention, he nevertheless gives Mickey a CD with a virus that will destroy every mention of him. Unfortunately, either Mickey never uses the CD or the virus doesn't work, because, as we'll see, the Doctor is going to remain very well known indeed.

The Doctor and Rose In the pair's first interaction with characters from present-day Earth, there's a lot of forced confrontation about their relationship, from Jackie stating outright that Rose is infatuated with the Doctor to the police officer asking if their relationship is sexual. They both vehemently deny this, but their denial is so hurried that you can tell at least one of them wishes it were so. There's also the Doctor's pseudo-macho rivalry with Mickey (although they come to an understanding by the end of the story) and Jackie asking if Rose will always be safe with the Doctor. He doesn't answer the latter question, but it informs events later in the season.

Monster of the Week The Slitheen family, from Raxacoricofallapatorius. They're green, eight feet tall, with infant-like faces, eyes that blink sideways and claws with talons that pop out. They need to fit inside big humans, but have trouble with the gas exchange, which makes them fart.

Stand Up and Cheer In amongst all the fun of farting, baby-like aliens and the jokes about the contents of Mickey's kitchen, the deadly serious standoff between the Doctor and Margaret Blaine — "What, you trapped in your box?" — is riveting. The surrounding comedy makes the contrast stronger and Eccleston's conviction sells the moment.

Roll Your Eyes The CGI of the Slitheen running through Downing Street is quite good . . . but it looks nothing like their movements in close-up. The CGI draws attention to itself, which it should never do.

You're Not Making Any Sense The Slitheen's entire plan is predicated on somehow blocking the 20 or so people ahead of Joseph Green in prime ministerial succession. He's initially appointed acting prime minister only because the traffic is gridlocked and no one more senior can reach Downing Street. Why doesn't someone more senior assume the role once the traffic clears? Why don't they airlift the most likely successor into London? Or videoconference?

Interesting Trivia The Slitheen are huge, they're green and (dodgy CGI shots aside) they're played by actors in costumes. And if you're new to the series, then you could easily assume they're a Classic Series monster dropped right into the New Series. They're not, and a few details indicate that they're a world apart from classic monsters of the previous century: they're not a race, they're a family; they don't want to invade Earth, they want to sell it; and they don't invade steathily, they crash their alien ship live on television. Instead, the Slitheen are very much a parody of the sort of Classic Series monster we saw every Saturday at teatime in the '70s, with a postmodern twist.

Who's the murdered prime minister? We're never told, although the body on the floor has a similar build to Tony Blair. The production team actually hired a Blair look-alike to play the role. However, the actor didn't look enough like the then-PM, so it was decided to just shoot him from behind and leave it as a hint. With Harriet Jones becoming the next prime minister, a chain of events is here set in motion that plays out in the next several seasons and marks the point where the *Doctor Who* universe and the real world start to diverge. The alien "invasion" may be dismissed as a hoax, but the political ramifications are going to be enormous.

The Doctor starts off thinking that Harriet Jones is vaguely familiar, reiterates that he knows her from somewhere and then at the end of the story he suddenly knows her entire biography. So what changed? Very possibly, history itself. It's likely that, originally, Harriet never ascended to PM but — either because of the Slitheen's presence or, more likely, the Doctor's — future history changes and now Harriet always was the four-term prime minister, architect of Britain's new golden age. This idea of history changing in front us is quite subtle, but it's a lovely theory. The only snag in this theory is that history tends to react to these kinds of changes, so Harriet's prime ministership may not be as stable as she'd hope. We'll return to this shortly . . .

When Rose says "you're so gay" to the Doctor, it opened up a huge minefield for the show: should it be setting the standards or should it be trying to reflect what society is like? "Gay" used as a pejorative is part of how teenagers speak. Davies' response to this issue was that sometimes these things need to be included in order to provoke outrage, which sounds like a case of wanting to have your cake and eat it too. He could have been deliberate when writing the line, but most likely he just included it for realism without thinking through the implications. Given that he never uses such inflammatory language again, it's likely that he wasn't actually trying to outrage people after all.

We meet a soon-to-be-familiar worldwide chorus of responses to an alien invasion, including Lachele Carl's first appearance as the U.S. newsreader (later named Trinity Wells), the invasion incorporated into television shows (a make-your-own alien spaceship cake happening on the children's show *Blue Peter*) and real-world personalities (*Blue Peter* presenter Matt Baker, and Andrew Marr, the BBC's political editor from 2000 to 2005). Davies is interested in investigating the world's response to an alien threat, rather than brushing the existence of aliens under the carpet.

Much of the Doctor's potted history of 10 Downing Street is historically accurate: Downing Street was marshland 2,000 years ago. In 1730, it was occupied by a Mr. Chicken ("Nice man," says the Doctor). By 1796, the cabinet room was in Downing Street. In 1991, a security system was installed: three inches of steel line every single wall and shutters close in across the doors and windows.

In 2005, the official BBC *Doctor Who* website produced a "Who Is The Doctor" mini-site that saw Mickey continuing the work of Clive in investigating the Doctor. It's never confirmed in the series, but Mickey certainly has become knowledgable about the Doctor's activities, and more computer savvy, during the year Rose is away.

Dr. Sato will later turn up in *Torchwood* as Toshiko Sato. She's the same character, except that there she's a computer expert, rather than a doctor. In her final *Torchwood* appearance, it's retroactively explained that she swapped places with Torchwood's doctor for this adventure, as he had a hangover.

The TARDIS Chronometer In the Powell Estate, 12 months after Rose left, which the missing persons poster dates as March 6, 2005. The Doctor then takes the TARDIS to a storeroom in Albion Hospital, before returning to the same spot in the Powell Estate.

Fantastic? (RS?) An iconic building is destroyed, leading to widespread fear, talk of martial law and the curtailing of human rights. A leader who wasn't properly elected and acts like a buffoon dismisses all advice from trained personnel in favour of his own agenda. Massive weapons of destruction that don't exist. The British provide absolute proof of their existence to the U.S. Votes are secured to launch a massive retaliation at a target that wasn't responsible for the attack. After the bombing, the target will be carved up for big business, because it was always, always about fuel.

But that's enough of the real world, what about *Doctor Who*?

All right, so here it is, the first two-parter of the New Series. Surely *the* epic showcase of the first half of the season? Something gritty and hardcore, with an utterly convincing sense of realism and aliens so terrifying they're guaranteed to have you behind the sofa?

Er, no. "Aliens of London"/"World War Three" goes for broad comedy, rubber aliens with inconsistent effects, cliffhangers, soldiers running about, UNIT, the entire fate of the planet being decided from one room and some allegory that's so close to its subject matter it barely qualifies as pastiche. Remind you of any classic television series you may be a fan of?

This two-parter is the one thing this new series hasn't been until now: a good old-fashioned *Doctor Who* story. But what's confusing about this story is that it tries to be so many things at once. It was so perfectly honed for its British election coverage timeslot that it became dated weeks later. It's the broadest — and at times funniest — comedy the show has seen in decades. It's loved and hated by fans in about equal measure. It's an extremely sharp allegory about the War on Terror and the Iraq invasion. It's a character piece, far more interested in the domestic happenings at the Powell Estate than the alien invasion A-plot. The entire setup with the crashed spaceship leads inexorably to an exquisitely planned trap. And all this in what is basically a four-part story, in the old money.

The engine that drives the story is the domestic material. Which is not only extremely well written, but brought to life with love and care by the director and cast. The 12 hours/12 months opener is astonishing and makes us wonder why we've never seen something like this before. It forces all manner of consequences to happen at once: the Doctor and Rose can't have a stealth relationship, Jackie has moved from flirting with the Doctor to being mad at him, and Mickey becomes a murder suspect. The latter occurs largely because he's a black man, which is subtle but pointed. Best of all, it brings the supporting cast into sharp relief. No longer there just for the comedic moments (although they provide those too), they're now characters we're invested in and care about.

Eccleston's slightly deranged laugh when the alien spacecraft almost crashes into the council estate is brilliant, as it conveys so much in that moment. Piper's "Oh, it's just not fair" gives the punchline some weight, but it's telling that whereas she has to say it, Eccleston can portray everything we need to know with just a laugh. The space pig should be ridiculous, given that it's a wobbly actor in a pig costume, but it's given surprising pathos. Dr. Sato assumes that this is what aliens look like, which is a nice line. However, what really sells the space pig is the Doctor's reaction: he's kind to it, he treats it like a shy cat and then he's outraged at the humans' treatment of it. He takes what should be something laughable and turns it into a comment on the military and on human xenophobia, making a rubber-suited pig sympathetic into the bargain.

In fact, the entire cast is giving it their all. David Verrey is particularly good as the acting prime minister, going from humour to chilling menace with remarkable aplomb. He's also one of the few actors who can cackle his way through a cliffhanger without ruining the tension. As Harriet Jones, Penelope Wilton is a delight, flashing her ID card at everyone and remaining cool under pressure ("Pass it to the left, first"). Her rapport with Eccleston is particularly good.

And Noel Clarke as Mickey is a revelation. His pratfall in the first part is a bit goofy, but by the time he faces down a Slitheen in his apartment, armed only with a baseball bat, telling Jackie to run, you want him to become a regular companion. The story's climax, in terms of both plot and character, relies heavily on him and, thanks to the work done here, it works. The final shot of Mickey on the pillar, still waiting, is poignant.

Then there are the farting aliens. Reactions to them have been pretty extreme, which is understandable. People have complained that *Doctor Who* shouldn't be silly, that it shouldn't have unconvincing aliens, it shouldn't do broad comedy and it shouldn't be aimed at children. I think they've misunderstood the series they're supposedly fans of. Personally, I loved the farting aliens.

I'll say that again: I *loved* them.

Like all good comedy, the joke works on multiple levels. For the kids, you've got aliens who fart, which is inherently funny. For the intelligent 14-year-old, the farting is used simultaneously as comedy and menace: the policeman visiting Jackie has an upset stomach, which tells you all you need to know. For the adult, you've got yet more allegory to raise a smile: politicians as gassy windbags. Oh yeah and they've got zippers on their foreheads. Actual zippers! Who couldn't love this story?

"Aliens of London"/"World War Three" is a delight. It's not what we were expecting, but it shouldn't be dismissed because of that. It's *Doctor Who* with something to say, so it's standing up and doing it, because no one else will. It has an utterly fabulous cliffhanger. It has some extremely affecting content, a study of some of the fundamentals of the Doctor, his relationship with his companions and those left behind. It also has hilarious aliens, comedy that ranges from the broad to the subtle with everything in between and a sense that this sort of *Doctor Who* is just as important as the gritty, men-with-guns story that's on next week. And it does all this, and more, while being non-stop entertainment from start to finish.

I don't know about you, but I'm shaking my booty.

Second Opinion (GB) The first episode, "Aliens of London," is certainly the closest the new *Doctor Who*, and Russell T Davies, ever gets to pastiching the Classic Series' most beloved writer, Robert Holmes: the broad, even grotesque, characters; the satirical flourishes; the bizarre aliens; the use of esoteric historical facts (the pig as Victorian mermaid); and the subversion of the alien invasion. Frankly, the farting Slitheen is just the sort of thing that Robert Holmes would have done had he thought he could get away with it.

Admittedly, the domestic stuff obscures this truth a little, but it's so fabulous we have to forgive it: the pre-credits sequence is absolute genius, and the implications of the Doctor accidentally taking Rose away for 12 months were really well thought through. Camille Coduri and Billie Piper really sell the difficult but honest love that this mother and daughter share.

That said, as political satire goes, this story is pretty much one note, no funnier or more sophisticated than a *Saturday Night Live* routine. The real weak links are Keith Boak's direction, which feels like a retrograde step after Euros Lyn's work, and, surprisingly, Christopher Eccleston, who is out of his depth in the lighter sequences, goofily grinning, mugging and generally making the viewer uncomfortable. His laugh when the alien spaceship flies past should be the capper on the scene; instead, it just seems like the sort of thing a manic-depressive does when he's off his meds.

Eccleston's on much surer ground with material requiring gravitas, so he makes the extremely slight "World War Three" happen by sheer force of will. Every serious scene he's in — most of them stuck in a room talking to the outside world via speakerphone — bristles with energy, excitement and, where necessary, pathos. And Penelope Wilton is superb.

The ending is wonderful, with the Doctor offering Mickey a chance to travel with them (and then covering for him with Rose when he declines). It's this that elevates the story above a fun romp, and we see what kind of an intriguing drama *Doctor Who* is on its way to becoming, gleefully switching between domestic drama and high action-adventure. Of all the episodes in the first series, "Aliens of London" and "World War Three" are the ones that deserve a second look. The story isn't perfect (internet-ready missiles, really?), but it's good, old-fashioned *Doctor Who* at its core.

1.06 Dalek

Written by Robert Shearman **Directed by** Joe Ahearne

Supporting cast Bruno Langley (Adam Mitchell), Corey Johnson (Henry van Statten), Anna-Louise Plowman (Diana Goddard), Steven Beckingham (Polkowski), Nigel Whitmey (Simmons), John Schwab (Bywater), Jana Carpenter (De Maggio), Joe Montana (Commander), Nicholas Briggs (Dalek voice), Barnaby Edwards (Dalek operator)

Original airdate April 30, 2005

The Big Idea The TARDIS follows a distress call to Henry van Statten's underground museum of alien artefacts, only to find the last Dalek in existence.
Roots and References *Die Hard*; *The Silence of the Lambs*; writer Robert Shearman's 2003 audio CD *Doctor Who* story "Jubilee" (a lone Dalek being tortured).
Adventures in Time and Space The Doctor makes an oblique reference to the

Daleks' creator, Davros, from 1975's "Genesis of the Daleks." Almost crowded out by the return of the Dalek is the appearance in van Statten's museum of a Cyberman head. For hardcore geeks, the head is from a Cyberman from several hundreds of years in the future that appeared in 1975's "Revenge of the Cybermen" (the little gun at the top of the head is the telltale sign — and, no, we didn't go out on any dates in high school). For the first time in the New Series, it's pointed out the Doctor has two hearts, a fact known in the Classic Series since 1970's "Spearhead From Space."

The Bad Wolf Effect The Daleks fought the Time Lords in the Time War; like the Time Lords, they were wiped out. The call sign for van Statten's helicopter is "Bad Wolf One."

Who is the Doctor? It turns out the Doctor was personally responsible for the genocide of both the Time Lords and the Daleks. (His being alive is "not by choice," indicating a profound sense of guilt.) For the Doctor, the Dalek embodies his own anger and guilt at being the sole survivor of his race; his hate toward the creature, even as it is changing into something more, shows a deeply ugly side to the Doctor.

The Doctor and Rose Rose insists to Adam that she and the Doctor are just friends. And yet the Doctor's feelings toward Rose have never been more passionately demonstrated. He's devastated when he thinks the Dalek has exterminated Rose, and when he finds out she's alive he lets the Dalek blackmail him into freeing it. The Dalek claims that Rose is the woman the Doctor loves — and it's true. She's the only person who can talk the Doctor back from the brink when his hatred of the Dalek threatens to consume him.

Monster of the Week The Daleks are the most famous monster to appear in *Doctor Who*. They appeared in *Doctor Who*'s second story in 1963 and subsequently became synonymous with the program. The Dalek has been both an icon and a joke in British culture, and this story uses the most seemingly ridiculous design feature — the sucker arm — to dramatic effect. And while Daleks have demonstrated their ability to navigate stairs in the Classic Series (namely 1988's "Remembrance of the Daleks"), this story shows that they can float effortlessly for lengthy periods. For the first time in *Doctor Who* history, we fully see the creature inside the Dalek casing.

Stand Up and Cheer The sequence where the Dalek takes out a whole squadron simply by activating the fire sprinklers to efficiently electrocute every human in the area — all the while elevated above the ground — is pretty much what longtime Dalek fans have wanted to see their entire lives.

Roll Your Eyes As we will see repeatedly, American accents in *Doctor Who* can really grate on the nerves of North Americans. Even actual Americans like Corey

Johnson don't sound quite right because they're pitching their performance to British audiences. Too often they hire non–North Americans, like Anna-Louise Plowman as Goddard, who do their best American accent and it sounds like fingernails on a chalkboard.

You're Not Making Any Sense Why is everyone, including the Dalek, prepared to accept the idea that the Dalek can be simply contained in the lower level of the bunker? Even if that were possible — perhaps van Statten has alien technology to enable that — you would think the Doctor and van Statten would have thought of doing that sooner.

Interesting Trivia The Dalek was first found in the Ascension Islands almost 50 years ago, or around 1963, which is when the Daleks first appeared on television. Curiously, the Daleks actually fought the Doctor in 1963 in London in "Remembrance of the Daleks."

Adam Mitchell, the young British genius who acquires items for van Statten's museum, is introduced as another love interest for Rose. He's a nerd and somewhat annoying, but Rose is clearly attracted enough to him to suggest he join her and the Doctor in the TARDIS — which seems to be entirely because he's a bit pretty (although, to be fair, he is). Bruno Langley, who plays Adam, was a reasonably high profile guest star; at the time he had just come off a lengthy stint on *Coronation Street* where he played Todd Grimshaw, the first gay character on the venerable soap.

Van Statten's company name is never stated onscreen, though on the official BBC website it was called Geocomtex. Apparently, van Statten "owns" the internet. Presumably he owns the entire electronic network that comprises the internet, though how that can actually be owned is not clear. The Dalek's download of the internet is odd: presumably it downloaded mostly porn, blogs and online discussion forums about TV shows. (Several drafts of the script had the Doctor asking the Dalek if it enjoyed reading *Buffy the Vampire Slayer* fan fiction. It's a shame that line got cut.) Van Statten's museum has a mixture of artefacts from the *Doctor Who* universe (the Slitheen arm) and pop culture science fiction (the mileometer from the Roswell spaceship) — and a hair dryer.

Robert Shearman's script went through multiple drafts (one of which didn't include the Dalek) and all of them began with a giant portrait of van Statten's face on the roof of a building that then opened into the hangar that received his helicopter. Once in production, the scene was immediately cut by director Joe Ahearne due to the expense.

The TARDIS Chronometer Van Statten's museum is located in an underground bunker in Utah (the nearest city is Salt Lake City). It's 2012.

Fantastic? (GB) The biggest challenge this new *Doctor Who* faced was in how it used the Daleks. In the Classic Series' mythos, these were the deadliest creatures in the universe, would-be galactic conquerors and the Doctor's greatest enemy. In the iconography of British pop culture, they were important enough to merit their own postage stamp. And yet, they were also derided for not being able to climb stairs, for having a sink plunger and for not really looking that credible as a threat. How then to honour the first two aspects and avoid the third?

It's a tricky balance. When American TV producers contemplated bringing back *Doctor Who* in the 1990s, they basically sidestepped the question by suggesting the Daleks could become spider-like robots, or even just be *Terminator*-esque androids. What writer Robert Shearman and executive producer Russell T Davies did was much more daring: they didn't change the Dalek at all, but demonstrated why these creatures, even with their quaint 1960s design, are the deadliest beings ever. How they achieved this was pure genius: they didn't show an army of them, they had the Doctor and Rose face a single Dalek and it nearly succeeded in destroying everyone.

It's the little details that make this work. While the basic shape is kept intact, Ed Thomas and his team of designers "bling up" the Dalek to make it seem more substantial. There are also new innovations, like the 360-degree gun section and a sucker arm that actually makes sense. (Even the "bumps" on the base are some kind of a weapon.) In short, it doesn't look like a guy in a fiberglass suit on ball casters any more. And, thanks to modern post-production techniques, they've added little servo noises to every movement the Dalek makes; it's precisely the sort of thing you wish they could have done with the Daleks in the 1960s.

The result is a Dalek that's lethal in every way. Cunning, resourceful and dangerous, it's more than a shrieking pepperpot, it's a genuine character. The Dalek shrewdly manipulates Rose to aid in restoring it and makes pointed remarks at the Doctor that shows a creature capable of understanding its enemy. There are all sorts of interesting character touches, starting with the idea that the only person a Dalek would talk to is the Doctor, which in one stroke adds a profound sense of pathos to this struggle between two old enemies. The moment where it opens itself up to reveal the actual creature inside shows us how truly vulnerable this Dalek is.

This episode is more than just a great action-adventure story. It's also dark psychological drama: both the Doctor and the Dalek end up defining themselves by what they most abhor and, in so doing, become more like the other. The Doctor goes to a place of hate so vicious the Dalek tells the Doctor he would make a good Dalek, while the Dalek literally reaches out to the light, becoming more human, to its utter disgust. The final confrontation between the two is stunning as, through Rose, both realize this similarity, before doing that which will restore them. The Doctor drops the gun and the Dalek asks for orders to self-destruct.

How lucky we all are, then, to have Christopher Eccleston on hand for this. The way Eccleston sticks his face in the Dalek's eyestalk, circling the Dalek in the cage, is riveting. The intensity of performance transforms a prop into an actual adversary: we treat the Dalek seriously because Eccleston as the Doctor does. The Doctor's reaction when the lights switch on and he realizes he's in a room with a Dalek illustrates this beautifully: the sheer terror on his face as he screams at them to open the door is something the viewer has never seen in him and instantly gives the Dalek credibility as an adversary.

Eccleston goes further than that, revelling in showing us a glimpse into the Doctor's private hell, a combination of uncovered anger and unresolved guilt. It's absolutely electric. Billie Piper is no less brilliant as she goes toe-to-toe with Eccleston in the climax. And Nicholas Briggs's voice work is superlative. He keeps the familiar sound of the Dalek, but imbues it with weariness and pain.

The main problem with "Dalek" is that there will probably never be another Dalek story as good as this. Once you show what an individual Dalek is capable of, it's all the harder to go back to a whole race shouting "Exterminate!" *en masse*. But at least we have this story to show that they can be much more than a mere punchline.

Second Opinion (RS?) One of the best things about this episode — among many brilliant things — is the direction. Joe Ahearne gives us a tenor that's distinct from what we've seen before. Part of this is seeing so much of the action through different viewpoints, literally: we have the Dalek's point of view, distorting facial features like a funhouse mirror, and the view through various monitors, but also the inscrutability of the Dalek's eyestalk. Then, at the end, when the Dalek opens up, we realize that it has a different view of the world again.

There are some superb camera angles: when the Dalek eyestalk swivels between Rose and van Statten, it does so in extreme closeup. And the scene of the Doctor screaming at the Dalek to just die is made so powerful by the close-ness of the camera to Eccleston's raw performance.

The director also knows how to bring out the best in his prize asset: Eccleston himself. When the Dalek says that it is alone and so is the Doctor, the camera is squarely on the Doctor's face so that we can watch the emotion play across it. This is an incredibly brave choice, because it lives or dies on the subtle shades of feeling passing across a man's features. This could have gone very badly indeed; here, it's brilliant, because the director and actor are working in tandem to bring out something astonishing. Best of all, it's done using only visuals.

The strength of "Dalek" is in the mirroring of the Doctor and the Dalek. The central character is a solitary survivor, a vulnerable creature wrapped in a hard shell (both physically and psychologically), fighting and killing but deep down yearning for freedom. And so is the Dalek.

The Psychic Papers: The Daleks

In 1963, a 33-year-old comedy writer named Terry Nation had a falling out with his boss, popular British comedian Tony Hancock, which left him unemployed. Nation decided to take up an offer he had previously rejected: writing seven episodes of a brand new family science-fiction series called *Doctor Who*.

Nation wrote a story that came to be known to *Doctor Who* fans by the title "The Daleks," which was broadcast from late December 1963 to early February 1964 as the series' second full story. Set on the planet Skaro, centuries after a neutron war, which created the Thals, Adonis-like pacifists, and the Daleks, hideous mutants who wish to exterminate the Thals and become the dominant form of life.

After a first episode spent exploring the setting, the second episode introduced the monsters at the heart of the story. In the script, Nation's description of the Daleks reads, "Hideous, machine-like creatures. They are legless, moving on a round base. They have no human features. A lens on a flexible shaft acts as an eye. Arms with mechanical grips for hands . . . The creatures hold strange weapons in their hands."

These were the Daleks.

Nation later stated he derived the visual idea for the Daleks from the Georgian State Dancers, who wore floor-length hooped skirts that gave the impression of gliding. Nation wanted an alien that could glide but didn't look like a man in a rubber suit.

The task of making Nation's description into the iconic figures we now know was down to BBC staff designer Raymond Cusick. (Curiously Cusick wasn't originally assigned the job. His fellow BBC designer, and future film director, Ridley Scott, was originally scheduled but was unavailable for the filming dates.) In 1963, the work on a series like *Doctor Who* was enormous: a single person not only designed the sets but also the props and the special effects. Cusick worked on the sets for the story during the week and the special effects over the weekend at home. It was over the course of one such Sunday that Cusick finished the design of the Dalek.

A round base was impossible, given the budgetary constraints, so Cusick used a series of fiberglass slats to form a skirt section, and decorated them with hemispheres. Budgetary constraints also meant making the arms fixed; they became a gun and a sucker arm in a middle section. The lens was now on a fixed shaft and attached to a top dome with lights that flashed to indicate speech.

An actor sat inside the device, pushing the prop forward and backwards on ball casters, operating the top lights, the gun and sucker arm. The prop obscured all human features; the actor saw out of a grille on the top dome. The final innovation came from BBC sound designer Brian Hodgson, who used a device known as a ring modulator to distort the voices of actors Peter Hawkins and David Graham to sound grating, metallic and electronic.

The result was something unlike any robot or alien created at the time for film or television, something that didn't look or sound remotely human. And while some people mocked the sucker arm that looked like a sink plunger or the lack of motive ability to conquer stairs, the fact is the Dalek design touched on something primal in the hearts of the *Doctor Who* audience, children and adults alike. It was unsettling, alien, a monster of metal. It brought to life Nation's characterization of the Daleks as pitiless xenophobes whose catchphrase (first uttered in "The Daleks" episode four) was "Exterminate." The Daleks were derived from Nation's fear of the Nazi menace growing up in Britain during World War II. The Daleks were Nazism incarnate: faceless, authoritarian killers who saw themselves as the master race. The Daleks' origins in an atomic war also appealed to the zeitgeist of nuclear fears in a world where the Cuban Missile Crisis was a mere 14 months earlier.

That the Daleks weren't robots, but a travel machine for an unseen mutant inside also appealed to the audience. The backstory was similarly shrouded: in "The Daleks," the only information given is that Daleks are the mutated descendents of a race called the Dals. (The closest thing the children of the 1960s had to an origin story for the Daleks was in the *Doctor Who* comic strip, which stated they were the creation of a blue-skinned scientist called Yarvelling.)

The effect the Daleks' first appearance had on the British public was electric. Word of mouth from their first appearance in "The Daleks" episode two — and this was in the days before the internet and even VCRs, so it was literally word of mouth — caused the audience to jump by two million viewers for the third episode. By the final episode, *Doctor Who* was in the top 30 television programs watched in Britain. Terry Nation was immediately asked to write a sequel; "The Dalek Invasion of Earth" was broadcast at the start of *Doctor Who's* second season in 1964.

Nation had shrewd representation at the time in the form of Beryl Vertue (who later became a respected television producer and, much later, mother-in-law to Steven Moffat), who worked out a deal with the BBC that saw Nation retain a portion of the rights to the Daleks. This was fortunate for Nation, as the Daleks were at the centre of the BBC's first major licensing boom, what is known by fans as "Dalekmania." The Daleks were featured in toys, comics (*TV21*), books and even two feature-film adaptations of Nation's first two Dalek serials: *Dr. Who and the Daleks* (1965) and *Daleks: Invasion Earth 2150 AD* (1966), both starring Peter Cushing as a human scientist named Dr. Who (who built a time machine, the *Tardis*, in his back garden). Nation became rich from the experience; designer Raymond Cusick was given a single ex-gratia payment from the BBC.

Onscreen, the Daleks changed substantially after their first appearance, which was designed as a one-off story. The Daleks went from being creatures trapped in their metal city to conquerors of Earth who travelled in spaceships; by their third appearance, in 1965's "The Chase," they had the ability to travel in time as well. By their fourth appearance, which comprised 13 episodes aired from October 1965 to January 1966, they were the undisputed galactic conquerors and the biggest enemy in the *Doctor Who* universe. By then, the Daleks had demonstrated their galactic dominance in the *TV21* comic strip and the *Dalek Annuals*, so a mythology had already taken shape. The Daleks' place in pop culture by that point was assured, even as Dalekmania started to cool.

By the time Patrick Troughton became the Doctor — his first story featured the Daleks, in order to smooth the transition from his predecessor, William Hartnell — Nation hoped to use the strength of the feature films to sell the Daleks as the basis for an American television series. The characters were written out of *Doctor Who* in 1967's "The Evil of the Daleks," with a "final end" as a humanized Dalek faction caused the Daleks to destroy each other.

Nation's plans for the Daleks to conquer the U.S. market never got past development, and the Daleks came back to *Doctor Who* in 1972's "Day of the Daleks," followed by two further appearances with Jon Pertwee's Doctor. But it was 1975's "Genesis of the Daleks" (during Tom Baker's first season as the Doctor) that changed everything. In that story, the Doctor was sent back by the Time Lords to possibly avert the Daleks' creation, and the viewer learned that the Daleks descended from a race called the Kaleds who were at war with the Thals. The chief Kaled scientist, Davros (crippled and disfigured from the war), had derived a mutated creature (which he believed the Kaleds would ultimately become), placed it in a Mark Three travel machine and called it a Dalek. A computer program inhibited these Daleks' emotional development, making them remorseless killers. The Daleks killed the remaining Kaleds and eventually Davros himself, before the Doctor entombed them in their city. (Presumably that detail was included to tie in with the original 1963 story.)

But Davros came back in 1979's "Destiny of the Daleks." In this story, the Daleks are seeking their creator, who is not dead but in suspended animation in the remains of the Kaled city, to aid them in a war. By the Daleks' final three appearances in the Classic Series, Davros is the mouthpiece for the Daleks and the Daleks are there to provide support. In the Daleks' last Classic Series story, 1988's "Remembrance of the Daleks," Davros has become emperor of one faction of the Daleks, who are now plunged into civil war. The Doctor uses the Time Lord weapon, the Hand of Omega, to destroy their home planet, Skaro. Curiously, this was also the first story to show the Daleks climbing stairs, putting the lie to a common joke about them that even the Doctor made in "Destiny of the Daleks."

Terry Nation died in 1997, but his creations lived on. Ironically, the Daleks almost didn't make it to the New Series. During pre-production, negotiations between Terry Nation's estate (which still manages the rights) and the BBC broke down. At one point, Robert Shearman wrote a draft of "Dalek" without the Daleks; the role they served in that story, and in the backstory of the New Series, would have been assumed by the deadly flying spheres that became the Toclafane in "The Sound of Drums"/"Last of the Time Lords." Fortunately, the BBC and the Nation estate were able to come to an agreement.

In the New Series, the Daleks are a key part of the mythology: because they were in the Time War, which resulted in the death of both the Time Lords and the Daleks at the hands of the Doctor, the very presence of the Daleks has a direct effect on the Doctor and impacts his motivation when dealing with them.

In some ways, after "Dalek," the Daleks became integral to *Doctor Who* in a way they hadn't since the 1960s: they made an appearance in every season of the New Series. While some may question the wisdom of this arguable over-reliance, what cannot be questioned is how, with the advent of the New Series, the Daleks took hold of the British public's imagination. The modifications made to their design, which made them more agile, and their ability to actually fly helped, as did the more personal link to the Doctor through the Time War. Advances in special effects also enabled whole armies of Daleks to be seen where groups of only four or five were shown in the Classic Series. They became convincing as galactic conquerors.

Fifty years on, the Daleks show no sign of going away. Not bad for a creation from a comedy writer who took a job he didn't want and a BBC staff designer working on his weekend.

1.07 The Long Game

Written by Russell T Davies **Directed by** Brian Grant

Supporting cast Bruno Langley (Adam Mitchell), Christine Adams (Cathica), Anna Maxwell-Martin (Suki), Simon Pegg (The Editor), Tamsin Greig (nurse), Judy Holt (Adam's mother)

Original airdate May 7, 2005

The Big Idea On Satellite Five, there's something about the TV news that is stunting the growth of human development in the year 200,000. However, Adam Mitchell is too busy failing as a new companion to notice.

Roots and References The advent of cable news (the constant packaging of news); *Max Headroom*; the works of William Gibson, especially *Johnny Mnemonic* (information storage and delivery through a human/cybernetic interface).

Adventures in Time and Space The Fourth Great and Bountiful Human Empire is probably a successor to the Earth Empire in the third Doctor's adventures, which began around the time of 1973's "Frontier in Space" in the 26th century and was in decline by the time of 1972's "The Mutants" in the 31st century. Kronkburgers are fast food in the alternate Earth where Rome never fell, mentioned in the 1979 *Doctor Who Weekly/Doctor Who Magazine* comic strip "The Iron Legion."

The Bad Wolf Effect One of Satellite Five's channels is Bad Wolf TV (which airs a story on the Face of Boe giving birth to Boemina).

The Doctor and Rose Even Adam can see that when given a choice between involving herself in the Doctor's investigation and helping Adam adjust to being in the future, Rose would rather be with the Doctor.

Monster of the Week The Editor in Chief, controlling operations on Satellite Five, is the Mighty Jagrafess of the Holy Hadrojassic Maxarodenfoe ("Max" for short). The Jagrafess is basically a giant amorphous slug living on the ceiling of Floor 500. He speaks in a language only comprehensible to his human agent, the Editor.

Stand Up and Cheer The opening scene is hilarious. It's basically a take-off of the opening of "The End of the World" only with Rose (assisted by the Doctor) playing the part of the knowledgeable traveller who leads the neophite companion to the reveal of the future Earth from orbit. Only this time, Adam faints dead away, a comic stroke that encapsulates the spirit of the episode brilliantly.

Roll Your Eyes Cathica tells the Editor that he'll regret not promoting her. It's said without a trace of irony, which seems odd given that everyone promoted wound up dead.

You're Not Making Any Sense While one aspect of the Doctor's naiveté at the end of the episode is revisited in "Bad Wolf," his decision to evict Adam while leaving his infospike chip active seems similarly ill thought out. Yes, Adam could just live out his life in mediocrity in the hope that he doesn't get noticed and dissected. Or . . . Adam could get noticed, dissected and someone could have technology from the far future in their hands. Or . . . Adam could still use the infospike chip for his own gain in 21st-century Earth.

Interesting Trivia "The Long Game" shows definitively that history in the *Doctor Who* universe can be massively changed. Earth is supposed to be in the Fourth Great and Bountiful Human Empire, a harmonious time where humans and aliens get along; Earth sustains a huge population and even has power over spatial engineering (having created multiple moons). And yet, none of this actually exists, because the Jagrafess (or someone behind the Jagrafess) has changed it, leaving an insular and paranoid society, addicted to their personal technology devices. (See if you can spot the subtle allegory going on here.) This is the flip side of the resolution to "World War Three," where history apparently changed and resulted in a new golden age. We're used to seeing history as immutable — the Classic Series never consciously altered the timeline — so this is new territory.

Right from the early stages of development of the season, Russell T Davies had it in mind to introduce a companion who would fail at travelling with the Doctor in an episode originally titled "The Companion Who Couldn't." Davies piggybacked this on an idea he submitted to the *Doctor Who* production office in the 1980s, about a space station where aliens were controlling Earth through news transmissions. Davies submitted the idea just as the series was going off the air, so it was never seriously looked at by the production team.

The TARDIS Chronometer It's the year 200,000, according to the Doctor.

Fantastic? (GB) You have to wonder about Rose Tyler. Why on Earth did she even suggest Adam accompany her on her travels with the Doctor? There is nothing in "Dalek" that indicates his suitability at all; he distinguishes himself by bragging about nearly starting World War III as an eight-year-old. He's smart (he makes the observation about the lack of aliens on Satellite Five that gets the Doctor thinking), but he's also arrogant and narcissistic. Yet Rose proposed he travel in the TARDIS. The Doctor actually called it: Adam is very pretty. And Rose is apparently that shallow.

If Rose's mistake sets up the episode — a companion who makes an epic fail on his first adventure with the Doctor — she also makes up for it with her courage, tenacity and curiosity. Adam, on the other hand, realizes the potential of Rose's phone being able to dial back to his own time, and immediately manipulates Rose to go with the Doctor so he can exploit this to his own ends. It's not just that Adam commits this one act of selfishness. It's that again and again he makes bad choices, getting himself deeper into trouble until he ultimately endangers everyone. Bruno Langley does a superb job conveying his character's hubris as he consistently makes terrible calls that jeopardize more than the lives of the Doctor and Rose. His comeuppance at the end is delightful.

There's not a lot else to "The Long Game" beyond the companion-who-failed storyline. There is the dystopian satire of the 24-hour news cycle, where events and information are packaged and broadcast without real analysis, but Russell T Davies' potshots at current trends aren't particularly subtle. The idea of a future where the media is a key apparatus of keeping people enslaved isn't particularly new — George Orwell did it back in 1949 in *Nineteen Eighty-Four*. Davies adds some new and interesting spins, where "journalists" become extra processing RAM for a media packaging system that has filtered out the need to ask questions. And yet, as these things go, it's a pretty gentle satire. This story is crying out for something with the Juvenalian sharpness of *Max Headroom* or the bite of a Classic *Who* story like "Vengeance on Varos." It doesn't help that the concept of a civilization hindered from growth by its media is only illustrated by the existence of a Kronkburger stand.

It's been said this story was designed to give Christopher Eccleston and Billie Piper a bit of a break from the rigours of filming (a precursor to the "double banked" Doctor-lite episodes starting in Series Two). The fact that one doesn't notice this immediately is a credit to the scripting, but also to the wonderful guest performances. Simon Pegg is probably the best bit of stunt casting thus far. He's unbelievably creepy, acting like he's the smartest, most stylish and funniest guy alive, even though he's an accountant working with desiccated corpses and taking orders from a piece of meat hanging from the ceiling. And the extended cameo by Tamsin Greig, from the Britcom *Black Books*, is great fun.

Based on the DVD commentary and the shooting script, one has the sense that more was made of Rose's relationship with Adam and that there was more to Adam's motives originally (he wanted to help alleviate his father's arthritis), but this was cut. It's a shame the rationale for Adam's actions were edited from the script, because his messy motivations would have been more real. And, as broadcast, Rose pretty much cuts ties with Adam the moment he faints, which only makes her shallower. Take out the Adam plotline and the additional star turns, and "The Long Game" is rather flimsy. Fortunately, both of those are in place and the result is something entertaining, if unspectacular.

Second Opinion (RS?) I can't help it. I love "The Long Game."

What my co-author misses above is that satire doesn't have to be subtle to be effective — and the degeneration of media in the years following this story indicates that it wasn't misplaced either. When Fox News is the most watched TV news program in the world's largest economy, we need more television to stand up and point out the obvious limitations inherent in the media. "The Long Game" does a fine job.

Kronkburgers aren't the only indication that something is terribly wrong with the human race; there's the startling lack of aliens in all the early scenes, and there's Cathica's almost willful blindness. News media has always pretended it's objective while never able to shake off the cultural norms of the society it hails from. Here we see that taken to an extreme: people think they're individuals and free, but are manipulated into voting against their own interests via a complicit media. Actually, that's not taken to much of an extreme at all . . .

What's fascinating about "The Long Game" is that it gives us the manifesto of the season explicitly. Despite his tough exterior, the ninth Doctor isn't a man of action but is an inspirational figure. He and Rose are in manacles, their other companion both a sellout and trapped by the machine . . . and yet it doesn't matter in the slightest, because the Doctor can inspire Cathica to do the right thing. He does this by challenging her throughout, never allowing her to take the easy route but forcing her to make the right decision. This season isn't about watching a superhero do impossible things; it's a call to action for us, the viewer at home, to stand up for what's right, even if it's hard.

If "The Long Game" gives viewers a healthier skepticism of the news media, then it's a huge success. The complexities of media manipulation aren't easy to convey to a general audience. But this story lands some effective punches and is entertaining to boot. I won't hear a word said against it.

1.08 Father's Day

Written by Paul Cornell **Directed by** Joe Ahearne

Supporting cast Camille Coduri (Jackie Tyler), Shaun Dingwall (Pete Tyler), Julia Joyce (Young Rose), Christopher Llewellyn (Stuart), Frank Rozelaar-Green (Sonny), Natalie Jones (Sarah), Eirlys Bellin (Bev), Rhian James (Suzie), Casey Dyer (Young Mickey)

Original airdate May 14, 2005

The Big Idea The Doctor takes Rose back in time to be with her father when he dies, but she saves him, creating a wound in time that must be sterilized.

Roots and References Ray Bradbury's *A Sound of Thunder* (small changes to the past having big effects); *Back to the Future* (time travel to change one's family); *Only Fools and Horses* (Rose calls Pete a "Del Boy"). The songs "Never Gonna Give You Up" by Rick Astley and "Never Can Say Goodbye" by the Communards are part of the '80s soundtrack; "Don't Mug Yourself" by The Streets bleeds into the past.

Adventures in Time and Space Though it's not explicitly named, Rose touching the baby is an example of the Blinovitch Limitation Effect (1983's "Mawdryn Undead").

The Bad Wolf Effect A poster for a rave called "Energize" (dated 20.11.87) has "Bad Wolf" graffitied on it; it's the lower of the two yellow posters where the second version of Rose and the Doctor stand. There used to be laws protecting time, and the Doctor says that his people would have stopped the Reapers, but the Time Lords are all gone.

Who is the Doctor? The Doctor's anger and disappointment at Rose for averting her father's death probably speaks more to his own sense of regret — having watched his entire planet die, including his family — than to Rose's action. He tells Rose he thought of going back to save his family but never acted on it.

The Doctor and Rose The Doctor and Rose's relationship is never stormier, as the Doctor accuses Rose of wanting to travel with him solely to go back in time and save her father. He even demands the TARDIS key back. Rose's retort — that she knows how sad he is and that he'll be back — is the sort of ugly but true remark made in relationship breakdowns. Growing up with a legacy of stories of her adventurous father suggests that Rose might have a psychological predisposition for her attraction to the Doctor. Does Rose see the Doctor as a father substitute, or is she looking for a potential partner who personifies her childhood influences?

Monster of the Week The Reapers (never named onscreen) are huge flying monsters, which look part insect and part bat, and function like bacteria sterilizing a wound in time. Anything new, any disturbance in time, such as a paradox, makes them stronger. They devour people.

Stand Up and Cheer Pete's realization that he wasn't there for Rose is heartbreaking, because he sees right through Rose's tale of future him reading bedtime stories and taking her on picnics. It's also triumphant because he gets to be the father she never had, saving the world by sacrificing himself. His line "I've had all these extra hours!" causes Rose to dissolve in tears and probably has the same effect on most of the audience.

Roll Your Eyes The period detail on the costuming is well researched and quite faithful to the 1980s, particularly the bridal party dresses. Unfortunately. It makes our eyes bleed . . .

You're Not Making Any Sense We're told that the older something is, the stronger it is. So why do the Reapers continually attack older people? They take Mickey's mum, but not Mickey. They attack Stuart's dad but not Sarah, pausing in front of her before moving to attack the much older vicar.

Interesting Trivia Rose seems to have swallowed Jackie's hype regarding her father wholesale, enthusing that he won third prize at bowling at Didcot. Didcot is a town in Oxfordshire whose claims to fame are a nuclear reactor and railway museum, though Rose speaks of it as though it were Wembley Stadium. In actuality, it's an unremarkable achievement in a parochial competition.

Jackie's full maiden name is Jacqueline Andrea Susette Prentice. Pete doesn't get it right at their wedding and Jackie says, "If it's good enough for Princess Di," a reference to Diana mangling Charles's name in their 1981 wedding.

When history is changed, the car radio plays music from the 21st century and the words "Watson come here, I need you" are heard through the phone lines. That's Alexander Graham Bell's voice from the very first phone call (although historical records suggest that he actually said, "I want you").

One of the themes of this episode is "what's meant to be." We see this through Pete's predestined death, young Mickey's instinctual attraction to the older Rose, and Stuart and Sarah's tale of how they met. Interestingly, the Doctor's response to their story is that he's never had a life like that, suggesting that he doesn't play by the fatalistic rules.

The title of this episode was kept under wraps for longer than usual before its airdate, because the title made it easy to guess it was about Rose's father.

Russell T Davies' initial idea was that this episode would be cheaper to produce and take its cues from *The Twilight Zone.* It was originally meant to be a small character piece where Rose and the Doctor investigated the death of her father. Writer Paul Cornell suggested adding the Reapers to the mix. BBC head of drama Jane Tranter enthusiastically agreed to this, as she felt the stories in development needed more monsters. Consequently, the cost-saving episode became quite expensive because of the CGI!

The TARDIS Chronometer Various locations around the Powell Estate and an unnamed London church on November 7, 1987.

Fantastic? (RS?) The power of this story is in its emotion. Indeed, it's almost purely emotionally driven from start to finish. The Doctor agreeing to take Rose to see her father's death indicates just how off his filters are. That he does it a second time is astonishing. Nearly every interaction Rose has with her father is a Catherine wheel of emotional energy; she's all over the psychological map, with almost no ability to be tactful or to lie gracefully.

The viewer gets caught up in the emotion too, because every one of us has probably wondered about having the perfect parent, instead of the flawed humans we all have. And then, when our own turn rolls around, we realize that, as much as we'd like to be the perfect parent every child wants, we're just as flawed as our own parents were. The tiny clues that Pete amasses — Rose's silence when he asks about himself in the future, her lie about him being the perfect father — are the sort of thing that would usually be there just as asides for the viewer to notice; that Pete picks up on them is an indication that the episode isn't playing by the usual rules. Because so much preliminary work is put into developing Pete, we can see that he immediately knows Rose's imagined version of him is fiction through Shaun Dingwall's performance, rather than any heavy-handed dialogue.

As a result, the central dilemma is fabulous. The argument between the Doctor and Rose feels real, especially because it doesn't end when he returns, but only when she apologises. We know intellectually that the Doctor's right, but in our hearts we'd probably all do what Rose does. As a result, their disagreement doesn't feel contrived; both sides make sense.

However, the real brilliance of this story is that Pete is able to read Rose like a book, piecing together what should be outrageous ideas. The ostensible mystery — how to put time back the way it was — isn't given more than a cursory glance, because it's not the point. Everyone knows how to put time back the way it was, but nobody wants to take that action, not even the Doctor. Despite this, Pete works out how to reset time and does what must be done, because somebody has to be the adult in the room. In many ways, this is the story of an ordinary man learning to deal with the extraordinary, simply by using his brain.

The only downside is that, in order to make the climax work, the Doctor has to be removed from the plot. Having him eaten by the Reapers is an effective moment, but it does rob the story of some of its power, implicitly acknowledging that the Doctor would have solved the problem in some other way. Instead, he has to be taken out of the picture so that it can be Pete who makes the final decision. This is a structural flaw that was probably avoidable, but only by rewriting from the ground up, so you can see why they stuck with it.

Pete hitting on Rose is deeply uncomfortable and not just because he's her father; he's a 33-year-old man trapped in a bad marriage who's just met a beautiful 19-year-old girl. And then, just to muddy the waters further, after rejecting his advances outright, she proffers her arm in the same way the Doctor does to her. Does that make the Doctor a slightly creepy old man or does it indicate a purer form of love, one unsullied by sex? The story leaves it to us to decide.

There are also some very effective images, thanks to the strong — and at times unusual — direction. The Doctor in the church pulpit is a fabulous visual, while it's notable that Pete's vase only cracks when he dies. Rose's smile when she hears the Doctor coming back for her — even if he is warning her of imminent danger — is fantastic. And the TARDIS being just a police box is very effective indeed, undercut slightly by the fact that it's never explained.

The only bit that doesn't work for me is the "Who said you're not important?" scene, where the Doctor tells two ordinary people how impressive their ordinary lives are. It's too cheesy and disconnected from the rest of the story, which grinds to a halt so the scene can take place.

"Father's Day" is one of the standout episodes from the first series. It packs an astonishingly potent punch with an immensely effective and likeable guest star in Shaun Dingwall, Rose on a mental roller-coaster and the Doctor both harsh and full of sadness. The tone is somewhat odd but that just adds to the atmosphere. The most emotional *Doctor Who* story yet.

Second Opinion (GB) The moment you hear Rose talking about her dead father, over a picture of him, you know you're in for something different and possibly special. "Father's Day" is both. The wonderful pre-credits sequence feels like nothing *Doctor Who* has done before and that sense of ambition permeates the whole production.

Unlike my co-author, I didn't think much of Joe Ahearne's work on "Dalek." It wasn't as compelling as the other television projects he's directed, like the 1999 British series *Ultraviolet*. However, his work on "Father's Day" is wonderful. He takes the small scale of the story and uses it to his advantage, setting it in a creepy, empty world that has a nightmarish quality to it. He makes the story profoundly eerie with the visuals — the car that killed Pete doing a ghostly lap around the church again — and the Reapers only add to the off-kilter feel of the story.

Paul Cornell's script is sublime. On the surface, the episode plays like pure science fiction — the undiluted time-travel story that *Doctor Who* never normally touches — but, after showing some nifty and elaborate time rules (that are later broken!), it becomes clear the story is not about time travel really. That's just an elaborate camouflage for a drama centred on the complexity and messiness of family: how they fail to live up to expectations one moment and exceed them the next.

There's so much more to love: the 1987 setting, which feels absolutely right, down to the Rick Astley on the car radio; Murray Gold's main theme, which is a cunning riff on "Someday My Prince Will Come"; the punch-the-air moment where the Doctor tells Stewart and Sarah that their first meeting at a pub makes them unique; the heartbreak in every scene where Pete dies.

"Father's Day" is creepy, sad, haunting and gloriously redemptive. It's also profoundly courageous in its themes and its storytelling. It may be the best story this season.

· ·

Billie Piper

Despite being just 23, Billie Piper was already a major celebrity in the U.K. before *Doctor Who*. With a record deal at 15, she was the youngest artist to debut with a U.K. number one single, "Because We Want To" (under the name Billie) in 1998. By 2005, she had recorded several successful albums and been in a highly publicized marriage to TV presenter and DJ Chris Evans (they had separated before she began filming on *Doctor Who*). Piper was looking to break into acting and did so with a critically acclaimed turn in a contemporary adaptation of *The Canterbury Tales* shown on the BBC in 2003 before getting the role of Rose Tyler.

Piper stayed for two seasons, although she would reprise the role several times.

Following *Doctor Who*, Piper played Sally Lockhart in the 2006 BBC adaptation of Philip Pullman's *The Ruby in the Smoke* (her co-star was future Doctor Matt Smith) and its 2007 sequel *The Shadow in the North*. From 2007 to 2011, Piper played escort Belle Du Jour in the ITV drama series *The Secret Diary of a Call Girl*.

1.09—1.10 The Empty Child / The Doctor Dances

Written by Steven Moffat **Directed by** James Hawes

Supporting cast John Barrowman (Captain Jack Harkness), Richard Wilson (Dr. Constantine), Florence Hoath (Nancy), Luke Perry (Timothy Lloyd), Albert Valentine (The Child), Cheryl Fergison (Mrs. Lloyd), Damian Samuels (Mr. Lloyd), Robert Hands (Algy), Joseph Tremain (Jim), Jordan Murphy (Ernie), Martin Hodgson (Jenkins), Vilma Hollingbery (Mrs. Harcourt), Noah Johnson (Voice of the Empty Child)

Original airdates May 21 and 28, 2005

The Big Idea An empty Chula ambulance has been brought to London at the height of the Blitz by rogue Time Agent Captain Jack Harkness. What does it have to do with a child in a gas mask looking for his mummy?

Roots and References Romantic comedies, including Steven Moffat's own British TV series *Coupling*; World War II movies about the home front, like *Mrs. Miniver*; zombie movies, particularly *28 Days Later* (which features Christopher Eccleston); *Oliver!* and *Annie* (the gang of kids out of a West End musical); the 1964 pilot to *Star Trek*, "The Cage" (aliens reconstructing a human being without a template). Glenn Miller's "In the Mood" and "Moonlight Serenade" both play.

Adventures in Time and Space The Chula ambulance is jumping time tracks, one of the oldest pieces of technobabble in *Doctor Who*, dating back to 1965's "The Space Museum." Albion Hospital appears for the second time this season (although in "Aliens of London" it was close to Central London; now it's in the East End). Captain Jack is a Time Agent from the 51st century, a shout-out to the Time Agents who pursued the mad scientist Magnus Greel from the 51st century in 1977's "The Talons of Weng-Chiang." (Writer Steven Moffat sets a number of his adventures during this period.)

The Bad Wolf Effect If you use the pause and zoom functions on your DVD player when Jack is straddling the bomb in the tractor beam, you can see on the side of the bomb the German phrase "Schlechter Wolf," which translates to "Bad Wolf." (Actually the translation is somewhat dodgy; it's probably closer to "Unsatisfactory Wolf"!)

Who is the Doctor? The second episode in particular poses the question: does the Doctor "dance" (with all the subtextual glory that "dancing" implies)? For a long time, this question was anathema to old-time *Doctor Who* fans. Aside from a couple of kisses with Grace Holloway in the 1996 TV Movie, the Doctor in the Classic Series was about as asexual as they come. This story opens the door to the possibility the Doctor has a sex life.

The Doctor and Rose The whole story is predicated around the idea that the Doctor finds a rival in Captain Jack, who sweeps Rose off her feet. The Doctor is annoyed that Rose assumes the Doctor can't "dance," which is probably the first example of a sustained double entendre in the entire history of *Doctor Who*. On the literal level, Rose challenges the Doctor to show he can dance. He's awkward and unwilling to do so, until the opportunity comes to demonstrate the universe's greatest example of cock-blocking with Jack at the end of the story, appropriately during Glenn Miller's "In the Mood."

Monster of the Week The titular Empty Child is a four-year-old boy named Jamie, who died after a bombing raid. He was reconstructed and brought back to life by nanogenes from the Chula ambulance; the nanogenes had never encountered a human before and so put it together as they thought it should be, complete with gas mask. Jamie then became a carrier of nanogenes that "repair" any human it encounters according to Jamie's template, making them undead zombies with gas-mask faces, made of skin and bone, and the mind of a child, all wanting their mummies.

Stand Up and Cheer The climax is not only the stand up and cheer moment of the episode, but perhaps the whole series. The solution — for Nancy to admit to the child that she's his mother — is remarkably elegant, but it's also deeply affecting. Watching the emotionally damaged Doctor then exultantly restore everyone, revelling that everybody lives, brings tears to the eyes.

Roll Your Eyes The scene where Nancy puts Mr. Lloyd in his place is supposed to demonstrate how smart and resourceful Nancy is, but it seems superfluous to the story.

You're Not Making Any Sense Leaving aside the fact that the barrage balloon is historically inaccurate (they were tethered with wire cable, not rope) and the fact that this particular untethered barrage balloon seems to descend to rooftop height only to go upward once something as heavy as a human female grabs hold . . . just what the heck is the child doing on the roof in the first place?

Interesting Trivia This story introduces Captain Jack Harkness, who goes on to be a major player in the *Doctor Who* universe (and beyond). He's an omnisexual flyboy in the shape of a square-jawed macho hero, with an unlimited talent for innuendo. His background — Time Agent, con man, missing two years of his life — is clearly a setup for an ongoing mystery that needs to be solved . . . only it never gets looked at ever again. Fortunately the character's going to far more interesting places soon enough.

Jack's unashamedly bisexual, actively revelling in all the innuendo while also being there as someone who can wield a gun when the Doctor can't. He might very well be TV's first queer action hero. Rather than being a token, what makes Jack work is that he's so much fun. Where this works best of all is within the confines of *Doctor Who* as a family show; it puts the brakes on how far the innuendo can go, which only makes it more amusing. Thus, in the 51st century, we're all going to be impossibly good-looking and have sex with everything that moves. It's good to know our future is heading somewhere fun . . .

This is the first time the phone on the police box exterior of the TARDIS is ever used, though the inside panel should be white, not blue.

Naturally, this being *Doctor Who*, historical inaccuracies abound; along with the aforementioned barrage balloon, wire recordings or recordable gramophones would have been used in the hospital, not tape-recording technology, which wasn't available in Britain at this time. (Magnetic tape was invented in the 1930s, but it was German technology.)

The TARDIS Chronometer It's 1941, the height of the London Blitz. According to RAF records in the first episode of *Torchwood* ("Everything Changes"), Captain Jack Harkness disappeared after January 21, 1941, so presumably this story takes place around then.

Fantastic? (GB) One of my favourite songs happens to play throughout "The Empty Child"/"The Doctor Dances." "Moonlight Serenade" by the Glenn Miller Orchestra has a pretty melody, but the big band sound adds such lushness that it evokes feelings of romance and visions of bygone places. The result is one of the most gorgeous songs ever recorded. To create that sound, you need a full orchestra in, quite literally, perfect harmony.

"The Empty Child" and "The Doctor Dances" are like that.

Never mind the stunning flight by barrage balloon over Blitzed London, the Doctor's exchanges with Nancy and the kids ("I don't know if it's Marxism in action or a West End musical"), the charming first appearance of Captain Jack or the creepy first appearance of the child. Moffat had me at hello, with the Doctor and Rose bantering about the need to come to Earth for milk and Rose's frustration that the Doctor won't give her some Spock.

It would be easy to reduce Steven Moffat's first script for *Doctor Who* to the building blocks that will serve him in good stead for the next five years: a witty, bordering on mouthy, female supporting character; horror in something otherwise commonplace; a world of mystery created with thoughtful precision; funny dialogue and a gentle mocking of the series mythos. (I love the Doctor's exchange with Jack about the utility of creating a sonic screwdriver.) All of this is certainly on display in these two episodes. But what makes this story so utterly wonderful is that it's so much more.

First, it's a horror story. The use of the child here is sublime: that all this fear and terror is caused by four-year-old is a frightening concept. The revelation that the patients *aren't* wearing gas masks is deeply unsettling, but it's the logical extension of a favourite theme in British genre television, body horror, as well as Steven Moffat's favourite Classic Series story, "The Ark in Space." It adds a cunning, chilling nuance: the horror is now in becoming something alien, even though it looks commonplace. Furthermore, Moffat and director James Hawes are observant of the cardinal rule: don't show as much as you think you should, but when you do, go for the jugular. All of this together is why Dr. Constantine's transformation is so scary.

Secondly, it's a comedy — and a romantic comedy at that. Jack is what the Doctor would be if he were reimagined as a Hollywood hero: he carries a sonic weapon, flies a cool spaceship and uses psychic paper as a means of flirting. Jack's the dashing guy that our outsider-nerd hero has to beat in order to win the affections of Rose. Naturally, this being *Doctor Who*, it subverts as much as it borrows from other genres. For a romantic comedy to truly work, the men need to be able to "dance," and the best this story can do is have the Doctor articulate the question and boogie-woogie to "In the Mood." But that alone is charming, particularly with dialogue that crackles.

Third, it's great science fiction. It establishes rules for its world and then delivers a giant surprise in how the world interacts with these rules. Everything is laid out in "The Empty Child" to solve the mystery in "The Doctor Dances." Nancy's relationship with Jamie and the other children, the Chula ambulance, the nanogenes . . . it's all there. The twist is in how all those elements come together. It's the best sort of science-fiction writing, the sort created by a comedy writer who understands that good science fiction is good gag writing.

But really, all of these things would fall flat if "The Empty Child"/"The Doctor Dances" wasn't a full-blooded character-driven drama in the first place. The key to the mystery is Nancy, who is haunted by her failure to save her son. When the Doctor meets her, she's parenting other orphans, pretending to be their mother in "family" dinners in someone else's house. The only way forward for her is to admit what she really is. Nancy admitting she's Jamie's mother not only stops the jeopardy, it provides emotional resonance.

However, the success of this two-part story, what pushes it from the very good to the unbeatable, are all the other elements working in concert with the script. Director James Hawes gives everything a cinematic gloss, creating the most romantic-looking wartime London possible, and builds on the creepiness of the child by only showing him in partial views or from a distance, until the horror of what he's capable of is fully revealed. The cast brings their A game as well. Richard Wilson's brief turn as Dr. Constantine is particularly memorable, while John Barrowman is charming, dashing and very funny.

And if that weren't special enough, we have kindred spirits in the Doctor and Nancy: people who never talk about the loss they've experienced, who try to help others while exchanging barbed witticisms. Both Eccleston and Florence Hoath relish the opportunity given them. The climax, where the Doctor triumphantly proclaims that everybody lives, is Christopher Eccleston's greatest moment in the role of the Doctor.

Like "Moonlight Serenade," "The Empty Child"/"The Doctor Dances" is amazing precisely because it's written, directed and performed by people at the top of their game. Any one of the story elements would make for good television. All of them together is perfection, giving you everything you want, and more. To paraphrase the Doctor, we all need more days like this.

Second Opinion (RS?) The Time War has been a rather subtle element to the arc that's played out through the season. Rather than seeing the epic battle between the Time Lords and the Daleks, complete with a dramatic regeneration, we started with the immediate after-effects and moved on from there. The Time War was undoubtedly a huge, universe-shaking event, but it's the effect on the Doctor that's most important.

The emotionally damaged Doctor forces jollity into situations where it isn't quite appropriate, he lacks tact and he never quite succeeds at what he does best. He's largely been going through the motions, while Rose's humanity has slowly broken through his defences.

This story is, in many ways, the culmination of his character arc. After a season of continual failure — he accidentally kills the Nestene, he coldly watches Cassandra die, he can't save Pete Tyler — we see a rare and total victory for the Doctor, against the odds.

What's clever is the Doctor's praise for the British role in the war: there's an unstoppable war machine, rolling over everything in its path, until a tiny damp island stands up and says no. Coming from a Doctor who insulted humans for their beans-on-toast ordinariness at the start of the season, this is a remarkable turnaround, rather than the British jingoism it initially appears to be. It's a clever metaphor for the Doctor himself (and similar to what Rose will say about him in the season finale). No matter how terrible the threat or how small you are in comparison, what matters is standing up and saying no.

Even the Doctor's interactions with Captain Jack reflect this new softening:

whereas the Doctor previously dismissed people, like Adam, who made mistakes, here he tolerates Jack's error, giving him space to redeem himself, and earn a place on board the TARDIS.

The only downside is that the show hasn't quite caught up with reality. Rose is utterly shocked that a 51st-century guy would be into other guys. Rose is a modern 21st-century woman; she's probably seen this every Friday night down at Club Babylon. Jack's pan-sexuality is definitely something worth exploring on TV — as *Torchwood* will go on to do — but its introduction here doesn't quite resonate.

But that's just a tiny misstep in what is otherwise a sublime story, one that has everything from actual character development for the Doctor to the ability to scare the living daylights out of you. Just this once, everything works.

John Barrowman

Before he was cast as Captain Jack Harkness, John Barrowman had a burgeoning career in musical theatre in London's West End, though his best known role in film and television was a small part in the 2004 film *De-Lovely*, where he sang a duet with Kevin Kline's Cole Porter. (Barrowman was almost cast as Will in *Will & Grace* before losing out to Eric McCormack because he wasn't "gay enough"; the irony, of course, being that Barrowman is gay while McCormack is straight.) Barrowman, though born Scottish, was raised in the United States and picked up an American accent while he lived there.

Barrowman's Captain Jack is the lead in the *Doctor Who* spinoff *Torchwood*, which has had four seasons (in varying forms) from 2006 onward. Barrowman has performed in other roles on series such as *Desperate Housewives* and has released several albums.

The Sonic Screwdriver

The Doctor's trusty gadget first appeared in 1968's "Fury From the Deep" where it did just what the name implied: it raised or lowered screws using sound waves. In the 1970s, the device's abilities were expanded to include unlocking doors, detonating landmines and even burning a hole through metal. Throughout the Classic Series, it was unable to work on wood, and in the New Series it is established that it cannot open anything with a deadlock seal. The original was destroyed by the Terileptils in 1982's "The Visitation" and wasn't used again until it resurfaced in the 1996 TV Movie. In the New Series, the device is actually a sonic probe capable of many more things than just loosening screws . . .

1.11 Boom Town

Written by Russell T Davies **Directed by** Joe Ahearne

Supporting cast John Barrowman (Captain Jack Harkness), Noel Clarke (Mickey Smith), Annette Badland (Margaret Blaine), William Thomas (Mr. Cleaver), Mali Harries (Cathy), Aled Pedrick (Idris Hopper), Alan Ruscoe (Slitheen)

Original airdate June 4, 2005

The Big Idea The Doctor foils a plan by the last Slitheen to destroy Cardiff, but must then take her home to face the death penalty.

Roots and References *Buffy the Vampire Slayer* (a monster as mayor, mortal enemies having civilized conversation, relationships being as important as murderous creatures).

Adventures in Time and Space Rose has been to Justicia, in the tie-in novel *The Monsters Within*. The Doctor tells the others he landed in the 1960s where the TARDIS disguised itself and got stuck, which happened in 1963's "An Unearthly Child." Margaret says that if she'd refused her first kill, her father would have fed her to the venom grubs, which appeared in 1965's "The Web Planet." Tribophysics was mentioned in 1975's "Pyramids of Mars." Rose describes the chameleon circuit as a cloaking device, as was done in the 1996 TV Movie. William Thomas (playing Mr. Cleaver in the teaser) is the first actor in the New Series to have previously appeared in the Classic Series (he was the undertaker in 1988's "Remembrance of the Daleks").

The Bad Wolf Effect Margaret Blaine's project is called *Blaidd Drwg*, Welsh for bad wolf, although she chose the name at random. The Doctor speculates that two words could be following them around through space and time, but then dismisses the idea. Rose says that she's heard those words lots of times before.

Who is the Doctor? Margaret infers from the Doctor's insights that he's a killer, just like her. The Doctor doesn't answer that charge, but he nonetheless is willing to take her to her execution and even has the stomach to accompany her to her last meal, an indication that he's been to some pretty dark places.

The Doctor and Rose Mickey confronts Rose regarding her ambivalence toward him, saying she effectively keeps Mickey on standby and will always do so while the Doctor is around. The Doctor, meanwhile, tells Jack he has no interest in Rose and Mickey's relationship, though the fact that he's saying this while watching the pair on the TARDIS monitor suggests he's lying to Jack . . . or himself.

Monster of the Week Margaret Blaine, a.k.a. Blon Fel-Fotch Passameer-Day Slitheen (previously seen in "Aliens of London"/"World War Three"). When her life is in danger, a female Raxacoricofallapatorian can manufacture a poison dart within her own finger. Excess poison can be exhaled through the lungs.

Stand Up and Cheer The dinner and bondage scene is electrifying. The Doctor is forced to have dinner with someone he's about to kill, and she starts off trying to murder him, moves into pleading for her life and then turns the tables on the Doctor, exposing his lifestyle as that of a killer who runs from the consequences of his actions. And every one of her points is legitimate. It's a deeply uncomfortable scene, because we don't like to think of our hero as being flawed, but it's enormously effective because we've never seen anything like this before. The rapport between Christopher Eccleston and Annette Badland is superb.

Roll Your Eyes We saw Rose's first trip in the TARDIS and her first step into the past. Not letting us see her first trip to an alien planet, but just telling us about it, was an enormous oversight.

You're Not Making Any Sense Margaret Blaine manages to become Lord Mayor of a major city without ever being photographed or seen on TV, unlike every politician in the last 50 years. At the reception, the photographer snaps a single photo of her and she puts her hand up in front of her face in reaction. However, in the photo in the paper, her hand is already in front of her face.

Interesting Trivia The TARDIS needing to refuel is rather mundane for such a fantastic and magical vehicle (as well as something never mentioned before). We're also given a potted history of what a police box was originally for (as a temporary lock-up for criminals, although this is actually inaccurate; it was mostly used for communication with the station and as a mobile base for police officers). These properties bring the TARDIS down to Earth, by making it seem like a police car stopping for petrol (taking advantage of the Rift introduced earlier in the season), with a criminal locked in the back. However, the final property of the TARDIS goes in the other direction: it has even more magical properties than even the Doctor was aware of, thus counterpointing the earlier mundanity.

The TARDIS's materialization in this episode has implications for the spinoff series *Torchwood*, as it creates a paving stone with a perception filter on the landing spot. The Torchwood hub will have a second entrance via this paving stone, allowing people to enter and exit unnoticed.

Does your background matter? That's one of the central questions this episode asks and the answer appears to be yes. If you're forced to make your first kill at age 13 (or be killed yourself), then killing could become fairly normalized. Margaret is the way she is because she was brought up that way and, in a sense, it's the only life she knows. Regressing her to an egg gives her a chance to start anew with a different family, so that killing isn't part of her repertoire. Compare that to the Doctor: he's simultaneously unable to cause death in the name of justice and identified as a killer, one who dare not look back. Where Margaret is a prisoner of her upbringing, the Doctor desperately flees his background: he never discusses his early history, his childhood or even his name. So if he'd looked into the heart of the TARDIS and regressed to a baby, would he grow up to be the same Doctor?

We know what the extrapolator does — it allows you to surf your way out of a nuclear meltdown thanks to its forcefield — but where did it come from? We're never told. Given its importance in future episodes, it's bizarre that this is just handwaved away.

The TARDIS Chronometer A caption states that it's six months after the events of "Aliens of London"/"World War Three," making it September 2006. The TARDIS has stopped in Cardiff to refuel. Immediately after the story ends, they're heading to Raxacoricofallapatorius.

Fantastic? (RS?) "Boom Town" might look somewhat light and fluffy, but it has weight. Plotwise, it's a crucial story in setting up *Torchwood* and the two-part season finale. Arcwise, it's the episode when the season-long Bad Wolf references start to come together. Character-wise, it's interested in examining both Rose and Mickey's relationship and the Doctor's morality.

But, in another sense, it *is* somewhat light and fluffy — and all the better for it. The comedy flows from character, as all good comedy should: the rapport between the Doctor, Rose and Jack that's undercut by Mickey's "My God, have you seen yourselves?"; the "accidental" deaths of all the safety inspectors on the Blaidd Drwg project; Jack's oh-so-serious plan turning out to be mobile phones; Margaret realizing she's gone native; the teacup smashing in the next room after the Doctor announces his presence.

This episode is incredibly disjointed. First it's the TARDIS crew having a fun day, then it's a comedic chase, then there's the most serious arc scene yet, then it's a deadly serious moral debate and finally it's a character piece about Rose's relationship. But what's great is just how much attention each of these facets receives. The moral debate is as serious as the comedy is funny, while the character stuff feels achingly real. This is what it would be like to live in the Doctor's world, especially if you were the boyfriend left behind.

The operative word for this episode is "consequences." Which automatically makes it an inversion of almost every other *Doctor Who* story, because *Doctor Who* is fundamentally uninterested in consequences. "Boom Town" pinpoints that brilliantly: a life where you do what you want and then swan off afterwards is no different from being a murderous green monster. That's a courageous and unpopular viewpoint and the prime reason this story isn't better loved, but it also makes for fascinating television.

Mickey is deeply upset that Rose left him, feeling like he's nothing and can't even go out with a girl from the shop — whom he's only dating for her stability — because when Rose calls he comes running. At the end, Rose says he deserves better — and she's partly right. What's great about this scene is that it takes the Mickey from "Rose" and makes him into a real person. Where "World War Three" turned him into a hero, this story turns him into a human being. This is where TV succeeds enormously: recurring characters have the ability to grow and deal with the consequences of earlier actions. Meanwhile, in another development from a previous episode, Margaret becomes a sympathetic and surprisingly affecting character when she decides not to kill Cathy upon realizing Cathy is pregnant. You actually feel sorry for an enormous silly green monster sitting on a toilet, which is an incredible feat unto itself.

The Blaidd Drwg scene is haunting and creepy as you start to ponder the implications . . . before the Doctor's quick dismissal of it as a coincidence. It's also an excellent setup for the finale, letting us know that this is going somewhere, but defying us to figure it out.

The Doctor orders steak in the restaurant, which might have seemed innocuous to new fans, but not to those of us who remember that he was explicitly a vegetarian from 1985's "The Two Doctors" onwards. It's not remarked upon here, so it's possible the production team weren't even aware of this detail. As to whether the Doctor would naturally be a vegetarian or not . . . it's a thorny one. If he wants to avoids deliberate cruelty and harm to living beings, then shouldn't he be a natural vegetarian? Many of us fallible humans would like to avoid cruelty, but we also have to live in the world in the way the Doctor doesn't (and we're also subjected to a lot of propoganda by the meat and dairy industry). Talk to any vegetarian (like myself) and they'll argue fervently that the Doctor should be. Talk to any non-vegetarian (like my co-author) and they'll argue the opposite. But what's most frustrating of all is that the production team didn't pick up on the fact that this is the first time in the new series that he isn't, as this dichotomy would resonate with this episode's themes quite nicely.

Aside from dealing with consequences, there's another reason this story isn't better liked, and it's the *deus ex machina* climax. It's really a setup for the season finale, but is somewhat unsatisfying for this episode. A hitherto unmentioned power from the TARDIS saves the day? Say what? If only we'd had some clue — anything, anything at all — that the TARDIS was a telepathic, living machine with incredible powers that even the Doctor was unaware of!

The Doctor's "Off we go then, always moving on" line reflects Margaret's earlier charges, demonstrating that her points really did resonate: the Doctor isn't sticking around, he's left devastation in his wake and ruined lives (not least of which is Mickey's). So off he goes, not looking back.

"Boom Town" is a fascinating episode with a lot to say. And it's highly entertaining, to boot. This isn't a watertight script plotted within an inch of its life, but a thoughtful piece, interested in raising questions about our hero. If you like your *Doctor Who* funny, serious or romantic — or if you just like big green monsters — there's something here for you.

Second Opinion (GB) At the risk of sounding like Simon Cowell, let's come back to planet Earth for a moment. With the utmost respect to my colleague, "Boom Town" is good, but not *that* good. Yes, it makes a virtue out of its budget constraints to create some superb character pieces. Yes, the sequence where the Doctor and friends block Margaret's escape is very funny. And yes, Christopher Eccleston and Annette Badland are thrilling to watch in a dinner scene with comedy for an appetizer and serious, meaty drama for a main course.

But there's no real story here. The mood of the piece defines it, in an attempt to veil the fact that the plot is something out of a cartoon. A Slitheen miraculously becomes mayor so she can inexplicably demolish a major Cardiff landmark to create a nuclear reactor (one in the *centre of the city*, I hasten to add) and then, several years down the road when it's built, blow it up so she can activate the device she handily hides — wait for it — *under the architectural model of the reactor*. The Doctor might as well have pitched up in Cardiff in the Mystery Machine — though, frankly, Shaggy could have solved this case without the aid of Scooby snacks.

The counter-argument my co-author might make, were he not too busy ascending to rapturous heights after watching this, is that the plot serves as a placeholder in order to enable the powerful character set pieces to happen. To which I say, nonsense. A departure from the format of *Doctor Who* like "Boom Town" should honour the serious drama more by making the story actually credible. But what we have here is either lazy, cynical or both.

And all that superb drama leads nowhere. For the third time this season, a serious moral dilemma for the Doctor is rendered moot by taking the decision out of his hands; here, he doesn't have to deliver Margaret to be executed because she's magically made into an egg. Rose, confronted by her selfishness and lack of consideration for Mickey, just resigns herself to thinking that Mickey deserves better. The promise that the characters will change in some significant way is left empty. In the end, it's just the illusion of change: everyone's soulful and reflective, but nothing has made any long term impact outside of the story's confines.

"Boom Town" has its enthusiasts — my co-author is not only enamoured with it, he's clearly planning to buy it flowers and take it out for dinner, dancing and possibly bondage — and while I rate the weighty character scenes and adore Murray Gold's score, I'm not one of them. It's a fun romp. Nothing more than that.

1.12—1.13 Bad Wolf / The Parting of the Ways

Written by Russell T Davies **Directed by** Joe Ahearne

Supporting cast John Barrowman (Captain Jack Harkness); Jo Joyner (Lynda Moss); Jamie Bradley (Strood); Abi Eniola (Crosbie); Davina McCall (Davinadroid); Patterson Joseph (Rodrick); Jenna Russell (floor manager); Anne Robinson (Anne Droid); Trinny Woodall (Voice of Trine-E); Susannah Constantine (Voice of Zu-Zana); Jo Stone Fewings, Nisha Nayar (programmers); Dominic Burgess (Agorax); Karren Winchester (Fitch); Kate Loustau (Colleen); Sebastian Armesto (Broff); Martha Cope (controller); Alan Ruscoe, Paul Kasey (androids); Barnaby Edwards, Nicholas Pegg, David Hankinson (Dalek operators); Nicholas Briggs (Dalek voice)

Introducing David Tennant (the Doctor)

Original airdates June 11 and 18, 2005

The Big Idea The TARDIS crew is trapped in a series of reality TV shows, which leads them to discover an enormous Dalek fleet on the edges of the solar system.

Roots and References Reality TV, especially U.K. versions of *Big Brother*, *The Weakest Link* and *What Not to Wear*; the 1960s Dalek comic strip in *TV21* (the iconic look of the Dalek space fleet).

Adventures in Time and Space The Face of Boe (introduced in "The End of the World") is the oldest inhabitant of the Isop Galaxy (1965's "The Web Planet"). There's a lunar penal colony (1973's "Frontier in Space"). Delta waves were used in 1982's "Kinda." The guards' guns use Bastic bullets (1985's "Revelation of the Daleks"), which can destroy a Dalek if they hit its eyestalk directly. The Dalek Emperor previously appeared in 1967's "Evil of the Daleks" (an emperor also appeared in 1988's "Remembrance of the Daleks," but was Davros in disguise). When Rose says that the Daleks are half human, the Daleks chant, "Those words are blasphemy!" which is a reference to the 1996 TV Movie (where the Doctor was half human) and fandom's response (who, let's just say, weren't pleased).

The Bad Wolf Effect All the elements of this season's story arc come together as the "Bad Wolf" meme (seen in this story on a poster in the chip shop and in enormous letters in a playground) and the Time War finally connect. "Bad Wolf" is a message for Rose, telling her she could get back to the Doctor. When she does this, by looking into the heart of the TARDIS, she becomes the Bad Wolf. Now possessing godlike powers, Bad Wolf Rose pronounces that "the Time War ends" and destroys the Dalek fleet. From this point forward, the Time War, which drove many of the stories this season and provided motivation for the ninth Doctor's character, becomes backstory.

According to *The Weakest Link*, the great cobalt pyramid is built on the remains of the Torchwood Institute. Keep that name in mind for next season . . .

Who is the Doctor? In the ancient legends of the Dalek homeworld, the Doctor is called the Oncoming Storm. The Doctor's legendary status continues to grow from this point. Faced with the opportunity to repeat the circumstances of the Time War by destroying the Daleks and humans, the Doctor finds he cannot do it again. It's the final step for the Doctor to come to terms with his actions in the Time War, as he refuses to let his hatred of the Daleks provoke him to mass extermination. The ninth Doctor's last words speak to his love of Rose and his acceptance of himself after so much self-loathing: "I just want you to know, you were fantastic. And you know what? So was I."

The Doctor and Rose The situation on the Game Station leads the Doctor and Rose to take desperate steps for each other. The Doctor, having already suffered a near catatonic breakdown when he thought Rose was killed by the Anne Droid, forcibly sends her and the TARDIS back to Earth (where he begs her in a holographic message to "have a fantastic life"), because he wants to spare her what is to come. (Note that he doesn't do this for Jack or for Lynda, whom he flirts with throughout.) Rose refuses to accept this and risks everything to open the heart of the TARDIS, telling Mickey there's nothing for her on Earth without the Doctor. The Doctor and Rose share a brief kiss, ostensibly to remove the time vortex energy that is killing Rose, but, given that this act has the ninth Doctor sacrificing himself for Rose, it's hard not to read more into it than mere exsanguinations of chronal energy.

Monster of the Week The Dalek Emperor survived the Time War, his ship falling through time, crippled but alive. He's housed in giant, immobile tank. The Emperor is now the object of worship by a new breed of Daleks he created by harvesting the waste of humanity. It's blasphemy to call these Daleks "human," though they are human-Dalek hybrids.

Stand Up and Cheer "No. 'Cause this is what I'm going to do. I'm gonna rescue her. I'm gonna save Rose Tyler from the middle of the Dalek fleet, and then I'm gonna save the Earth and then, just to finish off, I'm gonna wipe every last stinking Dalek out of the sky!"

"But you have no weapons, no defences, no plan!"

"Yeah. And doesn't that scare you to death? Rose?"

"Yes, Doctor?"

"I'm coming to get you."

Need we say more?

Roll Your Eyes While the satirical element is well observed, we do have to ask if

British game shows and television from 2005 would be so fondly remembered 198,095 years in the future.

You're Not Making Any Sense After the events of "The Long Game," Earth's government and economy collapsed and the entire planet froze, simply because they weren't able to get prepackaged news reports. This beggars belief, as though the U.S. would collapse if Fox stopped broadcasting news.

Interesting Trivia The Emperor survived the Time War, so it's very likely this time-active status allowed him to change history, 90 years before "The Long Game." These aren't quite the Daleks of old, because they're made from human cells. As the Daleks are the ultimate racists, this makes them self-hating and thus more dangerous than ever. It also means that the single Dalek we saw in "Dalek" really was the last proper Dalek.

We see a Dalek with an attachment other than the sink plunger. The Classic Series occasionally had Daleks with different attachments, such as a flame-thrower, and so did the two Cushing movies, all in the '60s. The Dalek we see here with the cutting tool is a lovely throwback to an earlier era. Okay, so it's a little odd that the default factory setting is the sink plunger, but we've had 50 years to get used to it. It's probably time to accept it and move on . . .

You can have full-frontal nudity in prime time, as much violence as you can imagine — and yet, you can't swear. So it's reality TV taken to its logical extension, basically about five years into the future. The programs mostly have the same titles as contemporary shows (*Call My Bluff, Ground Force, Stars in Their Eyes*) only with added violence (real guns, getting turned into compost, being blinded). This is obviously a commentary on our obsession with violence on TV (and, to a lesser extent, sex), but it works so well because the commentary is so close to its source.

The Daleks make one fatal mistake. They monitor everything on Earth, only they don't watch the programs. This is classic Russell T Davies: identify an issue in society, shift it a few degrees into allegory, show us how horrible it is — and then ensure that we can't actually dismiss it entirely. Rather than undercutting Davies' argument, the Doctor interrupting his own diatribe about reality TV to praise *Bear With Me* provides a counterpoint to make us think. It's true that reality TV dulls your brain, subtracts from quality drama and manipulates people into making idiots of themselves in public. On the other hand, it might just save us from a Dalek invasion in 200,000 years' time.

The line "They've had to cut back; it's not what it was" is a parody of a scathing fan complaining about his favourite show not being as good as it used to be, despite it being a massive success by any reasonable measure. We suspect Russell T Davies had some specifics in mind when he wrote this . . .

You get executed if you don't pay your licence fee, which is quite amusing. In Britain, the licence fee is the way the BBC is funded as a public broadcaster and effectively avoids being a state broadcaster. If you own a television, you have to pay the fee (whether or not you watch the BBC) and licence fee inspectors have the right to enter your home to determine whether you have a set. From a North American point of view, it's both incredibly invasive and a stunningly brilliant way to operate a broadcaster: the idea of a national bureaucracy being able to enter your house to check whether you have a television or not is very, erm, Big Brother, but it's also a clever way of ensuring independence from government interference in the media or corporate advertising.

A scene with a bare-bottomed Captain Jack was cut; it's the only scene in the entire season that was censored. But don't worry, Jack fans. We will eventually get to see what you're all hoping for . . .

It's confirmed here that the TARDIS can't go back to last week with warnings of the future because as soon as it lands it becomes part of events. This is the working theory of time travel from the New Adventures line of books (one of which was written by Davies). There it was posited that the Doctor was on a treadmill, forced to continually uphold history, because he'd become part of it just by landing the TARDIS. We don't quite go into as much depth here, but the fundamental theory is such a good one that it makes perfect sense to adopt.

The use of *Big Brother*, *The Weakest Link* and *What Not to Wear* was fully licenced from the various companies who own those shows. The *Big Brother* production team joined in the fun by designing a futuristic version of their logo. The actual hosts provide the voices, with *Big Brother*'s Davina McCall playing Davinadroid, *The Weakest Link*'s Anne Robinson as the Anne Droid and *What Not to Wear*'s Trinny and Susannah voicing Trine-E and Zu-Zana.

The Doctor even uses Davina McCall's catchphrase for ejected *Big Brother* housemates when he says to Rose, "I'm coming to get you." In the British version of *Big Brother*, when a houseguest was evicted, Davina announced this to the evictee over the intercom. Davina then greeted the ejected contestant, often bewildered and upset after being voted out on national television, with a huge hug and whispered reassuringly, "It's all panto, love; it really doesn't matter." It's the reality behind the catchphrase that Russell T Davies is trying to get at when the Doctor says he's coming to get Rose. Earlier, the catchphrase is horribly parodied — the Davinadroid is coming to get house guests by disintegrating them — but here the Doctor is coming for Rose to take her away and reassure her that everything's all right.

Christopher Eccleston's departure was supposed to be kept quiet, so the regeneration at the end would be a total surprise. Two endings were filmed:

the regeneration, and a false one (to use at press screenings) where the Doctor looks at the TARDIS scanner to discover that Rose is dying. When the BBC announced Eccleston's departure mere days after "Rose" was broadcast, the need for such secrecy was blown out of the water.

The details of why Eccleston left *Doctor Who* are still shrouded in secrecy. None of the executive producers has ever gone on record to speak about it. The BBC's 2005 press announcement stated that Eccleston feared typecasting, but it was later retracted. Eccleston stated, in an interview with the *Daily Mail* in 2011, "I left *Doctor Who* because I could not get along with the senior people. I left because of politics. I did not see eye-to-eye with them. I didn't agree with the way things were being run. I didn't like the culture that had grown up around the series. So I left, I felt, over a principle."

While the casting of the tenth Doctor was a surprise to some, there were early indications which way things were leaning: mere hours before *Doctor Who* debuted on British television on March 26, 2005, BBC1 aired *Doctor Who: A New Dimension*, a documentary on the Classic Series and the then-forthcoming New Series. The narrator of that documentary? David Tennant.

The TARDIS Chronometer It's the year 200,100. The TARDIS is parked in Archive Six on Floor 500 of the Game Station.

Fantastic? (RS?) This two-part finale is marvellous right from the opening scene, where the Doctor is viewed from above in a box while the camera turns, disorienting the viewer until the Doctor stumbles out into an episode of *Big Brother*. From there, the story moves from strength to strength. The Doctor's "Here's the latest update from the Big Brother house" speech to the camera would be the highlight of any other episode. When Lynda tells him that he'd need a nuclear bomb to get through exoglass, his response is "Don't tempt me" — and you believe, absolutely and totally, that he'd be capable of it. He concludes by not only getting out of the house, but convincing Lynda to come with him, using the sheer power of his personality. This takes the damaged and malfunctioning Doctor of this season and turns him into a hero.

The Doctor's catatonic arrest when he thinks Rose is dead is quite bizarre. We've seen him lose people before, but the one thing the Doctor has never been is out of ideas. Then, when he does escape, he's particularly nasty, slamming a guard's head into a wall, a shocking act for a hero who is usually anti-violence. When he points a gun at a group of hostages, it echoes him pointing a gun at the Dalek. However, what's different here is that he's able to redeem himself without Rose (by throwing the gun to one of them) despite the incredible loss he's suffered.

The Doctor's impassioned "It means no" speech to the Daleks is wonderful, mostly because he starts off looking awkward, tugging at his jacket as though preparing for a particular irksome job interview. But as soon as he says no — doing exactly what the entire season has built up to: standing up and saying no — he's in total command. Sublimely, everyone present swings their heads to him in unison, but you probably didn't notice that on first viewing, because the Doctor is so captivating. This is the ninth Doctor's greatest moment.

The entire season has been about the Doctor inspiring others while being unable to act himself, and this is the payoff: the Doctor, with no plan and no weapons, saying no to the bullies. What's clever is the Daleks' reaction: they go into a massive meltdown and accelerate their plans, stating that the Doctor has initiated hostile action, when all he's done is make a speech. Ordinarily, they'd just exterminate the hostage or blast the space station out of the sky, but this is the Doctor they're facing and they effectively wet themselves when he simply says no.

The second part is wholly unlike the first, but no less fabulous. It has some amazing touches, like the Doctor with his head against the TARDIS door, listening to the Daleks' never-ending chant of "Exterminate"; Jack kissing Rose and the Doctor (which works perfectly because he kisses them both in exactly the same way) or the sweetness of Lynda contrasted with her horrific death.

Despite the high-octane pace and the thousands of Daleks attacking, "The Parting of the Ways" is centred on the utterly captivating scenes on Earth that cut to the heart of the character development we've been watching all season long. After complaining last episode that all Mickey does is come running whenever Rose calls, here Mickey literally comes running when he hears the TARDIS engines. Jackie, who once hated the Doctor, now says she loves him because he kept her daughter safe. Rose decrying the mundane existence of a normal life after having been with the Doctor is nicely undercut by Mickey pointing out that this is what everyone else does. Most cleverly of all, this discussion is about chips, inverting the earlier joy found in chips in "The End of the World."

Rose's speech — "The Doctor showed me a better way of living your life. You don't just give up. You don't just let things happen. You make a stand. You say no. You have the guts to do what's right when everyone else just runs away." — is the perfect summation of the Doctor, but also a call to action to the viewer. We aren't just passive consumers of television; we're humans who need to make a stand against the bullies. Her words inspire Jackie and Mickey into action: first Mickey tries to use his car to open the TARDIS, then Jackie finds a truck. Even though neither of them want to lose Rose, they still help her fight for a bigger cause, because it's the right thing to do. And it's that spirit that makes the ending resonate. The heart of the TARDIS may be a *deus ex machina*, but it's the emotional cost the characters suffer that gives the story power. Every single guest cast member, plus about half the regular cast, are killed off. Which brings us back to another theme of the season: everything has its time.

Well, everything except Captain Jack Harkness. What happens to him here is incredibly profound, though we won't understand the implications for some time.

Everything has its time, and the ninth Doctor, who has led us on a journey of resurrection, who has worn his pain on his sleeve and who gave us a Doctor unlike any seen before or since, here meets his end. He faces a clinching moment: killer or coward? After surviving the Time War, and being responsible for the deaths of two species, he finally has his moment of redemption. And it's not the heroic fight of a soldier but the lovely realization that it's better to be a coward than to inflict pain, no matter the consequences.

Although regeneration has been a staple of the Classic Series, it's still an incredible shock to lose the Doctor after just one season. Despite the lost potential of further episodes with such an amazing actor in the lead, it makes for a very powerful emotional payoff to a superb debut season.

"Bad Wolf"/"The Parting of the Ways" is an excellent story both in its own right and as the cap to a season-long tale of redemption. The threat of a thousand Daleks is effective because we saw how powerful one alone could be in "Dalek." Rose's frustration at being locked out of the action works because she's been so well developed as an equal. And the Doctor's final choice is powerful because we've spent a season watching him take the unpredictable route, never quite knowing if we could trust him, but willing to go along for the ride anyway. There's only one word to sum up the magnitude of this experience: fantastic.

Second Opinion (GB) Wow.

If there's one thing Russell T Davies can do, it's end things, bringing all the different threads together and still throwing in surprises. "The Parting of the Ways" is 45 minutes of heart-stopping moments: the TARDIS avoiding Dalek missiles, rescuing Rose, meeting the Dalek Emperor and shipping Rose back to Earth. (Even after all these years, the holographic speech leaves me breathless when the Doctor turns to Rose and wishes her a fantastic life.)

I will never forget the first time I watched "Parting of the Ways": I said to myself, "I have no idea how this will end." And there's a part of me that wishes that could be the case every time I watch it. Because how it comes together is remarkable, drawing on disparate elements from many stories, including "The Long Game," "Father's Day," "Boom Town," "Dalek" and even "Rose," as Rose once and for all rejects the Doctor's judgement that humans should just work and eat and avoid all the terrors beneath the surface.

My favourite moment of all is when Jackie arrives with Rodrigo's truck.

That's the stand-up-and-cheer moment to end them all as Jackie and Mickey (I love his wink to Jackie!) prepare to stand behind Rose's mad dream even though it might kill her. It's a single, beautiful moment that underscores all the ways each character has grown as a result of knowing the Doctor.

Consequently, I've never felt cheated by Rose becoming the Bad Wolf. It brought everything together powerfully, delivered the Doctor just as he finally articulates his refusal to be a victim of the Time War ("coward, any day"), and gave us the Doctor and Rose's kiss that we all secretly wanted, even though it ultimately killed him.

And the ninth Doctor's final scene is beautiful, as he awkwardly tries to reassure Rose (and the viewer) while he breaks the news he's going to change. Christopher Eccleston is glorious here, as he has been all season. The truth of the matter is that the relaunch of *Doctor Who* would never have been treated seriously by the BBC, the press or the viewing public without an actor of Eccleston's calibre to bring the series out of the starting gates. While I'm still saddened, all these years later, that this is the final scene of Christopher Eccleston's Doctor, and that there are no more televised adventures of the ninth Doctor, his willingness to take his Doctor on an incredible emotional journey for 13 episodes made for a season of television that I will never forget.

The Psychic Papers: Regeneration

By 1965, ill health was taking its toll on William Hartnell, the first actor to play the Doctor. He suffered from arteriosclerosis, a condition that was making him infirm even in his 50s. The rigours of acting in a television show (for 48 weeks a year, as was the practice in the 1960s) were becoming difficult for Hartnell, and he was increasingly disagreeable on set. *Doctor Who* producers began pondering ways of replacing Hartnell with a new actor.

By 1966, the producers, BBC management and Hartnell agreed it was time for a change. In a decision that is likely responsible for keeping *Doctor Who* on the air for the next six decades, the powers-that-be decided not to replace Hartnell with a look-alike actor who would play the part as Hartnell had, but to do something radical. They would cast a very different actor, Patrick Troughton, in the role. Inspired very loosely by *Dr. Jekyll and Mr. Hyde*, they physically transformed the Doctor onscreen. At the end of 1966's "The Tenth Planet," a weakened Doctor, who had earlier stated, "This old body of mine is wearing a bit thin," staggered into the TARDIS. With the controls on the console acting automatically, the Doctor collapsed and a startling transformation took place as he literally became a new man.

In the following story, 1966's "The Power of the Daleks," this new Doctor explained the process as a "renewal," comparing it to the emergence of a butterfly from a chrysalis. There was an oblique explanation that it was also a property of the TARDIS. It was intended as a rejuvenation, the idea initially being that the Doctor simply became a younger version of himself.

Already quite radical, this concept went further when Patrick Troughton played the Doctor as a complete contrast to his predecessor. Beyond his broadly similar clothing, everything about the second Doctor was different: he was impish where the first had been haughty, childlike where the first had been authoritative. He was a completely new person.

The end of the second Doctor's era saw the introduction of his people, the Time Lords, who placed the Doctor on trial in 1969's "The War Games." Part of his sentence was a change of appearance, which they justified by saying, "Your appearance has changed before; it will change again." By this point, the process wasn't rejuvenation but a complete physical transformation. The third Doctor's personality was different again: he was more serious than his predecessors. With him came a change in tone for the series, as *Doctor Who* became Earthbound for much of his tenure, thanks to a complete turnover in behind-the-scenes personnel.

The concept wasn't formalized until the end of the third Doctor's era when, in 1974's "Planet of the Spiders," it was finally called "regeneration" onscreen. It was established as a facility Time Lords have to change their bodies — every single cell — when dying. This regeneration was accompanied by a "push" from a wiser Time Lord, who aided the Doctor's changeover.

The brilliance of regeneration lies not only in allowing the series to change the lead actor, but to send it spinning in new directions. Most regenerations mark the end of an era, not just the end of a Doctor's tenure. Companions usually depart within a few stories either side of a regeneration. Production teams often change as well, as a regeneration provides a natural "moving on" spot. The regeneration from the third to the fourth Doctor was another such opportunity, as the series changed stylistically to a more sophisticated tone and increased horror.

The fourth Doctor's changeover in 1981's "Logopolis" was aided by a future version of himself called the Watcher, who merged with the Doctor during the regeneration process. There was an emphasis that this was the end of an era: the fourth Doctor's regeneration featured images of past companions and villains speaking to him in his final moments.

Until the New Series, almost every regeneration was different. Some featured impressive special effects, others a simple cross-fade between the two actors. Most were followed by a period of disorientation, as the new Doctor found his feet. The fifth Doctor's debut story, 1982's "Castrovalva," added a new wrinkle to the process as the Doctor suffered post-regenerative trauma and had physical difficulty adjusting. This instability was further explored in the sixth Doctor's first story, 1984's "The Twin Dilemma," as the Doctor became mentally unstable, even violent, as a result of his transformation.

Most regenerations were a climactic conclusion to a Doctor's era, although the sixth Doctor's end came at the beginning of a new season and didn't even feature actor Colin Baker; instead, 1987's "Time and the Rani" opens with the Doctor's regeneration, achieved using Sylvester McCoy in a blond wig and some facial blurring during a pre-credits sequence. The seventh Doctor regenerated mid-story, in the 1996 TV Movie, his appearance forming an extended prologue before the eighth Doctor's single hour of television.

The transformation from the Doctor's eighth to ninth incarnation remains the only regeneration not shown onscreen. Unusually, the transition from the ninth to the tenth Doctor involved almost no other changes in the series, either in front of the camera or behind it. However, the tenth Doctor's regeneration into the eleventh was much more in the vein of the Classic Series: it marked the end of an era in more ways than one, with a change in production team, a new companion and a new tone for the series. The New Series' major innovation was to have the Doctor regenerate standing up; all previous regenerations involved the person lying down, usually having collapsed.

In the Classic Series, it was established that there were limits on the number of regenerations a Time Lord could have. According to 1976's "The Deadly Assassin," a Time Lord has 13 lives. The New Series has yet to tackle this, though with the Doctor currently in his eleventh incarnation perhaps it's only a matter of time. In the 2010 *Sarah Jane Adventures* episode "Death of the Doctor," the eleventh Doctor answers Clyde Langer's question of how many times he can change with "507." Perhaps he's being flippant. Perhaps not.

Regeneration is the gift that keeps on giving. Without it, *Doctor Who* would never have made it out of the '60s. It keeps the series fresh, by changing its leading face and allowing the series to reboot itself every few years. This is the miracle of *Doctor Who* and the secret to its incredible longevity.

SERIES TWO

Starring
David Tennant as the Doctor
Billie Piper as Rose Tyler

Executive Producers
Russell T Davies, Julie Gardner

Producer
Phil Collinson

2.X Children in Need Special

Written by Russell T Davies **Directed by** Euros Lyn

Original airdate November 18, 2005

The Big Idea The Doctor is a new man, but can he convince Rose that he's the same person?

Adventures in Time and Space The TARDIS Cloister Bell, a warning alarm that dates back to 1981's "Logopolis," rings when imminent disaster is about to befall the ship (or the universe).

Who is the Doctor? The Doctor is initially manic and garrulous after his regeneration (qualities that never entirely go away). He's fascinated by all the physical changes that have happened to him, including the big hair, bad skin and the mole between his shoulder blades (which he decides he'll come to love).

The Doctor and Rose Rose is completely freaked out, even after the Doctor proves to her that he's not an imposter by recounting how they first met. Rose asks the Doctor if he can change back, the first time a companion has asked this.

Interesting Trivia The Doctor's remark that Captain Jack is "busy rebuilding the Earth" in 200,100 indicates he's aware of his resurrection after his extermination. We'll come back to this in "Utopia."

The Doctor says he has a slight weakness in the dorsal tubercle, a nodule found on the forearm. Now that's knowing your anatomy.

Since 1980, the BBC has held an annual charity appeal in November called Children in Need, which has raised over £500 million for children's charities across the U.K. The highlight of the campaign is a special broadcast on BBC1 hosted by venerable BBC presenter Terry Wogan and featuring high-profile musical acts and special one-off programs designed to attract viewers who will then donate. It's one of the highest-rated nights of television in Britain annually. Since 2005, *Doctor Who* has contributed a segment to Children in Need, whether a special scene, a trailer or a concert for children.

Brilliant? (GB) It's a *scene* and not a mini-episode, which is an important distinction to make. There's no rising and falling action, no climax. It's just a six-minute scene, which is almost unheard of on modern television.

But it's a great six-minute scene that fills in an important gap: how does Rose, who has had such an intense relationship with the Doctor, trust him after he physically transforms into a completely different man? Writer Russell T Davies doesn't provide a pat resolution, but instead dwells on the wonder and the emotional fallout of a miraculous process like regeneration.

In some ways, the biggest shame about it is making it fit with the following episode, "The Christmas Invasion," with the Doctor scattered and reckless. On the one hand, it's a good way of adding a cliffhanger to the scene; on the other, wouldn't it have been nice to see the Doctor and Rose explore this situation just a little more? Still, being left wanting more is not bad for something so short.

Second Opinion (RS?) There's an absolutely brilliant introduction to the tenth Doctor, one that will resonate with viewers for years to come and that firmly establishes him as a force to be reckoned with. That happens in the next story, not in this one. Here, we have a lacklustre piece of filler that achieves nothing — it can't, because it has to leave the status quo exactly as it was, thanks to being inserted in the middle of two massive event episodes — and actively harms the big story it's leading into by undercutting the tension of that story's opening.

People at the time were quite excited because it featured an extended TARDIS scene, and fans thought it was radical because Rose asked the Doctor if he could change back. It isn't. David Tennant starts as he means to go on: doing his default schtick in a slightly irritating way. When he's challenged, Tennant can be excellent. But when he's left on autopilot, he hops on one foot and camps it up for the camera.

Yes, it's a scene for Children in Need. But time has not been kind to it. On your next rewatch, go straight from the ninth Doctor's regeneration to the iconic crash landing at Christmas and see if you notice anything missing. Trust me, you won't.

· ·

David Tennant

Born in 1971, Scottish actor David John MacDonald had to adopt a stage name because there was another David MacDonald in Equity, the U.K. actor's union. He took the name Tennant from Neil Tennant of the Pet Shop Boys' fame. His first major role was in the Scottish TV series *Takin' Over the Asylum* (1994). He developed his career in the British theatre, particularly the Royal Shakespeare Company. A *Doctor Who* fan since childhood, he had several small parts in Big Finish's range of *Doctor Who* audios, most notably Colonel Brimmicombe-Wood in *Doctor Who Unbound: Sympathy for the Devil*.

In 2004, Tennant played his breakout role as Detective Inspector Peter Carlisle in *Blackpool*. He followed this up with the lead role in Russell T Davies' 2005 adaptation of *Casanova*, which then led to his being cast as the tenth Doctor. He played the Doctor from "The Parting of the Ways" (2005) to "The End of Time, Part Two" (2010). Since leaving *Doctor Who*, Tennant continues to act on the stage (notably in an acclaimed Royal Shakespeare Company production of *Hamlet*), in film (including 2011's *Fright Night*) and on TV.

· ·

2.00 The Christmas Invasion

Written by Russell T Davies **Directed by** James Hawes

Supporting cast Camille Coduri (Jackie Tyler), Noel Clarke (Mickey Smith), Penelope Wilton (Harriet Jones), Adam Garcia (Alex), Daniel Evans (Daniel Llewellyn), Sean Gilder (Sycorax leader), Anita Briem (Sally), Chu Omambala (Major Blake), Sian McDowell (Sandra), Paul Anderson (Jason), Jason Mohammad (newsreader 1), Sagar Arya (newreader 2), Lachele Carl (newsreader 3), Cathy Murphy (Mum), Sean Carlsen (policeman)

Original airdate December 25, 2005

The Big Idea On Christmas Day, a giant spaceship looms over London, threatening a third of the world's population. Unfortunately for the world, the Doctor is in a coma.

Roots and References *Independence Day* (the giant spaceship); Russell T Davies' *The Second Coming* (the people on the roof); *The Hitchhiker's Guide to the Galaxy* (the Doctor calls the pyjama and bathrobe ensemble he wears throughout "very Arthur Dent"); Shakespeare's *The Tempest* (the Sycorax derive their name from Caliban's mother). The Doctor finds himself quoting from *The Lion King*'s "Circle of Life."

Adventures in Time and Space Major Blake tells Llewellyn they've seen Martians, which is either a reference to the Martian race known as the Ice Warriors, who made four appearances during the Classic Series in the 1960s and 1970s, or the alien ambassadors from Mars in "The Ambassadors of Death" (1970). Big Ben is seen to be under reconstruction after its mishap with the Slitheen ship in "Aliens of London." Harriet Jones, former MP for Flydale North, is now prime minister, as the Doctor noted in "World War Three" (charmingly, she still introduces herself with her title even though everyone, including the Sycorax, know who she is). According to the news ticker at the bottom of Jackie's TV during the Guinevere news item, her cottage hospital scheme is now available nationwide!

The TARDIS wardrobe, first seen in 1978's "The Androids of Tara," makes an appearance here, the first time we have seen another room in the New Series' TARDIS. There are a number of old costumes in this sequence; too many to list, but it's worth freeze-framing the long shot of the wardrobe to have a look.

The Torchwood Effect This season's arc gets started with Harriet Jones asking about Torchwood, a secret organization that neither she nor the United Nations is officially supposed to know about. Nothing much is known of Torchwood except that they possess alien technology capable of destroying the retreating

Sycorax ship. Over the course of the season, we'll discover how Torchwood came to be and what it's done throughout history.

Who is the Doctor? This new Doctor is trying to figure out his personality. (One of the — tragically — deleted scenes, available on the DVD, shows him attempting to say, "Fantastic!" but, with his new teeth getting in the way, he's left trying to come up with a new catchphrase.) He decides on "no second chances" as his defining credo (which mostly sticks; he'll generally offer his enemies a single chance). His eventual new outfit consists of a pin-striped suit, tie and trenchcoat. He apparently needs to wear glasses for reading.

The Doctor and Rose Rose is grieving for the loss of "her" Doctor, whom she calls the "proper" Doctor (causing Mickey to realize she really loves him). The loss of her Doctor leaves her unable to cope with the Sycorax invasion initially, but when the new Doctor emerges ready to challenge the Sycorax, she accepts him and is willing to travel with him anew. The Doctor is initially rude about this ("You gave up on me"), though the pair are holding hands, ready to travel again, by the episode's end.

Monster of the Week The Sycorax are a fearsome-looking, war-loving race, who wear the skulls of others over their faces. They kill without reason and have no desire for negotiation or peace. And yet, like many bullies, their biggest weapon is fear: they use blood control, a "cheap voodoo" trick according to the Doctor, to make the world think they can convince a third of the Earth's population to jump to their deaths.

Stand Up and Cheer The moment when the Doctor brings down Harriet Jones by just whispering six words in Alex's ear is chilling and incredible. It says everything about what this new Doctor is capable of doing and what will later lead to his downfall.

Roll Your Eyes Rose weeping and telling Mickey that "her" Doctor, the proper Doctor, wouldn't leave her like this makes her look like a blithering idiot. Even if she is grieving the loss of the ninth Doctor (which is only natural), "her" Doctor, the proper Doctor would in fact leave her like that if he were lying in a coma.

You're Not Making Any Sense The Santas may have the most harebrained scheme in the history of *Doctor Who*. Instead of, say, waiting til Mickey and Rose have left Jackie alone with an incapacitated Doctor, storming the flat and kidnapping him, what do they do? They follow Mickey and Rose, attempt to kill them in public and then, when that fails, they wait for them to get back to the flat where they attempt murder by Christmas tree . . . a tree they had delivered when the only people at the flat were, you guessed it, Jackie and an incapacitated Doctor.

Interesting Trivia The post-regenerative Doctor is still bursting with a golden glow that he exhales. Suffering from the effects of the regeneration, he winds up in a coma caused by a neuron implosion. He recovers thanks to the tannins and free radicals in the vapours from a thermos of tea that spills on a light below the TARDIS console.

Harriet Jones was the architect of Britain's golden age (implied to be occurring here via Jackie's pay rise). And yet, the Doctor takes her down anyway, creating a power vaccum at the story's end. This is actually a major turning point in the *Doctor Who* universe, as it sends the series down a much darker path, one that will culminate in "The Sound of Drums."

A third of the population is said to have type A+ blood. This is broadly accurate, although it varies: 26% for Iceland and 42% for Norway. The remaining non-O+ blood types are relatively rare. Llewellyn is clearly quite self-effacing by not including his own blood type in the sample to send to the stars. Perhaps he had a rare blood type and didn't want aliens to think that was representative.

What are the Santas? They appear to be robotic, but we learn almost nothing about them. They're only explained in metaphor as "pilot fish" (smaller fish who trail sharks and other big fish, eating leftovers from the bigger species), which is not entirely helpful. Perhaps next Christmas, we'll learn who and what they are . . .

The Guinevere One space program is tasked with finding life on Mars. The probe landing on Mars on Christmas Day (but ultimately failing) is "ripped from the headlines": the U.K. space program's *Beagle 2* probe was scheduled to land on Mars Christmas Day but failed to transmit and, ultimately, was presumed lost. This is not the only such moment; Harriet's response to the American president, "He's not my boss, and he's certainly not turning this into a war," was considered by many a sarcastic jibe at Tony Blair who was perceived by much of the British public to be George W. Bush's "poodle" in the Iraq War.

The firing on the retreating Sycorax ship may well be inspired by a controversial incident during the Falklands Crisis of 1982, where a retreating Argentinian ship, the *Belgrano*, was sunk by British forces. To this day, it's not clear whether the British chain of command was aware the *Belgrano* was in retreat, though many feel it was.

The TARDIS Chronometer Christmas Day, a short time after the events on Earth during "The Parting of the Ways."

Brilliant? (GB) The Doctor's capacity to regenerate and the show's ability to change lead actors (and, effectively, lead characters as a result) was a quirky part of *Doctor Who*'s heritage by the end of the Classic Series. In today's television environment, people invest more in the lead characters and the relationships they form, meaning that the prospect of regenerating the Doctor was, frankly, the most dangerous it's been since it first happened in 1966.

How Russell T Davies gets everyone on board for this change, and reintroduces — after only a year — the character of the Doctor, is really quite cunning. He has the Doctor out of the picture, unconscious for most of the episode. And everything goes to hell in a handcart. The characters (and by extension the audience) don't need to learn to trust the new Doctor; they just need the Doctor. By building the menace with something that neither Harriet, the Earth's defences nor even Rose can handle, it ratchets up our need for the Doctor.

And when the Doctor does finally show up — 34 minutes into the episode! — we're treated to 20 of the most exciting minutes in *Doctor Who*. It's one stand-up-and-cheer moment after another as the Doctor exposes the baddies (both Sycorax and human) and stops them in ways that are totally satisfying and even unexpected. It's an incredible sleight of hand Davies uses: we wanted the character to show up so much that we immediately accept him with relief and gratitude. That's genius.

"The Christmas Invasion" includes a 15-minute warm-up act as Rose and Mickey are terrorized by maruding Santas and a killer Christmas tree followed by the big show of the Sycorax coming to Earth. It's as though Russell T Davies had written a story called "The Sycorax Invasion" and then, given the holiday timeslot and an extra 15 minutes, bolted the Christmas material on with the robot Santas. In spite of the obvious lack of connection between the two parts, it works because it's just so entertaining. It's funny (particularly the Christmas tree) and goofy — as Davies having fun with iconic imagery usually is — superfluous though it might be.

Once the comic element is out of the way, "The Christmas Invasion" starts resembling Davies' earlier series *The Second Coming* (about the Son of God returning to Earth): giant, incredible events happen around ordinary people. Like *The Second Coming*, there's a real sense of dread and tension, contrasting the great force above with the scared and confused people below, created in part by the haunting crowd shots of people leaving their suburban homes. Director James Hawes was absolutely the right man for the job. Either the Christmas special had a bigger budget than an average episode of *Doctor Who* or Hawes makes it look that way. There's a grand scale to everything, from the Sycorax ship to UNIT's high-tech, high-security headquarters.

The supporting cast is superb, led by Noel Clarke who just gets better and better. He steals every scene he's in — of note is when Mickey gently mocks Rose for the way she gushes about the Doctor — and his character gets to demonstrate real kindness and bravery. We also see new facets to Jackie, who won't let an ailing Doctor get a word in edgewise, yet stays by his bedside all night while he lies comatose. Camille Coduri rises to the occasion. However, the real standout performance is Penelope Wilton. While Harriet Jones is still the kind, coffee-making, badge-flashing enthusiast she ever was, the character is now in a position of power that she wasn't in "Aliens of London," and it's fascinating watching her harder edge emerge from the dotty woman we know and love. Her final moments with the Doctor — as she goes from defending her position to threatening the Doctor to regretting everything — are totally riveting.

One can understand Harriet's position, but also see why the Doctor feels the destruction of the retreating Sycorax vessel was so wrong: the Sycorax really haven't demonstrated any weaponry; their great demonstration of superiority was, in fact, a giant con game. Harriet is acting out of fear; the Doctor understands how terrible this action really is. And, seeing what his friend has become, he feels he has no choice but to depose her; the six words are just showing off.

The only character who gets short shrift in "The Christmas Invasion" is Rose, despite her abundance of screentime. Rose is great with the killer Santas, but, once the Sycorax arrive, her despondence feels completely out of character. (Even Rose's claim that she's rubbish with menaces closer to home seems hollow in light of "The Parting of the Ways.") Billie Piper tries gamely to make Rose's grief and misery work, but a useless Rose is not a pretty sight.

With all eyes on him, David Tennant establishes himself as the Doctor in a five-minute monologue. He's smart. He's charming. He's sweet. He's goofy and manic (though in a very different way than Eccleston). As the episode progresses, we see other interesting facets develop, particularly when he finally confronts Harriet after shooting down the Sycorax ship. He's tough. The change in costume symbolizes the change in character: the ninth Doctor wore a leather jacket as though to protect himself; the tenth Doctor doesn't need such a carapace. He can handle himself.

If "Rose" re-established *Doctor Who*, "The Christmas Invasion" re-establishes that changing the lead actor doesn't kill the program but opens the series up to new excitement and new possibilities. David Tennant's performance indicates we're in for a very different kind of Doctor. What a Christmas present!

Second Opinion (RS?) There are a number of things about this story that don't sit quite right: the robot Santas are never explained, the story's way too intricate for the casual viewer, the first 15 minutes are clearly tacked on, the weepy and incompetent Rose is unrecognizable from her previous characterization, and the new Doctor is absent from most of it. But none of this matters a damn, because "The Christmas Invasion" is utterly fabulous.

It's a story that has it all: a proper, honest-to-goodness alien invasion, Christmas dinner, edge-of-the-seat tension (the A positives on the roof), UNIT, Torchwood, the Powell Estate, Harriet-Jones-Prime-Minister, a post-regenerative Doctor, hand-to-hand combat and a twist in the tail so delightful that they haven't tried to top it since, knowing they probably couldn't.

Taking the Doctor out of the picture is a brilliant move, as it allows us to see the sheer power of what he does by his absence. Harriet Jones's plea for the Doctor to come save us all underpins so much of what happens, from Rose's breakdown that destroyed her character in one fell swoop, to Harriet's actions at the end — and, indeed, the whole Torchwood arc of the forthcoming season.

The only real problem with "The Christmas Invasion" is that the subsequent stories of the season pale in comparison. "The Sycorax Invasion" would have been a far stronger opening than "New Earth." That they decided to base the tenth Doctor's character on the gabbling hyperactivity of "Ooh, a lovely big red button!" rather than the cold fury of "Don't you think she looks tired?" was a colossal mistake. And what it does to Rose is unforgivable. But those are all problems that the next season will amplify. Taken on its own, "The Christmas Invasion" is quite wonderful.

The Doctor's Costume

The costume for a Doctor in the New Series is a collaboration between producers, costume designer and star. For the ninth Doctor, Russell T Davies only specified in his script that the Doctor wore a battered leather jacket. Christopher Eccleston insisted in interviews in 2005 that he wanted the performance to matter more than the costume; his vision was for a more stripped-down look, quite different from the Victorian- and Edwardian-inspired Doctors of the Classic Series.

With the tenth Doctor, Russell T Davies was keen to see more modern clothes, but the long greatcoat was David Tennant's idea from the outset, drawing on Doctors from the 1970s and 1980s. Tennant worked closely with designer Louise Page before settling on the brown pinstripe suit.

The costume of Matt Smith's eleventh Doctor is mostly down to Smith himself. Smith had been watching his predecessors' stories on DVD and was particularly influenced by the performance and look of the second Doctor, Patrick Troughton (1966–1969). While the production team suggested a grander looking costume with a pirate-like coat, Smith insisted on something more professorial, with a tweed jacket and a bowtie like Troughton.

Briefly glimpsed in "Aliens of London," UNIT has its first full-on appearance in "The Christmas Invasion." UNIT is a top-secret paramilitary organization tasked by the United Nations to investigate the unknown and fight alien threats to Earth, introduced to the series in 1968's "The Invasion."

Piecing together disparate references across the Classic and New Series, the United Nations Security Council created UNIT as part of an alien first-contact policy in 1968. UNIT forces are comprised of seconded personnel from its signatory countries' military forces (in the U.K., from the British Army); its chain of command is through the United Nations and is headquartered in Geneva. In the Classic Series, UNIT soldiers wore modified army uniforms. In the New Series, standard issue appears to be a black uniform with a red beret.

The third Doctor (Jon Pertwee) was exiled to Earth by the Time Lords and was employed as UNIT's scientific adviser under Brigadier Alistair Gordon Lethbridge-Stewart. The era of *Doctor Who* that is now called "The UNIT family" began in 1970 with the Brigadier and UNIT soldiers Sergeant John Benton and Captain Mike Yates appearing as recurring characters. UNIT acted as a home base for the exiled Doctor, and UNIT's involvement with the alien and unknown provided a catalyst for stories in this Earthbound era of *Who*. After the Doctor's exile was lifted in 1972's "The Three Doctors," less and less was seen of UNIT; the Doctor had left his role as scientific adviser by 1975's "The Android Invasion." The final appearance of UNIT in the Classic Series was 1989's "Battlefield."

The period the Classic Series UNIT stories are set in is a source of controversy. In the late 1960s and early 1970s, they were meant to be set in the future, the 1980s. By the mid-1970s, they were set a few years in the future (still the 1980s). By the 1980s, it was decided the stories were, in fact, set in the 1970s. So far, the New Series has refused to take a stand on this (though the spinoff *The Sarah Jane Adventures* has implicitly confirmed it was the 1970s). Indeed, in "The Sontaran Stratagem," the Doctor says he can't remember which decade it was.

In the New Series, UNIT is still fighting alien threats and is still covert: its high-tech secret base is located underneath the Tower of London. They operate a flying helibase, the *Valiant*, that appears in a number of stories, starting with "The Sound of Drums." UNIT is at the forefront of the UN's Homeworld Security initiative.

After "Aliens of London"/"World War Three" aired (and a website for the fictional UNIT went live as part of the BBC's *Doctor Who* site) with the original UNIT acronym, United Nations Intelligence Taskforce, the real United Nations requested that *Doctor Who* no longer make the claim that UNIT was a United Nations organization. It wasn't until "The Sontaran Stratagem" that a new name was revealed: the Unified Intelligence

Taskforce. Within the *Doctor Who* universe, the change probably occurred some time before the New Series, as the only person who says "United Nations Intelligence Taskforce" in the New Series is the ninth Doctor, in "Aliens of London."

Under the new name, UNIT continued to appear in *Doctor Who* including in "The Stolen Earth" and "Planet of the Dead." UNIT has also appeared in *Torchwood* ("Reset," "Fragments" and "Children of Earth") and *The Sarah Jane Adventures* (the second-season finale "Enemy of the Bane" — which featured the final appearance of the Brigadier, as actor Nicholas Courtney passed away in 2011 — and "Death of the Doctor").

2.01 New Earth

Written by Russell T Davies **Directed by** James Hawes

Supporting cast Camille Coduri (Jackie Tyler), Noel Clarke (Mickey Smith), Zoë Wannamaker (Cassandra), Sean Gallagher (Chip), Doña Croll (Matron Casp), Michael Fitzgerald (Duke of Manhattan), Lucy Robinson (Frau Clovis), Adjoa Andoh (Sister Jatt), Anna Hope (Novice Hame), Struan Rodger (Face of Boe), Simon Ludders (patient)

Original airdate April 15, 2006

The Big Idea The Doctor is summoned to a hospital on New New York, where he finds a bodyswapping Cassandra, the enigmatic Face of Boe and cat nuns who can cure every known disease.

Roots and References Bodyswapping stories such as *Freaky Friday*, *Star Trek*'s "Turnabout Intruder," *The Prisoner*'s "Do Not Forsake Me Oh My Darling"; *Night of the Living Dead* (via the current metaphors of zombies as a disease); and the musical *Cats*.

Adventures in Time and Space This is a sequel to "The End of the World," featuring Cassandra, her robot spiders and the Face of Boe, a similar setting and the same theme ("everything dies"); the episode establishes continuity across two incarnations of the Doctor. It's the second of a three-part trilogy of adventures set in the year five billion and featuring the Face of Boe (the third will be "Gridlock" next season). In a callout to the previous season's arc, the words "Bad Wolf" are still visible in the playground, where they were last seen during "The Parting of the Ways."

Who is the Doctor? The Doctor is described by the Face of Boe as a "lonely god" for the first time. It's a phrase that recurs throughout the tenth Doctor's tenure and in many ways epitomizes this Doctor, who shows great power and hubris — in this story, he single-handedly cures the plague carriers — but will inevitably wind up alone. He also utters his soon-to-be frequently repeated phrase "I'm sorry . . . I'm so sorry" when he sees his first intensive-care patient, showing how this Doctor frequently wears his hearts on his sleeve.

The Doctor and Rose Rose appears to have moved on from her initial reluctance about the Doctor's change of form. The pair act like two gadabout honeymooners, unable to stop smiling at each other. Cassandra notes from her bodyswap that Rose has been surreptitiously looking at the Doctor's body.

Monster of the Week The hospital is run by the Sisters of Plenitude, bipedal cats in nuns' habits. They have extendable claws.

Stand Up and Cheer At the end of a fluffy and sometimes quite silly story, the scene where the human Cassandra unknowingly meets her future self in the dying body of Chip is heartwrenching. It closes Cassandra's arc perfectly, having her die at the feet of herself, on the last day she was called beautiful (by herself, as it turns out). The tragedy is in knowing that many thousands of years will then unfold, none of them happy. This captures the futility of overextending one's life, because it's the moments of happiness that make life worthwhile, not the number of years one accumulates. And, gloriously, as the elder Cassandra dies in the younger's arms, she collapses onto a piece of stretched animal skin on the floor, thus foreshadowing the latter's fate in an extremely understated way.

Roll Your Eyes The opening lovefest between the Doctor and Rose doesn't work at all. She's barely had a chance to get to know this new Doctor and suddenly, between stories, she's become infatuated with him? Instead of reassuring us that the Doctor is still the same man, it undercuts the character development by not letting us get to know this new guy along with Rose.

You're Not Making Any Sense The Sisters of Plenitude can apparently cure every known disease . . . except for any airborne diseases, because you're completely safe unless one of their intensive care patients touches you. The cat nuns have distilled cures for all these diseases into colourful plastic bags, which the Doctor then open and handles, which should have caused him to drop dead because the cures for many of these diseases would likely be as dangerous as the original infection. But . . . they aren't, and he doesn't. Instead, the Doctor sprays the cure onto the infected patients, healing some of them instantly (without so much as a scar), and they simply touch the others, thus "infecting" them with the cure. This is nonsense.

Interesting Trivia The Doctor notes that diseases have advanced along with humanity's progress, which makes an enormous amount of sense. What doesn't is most of the rest of the diseases. Imagine you're infected with every single (touch-transmitted) disease known to feline-kind. You'd imagine some of them might be fatal, wouldn't you? Yet apparently not a single one of them is because, according to the Doctor, plague carriers are "always the last to go." This isn't really robust logic on his part; while it's true that a small percentage of people transmitting an infectious disease may be asymptomatic carriers, it's ridiculous to imagine that they'd therefore be carriers for more than one disease, let alone every single one.

At one point, a quarantine is initiated, meaning that the elevators don't work. Yet, immediately afterwards, an exterior shot of the hospital shows the elevators sliding up and down. Perhaps the quarantine didn't extend to the external elevators, so visitors were trapped inside, pointlessly riding up and down in hopes of an escape. Or perhaps earlier footage was reused without thinking about it.

The TARDIS Chronometer The TARDIS is initially on Earth, near the Powell Estate (not where it was last time, suggesting further unseen adventures). It then travels to the far future to the planet New Earth, in the M87 Galaxy, on an applegrass hill outside of New New York. At the story's conclusion, the Doctor, Rose and Cassandra (in Chip's body) travel back in time many years, to a party Cassandra attended before she was in her trampoline form.

Brilliant? (RS?) It's the opening salvo of the new season, so we're in for some pretty hard-hitting, nail-biting stuff. There's going to be action and explosions and gripping death-defying scenes. It's backs-to-the-walls all the way through and no mistake. Right?

"New Earth" is many things, perhaps too many, but the one thing it isn't doing is taking itself seriously. Which might come as a surprise to anyone familiar with the broad details of the plot: death and disease on a grand scale, the morality of scientific experimentation and the twin themes of rebirth and knowing when to accept death.

Some have argued that the new season, if you start counting from "The Christmas Invasion," looks a lot like the previous one: first you've got to introduce the new Doctor, amid the domesticity of the Powell estate and an invasion in central London. Next you've got a visit to the far future, with robot spiders, the Face of Boe and Cassandra. Then it's back to the Victorian era for some old-fashioned scares.

The problem with that argument is that the counting is off. "New Earth" isn't the emotionally wrenching follow-up to the season opener, it's the one doing the introductory work. So instead of kicking off the season's arc, it's got the job of bringing back *Doctor Who* for the general audience, ensuring they have a good time while they're watching.

Like "Rose," "New Earth" isn't about its plot; both are showcases for the characters, which is far more important at this stage in the game. Talk to just about any thirty-something fan who's seen the episode and they'll list its faults until the cows come home. The plotting is a bit dodgy, logic is sacrificed for a good laugh, the disease stuff makes no sense, the Doctor's resolution is equally iffy . . . Talk to any eight-year-old who's watched the first third of the season, and they'll tell you that "New Earth" is by far their favourite and, more, the zombies were the scariest monster yet. Let me say that again: the disease zombies are scarier to kids than anything the next bunch of episodes can dish up, no matter how realistic the CGI monster looks in "Tooth and Claw."

Most deliciously of all, fan reaction actually mirrors one of the episode's themes. Do we know when our time is up, or do we keep hanging on some more? Please keep your answers to one side of the paper.

It's the acting that really makes this work. Tennant and Piper are hilarious, and Sean Gallagher is excellent. I have a lot of time for a flawed story if it can pull off humour, and "New Earth" does it masterfully. Rose announcing that she's a chav is final, clinching proof that you don't need to get the reference at hand for the joke to be funny. David Tennant swinging his hips and doing the twin-hearted samba is comic genius. The "textbook enigmatic" scene is a delight and it'll take you at least a second to get "I'm a walking doodle." The disinfectant scene is also amusing, even though it probably shouldn't be.

What's great is the way the comedy dovetails with the emotional scenes. The repartee on the ladder leads directly into "They just want to be touched," which is far more telling than it appears. It's the beginning of Cassandra's realization that culminates in the tear-jerking last scene, which is quite a feat given the laughs that came before it. There's a resonance between the "wanting to be touched" idea and a similar idea that'll crop up in the season finale, which is very nice indeed.

So what we've got here is an episode that's light-hearted, character-driven, fun, touching, intriguing and scary for the kiddies, often simultaneously. It's less of a cohesive narrative in its own right than a sampler for what's to come throughout the rest of the season. Which is precisely as it should be: for the first time in ages, this is televised *Doctor Who*, going about its business as usual. So sit back and enjoy the ride. You'll have a much better time if you don't analyze it too much. And so will the next generation.

Second Opinion (GB) The opening, with the new Doctor powering up the TARDIS and getting ready to take off, is stirring. The ending, where Cassandra in Chip's body tells her past self she was beautiful before dying, was poignant. What occurs between these two points doesn't measure up to either.

"New Earth" is, in its favour, fast moving, with some fun set pieces, great monsters-of-the-week in the cat nuns and some hilarious moments provided by both David Tennant and Billie Piper when Cassandra possesses the Doctor and Rose. But it also has a plot written on the back of a packet of crisps, science that, even by the standards of *Doctor Who*, seems ludicrous (and I would say that even if a mathematical epidemiologist wasn't co-authoring this book) and weird tonal shifts. Plus, the location work does the story no favours: filming at a modern building doesn't look futuristic; it instantly dates the episode instead.

Despite all this, "New Earth" is still likeable. The cast is all first-rate, putting their all into material that isn't meant to be anything more than a lightweight, undemanding fluff-fest designed to just kick the season into gear. Murray Gold provides some lovely, surprisingly delicate music. And Zoë Wannamaker is, as ever, a diva par excellence as Cassandra.

"New Earth" is like an attractive person who turns out to be not that bright. You appreciate them for what there is to appreciate for as long as you see them. Maybe a season opener could and should do more, but bright, colourful and fun isn't a bad mission statement.

2.02 Tooth and Claw

Written by Russell T Davies **Directed by** Euros Lyn

Supporting cast Pauline Collins (Queen Victoria), Ian Hanmore (Father Angelo), Michelle Duncan (Lady Isobel), Derek Riddell (Sir Robert), Jamie Sives (Captain Reynolds), Tom Smith (The Host), Ruth Milne (Flora)

Original airdate April 22, 2006

The Big Idea On her way to Balmoral, Her Majesty Queen Victoria is diverted to Torchwood House, which has been taken over by a cult that worships a werewolf.

Roots and References *An American Werewolf in London*; *Crouching Tiger, Hidden Dragon* (the opening "bullet time" fight sequence).

Adventures in Time and Space Deciding to convince Queen Victoria and her retinue that he is Scottish, the Doctor takes on the identity of Dr. James McCrimmon. Jamie McCrimmon was the second Doctor's companion, from the time of the Battle of Culloden in 1745 in "The Highlanders" (1966).

The Torchwood Effect At the end of this story, Queen Victoria decides to create an institute, in Sir Robert's memory, named after Torchwood House. This Torchwood Institute will defend the British Empire from further alien threats, the Doctor included. The Host can sense "a bit of the wolf" about Rose, a call-back to Rose's part as the Bad Wolf last season.

The Doctor and Rose The honeymoon continues for Rose and the new Doctor, as they lark about, riffing on their own private jokes.

Monster of the Week The Host is a werewolf or, as the Doctor more accurately terms it, a lupine wavelength haemovariform. It came to the Scottish moors 300 years before this story began and has survived by passing its lycanthropic form on to successive humans. Many of these hosts are children snatched by monks from the nearby St. Catherine's monastery. These monks turned away from worshipping God to worshipping the wolf and are now servants of the Host.

Stand Up and Cheer It's not just that Queen Victoria faces down Father Angelo with a service revolver. Nor is it that she kills him while correcting him on the proper form of address when speaking to the Queen. It's that, afterwards, she claims Father Angelo's murder was the work of Captain Reynolds. You simply do not mess with this woman.

Roll Your Eyes The £10 bet to get Queen Victoria to say she is not amused is a good running gag. However, honestly, when you're trapped in a room with the risk of death hanging over you, and there are dead bodies outside, now is not the time to try to win a bet, Rose.

You're Not Making Any Sense Between this and "New Earth," Russell T Davies seems to be going for some kind of a distance record in avoiding basic scientific concepts. There is no such thing as "moonlight": it's simply the sun's light being reflected on the surface of the moon. Even if it could be refracted and magnified by a tricked-up telescope — a dubious concept at best — it would be just the same as ordinary sunlight.

Interesting Trivia Aside from the poetic licence of bringing Queen Victoria to Torchwood House to face a werewolf with a Time Lord, there is surprisingly little to quibble with the story, historically. Victoria had, in fact, encountered six of her eight assassination attempts by 1879, she was obsessed with her late husband, Albert, and she frequently visited the royal residence at Balmoral Castle in Aberdeenshire (in fact, she was there in October 1879 to receive Major John Chard, a hero of the otherwise devastating Anglo-Zulu conflict). The Koh-i-Noor diamond did have a substantial portion of it (about 42% of its weight) cut to enhance its brilliance. Prince Albert supervised this and was still not pleased with the result. Where everything gets a little fanciful is that mistletoe, a parasitic plant that tends to grow on soft-barked trees, is not found in abundance in the Scottish moors. Where it gets very fanciful are the kung-fu monks in an era when martial arts were virtually unheard of in the West.

The Doctor is going to take Rose to see Ian Dury and the Blockheads at the Top Rank in Sheffield, November 1979. (The Doctor even plays a bit of "Hit Me With Your Rhythm Stick" to get in the mood.) While Rose calls the Doctor a punker, Dury was more a New Wave artist.

The TARDIS Chronometer The Scottish moors, somewhere south of Aberdeen, in 1879.

Brilliant? (GB) You kind of have to give Her Majesty some credit. Queen Victoria's banishment of the Doctor and Rose smacks of narrow-minded xenophobia and superstition, but she does have a point: the Doctor and Rose behave like first-rate gits for most of the story. The pair of them traipsing about with absolute smugness, with Rose trying to win a bet during a crisis, and both her and the Doctor treating the threat of the Host like some kind of a game. When Queen Victoria gives them a reality check by banishing them, they don't even seem the least bit bothered and saunter back to the TARDIS mocking the royal family. Don't get me wrong, flippancy in the face of danger is a beloved trait in *Doctor Who*, but here it just borders on being unlikeable.

With that out of the way, I have to say "Tooth and Claw" is one of the best amusement park rides *Doctor Who* has ever done. A fast-paced experience full of thrills and scares, "Tooth and Claw" keeps the pace going, the excitement level up and the viewer off-balance.

I like to picture Russell T Davies writing "Tooth and Claw," smoking a cigarette and typing while muttering to himself, "Screw you, Steven Moffat . . . screw you 'Empty Child' at the top of the DWM poll . . . screw all the fan critics who say, 'Russell can only write camp humour and soap opera and can't do horror . . .' I'll show you all." Because what he delivers is a story devoid of all the things he's usually famous for writing, instead giving us horror, suspense and historical drama. And it turns out Russell T Davies can write an old-school *Doctor Who* story with the best of them. All this is ironic as, judging from comments Davies made in *Doctor Who Magazine*, this was a last-minute replacement script, virtually written overnight.

What really makes everything sing, though, is the editing by Crispin Green, which is tight and pacey and reflects the verve with which Euros Lyn directs the episode, particularly the martial arts pre-credits sequence. Pauline Collins' standout performance as Queen Victoria takes it to the next level, as she uses Her Majesty's familiar imperious persona as a façade for something much more cold-blooded. Collins' Victoria is supported by lots of small but standout performances: Jamie Sives as Captain Reynolds is charming in his eagerness to fit in while dining with royalty; Michelle Duncan as Lady Isobel has this lovely, quiet transformation from shrinking flower to someone smart and brave enough to take on a werewolf; and Tom Smith is delightfully creepy in his one scene as the Host in human form. And David Tennant is so wonderful when he gets to use his own Scottish accent that it's a shame when he resorts back to his standard Estuary English.

After three event episodes in a row (the finale, Christmas special and season opener), "Tooth and Claw" is the first "regular" episode of *Who* we've had in a while. On balance, I'd say this was the good kind of regular.

Second Opinion (RS?) This is very nearly the incredibly awesome werewolf story it wants to be . . . but not quite.

The story moves rather glacially at first, but it's all a slow burn until the reveal of the wolf. From that point on, things rollick along, sadly let down only by the Doctor and Rose acting like smug idiots. If there's one thing the show should never do, it's make the Doctor unlikeable. Alien yes, annoying no. Fortunately, there are consequences: the season arc gets kicked off as a direct result of the Doctor and Rose being so irritating.

Plaudits should go to the CGI work on the werewolf itself. It's easy to forget just how much effort goes into the effects these days, but the werewolf's face is a thing of beauty. The fact that its movement isn't quite right — why exactly does it like to walk down a corridor on its hind legs? — doesn't detract from the sheer detail in the facial hair and snout. Plus, the lights are turned down, so even when it has to move down a corridor in that telltale CGI lumber, it doesn't look as awkward as it might.

It's a little bizarre that the monks are never dealt with. At the story's climax, they're surrounding the house, armed with rifles and shooting at anyone who tries to escape. Then they vanish completely, as though the death of the werewolf caused them to pack up and return to their monastery, no questions asked. It's a shame we don't get to see the Doctor and a bunch of unarmed women overpower ninja monks with rifles who somersault in slow motion. Taking it as read that this just happened, without even a line of dialogue, is simply lazy.

Despite its problems, "Tooth and Claw" has a lot to recommend it. The mood is excellent, the wolf is beautiful and the trap within a trap is delicious, a stunning way of building a mystery and its solution into the constraints of a 45-minute mood piece. Ironically, its pivotal role as the foundation of Torchwood works against it; if it had been a standalone story, it would probably be better remembered.

2.03 School Reunion

Written by Toby Whithouse **Directed by** James Hawes

Supporting cast Camille Coduri (Jackie Tyler), Noel Clarke (Mickey Smith), Elisabeth Sladen (Sarah Jane Smith), Anthony Head (Mr. Finch), Rod Arthur (Mr. Parsons), Eugene Washington (Mr. Wagner), Heather Cameron (Nina), Joe Pickley (Kenny), Benjamin Smith (Luke), Clem Tibber (Milo), Lucinda Dryzek (Melissa), John Leeson (Voice of K9)

Original airdate April 29, 2006

The Big Idea The Doctor has gone undercover, investigating strange happenings in a school and discovers someone else investigating: his old companion, Sarah Jane Smith.

Roots and References British children's television of the 1990s, particularly *The Demon Headmaster* and Russell T Davies' *Dark Season*, and U.S. television such as *Buffy the Vampire Slayer* (also starring Anthony Head) with nefarious goings-on at ordinary schools.

Adventures in Time and Space Sarah's litany of things she's seen with the Doctor are all references to her Classic *Who* stories in the Jon Pertwee and Tom Baker eras of the 1970s including mummies (from 1975's "Pyramids of Mars"), robots (particularly Tom Baker's 1974 debut adventure "Robot"), Daleks (in 1974's "Death to the Daleks" and 1975's "Genesis of the Daleks"), anti-matter monsters (from 1975's "Planet of Evil"), dinosaurs (in 1974's "Invasion of the Dinosaurs") and, finally, *the* Loch Ness monster (in 1975's "Terror of the Zygons"). Rose's list includes ghosts (actually the Gelth), the Slitheen, the Dalek emperor, gas-mask zombies and the werewolf.

The Doctor tells Sarah Jane he's regenerated "half a dozen times" since they last met. They discuss the ending of their last adventure together, 1976's "The Hand of Fear," and she reveals that the Doctor dropped her off in Aberdeen, not Croydon as intended at the time.

The Torchwood Effect Mickey's attempt to get more information about the UFO sightings around Deffry Vale School are repelled by a Torchwood firewall.

Who is the Doctor? The Doctor shows that his billing as a "lonely god" is partly of his own making. He can't bring himself to go back to Sarah Jane after leaving her behind, because, as someone who never really grows old but regenerates, he finds it hard to watch the ones he loves eventually wither and die. He calls it "the curse of the Time Lord." He continues with his resolution of no second chances, telling Finch, "I'm so old now. I used to have so much mercy."

The Doctor and Rose The honeymoon with Rose and the tenth Doctor abruptly comes to an end. Rose is deeply unsettled by Sarah Jane's presence and what it represents. Rose tells the Doctor, "I've been to the year five billion . . . but this . . . is really seeing the future. You just leave us behind. Is that what you're going to do to me?" Rose is hostile to Sarah Jane, partially because she sees Sarah's sad future ahead for herself (though the pair bond when they realize the extent of their shared experience). The Doctor assures Rose that he would never leave her behind, though Rose doesn't seem convinced.

Monster of the Week The Krillitane are aliens who take on the genetic traits of the races they conquer to form a composite species. They once looked human but with longer necks; now they look more bat-like and possess wings that were pillaged from another race, the Bessans, ten generations ago. They use a morphic generator to make people think they look human, though Brother Lasser, who poses as the school headmaster, Mr. Finch, has taken on an actual human form.

Stand Up and Cheer Sarah Jane and Rose's duelling lists of monsters not only reaches the highest geek quotient in the series to date, it's also a very, very funny scene, particularly when it reaches the punchline and Rose gets knocked off her high horse to admire Sarah Jane's encounter with the Loch Ness monster!

Roll Your Eyes The Doctor bemoaning that humans wither and decay and die, leaving him alone. Leaving aside that *Highlander* did that bit already, it comes across as a bit whiny. It's called life, Doctor, deal with it . . .

You're Not Making Any Sense Given that K9 doesn't work any more, why is Sarah Jane still carting him around in the back of her Volkswagen Jetta, particularly since he seems to take up most of the trunk space?

Interesting Trivia The oil, and its use in school dinners with lots of chips, is a cheeky reference to TV chef Jamie Oliver's campaign to bring more nutritious meals to British school lunchrooms around the time the program was made.

There isn't actually a Skasis Paradigm, but it's not dissimilar to the Grand Unified Theory in physics, which aims to unite three disparate forces in one explanation. An even bigger version is the Theory of Everything, which would like to add an explanation for gravity into the mix. Thus far, there isn't such an explanation; in fact, Einstein spent 30 years searching for one but was unsuccessful. If we did find one, then it would be an elegant description of the rules that underpin our existence, but it's rather unlikely to be useful in reordering the universe.

Several scenes in the script were cut during filming, including Milo's brain being shorted out by the Doctor's questions (which is still alluded to in the final episode). Several filmed scenes, building up Kenny's role as an outsider figure and giving him more to do, were cut, ostensibly for timing, but young actor Joe Pickley seems terribly awkward in the deleted scenes included on the DVD set.

The TARDIS Chronometer The story is set some time after the events of "The Christmas Invasion" (Sarah Jane mentions the Sycorax ship), at Deffry Vale School, a suburban comprehensive school presumably somewhere in or near London.

Brilliant? (GB) Back in the dark 15-year gap before the New Series, fans had a lot of time to assess why their beloved show had failed. A number of fans, this writer included, had determined that one of the reasons might have been the obsession the show developed in its later years with its own continuity. Many, including myself, felt that should *Doctor Who* come back, it should make a clean break from its past and never mention previous exploits except in the most oblique ways. To a certain extent during the first series, you can see some of this thinking at work: in "Dalek," the Daleks' creator is never named. Similarly, the Doctor never once mentions the name of his own home planet during the first two series.

"School Reunion" marks the first significant break from that thinking and, in a way, shows us why such thinking was flawed in the first place. The extensive past of *Doctor Who* can be used, accessed, even discussed in geeky detail (who imagined one would ever see the Doctor and Sarah Jane discussing the ending of "The Hand of Fear" on modern British television?), just so long as it is used to tell an interesting story. Here, the central conceit of treating a past companion as an ex-wife figure is excellent. The story offers a great insight into the Doctor's emotional attachment to his companions and how hard that must be; decades later, Sarah Jane is still struggling to put her life back together and K9 is going to rust. No wonder Rose is worried. You don't have to know who Sarah Jane is (or K9 for that matter) to get that, though it helps that they're using the Classic Series' two most iconic companions.

It also helps that Elisabeth Sladen is wonderful in "School Reunion." I have to admit, having loved her since I was a teenager, I was worried she would turn out to be an actress of a particular time and place who wouldn't work so well in a modern context. But she demonstrates precisely why I loved her so much in the Classic Series: she has her own unique charisma and charm. At the café, Sarah Jane asks the Doctor that question everyone who was ever dumped asks: was it me? Was there something I could have done? The fact that Lis Sladen can pull off this sort of emotional scene, which was never at the core of her era of *Doctor Who*, impresses me more than I can say.

Toby Whithouse writes with memorable flourishes of dialogue ("think how bad things could possibly be, then add another suitcase of bad") that make his later BBC series, *Being Human*, so delightful to watch. His script has great scenes for everyone, including Mickey, whose realization that he's the tin dog is priceless. The Doctor's confrontation with Finch by the pool is one of the standouts of this season. Anthony Head is delightfully playful, and David Tennant is chilling as the Doctor quietly tells Finch he will stop him. It's a shame the season thus far has shown more of the garrulous, bouncy Doctor, because when Tennant broods it is glorious to watch.

The school plot is lightweight, almost a comic-book story, but it's used to frame the supremely witty character drama within. And yet, I wish the episode succeeded at being a brilliant adventure story *and* a great emotional drama. Part of me wonders if it's the school setting; if it had been set in an army base (as originally intended), would it have had more gravitas?

As lightweight as the plot might be, I must concede that any story that can make the death and resurrection of K9 so emotionally powerful has to be doing something right. I also think this points to something bigger when it comes to revisiting *Doctor Who*'s legendary past: it's about heritage, not continuity. *Doctor Who*'s past is something that rightfully belongs to it, and it's perfectly fine to play with it, just so long as it makes it fun and worthwhile. Judging by the success of the story — and the spinoff series that came from it — the makers of the program were correct to embrace, rather than avoid the past.

Second Opinion (RS?) This is, in a sense, where it all went wrong. Until now, New *Who* had been (mostly) fresh and original. It was stripped down to its constituent elements: a man in a box, travelling in time and fighting monsters. Yes, there were the Daleks, but they were huge icons of the Classic Series and their absence would have been strange.

What the New Series needed at this point was its own monster for the 21st century. Something that was powerful, frightening and that couldn't have been thought of back in the 20th century. Something to give the show its own identity, to demonstrate that it isn't just trading on dusted-off old ideas, but that it has its own voice. In short, *Doctor Who* needed something like the Borg in *Star Trek: The Next Generation*.

But instead of moving forward, the show starts looking backward with this episode — and does it more so, as time goes on. The Classic Series was at its best when it was telling original stories and not gazing at its own navel; the same is true of the New Series. Most likely, the reason why the show keeps returning to the past is because it's being made by producers who grew up as fans. The score: originality 0, fandom 10.

As for "School Reunion" itself, there's merit in a story about staying young while watching your friends and lovers grow old. Of course, that story gets shown, rather than told, in the next episode, making this less powerful than it otherwise would be. Although the Doctor's logic — that watching someone grow old would be too painful, so he must therefore run away — is rather tenuous; a great many of us mere mortals are likely going to have to watch loved ones wither and decay, without the option of running away, which makes the Doctor look shallow and insensitive. Fortunately, we'll pick up the flip side of this issue in the next episode.

The Krillitane are reasonable one-off monsters, although Anthony Head is a shade too mincing as the villain and Kenny is awful, even despite having all his lines cut. And it's bizarre that Sarah Jane gets reintroduced via an inconsequential scene in a stairwell.

"School Reunion" is the pivot around which the remainder of the Davies era swings. From this point forward, *Doctor Who* will draw more and more on its past, shaking off the last confines of its now-anomalous first series. The payoff is a hugely successful series, in the eyes of the general public and fans alike. The price is the loss of originality and of the sheer angry power that drove so much of its amazing first season.

Doctor Who is dead. Long live *Doctor Who*.

The Psychic Papers: Sarah Jane Smith and K9

Elisabeth Sladen's Sarah Jane Smith is one of the longest running companions, having travelled with both the third and fourth Doctors for more than three seasons of the Classic Series. Sarah Jane met the Doctor (then played by Jon Pertwee) when she was a young journalist investigating the disappearances of scientists in 1973's "The Time Warrior." During that story, she stowed away on board the TARDIS and found herself whisked back to the Middle Ages, where she and the Doctor faced off against a Sontaran named Linx. After that, she and the Doctor (who was then UNIT's scientific adviser) adventured on contemporary Earth and in space while she continued her career as a writer with *Metropolitan* magazine.

Intelligent, quick witted and resourceful, Sarah Jane was initially written as a Women's Lib era feminist, though this was toned down as time went on. Fortunately, she continued to be a more proactive companion than her predecessors, and Sladen's charisma made Sarah Jane a much-loved character.

While the third Doctor's relationship with Sarah Jane was avuncular in nature (much like the Doctor/companion relationships leading up to then), when the Doctor regenerated in 1974's "Planet of the Spiders," Sarah Jane developed a close bond with the fourth Doctor (which reflected Elisabeth Sladen's own rapport with actor Tom Baker). The two had an easy, free-flowing relationship full of humour and respect. In many ways, Sarah Jane and the fourth Doctor seemed to have the first close friendship between a Doctor and a companion.

Soon after the Doctor's regeneration, he gave up working with UNIT, and the two travelled exclusively in the TARDIS during one of the most popular periods of the show. Sarah Jane's travels came to an end in 1976's "The Hand of Fear," when the Time Lords summoned the Doctor back to Gallifrey. Not permitted to bring an alien to his home planet, the Doctor returned Sarah Jane to her home in South Croydon, only she realized after the TARDIS left that he hadn't landed in South Croydon at all!

A year or so after Sarah Jane left *Doctor Who*, the Doctor's robotic companion, K9, first appeared in 1977's "The Invisible Enemy." K9 was the creation of Professor Marius, a physician at the medical facility the Bi-Al Foundation near Titan. Marius had to leave behind his own pet canine on Earth, so he made the next best thing: a mobile computer shaped like a dog, with ear and eye sensors, and a nose laser for good measure. At the end of that story, Marius is dispatched to Earth; unable to take K9 due to weight restrictions, he offered the tin dog to the fourth Doctor, who took K9 on board the TARDIS.

Voiced mostly by actor John Leeson, K9 was a fussy know-it-all but was also adorable. Critics scoffed, saying it was part of a zeitgeist of cute robots that included R2D2 from the *Star Wars* films. The rest of the audience — among the largest the Classic Series had seen — was delighted by the tin dog.

Over the next four seasons, the Doctor gave K9 to a departing companion, built a Mark II version, and then later gave that to another departing companion. But you can't keep a good tin dog down. In 1981, the *Doctor Who* production team made a pilot for a potential spinoff of *Doctor Who* called *K9 and Company*, which saw Sarah Jane, once again working as an investigative journalist, receiving a gift from the Doctor: K9 Mark III. The one-off story (in which Sarah Jane, K9 and Sarah's nephew, Brendan, investigated satanic cults) was never made into a series. Sarah Jane appeared in *Doctor Who*'s 20th anniversary story, 1983's "The Five Doctors," alongside the third Doctor (with a cameo from K9). Curiously, Sarah Jane doesn't remember the events of this story at all in "School Reunion," which suggests the experience may have been erased from her memory.

In 2007, Sarah Jane succeeded where she hadn't in 1981. *The Sarah Jane Adventures*, created by Russell T Davies for CBBC, the children's division of the BBC, shows what happens to Sarah Jane after "School Reunion." Now living in a house on Bannerman Road in Ealing, Sarah Jane investigates the unknown and fights alien invaders along with her adopted children, Luke and Sky, and Luke's school friends Clyde, Rani and Maria, aided by a super-computer called Mr. Smith. (A non-BBC spinoff series was made with K9 by the dog's creator Bob Baker; K9 Mark IV was sent off to space to seal a black hole, but he came back in *The Sarah Jane Adventures*' third season.) Several *Doctor Who* monsters have appeared in *The Sarah Jane Adventures*, including the Slitheen, the Sontarans and the Judoon; the tenth and eleventh Doctors have appeared as well. The series was among the most popular shown on CBBC. Sarah Jane, meanwhile, returned to *Doctor Who* in "The Stolen Earth"/"Journey's End" and "The End of Time, Part Two."

Elisabeth Sladen died of cancer on April 19, 2011, aged 63. At the time of her death, she had completed the first half of *The Sarah Jane Adventures*' fifth season, which aired in the following autumn. *Doctor Who* fans everywhere still mourn the loss of Elisabeth Sladen and Sarah Jane Smith.

2.04 The Girl in the Fireplace

Written by Steven Moffat **Directed by** Euros Lyn

Supporting cast Noel Clarke (Mickey Smith), Sophia Myles (Reinette), Ben Turner (King Louis), Jessica Atkins (Young Reinette), Angel Coulby (Katherine), Gareth Wyn Griffiths (manservant), Paul Kasey (clockwork man), Ellen Thomas (clockwork woman), Emily Joyce (alien voice), Jonathan Hart (alien voice)

Original airdate May 6, 2006

The Big Idea A spaceship from the 51st century is stalking Madame de Pompadour in the 18th.

Roots and References *Dangerous Liaisons* (romance amidst pre-revolutionary French aristocracy); *The Lion, the Witch and the Wardrobe* (the fireplace as a portal to another world); Audrey Niffenegger's novel *The Time Traveller's Wife* (though inverting the story and focusing on the time traveller; Niffenegger's next novel, *Her Fearful Symmetry*, returns the favour by having the protagonist watch "The Girl in the Fireplace"); Philippa Pearce's children's book *Tom's Midnight Garden* (with a protagonist who meets a girl from the past at various stages of her life through a portal in his aunt's garden).

Adventures in Time and Space The Doctor says, "Bananas are good," and dancing is used as a metaphor for sex, callbacks to "The Doctor Dances," also written by Moffat. Rose references the Daleks and their name for the Doctor, the Oncoming Storm, which was mentioned in "The Parting of the Ways." Mickey names Sarah Jane Smith among the Doctor's past love interests ("School Reunion"). The Doctor mentions zeus plugs (1976's "The Hand of Fear").

Who is the Doctor? With Reinette, the Doctor finds a degree of intimacy he has not found with any of his human companions, even Rose. Reinette is precocious enough to use their shared mindlink as a means of seeing into the Doctor's mind to discover the lonely little boy that he is. Her suggestion that it's time that the Doctor learn to dance, laden with the subtext from "The Doctor Dances," implies that there is perhaps some sexual encounter between the two, though this is not seen onscreen. Regardless, the Doctor is profoundly shaken when he discovers Reinette has died.

The Doctor and Rose The Doctor falls in love with someone else, and Rose, while initially jealous, actually stands aside to let it happen. She delivers Reinette a crucial message and is willing to let her join the TARDIS crew. Her question at the end ("Why her?") is quite impressive in its subtlety: it's there to set up the final reveal, but it's also a question about so much more than that. And, tellingly, it goes unanswered.

Monster of the Week Repair droids from the S.S. *Madame de Pompadour*. When the ship faced systems failure following an ion storm, the repair droids harvested the organs of the crew, wiring them into the ship. They have clockwork gears inside a glass dome, but they wear jesters' masks and costumes as a disguise. They have an inbuilt short-range teleport.

Stand Up and Cheer When the Doctor bursts through an 18th-century mirror on a horse, sacrificing his only way home in order to save Reinette and the assembled hostages . . . it actually does make you want to stand up and cheer.

Roll Your Eyes When Reinette says that her companion is the king of France, the Doctor replies, "Well, I'm a Lord of Time" so rudely that you wonder what the king did to offend him. This is particularly strange, since the king is seen to be sensitive and polite. Perhaps he's just jealous.

You're Not Making Any Sense Reinette broke the link with the ship when she moved the fireplace, so it was offline when the mirror broke. However, minutes before the mirror broke — and while the fireplace was in its new location — she called out through it. So in what sense was it offline? The Doctor does say that the link is basically physical, although it's hard to determine what it being offline then means.

Interesting Trivia David Tennant and Sophia Myles's onscreen chemistry has another layer to it when you're aware that they became a couple around this time and dated for two years.

Jeanne Antoinette Poisson, Marquise de Pompadour, also known as Madame de Pompadour, *maîtresse-en-titre* of the king of France, was as fascinating a character in real life as she is onscreen. The Doctor's summary of her in the story — "actress, artist, musician, dancer, courtesan, fantastic gardener" — is accurate, though according to Madame de Pompadour's own recollection she was not nicknamed Reinette until she was nine years old (the result of a visit to a fortune teller who claimed she would "reign over the heart of a king"), two years after the Doctor's first visit to her in 1727. (Curiously, by 1758 — when the climax of this story is set — Reinette had not had sexual relations with the king in seven years, though the two remained extremely close friends.)

The TARDIS Chronometer Reinette's story starts in 1727 when she's seven, picks up months later, then jumps ahead to when she's 23, 32 and 37. It ends just after her death at age 43 in 1770. The TARDIS materializes on board the S.S. *Madame de Pompadour*, 3,000 years after 1764 according to an onscreen title. The Doctor claims it's 3,000 years into Rose's future and later mentions that it's the 51st century. These dates only add up once you realize the onscreen title must be rounding up wildly. Which is odd, but the jolting effect of "3,000 years later" is quite superb, so we'll let it go.

Brilliant? (RS?) Oh indeed, yes! In fact, part of what's great about this episode — whether planned from the outset or not, I have no idea — is that it's paired with "School Reunion." In that story, we were simply told about the Doctor's fear of romance, because he'd be forced to watch his lovers grow old and die. Here, we get to watch it happen — and it's heartbreaking.

"The Girl in the Fireplace" is the show's first actual romance. Previously, we've had hints and subtext, but here the romance is on the screen and proud of it. This is the point when the old guard had to adapt or die and when the shippers — a term used to describe (primarily female) fans who are in it for the relationships — finally knew that this was their show as well.

The effect on the Doctor is magnificent. For once, we see the cracks in the lead character's armour. The Doctor hurriedly whipping off his glasses when he spies the adult Reinette is a marvellous moment. The final scene shows just how deeply affected he is by Reinette's death and the extent to which tiny human lives come and go like fireflies. And his response to Rose, "I'm always all right," is delivered with just enough bravado that both we and Rose know full well he's lying.

That the Doctor very deliberately chooses to sacrifice his lifestyle for Reinette — trapping himself 3,000 years from his TARDIS and companions — is a testament to just how strong their connection is. Where the threat of death is usually an empty one in drama, the reality of having to take the slow path is a brutal one for the Doctor, and we're made to feel just how big a sacrifice it is.

Popping off and forgetting all about the time differential between the realities is completely typical of this incarnation of the Time Lord: he wants Reinette to come with him, but he hasn't thought everything through. The script recognizes the tragedy of this, rather than trying to sweep it under the rug. It takes the Doctor on an emotional arc from brave to romantic to emotionally vulnerable and finally to wisdom, earned at a steep price.

And yet, instead of transplanting the Doctor into a romance, it makes the story fundamentally about him. The teaser sets the tone, with Reinette pleading into the fireplace, calling out to the man who has saved her throughout her entire life, ending on the word "Doctor" before the credits crash into your disbelief. This is a beautiful use of the show's mythos. Not its continuity (although there's a fair smattering of that), but its very essence.

Fundamentally, it's a story about mirrors. It's a reflection of the previous story; it's a science-fiction tale of a spaceship looking for its mirror image; many of the portals are literal mirrors, one of which is dramatically smashed at the climax; and it stars two characters who are reflections of each other. The first time the Doctor sees young Reinette, she's framed in her bedroom mirror.

And when adult Reinette looks back into the Doctor's mind, she not only sees into his soul, she grasps the fundamental nature of what it means to be the Doctor.

We see this play out as the action draws to a typical *Doctor Who* climax: the monsters arrive and only the Doctor, using an unexpected approach, can defeat them. And yet, along the way, Reinette realizes that the monsters and the Doctor have to coexist, that you can't have one without the other. She states that "one may tolerate a world of demons for the sake of an angel" and finally realizes, "The Doctor is worth the monsters." Thus, the Doctor and the monsters are also reflections of each other. She even stands up to the monsters herself in his absence, saying, "The answer is no," which demonstrates just how much like the Doctor — especially the ninth — she's become.

In short, this is one of the best stories that New *Who* has to offer. It makes amazing use of its 45-minute running time; it manages to be oddball, heroic, surprising and romantic with time-travel malarkey and killer droids; and it's a deep and fundamental comment on the nature of the Doctor. The time portals are astonishingly effective, despite the fact that the production team simply built the sets side by side, breaking the fourth wall using nothing more than a rotating floor, a tapestry and a one-way mirror. This episode cemented Moffat's position as someone who could deliver the goods over and over again, and it's endlessly rewatchable. Glorious.

Second Opinion (GB) Given the fact that "The Girl in the Fireplace" has won writer Steven Moffat a Hugo Award, a *Doctor Who Magazine* award and every other conceivable plaudit, I'm not going to talk about the writing on this episode — which is really as good as everyone says it is — and will instead focus on other aspects.

Like Murray Gold's score, which is among his best for the entire series, particularly the music in the last five minutes, which is so haunting it stays with you for weeks afterward. Or the performance of Ben Turner, who plays the king and is absolutely sublime in his final scene where he talks fondly of Reinette with his rival, the Doctor. There's the wonderful work of Sophia Myles, who plays to perfection someone you can believe the Doctor would totally fall in love with in the space of a few hours. And let's not forget David Tennant's virtuoso performance, showing the Doctor actually falling in love with someone and then his heartbreak when he knows he's too late to be with them.

All this ignores the sublime design: the clockwork robots are gorgeous to look at. Or the practical and effects work. (I had no idea while watching that the horse wasn't actually in the ballroom during filming!) Or Noel Clarke and Billie Piper's entertaining (and thankless) double act. Or the way the story is beautifully set up in the same clockwork fashion as the wind-up droids and yet what actually propels it is the relationship, nay the romance, between the Doctor and Reinette, resulting in an episode that pleases the mind and heart.

Oh dear, I wound up talking about the writing, after all. Damn you Steven Moffat!

2.05—2.06 Rise of the Cybermen / The Age of Steel

Written by Tom McRae **Directed by** Graeme Harper

Supporting cast Camille Coduri (Jackie Tyler), Noel Clarke (Mickey Smith), Shaun Dingwall (Pete Tyler), Roger Lloyd Pack (John Lumic), Andrew Hayden-Smith (Jake), Don Warrington (The President), Colin Spaull (Mr. Crane), Mona Hammond (Rita-Anne), Helen Griffin (Mrs. Moore), Paul Antony-Barber (Dr. Kendrick), Adam Shaw (Morris), Paul Kasey (Cyber-Leader), Nicholas Briggs (Cyberman voices).

Original airdates May 13 and 20, 2006

The Big Idea The TARDIS falls into a parallel universe where a mad genius has invented a way for humans to extend their lives: by becoming Cybermen.

Roots and References The 1975 *Doctor Who story* "Genesis of the Daleks" (a mad genius in a wheelchair creating one of the Doctor's most terrifying enemies); *Star Trek*'s "Mirror Mirror" and its various descendents (Mickey is immediately familiar with parallel universes, referencing films and comics); *A Clockwork Orange* (a happy song plays over extreme violence). Mr. Crane plays Tight Fit's 1982 cover version of "The Lion Sleeps Tonight."

Adventures in Time and Space The Cybermen say, "You will become like us," a line from 1967's "Tomb of the Cybermen." Lumic's dummy company is called International Electromatics, the name of Tobias Vaughn's company in 1968's "The Invasion." Lumic is designated as the Cybercontroller, similar to the one seen in "Tomb of the Cybermen" and 1985's "Attack of the Cybermen."

The line "We attack on three sides: above, between, below" is a reference to the approaches to Rassilon's tower in 1983's "The Five Doctors."

Rose remembers seeing the Cyberhead in van Statten's museum ("Dalek"). Mickey refers to himself as the tin dog ("School Reunion") and says he once saved the universe with a big yellow truck ("The Parting of the Ways").

The Torchwood Effect Rose's phone downloads the latest news and, just before she switches it off, there's a mention of Torchwood. At Jackie's party, Pete makes an excuse to stop talking to Rose by calling out to someone named Stevie, saying, "How's things at Torchwood?" suggesting that, in the parallel world, Torchwood is an organization known to the general public.

The Doctor and Rose When faced with the choice of whether to run after Rose or Mickey, the Doctor chooses Rose, every time.

Monster of the Week The Cybermen, creations of John Lumic, CEO of Cybus Industries. They're a human brain in a cybernetic body, described as "human-point-two." Cybermen have artificially grown flesh inside their metal armour, which responds like a living thing. They have emotional inhibitors because emotions hurt.

Stand Up and Cheer The scene where the Doctor and Mrs. Moore encounter the lone Cyberman is amazing. With its emotional inhibitor broken, the Cyberman reveals that she used to be Sally Phelan, supposed to be getting married to Gareth in the morning, and we feel the pain of her fate. It's a heartwrenching scene, all the more for the depth of emotion pouring out of a motionless metal body in an electronic monotone.

Roll Your Eyes When the Doctor says, "I'd call you a genius except I'm in the room," it's a wonder someone doesn't slap him. And it makes no sense; if Stephen Hawking travelled back and met Einstein, would one of them have to give up the title of genius, because you can only have one at a time? What happens at MENSA meetings?

You're Not Making Any Sense Why do the Cybermen start killing people immediately after they kill the President? Nobody else has explicitly refused upgrading. Did they consider the President to be the only useful stock in the room? And it turns out that they can harvest brains from dead bodies anyway, so why bother giving the President the choice?

Interesting Trivia With the loss of the Time Lords, the question of what powers the TARDIS has been left unanswered. In the Classic Series, it drew its power from an artificially created black hole, the Eye of Harmony, that was captured and placed beneath the Time Lord citadel on Gallifrey (although it was — strangely — located inside the TARDIS itself in the 1996 TV Movie, though many have postulated this is simply a link to one on Gallifrey). With Gallifrey gone and the Eye of Harmony with it, the TARDIS should presumably be unable to function. However, in "Boom Town," we saw the TARDIS refuel on the Cardiff rift. Here we're told that it draws power from our universe, and, indeed, it shuts down almost entirely once it's in the alternate universe. Presumably, the Doctor jury-rigged it after the Time War so that it was still functional.

Mickey mentions Tony Blair being prime minister, making him either the PM who was killed in "Aliens of London" or the one between Harriet Jones and Harold Saxon.

Alt-Mickey is named Ricky, which happens to be the ninth Doctor's nickname for Mickey. Some have speculated that this is a grand confluence of events, that the Doctor was precogniscent or had already travelled to the alternate universe (despite the impossiblity of this). The trouble is, the more you dig for an explanation, the sillier this seems. It's much more likely that it's a cute reference on the part of the writers, nothing more.

The TARDIS Chronometer The TARDIS falls through a crack in time (purely by accident) and lands in a parallel London. Mickey finds a newspaper and says the date is "the first of February, this year." Because of the "lost year" from "Aliens of London," the writers don't tell us outright what year it is. Jackie's desire to align herself age-wise with Cuba Gooding Jr. (he was 39 in 2007) would suggest we're still at current-year-plus-one and it's February 1, 2007.

Brilliant? (RS?) In the time that we've known him, Mickey Smith — the first non-white companion in televised *Doctor Who*, incidentally — has gone from zero to hero. Originally the comic relief, with little to contribute beyond pratfalls, Mickey has grown magnificently and now finds himself the centrepiece of the action.

And yet, that action always seems to involve watching his girlfriend with another man, one who has infinitely more to offer her than he does. He's tried railing against the situation and he's tried joining them, but here he finally realizes that Rose will never look at him the way she looks at the Doctor.

What's more, Mickey finds an actual purpose in the alternate world. Not only is his grandmother alive here, but he meets a version of himself who's everything he isn't: rebellious, tough and brave. In this alternate universe, Ricky Smith isn't the idiot, he's the hero. And that proves to Mickey that he can be so much more than he thinks.

Following Ricky's death, Mickey starts to change. He reprograms the villains' technology against them, he refuses to let Jake kill the partially cybernized sentries — on the grounds that this would make them no better than Lumic — and he won't let the Zeppelin leave until his friends are safe. In short, he becomes the Doctor. At the end, his transformation is complete: he leaves behind everything he's known and heads out into the unknown to liberate the world from oppression. This is utterly superb.

It's a pity about the rest of the story, though.

One of the central problems is John Lumic. Roger Lloyd Pack hams it up at every opportunity, turning a potentially menacing villain into a cartoon. In the Classic Series episode "Genesis of the Daleks," which this so desperately wants to be, the evil genius in the wheelchair was mesmerising, because he oozed quiet menace and dangerous insanity, punctuated by moments of incredible instability. Here, Lumic leaves no rant unturned, melodramatically turning all his lines into buffoonery. And when the Cybermen turn on him, it's not the story's climax (as in "Genesis") but rather a minor scene where Lumic reveals himself to be completely ineffectual and with no backup plan.

Another problem is the Cybermen themselves. They're saddled with not one but two ridiculous catchphrases ("Delete" and "You will be upgraded"), which serve to entirely undercut any menace they might have had. Computers aren't terrifying, they're frustrating. Trying to evoke primal terror with the delete button was a colossal mistake. Microsoft's auto updates might be evil incarnate, but they embody the banality of evil, which doesn't make for very good television.

Then there's the plot, which has all the right ingredients but an appalling cook. Key revelations, like the identity of Gemini, are thrown out so haphazardly you wonder why they bothered with the entire subplot. The world being enslaved via earpods is one of those classic Russell T Davies ideas that could have been brilliant in his hands, but it fails miserably when another writer tries to make it work. Wouldn't all those people who are driving when the daily download comes crash into hundreds of pedestrians, because they're immobile for two minutes?

Even the arc of Rose meeting her alternate parents is lacklustre. It's great to see Shaun Dingwall again, but his character has very little of substance to contribute, other than a clumsy revelation and running away from a conversation at the end.

Playing "The Lion Sleeps Tonight" over scenes of implied violence is good, but it would have been infinitely more powerful without Mr. Crane explicitly putting on music to drown out the screams. If ever there was time for a postmodern televisual trick, this was it. It's hard to believe this and "Love & Monsters" were made in the same year. And the masses of Classic *Who* continuity only serve to make this seem even more like a fan-fiction story that accidentally found its way onto TV.

The direction, however, is fantastic. This was Graeme Harper's return to New *Who*, and he doesn't disappoint. The way he lights the Cybermen is particularly effective: throughout the entirety of the first episode, they're always out of focus or in front of extremely bright light so we have no idea what they look like. Sometimes they're in such extreme closeup that we only see a shadow pass in front of the camera, or we just see boots marching in lockstep. We know from the title that they're the Cybermen, but we haven't seen their redesign, so this gives their entrance at the cliffhanger even more impact.

There are a few really good moments in the story: the Doctor guiding Mickey at the conclusion by calling him an idiot; Jackie naming her tiny dog Rose; the reason for Ricky being London's most wanted and his cheeky response; the Cybermen marching in synch; the dormant Cybermen in the cooling tunnels;

the gay subtext between Jake and Ricky/Mickey; and Alt-Jackie's class dismissal of Rose.

However, good moments do not a good story make. Despite an excellent throughline in Mickey's character arc, "Rise of the Cybermen"/"The Age of Steel" is a huge disappointment. What could have been scary and resonant is instead cartoonish and often nonsensical. It's a hodgepodge of amateurish social commentary, pointless continuity and lacklustre villains. The only reason it has any resonance is because of its links to the season finale, which shows how a Cyberman story should be done.

With this second season clunker, we realized that the first two-parter of a season in the Davies era was always going to be the kiddie two-parter. Depressingly, each would be worse than the previous one. Despite the obvious difficulties that posed.

Second Opinion (GB) Until "Rise of the Cybermen" and "The Age of Steel," this new *Doctor Who* had never produced anything that was actually bad. Underdeveloped, yes. Ordinary, yes. But bad? This is where it all goes seriously pear-shaped.

One of the problems with this story is that it undercuts every single strength it has. Mickey's growth in the second episode is thrilling to watch; however, Clarke distinguishes Ricky from Mickey by sneering like an 11-year-old. They bring back Shaun Dingwall as Pete Tyler, but they've jettisoned all the subtlety that made us love him in "Father's Day" (the revelation that Pete's been on the side of the angels all along seems to be for dramatic convenience more than anything). The body horror of the Cybermen is nicely touched on in two scenes — the Doctor and Mrs. Moore talking to the cybernized bride-to-be, and Pete and Rose losing the converted Jackie to a room full of Cybermen — but it too is undermined by a climax that glosses over the full horror of the mass murder taking place. The idea that in the parallel world Mickey/Ricky is the leader of a resistance cell and London's most wanted is actually kind of cool, but then it turns out his only crime is unpaid traffic fines. Ho ho ho, we're supposed to laugh, but in fact it makes the character (and the Preachers) look weak and ineffectual.

Which brings us to problem number two with this story: the tone is completely off-kilter. It should be scary, doom laden and emotional — not unlike last season's "Dalek" — but instead it's broad and overplayed. Roger Lloyd Pack's Lumic is a cartoon. There's nothing remotely scary or compelling about him, and Lloyd Pack is quite happy to cackle (he's even worse as the Cybercontroller). In the Classic Series, the Cybermen reflected the dread of organ transplants and computers. Here they represent what? The need for upgrades? People's need to check their BlackBerrys? It's as though the production team got genuinely gunshy about showing where the story's real potential lies in something full of body horror and a genuine dystopia, rather than a world like ours only with more Zeppelins and Bluetooths.

I really wanted to like this story. I love the new Cybermen design, I thought Mrs. Moore was a wonderful character, Mickey gets (after some needless ill treatment by the Doctor and Rose) a good send-off and Graeme Harper's direction is superb. But those things are not enough. This is *Doctor Who*'s first big failure.

The Psychic Papers: The Cybermen

First seen in 1966's "The Tenth Planet," William Hartnell's final story, and appearing opposite almost all the Doctors, the original Cybermen were the Classic Series' second-most-featured monster.

The Cybermen were the creation of writer Gerry Davis, who was then script editor of *Doctor Who*, and Kit Pedlar, a physician and scientist who was acting as an unofficial scientific advisor to the series. One idea suggested by Pedlar was an evolution of the then relatively new procedure of organ transplantation: if human organs could be transplanted, why not create completely artificial implants? (Pedlar was decades ahead of his time.) And if organs can be transplanted, why not a skeleton? Why not replace the human body with a robotic one? With that, the Cybermen were born.

In "The Tenth Planet," the Cybermen were humans from Earth's twin planet Mondas who slowly replaced their body parts with cybernetics, eventually becoming completely mechanized creatures. Over the course of nine stories in two decades, the Classic Series Cybermen battled the Doctor and his companions mostly in space and in the future (though they had some limited capacity for time travel). During this time, the Cybermen relocated to the planet Telos and, later, developed a weakness to gold.

The design of the Cybermen evolved but retained the basic silhouette, which included "jug handles" on both sides of the head and a blank expression with circular eyeholes. Some stories featured a stylized "teardrop" indentation on the sides of the eyeholes. The New Series Cybermen retain the jug handles and the teardrops.

As well as regular Cybermen, stories often featured a Cyberleader (distinguished by black handles); a Cyberleader first appears in the New Series in "Army of Ghosts." All Cybermen are controlled by a Cybercontroller (a larger Cyberman with a bulbous head through which his brain showed) and used mobile weapons called Cybermats. Their origins were only broadly summarised on television, and a creator was never mentioned.

Genesis of the Cybermen stories have appeared for years in the comics (most notably "The World Shapers" by popular comics writer Grant Morrison, who postulated that they evolved from the Voord from 1964's "The Keys of Marinus"), and the subject was even a proposed television story by Cybermen co-creator Gerry Davis in the 1980s. In 2002, Big Finish (makers of a series of audio *Doctor Who* adventures) released an adventure called "Spare Parts," detailing the origins of the Cybermen (consistent with their history in "The Tenth Planet"). In that story, Mondas is a dying planet and a collection of scientists create the Cybermen to enable people to live in its hostile environment.

When creating the New Series, the decision was made to create a new race of Cybermen rather than continue with the same monsters that appeared in the Classic Series (as they had with the Daleks), and furthermore to give this new race an origin story. "Rise of the Cybermen"/"The Age of Steel" was supposed to use the background established in "Spare Parts" (which explains the credit for its writer, Marc Platt), although the only things that explicitly come from that story are the meeting with cybernized Jackie and the remark about why emotions are taken away.

Later stories such as "The Next Doctor" and "A Good Man Goes to War" suggest that these parallel-world Cybermen escaped into our universe and then evolved to develop space-travelling abilities and giant walking robot base stations.

The Cybermen will continue to loom large in *Doctor Who*'s history, representing the side of humanity that concedes more and more to technology. Gerry Davis and Kit Pedlar's nightmare scenario may yet happen.

2.07 The Idiot's Lantern

Written by Mark Gatiss **Directed by** Euros Lyn

Supporting cast Maureen Lipman (The Wire), Ron Cook (Magpie), Jamie Foreman (Eddie Connolly), Debra Gillett (Rita Connelly), Rory Jennings (Tommy Connelly), Margaret John (Tommy's Grandma), Sam Cox (Detective Inspector Bishop), Ieuan Rhys (Crabtree), Jean Challis (Aunty Betty), Marie Lewis (Mrs. Gallagher)

Original airdate May 27, 2006

The Big Idea The Doctor and Rose visit 1950s Britain, where a noncorporeal entity who lives inside televisions is stealing people's faces.

Roots and References The Coronation of Queen Elizabeth II and its historical effect on television sales; the 1930 film version of *Frankenstein* (lightning striking the television aerial and fears of new technology); *Coronation Street* (domestic drama; Florizel Street was the original name for *Corrie*).

Adventures in Time and Space The prominence of the transmission tower, especially at the story's conclusion, is a clear visual reference to 1981's "Logopolis" (a scripted comment about the Doctor's fear of towers because he fell off one once was cut). The Wire's continual screams of "Hu-u-ungry!" are unfortunately reminiscent of the Great Architect in 1987's "Paradise Towers."

The Torchwood Effect Detective Inspector Bishop mentions that if they mess up while the Coronation is on, they'll have Torchwood on their backs.

The Doctor and Rose When Rose's face is taken, the Doctor is as angry as we've ever seen him, saying, "No power on this Earth can stop me." His fury motivates the interactions that follow with Mr. Connelly and Magpie. Rose, even while trapped, keeps the faith: while all the other faces on the TV screens mouth, "Help me," Rose mouths, "Doctor!"

Monster of the Week The Wire. She was executed by her own people but escaped in noncorporeal form. She needs to regain a body but is trapped within the television, using the image of a BBC presenter. She feeds off electrical activity of the brain, taking her victim's faces and leaving them minimally functional.

Stand Up and Cheer The interrogation scene starts with the Doctor sitting and Bishop standing, questioning him. However, the Doctor quickly deduces Bishop's identity (thanks to his name being sewn into his collar) and his superior knowledge of the situation means he turns the tables on his interrogators. The scene ends with the Doctor standing and Bishop sitting, their role reversal complete. It's great, although it could have stood to be a little bit longer.

Roll Your Eyes There's no other way to put it: the Doctor and Rose act like complete knobs when they enter the Connelly house. The Doctor shouting at Connelly ("I'm not listening!") is cringeworthy, and Rose is so smug about the Union Flag that you want to throw something at the television.

You're Not Making Any Sense The Wire steals people's faces . . . for what reason, precisely? She doesn't devour them, despite being hungry, as they're returned at the end. Meanwhile, the faceless bodies operate on minimal life signs, but it's hard to sustain life when you can't eat, drink or breathe. How do the bodies stay alive for what seems like weeks in some cases?

Interesting Trivia Mr. Magpie is selling television sets for a fiver, which is a great deal considering television sets cost £70 in 1953. Despite his impending bankruptcy, his inheritors must be gifted businesspeople, because we see Magpie Electricals still producing TV sets in the present day ("The Sound of Drums") and even on *Starship UK* in the far future ("The Beast Below").

Jackie and Rose are wrong when they talk about the difference between the Union Flag and the Union Jack. Naval regulations state that the flag can be referred to by either name on land; Rose herself spoke of her Union Jack shirt in "The Empty Child."

The historical aspects are actually pretty accurate: except for the anointing and communion, the entirety of Queen Elizabeth II's Coronation was televised. The coverage was instrumental in boosting the medium's popularity, with 20 million viewers (more than half the country) watching it on TV. The Doctor convincing the guards through the psychic paper that he's the king of Belgium is a reference to an apocryphal story: during the Coronation, a royal personage (the country varies) came to Alexandra Palace, then the BBC's main transmitting centre, believing the coronation was taking place there. And yes, back in the olden days of British television, continuity announcers, like the one the Wire bases her form on, were seen onscreen, dressed to the nines.

Not only does the Doctor favour Betamax for his video needs, but the tape he uses has a label that's been scribbled over several times. Clearly, like most of us used to, he's taped half a dozen programs over each other and keeps rewriting what's on it! What's amusing about this is that the writing is in the "clockface" Gallifreyan lettering.

The TARDIS Chronometer The Coronation was June 2, 1953, which means this story is set June 1 and 2 of that year.

Brilliant? (RS?) There's nothing inherently wrong with this story. Unfortunately, there's nothing that particularly stands out either. *Doctor Who* had been back on television for a year and a half by the point this aired, and this episode is precisely the moment when it stops being special.

Every story of the first season tried to be something special. Thus far this season, we've had a bunch of middling stories, but they were all trying. Sometimes they failed, but they failed in reaching for something and not quite getting there. And the successes all had something to say. "The Idiot's Lantern" is a formulaic runaround. And that kills it.

Doctor Who is a series that can be anything except boring. Its failures can be epic, but it can survive those. Like a shark, it's only when the series stops moving that it dies. Nobody's even trying here; it's finally sunk in that this show is a huge success and the production team has no idea what to do with that. The show isn't the loud, angry revolutionary of last year; instead, it's become the comfortable suburban success story and that's taken away its edge.

This comfort is also reflected in the Doctor and Rose's relationship. The Doctor has morphed into the generic heterosexual action hero, vowing vengeance upon his enemies only when his girl's life is threatened, not when anyone else is in trouble. The Doctor of old didn't distinguish between the plight of his friends and the plight of innocents, but here the message is clear: some people matter more than others.

This is a huge sea change for the series and not a pleasant one. Shading in undercurrents of flirtation in the Doctor and Rose's relationship was an excellent addition to the show. Rose as the humanizing influence on his alienness was a great setup. The Doctor as a bland, straight hero borders on criminal.

Furthermore, the Doctor and Rose have taken their obnoxiousness from "Tooth and Claw" and turned it up to 11. Their antics in the Connelly house are atrocious, and someone should have stepped in and put a stop to it.

The real problem here is that there are huge developments in their relationship . . . only all those developments are being held back for the season finale. Like the good formulaic television it is, *Doctor Who* has become a victim of its own success. All the stories between "Tooth and Claw" and "Doomsday" have nowhere to go; they're sitting in a holding pattern, unable to advance the central relationship, so instead lumber us with stereotypes and cul de sacs.

That isn't to say that this story is bad. Far from it. The small scale drama is a nice idea. There's a gay undercurrent to Tommy (clearly a Mary Sue character), which would have worked better by being not quite such an undercurrent, but it's still quite effective. And contrasting the pride of World War II veterans with generational fascism works well.

Sadly, the ending devolves into a very TeeVee runaround, with an unthrilling climax on the tower punctuated by the Wire screaming "Hu-u-ungry!" every three seconds. The entire plot is resolved by Tommy rewiring a circuit, a solution that may well have been in Gatiss's notes from the version he doubtless penned in primary school, starring himself.

Mrs. Connelly throwing Eddie out at the end is dramatically satisfying, but none of the hard questions are asked. How is she going to support herself and two dependents, given that Eddie's very likely the sole breadwinner? Why does he just meekly accept it? Then there's the casual shot of black characters in the conclusion, being fully integrated into the street party that otherwise consists of white suburbanites. In what version of 1950s Britain does this occur, then?

The answer is: the TeeVee version. "The Idiot's Lantern" is steeped in the conventions of TV. It's got mysterious men in black abducting people and hiding them in a disguised factory, because that's exactly the sort of thing you expect to see on TV. The Wire turns her black-and-white picture to colour for no particular reason and with no scientific basis whatsoever (she does this when she's in one of Magpie's sets, not her specially constructed portable TV; you try broadcasting a colour signal on a 1950s TV and see how far you get), simply because it's a neat-looking visual.

Thus, the effective parts are those that television naturally does well: the spookiness of the mystery upstairs, dramatic two-handers like the interrogation scene, the unsettling power of a reassurring face intruding into your living room. The parts that don't work are precisely those for which generic television has found no solution: the inability to show two people enjoying themselves in the absence of dramatic tension, the refusal to ask hard questions about the world it inhabits, the twee "lesson" Tommy learns at the end.

"The Idiot's Lantern" is desperately torn between wanting to tell a coming-of-age story about a real family in an oppressive time and drawing so heavily on the dramatic conventions of television that all the edges are filed off before it begins. By being so steeped in TV's roots, it's unable to ask anything meaningful about its environment. It seems as though there could have been more here, but there's also a very real sense in which there actually couldn't.

Second Opinion (GB) I'm honestly not entirely sure why this story vexes my co-author so. I could spend my allotted word count answering several of his charges (I don't quite see how the Doctor being emotionally affected by seeing his friend violated makes him a heterosexual action hero, any more than I see how the Doctor is a git for putting down a man who, only moments before, was volubly demeaning his wife and son), but instead I think I'll vex him further by simply stating I think "The Idiot's Lantern" is an underrated gem from this season. It's fun, inventive and entertaining.

The great thing about "The Idiot's Lantern" is how wonderfully charming it all is. Tennant and Piper get some great (and much-needed) comedy scenes. My collaborator thinks it's embarrassing, but I disagree. It was delightful watching the Doctor and Rose put Mr. Connelly in his place, though I agree the Doctor literally turning his interrogation around was one of the funniest scenes this season. (Watch the other officer in the background attempt to touch his own elbow!)

I love the premise, which is delightfully off-the-wall: a being that lives in television who literally rips your face off. Moreover, I think the Wire is one of the best ideas for a *Doctor Who* villain, ever. What better menace could *Doctor Who* have than a 1950s continuity announcer? Upper-middle class, Received Pronunciation, all perfectly coiffed and yet belying great misery underneath. (Which pretty much sums up life in the 1950s.) What's even better is that Maureen Lipman is absolutely delightful in the role.

Writer Mark Gatiss loves creating grotesques, and they're rooted in a sense of pathos: Mr. Connelly is a jerk, but ultimately he's a character to be pitied, not sneered at. All the same, you can't help but cheer for Mrs. Connelly when she shows him the door. (I think she'll do just fine, incidentally.)

I harbour no delusions that "The Idiot's Lantern" is the best story of the season. Perhaps, as Robert argues, the story is a bit generic at points (Tommy in particular is as bland as they come). But I also think there's a place for entertaining, escapist fantasy and a story about a monster who eats the faces of people in Coronation-era Britain isn't necessarily the place to ask the hard questions. (Though I concede that on-the-nose speeches about why people fought in the war may invite the expectation that such questions will be addressed.) I finished "The Idiot's Lantern" with a huge smile on my face, having been delivered some scares, some comedy and a great villain. For me at least, that'll do nicely.

2.08–2.09 The Impossible Planet / The Satan Pit

Written by Matt Jones **Directed by** James Strong

Supporting cast Danny Webb (Mr. Jefferson), Shaun Parkes (Zachary Cross Flane), Claire Rushbrook (Ida Scott), Will Thorp (Toby Zed), Ronny Jhutti (Danny Bartock), MyAnna Buring (Scooti Manista), Paul Kasey (The Ood), Gabriel Woolf (Voice of the Beast), Silas Carson (Voice of the Ood)

Original airdates June 3 and 10, 2006

The Big Idea Rose and the Doctor are trapped on a planet in orbit around a black hole. Could it be the work of the Devil?

Roots and References *Pitch Black*, the *Alien* trilogy and other thrillers set on alien planets; *Doom* the video game (it even has the door sound effect); the look of the Beast is influenced by Ridley Scott's 1984 film *Legend*.

Adventures in Time and Space The Doctor claims that his people invented black holes, which, according to the mythos of the series, is actually near enough true (as mentioned in 1972's "The Three Doctors" and 1976's "The Deadly Assassin"). The Doctor mentions that there are black holes that are gateways to other universes, something he personally encountered in "The Three Doctors." The Doctor's listing of civilizations whose religions feature the horned beasts includes Draconia (home of the Draconians, from 1973's "Frontier in Space"); Daemos, home of Azal from 1971's "The Dæmons"; and the God of War of the Kaleds, a race from the planet Skaro, whose mutant offspring became the Daleks. In a bit of a metatextual nod, Gabriel Woolf, who was previously employed to voice the Classic Series' personification of evil, Sutekh, in 1975's "Pyramids of Mars," provides the Voice of the Beast.

The Torchwood Effect Sanctuary Base 6 is an exploratory mission for the Torchwood Archive, which hints at what the Torchwood Institute might evolve into in future. The Voice of the Beast tells Rose she is "the valiant child who will die in battle soon."

Who is the Doctor? We get an insight into the Doctor's own beliefs here. While he's abseiling into the pit, the Doctor has a personal epiphany and comes to realize that, like everyone else, he has his own set of "rules" about what can and can't be true. He learns from this realization, though, saying, "That's why I keep travelling. To be proved wrong."

The Doctor and Rose With the TARDIS lost, the Doctor and Rose awkwardly discuss what they'll do in the future, joking about the prospect of settling down, all the while avoiding talking about living together, even though the whole conversation is about just that. Their relationship looms large across the story: Rose kisses the helmet of the Doctor's astronaut suit before going into the pit, while the Doctor tells Ida, "If you talk to Rose, just tell her . . . " and then breaks off, muttering, "Oh she knows." When faced with the Beast, the Doctor tells it he believes in Rose enough that he can sacrifice her along with himself to destroy the Beast once and for all.

Monster of the Week The Ood are a slave race, and are apparently born wanting to serve. This will be examined more critically in "Planet of the Ood," but the human inhabitants of Sanctuary Base 6 take it as read, referring to the Ood as "livestock" (their scanners don't even register the Ood as a lifeform). The Ood exert a low-level telepathic field and communicate through a translation device attached to them.

Stand Up and Cheer The Doctor abseiling into the darkness is one of the most beautiful images in the entirety of *Doctor Who*. But what's even lovelier is the quiet conversation during that time the Doctor has with Ida, where they discuss faith and the Doctor's own limitations in his outlook. It's lovely watching the Doctor as he almost makes a quiet conversion to agnosticism, capping it off with the credo about why he keeps travelling. David Tennant is wonderful here, demonstrating the amazing power that can come out of a quiet, minimal performance.

Roll Your Eyes How convenient that the first two fatalities by the Ood — you know, the ones that demonstrate that they mean business and really are homicidal — are the only two non-speaking parts. The same sort of lazy shorthand of storytelling comes back at the end of the story when the Doctor conveniently finds the lost TARDIS just before the planet falls into the black hole.

You're Not Making Any Sense The pit was designed by the Beast's jailers to allow any visitor to potentially destroy the power source, the planet and the Beast. Leaving aside the fiendish over-complexity of that, there's still the question of why the Voice of the Beast, who has already escaped and possessed Toby and the Ood, makes such a big deal of the pit being opened. And why does the Beast prevent Ida and the Doctor from coming back to the surface — and away from the means of its destruction?

Interesting Trivia "Bolero" plays prominently throughout the episode. Ravel always thought of the piece as being very mechanical, which is appropriate for the base setting. There's also a sexual element to the song, which suggests a further layer to the relationship between the Doctor and Rose.

Matt Jones is credited as the writer, but Russell T Davies acted as an uncredited co-writer. (While Davies does tend to polish many other writers' scripts, in his book *The Writer's Tale*, Davies states this is the only story he probably should have taken a co-writing credit.) Davies' own work began many drafts back, since he owns copyright on the Ood, according to "The Doctor's Wife." Jones' original choice of servant race was actually the disgraced Slitheen, who were looking to redeem themselves. The Ood will go on to be the first monster to appear in more than two stories since the Sontarans of the '70s.

The TARDIS Chronometer Sanctuary Base 6 is on a highly anomalous planet orbiting a black hole. The date is unspecified, though its sequel, "Planet of the Ood," is set in 4126 and it's likely contemporary with that.

Brilliant? (GB) What's great about "The Impossible Planet" and "The Satan Pit" isn't what's said, it's what's not said. Any other story, some kind of effort would have been made to explain just what happened with Jefferson's wife, or why Ida is "running from Daddy" or how Danny is the "little boy who lied." But here we're just left with these tantalizing suggestive phrases that say so much about the dark places these people have been.

So much of this story can be seen in this light. What was the Beast? Was it the *ur-source* of all Devil myths from before time existed or just a jumped-up alien menace? The story makes no definitive conclusion, though the Doctor, rightly, provides the sceptical viewpoint. The conflict is neatly summed up by the Doctor having to talk to himself and puzzle out the nature of the Beast's jail: it's something bigger than the Doctor, bigger than anyone. But that's good, this story tells us. We shouldn't have all the answers, much less easy ones. One of the best moments of the story is when the Doctor disputes the Beast's assertion he comes from before time existed. "Is that your religion?" asks the Voice of the Beast. "It's a belief," the Doctor responds. Even the Doctor should be challenged.

There's a warm humanism at the heart of this story. When the survivors are confronted with the dark places they've been and it ramps up into the possible spread of superstition, the Doctor reframes the conversation to remind them what makes them great as human beings: they're always exploring, asking questions, never being satisfied with what's easy.

All this talk about the thematic content, though, is an easy distraction from the basic fact that this is a very, very scary story, particularly the first episode. "The Impossible Planet" succeeded in being the first *Doctor Who* episode ever to seriously creep me out and it continues to do so even today. The scariest scene in the whole first 45 minutes is the one where the Voice of the Beast tells Toby not to turn around. It's a gloriously tense scene, and director James Strong amps up the tension by keeping Toby in closeup, shot from the back, the whole time. Add to this the genius vocal casting of Gabriel Woolf (not just because of his fabled connection to the Classic Series, but because he has the perfect voice) and we have something that creates a genuine sense of dread and fear.

This scene also works because everyone took the time to establish the Sanctuary Base and the people who populate it so that when everything goes wrong it has a real impact. I refuse to watch the *Doctor Who Confidential* on the making of this story because I honestly don't want to know how much of the base was done on location and how much was done in studio. For me, Sanctuary Base 6 is a fully realized environment, claustrophobic, harsh and yet compelling, with believable people populating it; not just ciphers, but people with honest-to-goodness fears, anxieties and relationships (watch how Ida interacts with Scooti, Zack and Jefferson in the scene where everyone is introduced). We believe these characters have a close working relationship. I love how Ida's immediate response to the loss of the TARDIS is to put the Doctor and Rose on the laundry rotation.

What's better is that we get to see all these characters blossom as the story develops: Zack coming to terms with being a leader; Jefferson atoning for whatever happened with his wife by dying with honour; Ida, trying to be the smartest, bravest person in the room but so vulnerable when finally left alone. All these characters are uplifting in how flawed but wonderful they are, and the performances have real verisimilitude. Indeed, I'm genuinely disappointed the Doctor never fulfilled his promise and revisited Ida, because Claire Rushbrook was simply wonderful here (as are Danny Webb and Shaun Parkes).

The Doctor and Rose also have some wonderful moments. Indeed, the pair of them are never better this season. They get the smarmy double-act out of their system in the first minute or so and then act as an intimate team for the rest of the story. The real tragedy of this season is that, perhaps to establish David Tennant's Doctor, they ignored a lot of the relationship with Rose, giving the Doctor others to interact with (Sarah Jane, Reinette), expanding the team (Mickey) or split-ting Rose and the Doctor up. Here, they finally correct this problem, with the Doctor and Rose having some emotional, even sexual chemistry, after a very long holiday earlier this season. What's even better is that both characters shine. While the Doctor puzzles out what's in the pit, Rose takes charge of the crisis with the Ood. But even while facing separate dangers, the connection between the two characters is paramount: Rose sees defeating the Ood as a means to saving the Doctor; the Doctor is prepared to sacrifice both of them, because to do anything less portrays her as just a victim. It's mature and complex and, frankly, welcome.

At its core, everything that's so scary or great about this has been done before in *Doctor Who*: possession, doom-laden relics of an ancient civilization, the gloomy base under siege and the TARDIS being seemingly lost. But what makes it all work so magnificently here is that it breathes new life into these tropes. The script, the direction and the actors are not afraid to connect to it all with very real emotions. Thus, the possession is genuinely creepy, the ancient civilization is hugely ominous and the gloomy base under siege is populated by people with real hopes and fears. "The Satan Pit" in particular gives us base under siege, 2006-style, where Rose's party needs to get from point A to point B (through ventilation ducts, though cleverly ones that have no air!) to stop the monsters. It sounds like episode three of just about any *Doctor Who* story in 1975, but describing it that way doesn't begin to capture how brilliantly it actually works (or how incredible Toby gesturing to the Ood to be quiet is).

Given the brilliance of "The Impossible Planet," "The Satan Pit" probably never stood a chance at bettering it, but it certainly comes close. The climax perhaps leaves too much for the Doctor to solve through dramatic monologue, especially when it has to establish that the Beast has severed its consciousness from its physical form, what the power source is, what the consequences of destroying it are, and what the motivations of the Beast's jailers were. (The cross-cutting with the possessed Toby on the rocket helps mitigate this somewhat.) And yet, the rest of the episode is a taut little thriller with some wonderful, quiet soul-searching scenes, so the climax is easily forgivable.

I honestly don't know if we'll ever see a story as smart, or as brave, as "The Impossible Planet"/"The Satan Pit." It takes just about every conceivable risk a show like *Doctor Who* can take. It's genuinely frightening, mature, thoughtful and intelligent. If there have been episodes this season that the kids can appreciate more than the adults, here's the story that grown-ups will love, think about and hide behind the sofa while watching.

Second Opinion (RS?) This story has a lot of good elements: the setup is intriguing, it features the New Series' first truly recurring monster in the Ood, the lights are low and there's some meaty stuff beyond the action. These elements, taken on their own, work to varying degrees. But I must disagree with my co-author: the story as a whole simply doesn't hang together and ultimately leaves a nasty taste in the mouth.

The fundamental problem is the Beast itself. We spend an episode and a half building up to something in the pit, something that can possess people and Ood alike, that can allow a human body to survive the vacuum of space (how, exactly?) and that apparently existed before the universe . . . only to discover it's a piece of poorly rendered CGI that does nothing but snarl. Any time an effect would be significantly improved by a man in a hairy suit, you know you've got problems. It's a shame, because the CGI for the black hole is excellent.

The Ood don't fare much better. They're a slave race, who supposedly live to serve. While Rose tries to befriend them and the Doctor offers some platitudes, what we don't see is any real questioning of this setup. What's worse is that at the end when the Doctor only has time for one trip, he chooses to save a single human rather than 50 Ood. This goes against everything that *Doctor Who* is fundamentally about. Why isn't the Doctor ferociously condemning the humans for their use of slaves with every fibre of his being? Why does he treat the Ood as second-class citizens, just like everyone else does?

The theology is a brave choice (though Tennant's gravitas is questionable), but it's something that really needs to be done carefully, because it's questioning one of the core principles of the series (its secularism). And it's all predicated on a rather flimsy premise: because the Beast claims to be from before the universe existed, that somehow rocks the Doctor's belief system to its core, in a way that 1983's "Terminus" (featuring a dead alien from before the universe existed) never did.

I can see why people like this story. It ticks a lot of the boxes for what makes a *Doctor Who* story exciting, scary and thoughtful. Unfortunately, it doesn't cohere and that does it some serious damage. I'll never love this story, but I don't begrudge those who do.

. . . .

Doctor Who Confidential

The first six seasons of the New Series had a companion program on BBC3, *Doctor Who Confidential*. *Confidential* aired just after *Doctor Who* on Saturday nights and showed behind-the-scenes details on how that week's episode was made. Cut-down versions, which usually excised material from the Classic Series and montages set to pop music, appeared on the DVD boxsets for Series One through Six. The series was mostly narrated by Simon Pegg (Series One), Mark Gatiss (Series Two), Anthony Head (Series Three and Four), Alex Price (Series Five) and Russell Tovey (Series Six).

. . . .

2.10 Love & Monsters

Written by Russell T Davies **Directed by** Dan Zeff

Supporting cast Camille Coduri (Jackie Tyler), Marc Warren (Elton Pope), Peter Kay (Victor Kennedy/The Abzorbaloff), Shirley Henderson (Ursula Blake), Simon Greenall (Mr. Skinner), Moya Brady (Bridget), Kathryn Drysdale (Bliss), Paul Kasey (The Hoix), Bella Emberg (Mrs. Croot)

Original airdate June 17, 2006

The Big Idea A group of fans of the Doctor are infiltrated by an alien who wants to absorb them.

Roots and References *The X-Files'* "Jose Chung's 'From Outer Space'" and *Buffy the Vampire Slayer*'s "The Zeppo" (supporting characters are seen from a radically different perspective); *Scooby-Doo* (the Doctor and Rose chasing the monster). The Electric Light Orchestra songs "Don't Bring Me Down" and "Mr. Blue Sky" are featured.

Adventures in Time and Space This story recreates the shop window dummies scene from "Rose," the Slitheen crash-landing from "Aliens of London" and the arrival of the Sycorax ship from "The Christmas Invasion." Most of these scenes were re-filmed for the episode. The Abzorbaloff is related to the Slitheen, coming from Clom, the twin planet of Raxacoricofallapatorius.

The Torchwood Effect Victor Kennedy has access to the Torchwood files and looks through their old databases. When it comes to Rose, the Torchwood files are strangely lacking, with the evidence corrupted by the Bad Wolf virus. There is also a hint of events to come next season with *The Daily Telegraph* headline: "Saxon leads polls at 60%."

Who is the Doctor? LINDA provides a rare opportunity to see how the Doctor is viewed by people who are not close to him; in particular, a fan group of sorts. For Elton, he's a dark figure in his past; Skinner has an academic analysis that posits the Doctor as a form of archetype: King, Stranger, Thief, Fool, Doctor (represented by a question mark); Bliss sees him as an artistic abstraction; Bridget looks for his footprint in history and culture. It's an odd assemblage of the Doctor and yet an absolutely correct one.

Monster of the Week The Abzorbaloff, although that's likely not its real name (since various people call it Abzorbathon, Abzorbaling, Abzorbatrix and Abzorbaclon, before it decides it likes "Abzorbaloff"). It absorbs people, enjoying the taste. Once absorbed, the Abzorbaloff's victims are kept alive and sentient inside its body, the outline of their face visible through its skin.

Stand Up and Cheer The final scene ("We forget because we must"). Coming on the heels of a very funny episode, this is a bittersweet ending, made incredibly powerful thanks to Marc Warren's acting. The scene ostensibly reflects on the Doctor's involvement in Elton's life, but it's actually about growing up and leaving childhood behind. Elton admits that he's had the most terrible and the most wonderful things happen to him, but that he can't tell the difference. And even though the Doctor might be wonderful, it was the LINDA group that Elton valued most, but it was destroyed, albeit inadvertently, as a result of the Doctor. Elton's final line — noting that when you're a kid you're told to grow up, get a job, get married, get a house and have a kid, only to discover the world is so much stranger, darker, madder and better than that — is a beautiful paean to rejecting the ordinary and choosing your own path in life. For anyone who was ostracised for not fitting in, but who nevertheless stuck to their own oddities and made a life for themselves, this is glorious.

Roll Your Eyes The Abzorbaloff's tiny black loincloth, while admittedly giving Bliss a clear rearview vision when it runs, is the only joke that really misfires.

You're Not Making Any Sense How does Victor Kennedy make the lights switch on for his dramatic entrance into LINDA's lair?

Interesting Trivia LINDA stands for London Investigation 'N' Detective Agency; Elton says he thought of the acronym years ago and has been wanting to use it for ages. Elton wasn't the only person to think that LINDA was a good idea; Russell T Davies nicked the acronym from his work on the children's series *Why Don't You* in the early '90s (although the L stood for Liverpool then).

The Abzorbaloff was created by nine-year-old William Grantham in a draw-a-*Doctor-Who*-monster competition on the long-running BBC children's series *Blue Peter*. It was supposed to be the size of a bus, but no one told the production staff.

This episode begins a tradition of "double banking," which will continue for the next few years: two episodes are filmed simultaneously with the main cast appearing only minimally in one of them. This was done to accommodate the Christmas special, which increased the season's episode count from 13 to 14, while keeping the tight production schedule for *Doctor Who*.

The TARDIS Chronometer The bulk of the story takes place in the present day, but there are flashbacks to Elton's childhood (in the late '70s or early '80s; we hear the TARDIS materialize), as well as to the Nestene invasion of 2005, and the Slitheen and Sycorax invasions of 2006.

Brilliant? (RS?) When Victor Kennedy says his skin complaint is Eczema, he uses the American pronunciation, "Exzeema" and Elton corrects him, saying, "You mean 'Exma'?" (the British pronunciation). This is brilliantly and hilariously turned on its head by Victor saying, "This is worse. Much, much worse." This is exactly the kind of pissing match that actual fans get into, involving as it does accuracy of pointless things, strange bodily functions and the intense need to be right, at the expense of social relations. That's an astonishing throwaway line.

Actually, that's not where I started with "Love & Monsters" — oh no! — but I just put that bit first because it's a brilliant opening. First though, a bit about me: I'm Robert Smith? —

"I don't care if Monday's blue, Tuesday's grey and Wednesday too . . ."

— No, not that one, I'm the one with the question mark. I like biking, swimming, reading and writing. I like to hang out with friends and travel the world. But if there's one thing I really love, it's *Doctor Who*.

Dum de dum, dum de dum, dum de dum. Whooo-eee-oooo dum de dum, de dum de dum.

Don't worry, it's not just all me talking. Just wait til the bit about Elton's lean. But this is the story of how I came to know "Love & Monsters," with all its weirdness and its hilarity and its strangeness. This is a story about growing up, but it's also about community and the power of *Doctor Who* in our lives. In short, it's about us.

"Love & Monsters" is an incredibly personal story. There are no sneering stereotypes of fandom, just a celebration of its ability to bring people together, initially for a common purpose, but subsequently to create friendships and relationships. If you can't see yourself in this story, then it's probably because you're a Victor Kennedy, wanting everything quantified and rigid but fundamentally missing the point of fandom.

Most of this season has been a victim of Second Album Syndrome. Having made it big with the first hit (the Eccleston year), how do you top that for an encore? Worse, when you start to overthink it, you lose the magic that made the first album so brilliant. So much of this season has been in a holding pattern, not knowing what to do with the success it inherited and terrified to rock the boat in case that success disappears. "Love & Monsters" is the only story this season that has something to say. It's powerful, kicking and desperately angry. For once, this isn't formula television — and the results couldn't be more satisfying.

Much of this story's success comes from the unconventional approaches to television. From the musical cutaways (complete with Elton dancing on the bed to ELO) whenever he gets good news to the smoke coming out of his computer when the internet goes into meltdown over the Doctor's antics, this episode is using narrative interruptions to comment on *Doctor Who* at large, add character background to Elton (so that he can carry a Doctor-lite episode) and make the story personal by having it work the same way as somebody's shaggy dog story down the pub.

I'll get back to talking about the narrative interruptions in a moment, but first I really want to tell you about Elton's lean. Yes, that's right, his comedy lean, which is utterly brilliant. At one point, Elton amusingly leans into the camera because he doesn't have a remote-control zoom. This is reminiscent of early *Doctor Who*, when the cameras had to be physically pushed for a zoom effect. It's also a metaphor for the fact that Elton's stuck in his development; he can't zoom in on the source of his issues, because he's too scared to look too closely at his childhood trauma. He can only approach it from the outside. By the story's end, though, he's bought a remote-control zoom, symbolising both the advances in technology and the growing up that's occurred as a result of his confronting his inner demons, thanks to the Doctor. In any other story, the

Doctor would simply have taken him back in time to witness the past events firsthand. Here, however, Elton has to do the emotional work on his own. And all this in a comedy lean.

Where was I? Oh yes, interruptions to the narrative. These include the out-of-sequence placement of the opening scene (and Elton's explicit commentary on his reasons for doing that); the fact that the sight of the monster doesn't make Elton run, but the Doctor saying "Don't I know you?" does; the out-of-left-field appearance of Elton John; and the way the opening scene is later summarised via a fast-forward visual, complete with screeching noise to indicate film at high speed. The story ends with a dreamscape of Elton metaphorically farewelling his mother, in an overexposed sequence, demonstrating that he's finally come into the light. Credit must go to Russell T Davies for the concept, but also to Dan Zeff for his outstanding direction, without which this could easily have flopped.

Then there's the comedy, almost all of which is laugh-out-loud funny. The *Scooby-Doo* corridor running is brilliant, hilarious and not a million miles from the sort of thing Patrick Troughton used to do. The next bit you already know: Victor Kennedy; eczema; much, much worse; screech. The entire sequence with Elton infiltrating Jackie's flat is comic genius. Victor's training sessions are run just like a school, complete with Elton raising his hand to ask a question. (Not to mention Victor's "I could kiss you! Except I can't. Eczema.")

And when Elton asks the Abzorbaloff where Mr. Skinner is, his answer — "He's in the toilet" — is utterly hilarious. It shouldn't be, but it's the kind of thing that gets funnier the more you think about it because a) it's an attempt at a perfunctory answer, contrasted with b) the fact that people simply don't use the toilet on *Doctor Who* while c) it's delivered by an off-camera voice belonging to something unseen that's revealed to be d) holding an enormous newspaper that covers its features entirely, except for e) green alien hands.

The paving stone joke (suggesting that Ursula and Elton manage a love life, despite the fact that she's just a face in a stone, sitting suspiciously in his lap) is the crowning achievement of all the comedy. It's this story in a nutshell: uncomfortable, too personal and utterly hilarious. This has made a lot of people very upset, which only proves how powerful this story is. The joke itself is actually much more benign than is remembered, but it's still surprising to see what could be a fellatio joke in *Doctor Who*, even if that might not have been wholly unexpected from the man behind *Queer as Folk*.

"Love & Monsters" also features the redemption of Jackie Tyler. Her "Because it's hard" speech is Camille Coduri's best acting in the series bar none. Elton works extremely well as a surrogate lead character largely because he's so charming, but it's Jackie who's our connection to the regular cast. Coduri infuses her scenes with comic brilliance, wistful reflection and raw anger, all in the space of several minutes. For a character that most had dismissed as the weak link of the series, this is incredible. With Jackie, the story takes an apparently throwaway comic relief character and both keeps the humorous elements intact and shows us the bittersweet pain that underpins it. That's "Love & Monsters" all over.

It's even been speculated that the entire story is just a made-up anecdote by Elton and that the only things that were "real" were on his camera. Which is an amusing way of twisting yourself in knots, because none of it is actually real anyway, and everything that we understand to be "real" in any other story is communicated via camera. The evidence for this is that we only see the back of Ursula's paving stone on Elton's camera, although we do hear her voice, leading to elaborate theories about her standing just off camera and being part of the hoax, or something. These theories probably fulfil a deep-seated need in fandom to deny aspects of the show we don't like. It's interesting that one of the most violent objections to content in our favourite show is the idea of a *Doctor Who* fan having a love life. Despite the fact that this happens at conventions everywhere (increasingly so, thanks to the show's revival), we're clearly still a deeply repressed bunch.

Because, you see, "Love & Monsters" might have been a throwaway comedy story without the Doctor, only it reached out and touched me personally. It has the most wonderful and the most terrible things, but I find I can't tell the difference. It's full of themes about friendship, community, growing up and being different. But it's also a fabulous story, conveyed with unconventional techniques, making it one of the highlights of the show's revival. And it's hilarious, to boot. "Love & Monsters" is Russell T Davies' love letter to fandom, in all its ungainly glory. Fandom might seem like it's a bunch of weirdos sitting around debating a time traveller, but it's actually so much stranger, so much darker and so much madder than that — and so much better!

Second Opinion (GB) What he said. Though without the disdain towards the second series.

2.11 Fear Her

Written by Matthew Graham **Directed by** Euros Lyn

Supporting cast Nina Sosanya (Trish Webber), Abisola Agbaje (Chloe Webber), Edna Doré (Maeve), Tim Faraday (Tom's dad), Abdul Salis (Kel), Huw Edwards (commentator)

Original airdate June 24, 2006

The Big Idea A lonely alien possesses a young girl, giving her the ability to convert people to drawings.

Roots and References *The Twilight Zone*'s "It's a Good Life" (scary child with godlike powers that most people are afraid of), "The Monsters Are Due on Maple Street" (paranoia on an ordinary street) and "Little Girl Lost" (children lost to another dimension); *Inspector Morse* (the Doctor pretending to be a detective with an assistant named Lewis); Catherine Storr's children's novel *Marianne Dreams* (drawings coming to life); *Brookside* (soap operaic interactions that take place on a small street). Trish and Chloe sing "Kookaburra."

Adventures in Time and Space The Doctor requests parlay in accordance with the Shadow Proclamation, just as he did with the Nestene Consciousness in "Rose." He also states that, after being threatened by cat nuns in "New Earth," he isn't really a cat person.

The Torchwood Effect It's been speculated that there might be a faint line in the Olympic commentary that references Torchwood, but it could just as easily be a line saying, "the [Olympic] torch would . . . ," so it's hard to be sure if this counts. Or, for that matter, why a secret organization devoted to fighting aliens would be referenced by a sports commentator.

Who is the Doctor? The Doctor has insight into children by virtue of having been a father once himself (although he doesn't elaborate on when or how this took place).

The Doctor and Rose In foreshadowing for the season finale, Rose says, "They keep trying to split us up, but they never will."

Monster of the Week The Isolus, empathic beings of intense emotion. The Isolus mother drifts in deep space, jettisoning millions of fledgling spores. The Isolus children travel inside a pod, riding the heat and energy of solar tides and being sustained by the need for each other. It takes thousands of years for them to grow up, so they play games while they travel, using ionic power to create make-believe worlds.

Stand Up and Cheer The TARDIS materialising sideways between two sheds then immediately rematerialising the right way round is quite fun. It's the sort of thing you imagine must happen all the time.

Roll Your Eyes The Doctor running with the torch to light the Olympic flame, intercut with scenes of people cheering insanely, and Rose's "Feel the love" line are incredibly cheesy. And that's the episode's climax.

You're Not Making Any Sense Why does everyone's breath mist at the height of summer even after the Isolus pod has left the street?

Interesting Trivia How exactly does the scribble work? The drawings that come to life have otherwise been within a page, so a moving scribble in a piece of paper might have made more sense. But what's really bizarre is that the scribble can be erased from reality altogether using an eraser. Nothing is done with this, but we're left to wonder if perhaps there was a simpler solution to the entire problem . . .

The *Shayne Ward Greatest Hits* poster is a bit of a joke for the British audience: Ward won the British version of *X-Factor* in 2005.

The TARDIS Chronometer It's London, July 2012, coincident with the 30th Olympiad.

Brilliant? (RS?) Alas, no.

You're tempted to ask, "What the hell were they thinking?" but ironically you can see what they were thinking quite clearly: a small-scale story, dealing with emotional trauma amplified by an empathic alien and resolved by collective goodwill. That's a great premise. Unfortunately, just about every aspect of the production works against that goal: the writing, the performances, the cowardice, the sheer awfulness of the writing, the dialogue, did I mention the writing?

Actually, to be fair, there are only two performances that aren't very good. Unfortunately, one is Chloe and the other is the Doctor. The former you can at least understand, since child actors are notoriously variable (although expecting a child actress to carry your entire story might have been a bit of a mistake). However, Tennant's attempts to be eccentric fall incredibly flat. Some people like the "fingers on lips" scene, but I found it risible. His antics while looking for the residue are just irritating. The only amusing moments were the marmalade eating (because for once it isn't overplayed) and the moment when his bog-standard "Ohhhh!" exclamation is then immediately followed by a confused "What?," which was actually quite funny.

The dialogue during the Olympic scenes is atrocious. ("Feel the love!" and "It's a beacon of hope" are two lines that should have set off some sort of cliché alert on the writer's computer.) Until that point, the episode is a small-scale horror story, but it then descends into camp nonsense. Why is no one overly bothered by the disappearance of 80,000 people? Why is it day in the street but night in the stadium? How does the Doctor get into the Olympic stadium? If I tried to grab the Olympic torch during its run, I'd be arrested on the spot.

There are people who firmly believe that *Doctor Who* is a horror series. It's not, but you can understand why if you were watching during the late '60s or mid-'70s, two fondly remembered eras of the show. This episode is predicated upon that belief, as the title demonstrates. There's nothing inherently wrong with this — and, to its credit, the episode is actually quite scary on first viewing, if watched with the lights out.

However, the problem with this episode is that it doesn't have the stomach for its premise. Horror isn't scary just because the lights are low and there's something lurking around the corner; it's scary because it ties into one of the primal fears that we as humans struggle with. (Hint: people turning into drawings isn't one of them.) Instead, what powers the episode is Chloe's relationship with her now-dead father — and that's also the episode's biggest flaw.

There's an alternate universe where this episode actually carried through its vision and produced a story predicated around a child traumatised by her abusive father, amplified by an alien whose loneliness made it identify with Chloe but caused untold fear and destruction because it couldn't contain that power. Had we actually had that episode, it would still be talked about and would likely even have done some good, with a helpline number attached to the end for abused kids to call. Instead, every time the episode wants to deal with its issues, it stops short of saying something profound, because it's so afraid of its own subject matter.

You can see it all going terribly wrong from the first scene: the shocking moment that leads us into the credits is . . . a badly drawn cartoon. And the episode proves just how uninterested it is in its own premise when it doesn't bother to show moving drawings ever again. It also glosses over the implications entirely: Chloe's bedroom should be alive with moving pictures, yet the only subsequent movement is an offstage sad face and a pointing arm.

That said, the scary father booming, "I'm coming to hurt you, Chloe" is still pretty disturbing. Unfortunately, contrasting that with feel-good Olympic nonsense doesn't work at all. The episode should be about Trish coming to terms with the fact that it's her own refusal to address the issue that's keeping Chloe in pain, long after her abuser is dead. Substituting that with a song about kookaburras isn't exactly satisfying dramatic payoff.

There are a couple of redeeming features. The cast is quite diverse, reflecting the multi-ethnic makeup of an actual London street in the 21st century (although the early paranoia where white residents blame Kel, the council worker, sits rather uncomfortably). The scribble monster is cool, both in concept and execution. And the final scene is gorgeous: although it isn't a literal lead-in to the finale, the approaching storm is a nice way of setting the mood.

"Fear Her" is easily the worst episode of the New Series thus far. The tragedy is that the damage is all so close to the surface, because underneath you can still glimpse the powerful story it could have told. It's rare that the process fails so badly, in so many ways simultaneously. It's a shame, because this could so easily have been something very special.

Second Opinion (GB) Submitted for your approval: one Chloe Webber. A little girl coping with the flotsam and jetsam of a difficult childhood encounters some flotsam and jetsam from space and puts her whole street into . . . *The Twilight Zone.*

That's really how it should have happened. (Though perhaps without the Rod Serling narration.) The idea of something as grand and operatic as *Doctor Who* doing something as small-scale and nuanced as *The Twilight Zone* is quite novel. Does it work? I feel like I should be David Tennant tilting his head and saying, "Eehhhh." It sort of does. The *idea* of Chloe Webber drawing people out of existence with her crayons is actually scarier than what we see onscreen.

You only have to watch *Life on Mars* to see that Matthew Graham is a great writer who's not afraid of going to dark and interesting places. I get the sense watching this episode that there was a far darker story there before it had all the edges sanded off in rewrites. There's no point to keeping in anything to do with Trish and Chloe's abusive relationship with Chloe's father if all they're going to do avoid the issue all together. Worse, that they sidestep all this by fending off the menace singing "Kookaburra" together indicates how gutless this story really became. Add to this the discordant touches like the annoying Olympics coverage and you have a right old mess.

What we have is have a story where Rose returns the favour the Doctor gave in "The Idiot's Lantern" by rescuing him after he's been taken out of play for the last 15 minutes. Billie Piper is charming and delightful in the spotlight ("That's not a council spaceship"). I'll even go on record to say I'm probably the only *Doctor Who* fan in the world not annoyed by the Doctor carrying the torch. But the problem is the story should be with Trish and Chloe, and better developing that relationship instead of hamfistedly foreshadowing the Doctor and Rose's.

To this day, I don't understand why, looking at the production schedule for the season, the team decided to film a story set in July in February. The amount of breath showing says this is more than a drop in a few degrees caused by some technobabble; these people are on the verge of suffering from hypothermia! If they had just dropped the tie-in to the 2012 Olympics, they would have done away with the beacon of hope, the July setting and a lot of other nuisances. That said, we still would have been lumbered with "Kookaburra" and all the cowardice and bad ideas that led to it, so there wouldn't have been much improvement.

2.12–2.13 Army of Ghosts / Doomsday

Written by Russell T Davies **Directed by** Graeme Harper

Supporting cast Camille Coduri (Jackie Tyler); Noel Clarke (Mickey Smith); Tracy-Ann Oberman (Yvonne Hartman); Andrew Hayden-Smith (Jake Simmonds); Raji James (Rajesh Singh); Freema Agyeman (Adeola Oshodi); Hadley Fraser (Gareth); Oliver Mellor (Matt); Barbara Windsor (Peggy Mitchell); Derek Acorah, Alistair Appleton, Trisha

Goddard (themselves); Nicholas Briggs (Dalek and Cyberman voices); Catherine Tate (the Bride/Donna Noble)

Original airdates July 1 and 8, 2006

The Big Idea The Torchwood Institute is finally revealed to the Doctor and Rose, just in time for them to find that Torchwood has brought the Cybermen and the Daleks to Earth.

Roots and References The ending of Philip Pullman's *The Amber Spyglass* (two lovers forced to live separately on parallel worlds in order to save them) and, in the Dalek/Cybermen battle, the fantasy of just about every *Doctor Who* fan for 40 years.

Adventures in Time and Space Mickey, Pete, Jake and the Cybermen have come through from the parallel world in "Rise of the Cybermen"/"The Age of Steel." The Doctor modifies Jake's gun so it can penetrate the Dalek's "bonded polycarbide armour," a piece of technobabble that goes back to 1988's "Remembrance of the Daleks" (generations of kids prior to that called it Dalekanium). On the parallel world, Harriet Jones ("The Christmas Invasion") is the new president of the Republic. Rose is aware of what she did to the Emperor Dalek in "The Parting of the Ways." The void was where the Eternals lived (1983's "Enlightenment").

The Torchwood Effect After seeing how it was created, what it does and what it will become, we finally meet Torchwood. The Torchwood Institute, run by Yvonne Hartman, secretly owns the tower at Canary Wharf. They work on behalf of the Crown stopping alien invasions and using alien tech for the benefit of the British Empire. Torchwood is creating the "ghostshifts" that are causing the world to be populated by "ghosts."

Who is the Doctor? We have a reminder of the battle-damaged Doctor of old as he tells the Cult of Skaro Daleks, "Some day I might come to terms with it." Though he doesn't finish his final message to Rose, he is visibly crying onscreen, a first for the character.

The Doctor and Rose The Doctor and Rose's journey together ends here, as the pair are separated on parallel worlds when the void is closed. The pair's final conversation is bittersweet in the extreme, as they joke about their friends and Rose finally tells the Doctor she loves him. The Doctor responds, "Quite right." He stalls a little before telling Rose, "Rose Tyler, I . . ." but the transmission through the dimensions ends. Both are devastated by this.

Monster of the Week We've seen Daleks, and we've seen Cybermen. But we've never seen them together. The Daleks are led by the Cult of Skaro, an outside-the-box initiative of the Daleks during the Time War. These Daleks were tasked to think like the enemy and therefore have individual names: Dalek Sec (whose armour is black and is the leader), Dalek Thay, Dalek Caan, Dalek Jast. They survived the Time War and recovered the Genesis Ark, a Time Lord prison containing millions of Daleks, from the void. By using an emergency temporal shift, they escape being sucked back into the void.

Stand Up and Cheer There are so many moments (Pete and Jackie finally coming together certainly gets a vote, as does the Doctor's discussion of Daleks and touch), but in the end it has to be watching the Daleks talk smack with the Cybermen. Who knew the Daleks could be so delightfully bitchy? "This is not war. This is pest control."

Roll Your Eyes We understand the intent that the Cybermen invasion was affecting ordinary people in their ordinary homes. However, there is nothing impressive whatsoever about watching the Cybermen stomping around undamaged suburbs.

You're Not Making Any Sense The Time Lords are fighting the deadliest of enemies who would exterminate them in a second and are relentless and determined. Even with the safeguards of requiring a time-travelling humanoid to unlock it, in what reality is simply imprisoning a million Daleks a good idea?

Interesting Trivia In "The Satan Pit," the Beast prophesized Rose's death. Here, we learn that she survived in an alternate universe but was listed among the dead in our universe. So the Beast, the embodiment of all that is evil, didn't actually make a doom-laden prediction of the future, but rather . . . looked up a factoid on Wikipedia?

How does the Doctor see void stuff with 3D glasses? No, really, we'd genuinely like to know. Did people at IMAX-3D wonder why their film was being interrupted by tiny particles, shortly before being gunned down by Cybermen?

This story begins a tradition during Davies-era finales of showing how enormous events are instantaneously accepted in British pop culture. Here, we have the ghosts as the subject of Trisha Goddard's daytime talk show and a ghost being used in a plot in the popular soap *EastEnders* (the ghost is supposed to be deceased villain "Dirty" Den Watts; curiously, he was killed by his wife, who was played by Tracey-Ann Oberman, who plays Hartman here). The ghostshifts are covered on a program called *Ghostwatch*, a reference to an infamous 1992 BBC program Hallowe'en broadcast where BBC news personalities "investigated" a haunting "live" on television; a sort of *Blair Witch Project* featuring actual journalists, only not particularly good.

We discover that the beach where the Doctor and Rose say goodbye is a place in Norway called *Dårlig Ulv Stranden*, which roughly translates as "Bad Wolf Bay." In "Parting of the Ways," the Bad Wolf Rose, who has the powers of a god and can see all of time and space, says, "I create myself" and she creates the name/meme "Bad Wolf." There is an interesting implication to this: she could have come up with the name Bad Wolf because she knows the name of the place where she will last encounter the Doctor.

The TARDIS Chronometer On the Doctor and Rose's Earth, the timeline follows contemporary events from "The Christmas Invasion" and "Love & Monsters." On the parallel Earth, three years have passed since "The Age of Steel." (Given that the events of that story were in the same year Rose and Mickey came from, it can be speculated that travelling through the void involves some minor amount of time travel.)

Brilliant? (GB) In so many ways, this story, and indeed this season, was just a lead-up for the ending, which is utterly heartbreaking and powerful. The Doctor and Rose, forever separated, talking one last time on a beach. Rose finally says how she feels and the Doctor . . . doesn't. It's probably the finest moment of tragedy ever filmed in *Doctor Who*.

It's funny, because while this two-part series finale is quite brilliant, it also feels more like an addendum to the first season, complete with Time War references, Daleks and the Doctor/Rose relationship front and centre. There's even closure for the Bad Wolf mystery. In this respect, it puts in sharp relief that all these elements were missing from so much of Series Two. While it's great to see all these elements finally revisited for the Doctor and Rose's last outing together, it's also frustrating that these weren't touched upon sooner.

Meanwhile, this season's story arc gets resolved, and it turns out it's not about the revelation of the modern-day Torchwood at all. Series Two's story arc is about the hubris of the Doctor and Rose, and the tragic consequences it brings. Their arrogance and high-handedness with Queen Victoria created the very instrument of their separation. Rose became a better, more independent person through the Doctor, but she also became increasingly overconfident and more reckless to the point where, in this story, she gleefully tells an armed Dalek she killed its emperor. Jackie absolutely calls it when she tells her daughter that she's losing herself, that the thrills of travelling with the Doctor have made her lose sight of her own humanity and vulnerability. And Rose pays the price for that. The Doctor pays the price too. In "School Reunion," he sees, through Sarah Jane, proof that the companions who travel with him burn brightly and then go away — and he still tells Rose he won't leave her behind. He can't make that sort of a promise. He knows that. But he does anyway.

However, talking about the season arc and the ending eclipses what is actually a thrilling story that routinely changes what you expect it to be about. Russell T Davies starts out with a deliciously satirical premise: what if we could suddenly see ghosts as a regular everyday occurrence? We'd make them plot-lines on *EastEnders* and fodder for talk TV and dodgy advertising . . . but mostly we'd put all our faith in them, even if there's really no proof for what they actually are. In other circumstances, this might have made a lovely story all its own, but what's surprising here is that it's just the first seven minutes. We then get our first glimpse into Torchwood, but instead of being run with military precision by a Picard-like leader, we have Yvonne Hartmann, who acts more like a life coach than the director of a super-secret organization. And then, just when you think you're headed into a Cybermen invasion story, we have . . . *that* cliffhanger.

"Doomsday" is 45 minutes of non-stop action, emotion, poignance, drama and apocalypse. There are so many wonderful moments: the proposed Dalek/Cybermen alliance that turns into monster-oh-no-you-didn't; the Cyber-Hartman's tear; Jackie and Pete reuniting; the Doctor's gut-wrenching scream as Rose falls toward the void; the Doctor pressing his face against an empty wall.

Here we are, back at the ending. And it's devastating from the moment the void closes. Billie Piper is astonishing at capturing the reality of someone whose world suddenly, finally collapses. David Tennant does that too, but he does it without histrionics, just intense silence, putting his head to a wall. It conveys the emotion, the humanity and yet the alienness of the Doctor all at once. The thing about "Doomsday" is that it takes the Doctor to an emotional place where we've never seen him before: to tears. Some might have thought it couldn't have been done, given the nature of the Doctor's character as aloof outsider. But David Tennant made it happen.

The rest of the cast is glorious. Shaun Dingwall and Camille Coduri make the scene where Pete and Jackie reunite — yet meet for the first time — sing joyously. And Noel Clarke is wonderful; at last, Mickey is flirtatious, smart and dashing. Behind the camera, there's much to praise. Murray Gold captures the devastation of the loss of Rose with a superb musical cue and Graeme Harper's direction is pitch-perfect; having the Doctor shot almost entirely in closeup on the beach was a stroke of genius.

It all comes back to the conversation on the beach. Imagine being able to have a two-minute conversation with a person you love more than anything who had died in an untimely fashion and it was the only chance to say any-thing; that's what Rose and the Doctor are doing here. The emotion of it feels absolutely real. What I love most about "Doomsday" is that, in the midst of all the cosmic drama, it still knows that the real drama is separating the Doctor from the companion who defined the New Series.

The whole series' identity up until this point was bound in Billie Piper's portrayal of Rose, who was the identification figure going in and was the point of stability when the series' lead changed after the first year. The Doctor and Rose's relationship defined the whole first series and much of the second. From this point onwards, *Doctor Who* ventures into territories unknown.

Second Opinion (RS?) Right from the opening voiceover, this finale grabs your heartstrings and never lets them go. Torchwood's honing in on the Doctor suddenly makes the Powell Estate mythic, in a way you never imagined it could be. And, in a nice touch, Yvonne's reaction to seeing the TARDIS is almost precisely the reaction the Daleks have upon hearing the Doctor's name at the start of "Doomsday."

Indeed, Yvonne might be one of my favourite *Doctor Who* villains yet. Her superciliousness with the Doctor is perfectly pitched and her final fate, although subtle, actually works a treat. It's a scene that isn't trying to be spectacular, since everything is spectacle by that point, but which — at least once you put the pieces together — is incredibly haunting and more plausible than it seems at first. And the teardrop is astonishing.

Rose is incredible here. When facing the Daleks, she shows the kind of steel she should have shown in "The Christmas Invasion." Suddenly, the Rose we knew and loved is back with a vengeance. However, the big problem with the Doctor is that once he enters Torchwood, he never leaves it. Which makes him entirely disconnected from the CGI carnage happening beneath him. The ghosts started off as something you watched on TV and they basically never progress beyond that point. We're told that hundreds of people are dying, but we don't feel it. It makes the big war irrelevant, when it didn't need to be.

Fortunately, everything else is firing on all cylinders. From the moment the psychic paper fails, you realize that the rules have changed. The tension ramps up between this point and the cliffhanger, with revelations — both major and minor — coming thick and fast.

Then there's the epilogue, which is just heartbreaking. Watch it and weep, especially when you realize which character has moved on with their life and is joking around, versus which is going to the ends of the universe for the other. What's astonishing is just how much payoff we get — and just how little there was in the rest of the season. The mishmash that was the Cyberman two-parter? The Doctor and Rose acting like knobs all season long? The fact that their relationship has been in a holding pattern ever since the Doctor's regeneration? All sacrifices so that this slam-dunk of a finale could work.

Overall, this is a winner, no question. Perhaps one of the best things ever, but boy was there a high price paid to get here. When a whole season has to be sacrificed in order to make way for a spectacular finale, it's hard to know whether it was worth it or not. I'll go with a cautious yes, but it's not an experiment I'd be keen to repeat.

. . . .

Torchwood

In the *Doctor Who* spinoff series *Torchwood*, it is revealed that there were four offices of the Torchwood Institute in the countries comprising the United Kingdom. There was Torchwood One, the head office in London, which is destroyed in the Battle of Canary Wharf. Torchwood Two in Glasgow is run by a "very strange man" and little is known about it (though an onscreen graphic in *Torchwood: Children of Earth* indicates it closed some time before the events of that story). Torchwood Three is based in Cardiff, with its headquarters below Roald Dahl Plass (the place the TARDIS landed in "Boom Town"); it regulates the flow of the time and space rift under the city ("The Unquiet Dead"). There is a Torchwood Four, which is currently "missing" and its original location is unknown (though the presence of Torchwoods in England, Scotland and Wales suggests Northern Ireland as a possibility).

Torchwood Three is led by the Doctor's former companion, Captain Jack Harkness, who changed the focus of the organization to honour the work of the Doctor and to turn away from the more jingoistic goals of old. Captain Jack's Torchwood team (who star in the spinoff series *Torchwood* and some of whom appear in "The Stolen Earth") investigated alien menaces in the Cardiff area and beyond.

SERIES THREE

Starring
David Tennant as the Doctor
Freema Agyeman as Martha Jones

Executive Producers
Russell T Davies, Julie Gardner
Phil Collinson (3.08–3.09)

Producers
Phil Collinson
Susie Ligatt (3.08–3.09)

3.00 The Runaway Bride

Written by Russell T Davies **Directed by** Euros Lyn

Supporting cast Catherine Tate (Donna Noble), Sarah Parish (Empress), Don Gilet (Lance Bennett), Jacqueline King (Sylvia Noble), Howard Attfield (Geoff Noble), Trevor Georges (Vicar), Krystal Archer (Nerys), Rhodri Meilir (Rhodri)

Original airdate December 25, 2006

The Big Idea The last of the Racnoss is using bride-to-be Donna Noble as a key to restoring the creature's children from the centre of the Earth . . . so that they can devour all of humankind.

Roots and References Screwball comedies (*Bringing Up Baby, It Happened One Night*); *My Fair Lady* (via the song "Get me to the Church on Time"); *Journey to the Center of the Earth* (Donna mentions dinosaurs being underground, "like in that film").

Adventures in Time and Space "The Runaway Bride" starts with the same crash zoom from Earth's orbit that "Rose" starts with. The Doctor references the Slitheen when asking if Donna's fiancé is overweight with a zip on his forehead ("Aliens of London"). The extrapolator is used to stabilize the TARDIS ("Boom Town"). The robot Santas from "The Christmas Invasion" return (called Roboforms here), although they're now under control of the Racnoss. They once again have weapons shaped like musical instruments, and they also employ a deadly Christmas tree, although this time the ornaments explode.

The Doctor asks Donna about last Christmas ("The Christmas Invasion"), but she missed seeing the Sycorax spaceship because she had a hangover. He references the Battle of Canary Wharf ("Doomsday"), but she was scuba diving in Spain. We also get a few flashbacks to "Doomsday" when the Doctor is remembering Rose, with a number of reflections on the ending ("She's lost, but is very much alive").

The Saxon Effect Orders to fire on the Racnoss Webstar come from a Mr. Saxon. Who this Mr. Saxon is, and how he came to be, will form the basis of much of this season's story arc.

Who is the Doctor? The Doctor confirms that his pockets are bigger on the inside, something fans have long suspected, and, for the first time in the New Series, he acknowledges that the name of his homeworld is Gallifrey (originally named in 1974's "The Time Warrior").

The Doctor and Donna The Doctor and Donna do not initially warm to each other, but gradually Donna learns to trust him. The Doctor frightens Donna, so she rejects his offer to travel with him but acknowledges that he shouldn't be travelling alone.

Monster of the Week The Racnoss are centaur-like giant spiders, with many eyes. They came from the dark times, billions of years ago. They're omnivores ("born starving") and have devoured whole planets. The fledgling empires (including the Time Lords) went to war against the Racnoss, and they were wiped out. However, the Empress's children were in a ship that became the first rock that pulled together others to form the Earth.

Stand Up and Cheer The stroppy Donna of the first half is an astonishing breath of fresh air. Instead of being wowed by the Doctor, she screams at him for kidnapping her, slaps him when he starts gabbling technobabble and calls him on his crap. She lights up the screen and every time she yells (surprisingly accurate) insults at the Doctor, we love her a little more. It's a shame she doesn't join the Doctor in his travels, she would have made a really great companion . . .

Roll Your Eyes The Empress of the Racnoss is dire. Her speech patterns are annoying, rather than alien; her costume looks silly, rather than magnificent; and her acting is bad, rather than mannered. Where Donna lights up every scene she's in, the Empress drags her scenes down to the centre of the Earth. That said, we should give an honourable mention to "This time it's personnel!" As bad puns go, this is about as awful as it gets.

You're Not Making Any Sense You're driving along on the motorway when a box that's about the size of your car (if it stood upright) suddenly bounces directly in front of you. Do you a) swerve, b) slam on the brakes or c) continue driving as though the box were an imaginary computer effect that isn't actually there? If you answered c), congratulations! You're pretty much every driver on the motorway in "The Runaway Bride"!

Interesting Trivia The Doctor confirms here that it's impossible to go back along someone's personal timeline and change things. This isn't strictly true, as we saw Rose's timeline change subtly in "Father's Day"; however, broadly speaking, it's consistent with the rules of time travel that we see elsewhere in the series.

It's clear that Torchwood had a number of projects on the go before the Battle of Canary Wharf in "Doomsday." They own H.C. Clements as a front for what was presumably advanced research in Huon particles, but this involves tunnelling to the centre of the Earth so that the Racnoss spider-babies can come forth and devour every living thing. Including, presumably, the staff of Torchwood (only the Daleks and Cybermen got there first). So, erm, what was in it for them?

The music played as Donna walks down the aisle is Mendelssohn's "The Exit March," which is traditionally played at the *end* of a wedding service (but is rather funny when you realize that she is indeed exiting at that moment).

The TARDIS Chronometer London, Christmas Eve, 2007, the year after "The Christmas Invasion." The Doctor and Donna also travel back in time 4.6 billion years to the creation of Earth.

Brilliant? (RS?) It's the second Christmas special, one that showcases big-name stars and that sees the Doctor freed from the baggage of a companion. It's playing to a larger-than-usual audience who don't care about the ongoing story, they just want to see a fun adventure on Christmas afternoon.

It's not very good though, is it?

There are three things that keep this story from becoming the disaster it otherwise could have been. The first is Donna, who is superb. I loved her long before it was cool to do so. From her wonderfully sassy character at the beginning to her gentle, human side at the end, she lights up the screen and almost single-handedly saves this episode from itself. Getting popular British comedienne Catherine Tate to appear in the show was a huge coup. That she's such a brilliant character is incredible.

The second is the pacing of the first half, which runs like lightning. It's a madcap, screwball comedy and that's just so different from what *Doctor Who* normally is that you just have to sit back and laugh. This shouldn't work, but it does.

The third is the Doctor dealing with the aftermath of Rose's departure. Which is subdued, but it's necessary, touching and perfect . . . so it's a shame they didn't leave it at that and move on. That would not only have improved the season to come, it would have made this story more important in retrospect. Still, the little flashbacks at quiet moments and the Doctor's reluctance to discuss Rose with Donna are quite lovely.

Where the sexless romcom stuff works a treat, the scary sci-fi monster is a huge letdown. Dear god, Sarah Parish is unwatchable. She drags down every scene she's in, which is unfortunately quite a few. The entire second half is saddled with the Racnoss and it's just awful.

In fact, the entire story is upside down. The fast-paced, climactic chase occurs at the beginning, while the info-dump exposition takes place at the end. The story actually starts inside the TARDIS, something we thought would never happen again after the 1996 TV Movie did it so badly. This leads to an inversion of the usual scene, where Donna discovers not that the TARDIS is bigger on the inside, but that it's smaller on the outside.

The Doctor coldly destroying the Racnoss isn't bad, although it does come a bit out of left field. We haven't seen the Doctor with this kind of edge before, but it's not unwelcome. In fact, it doesn't go nearly far enough: how much better would it have been to have Donna utterly horrified by what she saw, unable to look this monster in the eye and bringing the sheer horror of what it means to be the Doctor home to us? Surprisingly perhaps, we will actually get there, but it's going to take some time.

This is the start of the tenth Doctor's "Lonely God" arc that plays out in the background of a number of stories to come, most notably when he's travelling alone. Donna's absolutely right when she says that the Doctor needs someone to stop him, but, ironically, she's one of the few who can, largely because she's not in love with him.

However, there's some real laziness in "The Runaway Bride." Why on Earth are the robot Santas in this story? Answer: because they were here last Christmas. They weren't explained then either, but the first time you can get away with it, the second you can't. They've become the *Doctor Who* equivalent of stocking stuffers: they're what you expect to see in *Doctor Who* at Christmas, explanations be damned. The show is now relying on narrative shorthand instead of actual plotting; since the Christmas episodes get higher ratings than the rest of the series, there must be a segment of the population who only know *Doctor Who* as a show where an alien fights robot Santas at Christmas.

The scene with the TARDIS on the motorway is, in theory, not a bad idea, if a little goofy. In the middle of the fast-paced first half, the plot's still moving quickly enough that its flaws aren't quite so apparent. And Donna having to trust the Doctor and jump is a great conclusion.

Unfortunately, that's not the conclusion at all. Instead, we're saddled with those kids in the back of the car. You know the ones, because you've seen them in every kid-friendly show ever: their parents are oblivious (despite the kids apparently shouting at the top of their voices), but the kids can see the magic that's happening and cheer it on. When the scene is finally resolved, they fist-pump the air, secure in the knowledge that they've experienced something of a world their parents know nothing about.

Except that the Doctor isn't a troll who lives in a secret garden that only pre-pubescents can see. He's got a ruddy great box bouncing around the motorway, and we're expected to believe that no one would pay any notice if that actually happened. This isn't about what is actual any more, it's about the fantasy. *Doctor Who* has always prided itself on having one foot on the ground so that even when there was weird sci-fi stuff going on, it was rooted in the theoretically possible.

Remember how the first season was, as Rose explained in the café, about standing up and saying no? Now the message is "Be magnificent." Do you see the difference? One is angry and subversive; the other is about fitting in and being a part of society. Being a good consumer. Unfortunately, "be magnificent" doesn't work at all. *Doctor Who* is a wonderful show, but it simply doesn't work when it's lazy.

Against all expectations, "The Runaway Bride" turns out to be quite important. But that's only happenstance, due to behind-the-scenes factors. This is a story that could have been big and brilliant but sabotages itself over and over again. Catherine Tate almost single-handedly holds the whole thing together, which is a very precarious position for the episode to be in. Fortunately she turns out to be up to the task, but with no thanks to the story itself.

Second Opinion (GB) First of all, I want to apologize to all of our readers because it's quite clear my co-author has recently had his soul surgically removed. The TARDIS chasing the taxi down the motorway is the best scene ever! It's what every kid (or the kid inside every adult) has ever wanted to see. It's a great little set piece with beautiful effects and a nice character beat as the punchline. The kids' cheering only makes the scene funnier. Normally I rate Robert quite highly, because he's discerning, funny and cool with the ladies. However, when he says he can't stand the TARDIS motorway chase in "The Runaway Bride," I fear something may be wrong with him.

"The Runaway Bride" is a great little lark of a story. I love the basic comic idea of a bride suddenly showing up in the TARDIS. And a bridezilla at that: stressed out, hostile with everyone and ready to kill anyone who gets in her way. Get Catherine Tate to play her, put her in the milieu of science fiction and the TARDIS and — Shazam! — instant comedy. Euros Lyn's direction excels in the first half of the story, using swooshing cuts and handycam shots to deliver breathless action sequences, madcap comedy and some lovely character moments at breakneck pace.

Russell T Davies tries to set up Donna as the sort of everywoman the Doctor would never normally travel with — shallow, self-absorbed and sarcastic — who is then transformed by her encounter with the Time Lord. Tate is lovely playing both the whirling dervish of narcissism and the reflective woman now aware of what an incredible place the universe is. The trouble is, Lance's betrayal is played for laughs (his tirade about Donna's constant chatter is the funniest speech in the whole special) and consequently the transition between the two Donnas doesn't quite work, no matter how beautifully the TARDIS-as-planetarium scene plays out.

There are other frustrations. On the one hand, I like that the Empress is played like a four-year-old (her favourite word is "funny"). On the other, I find it bizarre that Sarah Parish, an actress with a history of amazing chemistry with David Tennant — see *Blackpool* and *Recovery* for proof — would put herself under a tonne of latex to play a monster that is otherwise so banal.

There's no sin in being fun, though, and "The Runaway Bride" is just that: fun. The deficiencies are far outweighed by the stand-up-and-cheer moments, like the Doctor draining the Thames, or the TARDIS chasing the cab. (Shut up, Robert.)

3.01 Smith and Jones

Written by Russell T Davies **Directed by** Charles Palmer

Supporting cast Adjoa Andoh (Francine Jones), Trevor Laird (Clive Jones), Gugu Mbatha-Raw (Tish Jones), Reggie Yates (Leo Jones), Anne Reid (Florence Finnegan), Roy Marsden (Mr. Stoker), Kimmi Richards (Annalise), Ben Righton (Morgenstern), Vineeta Rishi (Julia Swales), Paul Kasey (Judoon captain), Nicholas Briggs (Judoon voices)

Original airdate March 31, 2007

The Big Idea A Plasamavore on the run hides out in a hospital that's taken to the moon by the Judoon.

Roots and References The New Adventure *Timewyrm: Revelation* (a building is transported to the moon); *The Great Train Robbery* (the Doctor references Ronald Biggs hiding in Rio de Janeiro); *Dracula* (the plasmavores; Stoker is named after the author, Bram Stoker).

Adventures in Time and Space When demonstrating her knowledge of extra-terrestrials, Martha references the spaceship crashing into Big Ben ("Aliens of London"), Christmas (likely "The Runaway Bride") and the battle of Canary Wharf ("Doomsday"). Adeola, whom we met there, was Martha's cousin (perhaps not surprising, as both characters were played by Freema Agyeman). The Doctor mentions Rose, saying she's with her family now ("Doomsday" again). The Doctor is pleased that the Royal Hope Hospital has a shop, referencing his obsession from "New Earth." He uses John Smith as an alias (reflected in the title), something he did quite frequently in the Classic Series, starting in 1968's "The Wheel in Space."

When preparing to take off, the Doctor fires up the gravitic anomalizer (1979's "The Horns of Nimon"), the helmic regulators (1975's "The Ark in Space") and the handbrake (the 1996 TV Movie).

The Saxon Effect During a radio interview after the hospital has been returned to Earth, Morgenstern says, "It all just proves Mr. Saxon right; we're not alone in the universe. There's life out there." There's a "Vote Saxon" poster near where the TARDIS has landed at the story's conclusion.

The Doctor and Martha Martha pretty much falls for the Doctor right from the start. It's really noticeable once he kisses her, though the Doctor insists that it was simply a genetic transfer of nonhuman DNA to her (like she hasn't heard *that* one before). The Doctor gives her mixed signals: though he insists he has no interest in Martha, he's happy to flirt with her when they first meet and is certainly interested in impressing her with time travel.

Monster of the Week The Judoon are rhinoceros-like aliens who walk upright. They're interplanetary thugs, acting as a police force for hire. They can lay charges, assume a verdict and carry out punishment, all in one go.

Stand Up and Cheer The hospital on the moon is a gorgeous image. The camera lingers on the view for a while, and you can understand why: it's absolutely lovely, with the moonscape under the Earthlight and the incongruity of an entire hospital sitting in a crater. And then the Judoon ships land, capping it off perfectly.

Roll Your Eyes The stakes are incredibly high: the hospital's MRI machine is about to overload and the lives of half the world's population are at stake. And this is resolved by . . . the Doctor pulling a plug. This was bad enough in "School Reunion," but at least there it was played for comedy. You can just imagine Russell T Davies seeing the script of that one and thinking, "I must add that to my repertoire! Now where's that file called 'Convincing Episode Endings'?"

You're Not Making Any Sense How does a hospital MRI have enough power to kill everyone in a 250,000 kilometre radius? That's without even asking where the electricity to run the lights and machines in the entire hospital is coming from. Yes, there's probably a generator, but that's one hell of a backup the Royal Hope carries.

Interesting Trivia The Judoon language appears to consist only of monosyllables that end in "o." If you count all the consonants, plus any combinations like "th" or "fr," then you get a language that consists of . . . about 50 words. This doesn't seem like much of a language to us. How do they book an airline ticket or have a domestic argument about the subtleties of precisely what was said to their in-laws over dinner? No wonder they all became cops.

The Doctor whipping up a new sonic screwdriver is a change from the '80s, when the sonic screwdriver was destroyed in 1982's "The Visitation" and not replaced for the remainder of the Classic Series. It makes sense that the Doctor could whip up another in the TARDIS lab, but it illustrates the pacing limitations of the New Series: the Doctor without the sonic screwdriver would slow the plot down too much.

The TARDIS Chronometer Initially, it's parked near the Royal Hope; later it's in an alley where the Doctor takes it to visit Martha earlier in the day to show off time travel. The date isn't specified, but it must be 2008.

Brilliant? (RS?) As a season opener, this is just about perfect. It does everything right: it introduces a new companion in an Earth-based plot, incorporates her family and makes her instantly likeable. It also relocates the action to a place of wonder, based on a central image (the hospital on the moon) and has no less than three sets of competing aliens, one with excellent comedic value.

After the heaviness of last season's finale and the questioning of the Doctor's methods in "The Runaway Bride," it's refreshing to see a fun story with a Doctor who doesn't know everything and is just along for the ride. There's no pre-credits teaser here, which actually works in the story's favour. It's more of a slow burn and introducing a contrived crisis would have lessened Martha's careful introduction. The only downside to Martha is her family: there are simply too many of them (five, including Annalise). This makes them impossible to keep track of and inevitably means that some are going to get more attention than others.

The Doctor's trick with the tie, where he shows that the random meeting with Martha at the start of the episode was, in fact, proof that he could travel in time, is superb. It's a great use of time travel and is capped with a killer punchline: when Martha asks why the Doctor didn't warn her not to go into work, he says that crossing timelines is strictly forbidden . . . except for cheap tricks. Tennant delivers this line with an indulgent smile, as opposed to his usual smugness, and it works a treat.

The character of Martha is hampered, though, by her instant crush on the Doctor. She's established as an extremely likeable, competent career woman, but that's immediately undercut by having her make puppy-dog eyes at the Doctor. Martha's going to spend almost the entirety of her tenure being defined by which guy she's interested in, which — whether the producers intended it or not — sits uncomfortably with her race and her gender. Martha is so smart and so independent, but in a stroke she's not only dependent but desperate to please the lead male character, who happens to be white. It takes away the autonomy of the character, it wasn't necessary — in a show with a 900-year-old Time Lord, Martha was never going to upstage the Doctor in knowledge or competency — and it deprives the character of some basic dignity.

Unpleasant subtext aside, "Smith and Jones" is absolutely wonderful. It's not as well remembered as it should be, partly because it's a fluffy season opener, but it's delightful viewing that's pitched exactly right. Oh, and it finally gets Tennant out of that hideous brown suit! What more could you want?

Second Opinion (GB) Rose is gone and her departure sees the series not only lose a fantastic actress in Billie Piper, but the central character around whom the New Series was based. The task before Russell T Davies was not just to replace Rose but to replace the backstory and a whole supporting cast as well as the companion's relationship with the Doctor and . . .

Never mind all that. "Smith and Jones" adroitly reinvents the show with a new companion and makes it all seem effortless.

Russell T Davies knows the audience has to fall in love with Martha, and he's written a showcase for her that does just that. Freema Agyeman nails it absolutely and totally. She sparkles. There's no other word for it. (And, oh my word, does director Charles Palmer know how to make her look gorgeous every moment she's onscreen.) Martha is absolutely delightful: charming, charismatic and confident, but completely grounded. She works really well with David Tennant's Doctor, providing a foil to his quirkiness in a way that Rose never did. She starts out regarding the Doctor as a relative equal, intellectually — and then falls for him the more she realizes she's not his equal. The chemistry is totally fissionable as a result.

Which is great, because the plot doesn't have much beyond the brilliant premise of transporting the hospital to the moon. It's designed to introduce Martha to the audience and to the Doctor. Which is absolutely fine because the story is big, colourful, fun and grandly entertaining. The Judoon are officious, imposing and awesomely designed, while the real threat turns out to hide behind the most banal disguise of all. (Oh, how I love Florence and her drinking straw!)

David Tennant, quite simply, rocks. The scene where the Doctor tries to convince Florence that he's actually a patient in to have a foot operation is a scream, as Tennant delivers the Doctor's make-it-up-as-he-goes-along dialogue letter perfect: "You'll have to excuse me, I'm a bit out of my depth, I've spent the past 15 years working as a postman, hence the bunion." But he also excels at the quieter moments too, such as the final five minutes that take every ounce of romance in Russell T Davies' script and put it onscreen. Murray Gold provides the gorgeous music, Charles Palmer gives us lush and beautiful pictures, and Freema Agyeman and David Tennant do the rest. Breathtaking and lovely.

"Smith and Jones" shows the New Series at its most confident, which is an astonishing feat when you consider it was starting from what is, by every other measure, a position of weakness in losing the lynchpin of the first two seasons. And this is only the season's opening episode.

· ·

Freema Agyeman

Like many jobbing actresses early in their careers, Freema Agyeman played a number of small roles in TV series like *Silent Witness* and *The Bill*. In 2005, 27-year-old Freema auditioned for Sally in "The Christmas Invasion" and a part in "Army of Ghosts" (that was ultimately cut). Agyeman was ultimately given the role of Adeola in that same episode, but *Doctor Who*'s producers were impressed with her versatility. When Billie

Piper departed from the series, Agyeman was in a shortlist of candidates to become the next companion.

Agyeman appeared as Martha Jones in every episode in Series Three and returned to the role for four more in Series Four (and a further three episodes of *Torchwood*). Following *Doctor Who*, Agyeman played in the BBC's 2008 adaptation of *Little Dorrit* and gained further fame playing crown prosecutor Alesha Phillips in *Law & Order: UK*.

· ·

3.02 The Shakespeare Code

Written by Gareth Roberts **Directed by** Charles Palmer

Supporting cast Dean Lennox Kelly (William Shakespeare), Christina Cole (Lilith), Sam Marks (Wiggins), Amanda Lawrence (Doomfinger), Linda Clarke (Bloodtide), Jalaal Hartley (Dick), David Westhead (Kempe), Andree Bernard (Dolly Bailey), Chris Larkin (Lynley), Stephen Marcus (jailer), Matt King (Peter Streete), Robert Demeger (preacher), Angela Pleasence (Queen Elizabeth I)

Original airdate April 7, 2007

The Big Idea Audiences at the Globe Theatre eagerly await William Shakespeare's new play, *Love's Labour's Won* — and so do aliens who want to use it to escape their imprisonment.

Roots and References *Shakespeare in Love* (an "origin" story for Shakespeare); *Blackadder the Second* (homicidal Queen Elizabeth); Dan Brown's *The DaVinci Code* (the title). The Doctor claims Martha comes from Freedonia (from the Marx Brothers movie *Duck Soup*). The mechanics of the temporal flux are explained using *Back to the Future* (the film, not the novelization), while the Doctor dismisses the ending of Ray Bradbury's time-travel short story "A Sound of Thunder." The Doctor and Martha talk about J.K. Rowling's Harry Potter books and, of course, the whole episode is about the plays of Christopher Marlowe (just kidding . . .).

Adventures in Time and Space This is the first onscreen meeting between the Doctor and Shakespeare (and presumably the first chronologically), though the Doctor's offscreen interactions with the Bard have been mentioned throughout the Classic Series, most notably in 1979's "City of Death" where the Doctor claims that a first draft of *Hamlet* was written in his own hand as Shakespeare had sprained his wrist writing sonnets. The Doctor uses his royal title, Sir Doctor of TARDIS, conferred upon him by Queen Victoria in "Tooth and Claw." We'll find out more on how the Doctor became a mortal enemy of Elizabeth I in "The End of Time, Part One" and "The Wedding of River Song."

It's not stated onscreen, but the Carrionites' method of using words to change physical reality is quite similar to those of the Logopolitans in 1981's "Logopolis." The Carrionites claim to have been banished by the Eternals, who appeared in 1983's "Enlightenment."

Who is the Doctor? Upon discovering she does not know the Doctor's true name, Lilith asks, "Why would a man hide his title in such despair?" While it's hinted at in other stories (including "The Girl in the Fireplace"), this is the first direct reference that the Doctor has a true name that no one knows.

The Doctor and Martha Shakespeare tells Martha, "The Doctor will not kiss you." Admittedly, Shakespeare was on the make at the time, but it certainly seems true: when lying next to Martha in bed, the Doctor starts reminiscing about Rose.

Monster of the Week The Carrionites resemble stereotypical witches. They use an advanced super-science that seems like magic and uses words to manipulate the physical universe.

Stand Up and Cheer The Doctor and Martha's first five minutes in 1599 is a marvel of location work, CGI and really funny dialogue. You come for the gorgeous evocation of Elizabethan London, but you stay for the witty lines, particularly the Doctor's responses to the science-fiction tropes about the butterfly effect and the grandfather paradox.

Roll Your Eyes The Doctor saying he misses Rose is tolerable, but he becomes a complete and total insensitive ass when he launches into all the ways that Rose would have been better at handling the situation while Martha lies a foot away from him in the same bed.

You're Not Making Any Sense The earnest hand-waving to prove the Carrionites are practising superior science that adheres to Clarke's Laws doesn't make a lick of sense. Words are like mathematics, which can change the physical universe. Er . . .

Interesting Trivia In terms of historical accuracy, the play's the thing here, so there are many liberties taken. *Love's Labour's Won* is indeed a "missing" Shakespeare play: it was listed among his works but no extant copy exists. (Although there are some who say the title was simply a misnomer and it either never actually existed or was an alternative title for another of Shakespeare's plays.) However, it was performed in 1598, a full year before construction of the Globe Theatre's completion in 1599. Also, in ye olden times before electric lights, theatre was performed in the afternoon. (Production convenience may have trumped historical accuracy here: the story was shot at the replica of the Globe Theatre in London, which is a working historical site during the day and therefore night shooting was required.)

Appropriate for a historical story like this, there is a running gag where the Doctor and Martha, paradoxically, give Shakespeare ideas he would use in later works, including "to be or not to be" (which Shakespeare initially judges as pretentious), "all the world's a stage," "a winter's tale" and the Sycorax. Shakespeare also likes "Rage, rage against the dying of the light," but the Doctor informs him it's not his (it belongs to Dylan Thomas). It is also implied that events of this story inform Shakespeare's later work: the Carrionites resemble the three witches Shakespeare later put into *Macbeth*, while the Elephant pub features in *Twelfth Night*. The story ends with Martha turning out to be the "dark lady" Shakespeare wrote "Sonnet XVII" for ("Shall I compare thee to a summer's day . . ."), though he does flirt with the Doctor as well, leading the Doctor to remark, "Fifty-seven academics just punched the air." Jokes are also made about Shakespeare's impending baldness and the ruff he eventually wears in portraits.

The TARDIS Chronometer London, 1599, according to the onscreen title caption.

Brilliant? (GB) Shakespeare matters. He really does. It's estimated that his works added two to three thousand words to the English language. His plays beautifully, often achingly, portray all the facets of the human condition: love, exultation, arrogance, ambition, pride, humour, anger, confusion, rage, madness, despair. He does all this with language that, even over four centuries later, still excites and captivates the heart and mind.

I say all this because, in the world of "The Shakespeare Code," Shakespeare matters only because the Doctor and the Carrionites tell us that he matters. Onscreen, Shakespeare is a perceptive soul who can see through the psychic paper, the ruse that Martha hails from Freedonia and Martha's self-deception of the Doctor's love. But what makes Shakespeare great, what sees his plays repeated again and again is never touched upon. In fact, aside from the last 30 seconds of *Love's Labour's Lost*, the only play of Shakespeare's we see during the entire episode is the one made up by writer Gareth Roberts, *Love's Labour's Won*. With other "celebrity" historical figures in the series — Charles Dickens, Queen Victoria, Agatha Christie, Vincent van Gogh — you really get a sense of who they are and why they were important. Shakespeare historically is a bit of a cipher and not much is done to add to the picture here: he's a bit of a wide boy, a bit of a jack-the-lad, a bit of a genius, but never a full character. That's a shame.

The Carrionites are great villains and, given their need to make magic — er, science — with words, are literally made for an adventure with Shakespeare. But the problem is that all the CGI in the world can't convincingly illustrate that sort of a super-science. In the end, stuff happens because people speak nonsense, and not even clever nonsense but the sort of technobabble you'd find on *Star Trek: Voyager*.

Fortunately, there are a lot of other things to like about "The Shakespeare Code." Gareth Roberts' script uses the familiar trope from comedy-sketch writing that olden times are not much different than our own but does it with great panache. (My personal favourite is his example of global warming.) The Doctor seems oddly juxtaposed in what is otherwise an exciting comedy adventure: he seems especially dark, to the point where you wonder if David Tennant is working from a much grimmer script. Fortunately, Dean Lennox Kelly is there to balance the scales. Given how much of a blank canvas the character is, Lennox Kelly is really quite likeable as Shakespeare, approaching things with an honest practicality. Confronted with the barbarism of Bedlam, Shakespeare tells Martha of his own madness and how the fear of the place kept him sane. Lennox Kelly nicely underplays the scene, where other actors might try to wring it for all the pathos it has.

Unfortunately, Martha is still mooning after the Doctor, and the Doctor is either wilfully ignoring her or he's just that stupid. Somewhere in between, I suspect. However, it's not a good sign that in only the second episode of the season the unrequited love angle is getting tiresome.

What really makes "The Shakespeare Code" come alive are the visuals. The location work (and full points to the production team for getting access to the replica of the Globe Theatre) and the CGI embellishments really give an impressive sense of place. Charles Palmer is probably the best director working on Series Three, and his visuals here are lush and romantic and perfect for this story.

"The Shakespeare Code" wins out because it's funny — the running gag of quoting Shakespeare's future work is actually really well done (particularly when they throw in other poets' work and then work the Bard himself already wrote) — and it's charming and exciting. It's a shame, with the title character so poorly drawn, that it's ultimately sound and fury, signifying nothing.

Second Opinion (RS?) Welcome to this week's attempt at race politics. A large number of racial epithets are thrown Martha's way and we're supposed to laugh because they're from ye olde worlde and dismissed by the Doctor as "political correctness gone mad," rather than, say, racism going on as usual. Martha (rightly) worries about being carted off as a slave, but the Doctor dismisses her concerns by saying that he's not even human. Right, and so not being human but looking like a white male is exactly the same as being a woman of colour, is it, Doctor?

The story wants to address the race issue head-on, which results in the initial discussion, but it has no answers to give. So, rather than deal with the actual consequences of being a woman of colour trapped in a terrifying and dangerous place, they sidestep the issue almost entirely.

How much more dramatic would it have been to have Martha forced to confront the reality of time travel? And the Doctor could have learned a much-needed lesson about his own whiteness, to boot. There's a story with actual emotional heart to be found in there, but it's far too dangerous an idea to be explored. Race has always been a thorny issue for *Doctor Who*, largely due to travelling into history. However, pretending it isn't an issue isn't actually a workable solution.

The real problem isn't in front of the camera; it's behind. While you don't have to be part of a minority to understand the minority experience, it sure does help. And if you're not, then what you need is sensitivity, and that's a notoriously difficult thing to grasp. So when the vast majority of writers, directors, executives, producers and script editors are white, there's a tendency to collectively ignore the power that stereotyping and under-representation can have. When you amplify that with the power of television, what you get is the status quo being reinforced, yet again.

We're often told that *Doctor Who* is a show that can be anything, but it's times like this when we realize just how untrue that statement actually is. At least while the show is being written, produced and directed almost entirely by white people.

3.03 Gridlock

Written by Russell T Davies **Directed by** Richard Clark

Supporting cast Ardal O'Hanlon (Thomas Kincade Brannigan), Anna Hope (Novice Hame), Travis Oliver (Milo), Lenora Crichlow (Cheen), Jennifer Hennessy (Valerie), Bridget Turner (Alice), Georgine Anderson (May), Simon Pearsall (Whitey), Daisy Lewis (Javit), Nicholas Boulton (businessman), Erika Macleod (Sally Calypso), Judy Norman (Ma), Graham Padden (Pa), Tom Edden (pharmacist #1), Natasha Williams (pharmacist #2), Gayle Telfer Stevens (pharmacist #3), Struan Rodger (The Face of Boe)

Original airdate April 14, 2007

The Big Idea And you thought your morning commute was awful: thousands of people are beneath New New York, spending decades just to travel five miles.

Roots and References The British comic book *2000 AD* (Sally Calypso is patterned after a similar character in Alan Moore's *Halo Jones* and the Businessman looks like *Judge Dredd* character Max Normal). The couple in the pre-credits teaser look like the couple in Grant Wood's painting *American Gothic*. The hymns "The Old Rugged Cross" and "Abide With Me" are sung at various points in the story.

Adventures in Time and Space This story (along with "The End of the World" and "New Earth") completes a loose trilogy of stories set in the year five billion that feature the Face of Boe. The cat nun Novice Hame from "New Earth" returns (and the green crescent medical symbol also appears on the mood patches). The Doctor's description of his home planet is pretty much how it was described in 1964's "The Sensorites."

The Saxon Effect The Face of Boe's dying words to the Doctor are "You are not alone." We'll come back to these words later.

Who is the Doctor? The Doctor has compartmentalized his feelings about being a survivor. He reveals his reason for lying to Martha about his planet not being destroyed: "I could pretend, just for a bit, I could imagine they were still alive underneath the burnt orange sky." It's only at Martha's insistence that he finally opens up about his loss.

The Doctor and Martha Martha tries to draw the Doctor out and talk about his home planet, but he balks and instead takes her to places he visited with Rose. Martha says that he likes the idea of a companion more than he actually likes her, and the Doctor begins to realize he's keeping her at arm's length on purpose.

Monster of the Week The fast lane is stalked by Macra, crab-like beasties that made their first appearance in 1967's "The Macra Terror." There, they were the big bad nasties enslaving humans in a space colony. In the ensuing billions of years, they've devolved and become many times larger but have lost their intelligence.

Stand Up and Cheer In what must be the most bittersweet and moving scene this season, everyone on the motorway stops and sings "The Old Rugged Cross." It's a moment when everyone on this endless journey stops and acknowledges each other and what they have, while underscoring both the futility of the journey and their strength. There's never been a moment in *Doctor Who* that better illustrates the contradictions of the human condition.

Roll Your Eyes As much as we'd hate to argue with the Doctor's gravitas, we suspect Pharmacy Town cleared out to go sell their goods on the repopulated surface rather than to avoid the Doctor's fearsome retribution.

You're Not Making Any Sense The mutated virus wiped out every living being on the surface of New Earth in seven minutes. Yet, during this time, the senate (comprising dozens of members, judging by the corpses) were able to enact a 100-year-long quarantine and seal the entire lower city. So they analyzed the problem, came to a decision and put it into practice all within a matter of minutes. It's good to know there'll be great progress in the future in at least one area. Most of the senates we've encountered take that long just to argue about their coffee allowance . . .

Interesting Trivia This is the third and final episode in the year five billion trilogy, all of which feature the Face of Boe, a variety of fantastical aliens, the far-future setting and the theme that everything dies. Other recurring motifs that feature in at least two of the episodes include the Doctor confessing the loss of his home planet, the city of New New York, cat nuns, rampant disease and ruminations on the class divide. They're visually quite similar, despite being helmed by three distinct directors. They also occupy positions one, two and three in the first three seasons, albeit not in that order.

Two years before this story aired, Russell T Davies' notes on the Face of Boe for *Doctor Who Magazine* (and reprinted in the 2005 non-fiction book *Monsters and Villains*) stated that the Face was said to live forever and is known as "the creature that God forgot"; legend says that he holds one final secret that he will speak with his final breath to a homeless, wandering traveller. Davies' essay states that when the Face of Boe dies the sky will rip open, which is precisely what happened for the people trapped underground on New New York's motorway. (Davies had apparently forgotten this when he had written the ending of "Gridlock"!)

The Cassini "sisters" are the first same-sex married couple to appear in televised *Doctor Who*.

The TARDIS Chronometer New New York in the year five billion and 53.

Brilliant? (GB) Once upon a time, before there was such a thing as "science fiction," there were parables, allegories and fables where our world was dressed up in another way in order to make a point about the human condition.

While there have been lots of allegories employed during *Doctor Who*'s history — the Daleks as an allegory for Nazism would be the number one example — "Gridlock" is *Doctor Who*'s first sustained foray into the world of allegory. The whole construction of the story is allegorical. In the same way that Bunyan's pilgrim travels through a world that is a representation of the Christian soul in the 18th century, so does Russell T Davies plumb the depths of 21st century culture: our travellers start in Pharmacy Town and make their way into a quarter-century-long traffic jam where five miles is travelled in decades. No matter who you are, everyone inevitably winds up on the motorway . . . til the journey's end.

That's why the "science" of "could there really be a world where people are stuck in their cars for decades?" matters absolutely not one whit. "Gridlock" is not meant to be realistic, any more than Swift's *Gulliver's Travels* or Beckett's *Waiting for Godot* are meant to be realistic. Like the room that is Hell in Sartre's play *No Exit*, the whole world the Doctor and Martha find themselves in is part of a larger allegorical meditation on the human condition.

The most powerful scene in the episode finds the Doctor desperately trying to convince Brannigan and his wife that there is no help coming from outside and their journey is futile just as the perky hologram Sally Calypso leads everyone on the motorway in singing "The Old Rugged Cross." Brannigan tells the Doctor, "We're not abandoned. Not while we have each other." As everyone sings the hymn, suddenly the message becomes clear. We're seeing a world where human progress has taken its people so far and not only do they not see a way out, they're pretty much content with their dismal lot. They just keep blindly believing in the possibility of help from outside — even though there's no evidence whatsoever that there is any help, much less any outside — while holding on, in whatever ways they can, to the communities they have from within.

Then it hits home: that world is our world too. Seen that way, "Gridlock" is an existentialist fable for our postmodern age. Bunyan's *Pilgrim's Progress* without God. Camus's *The Plague* without the pus and suffering. What happens in the motorway is true of the human condition here and now. Truly, we are stuck in gridlock, too.

That alone is enough to make "Gridlock" great, but the episode is more than just that. It's a fun, fast-paced story with lots of comedic set pieces (the Doctor jumping from car to car), developments for the ongoing story arc (like the Face of Boe) and some really affecting scenes and standout performances, particularly Ardal O'Halnan and Anna Hope's cats. (I love how Novice Hame bursts into Brannigan's car armed with a machine gun. Nuns with guns are great; cat nuns with guns are simply awesome.)

"Gridlock" covers similar territory as "The End of the World," revisiting how the ninth Doctor revealed to Rose his identity as the last Time Lord, only with the tenth Doctor and Martha. You would think that would play as terribly stale and yet they manage to make it work. In the scene where the Doctor admits to Martha he's the last of his kind, David Tennant knocks it as far out of the park as Christopher Eccleston did back in Series One. Part of the reason the last scene is so moving is that there's a progression as well. In "The End of the World," the Doctor was just naming who he was (a big step for the ninth Doctor); here, the Doctor is recalling his home and how much he misses it. We see how the Doctor has changed in the past two years in that scene alone.

Plus, the Macra are a great little treat for longtime fans. If you're going to have a big alien menace for a few minutes, why not pick one from *Doctor Who*'s rich 40-year heritage? Fans get an extra thrill from the easter egg of an old foe while casual viewers just get to see cool-looking crab monsters.

If asked to name the best story of Series Three, most people will probably choose "Blink" or "Human Nature"/"The Family of Blood" or maybe the finale. But I'm convinced that, with its fun and exciting storyline, fascinating ideas and themes, and powerful emotional undercurrents, "Gridlock" might well be the worthiest candidate for this season's best story.

Second Opinion (RS?) People spending their lives in their cars. Traffic that moves slower than walking pace. A transit lane that's almost entirely empty, because people can't cooperate enough to share a vehicle. Whole stations dedicated to traffic updates. Police that are nowhere to be seen. Exhaust fumes so intense you can't breathe. Still, that's enough about the year I lived in Los Angeles; what about "Gridlock"?

Take the setup of "New Earth" but subvert it, because the seedy underbelly of society is always more interesting than the glam and glitter of the rich. Reveal the Face of Boe's secret, but use it to further the season arc. Throw in a returning monster but invert the stereotype entirely. What you get is something that's ostensibly simple, even Spartan in its minimalism, but which reveals layer upon layer the closer you look.

David Tennant is excellent here. Let me state that again: he's excellent. I'm not the tenth Doctor's biggest fan, so I want to go on record to say how much I'm enjoying this year's version. Part of it is reining in the hysterics (with the sole exception of the embarrassing "Maaaarrrr-ttthhhhaaaa!!" but that seems to have been inserted solely so it could appear in the previous episode's "next time" teaser). Part of it is that Tennant's actually given some emotional material to work with (his response to questions about Gallifrey). He can't do anger, but he's excellent in the small, quiet moments.

Freema Agyeman, too, is great. She gets to be the rebound in more ways than one: she has to repeat many of the same scenes as her predecessor — she discovers the Doctor's the last of his kind, she admits she left Earth with a perfect stranger without thinking, she visits her first alien world — but she's note perfect. She's especially good when dealing with the aftermath of her kidnapping and carries scenes that could easily be ruined, like the "I have faith" speech.

"Gridlock" is far sadder and far cleverer than it first appears, but it's also funny and has big things to say both about character and our own society. The jokes are mainly visual (the kittens, the nudists, the Doctor simply pointing at the red guy), but they work a treat, without overwhelming the otherwise serious points that the episode is making. Did you catch the way the Doctor leaps out of the second car without actually checking to see if there's one underneath? I have yet to see a better illustration of the character.

"Gridlock" is one of the best episodes of the New Series. If you don't believe me, go check it out again and see if it doesn't make you cry.

3.04–3.05 Daleks in Manhattan / Evolution of the Daleks

Written by Helen Raynor **Directed by** James Strong

Supporting cast Miranda Raison (Tallulah), Ryan Carnes (Laszlo), Hugh Quarshie (Solomon), Andrew Garfield (Frank), Eric Loren (Mr. Diagoras/Dalek Sec), Flik Swan (Myrna), Alexis Caley (Lois), Earl Perkins (man #1), Peter Brooke (man #2), Ian Porter (foreman), Joe Montana (worker #1), Stewart Alexander (worker #2), Mel Taylor (dock worker), Nicholas Briggs (Dalek voices), Paul Kasey (hero pig)

Original airdates April 21 and 28, 2007

The Big Idea In the heart of the Great Depression, who is helping with the building of the Empire State Building? The Daleks!

Roots and References The original *King Kong*; James Whale's 1930 film of *Frankenstein* (the human Daleks on pallets, the art direction generally); Woody Allen's *Manhattan* (the use of Gershwin's "Rhapsody in Blue"); *The Island of Dr. Moreau* (genetic experimentation); the 1930s musicals of Busby Berkeley.

Adventures in Time and Space The Doctor traces the genetic makeup of the attempted Dalek embryo back to the planet Skaro, which marks the first time in the New Series that Skaro is explicitly named as the Dalek homeworld. The Cult of Skaro Daleks return (after using an emergency temporal shift in "Doomsday"). The Doctor and the hybrid Dalek Sec discuss the Daleks' creator, once again not naming him. The Daleks' armour is finally described as being made of Dalekanium, which is what it was called back in 1964's "The Dalek Invasion of Earth." The Daleks have visited the Empire State Building before: they briefly landed there while tracking the Doctor and his companions in 1965's "The Chase."

Who is the Doctor? The presence of the Daleks brings out the Doctor's survivor guilt. Upon seeing the Daleks' return, he laments, "I lose everything, while they still survive." He even becomes reckless, repeatedly challenging the Daleks to shoot him.

The Doctor and Martha Martha confesses her love of the Doctor to Tallulah, but she also knows the Doctor hasn't gotten over Rose, saying, "Sometimes I think he's not seeing me, he's just remembering her." The Doctor continues to be an insensitive jerk when he proclaims he should never waste time for a hug after missing the elevator because he was hugging Martha.

Monster of the Week Dalek Sec decides that the only thing the last four Daleks can do is to attempt to replicate themselves in the human race. To that end, Dalek Sec absorbs the body of Diagoras, a human, and uses Dalek technology to become the first Dalek/human hybrid. The hybrid is bipedal but has a tentacled, cyclopean head.

Stand Up and Cheer The funniest thing the Daleks ever have done, and will ever do, happens when one Dalek, while talking to another in hushed tones, rotates its eyestalk to see if it is observed.

Roll Your Eyes The Doctor's almost suicidal rage towards the Dalek worked back in "Dalek," because of the wounded nature of the ninth Doctor and because the story was about exploring his psychological state. Here, both instances of it look like random bipolar incidents.

You're Not Making Any Sense We may have a winner in the much-disputed competition for worst use of science in *Doctor Who*. Gamma radiation from solar flare activity is, well, radiation. The energy from it radiates from the sun to the Earth. It wouldn't come down as lightning and almost certainly wouldn't transmit the DNA of anyone it passed through.

Interesting Trivia The historical knowledge on display here is about as dodgy as the science: a Hooverville (the generic term given to the shanty towns that sprang up all over the United States during the Depression, named after the 31st president of the United States, Herbert Hoover) didn't exist in New York in 1930; the first signs of one began a year later, in 1931. It didn't exist in Central Park itself, but in the nearby reservoir that was drained at the time. Production expedience probably had much to do with the fudging of the historical record: while background plates of the Manhattan skyline for special effects were shot in New York in 2006 (the first foreign filming for the New Series), it was simply cheaper and easier to film in a park in Wales rather than fake a drained reservoir or recreate tenements where the vast majority of New York City's poor actually lived.

Radio Times, the BBC's own listings magazine, featured the human hybrid Dalek Sec on the front cover of the issue the week before "Daleks in Manhattan" was broadcast. Fans complained that this spoiled the cliffhanger at the end of the first part; Russell T Davies countered that the *Radio Times* cover helped offer a new publicity spin for the Dalek's third appearance in three years.

Why exactly are the Daleks crossing humans with pigs? No reason, they just are. Why is wiping the mind of the subject the last thing on the agenda, rather than the first? Simple plot contrivance so that Laszlo can remain intelligent. Why do they only live a few weeks, when both pigs and humans live much longer than that? Ask writer Helen Raynor, it must be in her notes somewhere. Right?

The TARDIS Chronometer New York, New York, November 1, 1930.

Brilliant? (GB) The American accents seem to be as good a place as any to start, as they pretty much serve as a metaphor for the story as a whole: highly variable. On the good side, you have Andrew Garfield's decent Tennessee accent, and

Ryan Carnes is actually American. Hugh Quarshie's accent is pretty serviceable. There are the accents that are tacky but enjoyable, like Miranda Raison's *Bugsy Malone*–esque Brooklyn accent for Tallulah. And then there are the accents that grate like fingernails on chalkboards: some of the workmen and human Daleks, Tallulah's dance partners and Eric Loren as Diagoras. Loren is an American, but his accent is so broad here it drives me batty.

Guess which actor ends up being the human/Dalek hybrid?

Instead of intoning the hybrid Dalek Sec so it sounds a bit like a Dalek, or even distorting its voice mildly, Dalek Sec talks in an accent somewhere between Brooklyn and New Jersey. The prosthetic design is already bordering on laughable, with the ludicrous one eye and the protruding tentacles that are shaped like . . . um . . . fingers. The fact he's still wearing the sharp suit and two-tone wingtips is utterly absurd. On top of it all, every time he opens his mouth, it makes you want to reach for the mute button on the remote.

In some ways, the dreadfulness of the hybrid Dalek Sec is the least of this two-parter's problems. The world it creates is absolutely bogus, the sort of only-on-TV world Robert complained about in his review of "The Idiot's Lantern": the poetic licence in terms of the location and timing of the New York Hooverville is one thing, but the portrayal of it as some sort of a commune where all creeds and colours live in harmony by a code of honour while bemoaning the evils of capitalism is not only ahistorical, it's downright ridiculous. It's the same phony world where aliens could create a giant base under the Empire State Building and never be detected.

Then again, the whole plot seems like a loose assemblage of all the ideas given out during the initial brainstorming: New York during the Depression! Showgirls! A musical number! Pigs crossed with humans! Plucky humans from the wrong side of the tracks! The Empire State Building! The Doctor on top of the Empire State Building getting hit by lightning! Daleks re-enacting *Frankenstein*! Human Dalek soldiers marching with Dalek machine guns! The creature inside a Dalek on someone's head! All the bullet points are there, but there's nothing to make it cohere. Likewise, the human supporting characters are completely dispensable. Laszlo's death throes are there to give the Doctor a "give me a day like this" scene like he had in "The Empty Child," but it just rings false and fails in its attempt to manipulate the heartstrings of the audience.

Some attempt is made to bridge both these problems with Dalek Sec's futile attempt to bring humanity to the Daleks. Here, the story grasps at worthiness by trying to evoke the internal struggle of the Dalek in "Dalek" and a spin on *Frankenstein* at the same time, where a Dalek creates new life that is abhorred by other Daleks because it is human. It's a really clever idea, and there are some great lines that come from it. ("You told us to imagine — and we imagined your irrelevance.") But not enough is done to develop it. Part of the problem is that the remit of the first two-parter of the season — to be a big, colourful adventure with monsters for the kids — isn't the place for that sort of a story. We're stuck with these momentary glimpses of depth in the midst of a story with a cuddly looking hybrid Dalek in a zoot suit.

It's not all bad. Tallulah (three l's, one h) is one of those cartoony characters who's just plain fun to have around. Miranda Raison steals the show in every scene she's in. She's adroit at the broad comedy but also brilliant at conveying the hardened vulnerability at the core of the character. There are some great moments as well, particularly Solomon's impassioned speech that ends in his extermination, and Dalek Caan's conversation with Diagoras, where Caan talks about the human race's propensity to survive and grooms Diagoras as the hybrid Dalek. Here we see Eric Loren use some subtlety and it's astonishing how well it works. It's a shame no one kept this in mind for the whole story.

All that said, I kind of want to see a sequel with Tallulah and Laszlo living in a duplex in the suburbs in the 1950s. Call me crazy, but I think that would be fun.

Second Opinion (RS?) This is bad, bad TV. Its problems are legion (and accurately outlined by my co-author above), so I'm going to focus on just one: Diagoras. He's the most important person in the narrative, the man the cliffhanger hinges on — and yet he never actually meets the Doctor. We see him yell at a few staff, never get his hands dirty and are simply told how important he is; we're never once shown it. As a result, we're awkwardly brought into a cliffhanger that features a man the Doctor's never spoken to and . . . he's wearing a Dalek hat.

After that, the story goes into a bit of a decline.

Everything about it is too pat. From the Doctor losing his sonic screwdriver on top of the tallest building in the world (only to recover it moments later, rescued offscreen in a moment of trite convenience) to Hybrid Dalek Sec simply switching sides (rather than deal with the complexity that is human morality), this is a hodgepodge of poorly realized big ideas.

Interestingly, the Doctor defines "not genocide" as "one member of the species left." He does this twice: with Dalek Caan and with Laszlo, clearly reflecting his innermost feelings about his own race's survival via himself. It's a subtle point and one I suspect came from Russell T Davies, as part of the season's arc, because it's so out of place with the sledgehammer tactics of the rest of the tale.

Overall, "Daleks in Manhattan"/"Evolution of the Daleks" commits the worst crime a *Doctor Who* story can commit: it's boring. None of the big ideas gel, the worthy discussions never threaten to turn into actual drama and,

Solomon aside, the characters are broad without being interesting. A waste of the Daleks, who have gone from terrifying to cartoonish in just four stories, a waste of a good premise (just how far would the Daleks go to ensure their own survival?) and a waste of everybody's time.

3.06 The Lazarus Experiment

Written by Stephen Greenhorn **Directed by** Richard Clark

Supporting cast Adjoa Andoh (Francine Jones), Gugu Mbatha-Raw (Tish Jones), Reggie Yates (Leo Jones), Mark Gatiss (Lazarus), Thelma Barlow (Lady Thaw), Lucy O'Connell (olive woman), Bertie Cavell (mysterious man)

Original airdate May 5, 2007

The Big Idea Professor Lazarus has invented a way to regain his youth, but it turns him into a big scorpion.

Roots and References Stories where humans transform into monsters (beginning with Robert Louis Stevenson's *The Strange Case of Dr. Jekyll and Mr. Hyde* and including *The Incredible Hulk* and *The Fly*, particularly David Cronenberg's 1986 remake); the original 1952 version of *The Quatermass Experiment* (the final confrontation in the cathedral); *This Is Spinal Tap* ("We need to turn this up to 11"). Lazarus is named for a man Jesus raised from the dead in the Gospel of John. The Doctor and Lazarus quote from T.S. Eliot's poem, "The Hollow Men."

Adventures in Time and Space The Doctor reverses the polarity of the hypersonic chamber, recalling the third Doctor's propensity to reverse the polarity of things, such as the neutron flow.

When Francine slaps the Doctor, he says, "Oh, the mothers, every time," referring to Jackie slapping him in "Aliens of London." The Doctor mentions being at the Blitz, referencing "The Empty Child"/"The Doctor Dances." The Doctor doesn't like black-tie events, saying that something bad always happens, a reference to "Rise of the Cybermen"/"The Age of Steel."

The Saxon Effect Lady Thaw twice notes Mr. Saxon's interest in Lazarus's experiments. Francine is approached by one of Saxon's representatives, which spooks her into leaving Martha a voicemail saying that she knows the Doctor is dangerous and that this information comes from Harold Saxon himself.

The Doctor and Martha The Doctor is as casual as ever, returning Martha to her flat and only staying on because he's seen Professor Lazarus on TV. At the end, he offers Martha another trip, but Martha finally asserts herself and refuses to travel with the Doctor unless she's in for the long haul. He accepts.

Monster of the Week Lazarus transforms into a creature using abandoned blind alleys of evolution, including a scorpion. His original face is intact, but his lower jaw can split wide open. The stinger can drain life energy in seconds. He can walk sideways or on the ceiling. Dormant genes in Lazarus' DNA were reactivated by the energy field chamber, but the DNA won't stabilize. When he's killed, he reverts to his original, aged form.

Stand Up and Cheer Professor Lazarus reminiscing about being a boy in the Blitz. It's both disconcerting and highly effective having a thirty-something-year-old man comparing notes about the Second World War with an elderly woman.

Roll Your Eyes The story is resolved by the Doctor playing the organ very, very loudly. When Martha asked him where he learned to play, he says that it came from hanging around Beethoven. She then responds — wait for it, wait for it — that this must explain his playing so loud. Then — heh heh heh — the Doctor says, "What?" and suddenly can't hear a word she says! Oh my sides!

You're Not Making Any Sense We're told that Lazarus becomes an enormous scorpion not due to some alien influence, but by dormant human genes being activated. Turning into a giant scorpion-like creature is apparently an option that evolution rejected millions of years ago. So why would those genes be passed on from generation to generation if they never had any sort of selective advantage? Evolution doesn't store all its choices in someone's DNA, like a closet of rejected outfits.

Interesting Trivia The Doctor tells Martha that setting 54 on the sonic screwdriver unlocks doors. The only other time the Doctor suggests there's an actual setting to the screwdriver is in "The Doctor Dances" where setting 2428D reattaches barbed wire. Still, it raises the question of how one adjusts the screwdriver to such settings? In "Let's Kill Hitler," it's suggested that the screwdriver works psychically. Perhaps all Martha has to do is simply think "setting 54" to unlock a door.

The TARDIS Chronometer The TARDIS lands in Martha's flat the morning after she left. The Doctor dematerializes and then rematerializes immediately afterwards. The rest of the action takes place that same evening.

Brilliant? (RS?) There's a brilliant story just waiting to be told about a mad scientist who creates a way to regain his youth and has to deal with the consequences. Unfortunately, "The Lazarus Experiment" isn't it.

The essence is there, but hardly anything is done with it. Lazarus hits on Tish as an old man, but she rejects him entirely; later, she's willing to snog him when he's young, even though she knows he's the same man. He seems to find Lady Thaw unappealing after he's regained his youth, although it's unclear whether that's an age or a personality thing; she's quite willing to be de-aged herself, but he says, "Do you think I would waste another life on you?"

Then, at the end, the Doctor gives a speech about longevity, saying that if you live long enough, then the only certainty is that you'll end up alone. Which, of course, isn't a certainty at all in the Doctor's case, because he's almost never alone. These moments are an attempt at examining the issue, but they're all rather superficial and none are integral to the story itself. The story wants to have a theme, but has no idea how to achieve it.

It's too bad, because there's a lot of depth that could be mined here, particularly in the comparison between Lazarus and the Doctor. Though the Doctor is the one to tell Lazarus that a longer life isn't always a better one, the complexity of that statement goes unexamined. The Doctor's long life actually is better: he has both youth and experience, he makes the world a better place and he does so with a bevy of pretty young things surrounding him. That's exactly what Lazarus wants.

Unfortunately, instead of having an actual debate or using the power of the theme to resonate inside the narrative, we're shown that wanting eternal youth is bad, because it'll turn you into a big scorpion. And, er, that's about it.

The scorpion isn't even a metaphor. It's just there to say "bad stuff will happen to you if you mess with science," à la every mad scientist ever shown in drama. Little wonder the Doctor defeats the villain by use of a church. It's *Frankenstein* all over again, only with bio-babble about DNA instead of electricity, and minus the originality and cleverness.

Instead, what we get is CGI substituting for story and that's simply unacceptable. Especially when the CGI isn't actually all that impressive; the tacked-on face looks particularly poor (and nothing like Mark Gatiss). About the only decent use of the scorpion is the way the camera turns when it runs sideways and upside down, although a) that's credit to the director and b) why, and how, exactly does Lazarus do this? Insects can run upside down because they can stick to a surface and their body mass is light enough to overcome gravity. The Lazarus scorpion would have to be making enormous holes in the walls and the ceiling — which it patently isn't — and that still wouldn't be enough to overcome its weight, even if said weight were only as much as Mark Gatiss. Just try crawling along the ceiling and see how far you get. And is it really better to run in a spiral when your prey is moving in a straight line? No wonder evolution rejected this option.

Bizarrely, the entire thing is over and done with at the 30-minute mark. The monster is dead, the guests are safe and the cleanup is underway. But then the story restarts and what we get is exactly the same thing — a big scorpion hunting the Doctor and friends in an enclosed space — only in a cathedral this time. It's not only stock horror cliché #57 (supposedly dead monster wakes up for one more killing rampage just when you thought it was all over), but the entire thing is there only to force the action to the musical denouement. Which isn't a bad conclusion per se, but the episode has twisted itself in knots to get there and you wonder why the Doctor didn't just pipe some Beethoven through the Lazarus Laboratories' speaker system instead.

The one saving grace in this story is Francine. Everything that happens to Martha's mother is utterly fascinating. She's immediately frosty to the Doctor, and it's not hard to guess why. Look at the Doctor's nonspecific dialogue with her: when she asks what they've been up to, he says, "Busy." When she asks for more details he says, "Oh, you know — stuff." Very likely, she thinks he's having sex with her daughter, which isn't a good start.

Then the Doctor rushes off and spills Francine's drink all over her, without even realizing. Finally, she's approached by one of Saxon's representatives, who tells her the Doctor is dangerous and whispers things she should know about him. This is a wonderful setup, because you can see how Francine gets to where she is and it only takes — literally — a small whisper in her ear to put her over the edge into outright hostility.

This is a great development in the season arc. Surprisingly, "The Lazarus Experiment" is the only mid-season story of Series Three to be set on present-day Earth ("Blink" doesn't count), so the majority of the arc's development has to go here. It also explains why the next story is going to have to force itself to reconnect with the present, because there's no other way to get the arc moving. It's a pity, because the arc could have used more attention, and there's likely an entire story that could have been built around Francine's hostility to the Doctor. I have no way of knowing, but I suspect Russell T Davies wrote the Francine stuff while Stephen Greenhorn perpetrated the big scorpion.

As far as the A-plot is concerned, "The Lazarus Experiment" is your bog-standard cliché of a horror story, with poor CGI substituting for drama. The B-plot is fabulous, but there's too little of it. This could have been an insightful treatise on the power of youth. Instead, the experiment, like the scorpion, is one big failure.

Second Opinion (GB) Let me be honest here: I think Freema Agyeman is a beautiful woman. In "The Lazarus Experiment," Martha wears an aubergine cocktail dress, and I think Freema is gorgeous in it. (Not to be exclusionary: Gugu Mbatha-Raw also looks great in her midnight blue frock for those who prefer her, while Reggie Yates and David Tennant also fill out their tuxes rather splendidly.)

I say this because, frankly and truthfully, I think Freema Agyeman in an aubergine cocktail dress and those cute shoes is the best thing about "The Lazarus Experiment."

I feel somewhat bad saying that I prefer the eye candy on display to the efforts made by the talent in front of and behind the camera. I love Stephen Greenhorn's adaptation of *Wide Sargasso Sea*. Mark Gatiss is a superb actor, and he turns in a great performance in both old age makeup and as an old man in a younger body. It's lovely to see Thelma Barlow demonstrate some range beyond Mavis on *Coronation Street*. The art direction is superb, and I would happily watch Adjoa Andoh remonstrate anyone, anywhere, anytime (it's a shame she looks dressed for a funeral). But, in the end, I'm there for the aubergine cocktail dress.

Part of the problem is that "The Lazarus Experiment" so badly wants to be a *Doctor Who* story from the early 1970s with an unscrupulous man challenging the laws of nature and being transformed into a monster as a result. The problem is, it doesn't have much of an original take on this trope, just something slightly better paced. It really wants Jon Pertwee wearing crushed green velvet and instead what it gets is something like the terrible chromakey monster effects. Worse, it doesn't know where to go with it, so it stops and restarts again someplace else, like the old six-part stories in the Classic Series. If that weren't bad enough, it repeats the "Doctor amplifying the sonic screwdriver" solution already used in "The Runaway Bride."

I want to like "The Lazarus Experiment," really I do. It at least makes an attempt to entertain, unlike lesser efforts this season. However, in the end, it's all about the dress.

3.07 42

Written by Chris Chibnall **Directed by** Graeme Harper

Supporting cast Adjoa Andoh (Francine Jones), Michelle Collins (Kath McDonnell), William Ash (Riley Vashtee), Anthony Flanagan (Orin Scannell), Matthew Chambers (Korwin), Vinette Robinson (Abi Lerner), Gary Powell (Dev Ashton), Rebecca Oldfield (Erina Lessak), Elize du Toit (sinister woman), Joshua Hill (voice of countdown)

Original airdate May 19, 2007

The Big Idea The Doctor has 42 minutes to stop a disabled space freighter from crashing into a living sun.

Roots and References Any number of film or TV productions where the narrative takes place in "real time" (and events unfold in the same amount of time the audience experiences them) including *24*, *High Noon*, *Timecode* and *Rope*. There are several visual homages to *2001: A Space Odyssey*.

Adventures in Time and Space The living sun is an update of the living planet in 1975's "Planet of Evil." The S.S. *Pentallian* may be named after the pentalium drive in 1975's "Revenge of the Cybermen." The Doctor upgrades Martha's phone in the same manner as he did Rose's in "The End of the World," enabling Martha to call anywhere in time or space (provided she uses the right area code). In the future, the Beatles are considered "classical" music, a conceit that was first used in 1965's "The Chase."

The Saxon Effect After Martha's first phone call to her mother is interrupted by the screams of Erina dying, Francine calls in people who work for Mr. Saxon, headed by an unnamed woman (listed in the credits as "Sinister Woman"). They listen in on Martha's succeeding calls to Francine and they even bag Francine's mobile phone as evidence afterwards. In the present day, it's Election Day in Britain. We'll see the result of it in "The Sound of Drums."

The Doctor and Martha The Doctor tries to shrug off upgrading Martha's phone and giving her a TARDIS key as "frequent flyer privileges," but Martha clearly believes these gestures mean something more. It's hard to discount Martha's point of view: it was clearly a big deal when the Doctor gave the TARDIS key to Rose in "Aliens of London."

Monster of the Week Crewmembers of the S.S. *Pentallian* are possessed by the sentient sunlight extracted by the ship's energy scoop. This raises their body temperature to over 100 degrees Celsius, replaces body oxygen with hydrogen and causes their eyes to burn intensely. More lethally, they can generate enough heat to completely vaporize a human being. The process usually burns out the consciousness of the possessed person, though echoes of the owner's mind exist, as with Korwin, and the Doctor can resist it to a point.

Stand Up and Cheer The scene where the shuttlepod detaches from the ship, leaving the Doctor and Martha each calling out to the other even though they can't be heard, is utterly haunting and utterly beautiful. It's a scene that's completely sold through the visuals, concluding with the camera slowly pulling back as Martha looks out the porthole to the shuttlepod freefalling towards the sun.

Roll Your Eyes It's bad enough that the technological MacGuffin enabling the Doctor to rescue the shuttlepod is on the exterior hull of the spaceship; do we have to have the Doctor struggling to hold on, failing to grasp it and saying trite phrases like "I can't reach"? (To add insult to injury, we have Scannell saying, "You have to do it!")

You're Not Making Any Sense The Doctor knows that the possessed humans can vaporize anyone. He doesn't know that Korwin is under attack by Scannell with the coolant. Given all this, why is he so interested in having Ashton open the visor to his helmet, particularly since it probably would mean the Doctor's instant vaporization?

Interesting Trivia This story purports to take place in real time and only really fudges this once: the sequence starting from the Doctor examining the wreckage of the engines to where he and McDonnell run to the med centre only takes two minutes and 16 seconds onscreen. In the narrative (as calculated by the time elapsed on the countdown clock before and after) all this takes five minutes and 55 seconds. Most other sequences, however, are reasonably accurate in their timing.

The second question that opens the door — find the next number in the sequence: 313, 331, 367, . . . (Answer: 379) — is to do with happy prime numbers, which is not made-up futuristic technobabble but an actual form of math. Happy numbers are when you take each digit in a number, square them, then add them together and then repeat the process until the answer is the number one. Prime numbers are numbers that are only divisible by themselves and one. Happy primes are numbers that are both happy and prime. We would speculate further about the mental state of the *Pentallian* crewmember who devised this question, but one of the co-authors of this book holds a Ph.D. in mathematics.

The episode features some superficial similarities to Danny Boyle's 2007 film *Sunshine*. These were entirely coincidental; the film was not released until a month before "42" was broadcast. However, one detail became a little too close for comfort when it was discovered both stories featured spaceships called *Icarus*, which necessitated a last-minute rechristening of the ship as the *Pentallian*.

The TARDIS Chronometer The cargo freighter S.S. *Pentallian* is orbiting a star in the Taraji system. Judging from the make of the spacesuits, this story is roughly contemporary with "The Impossible Planet"/"The Satan Pit."

Brilliant? (GB) The great thing, or so we're told, about *Doctor Who* is its flexible format which means that it can be set anywhere, take on any genre and do any kind of story. But here's the thing the sales brochure doesn't often discuss: while *Doctor Who*'s format means it's capable of doing anything, it's almost always done on its own terms. The series has, for lack of a better term, a house style, with its own visual and narrative grammar that will always be dominant, no matter the setting, genre or type of story.

This may seem a little abstract, but "42" makes the theory very practical. It's a real-time story, where events unfold during the 42 or so minutes the audience is watching. The best examples of real time in drama — *24* (mostly in its first season), *Rope*, *Timecode*, the *M*A*S*H* episode "Life Time" — employ specific techniques to create the immediacy of events unfolding at the same rate for the characters onscreen and the audience watching. A clock constantly onscreen, continuous takes, split screens: whatever might be needed to convey that the action is happening without dramatic compression.

"42" does none of this.

There is the fig leaf of cutting to a computer counting down to solar impact — an obviously fake-looking CGI construction added during post-production — but it's only flashed up at key points in the story and isn't referred to for long stretches (for over seven minutes at one point). What the story really needs is a countdown clock in the bottom corner of the screen at all times and for the camera, say, to follow the Doctor and McDonnell all the way from engineering to the med centre. There are practical reasons this didn't happen — there's only so far a production budget can go to dress a disused factory as a space freighter; it's hard to use an onscreen clock without making the episode look like *24* — but those decisions ultimately affect the immediacy. "42" doesn't feel like a real-time story. It feels like any other episode of *Doctor Who*, only we're supposed to accept that its events take place in the 42 minutes we're watching. Worse, it outright cheats early on, compressing the action by several minutes so it has enough time for a denouement.

And yet, on *Doctor Who* terms, "42" is an exciting episode. It's fast-paced and visually stunning. Chris Chibnall's script sticks to the tried and true (alien possession leading to homicidal rampage and a catchphrase; the captain in denial of the menace because it's using her husband's body), but the presentation is superb. "42" succeeds mostly because of Graeme Harper's direction, which is exquisitely paced and gorgeous to look at. It's an episode made even better by the editing: the rhythm to the cutting accelerates as the episode progresses.

It's also a great episode for Martha, and Freema Agyeman delivers her strongest work yet. It helps that the story finally takes all her unresolved feelings towards the Doctor and makes them subtext. We're not just talking about the look she gives the Doctor when he thanks Martha for saving his life and gives her the TARDIS key, either. The scene where Martha tries to get the Doctor into stasis is lovely, as she tries to keep him calm but is so terrified she isn't listening to anything the Doctor is trying to say. Martha's scenes with Riley are really sweet — Agyeman has great chemistry with actor William Ash — especially when they're trapped in the shuttlepod: two strangers facing imminent death, finding instant intimacy and opening up to each other.

That scene also has the phone call between Martha and Francine. Martha, expecting to die soon, just wants to find closure in a normal conversation with her mum. Francine, however, just can't let go of winning her war with her daughter over the Doctor, even to the point of betraying Martha to Saxon. The collision of these realities, neither party realizing what the other is doing, is heartbreaking. So much is said about Francine and Martha's relationship in this scene; connecting it to this season's arc only further enhances it.

"42" is a solid, traditional tale. It's so solid and so traditional it's a shame they didn't take more risks with how it was presented, especially given the opportunity of having the story unfold in real time. Fortunately, we're in for lots of risk-taking in the next few episodes.

Second Opinion (RS?) The DVD in the Complete Third Series boxset that features this episode is the only one that comprises four stories: "Daleks in Manhattan," "Evolution of the Daleks," "The Lazarus Experiment" and "42." By happenstance of episode placement, this may amount to the single worst *Doctor Who* DVD disc of all time.

"42" is the best of a bad bunch. It's not actively bad, but it's not actively good either. The best thing about it may be the pace: by evoking the premise of *24* (rather than *The Hitchhiker's Guide to the Galaxy*, as you might have been expecting), the real-time gimmick does mean that the action is forced to rollick along. This is helped immeasurably by Graeme Harper's direction, which might be papering over the cracks, but at least it's using high-quality paper and nice-smelling glue.

By far the most interesting parts are the bits that don't actually take place on the ship. Martha's calls to Francine are fantastic, and the shock reveal that she's having the phone traced is excellent. These have very little to do with the story at hand, but the arc needs them far more than the dull crew aboard the dull spaceship, so they're quite welcome. Martha's quiet conversation in the escape pod is also well done.

Sadly, it's the ending that's the biggest disappointment. Although the revelation that the sun is alive is a decent one, the Doctor being possessed is about the point where it all goes downhill. Which is a shame, because this should be the highlight of "42," but, in order to get to this, we learn that the possessed creatures can be overpowered by a simple punch to the stomach and that there's a handy machine that can freeze temperatures down to absolute zero that won't harm you in the slightest if you're standing right next to it. Despite — and I cannot stress this enough — the fact that it operates with the door open. Until this point, the story had been tense and gripping, but the entire last third involves frantic running down corridors to tell people things that could have been mentioned on the intercom.

There's a good idea at the heart of "42," albeit one that wouldn't have looked out of place on *Star Trek: Voyager*. The arc scenes help to make this more important than it should be, and the direction compensates for a multitude of sins. However, the actual story, filled with unmemorable characters and a threat that's too easily defeated, is a letdown. But don't despair: if this is the worst *Doctor Who* DVD disc of all time, the next one is very likely the best. Get ready for the good stuff.

3.08—3.09 Human Nature / The Family of Blood

Written by Paul Cornell **Directed by** Charles Palmer

Supporting cast Jessica Hynes (Joan Redfern), Rebekah Staton (Jenny), Thomas Sangster (Tim Latimer), Harry Lloyd (Baines), Tom Palmer (Hutchinson), Gerard Horan (Clark), Lauren Wilson (Lucy Cartwright), Pip Torrens (Rocastle), Matthew White (Philips), Sophie Turner (vicar)

Original airdate May 26 and June 2, 2007

The Big Idea The Doctor becomes human in a village in 1913 in order to hide from a marauding, time-travelling family.

Roots and References This is adapted from the Virgin New Adventure novel *Human Nature*, which featured the seventh Doctor deliberately choosing to become human in a similar setting with many of the same characters. *Superman II* (a superhero becoming human); *The Last Temptation of Christ* (Jesus being tempted by a vision of an ordinary life, completed with wife and children); James Hilton's *Goodbye, Mr. Chips* (World War I's effect on a public school); R.F. Delderfield's *To Serve Them All My Days* (military training in a school and a romance between a teacher and a nurse); Joseph Campbell's *The Hero with a Thousand Faces* (Smith's hero arc); Neil Gaiman's *The Sandman* graphic novels (Daughter of Mine's fate, being trapped in every mirror, is similar to Despair's).

Adventures in Time and Space Smith's *Journal of Impossible Things* features illustrations of the TARDIS console, the sonic screwdriver, gas masks ("The Empty Child"), a Dalek, the Moxx of Balhoon ("The End of the World"), Autons ("Rose"), the werewolf ("Tooth and Claw"), the pocket watch, clockwork droids ("The Girl in the Fireplace"), Cybermen, the police box, images of his former selves, buildings with the note "I can't remember this" (which are probably meant to be on Gallifrey), a Slitheen and Rose.

When Timothy opens the watch, he hears voices saying, among other things, "You are not alone." He also sees flashes of the Doctor using the sonic screwdriver held out before him ("The Lazarus Experiment"), a Dalek in chains ("Dalek"), marching Cybermen, an Ood, the werewolf ("Tooth and Claw"), the Sycorax ("The Christmas Invasion"), the Racnoss ("The Runaway Bride") and Professor Lazarus ("The Lazarus Experiment"). Later, we also get a flash of the Doctor amid the flames, from "The Runaway Bride."

Joan says, "A girl in every fireplace?" ("The Girl in the Fireplace"). When Joan asks if Gallifrey is in Ireland, the Doctor says he supposes it must be, following a running gag since 1976's "The Hand of Fear" where people naturally assume Gallifrey is Irish.

When Timothy runs away from the fighting, Hutchinson says, "Latimer, you filthy coward," to which Timothy responds, "Yes, sir, every time," echoing the ninth Doctor's line in "The Parting of the Ways." The Family stole a Time Agent's vortex manipulator (like Captain Jack's, as we'll see in "Utopia").

Lucy Cartwright's music theme is similar to the one from 1988's "Remembrance of the Daleks" (played during the scenes with the girl). Father of Mine is bound in unbreakable chains forged in the heart of a dwarf star, likely a reference to dwarf star alloy from 1981's "Warriors' Gate."

The Saxon Effect The Doctor uses the TARDIS's Chameleon Arch to turn himself into a human to avoid being detected by the Family. It takes the form of a pocket watch, which has a perception filter, so Smith won't think anything of it.

Who is the Doctor? Timothy is scared of the Doctor because he's seen him: "He's like fire and ice and rage. He's like the night and the storm in the heart of the sun. He's ancient and forever and he burns at the centre of time and he can see the turn of the universe. And . . . he's wonderful." The Doctor's human self, John Smith, dreams of his life as the Doctor, but he's cowardly when actually faced with the menaces the Doctor encounters. The Doctor anticipated every eventuality as a human except falling in love, which suggests how limited the Doctor's understanding of humanity can be.

The Doctor and Martha The Doctor's instructions for Martha in his video message ensure that he doesn't abandon her. But Martha is heartbroken to discover that, as a human, the Doctor falls in love with another woman. In spite of this, Martha is prepared to admit her love for the Doctor so Smith can realize how wonderful he is.

Monster of the Week The Family of Blood. They're gaseous entities who reside in globes. They have limited lifespans, no more than a few months, so they want to steal the Doctor's existence. They possess the bodies of humans and can access their memories, although they can also die in their new bodies. They fly an invisible spaceship and have soldiers made of straw, dressed as scarecrows and brought to "life" with molecular fringe animation.

Stand Up and Cheer It's the very last moment that finally does us in. The segue from World War I to the final scene, with the vicar reading the memorial to those fallen, makes us cry, every single time. After all the heartache and the emotional rollercoaster we've been on, this sequence shows us the sheer power of the passage of time. It draws on our knowledge of history, our sense of the futility of war and the power of memory. Having an unaged Doctor and Martha standing by in contrast to the line saying "as we grow old" is incredibly powerful television and the final culmination of something truly special.

Roll Your Eyes "You had to go and fall in love with a human — and it wasn't me," says Martha, in a bid for this week's bad American TV movie moment.

You're Not Making Any Sense Wouldn't it have made more sense to have Martha hold onto the watch instead of leaving it around where it could be easily detected by the Family? Or, as the case might be, stolen by a passing student?

Interesting Trivia John Smith's parents, Sydney (a watchmaker) and Verity (a nurse), are named after Sydney Newman and Verity Lambert, the creator and first producer of the show, respectively. In a very real sense, they were *Doctor Who*'s father and mother: one who created a time-traveller (the "watchmaker"), the other who brought the show into being (the "nurse").

The Doctor records a video message for Martha with numbered instructions for dealing with Smith. There are at least 23 of them. Number seven, which was cut from the episode, had the Doctor saying, "Don't let me eat pears" (which was also in the list in the original novel). It's unfortunate that this was deleted, as the Doctor says this over a scene where Smith eats a pear.

In terms of the actual historical content, Joan's husband died in the battle of Spion Kop, a disastrous battle during the Second Boer War (1899–1902) which left 200 dead and over 1,000 wounded. And, yes, in pre-suffrage days, women were not permitted inside public houses and had to drink outside the pub, even in November.

The televised episode adapts the broader story beats of Paul Cornell's 1995 novel wherein the Doctor becomes human John Smith in a pre-war school and falls in love with Joan while aliens seek to possess the Doctor's abilities as a Time Lord, only Tim has stolen the means for Smith to change back. The TV adaptation alters the Doctor's motivation for changing (it's an emergency measure; in the book it was voluntary), cuts down the supporting cast and simplifies the threat. Also, the device to change the Doctor back looked like a cricket ball, not a pocket watch. In the novel, Smith is Scottish (the seventh Doctor, played by Sylvester McCoy, had a Scottish accent), but, in spite of being a Scot himself, David Tennant requested that Smith, like his Doctor, retain an English accent. Thus, Smith's backstory moved from Aberdeen to Nottingham.

The TARDIS Chronometer A newspaper reveals that it's Monday, November 10, 1913, in the village near the Farringham School for Boys. The TARDIS has been there for two months (with one to go), hidden in a shed and on emergency power so it can't be detected. The Doctor and Martha later visit Latimer as an old man on Remembrance Sunday (probably sometime in the late 1990s, given Latimer's age and the female vicar).

Brilliant? (RS?) *Doctor Who* has been around for almost 50 years. During that time, it's been a TV show, a comic strip, radio plays, a series of novels, audio stories and novellas, and it has spawned a variety of spinoffs. Across all these media, the one thing it has always done is tell stories. Sometimes cleverly, sometimes awkwardly, sometimes on a wing and a prayer.

In 1995, the New Adventures reached their pinnacle with a lyrical tale of a simple man wanting to live a simple life. Turning a rich and complex novel into an episode of television was a very risky move. But it paid off brilliantly, because "Human Nature" is the best story that *Doctor Who* has ever told. Not just in the New Series but in its almost 50-year history.

Everything about this episode comes together: David Tennant is at the top of his game, the period setting is lovely, the threat is credible, there's a heart-breaking romance at its core and a brilliant theme, the episode isn't afraid to ask the hard questions, and, best of all, this is an episode that plays every emotional beat to perfection, culminating in a glorious finale that will make you weep buckets of tears. Even throwaway things, like Smith's aged makeup, have an astonishing level of detail and love put into them.

I've complained previously about white male writers dealing with how Martha would be treated in certain historical periods, but this shows how it should be done. Instead of running from it, "Human Nature" faces the problem head on and shows us just how agonizing it would be to be a woman of colour living in even the recent past. Better still, it brings issues of sexism and classism into the bargain. And, brilliantly, it doesn't just make unlikeable characters racist to show how evil they are, it imbues even the story's heroes with these attitudes and shows us how prevalent and how uncomfortable this is.

That Joan is able to accept aliens and time travel before she can accept a black woman being a medical doctor speaks volumes about the power of racism. The boys make openly racist jokes, Martha and Jenny have to sit outside the pub in the cold, and Smith is incredibly patronizing to Martha. But rather than making Martha powerless, all this makes her seem even more heroic, as she has to overcome almost insurmountable odds, just to get people to listen to her.

The high-energy flashbacks are very effective at explaining the setup without being contrived, and they contrast wonderfully with the sedateness of 1913. Timothy's flashes of the Doctor and Martha, as well as of his own future, serve to make this sit in context. Adding in Smith and Joan's alternate future flash and you have a story that goes backwards, forwards and sideways, each element complementing and adding to the story at hand.

The scene with Smith saving the baby is a clever idea . . . made absolutely brilliant by juxtaposing it with his outward uncertainty and his halting mono-logue about the need to find heroes. Even afterwards, he doesn't know what to make of his abilities, equating them with his waltzing skills and saying that he's full of surprises today.

But the core of the story is the romance between Smith and Joan, which unfolds beautifully. It's slightly less powerful than the novel's version, since the tenth Doctor is a romantic Doctor to begin with, kissing companions and guest stars with some regularity. However, it's sold here by Smith's virginal uncer-tainty, which is superb. David Tennant has never been better, nor will he be again in the remainder of his tenure. This is an actor who's revelling in being forced out of his comfort zone. Freed from having to shout at people or spout technobabble at high speed, he allows the human side of Smith to emerge and it tugs at our heartstrings.

Prefiguring World War I is excellent. Timothy has a glimpse, the Family knows, Martha knows and, most importantly, so does the viewer. Baines's speech at the school is accompanied by sounds of war, which is astonishingly effective. The battle itself, with a boy crying in anticipation of using a gun and slow-motion shots of scarecrows being gunned down, emphasizes the horror of war even from the victor's point of view. When Martha tells Timothy that he doesn't have to fight in the coming war, he responds, "I think we do," which leads into the extremely powerful voiceover given by the Doctor.

The central debate over whether or not Smith is real has immense potency. We know that he's not, but nevertheless we're on the side of the humble, uncer-tain human, rather than wishing for our time-travelling superhero to return. That's an astonishing feat on behalf of the entire production team. Joan's sum-mation ("He was braver than you. You chose to change; he chose to die.") tells us that there are no easy answers and that her world is a sadder place for having met the Doctor. Her final question for the Doctor — if he hadn't visited on a whim, would anyone have died? — is incredibly mature, the sort of thing *Doctor Who* is usually uninterested in asking.

And then there's the resolution. Having the central character's climactic decision take place offscreen should be a textbook crime against drama, but here it allows both the Family and us to be fooled. This leads into the defini-tive statement of who the Doctor is: a man who hid from a desperate family of hunters and whose actions caused many innocents to die . . . because he was being kind to his enemies. Their antics then unleash the fury of the Time Lord and it's a cold fury indeed.

This is a view of the Doctor that isn't comfortable, but it's necessary. "Human

Nature" is a two-part story that barely features the Doctor as himself, but it's all about who he is. We know that the Doctor is a mass of contradictions, but "Human Nature" turns this into an asset. From the mythic power and terror to the trickery and the wonder, we witness through the eyes of so many characters — Martha, Timothy, the Family, even Joan — just what makes this character tick. It might not be comfortable, but it is brilliant.

"Human Nature" is the jewel in the crown of the Russell T Davies era. Davies subsequently stated that they would never attempt this kind of story again. You can partly see why — so rarely do things come together this perfectly that you could spend the rest of your days trying to recreate them in vain — but another part is probably screaming with frustration that they never even tried. The novel was the best *Doctor Who* book ever written but, astonishingly, the television episode has gone and done the impossible: made the adaptation even better than the original.

"Human Nature": the best *Doctor Who* story ever told.

Second Opinion (GB) You would think from the premise that the Doctor will learn how to be the Doctor when what makes him a Time Lord is taken from him. But what interests writer Paul Cornell is the ordinary courage that scared, frail human beings can muster in the face of monstrous evil. Martha, the headmaster, Joan, Tim — even Hutchison — all demonstrate real bravery.

John Smith, on the other hand, doesn't show any such greatness. Martha even tells him, "You're rubbish as a human." His response to the impending threat of the Family is about as un-Doctorly as you can get: he unquestioningly accepts the jingoism around him and arms children to fight his battle for him. But for all his dithering and anguish, Smith does all right in the end. Indeed, he does the most heroic thing anyone can do: he sacrifices himself.

To make that sacrifice real and truly meaningful, Cornell and company do two things. The first is to show us what Smith will have to give up. The second is to show us what comes next: the scene with the Doctor and Joan is truly heartbreaking as we experience the absence of Smith. Gone is the absent-minded, dotty but loveable teacher; in his wake is an alien who doesn't fully comprehend why Joan is grieving.

David Tennant is sensational. Having seen him play the confident Time Lord for a season and a half, it's bizarre and yet awe inspiring to see him play an ordinary man completely out of his depth. Smith is so totally different from the Doctor that it astounds: his very posture, his mannerisms, his voice; it's a wholly distinct performance, with marvellous subtleties. And if you only know Jessica Hynes' work in comedies like *Spaced*, her performance as Joan is an absolute revelation. Hynes understands the desperation of someone considered, in that era, an "off the shelf" widow, who senses a kindred spirit in Smith. Hynes is playing a character of a particular time and place, and yet you feel for her and her plight. The scene where she forces Smith to see the truth of his cowardice is extraordinary.

But then all the performances are incredible. Harry Lloyd as Baines becomes unbelievably creepy just by lowering his voice, slowing his speech, cocking his head and sniffing. Thomas Sangster has an other-worldly quality to him that belies his few years (his Doctorish response to the headmaster is lovely). And best of all is Pip Torrens' headmaster, who seems at first to be a typical Empire-supporting jingoist but then brings new shadings of resoluteness and compassion with every scene he's in.

"Human Nature" is like fire and ice and rage. It's like the night and the storm in the heart of the war. It's ancient and forever and it burns at the centre of England and it can see the turn of the Whoniverse. And . . . it's wonderful.

The Psychic Papers: The Wilderness Years

On December 6, 1989, the last Classic Series episode of *Doctor Who* was broadcast. There were brief returns to television: the Children in Need sketch "Dimensions in Time" in 1993; the TV Movie in 1996; an evening devoted to *Doctor Who* in 1999 (featuring *Who*-themed sketch comedy from Mark Gatiss and future *Little Britain* star David Walliams); and a *Comic Relief* sketch with Rowan Atkinson as the Doctor in 1999. However, these were small glimmers. For the most part, it was a decade that seemed to *Doctor Who* fans like Narnia: always winter and never Christmas.

Gradually, fans of the Doctor began to realize that other media would have to fill the void and provide their fix of New *Who*. In the summer of 1991, Virgin Publishing (which had been releasing novelizations under the Target imprint) started a line of original *Doctor Who* fiction, called the New Adventures. Initially, the same authors who wrote the TV novelizations produced similarly well-worn adventures. But the fourth book in this series, *Timewyrm: Revelation* by Paul Cornell, changed things in ways that still affect *Doctor Who* today.

With Paul Cornell came the first wave of a new generation of authors: fans of the show in their early 20s who were interested in pushing the boundaries of prose fiction using *Doctor Who*. *Timewyrm: Revelation* explores in literary terms what makes *Doctor Who* so compelling, featuring characters who seem achingly real. At the time, it was radical but caught on with a demographic of fans who were largely entering adulthood and wanted a *Doctor Who* for themselves.

With no TV show on the air, the New Adventures were the officially licenced continuation of the *Doctor Who* saga and initially featured the seventh Doctor and Ace, who were seen in the final episode in 1989. Soon the book series introduced its own companions, the first of whom was Bernice Summerfield, a witty archaeologist from the future, created by Cornell.

The brilliance of the NAs (as they were fondly known) was twofold. First, they were, at the time, the only game in town. If you wanted new *Doctor Who*, for several years this was the only place to find it. Second, they were forward-looking. Rather than slot adventures into established gaps or tell the same type of *Who*-ish story over and over, the NAs marched off boldly in their own direction. They were interested in issues of the '90s: cyberspace, environmental decay, moral complexity. Their stories were noticeably more adult than the Classic Series, and they often featured sex and swearing.

While some fans resisted this direction, the NAs became a publishing success in the middle of a recession, doubling their output several times and even managing to bring new fans to a series that no longer had a TV show to support it. A third secret to their success was the "slushpile": the publishers invited aspiring authors to send in submissions and every submission was considered.

This produced a significant number of new authors, many of whom went on to write novels and for television. Paul Cornell, Mark Gatiss, Gareth Roberts and Matt Jones each had their big break with the NAs before moving into television. Another author was Russell T Davies, who in 1996 wrote a New Adventures novel called *Damaged Goods*, which featured a tightly written setup, kitchen-sink drama, gay sex for the Doctor's male companion and a hot mess of an ending.

The NAs gave way, inevitably, to new ranges of fiction. The first of these were the Missing Adventures published by Virgin, novels set within the "gaps" in the TV series and featuring past Doctors. These stories were told in the style of their particular era and often functioned as sequels to favourite episodes. In 1997, the BBC reclaimed the licence for prose *Doctor Who* fiction and published a range of novels featuring the eighth Doctor (who had just appeared in the 1996 TV Movie) and one featuring past Doctors. (Virgin continued publishing New Adventure novels without the Doctor, featuring companion Bernice Summerfield.) The BBC's *Doctor Who* novels weren't as successful as the NAs but lasted twice as long: the final books were published just as the New Series was first broadcast.

By 1999, there was a new game in town: original adventures on audio featuring several actors who had played the Doctor such as Peter Davison, Colin Baker, Sylvester McCoy and Paul McGann. Made by Big Finish Productions, these were essentially radio plays released on CD, featuring a full cast, music and sound effects. In the same way the NAs came out of the fan-fiction movement of the late '80s, the audios came out of fan audios produced by Gary Russell and starring Nicholas Briggs as the

Doctor. For fans starved of actual dramatic productions of *Doctor Who*, this was the development they had been waiting for. Soon people were pledging their allegiance to the audios.

Though they mostly stuck to the format of the Classic Series, with four-part adventures like on television, the audios pushed the boundaries of the sound-only medium, particularly the ones by Robert Shearman. Like the novels, they were successful enough to spin off into new ranges, including ones devoted to the Daleks (*Dalek Empire*), the Cybermen, Sarah Jane Smith and UNIT, the latter featuring David Tennant.

Others got in on the act: in 2001, another company, Telos, launched a series of novellas featuring any Doctor (including some future Doctors). Virgin, the BBC and Big Finish also published a few short-story collections featuring past Doctors (and a few sideways ones). There were a host of independent companies that produced stories that didn't feature the Doctor but starred official monsters and companions, as well as Classic Series actors. These ranged from video productions like the *Stranger* series (starring Colin Baker playing not-quite-the-sixth Doctor) and companion-centric spinoff videos (like *Downtime*, which featured Sarah Jane Smith and the Brigadier) to audio adventures like the *Dominie* series (starring Sylvester McCoy playing not-quite-the-seventh Doctor). There was also the *Doctor Who Magazine* comic strip and a series of webcasts produced for BBC online, culminating in 2003's "Scream of the Shalka," which featured Richard E. Grant as the voice of the Doctor in an animated cartoon written by Paul Cornell.

The effect of the novels and audios on the New Series cannot be overstated. First of all, they featured the first *Doctor Who* work by both of the New Series' head writers, with Russell T Davies' *Damaged Goods* and Steven Moffat's short story "Continuity Errors" in the 1996 anthology *Decalog 3*. Series One's contributors were something of a "dream team" of writers from the '90s tie-in fiction, including Davies, Moffat, Cornell, Gatiss and Shearman. Davies also cast Nicholas Briggs to voice the Daleks in the New Series based on his work on the *Dalek Empire* audios (which Briggs also wrote). In the coming years, Gareth Roberts and Matt Jones also contributed; behind the scenes, former Big Finish audio producer Gary Russell became a script editor on the TV series.

Secondly, the books and audios produced between the Classic and New Series provided material for adaptation, particularly in the first three seasons. Some of the material was mined for innovations rather than actual content. Robert Shearman's 2003 audio "Jubilee," a political satire on the banalization of evil using the Daleks, became the basis of "Dalek" purely on the strength of Shearman's scenes where the Doctor's companion Evelyn faces a lone imprisoned Dalek. Even less was taken from Marc Platt's 2002 audio "Spare Parts," an origin tale for the Cybermen, though Platt was credited on "Rise of the Cybermen"/"The Age of Steel."

It's with the adaptation of Paul Cornell's 1995 novel *Human Nature* that we see the first true literary adaptation of *Doctor Who* from another medium. In the novel, the Doctor visits alien bodysmiths to be turned into a human in order to better empathize with the grief his companion Bernice Summerfield is experiencing. The major change made was in turning the alien Aubertides, a race of shapeshifters, into the Family of Blood. However, it's amazing how many things in the novel made it through to the final TV version — the ending at the war memorial, the girl with the balloon and Joan's casual racism — and *The Journal of Impossible Things* is an adaptation of the children's story written by Smith about a character named Doctor Who (these parts of the novel were written by Steven Moffat). Paul Cornell has noted in interviews that he intended to make a much more radical adaptation — even opening it with Joan and Smith married and in bed — but Russell T Davies kept moving it closer to the source material.

Other little bits and pieces from the NAs have made their way into the New Series. In Series One, "Father's Day" draws on the same idea of a church as sanctuary as Cornell's 1991 NA *Timewyrm: Revelation*. "Bad Wolf" mentions a dish made on Lucifer, from the 1993 NA *Lucifer Rising*. "The Parting of the Ways" (and subsequent stories) says that the Daleks call the Doctor the oncoming Storm; this was from Paul Cornell's 1992 NA *Love and War*, although there it referred to the Draconians' name for him (in the novels, the Daleks called him the *Ka Faraq Gatri*, the Bringer of Darkness). "The Parting of the Ways" also mentions the NAs' theory about time travel, which states that once the TARDIS materializes, events become fixed in the Doctor's timeline.

In Series Two, "The Girl in the Fireplace" has an exchange where the Doctor says that monsters have nightmares about him, which is a line from *Love and War*. In Series Three, the building on the moon, complete with everyone inside, is straight from Cornell's *Timewyrm: Revelation*. The alliance of old enemies in Series Five's "The Pandorica Opens" includes the Chelonians, turtle-like monsters from Gareth Roberts' NA *The Highest Science* (echoes of which, including the bus, featured in "Planet of the Dead").

In the 15-year gap between the end of the Classic Series in 1989 and the beginning of the New Series in 2005, there was a grand total of one official televised episode of *Doctor Who*, the 1996 TV Movie. However, during this time, *Doctor Who* output was far from dormant. The wealth of product during these wilderness years kept the flame alive for diehard fans and nurtured the talent that created the New Series.

When the New Series eventually ends — as it surely must, someday — the non-televised products of the next wilderness era will once again be there to pick up the torch for the next generation of *Doctor Who* fans. That's the true legacy of the wilderness years, in all their complexity: they not only kept the flame burning, they kept the love alive.

3.10 Blink

Written by Steven Moffat **Directed by** Hettie MacDonald

Supporting cast Carey Mulligan (Sally Sparrow), Lucy Gaskell (Kathy Nightingale), Finlay Robertson (Larry Nightingale), Richard Cant (Malcolm Wainwright), Michael Obiora (Billy Shipton), Louis Mahoney (Old Billy), Thomas Nelstrop (Ben Wainwright), Ian Boldsworth (Banto), Ray Sawyer (desk sergeant)

Original airdate June 9, 2007

The Big Idea Sally Sparrow visits a spooky house with moving statues and finds messages left in 1969 from a time traveller called the Doctor.

Roots and References Steven Moffat's short story for the 2005 *Doctor Who Annual*, "'What I Did on My Christmas Holidays' by Sally Sparrow"; the *Doctor Who* internet forum Outpost Gallifrey (now Gallifrey Base); the children's game "Statues" and DVD easter egg features.

Adventures in Time and Space The Doctor appears to Sally and Larry in a security protocol hologram much like the Emergency Program One hologram of the Doctor that appeared to Rose in "The Parting of the Ways."

Monster of the Week Looking like ordinary statues of angels, the Doctor describes the Weeping Angels as "the only psychopaths in the universe who kill you nicely." They displace their victims in time and space and let them "live to death" in the past while they consume the energy from the potential moments their victim might have lived had they continued in the present. Their existence is quantum locked so that they can only move — and they can move quickly — during the times when not observed. In order to avoid being caught in the gaze of one of their own, they tend to cover their faces, which make them look as though they're weeping.

Stand Up and Cheer The Doctor's "conversation" with Sally and Larry via the DVD easter egg may be one of the cleverest scenes in *Doctor Who*. It's both funny and intellectually captivating to watch, as they suddenly discover their conversation perfectly synchronizing with the Doctor's. It's a great scene that plays on different levels: the conversation happening in real time and the understanding it's with a recording made 37 years earlier.

Roll Your Eyes Surely Billy could have come up with a better line than "Life is short and you are hot"?

You're Not Making Any Sense The Weeping Angels move fast but, even so, how could they have moved the TARDIS from a police station on a busy London high street all the way back to Wester Drumlins without being seen?

Interesting Trivia In Kathy's letter to Sally, she mentions that she named her daughter Sally. Kathy's grandson Malcolm looks around 30, suggesting that Kathy was having children reasonably late for that time period. So it's conceivable that young Sally could be around 35 in 1969. Why does this matter? Because old Billy mentions that he married someone also called Sally. We see a photo of her and she's a white woman, so it's quite possible that the two other Sallys were one and the same. Interestingly, assuming that Sally Sparrow and Larry Nightingale get married at some point, then Billy would be Sally Sparrow's not-so-distant relative (via a number of marriages and time travel).

In Steven Moffat's original short story, Sally is 12 years old and encounters the Doctor, who has been separated in time from his TARDIS and is leaving Sally notes from 20 years earlier. It includes elements such as the note behind the wallpaper and the "conversation" with the Doctor on video. (There, the loop is closed when Sally writes up her homework assignment describing what happened and giving it to the Doctor when she grows up to become a spy.) Adding the Weeping Angels and making Sally an adult were the chief changes in adaptation.

In the broadcast version of the episode's denouement, a "One Year Later" title card comes up in the establishing shot of Sally and Larry's store. This does not appear on either the DVD release or syndicated version. The Complete Third Series DVD features the entirety of the Doctor's half of the conversation as an easter egg.

The TARDIS Chronometer The story is mostly set in 2007 (Kathy's letter to Sally notes the year when she was taken) at a house called Wester Drumlins in London, with brief visits to 1969 and 1920. Curiously, the story is set in the year it was broadcast, as opposed to the present-day-plus-a-year seen in most contemporary stories since "Aliens of London" (although the ending takes place in 2008).

Brilliant? (GB) "Blink" was deemed the best story of the season by a *Doctor Who Magazine* poll (and ranked number two in the magazine's poll of the all-time greatest *Doctor Who* stories ever made, the highest placing for a New Series story). It won the Hugo Award for best short form drama. And it has the biggest demonstration of jazz hands ever seen in *Doctor Who*.

The whole story makes a superhuman effort to keep the viewer paying attention to what's in front of them, and never pause to think about the internal logic of the story. If the viewer did pause, they might find themselves asking all sorts of niggling questions: How did the TARDIS get back to Wester Drumlins? Why did the Weeping Angels not follow the police when they impounded the TARDIS in the first place? How was it that the Angels didn't fall in line of sight of one another sooner? Why not, as demonstrated by Amy Pond in the sequel, try blinking with alternating eyelids?

Those questions don't get asked because the story happens with such breakneck speed, and the episode's world has such tantalizing rules (if you so much as blink, a statue will kill you) that you don't notice. And you simply don't care, because the story is so incredibly scary.

"Blink" gets the maximum amount of fear out of the simplest of means: essentially turning around and having something scream "Boo!" There should be nothing less scary than a statue. After all, it can't move. Having its motion implied by sudden changes in position while remaining stationary is unbelievably unsettling. It's about horror that's implicit rather than explicit — and that's how Steven Moffat and director Hettie MacDonald get you heart and soul.

Russell T Davies solved the problem of an episode without much of the Doctor in "Love & Monsters" by writing something closer to his non-*Who* work; Steven Moffat does much the same here. "Blink" gives us the quintessential Moffat heroine in Sally Sparrow: forthright, witty, confident and much smarter than every man in the room. It's a very different surrogate lead character than Marc Warren's innocent Elton in "Love & Monsters" and a more proactive one to be sure. Isn't it great that we have a before-she-was-famous Carey Mulligan to play Sally? Mulligan has the right sense of irony crossed with sweetness to pull it off. I love the way she exasperatedly tells the Doctor, "I'm clever, and I'm listening. Now don't patronize me, 'cause people have died and I'm not happy. Tell me." Nobody writes someone talking smack to the Doctor better than Steven Moffat, and nobody could deliver those lines better than Carey Mulligan.

Moffat's background in comedy and the sort of skills that enabled him to plot an episode of *Coupling* with incredible precision get a full workout as the episode follows the ontological paradox that drives it through to its logical conclusion: Sally gives the Doctor everything she's written about her encounter with him, which he will then use to guide her along. A lot of that paradox becomes head-scratching in the extreme if you think about it for more than a few seconds, but Moffat has jazz hands at the ready with "wibbly-wobbly, timey-wimey," the silliest piece of shorthand that says everything but explains nothing at the same time.

The ending is charming as Larry grows from the experience with the Weeping Angels to put it all in perspective and Sally becomes the obsessive. It's only in completing the loop that she can, at last, move on. Which brings to mind the other delightful thing about "Blink," and the other reason it so easily distracts the viewer: it has heart. In the same vein, Sally keeping vigil with Old Billy isn't just a discovery of a further wrinkle to the timey-wimeyness, it's a scene that wrings out every ounce of pathos it has.

The funny thing is, it's gone unnoticed, but this story has some remarkable similarities to "Love & Monsters." Both are stories about the power of being a fan of something. With "Love & Monsters" it was more affectionate as the LINDA gang find friendship and a sense of community. Here, it's a little more sardonic, as Larry and Banto stand in for the message-board-reading, T-shirt-wearing, essay-on-politics-at-the-ready sort of obsessive fan. Larry has the tunnel vision of a true enthusiast. (I love how he boggles at the idea that Sally can own only 17 DVDs!) The in-jokes — ranging from the commentary on the TARDIS windows to Banto's complaint while watching a DVD that no one ever goes to see the police in crisis situations — only reinforces this. While the message of "Love & Monsters" seems to be that the things you absolutely love can also ultimately engineer your downfall, with "Blink" it seems to be that nerds can be annoying but they're okay to have around.

The story ends with a reprise of the Doctor's speech about not blinking while flashing to shots of real statues. It's one of those sequences that really shouldn't work — what's so scary about real statues? — but the sense of unease built up throughout the episode comes tumbling back. That's "Blink" all over. Nothing about it should work, but it does. Exceptionally well.

Second Opinion (RS?)

- Making statues scary.
- The DVD easter eggs forming a coherent conversation.
- Having this work more than once.
- "Go to the police, you stupid woman."
- The heartbreak of "It's the same rain."
- The joy of Sally flirting with Billy Shipton.
- The bittersweet pain of Kathy's fate.
- The cleverness of the wallpaper message as a hook.
- Whatever you do, don't blink.
- Complicated.
- The final statue montage, which most definitely should not be watched with the lights out.
- Very complicated.
- The simplistic brilliance of the resolution.
- Sally's peaceful acceptance in the coda.
- "They kill you nicely."
- The way a technobabble explanation of time travel descends into "wibbly-wobbly, timey-wimey . . . stuff."
- Martha having to work in a shop to support the Doctor in 1969.
- The Doctor's apology to Billy.

- Larry's bemusement about what "Look to your left" means.
- The Lonely Assassins.
- The minimalist incidental music.
- "You live in Scooby-Doo's house."
- The Angels on the church.
- The way Sally so touched everyone's life that they married and had children with the same name.
- "You only own 17 DVDs?!?"
- The way you keep waiting for the Doctor to appear, only to realize the brilliance of why he doesn't.

But not necessarily in that order.

3.11 Utopia

Written by Russell T Davies **Directed by** Graeme Harper

Supporting cast John Barrowman (Captain Jack Harkness), Derek Jacobi (Professor Yana), Chipo Chung (Chantho), René Zagger (Padra), Neil Reidman (Lieutenant Atillo), Paul Marc Davis (Chieftain), Robert Forknall (guard), John Bell (Creet), Deborah MacLaren (Kistane), John Simm (the Master)

Original airdate June 16, 2007

The Big Idea The Doctor, Martha and Captain Jack travel to the end of the universe to find the last surviving humans — and they find a bit more than they bargained for.

Roots and References Post-apocalyptic movies, particularly the *Mad Max* series. Professor Yana's costume is modelled on William Hartnell's costume as the first Doctor (and it could be argued that his manner is modelled on Hartnell's Doctor as well).

Adventures in Time and Space The TARDIS takes a pit stop on top of the rift in Roald Dahl Plass in Cardiff as in "Boom Town" (Martha asks about the earthquake that happened then). There's a callout to Rose's final fate in "Doomsday" and flashbacks to Jack's death and resurrection in "The Parting of the Ways."

The Doctor's hand, preserved in a jar, was in the background of the Torchwood Hub during the first season of *Torchwood*. At the end of the *Torchwood* season one finale, "End of Days," the hand started to glow and the TARDIS materialization sound could be heard. Jack was last seen grabbing the jar with the hand and running out of the Hub, which continues with Jack's run for the TARDIS at the start of this story. (The Doctor also notes that the rift had been recently active, a shout-out to the events of "End of Days.")

Yana comes from the Silver Devastation, also where the Face of Boe hails from according to "The End of the World." Among the things Yana hears while holding the watch are the chuckling of Anthony Ainley's incarnation of the Master from 1980s *Doctor Who* and a quote from 1971's "The Dæmons."

Oh, and Yana turns out to be the Doctor's oldest enemy, the Master, a rival Time Lord who last appeared in the 1996 TV Movie. He's the Classic Series' most recurring villain, having faced off against almost all the Doctors over the years.

The Saxon Effect It all starts to come together. It turns out that in "Gridlock" the Face of Boe was not only informing the Doctor that he was not alone, the Face was giving the Doctor the identity of the Time Lord in question, YANA being an acronym for "You Are Not Alone."

Martha realizes Professor Yana is holding a fob watch exactly like the one John Smith had in "Human Nature"/"The Family of Blood." The Master used a Chameleon Arch to become Yana to hide from the Time War at the end of the universe, beyond where the Time Lords had ever been. Martha's questioning prompts Yana to see past the perception filter and finally open the watch, restoring his Time Lord nature. Once the Master has regenerated, Martha says she knows his voice . . .

Who is the Doctor? As a Time Lord, the Doctor can see that Jack has become a fixed point in time (see "The Fires of Pompeii") and he's consequently prejudiced about Jack's current state. He's in utter denial at the possibility that there's another Time Lord.

The Doctor and Martha Martha recognizes all too well the parallels in Chantho's relationship with Professor Yana: Chantho has stayed faithful and devoted to Yana for 17 years, even though he never notices her romantically. And yet, Martha is still awestruck when she finds out the Doctor can regrow his hand. The girl can't help herself, it seems.

Monster of the Week The Futurekind are feared to be what humanity might become: they're cannibalistic humanoids with sharp teeth and they're very hungry. They hunt humans.

Stand Up and Cheer The moment when all the pieces of the puzzle come together is truly exciting as the ship launches, the Doctor realizes the true meaning of the last words of the Face of Boe, Martha admits she may have caused Yana to see past the perception filter and Yana opens the watch. Nobody writes an all-important climax better than Russell T Davies, while Graeme Harper's direction and Murray Gold's music pushes it even further. All this is then topped off by a wonderful performance by Derek Jacobi as he abandons the doddering old professor persona and truly becomes the Master.

Roll Your Eyes John Bell's Creet is adorable but he gets one too many scenes that almost scream out, "He got the role in a *Blue Peter* contest!"

You're Not Making Any Sense Jack's immortality, as seen throughout the episode and *Torchwood*, works by virtue of him dying and resurrecting himself. If the room is flooded with Stet radiation so dangerous it disintegrates someone wearing protective clothing, shouldn't Jack be disintegrated and resurrected a few times in the course of the long conversation he has with the Doctor?

Interesting Trivia The year 100 trillion is further than the TARDIS crew has ever gone before. But so was the year five billion in "The End of the World." Indeed, both featured the end of the human race, despite being separated by an unimaginably long timespan. What we're seeing here is one of Davies' interests: important moments in the future history of humanity. What powers both stories is humanity facing down its own mortality. The only nod to the massive timespan between the two events is the line about humanity spending millions of years as gas clouds or downloads before reverting to the same basic shape. However, we suspect that we won't be seeing too many adventures set among the lives and loves of human downloads.

The Doctor says utopia means "the perfect place." He's wrong; it literally translates from Latin as "no place," though it has become synonymous with an ideal society thanks to the 1516 novel of the same name by Thomas More.

John Bell, a nine-year-old from Ireland, plays Creet. He won the role through a competition that unfolded over several episodes of *Blue Peter*, a BBC kids' current affairs program that's been running even longer than *Doctor Who*. The two shows have often had a symbiotic relationship. *Blue Peter* has frequently featured *Doctor Who* stars and counts among its hosts a former *Doctor Who* companion; conversely, *Doctor Who* has featured competition winners, such as Bell here, William Grantham's Abzorbaloff ("Love & Monsters") and Susannah Leah's junk TARDIS ("The Doctor's Wife"). Clips from *Blue Peter* appear in a great many Classic Series DVDs.

The TARDIS Chronometer The TARDIS initially lands to soak up some energy from the Cardiff rift in the present day. Once Jack grabs hold of the TARDIS (while dematerializing!) the TARDIS tries to shake him off by going to the planet Malcassairo in the year 100 trillion.

Brilliant? (GB) I think it would have been absolute genius had they just ended the pre-credit sequence with Jack holding onto the TARDIS in the time vortex and then done the *Doctor Who* main titles with Jack still attached to the side of the box, periodically screaming "Doctor!" over the theme music. Who's with me on this? Anyone?

Who knew that John Barrowman's Captain Jack would make such an amazing companion to David Tennant's Doctor? I thought David Tennant and Freema Agyeman were pretty good together (though I've been more a fan of Martha as a character than of her relationship with the Doctor), but the chemistry between the Doctor and Captain Jack is positively fissionable. Watching the pair banter and flirt with each other was one of the greatest surprises and delights of this story. The scene where the Doctor and Jack talk on either side of the reactor door is fairly straightforward — one character informs the other of ongoing events in the series — but it's written and performed as though it's between two old lovers thrown back together. Tennant and Barrowman are outstanding in the way they banter (the Doctor telling Jack the only man he'd ever be happy with is another Jack) and talk about their most intimate pains (the Doctor talking about Rose, Jack addressing whether he wants to die). When Jack describes how he's been inspired to live through the example of the last humans, he says, "That's fantastic"; Barrowman inflects it just subtly enough to make you think of someone else who used to say that.

It's just great to see Jack, period. He's such a superb companion, flirting with everything that moves (Chantho's reaction in particular is awesome: "Chan/I do not protest/Tho") and running around, exhilarated by the danger. He leavens every scene he's in (it is hilarious watching him strip down to enter the reactor, just so he can look good). I wish they had made this discovery sooner; *Torchwood*'s first season would have been a lot more bearable.

There's a lot to enjoy with "Utopia" that doesn't involve Captain Jack. Derek Jacobi, for one. He plays Professor Yana with doddering energy but just a hint of an edge that will come to bear once the watch is opened. His scenes with David Tennant are wonderful, showing the respect and friendship the Doctor and Master once had for each other. And, when the watch is opened, Jacobi is, briefly, a wonderful Master, all wry remarks and ice-cold demeanour. It's a shame he has to regenerate, but John Simm's first scene is so delightful you quickly forget that Jacobi is gone.

And when the revelation of the season's arc finally takes centre stage, watch out. Yana holding up his watch merits the season's biggest "Oh my God" moment. It's here that the genius of this season's arc becomes clear. This isn't simply reiterating a meme like Bad Wolf or Torchwood. There is not only what is now the traditional puzzle, but the whole season is plotted as a tight little arc, with elements seeded across seemingly unrelated stories suddenly coming together as a coherent mass. In "Utopia" (and in the next two episodes), we see the storm finally break. It's spectacular and breathtaking. The Master as villain gains dramatic weight because you know he's been behind so much over the course of the season and, yet, in timey-wimey fashion, he's actually created by the events that happen this season too. Had the Doctor never been John Smith in "Human Nature," Martha wouldn't have known what the watch was in the first place, Yana would probably still be Yana and events in "Utopia" would have been vastly different. It's the collateral effect the stories have on each other that's interesting here, and that continues with the next episode as well.

Since its first broadcast, there has been minor controversy as to whether "Utopia" is a separate story that simply sets the stage for the finale or the first of a three-part story. In deciding that "Planet of the Dead" was the 200th story, the BBC suggested this was the first of a three-part story in order to make the math work. Obviously, in this publication we have taken a contrary position. Admittedly, "Utopia" functions more or less to bring together the various threads of the season's story arc, but it's enjoyable because it has such a believable backdrop with its assemblage of smelly human refugees struggling to survive, under siege from their own future (in more ways than one). The story is straightforward enough that it is thoroughly engaging and still thoroughly accessible in spite of the season arc-heaviness. Plus, there's the Doctor and Captain Jack trading quips about having had work done. What more could you want?

Second Opinion (RS?) Look, I'm a paranoid spoilerphobe. I avoid all pre-publicity, I don't watch the "next episode" trailers and I don't even know what the upcoming story titles are. This can be hard work each Easter, but I like to experience *Doctor Who* stories as fresh as I possibly can.

I should have seen it coming. Two warring factions, a distinguished old professor and a big rocket. It's about as generic a Classic *Who* setup as you're likely to see . . . only it was written by Russell T Davies. This should have been a clue that something big was in the cards, but I assumed it would be the emotional payoff of Jack's story, overriding all the character missteps from *Torchwood* in one fell swoop.

I was looking at the wrong companion. Instead, it's Martha who — along with the unsuspecting viewer — puts together half a season's worth of clues. I'll admit that for a short time I thought Professor Yana was another incarnation of the Doctor, but then he utters those words: "I. Am. The Master."

And so the season draws all the puzzle pieces together, many of which we didn't realize were actually part of the puzzle until this moment. Where the second season saved all its cards for the finale, this season plays a few of them early, in order to make the grand showdown even more spectacular.

What's particularly good is that this takes the best bits from before — this is the equivalent of "Boom Town" both in placement and drawing attention to the ongoing arc — but alters the structure. Previous seasons had a Classic Series monster showing up early on and returning for the big finale, but that

WHO IS THE DOCTOR

wouldn't really work here (unless you were hoping for a grand smackdown with the Macra).

In fact, the only disappointment is that Derek Jacobi isn't given more of a chance to play the Master. The clues leading us here have been excellent, probably the most confident arc of the Davies era, but it really needed a whole other season to play itself out, with two time-travelling enemies fighting each other across the course of an entire season. Sadly, there simply isn't room for that.

"Utopia" stands up well watching it today. But it's the "Utopia" of June 2007 that blew me out of the water. And that's exactly how it should be.

. . . .

What Happened to Captain Jack?

What happened to Captain Jack between "The Parting of the Ways" and "Utopia"? If you haven't seen *Torchwood*, here's a brief synopsis. (Don't worry, no real spoilers!)

Jack used his Time Agent vortex manipulator to travel back to the 21st century to find the Doctor but overshot the mark and wound up in 1869. He waited almost 140 years for a version of the Doctor that coincided with him to turn up. For the most part, he stayed based in Cardiff, hoping the TARDIS would visit the rift sooner or later.

He discovered his immortality some 13 or so years later, on Ellis Island in New York in 1892 when he survived being shot through the heart. Some time in the Victorian era (presumably after his first brush with death in 1892), he was recruited by the Torchwood Institute (as seen in the *Torchwood* episode "Fragments"). Though he disagreed with Torchwood's stance on the Doctor as a threat and was appalled by some of their methods, he agreed to become an agent of Torchwood when he discovered from a fortune teller that he wouldn't meet the Doctor for another 100 years.

Over the course of four seasons of *Torchwood*, several hints are given about the things Jack had been up to over the decades. He fought in Pakistan in Lahore in 1908 (according to "Small Worlds"). He was involved in World War I and World War II. He was sent to New York in 1927 on a mission to stop an alien parasite in the *Torchwood: Miracle Day* episode "Immortal Sins." In *Torchwood: Children of Earth*, Jack was involved in a mission on behalf of the British government in 1965.

At the turn of the 21st century, Jack became the leader of Torchwood Three in Cardiff. Over the next few years, Jack recruited a completely new team and, by the time the Battle of Canary Wharf happened in "Doomsday," he had distanced his Torchwood from the Institute, making it an organization that honoured the Doctor and his work. He collected the Doctor's hand after the Sycorax battle in "The Christmas Invasion" and used it as a means to detect the Doctor. This finally succeeded and they were reunited in "Utopia," after 139 years of waiting.

. . . .

3.12—3.13 The Sound of Drums / Last of the Time Lords

Written by Russell T Davies **Directed by** Colin Teague

Supporting cast John Barrowman (Captain Jack Harkness); John Simm (The Master); Adjoa Andoh (Francine Jones); Gugu Mbatha-Raw (Tish Jones); Reggie Yates (Leo Jones); Alexandra Moen (Lucy Saxon); Colin Stinton (President Winters); Nichola McAuliffe (Vivien Rook); Nicholas Gecks (Albert Dumfries); Tom Ellis (Thomas Milligan); Ellie Haddington (Professor Docherty); Sharon Osbourne (herself); McFly (themselves); Ann Widdecombe (herself); Olivia Hill (BBC newsreader); Lachele Carl (U.S. newsreader); Daniel Ming (Chinese newsreader); Elize du Toit (sinister woman); Zoe Thorne, Gerard Logan, Johnnie Lyne-Pirkis (Sphere voices)

Original airdates June 23 and 30, 2007

The Big Idea The Master has become prime minister of Britain and unleashed the Toclafane upon an unsuspecting populace.

Roots and References *Star Trek II: The Wrath of Khan* ("Revenge is a dish best served . . . hot"); *Lord of the Rings* (the Master calls the aged Doctor Gandalf); *V for Vendetta* (a fascist state with a TV hero called Storm Saxon); the *House of Cards* trilogy (a political conspiracy at 10 Downing Street); *Peter Pan* (asking the audience to wish Tinkerbell alive). The *Valiant* is equal measures *Captain Scarlet*'s skybase and the S.H.I.E.L.D. Helicarrier from Marvel Comics. The wizened, shrunken Doctor resembles Dobby the House Elf from *Harry Potter*. The Rogue Traders' song "Voodoo Child" plays as the Toclafane rains down from the sky, and the Master sings and dances to the Scissor Sisters song "I Can't Decide."

Adventures in Time and Space The Master says, "Peoples of the Earth, please attend carefully," just as he did in 1981's "Logopolis." He offers jelly babies to Lucy, in a nod to the confection eaten by Tom Baker's Doctor. We get a flashback to Gallifrey, showing its domed citadel as seen in the *Doctor Who Magazine* comic strips (and first named in 1977's "The Invasion of Time"). The Time Lords are wearing the ceremonial high collars first seen in 1976's "The Deadly Assassin," while the young Master is seen wearing the black-and-white surplices worn by the Time Lords in 1969's "The War Games." Above the entrance to the untempered schism is the seal of Rassilon. This symbol, first seen on Gallifrey in "The Deadly Assassin," was a key part of the Time Lords' design in the Classic Series, though this is the first time it's been used in the New Series.

The Master watches *Teletubbies*, an homage to Roger Delgado's Master watching the BBC children's series *The Clangers* in 1972's "The Sea Devils." The Master's laser screwdriver has isomorphic controls, a reference to 1975's

"Pyramids of Mars." The Cloister Bell rings inside the cannibalized TARDIS ("Logopolis").

Number 10 Downing Street is restored after being destroyed in "World War Three." Flashbacks include "Aliens of London" (Big Ben destroyed), "The Christmas Invasion" (the spaceship over London) and "Army of Ghosts" (the ghosts appearing). There are also references to metal men (the Cybermen, from "Doomsday"). The Master reminisces with the Doctor about the Daleks (1973's "Frontier in Space"), the Sea Devils ("The Sea Devils") and the Axons (1971's "The Claws of Axos"). The Master mentions that the Doctor once had companions who could absorb the time vortex ("The Parting of the Ways").

The President cites first-contact policy that was devised by the United Nations Security Council in 1968 (a nod to the date of the first UNIT story, 1968's "The Invasion"). Lachele Carl's AMNN presenter makes her annual appearance, first seen in "Aliens of London." (Fabulously, she gets to say, "It's 3 a.m. in the morning.")

Jack is revealed to be the Face of Boe ("The End of the World," "New Earth," "Gridlock"). Martha's TV has a Magpie Electricals sticker on the back ("The Idiot's Lantern"). The Master's statement, "Time Lords and humans combined; haven't you always dreamed of that, Doctor?" is likely a reference to the Doctor's half-human biology from the 1996 TV Movie.

The Saxon Effect In his guise as Harold Saxon, the Master has become prime minister and, using the Archangel network, has achieved dominance over the Earth's population via low-level hypnotic suggestion. This made people vote for him and keeps them scared once he assumes power. "Vote Saxon" posters and T-shirts are seen in the background.

The Master says that the Doctor sealed the rift at the Medusa Cascade, single-handed. We'll come back to the importance of the Medusa Cascade next season.

Who is the Doctor? The Doctor refuses to see the Master killed even after all his despicable acts. The Doctor is even willing to stop travelling in order to be the Master's jailer. The Master's refusal to regenerate is the ultimate revenge against the Doctor because it leaves him, once more, alone.

The Doctor and Martha Martha's year of journeying helps her come to terms with her feelings for the Doctor; she finally tells the Doctor that her unrequited love for him is holding her back and she's leaving him. And with that, Martha not only saves the world, she saves herself.

Monster of the Week The Toclafane are shrunken human heads inside metal spheres, which can extrude weaponry. There are six billion of them and they share each other's memories. They can't be damaged, but a lightning strike in South Africa brought one down. They're actually future humans, who found nothing at Utopia and instead cannibalized themselves as the end approached. They're returned to the end of the universe when the paradox machine is destroyed.

Stand Up and Cheer Martha's confrontation with the Master is superb. Having walked the Earth for a year, apparently assembling a gun that can kill a Time Lord, she reveals that the gun was just a ruse and that her real weapon is the story of the Doctor. What's brilliant is the way she punctures the Master's confidence with just a laugh. Although the Doctor adds, "Did you think I would send her to find a gun?" it's clear that he's just a bit player in this and the triumph belongs to her.

Roll Your Eyes The gnome Doctor. He's tiny, wears a miniature version of the Doctor's outfit and lives in a golden cage. Let me rephrase: he's a computer-generated elf. By the gods of CGI, what were they thinking?

You're Not Making Any Sense President Winters orders all armed personnel to leave the bridge of the *Valiant* before first contact occurs, under the terms of the U.N. security council resolution. However, immediately after he's killed, multiple people pull out handguns. Does "armed" only mean "visibly armed" in the resolution?

Interesting Trivia The Untempered Schism has three possible outcomes: it inspires you, it drives you mad or it makes you run away. This does retoactively explain why there were so many renegade Time Lords in the Classic Series, but it still seems like an odd thing for the Time Lords to show their kids. If only a third of their population are going to gain wisdom and they're going to spend much of their time fighting the other third who went insane and keep trying to take over the universe, then you have to wonder if it's really worth all the effort.

The concept of the Toclafane has been around since Series One, where they were to have been the replacement monster for the Daleks when negotiations with Terry Nation's estate briefly ran aground in 2004. (At that point, the monster was simply called "a sphere.")

The first part of this story derives its title from a line in the song "Voodoo Child" by Rogue Traders (which peaked at number three on the U.K. charts). Indeed, rights were obtained to play the song in the episode before the story was even written. Russell T Davies had to be reminded this had been done; he forgot to put it in the script originally!

Arthur Coleman Winters is president-elect of the United States, but, constitutionally speaking, the president-elect has no powers to act as head of state until they are inaugurated as president. The only way in which this might be possible is if Winters had been vice president and the current president incapacitated in some way; even then, he'd more likely introduce himself as either acting president or vice president.

Martha's brother Leo was supposed to be among the people meeting her on the beach, but actor Reggie Yates was only able to appear in a few short scenes in "The Sound of Drums," due to another acting commitment. Graeme Harper had to direct the sequence where Martha and her cohorts capture the Toclafane sphere after Colin Teague injured himself.

The TARDIS Chronometer The Doctor fused the coordinates when the Master hijacked the TARDIS in "Utopia," meaning that it can only travel between the year 100 trillion and present-day Earth, with 18 months leeway. (Presuming the U.S. election cycle is the same in the *Doctor Who* universe, Winters being president-elect suggests the story takes place between November 2008 and January 2009.) The TARDIS is parked on board the *Valiant*, although we discover that the Master previously returned to the year 100 trillion with Lucy.

Brilliant? (RS?) The first time I watched "Utopia," it struck me that there's something very odd about Professor Yana. Quite simply, Derek Jacobi's character doesn't belong in this show. He's an old man in a waistcoat. He's a scientist, working for the good of humanity. He's someone the Doctor immediately connects with, because they have a mutual love of science. He's a classic British thespian, the type who can convince you that what you're watching is Shakespeare, even though you've got an entire alien race made up of people with bits of gunk on their faces. Professor Yana doesn't belong in the New Series, because he's a relic straight out of the old one.

It's shocking just how often we used to get this type of character — and just how absent someone like him has been since the show came back. You can imagine my surprise when he turned out to be precisely that: a relic from the past. But it's not just that he's a returning character, it's that the actor playing him is — you know — old. At the end of "Utopia," the thing the Master seems to desire most isn't world domination. It isn't revenge. It isn't conquest over time. It's . . . youth and strength.

Which brings us to John Simm. But really, it bring us to the entire *raison d'être* of the New Series: this is *Doctor Who*, only with youth and strength. It's basically the same show as before, only it's a bit livelier and a bit faster than the creaky old show it used to be. And that's . . . it. That's everything and nothing, right there.

Look at this story. It's got fast-paced music, dancing, (pre-watershed) sex, it runs like lightning and it doesn't matter a whit that it makes very little sense when you stop to think about it, because thinking's for squares, granddad, we're just here to par-tay! Crank up the iPod and dance. Here come the drums. This is television for its timeslot. Anything else is a bonus.

Oh, and the very worst thing that can happen? You become old and feeble,

SERIES THREE

179

and you get pushed around in a wheelchair. (Or live in a birdcage, but it's much the same thing.)

On the other hand, it sure is slick. Not just in appearance, although that's a big factor, but the way that scenes are spliced and the manic way the plot unfolds. Then there's the songfic: writing a whole story just so you can play your favourite songs is, surely, every kid's dream.

Which brings us back, again, to the Simm Master. He's perfect for this, because he's a big kid, pretending to be an adult. He goes to work. He kisses his wife. But he also does precisely what any childhood bully would fantasize about doing as an adult: his work colleagues are stuffy, so he kills them. The U.S. president is pompous, so he makes fun of him (and kills him). He slides down banisters. He starts his day with pop music. He carves big statues of himself all over the world. And he keeps his worst enemy in a cage where he can taunt him all day long.

This Master is at a skewed angle to the show's reality. He's not the Master of old, but he's not the anti-Doctor either. He doesn't have Tennant's hyperactivity, his childlike jokes aren't actually funny (presumably they weren't intended to be) and he doesn't disarm his opponents with charm. Instead, he's more like an annoying goofball of a Time Lord, one who insists on making stupid comments just to annoy people, even though no one finds them amusing and they generally don't advance his agenda.

And yet, it works. Boy, does it work. Simm is excellent, which is part of it but only part. By not playing to the obvious expectation — he's the Doctor, only evil! — there's something deeply uncomfortable about the Master. Something subtly, textually, wrong. It sets your teeth on edge, because he almost fits but doesn't quite. And that's brilliant, because if the Master did fit, he'd be boring. Having the guy in the black hat automatically casts the Doctor in the white one and then you're not watching drama, you're watching chess. By twisting the Master out of shape, you open a gap for the show to explore. This Master isn't downright evil, he's actually somewhat likeable. He's still, fundamentally, doing the same work he was as Professor Yana: helping the Utopian people to reach the stars. He's not consumed with lust for power, he's troubled by the drumming.

By this point, the New Series has settled into its skin. It races along, dazzling the eye, the ear and sometimes even the brain. It knows how to avoid many of the obvious mistakes, and it also knows that when you can't avoid the corner you've painted yourself into, then you can at least disguise the problem if you go fast enough.

And the Master, despite all the inherent flaws in the character, fits into this new regime perfectly. If you're going to have the Daleks and Cybermen fight a war, then it had better be a big war. If you're going to bring back Sarah and K9, then at least create a moneymaking spinoff series in the process. If you're going to bring back the Master, then make him able to out-think the Doctor at every turn, take over the world and have the entire human race hate him.

Because, ultimately, what's the Master for? He's there as a distorted reflection of the Doctor. He's what the Doctor could be but chooses not to be. The power of the Doctor lies in the fact that he's a guy who's smarter than everyone else. By having him face an equal, you a) inject drama, b) level the playing field and c) show just how great the Doctor is, because he can even overcome someone as smart as him. The Simm Master fits the bill perfectly, perhaps better than any Master before him. Because the key isn't just in the reflection, it's in the degree of distortion.

After all, if the Master is somehow subtly wrong, doesn't that just seem oh-so-right? Now, bring on the music . . .

Second Opinion (GB) John Simm's amazing performance as the Master is a force to behold. While he is often delightfully over the top in the tradition of earlier portrayals of the character, he also brings great pathos to many of his scenes, such as his initial phone conversation with the Doctor about the destruction of Gallifrey.

All this, the gorgeous origin story of the Master on his home planet and the decent urban thriller that made up "The Sound of Drums," is just a warm-up act, though. In "The Last of the Time Lords," we're given the terrifying prospect of a world where the Master has won, and we see in disturbing detail how ugly and hideous that reality would be. The abuse and torture of Lucy Saxon only brings this home. Here we have a terrible mirror image to the Doctor and Martha; while Martha now travels the world telling people about the things the Doctor has done and how much she loves him and the incredible sights she has seen with him, Lucy is driven mad by her TARDIS travels and is physically beaten. As the hideousness of the Master's villainy both on a global and domestic scale becomes clearer, the Master is no longer the goofy comic figure of "The Sound of Drums." He truly becomes a monster. John Simm really understands the horrific side of his character and makes his performance more brutal to reflect it.

"The Last of the Time Lords" hinges on a *deus ex machina* plot device where the Doctor is miraculously able to restore himself, even make himself briefly godlike. It feels like a dip into a familiar well, and it is. But we need to go beyond the whats (though Docherty's discussion of Archangel's weaknesses covers that) to the whys. One of the great things *Doctor Who* has always extolled is optimism for humanity and what it is capable of. In one of the bleakest scenes in this story, the Master tries to argue that humans are fearsome destroyers. The point of the Doctor using humans to exploit the Archangel Network and restore himself from the psychic energy isn't just to get the Doctor "back to start" (though it is that); it's to reinforce the truth that ordinary people just like Martha can save the day.

The great thing here is Martha, as her story comes to a satisfying conclusion as she fulfils the potential shown in "Smith and Jones." Freema Agyeman does a brilliant job of conveying the changes Martha has gone through while keeping her optimism alive. And then Martha does the bravest thing imaginable: she leaves the Doctor. Let's hear it for the scene where she finally tells the Doctor why she really needs to leave him.

In spite of some slightly creaky plot devices and what must go down in the annals of *Who*-dom as the most bizarre method of making the Doctor feeble, "The Last of the Time Lords" brings to a close the most consistent, exciting and ambitious season of *Doctor Who* yet.

The Psychic Papers: The Master

In the 1971 story "Terror of the Autons," a Time Lord appears to the then-exiled-to-Earth Doctor with a message: "I came to warn you. An old acquaintance has arrived on this planet."

The Doctor replies, "Oh? One of our people?"

When the Time Lord says, "The Master," the Doctor's judgement is immediate. "That jackanapes! All he ever does is cause trouble."

The Time Lord replies that the Master will almost certainly try to kill him. The Doctor retorts categorically: "I refuse to be worried by a renegade like the Master. He's a, he's an unimaginative plodder." To which the Time Lord cheerfully points out, "His degree in cosmic science was of a higher class than yours."

This tells you almost everything you need to know about the Doctor and the Master.

Created to be the Moriarty to the Doctor's Holmes, the Master — a similarly academic-titled renegade Time Lord — was a regular adversary in the third Doctor's era, even featuring as the villain in an entire season of stories. Played by actor Roger Delgado, the character schemed to take over the world (and even the universe) or to destroy the Doctor (or both). In this cause, he often allied himself with various alien races, such as the Axons, the Sea Devils, the Ogrons and the Daleks.

Delgado's Master was suave, charming and had an almost gentlemanly rivalry with Jon Pertwee's Doctor (who, at the time, was going through a similar Renaissance-man phase). The Master smoked cigars, engaged in swordfights and impersonated vicars.

He spoke cordially to people, using their formal name and title. His trademark weapon was the tissue compression eliminator, which could shrink victims to an inch in height.

In 1972's "The Sea Devils," the Doctor reveals an important detail that has forever changed the dynamic of this Holmes-Moriarty relationship: in the past, on their home planet, the Doctor and the Master were once friends. This added a wrinkle to this adversarial relationship. Sherlock Holmes and Professor Moriarty never knew each other. That the Doctor and the Master did made it a much more personal relationship.

Delgado's untimely death in 1973 cut short plans for a final showdown with the third Doctor, and the character vanished from the screen for several years. He returned in 1976's "The Deadly Assassin," played by Peter Pratt in a withered form, having used up his full cycle of 13 regenerations. In 1981's "The Keeper of Traken," he resurfaced still in withered form (played by Geoffrey Beevers) and gained a new body from a member of the Union of Traken known as Tremas. In this new body, he was played throughout the '80s by Anthony Ainley; his Master faced no less than four Doctors and he was directly responsible for the fourth Doctor's demise in 1981's "Logopolis."

Ainley's Master was more of a psychopath, whose plans were dominated by revenge against the Doctor, arbitrary disguises and cackling laughter. He appeared about once a season through most of the '80s and was the villain in the Classic Series' final story, 1989's "Survival." In his final appearance, the Master was being consumed by a planet that turned anyone who went there into cheetah-like carnivores.

In the 1996 TV Movie, the Master was played by Eric Roberts, the movie's major guest star. The Master had been executed by the Daleks but still clung to life in the form of a morphogenic snake. He took over the body of Bruce, an ambulance driver from 1999 San Francisco. Roberts' Master was the first time an American had assailed the role, and he played him with a mixture of sneering intensity and sheer camp. At the end of that story, the Master was sucked into the Eye of Harmony, the black hole in the centre of the TARDIS.

The Master's great advantage is that he has so many of the attributes of the Doctor: he can travel in time; he's a genius; he can use his charm, wit and cunning to ingratiate himself into a society's power structure. Usually in possession of his own TARDIS, he can turn up in almost any story, often disguised as someone else. The danger is that he can be overused, a shorthand for not-the-Doctor that gives the show an easy antagonist.

Since *Doctor Who*'s return in 2005, fans and the media alike have been wondering when he would turn up. Executive producer Russell T Davies was determined to keep people off the scent and stated he didn't think he would ever use the character. In fact, by that point plans were already afoot to revive the character. This new Master (played by John Simm) was the same as ever, only bigger and better: he has managed to infiltrate British society to become prime minister. But the true genius in his revival was in giving him an origin story that explained the character and his motivations. We learn that, as part of his childhood initiation as a Time Lord, the Master was forced to view the Untempered Schism, the heart of the time vortex. This experience drove him mad, and a manifestation of that madness was that the Master forever heard the sound of drums in his own head.

This origin story was one of the first and only major examples of "retroactive continuity," or retconning, in *Doctor Who* with its implication that all incarnations of the Master — whether played by Delgado, Pratt, Beevers, Ainley, Roberts, Jacobi or Simm — all suffer from that same madness and hear the sound of drums in their own head. Watching the Master's first appearance in "Terror of the Autons" is fascinating in light of this revisionism. In "The End of Time," this origin is expanded considerably.

The New Series' emphasis on relationships is perfect for two former friends such as the Doctor and the Master (with the two of them being the last of their kind complicating matters even further), and much was done to bring this aspect out in both of John Simm's appearances in the David Tennant era. Whether the Master comes back to face Matt Smith's Doctor remains to be seen, but there is a lot of scope for him if, and when, that unimaginative plodder and jackanapes does return.

SERIES FOUR

· ·

Starring
David Tennant as the Doctor
Catherine Tate as Donna Noble

Executive Producers
Russell T Davies, Julie Gardner
Phil Collinson (4.03, 4.04–4.05, 4.07, 4.11)

Producers
Phil Collinson
Susie Ligatt (4.03, 4.04–4.05, 4.07, 4.11)

· ·

4.X Time Crash

Written by Steven Moffat **Directed by** Graeme Harper

Supporting cast Peter Davison (the fifth Doctor)

Original airdate November 16, 2007

The Big Idea Something goes wrong with the TARDIS, causing two incarnations of the Doctor to exist simultaneously.

Roots and References 1973's "The Three Doctors" and succeeding multi-Doctor stories from the Classic Series ("Snap!"). Murray Gold's music mimics the '80s synthesizer scores of the Davison era at key points.

Adventures in Time and Space The Cloister Bell rings (first heard in 1981's "Logopolis"). The tenth Doctor mentions the TARDIS's Helmic Regulator (1975's "The Ark in Space") and Zeiton Crystals (1985's "Vengeance on Varos").

The tenth Doctor reminisces about Nyssa and Tegan (the fifth Doctor's primary female companions), Cybermen (1982's "Earthshock"), the Mara (1982's "Kinda" and 1983's "Snakedance"), Time Lords in funny hats (1983's "Arc of Infinity") and the Master (intermittently from 1982's "Castrovalva" through 1984's "Planet of Fire"). That dates where the adventure takes place in Davison continuity: after the events of "Arc of Infinity" and "Snakedance" but before 1983's "Mawdryn Undead." In reference to the sonic screwdriver, the tenth says, "You mostly went hands-free," referring to its destruction in 1982's "The Visitation."

The fifth Doctor references LINDA ("Love & Monsters") and the tenth Doctor says that the Master just showed up again ("Utopia" through "Last of the Time Lords"). Both Doctors say "Wibbly-wobbly, timey-wimey" ("Blink").

Who is the Doctor? The Doctor is bemused seeing his fifth incarnation. He finds himself nostalgic for the gestures and actions he used to make. At the end, the Doctor expresses his fondness for that time in his life, noting he's kept a few of his past incarnation's affectations, like the reading glasses and the trainers, and even tells the fifth, "You were *my* Doctor."

Stand Up and Cheer "Brave choice, the celery. But, fair play to you, not a lot of men can carry off a decorative vegetable."

Roll Your Eyes Having the Doctors talk about *Doctor Who* technology in terms of our own ("You mostly went hands-free" for not having the sonic screwdriver or "You've changed the desktop theme. Coral? It's worse than the leopard skin" for the TARDIS interior) is extremely hokey.

You're Not Making Any Sense "Wibbly-wobbly, timey-wimey" manages to paper over a fairly serious, and ridiculous, paradox at the heart of the story. Also, if the TARDISes really have merged, why don't we see the Davison-era TARDIS converged with the Tennant-era one?

Interesting Trivia "Time Crash" is the 2007 contribution to the BBC's annual Children in Need charity appeal. It was shot over the course of a Sunday on the TARDIS set with stars and crew working for free. Writer Steven Moffat suggested that a Children in Need mini-episode would provide an excellent opportunity for the Doctor to meet a past incarnation. Davison, who was playing King Arthur in *Spamalot* in the West End at the time, was delighted to return, as his school-aged children were fans of the New Series (Davison and his kids had previously visited the London location filming of "The Christmas Invasion").

Peter Davison played the fifth Doctor from 1981 to 1984, and his tenure was a favourite of David Tennant and Steven Moffat, who knew Davison from the sitcom *Fear, Stress and Anger*, which Moffat's wife, Sue Vertue, produced. (Davison later became Tennant's father-in-law, but that's a tale to be told in "The Doctor's Daughter.") Past Doctors had previously teamed up in the Classic Series in "The Three Doctors" (1972), "The Five Doctors" (1983) and "The Two Doctors" (1985), but "Time Crash" is the first time where we have an in-story explanation that the "younger" Doctor now looks so much older: the meeting shorts out the time differential. No, it doesn't make sense, but it does acknowledge that Peter Davison is greyer, balder and thicker round the waist!

The TARDIS Chronometer The TARDIS is seen parked outside the Jones' house, in the reprise from "Last of the Time Lords." The rest of the action takes place in space, with the two TARDISes merged.

Brilliant? (RS?) After two installments of creeping horror, Steven Moffat puts on his comic hat and gives us a mini-episode that involves two men trading one-liners on a single set — and that may be one of the most satisfying short-form *Doctor Who* stories ever told. Indeed, despite his many evident talents, I'm convinced that Moffat's at his best in the short-story format and when forced to rely on dialogue.

The dialogue sparkles, from the description of the fifth Doctor saving the universe using a kettle and some string to the explosion blowing a hole in the space-time continuum the exact size of Belgium. Then there's the tenth Doctor attempting to high-five the fifth, and the latter just standing still and looking bewildered, a subtle nod to the passage of time.

However, it's the moment that the fifth Doctor figures out who the tenth must be that really had me. The tenth, along with the viewer, is waiting for him to put the pieces together; with a look of recognition, he suddenly announces, "Oh no!" and then, against all expectations, says, "You're . . . a fan!" This is brilliant, partly because it's a great punchline and partly because David Tennant is indeed a fan. But it's the subsequent exchange — "I'm not just a fan, I'm you!" "Okay, you're my biggest fan!" — that's sublime.

This mini-episode can afford to have all the in-jokes about the past that the new show can't do. However, what's astonishing is that this was, at the time, the second-most-watched episode of New *Who*, thanks to its inclusion as part of Children in Need. It also received critical acclaim from all quarters, making it the first solid piece of proof that there was no division between the old and the new.

There's only one moment that doesn't work: when the tenth Doctor says, "You were *my* Doctor" to the fifth. It's a sweet meta-moment, but it makes absolutely no sense in the context of the story. I might say to my 18-year-old self, "I enjoyed being you," but I would never say, "You were *my* Robert!" The line is a single entendre: it functions only as a moment between two actors, not between two characters, taking us out of the reality of the story altogether. But, fortunately, only for a moment.

"To days to come," says the fifth Doctor and for the first time we see that a rosy future lies ahead of his era. "All my love to long ago," responds the tenth Doctor, encapsulating the nostalgia for a bygone age that nevertheless lives on. The Doctor can travel in time in the fictional universe he inhabits but occasionally, with stories like this, so can we.

Second Opinion (GB): Sigh. The whole season spent regaining the good will I lost with my co-author over his curt dismissal of the motorway scene in "The Runaway Bride" . . . gone, in an instant. How can anyone not like the "You were *my* Doctor" scene? Once again, question-mark boy is smart, charming, great with the ladies — and still seems to have lost his soul. The whole mini-episode is leading up to that moment. It is a lovely moment that works on a meta-level and in the fiction of the story. Perhaps we wouldn't use such a term referring to our past version of ourselves (personally, I probably would say to my 18-year-old self, "You were *my* Graeme," because, honestly, it's mostly been downhill since then), but we're not a Time Lord whose past is made up of nine distinct and unique personalities. I think the tenth Doctor having a preference for the time in his life he liked the most and the incarnation he was at the time is rather sweet.

The strength of "Time Crash" is that it's equal parts charm, comedy (the Doctor on whether the Master still has a "rubbish beard": "No. Well, a wife . . .") and wonderful moments nerds will love, such as the stabs of 1980s Yamaha DX-7 snyth. It works because Steven Moffat takes the best part of multi-Doctor stories — the Doctors actually meeting each other — and expands it into something funny and clever and then gets the hell off before it has to become an ordinary *Doctor Who* story. The thing is, Peter Davison is so wonderful, and

Tennant is having a ball performing with his childhood hero, I'd have loved to see a full-length, two-part adventure with the pair of them that took place on more than one set. But then the very essence of good comedy is to leave the audience wanting more.

4.00 Voyage of the Damned

Written by Russell T Davies **Directed by** James Strong

Supporting cast Kylie Minogue (Astrid Peth), George Costigan (Max Capricorn), Clive Swift (Mr. Copper), Gray O'Brien (Rickston Slade), Russell Tovey (Midshipman Alonso Frame), Debbie Chazen (Foon Van Hoff), Clive Rowe (Morvin Van Hoff), Jimmy Vee (Bannakaffalatta), Geoffrey Palmer (Captain Hardaker), Bernard Cribbins (Wilfred Mott), Nicholas Witchell (himself), Paul Kasey (the Host), Jessica Martin (voice of the Queen)

Original airdate December 25, 2007

The Big Idea The Doctor finds himself on a starship orbiting the Earth that calls itself the *Titanic*. What could possibly go wrong?

Roots and References Disaster movies of the 1970s, particularly *The Poseidon Adventure*; *Passenger 57* (the Doctor's ID); the *Austin Powers* films (Max Capricorn's look and performance appears to be filched from Dr. Evil); *Max Headroom* (the Host stutters "Max"). The story shares the same premise (and, in early drafts, the same title) as Douglas Adams and Terry Jones' videogame and book *Starship Titanic*. It was also heavily influenced by a little-seen 1997 historical film starring Leonardo DiCaprio and Kate Winslet . . .

Adventures in Time and Space Earth is a Level Five society, a technological rating used as far back as 1979's "City of Death." The Doctor states that Gallifrey was in the constellation of Kasterborous (1975's "Pyramids of Mars"). The Doctor explains his knowledge of Earth by mentioning a period of time when he was "sort of made homeless" and "there was the Earth," a reference to the third Doctor's exile to Earth during the early 1970s.

Residents have abandoned London this Christmas thanks to "The Christmas Invasion" and "The Runaway Bride." The Doctor complains that his tuxedo must be unlucky ("Rise of the Cybermen"/"The Age of Steel," "The Lazarus Experiment"). The Doctor says, "One of these days it might snow for real," referring to the faux snow in "The Christmas Invasion" and "The Runaway Bride."

In "The Idiot's Lantern," the Doctor referenced Kylie Minogue ("It's Never Too Late"), which becomes retroactively metatextual with Kylie herself appearing in this episode. The Doctor finally gets to fulfil his desire (expressed to Rose in "Army of Ghosts") to say "*allons-y*" to someone named Alonso.

Who is the Doctor? Mr. Copper tells the Doctor, "If you could choose, Doctor, if you could decide who lives and who dies . . . that would make you a monster." The look on the Doctor's face indicates that this is a reminder of his own hubris.

The Doctor and Astrid: The Doctor develops an instant connection with waitress Astrid Peth, identifying with her wanderlust, telling her, "You dreamt of another sky." She's swept up with the unfolding adventure, flirts with the Doctor ("You should see me in the morning"/"Okay") and even snogs him at one point. Unlike Martha, where he remains aloof, the Doctor seems to enjoy the frisson of sexual tension.

Monster of the Week The Heavenly Host are robots dressed as angels (presumably to enhance the Christmas theme). The Host are on board the *Titanic* to provide tourist information and assistance. Once the meteorites hit the ship, they resort to orders given by Max Capricorn to murder the remaining passengers, using their razor-sharp halos.

Stand Up and Cheer When Bannakaffalatta saves the Doctor's party from the Host, it's a glorious moment: he not only sacrifices himself but does so in a moment of pride demonstrating who he really is. Then he dies flirting with a beautiful woman played by Kylie Minogue. You have to love someone for that.

Roll Your Eyes The Doctor says bombastically, "I'm the Doctor. I'm a Time Lord. I'm from the planet Gallifrey in the constellation of Kasterberous. I'm 903 years old and I'm the man who's going to save your lives and the lives of all six billion people on the planet below." It's a sentiment that seems to be made for a cinema trailer (in fact, it was used in a cinema trailer!), but in the episode it just seems overblown, pompous and redundant, especially following a genuinely funny and charming moment where the Doctor (literally) outlines his plan. We're pretty sure we saw Bannakaffalatta rolling his eyes afterward.

You're Not Making Any Sense If the Host can break through the deadlock-sealed bridge by punching through from below, why didn't they do that much earlier?

Interesting Trivia This is the first episode to use a new version of Ron Grainer's theme by composer Murray Gold. This version continues to sample Delia Derbyshire's original 1960s version while adding different instrumentation to the mix. The remake was necessitated by a BBC mandate to decrease the duration of opening and closing titles. The new version of the theme will stay for the remainder of the David Tennant era.

The currency system on Stow has an easy conversion. Mr. Copper puts 50 million credits on the credit card, which amounts to a million pounds. Foon also says she spent 5,000 credits on the voyage (about the price of a ticket), which Morvin says will take 20 years to pay off. Only, with the above conversion rate, the Van Hoff's tickets cost . . . £100. Which means they earn about £5 a year. That's quite the depressed economy they have there on Stow. No wonder they're in the process of giving cyborgs rights.

The part of Astrid was written specifically for pop star Kylie Minogue. Minogue's interest in starring in an episode of *Doctor Who* came to the attention of the producers through her creative director, Will Baker, who is himself a massive *Doctor Who* fan.

The story was dedicated to *Doctor Who*'s first producer, Verity Lambert OBE, who died a month before broadcast, on the eve of *Doctor Who*'s 44th anniversary.

The TARDIS Chronometer The space cruiseship *Titanic*, orbiting Earth, Christmas 2008. There's a brief visit to a deserted London as well.

Brilliant? (GB) Steven Moffat once said that every *Doctor Who* story is a promise to the viewer to deliver adventure, thrills, horror and comedy. If that's true, then the *Doctor Who* Christmas special is a specific promise to deliver something to a first-time audience watching it on Christmas Day. Indeed, "Voyage of the Damned" shows how the *Who* Christmas story should be done: it's less concerned with the broader ongoing story and more interested in huge spectacle, big laughs, maximum thrills and fast pace. What better way to deliver on that promise than with Kylie Minogue on the *Titanic* in space?

It's the maddest premise for anything since *Snakes on a Plane*, but *Doctor Who* is at its best with mad premises. It works even better when it steals from a whole genre while doing it. "Voyage of the Damned" allows *Doctor Who* to finally pilliage from that most honourable of genres (in many ways a Christmas staple), the disaster movie. The episode features a brilliant pastiche of Irwin Allen's 1970s oeuvre, which is apparent in almost every frame. They're all recognizable types from *The Poseidon Adventure* (indeed Foon is particularly reminiscent of Shelley Winters). Just about every character has a sympathetic backstory and gets a sweet moment to show them at their most intimate and vulnerable, solely to create maximum impact when they die: the bullied Van Hoffs; the closeted cyborg, Bannakaffalatta; and the sweet waitress who just wanted to travel, Astrid. Only Slade stays a cipher, which is a missed opportunity as clearly Gray O'Brien has something to offer as an actor. The Doctor gets to play the Paul Newman role from *The Towering Inferno*: the one who sees the impending disaster, is not listened to and has to lead the attempt to survive.

Like all disaster movies, "Voyage of the Damned" lives on elaborate set pieces where the characters struggle through the wreckage, avoiding deadly obstacles to survive (and the survivors crossing a chasm in the centre of the ship doesn't skimp on spectacle). It is here where *Doctor Who* subverts the genre and does what it does best: instead of deadly natural or man-made obstacles, the survivors face marauding killer robots dressed like angels and a mystery below decks.

It's also really funny. Russell Davies' dialogue is never smarter or more charming. The Doctor's plan as a numbered list that includes roman numerals is hilarious, and Copper's attempts to describe Christmas are genius. The running gag that the Doctor is rubbish with the Host's three question limit is a lot of fun. Plus there are great lines like "Never say 'trapped,' just 'inconveniently circumstanced.'"

It's the fusion of *Doctor Who* and disaster movie that makes "Voyage of the Damned" so compelling. You care about the plight of these people (well, perhaps not Slade) and the randomness of who eventually dies has genuine poignancy. This is particularly true of Bannakaffalatta's heroic death and Foon's gesture of loss and desperation that becomes something heroic.

The Doctor's part in this story may be heroic, but he also has to grapple with his own hubris. His experience with Astrid certainly gives him pause. Their first meeting pretty much demonstrates her suitability as a companion: someone, like Rose, who wants something better than her humdrum existence. Someone, like Martha, who is instantly charmed by the Doctor and his manner. Astrid's one-off presence here does provide a moving reminder that not everyone passes the audition to become a companion; some don't actually survive the audition.

Which is a pity, because Kylie Minogue is so winning as Astrid and David Tennant has real chemistry with her. (Just her saying "okay" may be the most brazen bit of flirting ever accomplished in *Doctor Who*.) Minogue doesn't get a lot to do, but you enjoy every second she's there. That counts for everything.

In so many ways, "Voyage of the Damned" demonstrates that the best way for a *Doctor Who* Christmas special to deliver on its promise to the audience is to fully deliver on its promise as an episode of *Doctor Who*. Play with other genre connections; give us genuine laughs, vivid characters and real thrills; and, just for a modern audience, have a bit of flirting as well. "Voyage of the Damned" does all this and gives us Kylie and a three-foot alien named Bannakaffalatta as well. I don't know about you, but that's one hell of a Christmas present.

Second Opinion (RS?) "Voyage of the Damned" is a story about expectations. In any big-budget action movie, you can usually tell in advance who's going to live, who's going to die a tragic death and who's going to die as punishment for their sins. "Voyage of the Damned" is a high-profile, fast-paced, big-budget action movie . . . that undercuts expectations at every turn.

So you expect female lead Astrid Peth and the likeable Van Hoffs to survive, Mr. Copper to die a redemptive death and Rickston to get his comeuppance, either in the form of gruesome death or at least in learning a valuable lesson.

Even Midshipman Frame looks like a red shirt, who's going to hang on just long enough to pass on crucial plot information, yet he recovers from his bullet wound and pulls through.

It's bigger than that, though. There's not a single promise the Doctor makes that he can keep, from keeping everyone alive to coming back for Foon. The inhabitants of London are expecting an alien invasion, the viewer at home is expecting a big Christmas disaster like the destruction of Buckingham Palace and we expect the Doctor to get his party across a bridge without losing half of them in the process.

Mr. Copper's expectations involve simple things: a house, a garden, a kitchen. We don't expect Max Capricorn, the info-dump hologram, to be behind it all. And, ultimately, we expect that a man who can choose who lives or dies would be a hero, not a monster.

The brilliance of "Voyage of the Damned" is that it plays with all these pre-conceptions, while still telling a rollicking good story that appeals to fans and the general public alike. Kylie Minogue is the biggest star to appear in the New Series and the ratings were consequently the show's best yet. All those viewers who don't normally watch *Doctor Who* but tuned in for Kylie were probably looking for a fun slice of Christmas adventure with romance, witty lines, dramatic action and a satsifying conclusion. Fortunately, in this case, they got exactly what they expected.

. . . .

The Theme Song

The original theme song for *Doctor Who* was written by Ron Grainer, a stalwart composer who, over the years, wrote most of the really great theme songs of 1960s British television (including those for *The Prisoner*, *Steptoe and Son* and *Man in a Suitcase*). But the person who made *Doctor Who*'s theme song the incredible, enduring, iconic piece that it is, even today, is Delia Derbyshire. Working at the BBC Radiophonics Workshop (a department tasked with designing music and sound effects for BBC productions using experimental techniques), Derbyshire was one of the progenitors of electronic music.

Before synthesizers were even commercially available, Derbyshire created the theme in 1963 by creating each individual sound electronically with an oscillator, recording it and then cutting the tape to the appropriate length to create each note. She then spliced the tape together to create the various elements — bass line, melody, swooping noises — and played them in various loops (the loop apparently extended across a room!) until the final theme was created. The result was something so unique-sounding, composer Ron Grainer apparently said to Delia Derbyshire, "Did I write that?"

In all three versions of the theme for the New Series, composer Murray Gold has sampled Derbyshire's original 1963 version (usually the melody line) but overlaid additional instrumentation and created a counter melody to enhance it.

. . . .

4.01 Partners in Crime

Written by Russell T Davies **Directed by** James Strong

Supporting cast Billie Piper (Rose Tyler), Sarah Lancashire (Miss Foster), Bernard Cribbins (Wilfred Mott), Jacqueline King (Sylvia Noble), Verona Joseph (Penny Carter), Jessica Gunning (Stacey Campbell), Martin Ball (Roger Davey), Rachid Sabitri (Craig Staniland), Chandra Ruegg (Claire Pope), Sue Kelvin (Suzette Chambers), Jonathan Stratt (taxi driver)
Original airdate April 5, 2008

The Big Idea The Doctor and Donna are separately investigating an Adipose plan to use human fat cells to reproduce.

Roots and References Our culture's obsession with weight (pretty much anything made in the last several decades); Tove Jansson's *Moomin* series of books (the Adipose); *Supernanny*'s Jo Frost (Miss Foster); the "Fat Fighters" sketches in *Little Britain*. The Adipose ship is reminiscent of the mothership in *Close Encounters of the Third Kind*.

Adventures in Time and Space The Doctor mentions that he's met cat people ("New Earth"). Wilf mentions Lance and that barmy old Christmas ("The Runaway Bride"). Donna believes everything, except for the *Titanic* flying over Buckingham Palace ("Voyage of the Damned"). The Doctor refuses to blow up the Adipose ship as the creatures are just children, which Donna says makes a change from last time ("The Runaway Bride"). There's a reference to the Shadow Proclamation (first mentioned in "Rose").

The Bees Are Disappearing Effect This season's arc has several disparate elements, many of which are identified here. First of all, Donna thinks the Doctor must be connected to the bees disappearing, although he has no idea what she's talking about. Secondly, the Adipose breeding planet was lost. And finally, the woman with whom Donna leaves instructions to give Sylvia about her car turns out to be Rose. All these aspects will feature throughout the season and eventually come together.

The Doctor and Donna The Doctor is clearly lonely; he's talking to himself in the TARDIS, but he initially refuses to let Donna come aboard, as things got complicated with Martha and now he just wants a mate. It's a sign of how Martha made him realize he needs to set boundaries in his relationships. Only Donna is quite clear she too just wants a mate and doesn't want *to* mate. She's spent the intervening months after "The Runaway Bride" trying to find him, and she even keeps her bags in her car, because she just wants to travel with him.

Monster of the Week The baby Adipose are tiny creatures made of living human fat. They have faces, arms and legs, and they tend to smile and wave at people. They're created when humans ingest a pill that attracts fat cells, binding the fat together to form a body, which is expelled and walks away. In a crisis, the Adipose can also convert bone, hair and internal organs, which consumes an entire person at once.

Stand Up and Cheer The scene where the Doctor and Donna first see each other through the window is hilarious. After a long buildup of the Doctor and Donna just missing each other, it's an enormously successful payoff that's laugh-out-loud funny. Catherine Tate's miming is particularly amusing, and it's capped by a brilliant punchline: Ms. Foster and her guards silently watching the interchange. Possibly the single funniest scene in all of New *Who*.

Roll Your Eyes When the Adipose switch off their levitation beam, there's an oh-so-funny-stop!-my-sides! pause while Ms. Foster hangs for a moment as though she's Wile E. Coyote, before plummeting to the ground.

You're Not Making Any Sense The Doctor, inside the office block, grabs Donna's ankles while she's hanging from a rope outside the window. A moment later, Donna is inside and dusting herself off. As opposed to, say, falling backwards and taking the Doctor with her, as physics might suggest.

Interesting Trivia In the Adipose, we see a monster that — despite being made from human fat — is cuddly and adorable. However, the Adipose cuteness isn't the only inversion of the usual alien plot: at the end, the Doctor notes that there was nothing really wrong with their scheme, which is essentially a win-win scenario. The only problem is the legal violation of a Level Five civilization. In theory, we could solve a number of humanity's problems by going through the proper channels and inviting the Adipose back willingly.

The journalist in the story, Penny Carter, was originally going to be the companion for the season before Catherine Tate indicated her willingness to return. Rose's appearance was kept secret even from the press screening and was seen only during broadcast.

The episode was dedicated to the late Howard Attfield, who played Donna's father, Geoff Noble, in "The Runaway Bride." Attfield initially returned to the cast as Geoff but was diagnosed with cancer. All of Wilf's scenes on the hill with Donna were originally shot with Attfield playing Geoff and are available on the deleted scenes of the Complete Fourth Series DVD set. Attfield's condition was so poor it was even mentioned in dialogue. It was determined that Attfield would need to be recast (and indeed he died not long afterwards). Bernard Cribbins, whose role in "Voyage of the Damned" was intended to be for an unrelated character, was subsequently recast as Donna's grandfather. Graeme Harper directed these scenes (along with the scene with Rose) during the making of "Turn Left."

The TARDIS Chronometer The TARDIS lands in an alley near Adipose Industries in early 2009.

Brilliant? (RS?) "Smith and Jones" might have been the perfect season opener, but "Partners in Crime" is a close second. It uses its twin strengths — the more serious theme of weight loss balanced by the out-and-out comedy — to provide us with the perfect vehicle to reintroduce Donna.

This Donna is a slightly milder version than the angry shouter we saw in "The Runaway Bride," which was probably a necessary adjustment for an ongoing companion, but thankfully she still retains some of her fire. She's not afraid to shout at the Doctor on a moment's notice ("I'm not mating with you, sunshine!") but also reveals her vulnerable side, in her regret at letting the Doctor get away. In fact, her sudden shift from desperately wanting to travel with the Doctor to berating him for an apparent come-on ("I'm not having any of that nonsense!") hints at a deeper trauma that we can only guess at, adding a further layer to the character, while keeping their relationship pleasingly nonsexual. After Martha's puppy-dog-eyes arc all but stripped away any other element of her character, Donna's lack of physical attraction to the Doctor is incredibly welcome.

Making Donna and the Doctor just friends and not star-crossed or unrequited lovers was a stroke of genius. It means the show is freed up to do what *Doctor Who* does best: explore new worlds with wonder, expound on the value of friendship and promote compassion, through the lens of the oh-so-human companion.

One of the cleverest but most underappreciated scenes is Donna sitting motionless in the kitchen while Sylvia nags at her, in a series of cross-fades. It's directorially brilliant, it establishes a key relationship of the season and it tells us everything we need to know about what happened to Donna since we last saw her, all without her uttering a word. Donna's clearly not the superficial person she was in "The Runaway Bride." She's now capable of infiltrating a corporation to conduct her own investigation and has thought ahead about what life with the Doctor might involve.

The humour is also top notch. As well as the (justly famous) miming scene, there's the Doctor awkwardly holding Donna's bags, her line "Planet of the hats, I'm ready!" and her dismissal of any potential romance: "You're just a long streak of nothing. Alien nothing." Even throwaway gags like "Hold on!"/"I am!" (when Donna is hanging on the end of a cable) are made much funnier than they have any right to be, thanks to Tate's delivery (in this case, screaming her line back at the Doctor).

The weight theme is one we've seen before from Russell T Davies, but it's one that gets a fuller exploration here. This is Davies playing to his strengths: taking one of society's hot issues, adding an alien component and running through all the permutations. So we have Stacey Campbell dumping her boyfriend, because she can do better than him now that she's lost a few pounds; we have Roger being a tried and true Adipose customer, despite the fact that he's quite thin by the time he meets the Doctor; we have the Adipose lecture extolling the marketing virtues of weight loss in pill form; and we have the Doctor's final assessment that, as a diet plan, it kind of works.

What's particularly interesting is that, for the first time in any medium of *Doctor Who* ever, we have a companion who isn't stick-thin. Thankfully, Donna isn't the least bit interested in the weight-loss program happening around her and explicitly rejects the Doctor as too thin to be attractive. There's probably something very profound in the fact that *Doctor Who* can have a non-white companion before it can have one who isn't Hollywood-thin. Of course, this only happened by accident because Catherine Tate is a big-name star in her own right; an unknown with the same body type would never have been cast in this role. We'll be charitable and gloss over the fact that the first New Series companion the Doctor isn't romantically interested in is also the first one who doesn't look like a model.

"Partners in Crime" hits most of its marks quite effectively. It's funny, it has an engaging theme, the monster is cute rather than terrifying and there's even a shock cameo at the end. Another successful season opener to add to the list.

Second Opinion (GB): For a non-British audience, the significance of Catherine Tate as a lead on *Doctor Who* is somewhat lost. In Britain, Tate is an A-list comedienne whose sketch comedy show is popular and thoroughly catchphrased in popular culture. Her presence in "The Runaway Bride" was stuntcasting, pure and simple. Tate joining the cast takes it to another level: it's like Tina Fey joining the cast of *CSI*.

The clever trick Russell T Davies has done here is establishing that Donna now wants to be the Doctor's companion and in so doing the viewer gets to see the other side of what seemed in "The Runaway Bride" to be the unsuitable companion. And Tate nails it. Her scenes with Bernard Cribbins show that, as well as being wonderfully funny, she's brilliant at these quiet, personal moments at the heart of New *Who*. Donna's frankness makes a nice dynamic with a Doctor more used to greater (though not unquestioning) devotion from his companions. Donna turns out to be a fascinating departure from the typical companion who promises to make for an intriguing season.

The story's chief strength is as a farce. From the Doctor and Donna's near misses and the laugh-out-loud hilarity of their first (inaudible) conversation to the running gag with the reporter being tied up to the scene where Donna finally gets to join the TARDIS (a scene that is the complete antithesis of the way the Doctor wooed Martha on board), great pains are made to ensure that if anything can get a laugh, it will.

The downside of this — and making the Adipose Moomin-esquely cute — is that there's not a lot of jeopardy. Adipose being created from fat people and wobbling up the street, smiling and waving all the while, is really silly. Dementedly silly, admittedly. Brilliantly silly, in fact. The problem is, instead of being macabre, it's played for laughs and everything seems off-kilter as a result.

As season premieres go for New *Who*, it seems the odd-numbered seasons introduce a completely new companion with a fast-paced journey into terror. The even-numbered seasons do a frothy romp with a wafer-thin plot using characters who have already been established. "Partners in Crime" is the latter, but it's enjoyable goofy. And when the person Donna talks to about her car turns around, you realize that the answer to the question "What could top the Daleks, Cybermen and the Master this season?" is, well, *her* . . .

Catherine Tate

Born in 1968, Catherine Tate was 40 when her episodes as companion Donna Noble were broadcast, making Tate the oldest actress to play a female companion on *Doctor Who*. Tate is arguably the most well-known actor to ever work as a regular on the Classic or New Series. By the time she first appeared in "The Runaway Bride," Tate had already worked on three seasons of her own BBC comedy series, *The Catherine Tate Show*; her character, Lauren Cooper, was hugely popular.

While many see Tate's *Doctor Who* role as a move to drama for the comedienne, she already had serious dramatic credentials, having worked with the Royal Shakespeare Company and in a number of more serious West End productions before her comedic roles. She continued to work in theatre following *Doctor Who*. In 2011, Tate appeared in the U.S. version of *The Office* as Nellie Bertram, a potential replacement for Steve Carrell's Michael Scott. Tate's character was so popular that she appeared in a recurring role during *The Office*'s eighth season.

4.02 The Fires of Pompeii

Written by James Moran **Directed by** Colin Teague

Supporting cast Peter Capaldi (Caecilius), Tracey Childs (Metella), Phil Davis (Lucius Petrus Dextrus), Sasha Behar (Spurrina), Francesca Fowler (Evelina), Lorraine Burroughs (Thalina), Victoria Wicks (high priestess), Francois Pandolfo (Quintus), Karen Gillan (soothsayer), Phil Cornwell (stallholder)

Original airdate April 12, 2008

The Big Idea It's Volcano Day in Pompeii, and the Doctor and Donna have different ideas about what to do when Vesuvius erupts.

Roots and References The HBO series *Rome* (soap opera developments in Roman times; the episode was also shot on *Rome*'s sets at Cinecittà studios); the Cambridge Latin curriculum used for secondary students in Britain (Caecilius and his family); *Asterix* comics, particularly *Asterix and the Laurel Wreath* (the cheeky Latinate names, particularly Lucius Petrus Dextrus, which translates as "Lucius Stone Right Arm"); *Spartacus* (both the Doctor and Donna declare, "I am Spartacus"); *Fawlty Towers* ("You must excuse my friend, she's from Barcelona.")

Adventures in Time and Space The Doctor references inspiring the Great Fire of Rome (1965's "The Romans"). The TARDIS translation facility not only translates verbal language (as established in "The End of the World"), it makes all written language look like English to Donna, explaining a curious translation convention that dates all the way back to 1963's "The Daleks." Caecilius purchases the TARDIS as a piece of modern art, a joke that references a famous scene where the TARDIS is appreciated by two art critics in a gallery (played by Eleanor Bron and John Cleese) in 1979's "City of Death."

The Doctor says it's Volcano Day, a phrase used for Vesuvius's explosion by Captain Jack in "The Empty Child." (There might be a rogue Time Agent around, working on a self-cleaning con.) Lucius tells Donna, "You have something on your back" (we'll find out what in "Turn Left").

The Bees Are Disappearing Effect For the second story in a row, a planet has been lost, this time the Pyrovile homeworld, Pyrovilia. Another recurring meme this season, the Medusa Cascade (previously noted by the Master in "Last of the Time Lords") gets a mention. Lucius warns the Doctor, "She is coming."

Who is the Doctor? The Doctor tries to explain to Donna that, as a Time Lord, he can see what events are fixed and what events are in flux because it's how he sees the universe every waking second: "I can see what is, what was, what could be, what must not. It's the burden of a Time Lord."

The Doctor and Donna Caecilius first takes the Doctor and Donna to be a married couple (a mistake that will be repeated by others throughout the season) and then brother and sister. She violently disagrees with the Doctor's refusal to intervene, and she prevents him from leaving until he saves just Caecilius and his family. At the end, the Doctor finally welcomes Donna aboard, stating that she was right in "The Runaway Bride": he does need someone to stop him.

Monster of the Week The Pyrovile are creatures made of rock that move thanks to the living magma inside them. Thousands of years before this story took place, an escape pod they were using crashed into Earth and the impact pulverized them at the base of what became known as Mount Vesuvius. They remained dormant until an earthquake 17 years before this story reawakened them.

Stand Up and Cheer The climactic moment where Donna gets in the Doctor's face and convinces him to go back to save Caecilius and his family is a stunning scene. Not only does Donna get past the Doctor's own self-loathing about the Time Lords' destruction, but Catherine Tate takes on David Tennant in full-on shouty mode, no less. Director Colin Teague radically departs from the usual formal composition of TARDIS scenes and shoots the scene close with a handheld camera, giving the sequence a raw intensity. It's nicely followed by the TARDIS's return to deliver salvation to just one family, which should be one of the iconic moments of the David Tennant era.

Roll Your Eyes It's coming to the point where any interior with amber-tinged marble instantly draws attention to the fact it was probably shot on location at the Cardiff civic building, the Temple of Peace, which has been used in "The End of the World," "Gridlock," here and, later, in "Cold Blood" and "Let's Kill Hitler" (where the exterior for the building also gets used). It's like the Willhelm Scream of *Doctor Who* locations: once you recognize it, you can't escape noticing it.

You're Not Making Any Sense The puzzle of why the soothsayers in Pompeii could accurately predict the future but couldn't predict Vesuvius's eruption is waved off with the explanation, "The explosion cracked open a rift in time. Just a second, that echoed back into the Pyrovilian alternative." This made things so much clearer. Thanks for that.

Interesting Trivia The story, surprisingly, keeps to the historic record: in AD 79 on August 23, Mount Vesuvius erupted, following several days of minor quakes. Where the story takes poetic licence is in the actual eruption: it actually took place over two days, starting around the 20th, with 16,000 people being killed in pyroclastic flows of superheated gas and ash which came down from the volcano about 18 hours after the initial eruption. (Donna tries in vain to get people to move to higher ground instead of towards the sea to avoid it.)

Writer James Moran borrowed Caecilius and his family from the Cambridge Latin Course textbooks, a popular curriculum for teaching Latin in British secondary schools. Those textbooks mostly focus on the story of Quintus, but Caecilius and Metella also appear. (There was no daughter, so Moran added Evelina to the mix.) Caecilius himself (in this story and in the Cambridge textbooks) is a fictionalized version of an actual Pompeii resident, Lucius Caecilius Iucundus, a banker who probably died in the earlier earthquake in Pompeii in AD 62.

Oh, and that tall, redheaded soothsayer who follows the Doctor and Donna as they search for the TARDIS? She's played by an actress named Karen Gillan, who will become important to *Doctor Who* in a little while . . .

The TARDIS Chronometer Pompeii, AD 79, the day before Volcano Day.

Brilliant? (GB) We've always been told that the companion is the audience surrogate. In practice, that's not totally true. The companion is a stand-in for the audience in the respect that she's an ordinary human who finds herself in the company of a Time Lord with a magic blue box, but most companions are happy to go along for the ride and don't put up much of a fuss. If most viewers had the opportunity to travel in the TARDIS, they'd ask the Doctor things like, "Where's the bathroom?," "Why don't people ever experience jet lag in time travel?" and "Why aren't you saving these people?"

Which brings us to Donna Noble, why she's so great and why "The Fires of Pompeii" is such a delightful story. Pretty much from the second she exits the TARDIS and walks the Pompeii streets with the Doctor, she's got lots of ordinary but interesting questions that would occur to most people if they got to travel through time in a police box. How is it she can see written English? What happens with the TARDIS translation facility if you use Latin phrases to people who speak Latin? There are lots of great moments for the audience to go, "I would have asked that myself!"

But where Donna does something really different from other companions is that, through her dispute with the Doctor about saving the people of Pompeii, she and the Doctor have the central conflict of the episode. The last time that happened was, sort of, in "Father's Day" and then you have to go back to 1964's "The Aztecs." With "The Fires of Pompeii," the conflict between Donna and the Doctor drives the whole episode, with Donna's attempts to tip off Evelina getting her noticed by the sisterhood, and her continuing to get in the Doctor's face and asking constantly why these people have to die. The great thing is that she refuses to take "just because" as an answer. Even after being given the temporal mechanics, she asks the Doctor how many residents of Pompeii die. Donna puts it down to human terms, always, and it's a nice pairing with the tenth Doctor who is very fallibly human in how he handles things.

The conflict between the Doctor and Donna also sets up an interesting frame for the Doctor to tell Donna he's the last Time Lord. With Rose in "The End of the World," the very act of naming his race was a huge thing for the Doctor. With Martha in "Gridlock," he moved to remembering. Here, the Doctor is forced to relive the choices he made as he condemns even more people to death. In the stunning climactic scene in the TARDIS, all his anger and pain about causing his own people to burn comes tumbling out; David Tennant is in top form performing this scene. However, where Rose and Martha greeted this revelation with sympathy, Donna doesn't let it drop. She insists that the Doctor not simply resign himself to how things have to be and begs him to go back and at least save the family they met. It's a powerful moment, and Catherine Tate is excellent in it. As she is for the whole episode.

It's fascinating the ways the story gets us ready for that explosive climax. The viewer instantly gets Caecilius' family because it's really a typical sitcom family: bumbling dad, domineering mum and rebellious son. It's only the soothsaying, petrifying daughter that reminds everyone they're watching *Doctor Who*. They're immediately identifiable and Peter Capaldi is a likeable milquetoast, so their imminent death becomes achingly real.

The problem for this story is that it employs a lot of other convenient television shorthand as well. The female cult of paranormals feels like a well-worn cliché by now (from Classic *Who*, for starters: they're almost a direct lift from 1975's "The Brain of Morbius"). While Phil Davis (and his scary overbite) is actually pretty good as Lucius, the character also feels like it's been borrowed from *The Life of Brian* and other Roman send-ups. The necessity for the convenient shorthand is because an awful lot is packed into this story. There are huge swathes of cosmology and the Pyrovile plan is needlessly complicated. I'm also not sure what is gained by having both the sisterhood and Lucius. At the same time, it could have been made a little more complex: the revelation that the Pyrovile are trying to cheat history so they can take over the world makes the moral dilemma faced by the Doctor and Donna far too easy.

And yet, I come to praise "The Fires of Pompeii," not to bury it. The character drama central to the story is brilliantly written, acted and directed by people at the top of their game. It's genuinely funny (the running gag of Latin phrases feedback looping into Welsh gets surprising mileage). The use of the Ancient Roman backlot at Cinecittà Studios gives it a much-needed boost of verisimilitude (though undermined a little when supplementing it with Cardiff locations). Where it really works is that it shows us the potential and power of a character like Donna Noble. Oi, Spaceman, you better watch out.

Second Opinion (RS?) What he said. Only without the disdain towards the Cardiff architecture.

As far back as 1964's "The Aztecs," the Doctor told his companion, "You can't change history, not one line!" Which always seemed strange because in stories set in the future, such as the next one, 1964's "The Sensorites," the Doctor and his companions changed events all the time. Isn't everything, as Donna points out to the Doctor in "The Fires of Pompeii," history at some point?

The immutability of history starts taking a kicking with stories like 1965's "The Time Meddler," which featured a rival Time Lord trying to prevent the Battle of Hastings in 1066. By 1975's "Pyramids of Mars," the producers decided to illustrate how the Doctor's time-travelling adventures can affect history. In that story, the Doctor and Sarah Jane fight the Egyptian demi-god Sutekh in 1912. Sarah notes that, in her time, Sutekh obviously hadn't won, so why are they worried? The Doctor takes Sarah back to her own time, where Earth is now a desolate wasteland. The meaning is clear: history can be rewritten at any time. It's a point reiterated in "The Unquiet Dead" (indeed, many drafts of the script featured a similar scene where the Doctor and Rose find the Gelth had destroyed Earth in the present day) and it's reiterated throughout the New Series.

However, the series was still quick to point out that certain events in Earth's history are still important, though it seems to be selective as to why, say, stopping a giant rat in Victorian England in 1977's "The Talons of Weng-Chiang" apparently has no impact on course of events while the Doctor is careful not to stop the Great Fire of London in 1666 in 1982's "The Visitation."

It's not until the New Series that we start to have an explanation for this. In *Doctor Who*'s cosmology there are events that are in flux and events that are fixed. The events in flux can be influenced and changed, but the events that are fixed are unchanging, immutable. Only a Time Lord, who can see what is, what was and what could be, is capable of discerning the difference.

Pompeii is a fixed event, though its cause turns out to be the Doctor and Donna interfering with the Pyrovile. In "The Waters of Mars," the destruction of Bowie Base One on Mars in 2057 is a fixed event that has serious repercussions on future events. In that story, the Doctor actually attempts to change fixed events, and the result is that history still wins: the events that needed to happen still happen, just in a different, more tragic, way.

Presumably stories like "The Aztecs" and "The Visitation" also deal with fixed events. One could also make the case that Pete Tyler's death in "Father's Day" was a fixed event, which is perhaps why it brings about the Reapers coming to sterilize the Earth.

Events appear to be in flux more than they are fixed. The Doctor points out that Agatha Christie could still die prematurely in 1926 in "The Unicorn and the Wasp," and the events of "The Shakespeare Code" could change Martha's present. The Doctor specifically notes in "Cold Blood" that an accord between humans and Silurians is possible precisely because it's an event that isn't fixed.

With changing personal timelines, it's a somewhat greyer area. The Doctor tells Rose in "The Parting of the Ways" and Donna in "The Runaway Bride" that once the TARDIS becomes a part of events he cannot go back in that timeline. That seems to be flatly contradicted at other points, such as "A Christmas Carol" or "Vincent and the Doctor." In those two cases, the intended interventions do not have the desired effect, which may be why it's avoided as a general practice.

Doctor Who seems to hold to the principle that time is, in many ways, a spatial dimension and the only reason humans see it differently is due to their perception of reality. In "Blink," the Doctor says, "People assume that time is a strict progression of cause to effect, but actually, from a nonlinear, nonsubjective viewpoint, it's more like a big ball of wibbly-wobbly, timey-wimey stuff." This means that history is constantly being rewritten, because it's not really history at all.

4.03 Planet of the Ood

Written by Keith Temple **Directed by** Graeme Harper

Supporting cast Tim McInnerny (Klineman Halpen), Ayesha Dharker (Solana Mercurio), Adrian Rawlins (Dr. Ryder), Roger Griffiths (Commander Kess), Paul Clayton (Mr. Bartle), Paul Kasey (Ood Sigma), Tariq Jorden (Rep), Silas Carson (voice of the Ood)

Original airdate April 19, 2008

The Big Idea The Doctor takes Donna to her first alien planet, only to discover it's the planet where the Ood are sold into slavery by a greedy corporation.

Roots and References Naomi Klein's *No Logo* (faceless corporation makes people into commodities); *Altered States* (Halpen's comeuppance); *Starship Troopers* (the ad that opens the story).

Adventures in Time and Space This story is a sequel to "The Impossible Planet"/"The Satan Pit." The Doctor notes that the Ood Sphere neighbours the Sense Sphere, home of the Sensorites, the eponymous race of 1964's "The Sensorites." The Sensorites look quite similar to the Ood and also possess telepathic abilities. (Much of this, according to Russell T Davies, was coincidence but when it came to light it was decided to emphasize the connection.) The giant brain is reminiscent of 1987's "Time and the Rani." The Doctor marvels that he finally gets to see real snow on the Ood Sphere, after several Christmas specials finding fake snow of various sorts.

The Bees Are Disappearing Effect Donna lists the bees disappearing among the global concerns of her era, and the Doctor briefly notes that all the bees disappearing is a bit odd. At the end of the episode, the Doctor is told, ominously, by Ood Sigma, "I think your song must end. Every song must end." We'll come back to this in "Planet of the Dead."

The Doctor and Donna Donna continues to subvert the Doctor's own expectations for a companion: when he expounds on the wonders of being on her first planet, she's gone back inside the TARDIS to get a coat! When he moralizes about the selling of Ood not being different than sweatshop labour, she asks him, "Is that why you travel round with a human at your side? It's not so you can show them the wonders of the universe, it's so you can take cheap shots?"

Monster of the Week We learn more about the Ood's physiology and development with this story. The Ood are three-brained creatures: they carry in their hands a second hindbrain with all the facets that give them individuality. During processing, this brain is cut off and the translator ball is installed instead. There is a third collective brain, a giant entity found beneath one of the glaciers on the Ood Sphere. The dampening field and the translator balls effectively lobotomize the Ood.

Stand Up and Cheer The scene where the Doctor allows Donna to hear the Ood song and she asks an unprocessed Ood to show what they're holding in their hands is one of the most heartbreaking scenes in *Doctor Who* this season. Part of the reason it works is how achingly real Donna seems, quickly asking for the ability to hear the song to be taken away. But credit must also go to the actors in the Ood masks (particularly Paul Kasey) who make the Ood distinctive through the subtlest of movements.

Roll Your Eyes Ryder's sudden reveal as a member of Friends Of The Ood is the sort of comical side-changing you'd expect at the climax of an *Austin Powers* movie.

You're Not Making Any Sense Halpen's transformation into an Ood seems reverse engineered to justify the cool visual — science, story logic and characterization be damned. How could the transformation be instantaneous? How did Ood Sigma come up with the quantities of the genetic MacGuffin needed to make such a transformation occur without being noticed? And why would he come up with such a scheme?

Interesting Trivia We were told that the Fourth Great and Bountiful Human Empire was scheduled for 200,000 in "The Long Game." Here we see the Second and it's 4126. This means there are at least two Great and Bountiful Human Empires unaccounted for. It doesn't seem as though we've had the first yet, so that means the First and Second are about 2,000 years apart. We have no idea when the Third is, but even if it's precisely in the middle of the Second and Fourth, that still leaves almost 100,000 years of dreariness and misery between

Great and Bountiful Human Empires. Why so long? We know of almost nothing between the 51st century and 200,000 and the little we do know (such as the solar flares that devastate Earth in 1975's "The Ark in Space") is dystopic.

This story genuinely feels like a natural progression from "The Impossible Planet" and "The Satan Pit" in our discovery of the Ood. Where the previous story shows a culture that has accepted the PR that the Ood are a natural servant race, here we go behind the PR to discover the truth is altogether more unsettling. We also learn new details about the Ood themselves: befitting a creature who has three brains, the Ood are more powerful psychics than previously realized; they deliver an ominous prophesy for the Doctor and even their designation, "TheDoctorDonna," has implications down the road.

The TARDIS Chronometer The Ood Sphere, 4126.

Brilliant? (GB) *Doctor Who* fans are always on the lookout for that episode which combines wit, intelligent plotting and quotable dialogue with gorgeous visuals and high production values. Think "The Empty Child"/"The Doctor Dances" or "The Caves of Androzani" or "The Deadly Assassin." All too often, we settle for an episode where the writing delivers more than the direction or the production values: "Rose" or "The Pirate Planet." With the New Series, we have an increasing number of episodes where, even though the story isn't quite up to scratch, it still looks stunning. Say hello to "Planet of the Ood."

Thankfully, "Planet of the Ood" isn't particularly bad. It just isn't particularly consistent (alcohol is banned in Ood Operations, but the visiting executives enthuse about an open bar). Plus, the Doctor actually contributes negligibly to the resolution. Ryder has done most of the job and the Ood have done the rest. All the Doctor has to do this episode is get chased by an admittedly cool CGI robot claw and then disable the most easily defusable explosive device in history.

Some of the disconnects are down to editing: the DVD release revealed the excision of several key scenes dropped for the sake of speeding the story up (hence how the Doctor knows the condition is colloquially called "red eye"). And yet, no amount of editing can cover how unbelievably generic it all is: Ood are seeing red (literally and figuratively) and rebelling. Guards in black are being mean. What's the secret in Warehouse 15? There are chases and there are emotional scenes that happen almost on schedule. It borders on being *Who*-by-numbers. The clumsy attempts at relevancy, by comparing Ood Operations with greedy corporate practices in a world of free trade, don't do the story any favours either. It's no wonder Donna smacks down the Doctor's only attempt to be explicit about this; globalization is a vast problem that won't be solved by freeing the third brain.

In many ways, the episode works in spite of, not because of, the story. There are several contributing factors to this. The first are the Ood themselves.

They have a magnificent prosthetic: even though it covers the actor's face, it is wonderfully expressive and evokes tremendous empathy. The second is the production design. The central irony of New *Who* is that stories set in cold climates are shot in the height of summer and hot climates are shot in the dead of winter. ("Planet of the Ood" was shot in August!) There are a couple of points where it doesn't work (if you look closely, you can see it's just a fertile landscape sprayed over white, and the brief glimpse of an unfrozen pond doesn't help), but, for the most part, the combination of CGI work, practical effects and the cunning use of location sells the Ood Sphere as an ice planet.

But as the story is directed by Graeme Harper, I wouldn't expect anything less. He not only imbues the story with a sense of place, he gives it a sense of scale, whether in the scenes where we see a massive line of Ood walking out during a shift change, or in the battle sequences between the corporate security goons and the Ood. As ever, Harper is a master of the well-used closeup: not merely content to point a camera in someone's face, he makes sure his performers bring out the right emotions as well.

Harper's sense of casting hasn't failed him, either. He's keenly aware of the satirical connotations within Keith Temple's script and populates it with suitable grotesques. Tim McInnery is delightful as Halpen, the cartoonish tycoon, but it's Ayesha Dharker who steals the show as Solana, the PR flack who wills herself to believe the talking points even when everything around her contradicts it: banal evil as 21st-century MarCom.

But the performance that makes this story really worth watching is Catherine Tate. The viewer believes the horror of the crime against the Ood because Donna's reactions are so honest. Her asking the Doctor to take away the singing from her mind is what any ordinary person would do, and her outrage with Halpen is spine-tingling. *Doctor Who* has enabled Tate to demonstrate her amazing range, which shows how pigeon-holed she'd been in her previous roles. And Donna's relationship with David Tennant's Doctor is awesome to watch, alternating between honest respect and bristling remarks.

In fairness to writer Keith Temple, nothing Harper, Tate or the rest of the cast does sprang up on our screens *ex nihilo*. The genius of "Planet of the Ood" is that they take the inspired bits of Temple's script and make it the dominant tone, then throw in dynamic and exciting visuals and performances on top of it. The story is also wonderfully cut together, as scenes where Solana markets the Ood are cut with scenes where the Ood are hunted down by Kess. The result is a highly entertaining 45 minutes of *Doctor Who*. The problem for me, though, is that the script should have been more than just a few incredible moments expanded and refracted by a brilliant director and cast.

"Planet of the Ood" is not particularly good or bad; it's just very generic. Highly entertaining, occasionally stunningly brilliant, but still very generic.

Second Opinion (RS?) This is a story that so desperately wants to be cutting-edge and relevant, yet fails almost entirely because it hasn't caught up to the century it's living in. Once upon a time, this would have been brilliant, because commentary on the evils of big business hadn't been done to death. However, in the 21st century, with the diffusion of media, television is no longer the only place where you or I will see a biting critique of corporate practices or slavery. And, without anything new to say, "Planet of the Ood" falls down rather badly.

Which is a shame, because it's actively trying to be more than throwaway entertainment. It has a message and it wants to get it out, only the story spends too much time on a cool CGI chase through a warehouse (that is admittedly spectacular, but that's largely because it's literally nothing more than spectacle) and not enough on the nuances of the Ood.

That said, Donna is absolutely fantastic in this one. It's the story that fleshes out her third dimension, and it shows that her belligerance can be put to shockingly effective use. Her "you idiot!" diatribe against Halpen is awesome. However, there's something very strange happening with what should have been the central moral debate: the Doctor raises an excellent point about slavery in our culture ("Who made your shoes?"), Donna slaps him down for making a cheap shot . . . and then he backs away. Huh? This had the makings of an excellent discussion of a thorny issue, one directly relevant to the story at hand and yet the writers scuttled away from it because it might frighten the horses. Had the Doctor not given in, we might have seen Donna forced to confront her own prejudices, inspired by the Doctor's beliefs, and question how close elements of our society are to that of the Ood. What's frustrating is that you can see the seeds sown in the story for exactly that and yet it's as though someone got cold feet, deleted the explicit parts of the argument and hoped we'd get it on its own.

That's "Planet of the Ood" in a nutshell. A promising story, working against its own limitations, ultimately producing something that's definitely interesting, but which should have been fabulous. Frustrating, in the extreme.

4.04—4.05 The Sontaran Stratagem / The Poison Sky

Written by Helen Raynor **Directed by** Douglas MacKinnon

Supporting cast Freema Agyeman (Martha Jones), Bernard Cribbins (Wilfred Mott), Jacqueline King (Sylvia Noble), Christopher Ryan (General Staal), Rupert Holliday Evans (Colonel Mace), Dan Starkey (Commander Skorr), Eleanor Matsuura (Jo Nakashima), Ryan Sampson (Luke Rattigan), Christian Cooke (Ross Jenkins), Bridget Hodgson

(Captain Price), Kirsty Wark (herself), Lachele Carl (U.S. newsreader)

Original airdates April 26 and May 3, 2008

The Big Idea The Sontarans have implanted half the world's cars with ATMOS, in a plan to turn the Earth into a new breeding world.

Roots and References *Invasion of the Body Snatchers* (Martha's clone assisting an alien invasion); *Revenge of the Nerds* (Rattigan and his academy); *An Inconvenient Truth* (the contribution of fossil fuels and motor vehicles to the impending environmental crisis); the nuisance of SatNav GPS systems in cars.

Adventures in Time and Space Martha calls the Doctor on her mobile, as she promised at the end of "Last of the Time Lords." She's engaged to Tom Milligan, her contact in the erased year during that same story, and she tells Donna that her family ended up in prison and tortured ("Last of the Time Lords" again).

Wilf and the Doctor reminisce about "Voyage of the Damned," while Sylvia remembers the Doctor from Donna's wedding ("The Runaway Bride"). The Sontarans "weren't allowed" to be part of the Time War ("Rose" et al.).

UNIT is now said to stand for "Unified Intelligence Taskforce," a change from "United Nations Intelligence Taskforce." UNIT is still located at the Tower of London ("The Christmas Invasion"), although journalists are now aware of it. The *Valiant* makes an appearance ("The Sound of Drums"/"Last of the Time Lords") and uses a weapon very similar to that seen in "The Christmas Invasion."

The Doctor recalls working for UNIT "back in the '70s. Or was it the '80s?" This is a reference to the notorious difficulties in dating the Classic UNIT stories. They use the callsign "Greyhound 16 to Trap 1," a nod to the UNIT callsigns of old. Brigadier Alistair Gordon Lethbridge-Stewart, the Doctor's old UNIT ally, is mentioned (currently in Peru and now knighted).

Staal says that females have a weak thorax, which was said in 1974's "The Time Warrior." The Rutans are mentioned (1977's "Horror of Fang Rock"). The Doctor dons a gas mask and asks, "Are you my mummy?" ("The Empty Child"). There's a reference to Martha knowing Captain Jack ("Utopia" et al.). Lachele Carl's AMNN reporter appears ("Aliens of London" et al.).

The Bees Are Disappearing Effect The Doctor lists places that he wants to take Donna, including the 15th broken moon of the Medusa Cascade. Rose appears briefly on the TARDIS scanner, mouthing "Doctor," but only Donna is in the TARDIS and she doesn't notice.

Who is the Doctor? The Doctor is vaguely embarrassed by his former cronies from UNIT, acting as though he's at a high school reunion he wants no part of: he doesn't like saluting, orders, being called "sir" or having people around him carrying guns. (Odd, since he didn't mind recommending Martha to UNIT.)

Monster of the Week Short and troll-like, the Sontarans wear armour and helmets that barely cover their heads. They're grown in batches and are dedicated to warfare. Their only weakness is the probic vent at the back of the neck. They take hypnotic control of humans, download a human's memory into a clone and chant "Sontar-Ha!" when victory nears.

Stand Up and Cheer The reunion with Martha is quite nice, when she calls the Doctor back to Earth. Her immediate bonding with Donna (who even notices Martha's engagement ring when the Doctor doesn't) is lovely. And Martha ordering the massive UNIT operation now that she's brought the Doctor in is magnificent.

Roll Your Eyes ATMOS may be the stupidest acronym in the world. It stands for Atmospheric Emissions System, and Rattigan keeps making the point that the S stands for System. So what does the O stand for? Or the M? Either it's ATMOspheric emissions System and we're supposed to ignore the word "emissions" or it's some weird selection of letters. If Rattigan's such a genius, why did he create such a rubbish brand?

You're Not Making Any Sense The Doctor's weapon solves the problem by igniting the unbreathable gas in the atmosphere (and somehow not setting the entire world on fire despite the fact that the gas is also down at ground level), leaving the rest of the breathable atmosphere intact (incredibly quickly, we note). He then takes his weapon to the Sontaran ship in order to ignite the air on board. Only the Sontarans don't breathe the gas, they breathe the same atmosphere as us. Rattigan and Donna spend significant time on the Sontaran ship and never have any trouble with their breathing. So why does the weapon even work?

Interesting Trivia We're given a retcon for Wilf's absence from Donna's wedding in "The Runaway Bride": he had Spanish Flu. If so, he's simultaneously incredibly unlucky and lucky. He's unlucky because Spanish Flu hasn't existed for about 90 years and, since 2007, only six samples of it exist in the world, all sealed away for research purposes. But he's lucky, because it was one of the deadliest natural disasters in history, killing as many people in six months as the Black Death did in 200 years. So if he did catch it, he was fortunate to survive.

Following the production team's tussle with the real-world U.N. after "Aliens of London," the United Nations Intelligence Taskforce has suddenly become the Unified Intelligence Taskforce. The official title should be spelled UNified Intelligence Taskforce, capitalizing the appropriate letters, but for some reason it's not done this way in the scripts or in any other documentation. (It's possible this was done to further distance the organisation from the U.N., but equally possible that nobody thought through the mechanics of the acronym carefully enough.) This means the organisation should really be UIT, but that sounds less like a global anti-alien incursion group and more like a small-town university.

The TARDIS Chronometer It lands in an alley near the ATMOS factory, not far from Chiswick, three days after Donna left with the Doctor.

Brilliant? (RS?) It's not quite as bad as "Evolution of the Daleks." But that's not for want of trying.

Did Colonel Mace kick the Doctor's puppy? The Doctor's rude to him in almost every interaction they have and with no provocation whatsoever. I personally don't much approve of the military and I hate guns, but I don't feel the need to act like a petulant teenager every time I speak to someone in uniform. The Doctor acts like a right-wing stereotype of a pious leftie. Not only is it deeply annoying, it makes no sense: Captain Jack carried a gun, K9 has one and the Doctor's worked happily alongside many people who've carried them. Including — and I can't stress this enough — members of the Unified Intelligence Taskforce.

Once upon a time, there was a draft of this story where this theme of guns made sense. Several drafts later, in the version that made it to screen, the Doctor goes on and on about how much he hates anyone who so much as carries a gun. Not just uses one without giving your enemies a choice, but simply carrying one. Which is fine, we rather agree with that. But then he goes and builds a kickass weapon that will destroy the atmosphere in the Sontaran ship and teleports aboard, fully intending to use it. So how is this not carrying a gun? Is it okay to do it if you made your firearm in your back shed, just so long as no profits went to Smith & Wesson?

In that draft, which might have approached watchable television, there was also a thoughtful story about the environment that examined the issue from all angles. As it is, we're left with Sylvia's ridiculous line, "All the things they said about pollution and ozone and carbon, they're really happening aren't they?" and that's about it. Hint to whomever abandoned that draft and wrote this version instead: if you actually want to examine an issue, you can't just insert one line of dialogue and assume that's enough.

The story is wrapped around the character of Rattigan, but he's deeply annoying and can't pronounce "cleverer." He's supposed to be the smartest person on Earth, but he gets hysterical at someone correcting his grammar. Hint for the next draft: truly smart people aren't insecure. Rattigan is a stereotype of a too-clever nerd, written by someone who's never actually met a human being. Oh, and his students wear godawful tracksuits and serve no purpose in the story whatsoever. None.

This story gave me new respect for Russell T Davies, because it shows just how badly his ideas can go in the wrong hands. ATMOS is pulled straight from the Davies holster: it's a slight extrapolation of a new, everyday technology; there's a worldwide threat; there are newscasts featuring Lachele Carl and images from around the world (the Sydney Opera House is seen wreathed in gas); and someone describes it as the end of days. There's even a "What?" coda.

And yet, everything about ATMOS is ridiculous. We're supposed to believe that it's programmed with UNIT's top-secret headquarters in the SatNav system, that trained soldiers dare not think to contradict it (Ross reacts with disbelief when the Doctor tells him to turn right when ATMOS said left) and that not a single scientist who examined it ever noticed that each box was storing enormous quantities of poisonous gas? These questions often arise in a Davies script too, but there the pace is so fast and the charm so great that you can smile and move on. Here, you can only grimace.

The Martha clone acts out of character, not caring for her own family and giving none-too-subtle signals that Something Is Wrong. The Doctor keeps glancing her way whenever one of these moments occurs and asks pointed questions for which she gives answers we know to be deeply out of character. And then the Doctor identifies her not because he fundamentally, emotionally knows the soul of Martha Jones . . . but because the clone has contracted pupils and thinning hair?! This is nonsensical.

Then there's that kiss between Colonel Mace and his female lieutenant. Where the hell did that come from and what is it still doing in this draft? It has no buildup and no connection to anything. Here's another hint: if you want an emotional payoff for a romance, then you have to actually give the characters in question some chemistry beforehand. Or dialogue.

Something clearly went terribly and horribly wrong with this story. Its heart is in the right place, but nothing else is. From 30,000 feet, this is a story featuring a hero who doesn't use guns, fighting an alien invasion alongside UNIT, saved by the heroic self-sacrifice of a mad scientist who saw reason in his final minutes. But if you look any closer, all these elements are deeply flawed and none of it joins up. The only parts that actually work are those with Donna and her family, which have nothing to do with the rest of the story. Everything else is a hideous mess.

Second Opinion (GB): You know the fan trope that even-numbered *Star Trek* films are better than odd-numbered ones. I think I've found the *Doctor Who* equivalent. Stories where David Tennant wears the blue suit are generally worse than ones where he wears the brown one.

Okay, there are exceptions: "Smith and Jones" is pretty good (though the Doctor reverts to the brown suit at the end of the story), and so is "Time Crash" (but that's not really a full story). Take those out of the equation and what do you have? "Daleks in Manhattan"/"Evolution of the Daleks," "The Lazarus

Experiment," "42." It's no wonder the Doctor got into a tux as quick as he could in "Voyage of the Damned." That tux is unlucky, but the blue suit is just dire.

"The Sontaran Stratagem"/"The Poison Sky" may well be the poster child for the "blue suit bad" movement. It takes two of the best things about the Classic Series (UNIT and the Sontarans) and one of the best things about the New Series (Martha Jones), and makes them all useless and, worse, dull. Christopher Ryan's Colonel Blimp–ish portrayal of Staal is a bad cartoon. The Doctor being prissy with UNIT is even more annoying than Robert says it is, but it would be almost bearable if Colonel Mace had even an ounce of charisma, or if any of the soldiers except Ross were actually competent. And is Freema Agyeman being punished for leaving her car in Julie Gardner's parking spot or something? Martha has absolutely nothing to do, and the only decent scene Agyeman has finds her acting opposite herself.

About the only thing that saves the story from outright direness is Donna, who is sublime super-temping the solution to the ATMOS factory mystery and then helping the Doctor remotely on the Sontaran ship. Sylvia's pragmatic solution to Wilf's dilemma (as opposed to the Doctor dramatically posing in the middle of the road) also gets a big cheer. Otherwise, the politics are heavy-handed (Helen Raynor, the 1990s called: they want their earnest environmental message back), the direction is ham-fisted, the art direction is lazy (and seems to boil down to "just use violet coloured floodlights on everything") and Rattigan and his tracksuited academy would have been rejected from *The Sarah Jane Adventures* for being too juvenile. There's so much to be angry at, I might as well just blame the blue suit.

The Psychic Papers: The Sontarans

The Sontarans are a race of militaristic humanoids, although they look anything but human. They were introduced in 1974's "The Time Warrior" when a single Sontaran crashed on Earth in the Middle Ages. The surprise at the end of the first episode was when it took off its neckless, semi-spherical helmet and revealed that its head was exactly the same shape!

The Sontarans value war above all else. They're a clone race (despite their appearance changing both subtly and profoundly over the succeeding decades) and they can breed millions of hatchlings at once. Their only weakness is a probic vent at the back of the neck; pressure to it can render them unconscious and a direct hit can kill them. Sontarans take pride in this, however, as it means the only way the weakness can be exploited is in retreat — and they never retreat.

They've been at war with the Rutans, a race of jellyfish-like shapeshifters seen only once in the Classic Series (in 1977's "Horror of Fang Rock"), for millennia. Indeed, they've fought for so long that, as the Doctor once stated, neither side can even remember how or why the war began. The Sontarans' second appearance, in 1975's "The Sontaran Experiment," was set thousands of years in our future and saw another lone Sontaran on Earth, this time performing gruesome experiments on the natives in preparation for a possible invasion. The Sontarans attempted to invade Gallifrey in 1978's "The Invasion of Time" and also appeared in 1985's "The Two Doctors." Both of these stories show the Sontarans, who have limited time-travel ability, seeking the secret of full time travel for a military advantage in their war with the Rutans.

The Sontarans aren't necessarily evil but are focused on winning their war, and they will do whatever it takes to achieve that aim. They value honour, especially in death. They come from a high gravity planet, explaining their stocky appearance, and fly in spherical ships. They're expert hypnotists and all appear to be male. Some versions have three fingers, others have five.

The Sontarans bear the dubious honour of being the last recurring monster (defined as a monster appearing in more than two stories) until the Ood in the New Series.

4.06 The Doctor's Daughter

Written by Stephen Greenhorn **Directed by** Alice Troughton

Supporting cast Freema Agyeman (Martha Jones), Georgia Moffett (Jenny), Nigel Terry (Cobb), Joe Dempsie (Cline), Paul Kasey (Hath Peck), Ruari Mears (Hath Gable), Akin Gazi (Carter), Olalekan Lawal Jr. (soldier)

Original airdate May 10, 2008

The Big Idea The Doctor becomes an instant dad and has to come to grips with his newfound daughter, Jenny, while sorting out a generational war between humans and the Hath.

Roots and References Walter Miller's 1960 novel *A Canticle for Leibowitz* (future society creates religion out of fragmentary knowledge relics); *Star Trek II: The Wrath of Khan* (the Source is basically a kinder, gentler Genesis Device).

Adventures in Time and Space Jenny exhales the same kind of energy the Doctor had after his regeneration in "The Christmas Invasion," which suggests perhaps that Jenny recovered from her fatal wound the same way the Doctor regrew his hand in that story: as a "new" Time Lord body, it has the capacity to repair itself after trauma without regenerating.

Speaking of the Doctor's severed hand, it's been hanging out in the TARDIS console room since the Doctor recovered it from the Master in "Last of the

Time Lords." The hand seems to have an affinity with the TARDIS and can even detect Jenny in a wibbly-wobbly, timey-wimey sort of way.

Who is the Doctor? The Doctor doesn't initially warm to Jenny and refuses to call her his daughter. When challenged by Donna about this, he admits it's not because he doesn't want to be a parent, but because he sees her as a reminder of all the Time Lords who are gone. The Doctor is also reminded of his violent past, warning Jenny, "The killing, after a while, it infects you, and once it does, you're never rid of it."

The Doctor and Donna When Donna finds out the Doctor has actually had children he has lost, she tells him, "You talk all the time but you don't say anything," a remarkably astute observation that few have said to the Doctor.

Monster of the Week The Hath are creatures with the body of a human and the head of a fish. They breathe using a tank of green-coloured liquid. They don't speak but make bubbly noises.

Stand Up and Cheer Pity poor Martha Jones, and actress Freema Agyeman, relegated to thankless and redundant guest parts this season (and in the second series of *Torchwood*). However, Martha's harrowing journey on the surface of Messaline with the Hath is exciting and surprisingly poignant. It reminds one how much Freema Agyeman is missed from *Doctor Who*.

Roll Your Eyes A science-fiction machine that takes a single cell and creates a fully grown woman with language, reason and fighting experience . . . who's *wearing mascara*?

You're Not Making Any Sense The whole "multiple generations created over a week" thing is a really clever twist. However, it doesn't bear close scrutiny: the entire original terraforming party would have to be dead, along with the initial generation products of the progenation machine, and there's nothing in the skirmishes with the Hath that shows the massive scale of annihilation necessary to have caused that. (And while we're at it, how, and why, is Cobb so old?)

Interesting Trivia Let's get the metafictional stuff out of the way first. Jenny, the Doctor's daughter, is played by Georgia Moffett, who is the daughter of the fifth Doctor, Peter Davison. After making this story, Georgia began dating David Tennant. She had a child with him in 2011, and they married later that year. So she's actually the Doctor's daughter, the Doctor's wife, and mother of the Doctor's daughter and granddaughter. Proof, if need be, that you *can* have too much of a good thing . . .

The progenation machine takes a single cell and creates a fully grown adult in seconds. It gives them language, tactical information, awareness and even clothing. This really makes them a clone of the machine, rather than a person. What would be lost here is genetic diversity, which can play havoc with a species' long-term survival. This machine is producing 20 generations a day, meaning Jenny is 140 generations into the cycle. Surely by this point the various generations would have suffered enormous genetic problems. It's a wonder Cobb's men don't all have six fingers and stand about two feet tall.

The TARDIS Chronometer It's 6012 according to the "giant space date" on the computer clock Donna finds (the Doctor identifies it as the New Byzantine Calendar but doesn't state whether it's actually the 61st century or not). The clock seems to use a North American standard mm/dd system, so whatever year it is, it's July 24 on the planet Messanine.

Brilliant? (GB) Last season, writer Stephen Greenhorn gave us "The Lazarus Experiment," a story that looked modern but felt like a traditional tale from 1970s *Doctor Who*, complete with mad scientists, experiments gone wrong, a bizarre-looking monster and a morality play. This time, with "The Doctor's Daughter," we have a tale that feels traditional but seems to be poaching the territory of early-to-mid 1980s *Who*: military characters with only one name, grim nasty fighting for its own sake and some smart conceits borrowed from literary SF to make it all go down easier.

If you've watched any of those science-fiction classics — or indeed watched any *Star Trek* over the past 40 years — you might feel a little let down by "The Doctor's Daughter," because you know the Source is going to be some ordinary bit of gadgetry long ago forgotten and the giant conflict is actually the result of office politics gone horribly wrong. The emotional journey the story follows is also pretty well trodden. By the time we get through the Doctor's objections that Jenny is not his daughter, we know this is going to lead to Jenny proving herself and then Jenny being taken away from him. It's about as well signposted as the average soap opera. But perhaps that's the point. There's nothing wrong with well-made melodrama that tugs at the heartstrings and thrills you as well. In this respect, perhaps the main flaw of the "The Doctor's Daughter" is that it has the wrong director working on it: someone like Graeme Harper or James Strong would milk these aspects for all its worth, while Alice Troughton makes it all seem pretty standard.

Even so, "The Doctor's Daughter" has some great moments. Most of them feature Georgia Moffett, who convincingly swings from military precision to wide-eyed innocence to moments of Time Lord–ish brilliance, sometimes in the same scene. It was wise to keep Jenny on as a character and there's a lot of potential for something interesting with her down the road.

The story also has a great, though sadly perfunctory, monster: the Hath are one of the oddest-looking, and yet most compelling, alien races the New Series has come up with. Who would have thought you could sympathize with an alien who says nothing and walks around with a water cooler strapped to its face? And yet, one of the most touching moments in the episode is watching the death of the Hath who accompanied Martha to the surface.

The impact on the Doctor of having a daughter is nicely measured, and one of the more surprising parts is why the Doctor finds the reality of Jenny difficult. It's not any of the obvious reasons but one that nicely connects with the Doctor's backstory: she reminds him of all the people he's lost, including his people and his past children. The Doctor describes being a Time Lord to Jenny: "A sum of knowledge. A code. A shared history. A shared suffering." Being confronted with someone with the biology but without all that is "Dad shock" on a different level.

It's also a lot of fun to watch how Donna solves the big mystery of the episode. Post-2005 *Who* makes a virtue of the ordinariness of the companion. Thus, Donna figures out the dating system just from common sense, observation, curiosity and work experience temping at a library. But the best scenes are with Martha who, after being sidelined in most of her *Doctor Who* and *Torchwood* appearances this year, finally gets some great scenes even if there really isn't a need for her to be in the story.

Like "The Lazarus Experiment," "The Doctor's Daughter" isn't going to set anything on fire but it's a good, solid tale that plays with familiar themes and, as a result, makes for refreshingly comfortable, and comforting, viewing.

Second Opinion (RS?) Almost everything about this story is either dull or absurd. From Martha's interminable trek across the planet's surface to Cobb's irrational hatred of the Doctor, almost nothing about this story works. If the soldiers are so desperate for new offspring, why don't they use Martha's or Donna's DNA? Especially when they said just seconds earlier that they would. Why is Cobb so old if he's been alive less than seven days? If the war eats up that many recruits that quickly, why don't we see any of them actually die? Why even bother with the seven day timeline if all it does is bend the plot out of shape for no good reason at all?

The story is saved by just one element: its title. This is Jenny's entire purpose: to give us a slam dunk of a title. The story then spends the entire 42 minutes trying to make it work. Mostly, it fails miserably. Where it succeeds is in the emotional connection between the Doctor and Jenny.

This is the first alien planet we've seen in the New Series that has no connection to us whatsoever, no deep importance in the future history of humanity. This planet has none of that; rather, it's Russell T Davies' human colony on the planet Zog, fighting the Zog monsters. Everything about it is generic, except for the bits that are downright stupid.

Instead, the story gives us a fundamental connection to a person. And it's here that the concept actually works: the Doctor and Jenny's relationship is straight out of the sitcom handbook, complete with jokes and an important lesson, but that's miles ahead of anything around it. It casts the Doctor and Donna as dysfunctional parents, and that works a treat. Why the story had to twist itself in knots to bring Martha along when she's confined entirely to a separate B-plot, I'll never know.

"The Doctor's Daughter" would likely improve significantly if the entire story had the Doctor, Donna and Jenny in that prison cell for 40 minutes, just talking out their issues. The emotional drama has legs, but the whole sci-fi premise that's constructed around it drags this down. Way, way down.

The Psychic Papers: The Doctor's Family

The very title of the series reminds us that the central character is still, in many ways, a mystery: Doctor Who? While we know many facts about the Doctor — including his planet of origin, his people, his contribution to the universe — there are still details that we don't know. His real name, for one thing. (Is it unpronounceable by humans, as the 1985 radio serial "Slipback" stated? Or is it something that can only be said by intimates, which is implied in "Forest of the Dead" and "Amy's Choice"?) And who his family is, for another.

At the start of the series, in 1963, the Doctor travelled with his granddaughter, Susan. The Doctor tells Ian and Barbara in the very first *Doctor Who* story, "An Unearthly Child," that he and Susan are "cut off from our own people." The pair have a familial bond: she takes care of the old man, while the Doctor occasionally gets exasperated by her behaviour and reprimands her. He only parts company with her when he sees that she's fallen in love with resistance fighter David Campbell in 1964's "The Dalek Invasion of Earth." Knowing that Susan will reject David, because she feels she must care for the Doctor, the Doctor locks her out of the TARDIS and leaves her in 22nd-century Earth in what must be the oddest display of tough love, ever.

For decades, Susan is the only explicit link to family for the Doctor. It became increasingly problematic as the character of the Doctor evolved from a grumpy old man travelling in time to a universe-saving hero. If the Doctor has a granddaughter, it means he fathered one of Susan's parents, which asked inconvenient questions and impugned the seeming asexuality of the character. In sources outside television, such as Terrance Dicks' novelization of his 1983 TV story "The Five Doctors" (which brought back Susan), it was stated that Susan merely "called" the Doctor grandfather, though in the TV version there is no attempt to make this distinction.

For a long time, the only other explicit reference to the Doctor's family was in 1967's "Tomb of the Cybermen." The Doctor's companion Victoria suggests that he's so old that he's forgotten his family, to which the Doctor replies, "I have to really want to, to bring them back in front of my eyes. The rest of the time they sleep in my mind and I forget."

This was the last word on the subject until near the end of the Classic Series when, in 1989's "The Curse of Fenric," the Doctor is asked, "Do you have any family yourself?" His response is "I don't know." In fact, there had been plans to make a story in the Classic Series' final season called "Lungbarrow" (written by Marc Platt), set in the Doctor's ancestral home where he would meet some of his strange cousins. This story was nixed by producer John Nathan-Turner, as it revealed too much about the Doctor's background.

The New Series enjoys far more oblique references to the Doctor's family than the Classic Series ever did. The Doctor says, "I was once a dad" in "Fear Her," something he reiterates in "The Doctor's Daughter." He could be talking about Susan's mother or father, or he could be talking about another child or a generated creation like Jenny. While the tenth Doctor didn't mind making these brief allusions, the eleventh Doctor is more awkward and changes the subject when asked about having children in "The Beast Below" and "A Good Man Goes to War." The latter story also features the Doctor's own cradle, which means he was once a baby himself. While it is not made explicit in the televised episodes, it is implied that the woman in white in "The End of Time" is, in fact, the Doctor's mother.

All these things are only partial clues. We may never have a complete sense of the whole puzzle. Understanding a person's family is a way to understanding that person. The Doctor remains a mystery. Doctor Who, indeed.

4.07 The Unicorn and the Wasp

Written by Gareth Roberts **Directed by** Graeme Harper

Supporting cast Fenella Woolgar (Agatha Christie), Felicity Kendal (Lady Clemency Eddison), Felicity Jones (Robina Redmond), Christopher Benjamin (Colonel Hugh Curbishley), Tom Goodman-Hill (Reverend Golightly), Ian Barritt (Professor Peach), David Quilter (Greeves), Adam Rayner (Roger Curbishley), Daniel King (Davenport), Charlotte Eaton (Mrs. Hart), Leena Dhingra (Miss Chandrakala)

Original airdate May 17, 2008

The Big Idea The Doctor and Donna wind up in the middle of an Agatha Christie mystery, aided by Agatha Christie herself.

Roots and References Too many works of Agatha Christie to count are mentioned, though onscreen we see Lady Eddison reading Christie's then-latest novel *The Murder of Roger Ackroyd* (1926). The 1957 reprint cover of Christie's 1935 novel *Death in the Clouds*, featuring a giant wasp looming over an airplane, is used as proof that the adventure lived on in Agatha's mind. (Not really: the cover art is supposed to be derived from looking at both objects in forced perspective.) The board game *Cluedo* (*Clue* in North America) is referenced (Professor Peach in the study, with the lead pipe). The story's title also shares a passing acquaintance with George Orwell's 1940 polemic *The Lion and the Unicorn*.

Adventures in Time and Space The Doctor wanted to take Martha to meet Agatha Christie at the end of "Last of the Time Lords." Donna compares their unlikely situation with having an adventure with Charles Dickens and ghosts on Christmas Eve, which, of course, happened in "The Unquiet Dead."

The Doctor's "C" chest contains a chest plate from a Cyberman, the ball containing the Carrionites from "The Shakespeare Code," a bust of Caesar's head and a facsimile edition of Agatha Christie's *Death in the Clouds* reprinted in the year five billion ("The End of the World" and its sequels). The flashback to the Doctor saving Charlemagne includes him with a bow and arrows, just as we saw in "Blink."

The Bees Are Disappearing Effect When Donna hears the buzzing of the wasp, it reminds her that there are still bees in the past.

The Doctor and Donna In an exchange that perhaps defines their relationship, Donna, lamenting Roger's obvious attraction to men, says, "Typical. All the decent men are on the other bus." To which the Doctor replies, "Or Time Lords." True to this, when the Doctor needs a shock as a part of his detox regimen to counteract cyanide poisoning, she gives him a full-on snog. The shock works. The Doctor says he should try that more often but then clarifies he meant the detox.

Monster of the Week The Vespiform are insectoid creatures that can transform into other species, in this case human form. Their insect form resembles a giant wasp.

Stand Up and Cheer The scene with the Doctor being poisoned may well be one of the funniest scenes in the entirety of the New Series, to the point where simply quoting excerpts can bring a smile to one's face. "A *Harvey Wallbanger*?!" "It's a song! Mammy!" "I'll give you a shock . . ."

Roll Your Eyes Donna noting that Davenport can't mourn the death of Roger is a nice little acknowledgement of the injustice of the historical period she's visiting; adding that it's like the Dark Ages indicates she's off on another tirade.

You're Not Making Any Sense If Reverend Golightly "apprehended" the ruffians who were robbing his parish, you would think more mention would have been made about the giant wasp attack.

Interesting Trivia As historical accuracy goes, this story is a bit of a red herring. Agatha Christie, in the midst of a scandalous marital breakup, did indeed disappear for 11 days in 1926 but, as one now expects of *Doctor Who*, the circumstances aren't quite as described in this story. For one thing, it happened in December, a little late in the year for a pleasant garden party. Christie had also left a note with the local constabulary saying she feared for her life. Opinion remains divided as to what happened when she reappeared in a Harrogate hotel registered under the name of her husband's mistress: some say she had suffered a nervous breakdown or from amnesia; others suggest it was a publicity stunt or an action designed to embarrass her husband. Christie herself never spoke of it. The Doctor was right about her works though. Only the Bible has sold more than the roughly four billion copies of her novels.

Future Christie works such as *Murder on the Orient Express* (1934) and Miss Marple (created in 1930) get namechecked, while many titles of Christie novels get referenced in the dialogue, some of them are charming ("I've called you here on this *endless night*"), some of them very clever ("N or M?"), and some of the absolutely atrocious ("Murder at the vicar's rage").

On the DVD, there are deleted scenes revealing a different opening and closing to the episode. These scenes are set in 1976, when Dame Agatha Christie is near death, trying to puzzle out her last mystery: the circumstances of her own disappearance and the identity of the man in the brown suit (another nod to a Christie title). The rest of the story as it appeared would have happened in flashback and, at the end, the Doctor and Donna visit Dame Agatha to tell her the mystery's resolution and to show her the edition of her novel from the year five billion. These bookends were removed because they reduced the immediacy of the story.

The TARDIS Chronometer It's 1926, the day of Agatha Christie's disappearance in the summer. (Though the "spinning headline" newspapers studiously avoid showing a specific date.)

Brilliant? (GB) If anything sums up "The Unicorn and the Wasp," it's the drawing-room scene. Traditionally, in a TV adaptation of an Agatha Christie mystery, this scene is where the protagonist methodically goes over all the evidence, churning up a few revelations before finally identifying the murder. Here, it starts with the hilarious reveal of the Unicorn (the criminal, in time-honoured tradition, actually has a dodgy lower-class accent) followed by the protagonists proceeding to accuse everyone of something before concluding with the lateral determination that Agatha Christie did it.

"The Unicorn and the Wasp" uses the bucolic conventions of a Christie mystery and upends it with *Doctor Who* parody. There's the sequence that lampoons the mystery convention of flashbacks establishing where the suspects were, only here it features lying suspects: the Colonel's bizarre flashback-within-a-flashback to the Moulin Rouge; Lady Eddison's flashback that continues to recount the (already witnessed) meeting with the Doctor and Donna; and, finally, the Doctor's complete non-sequitur flashback to rescuing Charlemagne from a crazed computer. Then there's the aforementioned drawing room scene at which point things go from bizarre to brilliant.

The real genius is that the parody is actually part and parcel of the story: the characters are in a pastiche of an Agatha Christie novel because the alien can only understand things in those terms. The Vespiform, for all its power, can't just kill; it's conditioned to conceal all its actions and keep up appearances as part of the affluent social class even though it's an insect from another galaxy.

Consequently, the episode takes all the standard tropes and milks them for all the comedy it can. The cast knows that great comedy is best done totally straight and when you have supporting actors as good as Felicity Kendal, Christopher Benjamin and Fenella Woolgar it makes it even better. The dialogue is cunning and witty; I love how Reverend Golightly asks, "What would Poirot do?" parodying a common 21st-century phrase about Golightly's own sky god. Add in some beautiful direction and period location filming (the hallmark of the British mystery television we've seen for decades) and it becomes sublime.

Catherine Tate's dramatic talents have been so mesmerizing this season that it's a surprise when she uses the comedic skills she's famous for. (Donna stuffing her face during the drawing room scene is a lovely touch.) Tennant and Tate's game of charades while the Doctor is being poisoned to death is so brilliant because both actors know the essence of good comedy is good timing.

My complaint about writer Gareth Roberts' "The Shakespeare Code" was that he failed to impart what made Shakespeare important. For the most part, he's been careful to avoid making this mistake twice. We may see Agatha Christie through a parody of the fictional genre she perpetrated, but in doing that Roberts lets us see what makes her and her work so vital: the mixture of the bucolic, the dark and the human. And Fenella Woolgar wonderfully captures a woman with considerable gifts who has been very hurt by the world but carries on nonetheless.

"The Unicorn and the Wasp" is a delightful change from the somewhat downbeat parade of endangered planets, slaughter, enslavement and historical tragedy that preceded it this season. No high stakes, no great angst, just a thoroughly charming murder mystery with lots of funny scenes written, directed and performed to perfection. It's topping, eh wot?

Second Opinion (RS?) It's the pacing that really makes this gem shine. Which is odd, because it lurches from a bog-standard murder to attacks by a CGI monster to a mystery revealed in the drawing room to a frantic vintage car chase in the dead of night. All wrapped around a plot that seems too clichéd to be believable . . . and that turns out to be precisely the point.

We should be suffering whiplash from these events crashing into each other, but instead the story effortlessly transitions from one to the next, without you pausing to wonder why, for instance, Lady Eddison kept her secret child's bedroom intact for 40 years or why Davenport simply disappears from the plot once Roger has been killed, despite being an obvious suspect.

Fortunately, very robust glue holds the episode together and that's the comedy. The flashback within a flashback is hilarious, even funnier if you grew up on the novels of that era that included such storytelling devices. The charades scene plays to Tate's comic strengths, with Tennant a very capable supporting act. And having all the flashbacks preceded by someone telling us they'll try to remember, before launching into either too much detail or not enough, is wonderful.

Despite all the wackiness, "The Unicorn and the Wasp" does one traditional thing: it makes this story fundamentally about character. The best of these historicals work when they're examining what makes their subject tick, rather than getting caught up in yet another alien invasion. The monster is used as an entry point into the psyche, not as an end unto itself.

I can't praise this story enough. It's simultaneously brilliant, hilarious, bizarre and lovely. Where most of the New Series has gone for angst and pain and attempts to pile an even grander threat on top of last year's, this makes you want to sip tea along with the suspects, even if it is likely poisoned and someone's going to expose your innermost secrets at any moment now.

4.08—4.09 Silence in the Library / Forest of the Dead

Written by Steven Moffat **Directed by** Euros Lyn

Supporting cast Alex Kingston (River Song), Colin Salmon (Dr. Moon), Eve Newton (The Girl), Mark Dexter (Dad), Steve Pemberton (Strackman Lux), Talulah Riley (Miss Evangelista), Jessika Williams (Anita), O.T. Fagbenle (Other Dave), Harry Peacock (Dave), Eloise Rakic-Platt (Ella), Alex Midwood (Joshua), Sarah Niles (Node 1), Joshua Dallas (Node 2), Jason Pitt (Lee)

Original airdates May 31 and June 7, 2008

The Big Idea One hundred years earlier, 4,022 people disappeared from the largest library in the universe, which may be located inside the mind of a little girl.

Roots and References *The Time Traveller's Wife* (River's relationship to the

Doctor); *Star Wars: The Phantom Menace* (a city filling an entire planet); the *Doctor Who Magazine* comic strip "War of the Words" (a library filling an entire planet). CAL watches *Pedro and Frankensheep* and *Ren and Stimpy* on TV. The Doctor references Jeffrey Archer, Bridget Jones and *Monty Python's Big Red Book*.

Adventures in Time and Space The library has a little shop ("New Earth"). The Doctor says, "Daleks: aim for the eyestalk; Sontarans: back of the neck." Emergency Program One is mentioned ("The Parting of the Ways").

River sends a message to the Doctor via psychic paper, just as the Face of Boe did in "New Earth." River looks through her diary and asks, "The crash of the *Byzantium*, have we done that yet?" No, but they will in "Time of the Angels"/"Flesh and Stone." River's sonic screwdriver is bulkier than the Doctor's, opens at the top and has red settings.

River also has a squareness gun that uses sonic technology to create square holes in walls (or the floor), just like Captain Jack's in "The Empty Child"/"The Doctor Dances" (it could even be the same gun). When the Doctor says history can be rewritten, she says, "Not one line!" a reference to 1964's "The Aztecs." She's seen whole armies turn and run away in the face of the Doctor, which might be a reference to something we'll see in forthcoming seasons.

Who is the Doctor? He doesn't trust River Song fully until she tells him his true name, the implication being that he would only tell it to someone he has an intimate relationship with.

The Doctor and Donna After losing River, the Doctor tells Donna the same thing he told Rose after losing Reinette in "The Girl in the Fireplace": "I'm always all right." But Donna asks, "Is 'all right' special Time Lord code for not really all right at all? Because I'm all right too." And the two friends stand together, holding hands, both having lost someone they fleetingly loved. That's friendship.

Monster of the Week The Vashta Nerada. Literally, "the shadows that melt the flesh." Most planets have them but usually in small clusters. You can see them as dust in sunbeams. They're piranhas of the air but only exist in the dark. They latch onto a food source, keep it fresh and eventually devour it. A clue that this has happened is that the person grows an extra shadow.

Stand Up and Cheer It might not be a moment to cheer, but the reveal of Miss Evangelista's distorted face is shocking and terrifying. We only see it for a few seconds, but it's an image that's incredibly powerful and lingers long after the story's over.

Roll Your Eyes In contrast to the above, the cliffhanger tries to be scary but fails miserably by overegging its pudding. The walking skeleton is a decent image and Donna's face on the Node is effective, but the dialogue each is given is rather poor. "Donna Noble has been saved" is slightly ominous, but "Hey, who turned out the lights?" is just cheesy. Put them together and you have competing catchphrases, becoming more meaningless with each utterance.

You're Not Making Any Sense The computer saved the original inhabitants because it had nowhere to send them once they were in the teleport. So why does it save Donna, when she was being teleported to the TARDIS? She had a destination that was sans Vashta Nerada and yet it pulled her out of the materialization and into its hard drive. And then why does her face appear on a Node if she isn't dead?

Interesting Trivia For a woman who's always on the hunt for a date, Donna Noble scores surprisingly little. Her only previous romance was her engagement to Lance, but he turned out to be a traitor. Here, she's finally given a romance and we see it in full bloom: she goes from first date to marriage to children with a sweet man, ostensibly what she's been looking for the entire time (even though we viewers know there's so much more to her). And although the punchline reveals that Lee is actually real, Donna never discovers this, leaving the poor woman to believe that her only two romances during her time with the Doctor were both tricks. That's a little bit cruel, actually.

River Song is the sort of character you imagine must turn up in the Doctor's life all the time: someone he meets out of order. With a time machine, there's nothing to stop the Doctor from meeting Napoleon in exile one day, as a kid the day after that, then at the height of the revolution. It gets even more likely when the other person has a time machine. However, the obvious danger is that the storyline can become needlessly complicated. The solution with River is to keep her enigmatic and, mostly, to only trust her in the hands of someone whose brain works like this as a matter of course. We'll pick this up again later. Or was it earlier?

It's the largest library in the universe and it's also a pinnacle of technology, with a supercomputer so powerful it can store living beings, in all their complexity. So why did they bother pulping entire forests to make books out of paper? Even when this story was being produced, Kindles were taking off, so it seems bizarre to have such a technologically oriented society not creating a digital repository of information. Perhaps fascimile books are, like so many anachronistic things in the future in *Doctor Who*, the latest fad?

The TARDIS Chronometer In the biography section of the library in the 51st century.

Brilliant? (RS?) This is . . . okay. It's got all the right ingredients: monsters based on primal fears, a small cast in a tight location, some trippy surrealism and a couple of moments of genuine terror. Unfortunately, it's all just a little too pat.

The most obvious problem is the Vashta Nerada: they're motes of dust and that's not scary in the slightest. Given that they're supposed to be, this is a huge liability for the story. Their connection to Earth is a big lead balloon as well. If your monster isn't scary in a base under siege with the lights turned down, then telling the audience that it's found on Earth too isn't going to save it. It doesn't ramp up the threat; it trivializes it. Oh, and why exactly do the archaeologists put on their helmets every time the Vashta Nerada turn up, when it accomplishes nothing?

Professor River Song is a nice idea, who's clearly there for future returns. Alex Kingston isn't bad (her first line is particularly well delivered) and the character has potential, although the constant explanations of "She knows you — but not yet!" grow a little tiresome. Just imagine how awesome these scenes could have been if they'd been played for broad comedy.

The use of "spoilers" doesn't really work either. It should be hilarious banter, but it falls flat (witness how the Doctor clunkily explains what spoilers are to Donna before he's even met River). What's interesting in hindsight is just how well formed River's character is here, yet she doesn't click with David Tennant at all. They have no chemistry whatsoever, which is another drag factor in a story that shouldn't have any but is full of them.

That said, the scenes that take place in the "real world" are excellent. It's here where the story really shines, especially early on when it throws you into a massive headspin. We also get some of the scariest scenes in the story in part two: the woman in the cloak is genuinely terrifying, even before we see her face. The bizarre thing about this is that she isn't meant to be scary, just mysterious, but the direction when Donna looks out the window is superb. The revelation of her face is also appropriately offputting. One almost wonders if entirely different directors handled the library and the real-world scenes.

Of course, this presents one of the greatest missed opportunities yet. Donna's domestic life is serviceable enough, but how much more interesting, and challenging, would the story have been if the Doctor and Donna had swapped places? You'd have the humans struggling to defeat a terror that puts them way out of their depth, you'd have Donna forced to take command and you'd have the Doctor being fish-out-of-water domestic. Do that and you'd have a "Human Nature" on your hands.

As it is, Donna's story is there basically for the stammering punchline at the end, while the Doctor's role is twofold: to establish his relationship with River and to have him defeat the menace in an incredibly pat way. While there's nothing to fault "look me up" technically, it's not exactly heroic or dramatically surprising. It's about as thrilling as watching Prince Charles convincing a waiter to give him a table by saying, "Don't you know who I am?"

Then there's the "Everybody lives!" epilogue. I mean, come on. Self-plagiarism is one thing, but — and this is an important point, Sally Sparrow fans — it should at least be from a source that the entirety of the audience isn't intimately familiar with. There's some attempt to disguise it with a nice mono-logue, but the outcome is still the same: a pale imitation of the author's own, and better, achievements, several years earlier.

There are two reasons "Everybody lives!" worked so well in "The Doctor Dances." First, it was the thematic end of the broken Doctor, one who had lost so much from the Time War onwards, so giving him one day's respite felt as though he'd earned it. Second, it was prefaced with "Just this once." Russell T Davies has talked about how the Doctor is intrinsically linked to death and that, wherever he goes — despite all his attempts to the contrary — people die. Terribly and horribly and often in great numbers. This is the tragedy of the Doctor and one of the things that sets him apart from what could easily be a superhero narrative. "Everybody lives!" is too sugar-coated, veering danger-ously close to the wearing of underpants on the outside of a brown-striped suit. And nobody wants that.

I've been harsher on this story than it probably warrants. None of the prob-lems are insurmountable and none, by themselves, are particularly destructive, but taken together they're a dead weight that the other elements can't compen-sate for. The good parts — the real world, the cloaked woman, CAL — are quite good. The way the story unfolds is quite good. The way the ending resolves everything into one neat package is quite good. Unfortunately, "quite good" isn't quite good enough.

Second Opinion (GB) The curse of the blue suit claims another victim and this time it's a Steven Moffat story. Since it's a Moffat story, the worst the blue suit can do is make it "very good" as opposed to "absolutely stunning." Even so, that's a significant fall from grace for the writer of "The Girl in the Fireplace" and "Blink."

There's a lot that does work with "Silence in the Library"/"Forest of the Dead." River Song has a fascinating emotional journey here: she's crushed to find the Doctor doesn't know her, but she still gets to be surprised by him. The significance of this becomes even more powerful with hindsight, but even in the present Alex Kingston takes that challenge and knocks it right out of the park. I would argue that River has no chemistry with the Doctor precisely because he's so awkward with her. David Tennant's final scene with Alex Kingston is so affecting you can see how, and where, the Doctor falls in love with River.

Equally compelling is the juxtaposition of the scenes with Dr. Moon and the girl, and the scenes in the library. The first episode creates a fascinating mystery of how the girl's world connects with the library's. In some ways, the insertion of Donna in that world in the second part is a bit of a letdown. Even so, it's a shame more isn't done with it to make the contrast between the two worlds more striking, even creepy.

I really don't know what happened with Euros Lyn's direction. I can't help but feel that, under another director, this story would have been actually suspenseful and the scenes with Dr. Moon odder. At the very least, we might have more creative uses of darkness to make the shadows actually threatening. In the end, the direction undercuts everything.

With the Doctor's final confrontation with the Vashta Nerada, we get to see a monster actually heed the Doctor's warning to stop what they're doing. Otherwise, what we have here is Moffat's standard checklist: an ordinary thing that becomes terrifying; a casual relationship with causality; a nifty gimmick; funny dialogue; a gorgeous and witty woman. The problem is, the viewer is now wise to this, and Moffat simply meets, rather than exceeds, expectations.

4.10 Midnight

Written by Russell T Davies **Directed by** Alice Troughton

Supporting cast Billie Piper (Rose Tyler), Lesley Sharp (Sky Silvestry), Rakie Ayola (Hostess), David Troughton (Professor Hobbes), Ayesha Antoine (Dee Dee Blasco), Lindsey Coulson (Val Cane), Daniel Ryan (Biff Kane), Colin Morgan (Jethro), Tony Bluto (Driver Joe), Duane Henry (Mechanic Claude)

Original airdate June 14, 2008

The Big Idea The Doctor's trapped on a bus with no escape and an unseen monster.

Roots and References *The Lord of the Flies* (the breakdown of social control); *The Crucible* (fear leading to hysterical paranoia); *The Twilight Zone* episode "Will the Real Martian Please Stand Up?" (paranoia created by an alien posing as a human); Dee Dee quotes from Christina Rossetti's 1862 poem "Goblin Market."

Adventures in Time and Space The Doctor tries out his standard alias, John Smith, to less success than usual. In testing the possessed Sky's synchronicity of speech, he names off his last three female companions: Rose, Martha and Donna. He talks to Sky about how Rose went to another universe in "Doomsday."

The Bees Are Disappearing Effect Dee Dee's thesis is on another lost planetary body, this time the lost moon of Poosh. The Medusa Cascade is mentioned yet again. And while the Doctor is trying to calm everyone, he has his back to the video screen just as Rose appears on it, silently yelling, "Doctor."

Who is the Doctor? With all the things that make the Doctor larger than life taken away from him, he's left to hold his own in a bus where people are scared, suspicious and xenophobic. He ends up desperately trying to explain to people what makes him special without having them rip him apart and is left impotently exclaiming, "Because I'm clever."

Monster of the Week There is an unseen creature on the surface of Midnight. It takes over passenger Sky Silvestri and assimilates the language and intelligence of everyone on the Crusader 50 bus. That said, it could be argued the real monsters here are, in fact, members of the human race, the Doctor's favourite species.

Stand Up and Cheer It's more of an "oh crap we're doomed" moment, but one of the most frightening things in the whole New Series is when the Doctor tells the passengers that if they want to kill Sky they'll have to go through him and the Hostess says, "All right." It's a sign of how truly vulnerable the Doctor has become, and it's quite chilling as a result.

Roll Your Eyes It's meant to denote the rising paranoia, but Val decrying immigrants on another planet seems, well, odd.

You're Not Making Any Sense For reasons we'll be able to get into in two episodes' time, Rose's random appearance on a video screen on another planet in the future is completely and totally inexplicable.

Interesting Trivia The Crusader 50's "retrovid classics" includes Italian singer Raffaella Carrà performing her 1977 English-language single "Do It, Do It Again" (a version of her international hit "*A far l'amore comincia tu*").

Hobbes may be named after the 17th-century philosopher Thomas Hobbes. In his 1651 book *Leviathan*, Hobbes theorized that individuals unite into political societies by a process of mutual consent. Without such a social contract, man's state of nature would essentially cause us to destroy each other. In many respects, the Crusader 50 passengers could be seen as a microcosm of Hobbes's social contract in action. Whatever the derivation of his character's name, the actor playing Hobbes has a special connection to the world of *Doctor Who*: actor David Troughton is the son of the second Doctor, Patrick Troughton.

The designation "50" was added to the Crusader when it was thought the episode would be the 50th episode of the New Series. In the event, its position in the broadcast order was switched around, though it was still the 50th episode made.

The TARDIS Chronometer The planet Midnight, sometime in the future.

Brilliant? (GB) "Midnight" is a deeply uncomfortable story to watch. It has no gore, no blood, no monster, no special effects (beyond a few CGI background shots) and yet it is one of the most disturbing stories in *Doctor Who*'s history.

It's a story that sees Russell T Davies at his most confident, stripping down *Doctor Who* to a single room with an unseen monster that turns out to be us.

In this respect, this episode (and the one that follows) is a dark inversion of Davies' own vision of *Who*. The warm, humanist optimism that shaped much of New *Who*, where the Doctor inspires humanity to new heights of courage, witnesses its reflection as humanity is ugly, scared, thoughtless and the Doctor can't do anything to inspire them to better things; in fact, he barely survives himself.

That's the other thing Davies' script does: it shows what it takes to truly render the Doctor vulnerable, by putting him in a locked cabin full of desperate people where his bravado and wit have no willing audience. He tries to do all the Doctor-y things we expect: inspiring others and allowing people like Dee Dee and Jethro to have a say, being cheery in the face of the unknown, trying to put himself between others and danger. But this time it fails. No one wants to listen to him; no one is cheered or inspired. Worse, we know it's all going to hell when the Hostess and Biff immediately challenge the Doctor after he asserts he won't let them kill Sky. His authority is gone.

David Tennant is stunning as he explores a Doctor who no longer has the easy charisma and arrogance that, in many respects, define the character. It's terrifying to watch because the Doctor has totally lost all control of the situation. This is, when you think about it, the bleakest thing that could ever happen on *Doctor Who*.

How we get into this position is a masterpiece of storytelling: lull everyone into a false sense of security where everyone gets to know and like each other. Then, bit by bit, the menace manifests itself. While this is happening, the Doctor tries to keep his control over the situation, but one by one everyone questions him and his motives. And then all hell breaks loose.

Lesley Sharp manages to be terrifying just through her body language while repeating what others say. When she finally emerges with the Doctor's voice, standing in an exultant posture, it only makes it scarier, especially as they keep cutting to David Tennant in closeup, his face a mask of fright, passively echoing what Sky is saying. Alice Troughton's direction is superb here. She studiously avoids closeups until this point, making the most of the claustrophobic setting and the theatricality of the piece, and then enhancing the maximum impact of the Doctor's total helplessness when she finally does go in close.

In the end, the sense of human optimism breaks through a little as the nameless hostess, the one who had been advocating for Sky's death and who had even threatened the Doctor, sees the true threat. But even in that sacrificial act, the Doctor is actually proven wrong and the Hostess proven right: his desire to protect Sky from destruction earlier was a futile gesture that almost led to his own death. The Crusader 50 tour ends with a mirror image of how it began: everyone sitting in silence, far from each other, their lives forever scarred. Perhaps they'll become better people. Perhaps not.

The basic premise of *Doctor Who* is about a larger-than-life figure exploring a universe full of darkness, but ultimately showing good can triumph and humanity can be better. "Midnight" removes all these things — as well as the monsters and the special effects — and shows us that, even without them, *Doctor Who* can still be scary, gripping, thoughtful and spectacular. And very, very disturbing.

Second Opinion (RS?) "Midnight," among its many other strengths, is interested in exploring its cast not as TV characters but as human beings, in all their complexity. And not just the individual characters, but the relationships between them. What's interesting is that the cast comprises a variety of sexualities, genders, races and class backgrounds — and yet these backgrounds have less weight than you might imagine, once the chips are down.

So we have the black, working-class Hostess, who never even gets a name, first suggesting killing Sky and then heroically sacrificing herself at the end. Is this racist, lazy television, where the unnamed black woman is both unlikeable and more disposable than the more developed white characters? Or does that not apply, because a) she's not the only character of colour in the cast and b) the lack of name is made into a focal point for the tragedy we've just witnessed?

Despite their very different backgrounds, the Hostess's insistence on following the rules means she has the most in common with Professor Hobbes and his repeated denials once the danger appears. What about Dee Dee, who's middle class, black and smart? Does she balance out the mix or is that just tokenism one step removed? Dee Dee's also young, putting her in the same league as Jethro, and both have a similar arc: they're the voices of reason for a while, even as the grownups around them devolve into threats of violence, but they too eventually succumb. Jethro comes from the same lower-middle-class-but-upwardly-mobile template as his parents, but his reasoning puts him into a different league altogether.

His insistence on sitting apart from them echoes Sky's wanting to be left alone. Sky's fondness for actual books parallels Hobbes's old-fashioned look, but it's her fundamental fear that prefigures the groupthink and also allows the threat to manifest by exploiting and reflecting that fear. Does fear of that which is alien keep you safe or does it do more damage in the long run? Where do you draw the line on what you define as alien?

Amidst all the differences on display, there's one difference that stands out more than the others: the alien known only as the Doctor. For once, our main character's background matters and the result is that he's relegated to a foreign element, feared and subjected to violence. Among the many notable inversions this episode undertakes, perhaps the most shocking is that he's able to connect to everyone when things are going well but is useless at claiming authority when the situation turns dangerous. His status as an outsider usually gives him some added experience or know-how; here, it's used against him and not by a sci-fi monster but by ordinary, terrified humans.

Are human beings just a collection of character background and traits? Or can disparate groups have more in common than they might think? Does this change if they're united against a common enemy? Is there even such a thing as a united group of people? Everything about "Midnight" defies the tropes of what we expect from drama. However, in doing so, it embodies — in a fundamentally complex and deeply painful way — what it means to be human.

4.11 Turn Left

Written by Russell T Davies **Directed by** Graeme Harper

Supporting cast Billie Piper (Rose Tyler), Bernard Cribbins (Wilfred Mott), Jacqueline King (Sylvia Noble), Joseph Long (Rocco Colasanto), Noma Dumezweni (Captain Magambo), Chipo Chung (fortune teller), Natalie Walter (Alice Coltrane), Lachele Carl (Trinity Wells), Clive Standen (Private Harris), Marcia Lecky (Mooky Kahari), Suzann McLean (Veena Brady), Bhasker Patel (Jival Chowdry), Ben Righton (Oliver Morgenstern), Loraine Velez (Spanish maid), Jason Mohammad (studio news reader), Sanchia McCormack (housing officer), Lawrence Stevenson (soldier number 1), Paul Richard Biggin (soldier number 2), Neil Clench (man in pub), Catherine York (female reporter), Terri-Ann Brumby (woman in doorway)

Original airdate June 21, 2008

The Big Idea Donna's past is changed so that she never met the Doctor.

Roots and References *It's A Wonderful Life* (a dystopic world created by the removal of one man); *Star Trek: The Next Generation*'s "Yesterday's Enterprise" (finding the past completely rewritten); *Sliding Doors* (a single decision changing a whole life). Donna's family and the Colasantos sing Queen's "Bohemian Rhapsody."

Adventures in Time and Space In the alternate world, Donna discusses events of "The Runaway Bride." There's also a flashback to the real history, featuring the Doctor amid the flames, the Racnoss screaming and water flooding. There's a reference to Donna's father (whom we saw in "The Runaway Bride") and an onscreen confirmation that he passed away some time before "Partners in Crime." The Royal Hope Hospital vanishes and reappears with only one survivor,

Oliver Morgenstern, who describes the Judoon ("Smith and Jones"). Martha Jones gave him one last oxygen tank then died. Sarah Jane Smith took control but was killed and her body recovered from the hospital. We see a brief retrospective of her life, along with photos, on the news. Luke, Maria and Clyde (*The Sarah Jane Adventures*) also perished. The following Christmas, the *Titanic* crashes into London ("Voyage of the Damned").

We get a reference to the Guinevere range of satellites ("The Christmas Invasion"), then see Adipose on the streets of the U.S. ("Partners in Crime"). Gwen Cooper and Ianto Jones (*Torchwood*) are killed when the Sontaran ship explodes, setting off the gas explosion in the sky ("The Poison Sky"). Captain Jack is transported to the Sontaran homeworld. Regular staples such as UNIT and Lachele Carl's AMNN reporter (named in the credits as Trinity Wells for the first time) both appear. The Cloister Bell rings (1981's "Logopolis" et al.).

In the regular history, the time parasite is said to be one of the Trickster's brigade, referencing the regular villain from *The Sarah Jane Adventures*. In "The Fires of Pompeii," Petrus Dextrus augured that something would be on Donna's back; here, that comes true.

The Bees Are Disappearing Effect When contemplating how bad things have become, Sylvia says, "Even the bees are disappearing." Rose returns, having crossed several universes in search of the Doctor. She says that the darkness is coming from across the stars and that nothing can stop it. Every single universe is in danger and the stars start going out.

Rose also whispers a message in the dying Donna's ear for the Doctor: Bad Wolf. Back in the proper universe, the Doctor and Donna discover that every piece of writing, including the TARDIS panels, now says "Bad Wolf." The Doctor says this means the end of the universe.

The Doctor and Donna Rose tells Donna that the Doctor thought Donna was brilliant and that Donna saw it in herself, just by being with him. Donna refuses to accept this and doesn't believe it when the Doctor tells her the same thing later on. Donna, for all her faith in the Doctor, does not have a lot of faith in herself, even as she elects to sacrifice herself to save the world.

Monster of the Week The time beetle feeds off time by making someone's life take a different turn. Usually the universe compensates around it, although in Donna's case it results in a whole parallel world.

Stand Up and Cheer It's almost the opposite of a cheer moment, but the scene where Rocco and his family are taken away on the back of the truck is astonishing television. Rocco is being his usual effusive self, finding the optimistic take on everything, Donna is trying to follow the thread of what's happening and Wilf works it out: they're carting away immigrants to forced labour camps, so that there'll be more room for Englanders. The exact moment of realization is conveyed to perfection by the look on Rocco's face, as he falters in his optimism and then salutes Wilf, who gives a shaky salute in return. Donna's subsequent running after the truck and impotent shouting is just heartbreaking.

Roll Your Eyes Ladies and gentlemen, welcome to the Planet of the Chinese People. Gasp! as you hear clichéd stock music in the background. Swoon! as you discover the only speaking part is that of "cunning dragon lady." Gulp! as everything is left cannily unexplained, drawing on the cliché of the mysterious East. Shiver! as you realize that the episode's need to condense these scenes results in horrendous stereotypes. Fast forward! next time you watch this on DVD.

You're Not Making Any Sense "Voyage of the Damned" explicitly states that the *Titanic* crashing into Earth will take out the entire planet with its nuclear storm drives. So why does it only destroy one city?

Interesting Trivia This season, instead of having a double-banked episode where the Doctor and companion effectively cameo in the story, the decision was made to have "Midnight" heavily featuring the Doctor, while this story primarily features Donna. Rose's presence in many respects provides a Doctor figure, someone more knowlegeable than Donna whom Donna can bounce off.

One thing this episode definitively proves is that the Doctor does much more good than harm. We're often invited to question the Doctor and his effect on the universe, but here we see (through his absence) that the death toll would be much, much higher — and the other consequences worse — if he wasn't around to save us over and over again.

History diverges at the point of "The Runaway Bride," and we see the effects of the Doctor's absence in present-day adventures such as "Smith and Jones." Because the Doctor never travels to Utopia, the Master never gets released and so Harold Saxon is missing from the present day. This is actually quite clever and has clearly been carefully thought through. But what about "The Shakespeare Code"? If the Doctor wasn't around in the past, then what's to stop the Carrionites from destroying humanity in 1599? In fact, the production team toyed with the idea of mentioning a backstory involving a UNIT soldier sent back in time to Shakespeare's day. It was ultimately dropped as distracting from the story at hand, but it does demonstrate the care with which this one was constructed.

The TARDIS Chronometer In a market on Shan Shen. In the alternate universe, the TARDIS is salvaged from under the Thames and brought to a UNIT base.

Brilliant? (RS?) Donna Noble was a companion designed specifically for one story, "The Runaway Bride." And she's amazing in that episode, far better than she seemed at first, because she continually breathes life into the story. Turning her into a regular companion could have been a disaster. But, sometimes, serendipity strikes. And, despite her comedic centre, the character of Donna succeeds by virtue of the fact that she's just so real.

Her family dynamic, while not looking like anything special on paper, is incredibly effective. Her mother could easily be a Jackie clone, but she's grittier and thus more unsettling. The death of Howard Attfield, the actor who played her father in "The Runaway Bride," also forced another serendipitous action upon the character: her grandfather is wonderful, all the more so for being played by Bernard Cribbins. There's a sense of uncomfortable realism here, partly from the acting and partly from the sense that the Nobles are living in Chiswick from paycheque to paycheque.

"Turn Left" is Donna's tour de force. It's an amazing story, taking what should be a science-fiction cliché and carrying it off with incredible aplomb. Watching her fall further and further in the alternative timeline, with her mother failing her and her grandfather's quiet sadness speaking volumes, it's impossible not to feel heartache at her family's plight. Her yelling at the singing immigrant family in Leeds is perfect, as it sets the stage for their subsequent deportation to a labour camp and some of the best acting seen in the New Series by far. The denouement, with her realization that the only special thing she can possibly do with her life involves that truck, is incredibly downbeat. This is a dark, dark story and it works entirely because the regulars are so strong.

It's also an episode driven primarily by women. Between Donna, Rose and Captain Magambo (and even Sarah Jane offscreen), this episode demonstrates that, in the absence of the Doctor, it's the women who step up. And though they do, about the best they can manage is to restore the status quo.

Because it's the status quo that this story is interested in examining. The Doctor isn't in "Turn Left," but his legacy is everywhere. Beyond being a continuity nerd's dream, all the links are there to make a serious point: that sometimes there are necessary deaths. Everywhere the Doctor goes, people die. Often tragically and unpleasantly, but one thing is for sure: he leaves a trail of bodies in his wake. By showing us the brutal effects of a world without the Doctor, this episode demonstrates that the deaths we see are far, far fewer than the deaths we'd be experiencing otherwise. Not just in number but in emotional intensity; that's why almost all the recurring cast are killed off, to make us feel the pain.

Unfortunately, the episode's not quite perfect. The plastic bug is so fake, it looks like a children's joke toy, only 15 times bigger. Mostly this is dealt with by featuring only eerie snapshots of a single leg or a blurry shot to emphasize the strangeness (and hide the fakeness). However, at the end, it lies on the ground and then on a bench in all its plastic glory, which rather undercuts the menace. The Bad Wolf ending is haunting, although in retrospect it's laughable, as it's going to go nowhere one minute into the next episode. And why does Rose speak like her mouth is full of cotton?

"Turn Left," despite a few problems, is easily the best story of the season and not just by default. By focusing on Donna, it brings together much of the past few years and examines them through a prism, taking the show to places that aren't comfortable but that show us the strength of the Doctor's methods in his absence. It's a story that may not be able to change the world by shouting at it, but it can certainly try.

Second Opinion (GB) The first thing that gets me about "Turn Left" is that it's not the Cybermen or the Daleks or the Master that ultimately destroy the world. It's the Judoon, the Adipose, the *Titanic*, all the menaces from the "frothy" stories — the Christmas specials and the season openers — that ultimately spell the end of things. (The only serious, intentional threat among them is the Sontarans.)

The second thing that gets me is that, even without the Doctor, human beings do at least minimize the damage: Sarah Jane stops the plasmavore at the Royal Hope Hospital; Captain Jack and Torchwood stop the Sontaran invasion; somehow, Midshipman Frame managed to minimize the effects of *Titanic*'s storm drive. All these things happen at great cost: everyone who attempted these things is dead (or imprisoned in the case of the immortal Jack Harkness).

What *really* gets me about "Turn Left" is watching Sylvia go from her usual domineering matron to a shell of a woman. Watch Sylvia in the room with everyone singing "Bohemian Rhapsody." Sylvia just sits there, wrapped in a blanket, sort of nodding, making a token effort but losing herself. And Donna knows what she must do long before she sees the stars go out; it's when she tries to reassure her mother, and she sees that Sylvia is completely dead inside. Jacqueline King's performance here just leaves me breathless.

However, the thing that not only gets me but also sucker-punches me in the gut is watching Donna. The scene when she's in the circle and she sees what's on her back and she screams at Rose, "You told me I was special!" is a stark, emotionally raw moment (there's no glamour to it; Donna isn't even wearing makeup at this point). And "Turn Left" has Catherine Tate in scene after brilliant scene like this.

There are things in "Turn Left" that still bother me (Rose's spurious presence as substitute Doctor) and things that trouble me (the fortune teller), but for me "Turn Left" is about those things I described above. It's a story of how the world ultimately gets destroyed by the silly things that populate a *Doctor Who* Christmas special and the ordinary people who then must live with the burden of being in a world without the Doctor. And how heartbreaking that must be.

4.12—4.13 The Stolen Earth / Journey's End

Written by Russell T Davies **Directed by** Graeme Harper

Supporting cast Freema Agyeman (Martha Jones); John Barrowman (Captain Jack Harkness); Elisabeth Sladen (Sarah Jane Smith); Billie Piper (Rose Tyler); Penelope Wilton (Harriet Jones); Gareth David-Lloyd (Ianto Jones); Eve Myles (Gwen Cooper); Noel Clarke (Mickey Smith); Camille Coduri (Jackie Tyler); Thomas Knight (Luke Smith); Bernard Cribbins (Wilfred Mott); Jacqueline King (Sylvia Noble); Adjoa Andoh (Francine Jones); Julian Bleach (Davros); Michael Brandon (General Sanchez); Andrea Harris (Suzanne); Lachele Carl (Trinity Wells); Richard Dawkins (himself); Paul O'Grady (himself); Paul Kasey (Judoon); Kelly Hunter (Shadow Architect); Elizabeth Tan (Anna Zhou); Nicholas Briggs (Dalek voices); Alexander Armstrong (voice of Mr. Smith); John Leeson (voice of K9); Amy Beth Hayes (albino servant); Marcus Cunningham (drunk man); Jason Mohammad (newsreader); Gary Miller (scared man); Barnaby Edwards, Nicholas Pegg, David Hankinson, Anthony Spargo (Dalek operators); Valda Aviks (German woman); Michael Price (Liberian man); Shobu Kapoor (scared woman)

Original airdates June 28 and July 5, 2008

The Big Idea Twenty-seven planets, including Earth, have been taken across the universe, where they form part of a machine to destroy reality itself.

Roots and References *Flowers for Algernon* (Donna's intellectual ascendance and fall). The Daleks surrounding the house and firing on it is lifted from the 1966 *Doctor Who* film *Daleks: Invasion Earth 2150 AD* starring Peter Cushing as Dr. Who and featuring a much younger Bernard Cribbins as policeman Tom Campbell.

Adventures in Time and Space There are flashbacks to "The Christmas Invasion" and quick flashes to Donna in all her stories. When Davros asks how many people have died in the Doctor's name, flashes include Jabe ("The End of the World"), the programmer and Lynda ("Bad Wolf"/"The Parting of the Ways"), Sir Robert ("Tooth and Claw"), Mrs. Moore ("The Age of Steel"), Mr. Skinner inside the Abzorbaloff ("Love & Monsters"), Bridget and Ursula ("Love & Monsters"), the Face of Boe ("Gridlock") and Chantho ("Utopia").

Part of the action is set in the Torchwood Hub, featuring *Torchwood* regulars Captain Jack, Gwen Cooper and Ianto Jones. There are references to *Torchwood* characters Owen and Tosh, as well as Gwen's husband, Rhys. Gwen confirms that she's from an old Cardiff family, going all the way back to the 1800s. The Doctor explains her similarity to Gwyneth ("The Unquiet Dead") as spatial genetic multiplicity (basically an explanation to allow that Gwyneth and Gwen are both played by Eve Myles). The Doctor says, "I told you, no teleport" to Jack, as he incapacitates his vortex manipulator ("Last of the Time Lords").

Another part of the action is set in Sarah Jane Smith's house in Ealing, featuring Sarah Jane Smith, Luke, K9 and Mr. Smith from *The Sarah Jane Adventures*. (One of the funnier gags is when it's revealed that the fanfare that plays when Sarah Jane activates Mr. Smith isn't incidental music but the computer's actual startup noise.) Luke references series regulars Clyde, Maria and Alan. Captain Jack says he's been following Sarah Jane's work and mentions her defeating the Slitheen (*The Sarah Jane Adventures* episodes "Revenge of the Slitheen" and "The Lost Boy").

The Doctor points out that Rose has previously met Dalek Caan, last of the cult of Skaro ("Doomsday"). The Doctor mentions losing a hand in a sword-fight with the Sycorax on Christmas Day ("The Christmas Invasion"). Harriet Jones stands by her actions in that story, as there are times (such as now) that the Doctor isn't present.

We see the Shadow Proclamation for the first time, after being mentioned here and there all the way back to "Rose." Security is provided by the Judoon ("Smith and Jones").

The Doctor notes that "someone tried to move the Earth once before," a reference to 1964's "The Dalek Invasion of Earth." Davros recognizes Sarah on sight, saying she was on Skaro at the creation of the Daleks (1975's "Genesis of the Daleks"). Davros's hand is a metal prosthetic because his original was shot off in 1985's "Revelation of the Daleks." The planets are moved using a Magnetron, which is how Earth was moved to a different constellation in 1986's "Trial of a Time Lord." The emergency temporal shift in "Evolution of the Daleks" took Dalek Caan into the Time War itself.

Martha teleports home to Francine ("Smith and Jones" onwards). The *Valiant* ("The Sound of Drums"/"Last of the Time Lords") is attacked and shot down. UNIT and Lachele Carl's Trinity Wells appear.

One of the missing planets is the uninhabited Callufrax Minor. (Callufrax appeared in 1978's "The Pirate Planet.") Others include Woman Wept (mentioned in "Boom Town"), Clom ("Love & Monsters") and the lost moon of Poosh (mentioned in "Midnight"). Mickey's gran ("Rise of the Cybermen"/"The Age of Steel") passed away peacefully in a mansion. Jackie, who was pregnant at the end of "Doomsday," had a boy called Tony.

The Doctor and Rose have their final conversation in Bad Wolf Bay in the alternate universe, just as they did in "Doomsday" (Rose says, "When I stood on this beach, on the worst day of my life …"). The Doctor says of his Blue Suit clone: "Born in battle, full of blood and anger and revenge. That's me, when we first met."

The Bees Are Disappearing Effect The bees disappearing is finally explained: some of the migrant bees are, in fact, aliens and they're going back home to Melissa Majoria. The TARDIS follows their trail, which ends in the Medusa Cascade, at the centre of a rift in time and space.

The missing planets were being used by the Daleks to construct their ultimate weapon, the reality bomb. The stars going out is due to the reality bomb, which has the potential to destroy everything in the universe, although in the end it barely gets activated.

Who is the Doctor? The Doctor leaves Rose with his blue-suited duplicate because he deems Blue Suit too dangerous to be left alone after he commits genocide. But the real reason, perhaps, is that he knew he had to remove Donna's memories and return her, broken, to her family. He has decided to avoid the company of others and resumes being a lonely god.

The Doctor and Donna The instant biological metacrisis that creates a human duplicate Doctor from Donna's DNA and the Doctor's hand also affects her, giving her Time Lord traits. The duplicate Doctor can see in her mind and knows, in spite of her brilliance, how worthless she feels. However, when Davros activates her Time Lord traits, she becomes fully alive, confident, able to take on Davros and the Daleks, and flirt with Jack. She begs the Doctor not to take away her memories in order to save her life, because she would rather die than have her experience of him taken away. The Doctor can't agree. He takes her memories and leaves Donna vain and shallow, just as she was when she first met him.

Monster of the Week Daleks, at the height of their powers. The Supreme Dalek is red, with extra slanted side panels. Davros, their creator, was rescued from the Time War. He created a new race using his own body: each Dalek was grown from one of his cells. Dalek Caan — referred to as an abomination by the Supreme Dalek — is insane. His casing is open and the mutant within speaks in prophecies.

Stand Up and Cheer It's the simple conversation at the end, with the Doctor talking to Wilf and Sylvia, that's the emotional payoff to this story. As Donna lies unconscious in the next room, her memories of the Doctor wiped, Wilf and Sylvia are forced to face the bittersweet truth: Donna was truly special, but she can never, ever know.

Roll Your Eyes The TARDIS towing the planet Earth across the universe should be a climactic triumph of the episode and the season, but it just looks ridiculous (and vastly out of scale).

You're Not Making Any Sense How did Rose know what she knew? In "Turn

Left," she knows so much she's almost prescient to the second about events that didn't happen in the original reality (such as Torchwood's suicide attack on the Sontaran ship). Here, we learn that she knew about the future because her world was slightly ahead, but this doesn't explain the sheer depth of knowledge she has about things she couldn't possibly know. And how did she appear on a TV screen in "Midnight," hundreds of years in the future?

Interesting Trivia Davros has been alluded to for some years, but unseen and unnamed in the New Series until now. He was a recurring villain in the Classic Series, first seen in 1975's "Genesis of the Daleks." He was originally a Kaled scientist, who was crippled during a war, but continued his work investigating the mutations of his people. He designed a travel machine for those mutations, which he named a "Dalek" (an anagram of his race's name). At the end of "Genesis" he was apparently killed, but the life support system in his chair sustained him and he was resurrected decades later to lead the Daleks. Throughout '80s *Who*, he was seen in every Dalek story, effectively functioning as their mouthpiece. The last time we saw him, he had ascended to Emperor of the Daleks. The power of Davros is the contrast between his crippled body and his articulate moral arguments.

This season's arc has been a lot more disparate than previous ones, combining a number of different elements: the lost planets, the Medusa Cascade meme, the Rose cameos, the talk about the bees disappearing and the stars going out in the parallel worlds. Then there are the things that are mentioned once or twice with payoff later on, like Donna having something on her back, or the ATMOS stickers on the cars in "Partners in Crime," or the Ood talking about "The DoctorDonna." Speaking charitably, the arc this season is really portents of doom. It's all about these different bad omens that are circling the Doctor and Donna: they finally come to roost, nearly leading to the end of the universe and certainly leading to the end of Donna.

In many ways, the arc this season is about Donna: we learn that — even on her first outing as a more selfish person — the whole world would have been different had the Doctor not met her; she's transformed and then has to have all of it taken away from her. And they even give a story reason for that aspect with the metacrisis, saying that all the coincidences, all of Donna's time with the Doctor, is leading to that happening.

The reality bomb is, when you think about it, the ultimate Dalek weapon: something that destroys any life form that's not Dalek. But the configuration of it is very odd. It needs the conjunction of 27 specific planets, but at least three of them — the lost moon of Poosh, Pyrovilia and the Adipose breeding world — are taken from the past, so they're not just moved through space but through time, which would have been a delicate operation, to say the least. Also, presumably the biomass on the planets was an important factor in the planetary configuration, or else why not exterminate everyone on Earth before moving it?

Russell T Davies' memoir of working on Series Four, *The Writer's Tale*, reveals many interesting paths not taken with this story. Early drafts had the Shadow Proclamation feature every alien from the New Series, including Midshipman Frame from "Voyage of the Damned" who now works for the Proclamation. In fact, Annette Badland had recorded dialogue as a regrown Margaret Slitheen (following the events of "Boom Town") before the sequence was cut down to a couple of albinos and some Judoon. Davies also originally had a more explicit explanation of why Rose couldn't stay with the Doctor: the void energy was poisoning her and would kill her if she left the parallel world. This had to be abandoned because Mickey was supposed to be in the third series of *Torchwood*, outside the parallel world, so the explanation didn't work. (Ironic since, in the event, Noel Clarke did not end up appearing in *Torchwood*.)

As is now traditional for a season finale, there are cameos by British celebrities, this time Paul O'Grady (apparently broadcasting his comedy chatshow live on a channel not airing nonstop news that Earth has been moved across space) and celebrity athiest Richard Dawkins, pointing out that it's the Earth that's moved. (Dawkins is married to Lalla Ward, who played Classic *Doctor Who* companion Romana.)

The TARDIS Chronometer The TARDIS lands on Earth and is then left hanging in space when the Earth vanishes (as the TARDIS's position is fixed). It travels to the Shadow Proclamation and then to the Medusa Cascade. Using the subwave network's phone call, it's pulled one second into the future and then lands somewhere in London, near a church.

It's transported to the Dalek Crucible and later tows the Earth back to its rightful position. In the coda, it lands in a London park and then in Bad Wolf Bay in the alternate universe. It's finally seen parked outside the Noble house.

Brilliant? (RS?) The very first thing this story does is undo the climax of the previous one: the TARDIS lands with its lettering restored, no mention of Bad Wolf and the Doctor declaring that everything is okay. This is not an auspicious beginning to the story.

What, exactly, is the plot of "The Stolen Earth"? The Doctor and Donna are stuck on the sidelines, achieving nothing, but follow a trail to the Medusa Cascade, whereupon the Doctor promptly gives up. It takes 36 minutes for the Doctor to arrive in the plot. He then lands on Earth and is shot by a passing Dalek. That's it. That's the entire plot of the first half.

Then, when he meets Davros face to face and Davros wants to hold him accountable for his actions, the Doctor refuses to defend himself. The central debate thrown out by this story concerns the children of time: the Doctor's companions, past and present. Faced with an overwhelming threat, they try to do what the Doctor would do, but they make the wrong choices, because they invariably go for weapons. Rose carries an enormous gun, Martha threatens to destroy Earth, and Sarah and Captain Jack hold the Crucible to ransom with a warp star.

The Doctor is understandably upset about this and Davros taunts him about it. His response is not to rise to the bait, which is admirable, but it makes for dull television. It's even more stark because Julian Bleach's Davros is something quite special indeed, lending his points even more gravitas. However, the core problem is that the Doctor never actually demonstrates what he would do that's better.

This is crying out for a counterpoint; some illustration of a third, brilliant option that only the Doctor's intelligence could think of. Instead, the Doctor does . . . nothing at all. Sheer happenstance means that Donna and the hand merge, creating a clone Doctor and thus saving the day. But even then, with three Doctors on the scene, all that any of them can manage is technobabble.

Worse, not only do Davros's claims go unanswered, but the one speech of outrage that the Doctor delivers is at himself. He's upset because the clone Doctor committed genocide and castigates him for it, sentencing him to a lifetime of hot monkey sex with Billie Piper. Which, we suspect, might not be the ultimate deterrent.

Fundamentally, what this story is grasping at is the idea of destiny. Dalek Caan speaks nothing but prophecy, Rose knows the future, Donna's destiny is retroactively preordained, Davros says the circle of time is closing and that this was meant to be. And yet . . . the event in question never comes to pass. Davros doesn't set off the reality bomb. So why were the stars going out and the walls between dimensions collapsing? Out of nervousness?

Donna becomes the most important person in the universe because she . . . walked too slow to a door. By a fluke of timing, she then merges with the Doctor, becomes part Time Lord and then has to have her memory wiped. Which means that her protestations that she's nothing special, just a temp, turn out to be true. Nothing about her made her special. This is the exact opposite of the message the story intends to tell, and it fails entirely because it's all so contrived. What's more, we understand that Donna has become part Time Lord because . . . she spouts lots of technobabble at high speed. Is that really what defines the Doctor?

David Tennant's impression of Catherine Tate ("That's wizard!") is very poor indeed. He captures none of her speech inflections and instead just overemphasizes a lot. Little wonder it appears once and is then dropped entirely from the narrative. And his interpretation of a part-human Doctor involves saying even more technobabble than usual, even faster and slightly louder; running on autopilot, in other words. Tate, on the other hand, subtly changes her whole demeanour, walking and standing with more confidence. The contrast is striking.

The reality bomb goes nowhere. It dissolves a few extras while the main cast escapes and then the bomb gets deactivated. This could have been huge; they could have killed Jackie and they could have unleashed it on an entire planet, so that we understood its power. Instead, it looks like a poor disintegrator gun, one that you have to convince people to stand under. And this is why the human race was spared? So that 12 of them could be guinea pigs in the bomb's test?

Plotwise, this is a mess. But emotionally, it packs a punch, entirely through Donna's fate. (Rose's is oddly unaffecting.) Taking Donna's memories away is horrific; instead of growing and learning from her time with the Doctor, she's reduced to the shallow version we saw initially, the entire season seemingly wiped away. This seems like a cheat and it seems unfair. What was Davies thinking?

The answer is that it's not about Donna; it's about Sylvia.

When we first met Sylvia, she was the nagging mum, who never believed in Donna. Even her depression in "Turn Left" saw her completely reject her daughter, despite Donna's attempts to keep the family together. She was the one who couldn't be told about aliens and whose reaction to the Doctor was hostile from the outset.

And now, at the end of Donna's story, when the Doctor sits in the living room and tells Sylvia that, for a brief time, Donna was the most important woman in the world, Sylvia snaps back, "She still is. She's my daughter!" It's clear that Sylvia doesn't look at Donna as she used to and that she fundamentally knows just how special her daughter is. When Wilf points out that Donna was better when she was with the Doctor, Sylvia rebukes him, saying, "Don't say that."

What's interesting is that this is part of a recurring theme throughout the New Series: Jackie, Francine and Sylvia are all initially hostile to the Doctor, but eventually and grudgingly learn to accept his influence in their daughters' lives; more importantly, they come to accept that their daughters are capable of making their own choices and learn to trust in them. This is subtle, but it's beautiful.

Series Four gives us the messiest season finale yet. The plot's all over the map, one of the central character beats (the Doctor and Rose) doesn't deliver, and the central moral issue is a damp squib. But the character payoff is magnificent for Donna and Sylvia (and, to a lesser extent, Wilf). It's fun to see all the old faces one last time, although even that will be undercut next season. You'll walk away from this incredibly heartbroken at Donna's fate, perplexed about Rose, thinking about Davros's accusations and with almost no memory of anything else.

Second Opinion (GB) The idea behind Series Four's story arc was brilliant and simple: Rose was back and big bad things were coming. Unfortunately, the execution wasn't quite up to the idea. Some hints of lost planets get dropped and some (in the end inexplicable) glimpses of Rose happen and the once-an-episode reference to the Medusa Cascade becomes more annoying than Torchwood references in Series Two.

And it all leads nowhere.

The much-built-up reunion of the Doctor and Rose doesn't really happen. Worse, the scene on the beach where the Doctor offers his human duplicate feels like he's offering Rose a consolation prize. (And, wouldn't you know it, the duplicate Doctor, who contributes to the worst part of this story, is wearing the blue suit.) You wish that the Doctor could have explained himself more, stated his responsibilities that would forever keep him and Rose apart, alluded to Donna's imminent collapse, or . . . something. Most damningly, the Doctor and Rose don't share a single scene alone the entire story. It's a season-long buildup for nothing.

"The Stolen Earth"/"Journey's End" is part sprawling mess, part sweeping epic. The first episode, which leaves Harriet, Rose and the heroes of the *Doctor Who* spinoffs trying to figure out how to contact the Doctor, is wonderfully tense, and Harriet's sacrifice is both poignant and funny. ("Yes. We know who you are.") Julian Bleach makes Davros creepy for the first time since Michael Wisher played him in 1975. The Doctor regenerating is one of the all-time great cliffhangers in the history of *Doctor Who*. The reality bomb not only has the coolest name of anything in *Doctor Who*, it is a brilliant idea for a Dalek weapon: something that destroys everything not Dalek, everywhere. And Daleks speaking German? That's just genius.

Ultimately, it's Donna's journey, and its end, that gives the season its overall cohesion and makes the story so very affecting (and there's a cost to this: Donna's development in "Journey's End" is at the expense of Rose's). Donna transforms from mouthy and annoying to someone with great passion and depth. Someone observant and thoughtful. Someone who not only saved the Doctor from himself but made him a better person. To watch all this get taken away is gut-wrenching in the extreme. It does raise the question: should the Doctor have granted her request and let her die? Of course you can see the Doctor trying to err on the side of living, however compromised. It's a far from perfect decision, and the result is a kick to the gut. But that's what makes the essence of drama.

This is Russell T Davies' swansong as writer and executive producer of *Doctor Who*. True, he comes back for four more encores in the mini-season of specials, but this story truly is the culmination of his tenure on *Doctor Who*. With Rose's story, you see the excesses of Davies' tenure, as the perfect ending of "Doomsday" gets completely undermined. But with Donna you see his brilliance. And in both, you find drama that isn't safe and that equally infuriates and delights. That's just wizard.

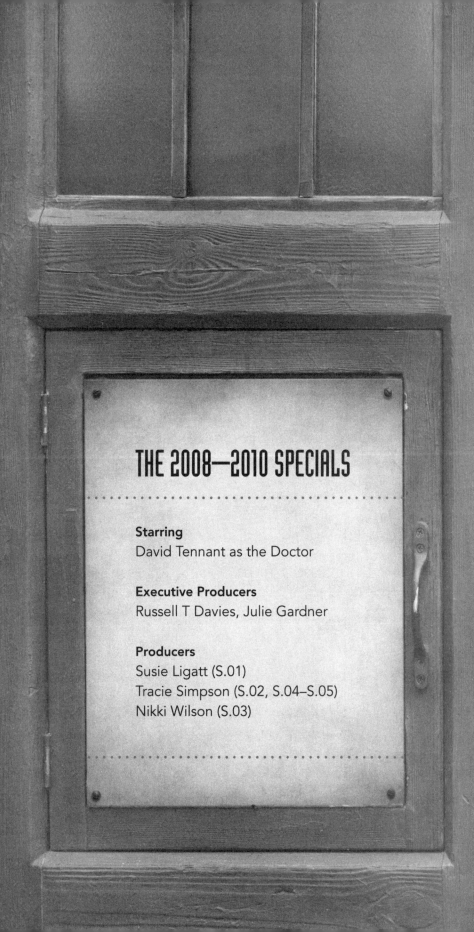

THE 2008—2010 SPECIALS

Starring
David Tennant as the Doctor

Executive Producers
Russell T Davies, Julie Gardner

Producers
Susie Ligatt (S.01)
Tracie Simpson (S.02, S.04–S.05)
Nikki Wilson (S.03)

5.01 The Next Doctor

Written by Russell T Davies **Directed by** Andy Goddard

Supporting cast David Morrissey (Jackson Lake), Velile Tshabalala (Rosita Farisi), Dervla Kirwan (Miss Hartigan), Edmund Kente (Mr. Scoones), Michael Bertenshaw (Mr. Cole), Jason Morell (vicar), Neil McDermott (Jed), Tom Langford (Frederick), Paul Kasey (Cyberleader), Nicholas Briggs (Cybermen voices), Jason Etheridge (Lad)

Original airdate December 25, 2008

The Big Idea The Doctor encounters another man who calls himself the Doctor, fighting the Cybermen in Victorian London.

Roots and References Works of Charles Dickens, including *Oliver Twist* (children in Victorian workhouses) and *A Christmas Carol* (the Doctor asking a boy what year it is); the super robot form of mecha found in Japanese anime such as *Mazinger Z* and what became known in North America as *Voltron: Defender of the Universe* (the CyberKing); the Robert Burns poem "To a Mouse" (Jackson refers to a Cybershade as a "timorous beastie," a phrase the Doctor also used in "Tooth and Claw").

Adventures in Time and Space It's snowing actual snow and the Doctor's delighted (referencing the fake snow at Christmases in "The Christmas Invasion," "The Runaway Bride" and "Voyage of the Damned"). "'Don't blink,' remember that? Blinking and the statues, Sally and the Angels?" "Blink." (Which is odd way to jog a memory, because the Doctor wasn't actually present for it.)

The Doctor tells Jackson and Rosita that the Cybermen were sent into a howling wilderness called the void ("Doomsday"). Everything inside the void perished. But the last of the Cybermen fell through the dimensions when the walls of reality broke down ("Journey's End"). They stole a dimension vault from the Daleks, which allowed them to travel in time. (This is quite similar to what happens to the Daleks in "Daleks in Manhattan.") Their information on the Doctor was likely stolen from the Daleks as well. Mickey also used the word "CyberKing" when speculating on the contents of the void ship in "Army of Ghosts."

Images of all ten Doctors are projected from an infostamp. Flashes of the tenth Doctor include footage from "The Runaway Bride" and "Rise of the Cybermen"/"The Age of Steel." Legend has it that the memories of a Time Lord can be contained within a watch ("Human Nature"/"The Family of Blood," "Utopia").

"The events of today will be history, spoken of for centuries to come." We'll revisit this in "Flesh and Stone." Jackson asks why the Doctor is alone and he says, "Because they leave. Some of them meet someone else. And some of them forget me. In the end, they break my heart." The former refers to almost all his companions while the latter refers specifically to Donna ("Journey's End").

Who is the Doctor? The Doctor seems initially bemused that there's a future incarnation of himself (he's more concerned that he regenerated for a good reason), which is odd given the Doctor's behaviour in the subsequent specials.

The Doctor and Jackson Lake The Doctor is quite jovial with Jackson when he thinks him to be a future Doctor. He's then compassionate in helping Jackson come to terms with the fact he's not really the Doctor. Because of his fugue experience assuming the Doctor's identity, Jackson knows the Doctor is often unrecognized for his exploits and makes sure he is cheered when he defeats the CyberKing. He also insists the Doctor join him for Christmas dinner when the Doctor tells him that he travels alone due to his recent heartbreak.

Monster of the Week The Cybermen are in the wrong century and don't have much power. They can plug infostamps directly into their chests and the projections then show in the eye. The Cybercontroller has his brain exposed, as he did previously, but he now has a black faceplate. They have no pity.

Stand up and Cheer Jackson realizing he has a son is a beautiful emotional payoff to the best part of this episode: Jackson's trauma in being forced to find escape in the world of the Doctor rather than face reality. In an episode featuring giant monsters stomping over London and the Doctor in a balloon defeating them to applause from the populace below, it's the quiet, human moments that stand out.

Roll Your Eyes Of all the hundreds of children in the workhouse, Jackson's son just happens to be the only child not to run out with the others and instead stands motionless on a high platform.

You're Not Making Any Sense When the Doctor and Jackson are being pulled through the window by a rope, they slide right through, but physics doesn't work like that. The rope was hanging down, so they should have caught at the window's edge or come through messily, not flown smoothly in.

Interesting Trivia Jackson Lake's outfit is that of "generic Doctor," with waistcoat, cravat and smoking jacket, in a deliberately retro look (albeit contemporary for the time the episode is set). This is the sort of outfit everyone assumed the Doctor would wear, until Christopher Eccleston and David Tennant came along and sported quite different looks. You can see this kind of generic Doctor outfit in Paul McGann's costume in the 1996 TV Movie and also Mark Gatiss's parody Doctor in the 1999 "Doctor Who Night," where Gatiss played a generic Doctor with exactly this kind of outfit, drawing on a race memory of the character as a fuddy-duddy professor type from a bygone age. The New Series has studiously avoided that, so it's interesting to note its appearance here, standing in as a shortcut for "Doctorish."

This is the first of five special episodes that were broadcast between Christmas Day 2008 and New Year's Day 2010. After four seasons, Russell T Davies was looking to leave. David Tennant was thinking of departing too, with new opportunities on the horizon, including playing Hamlet in a Royal Shakespeare Company production. Broadcasting a limited number of specials for 2009 meant that both star and producer could stay on a little longer (while enabling Tennant to play Hamlet) and allow the new production team to transition in smoothly while also ensuring that the BBC had at least some new episodes of *Doctor Who*. The practice of breaking up a run of regular seasons of a program with one-off specials is more common in Britain (*Absolutely Fabulous* has done it several times) than in North America, so it wasn't that unusual.

David Tennant announced he was departing as the Doctor in October 2008, which drove speculation about a story titled "The Next Doctor" into overdrive. Of course, within the first 20 minutes it was settled that David Morrissey was not the Doctor, which only fuelled further interest in who would be the eleventh Doctor. On January 2, 2009, that question was settled when, in a special episode of *Doctor Who Confidential*, it was announced that the next Doctor was an unknown actor named Matt Smith . . .

If you experience déjà vu looking at the layout of the workhouse set, there might be a reason for that: it's a cunning redress of the hub set from *Torchwood*!

The TARDIS Chronometer Near a market stall in 1851 London.

Brilliant? (RS?) "The Next Doctor" should be brilliant. It has a great hook — its bluff about the future Doctor — a popular old enemy, a suave and attractive villain, and a spectacular set piece in the CyberKing rising from the Thames to march over London. Unfortunately, although all these sound great on paper and are serviceable enough onscreen, they can't overcome one immutable fact: this story is almost entirely forgettable.

This will even become a plot point next season. Part of the problem is trying to make the episode too big; the CyberKing's march wants to be iconic, but instead it runs up against the problem that people should have noticed. Jackson's speech at the end about this event making history and being told for centuries to come is intended to address the problem via a joke, but it doesn't work because the problem is too big to be dismissed like this.

However, there's one aspect that really, soundly works: Jackson's trauma. ("They stole something so precious.") Fortunately, this drives a lot of the plot, but it suggests that Davies would be much happier writing "real" drama, as he simply isn't interested in the sci-fi mechanics of the story. In some ways, this is great, because I'd rather have a series with heart that didn't always make sense than the opposite. Unfortunately, sometimes the sci-fi logic problems muddle the story he's trying to tell.

The bluff about the future Doctor is very well done, convincing both us and the Doctor at first. The joke doesn't outstay its welcome, because it's used to further the plot. The Doctor's gentle explanation to Jackson and Rosita is fabulous — and his "whistling" the sonic screwdriver (remarkably in tune!) is hilarious.

Miss Hartigan is a worthy attempt at characterisation. Like the story itself, there's nothing intrinsically wrong with her; a woman used to manipulating men with a mind so strong she overcomes the Cybermen is a great throughline. "The Doctor: yet another man come to assert himself against me in the night" is a wonderful line. And her dressing all in red (complete with parasol) for a funeral is just fabulous. Unfortunately, despite all the great elements on display, they don't quite come together. Nothing actually sticks: Jackson's trauma is too small scale, the Cyberthreat is generic and there's no ongoing companion to add a connection for the viewer.

There's an attempt to make this socially relevant . . . if you can call mild commentary on Victorian work practices socially relevant in 2008. The children-as-a-workforce element is so half-hearted you wonder why they bothered. Part of it is that the story has to be so very careful to ensure none of the children are harmed, which results in a somewhat reduced menace. Instead, we're shown stock grimy, adorable kids in flat caps and brown waistcoats toiling briefly in a workhouse. Miss Hartigan speaks of a new industrial revolution, with children as its workforce, but nothing is done with the concept. It's set up to be biting commentary, but it lacks fangs.

"The Next Doctor" is surprisingly undercooked. It lacks the oomph of previous Christmas specials and instead feels like a fairly generic episode, which doesn't bode well for the forthcoming specials. The major redeeming feature is Jackson's trauma and its emotional payoff, but the rest struggles to be relevant or memorable. It's too bad, because all the ingredients were there, but somehow they just didn't mix.

Second Opinion (GB) What's fascinating about "The Next Doctor" is how Russell T Davies deconstructs the character of the Doctor through Jackson Lake: Jackson looks and acts the part the viewing public largely believes the Doctor to be (right down to the Victorian outfit he hasn't worn since 2005). But Jackson's Doctor, for all his cleverness, bravery and cocksureness, only connects with the Doctor (and the viewer) when we get past all that to the pain and emotion of the heart of the character. Which is, in itself, an interesting commentary on what makes the Doctor work in the modern series. It's a shame, though, that David Morrissey is playing such an archetype. You really want him to cut loose with David Tennant the same way the pair did in *Blackpool*, but when Morrissey settles for being charming and occasionally haunted, rather than his usual white-hot intensity, more's the pity.

Still, we have the compensation of Dervla Kirwan stealing the show as Miss Hartigan; she's probably the best villain New *Who* has ever seen. Kirwan is phenomenal playing a woman in Victorian times who has reached the edge of societal limits and now has the power to go beyond them. Her witty barbs are sublime. Her matter-of-fact manner while the Cybermen slaughter everyone except the people she's named is beautiful. The moment when the Doctor lets her realize the horror of what's happened to her — that she's merely being used and mistreated instead of being elevated to godhood — is frighteningly well nuanced. The real shame is that more isn't done with her.

The main problem with this story is the Cybermen. There's no good reason for their inclusion beyond their looks (although admittedly there's real iconic value to them marching through a snow-covered graveyard). They don't fit in the story at all, and the limitations of the New Series version of the Cybermen as domestic menace, as opposed to spaceborne threat, are no more evident than here. Another alien threat (or another past monster) might have worked better. (The Sontarans, for one.) That said, I still adore the battle between the CyberKing and the Doctor aboard Jackson Lake's TARDIS, even if the CyberKing makes little sense for the parallel-Earth Cybermen.

"The Next Doctor" has a great supporting character, a great villain and some poignant moments with both. The problem is, none of these elements actually connect to form a cohesive story. Fortunately, they're sufficient unto themselves.

5.02 Planet of the Dead

Written by Russell T Davies and Gareth Roberts **Directed by** James Strong

Supporting cast Michelle Ryan (Lady Christina de Souza), Lee Evans (Malcolm Taylor), Noma Dumezweni (Captain Erisa Magambo), Adam James (D.I. McMillan), Glenn Doherty (Sergeant Dennison), Victoria Alcock (Angela Whittaker), David Ames (Nathan), Ellen Thomas (Carmen), Reginald Tsiboe (Lou), Daniel Kaluuya (Barclay), Keith Parry (bus driver), James Layton (Sergeant Ian Jenner), Paul Kasey (Sorvin), Ruari Mears (Praygat)

Original airdate April 11, 2009

The Big Idea A London double-decker bus carrying the Doctor and a fleeing thief among its passengers gets sucked through a wormhole to an alien planet, leaving UNIT to contend with a possible alien threat on Earth.

Roots and References *Mission: Impossible* movies (Lady Christina's acrobatics);

The Pink Panther films and *Hustle* (the gentlewoman thief pulling capers); *Lawrence of Arabia* (the desert; Murray Gold even echoes Maurice Jarre's score at a couple of points); the original 1958 version of *The Fly* (the Tritovore design). The Swarm seem to have their origins in a variety of different marine-life thrillers, but we'll suggest the 1978 Roger Corman/Joe Dante film *Piranha*.

Adventures in Time and Space The Doctor and Malcolm reminisce about the giant robot from 1974's "Robot." UNIT's Captain Erisa Magambo was last seen in the parallel timeline in "Turn Left," when Donna was assisting Rose with her experiments on the TARDIS. This is Magambo's first appearance in the "regular" *Doctor Who* universe. The Doctor recalls the events of "Midnight" when he mutters, "Humans on buses, always blaming me." He admits to Lady Christina he stole the TARDIS (as established in 1969's "The War Games") and recalls how Donna used to call him "Spaceman."

The Song Is Ending Effect The last days of the tenth Doctor begin here, as Carmen repeats the Ood's phrase from "Planet of the Ood" as a warning to the Doctor, "Your song is ending." She tells him, "It is returning through the dark . . . he will knock four times." These two prophecies will dominate the next two stories.

The Doctor and Lady Christina The Doctor finds some connection with Lady Christina's sense of adventure. She claims she and the Doctor were made for each other and kisses him when he gets the bus back home, but the Doctor refuses to take her as a companion saying, "People have travelled with me and I've lost them. Lost them all. Never again."

Monster of the Week The Swarm are stingray-like creatures, vast in number, with metallic exoskeletons. They are mindless predators that devour everything on a planet's surface.

Stand up and Cheer The way Doctor averts another "Midnight" is really very sweet. He keeps everyone together by getting the stranded travellers to focus on what they were going to do that night back at home: "Far away, chops and gravy, Mike and Suzanne, watching TV and poor old Tina." It's a charming scene that not only shows in simple ways the lives of the other passengers, but the Doctor calms the fears of the passengers by connecting them to the basics: home, food and companionship.

Roll Your Eyes Is there now some kind of law that states the female guest star in a special must kiss the Doctor, no matter how little it makes sense? When Astrid grabbed a gratuitous snog with the Doctor in "Voyage of the Damned," you at least felt it was earned, based on the growing relationship between the two. Here, it just seems tacked on because it's deemed that Michelle Ryan and David Tennant ought to kiss.

You're Not Making Any Sense Four people guard the chalice *with their backs to* *it*?! The thief swaps it out with an object that makes noise and therefore alerts the guards?! Someone can bribe their way onto a London bus with a diamond earring?! Said bus doesn't stop when multiple police cars with sirens flashing are chasing it?! Just the bus goes through the wormhole?! That's only the first 10 minutes . . .

Interesting Trivia Malcolm Taylor is only the second scientific advisor to UNIT we've ever seen, the first being the Doctor himself in the '70s. The third Doctor's original companion, Liz Shaw, sort of fulfilled this role, but she was seconded to UNIT rather than made its scientific advisor. The position was probably created to give the Doctor some sort of official standing in the organization, but it makes sense that UNIT would need a scientific advisor, so we can surmise that they probably continued the role after the Doctor left and that Malcolm is just one in a very long line.

The bus is said to act as a Faraday cage, meaning that its metal cage insulates against electricity. This is why you're perfectly safe if lightning strikes your airplane in flight. However, the principle doesn't apply here, because the holes in a Faraday cage have to be significantly smaller than the wavelength of the electromagnetic radiation, and the bus has huge windows. It also doesn't protect you if you're in direct contact with the metal shell, which would be quite likely on a bus.

Malcolm's units of measurement include a "Bernard," named after Bernard Quatermass, the scientist from the pioneering BBC science-fiction series *The Quatermass Experiment* (1953) and its sequels that was, in many ways, a forerunner to *Doctor Who*. Interestingly, Malcolm doesn't indicate if Bernard Quatermass is fictional character in the *Doctor Who* universe, continuing a tradition of meta-fictional shout-outs to the *Quatermass* series in *Doctor Who* that began with 1988's "Remembrance of the Daleks" and continued in "The Christmas Invasion" with references to Quatermass's British Rocket Group, the space agency Bernard Quatermass led.

The bus was given the number 200 as a nod to it being the 200th *Doctor Who* story. Hardcore fans may debate the math employed to come up with this number (it excludes the incomplete 1980 story "Shada," counts the entirety of 1986's "The Trial of a Time Lord" as one story and counts "Utopia" and "The Sound of Drums"/"Last of the Time Lords" as a single story). Russell T Davies admitted to the spurious nature of the calculation, but he was happy for the opportunity for publicity nonetheless.

This was not only the first *Doctor Who* story to be filmed in the United Arab Emirates, it was also the first to be shot in the newfangled high-definition format. The bus was accidentally damaged in transit to the UAE, so the script was rewritten to incorporate its damage in the desert scenes. The London footage had already been shot, so the damage had to be added via CGI to the final scenes.

The TARDIS Chronometer London in the present day (the 2008 banking crisis has already happened) and the planet San Helios.

Brilliant? (GB) The great thing about *Doctor Who* is that it's like the weather: if you don't like what's here now, something else will be along shortly. It's something to keep in mind while watching "Planet of the Dead." People expecting it to be a super-serious kick-off to the final phase of the David Tennant/Russell T Davies era of *Doctor Who* will be very disappointed. It's a silly, inconsequential change-of-pace runaround.

Taken on that basis, there's a lot to enjoy. It's fast-paced, fun and frothy with some nice set pieces (the Tritovore ship) and some great comedy bits (the Doctor getting ready to take charge as he always does, only to find Lady Christina on the scene). The Tritovores are a fun monster, combining a kid-loveable, um, occupation, cool prosthetics and some funny (if implied) dialogue. On the other side of the wormhole, there's a delightful double-act in geeky fanboy Malcolm and the unflappable Captain Magambo.

David Tennant is clearly having a ball with the script, milking way more laughs out of any scene than it rightfully deserves. ("Before I die of old age, which would be quite an achievement, so congratulations on that.") The same is true for Lee Evans' infectious enthusiasm as Malcolm, only multiplied by a factor of 50 Bernards. Noma Dumezweni, who was delightful in "Turn Left," is even better here. Magambo's unflappable professionalism while never playing the fool reminds us of the glory days of a certain Brigadier.

It's a shame, then, that Michelle Ryan is thrown into the mix to stiffly play a Lara Croft clone. Her part is to conveniently provide us with a cat burglar who can steal the anti-grav clamp and provide the Doctor with a witty sparring partner. On paper, the role is written for a Diana Rigg as an Emma Peel type. The problem with Ryan's portrayal is that it's one note: smug.

Worse, there is zero chemistry between the Time Lord and the Lady. Compare it to the relationship with Donna in "The Runaway Bride" or Astrid in "Voyage of the Damned," and you see the romance of someone being drawn into an instant relationship with the Doctor. Here, Tennant and Ryan go through the motions. We're supposed to think they could be an item because they tell us they're made for each other, even though there's nothing compelling about her relationship with the Doctor. (Worse, thanks to the costume design, she's not even sexy. Here's the thing about Lara Croft: no one would ever dress like her, but that's not the point!)

The very setup of the story deprives it of much-needed substance. Even by the standard of *Who*'s frothy Christmas fare, this is remarkably lacking in actual danger or thrills. In a story that should be a cross between "Midnight" and "Voyage of the Damned," it studiously avoids all the things that made both those stories great. You're left wondering how much better it could have been with a more ordinary companion; if the Doctor and the passengers of the 200 bus had to struggle, as if on a Jules Verne expedition, for the things needed to get off San Helios. Having a professional jewel thief around speeds up the action, but it also puts the brakes on the drama. The result is very light on jeopardy. Worse, a bus full of well-established characters are left behind for 30 minutes doing nothing except occasional mobile phone calls to remind people they're there.

It would also help if there were, occasionally, some brains in the plotting. Once again, we have a story where calling events and plot devices random and unmotivated would be charitable. Lady Christina's gadget-filled rucksack would need to be carried by a linebacker. Why doesn't the Doctor just say he needs the anti-grav clamp? How do the Doctor and Lady Christina outrun a swarm that's supposed to be so fast they can rip the fabric of space and time? You could make a drinking game out of the holes in this plot, but you would die of alcohol poisoning in the process.

And yet, in spite of so many of my frustrations, it somehow seems churlish to criticize "Planet of the Dead" for not being more serious or dramatic; it's a bit like criticizing simple comfort food for not being gourmet enough. It's big. It's colourful. There are moments to cheer or laugh. That's all it really wants to do, ultimately. With a horror story on Mars and the big epic finale on deck, this little bit of frivolity might be the last time we see David Tennant doing silly things, and perhaps we should just enjoy it for what it is: a bit of a laugh with Lee Evans.

Second Opinion (RS?) In a parallel universe, there's a 45-minute version of this story that's the frivolous third episode of David Tennant's fourth full season. That story begins with a bus crashing in a quarry and ends with its triumphant escape home. What's missing from that version of the story is everything set on Earth and with UNIT. That version is competent, entertaining — and wholly forgettable.

The extra running time "Planet of the Dead" has as a special allows room for a B-plot, but it's the B-plot that outshines the twee A-plot on the planet. With the UNIT characters, we have amusing comedy (courtesy of Malcolm), actual tension (Magambo's threat) and a reason to care (the connection to Earth). Many stories set on an alien world, in a desperate bid for relevance, throw in a link to Earth. Think "Silence in the Library" or 1978's "The Pirate Planet." But what the writers of these stories fail to realize is that references alone do not a credible threat make.

"Planet of the Dead," while never going to suffer accusations of serious drama — Carmen must be the worst psychic in the world to get on that bus — nevertheless makes the threat posed to Earth feel real because it takes the time to set it up. The wormhole gives us a ticking clock (our heroes have until the swarm reaches it to escape or we're all doomed!), the Earthbound UNIT characters put a face on the potential victims and the disaster very nearly happens (some of the swarm making it through to Earth creates a more dramatic story).

This link allows the "planet" of the title to work, along with the brave choice to film in an actual desert. Instead of a quarry or a studio jungle, we have a location that doesn't look like anywhere in Britain, which is as alien as it's possible to get on British TV — and infinitely better than any CGI recreation could possibly be. Plus, with the link to Earth, it's not just Zog monsters on the planet Zog again.

That's the genius of "Planet of the Dead." It might be fun, frothy, throwaway fare, but — almost in spite of itself — it engages us and makes us care. That it's not more loved is largely due to the fact that it was the only story in a ten-month period. If it were episode three in that parallel universe, we would have simply shrugged and moved on.

5.03 The Waters of Mars

Written by Russell T Davies and Phil Ford **Directed by** Graeme Harper

Supporting cast Lindsay Duncan (Adelaide Brooke), Peter O'Brien (Ed Gold), Aleksander Mikic (Yuri Kerenski), Gemma Chan (Mia Bennett), Chook Sibtain (Tarak Ital), Alan Ruscoe (Andy Stone), Cosima Shaw (Steffi Ehrlich), Michael Goldsmith (Roman Groom), Lily Bevan (Emily), Max Bollinger (Mikhail), Charlie De'Ath (Adelaide's father), Rachel Fewell (Young Adelaide), Anouska Strahnz (Ulrika Ehrlich), Zofie Strahnz (Lisette Ehrlich), Paul Kasey (Ood Sigma)

Original airdate November 15, 2009

The Big Idea The Doctor visits the first human colony on Mars, knowing its inhabitants are about to die.

Roots and References The Mars trilogy by Kim Stanley Robinson; the David Bowie song "Life on Mars?" and the TV series of the same name (Bowie Base One); *The Abyss* (the water-based life forms) and *Short Circuit* (the cute robot).

Adventures in Time and Space The Doctor discusses the Ice Warriors, Classic Series villains from Mars who first appeared in 1967's "The Ice Warriors"; he says they built an empire out of snow.

The destruction of Bowie Base One is a fixed point in time and cannot be changed ("The Fires of Pompeii"). The Doctor tells Adelaide that there are laws of time and that once there were people in charge of those laws, but they died ("Father's Day"). The Doctor says he's saved some little people from historical events, likely referring to Caecilius's family in "The Fires of Pompeii." He also says, "Imagine you found yourself somewhere — Pompeii" and in trying to prevent a disaster you make it happen, referencing the same story.

We see a flashback to an incident set during the events of "The Stolen Earth"/"Journey's End," when a Dalek flies to young Adelaide's window. There are audio clips from past episodes of the Doctor saying he's the last of the Time Lords ("Rise of the Cybermen," "Doomsday," "Gridlock" and "Utopia"), that the Time Lords died (the Time War) and also that the walls of reality are closing ("The Stolen Earth"/"Journey's End").

There's a story of someone who once disguised a domestic robot as a dog, which the Doctor finds sweet, referencing K9 (first seen in 1977's "The Invisible Enemy"). The Cloister Bell rings twice at the end of the story; it first rang in 1981's "Logopolis." The Doctor wears the same orange spacesuit he wore in "The Impossible Planet"/"The Satan Pit." Ood Sigma previously appeared in "Planet of the Ood." After all his issues with people saluting him in "The Sontaran Strategem" and elsewhere, the tenth Doctor salutes Adelaide, the only person he ever formally salutes.

The Song Is Ending Effect The Doctor says that someone recently told him that he was going to die and that "he will knock four times." Instead, the Flood knock three times. After Adelaide's suicide, a vision of Ood Sigma appears and the Doctor says, "Is this it? My death? Is it time?"

Who is the Doctor? When he's asked his name, rank and intention, he answers, "Doctor, Doctor, fun." However, watching the plight of the doomed Bowie Base One crew brings him face to face with his guilt of being the surviving Time Lord, and prompts him to attempt to save them in spite of the fact that their destruction is a fixed point in time. Saving them, he declares that the laws of time are his and that they will obey him, and that he thought he was just a survivor of the Time War, but now believes he was the winner: the Time Lord victorious. Adelaide's suicide makes him realize his hubris.

The Doctor and Adelaide The Doctor and Adelaide have a conflicted relationship, to put it mildly. She's initially suspicious of him, but the Doctor is in awe of her and has always wanted to meet her. The pair eventually warm to each other, and the Doctor tells her she has starlight in her soul and even tells her the future history of her family as consolation for the fact that she's destined to die on Mars. She's appalled by the Doctor's decision to save her, saying that no one should have the Doctor's power. She kills herself to preserve future history and the legacy of her children and grandchildren.

Monster of the Week The Flood (named in a scene that was cut from the episode, though it is available on the DVD). It hides in water and infects people when as little as a single drop touches them. It can create water, sometimes in massive amounts. Infected humans have mottled faces, their jawlines cracked and grey. They can communicate telepathically, breathe water and don't need air. They can survive outside in the Martian atmosphere, thanks to internal fission, but can be immobilized by freezing.

Stand Up and Cheer The Doctor's walk away from the base, with the sounds of death playing over the intercom and him closing his eyes but still walking, is incredibly harrowing. It takes the tight action-adventure story of the base on Mars and integrates it with the larger story about the Doctor's foreknowledge of the base's destiny, making for very powerful television.

Roll Your Eyes When Tarak finds Andy, standing alone in the dark and dripping impossibly with water, why doesn't he report to Adelaide over the intercom, as specifically instructed? Instead, he walks right up to Andy, all alone, allowing himself to be within striking distance.

You're Not Making Any Sense Forty years earlier, in the midst of the extermination or capture of the entirety of humanity, a Dalek decided to spare young Adelaide and simply fly away because — somehow — it knew that she'd be important to the future history of Earth. Despite the fact that the Daleks spent the entirety of "The Stolen Earth"/"Journey's End" developing a reality bomb that would unravel all of non-Dalek kind. So they spared Adelaide to preserve a future history that, had it not been for the Doctor's involvement, they were hours away from wiping out themselves?

Interesting Trivia There's a concerted effort in this episode to illustrate the realism of space travel and colonization, from the nine-month flight time and every pound in weight equalling three tonnes of fuel to the attempts to grow vegetables and the base having been built by worker drones. Most future settings (in *Doctor Who* and elsewhere) skimp on these details, in the interest of plot expediency, which makes some sense given the constraints of television drama. However, many of the details are explicitly plot-related, which forces the story to confront the enormous difficulties that living off-Earth would entail. What it loses in expediency, it makes up for in the characters overcoming adversity, making their achievements seem even bigger in the audience's eyes.

The future website (modelled on the present-day BBC news site) is a clever way of imparting key information while avoiding characters explaining things to one another which they'd already know, or having the Doctor be ignorant of the setup (which isn't possible with this story's premise). Mostly, the important information is in the headlines, but pausing reveals all sorts of titbits about future history, from the Australian space race and Iowa's storms to NASA's development of a patch that overcomes symptoms caused by specific gravity measures. Perhaps the most intriguing is in the final flash, where a small boxout is titled "The Mythical Doctor," suggesting that Yuri and Gemma told people of their experiences, explaining how they came to be on Earth. Frustratingly, however, this detail is in the corner of the screen, so we don't get to read what it says about him!

The scheduling of this story was up in the air for a long time. Originally, this special would have aired on Christmas Day, 2009 (the original title was the frankly awesome "Red Christmas"), but a number of factors led to it ultimately being moved to a November airdate. This led to a "de-Christmasing" of the script, mostly changing references to Bowie Base One's accident happening in November 2059 instead of December. Echoes of the Christmas setting are still there, with conversations about the upcoming Christmas dinner and, in a deleted scene available on the Complete Specials boxset, an explanation that the snow is a "carbon wash," which would have continued the tradition of faux-snow in the Christmas specials.

This episode was dedicated to Barry Letts, producer for most of the Jon Pertwee era, who died in October 2009.

The TARDIS Chronometer The TARDIS initially lands on Mars, some distance from Bowie Base One, on November 21, 2059. It later materializes inside the base for a second, then lands on Earth, outside Adelaide's house.

Brilliant? (RS?) Before this half-series of specials, previous Christmas specials succeeded because they all offered something worth analyzing and discussing. This was largely due to their stunt companions: Harriet Jones, Donna Noble and Astrid Peth were all highly developed one-off (or, as it turned out, not-so-one-off) companions, the sort of people you got to know and connected with, even in a short space of time. This year's specials haven't offered much: David Morrissey's "next" Doctor had some pathos but wasn't really companion material, while Lady Christina was such a caricature that she's barely worth mentioning. What's more, those specials were fairly light and fluffy, lacking in any sort of ongoing arc or even having the decency to be scary.

Thankfully, none of this applies to "The Waters of Mars." The first time around, "The Waters of Mars" is a great standalone episode, with a few minutes of "arc" stuff tacked onto the end. But that one-off plot is fantastic. It has it all: a proper alien planet, supporting characters you can sink your teeth into and a threat that for once feels downright scary.

The possession effect is incredibly successful, despite — or possibly because of — its low-budget look. Good prosthetics beat CGI any day, and there's nothing to sell a threat like having a partial human face looking out at us. What's even better though is the idea: living water is primal. Water is patient. Water is unstoppable. We need water for survival, but we'll quickly die if we have too much of it. "The Waters of Mars" taps into these fears beautifully. It also turns down the lights, which helps enormously.

Then there's the last ten minutes. First time around, I hated it: tacked onto the end of an otherwise effective story, you have a last-minute panic that seemingly comes from nowhere. What's worse is that Tennant just can't pull off the scene on his own, which is a huge failing for the specials.

Which leads us to the obvious question about these specials: why didn't they include an ongoing companion? As we've seen, every story needs someone to fulfil the companion role, so what's the point of having the Doctor travel solo for so long? Once in a while, it's a nice change, but the series is vastly poorer for not having a second regular.

What's remarkable is just how different a story this is on second viewing. Second time round, knowing where it's all going, the various clues work magnificently. The flashforwards to the future news reports are great, an elegant way of providing exposition that doesn't involve the tenth Doctor explaining everything in a rushed garble, but does leave him (and us) with critical foreknowledge. The crew relationships are a lot richer than they seemed at first and even the threat seems scarier.

However, what's truly amazing is the tenth Doctor.

I've been critical of David Tennant before, but I want to be just as effusive now. He's really good here, in a way I just didn't notice the first time around. His fear when he hears three knocks is palpable, but it's his constant demeanour of quietness that really pays dividends. This is a Doctor who doesn't work at all when he's being shouty or gabbling, but who is incredible in the small, quiet moments.

What's more, the last ten minutes no longer feel tacked on. The Time Lord victorious feels wrong precisely because it's meant to, and the Doctor's instant switch from manic on Bowie Base One to calm on Earth is so unsettling that you sympathize entirely with the crew's reactions.

As far as the companion goes, "The Waters of Mars" is the exception that proves the rule: not only is Adelaide utterly fabulous, but the story twists your expectations at the end and what happens with her is truly shocking, even on a rewatch. It's still a shame we had to sit through Lady Christina, but if it meant this was the end result, then that's almost worth it. Almost.

Of course, it's still not perfect, even on rewatch. Despite succeeding emotionally, the ending still lacks logic. How do the survivors explain being on

Earth without the nine-month journey from Mars? Doesn't Adelaide ending up in her house mean the future text should be massively rewritten, not just changed by one word? Worse, Tennant still can't pull off that solo scene with the Ood. However, it's not the tacked-on ending I thought it was first time around, because you can see the logic of the story working throughout.

"The Waters of Mars" is a fabulous story. It has tight plotting, a fantastic guest star, excellent characterisation, a highly effective monster and is fundamentally built around the ongoing story. Plus, it gets better every time you watch it. Which is lucky, because it's the only one of the specials that you'll even remotely want to rewatch.

Second Opinion (GB) For me, the only thing that is really wrong with "The Waters of Mars" is its use of location. The corridors between the biodomes (shot on location) seem too large for credibility. Not even Graeme Harper can make it seem as claustrophobic as the studio sets for the bridge and the airlocks, which drains all tension from the chase sequences. However that's a small quibble, which I'll tolerate. I'll even tolerate the cute robot with flaming tire tracks.

Otherwise, "The Waters of Mars" is not only the best story of this shortened season of specials; it's one of the best stories of David Tennant's tenure as the Doctor. The genius of the script is that it plays on multiple levels: it's a brilliant base-under-siege thriller with a creepy monster, but it's also a dark meditation on power and responsibility in the *Doctor Who* universe. And it's a wonderful character piece for the tenth Doctor, as he starts out as his cheery, motormouth self and ends in the worst possible place, mentally and spiritually.

The great thing about David Tennant is that, unless you're Robert Smith?, you don't even worry any more that such a range is beyond him. He's that good. Lindsay Duncan proves "Planet of the Dead" false by showing the casting of the female lead is indeed crucial to the success of the episode. (Unlike my co-author, I think it's fine to do these specials without a recurring companion as they might well have got in the way of the Doctor's descent here.) Duncan's Adelaide is strong, grim and determined, but never — please take note, Michelle Ryan — one note. It's wonderful when she finally lets herself be swept up with the adventure and agrees with the Doctor that bikes are a good idea, as is her dramatic confrontation with the Doctor after his sin against the laws of time.

As expected for anything with the credit "Directed by Graeme Harper," the rest of the cast is just as great. You care for the plight of Bowie Base One because of all the vividly depicted characters onscreen. When everything goes to hell, the viewer ends up watching heartbreak after heartbreak: Steffi transforming while listening to her daughter speak in Swedish; Ed obliquely telling Adelaide she'd never forgive him while he detonates the rocket; Roman politely telling the crew he can't go on. It's no wonder the Doctor succumbs to temptation and decides to save them. The Bowie Base One's doom is otherwise unbearable.

All that said, the best thing about "The Waters of Mars"? In its final appearance, the curse of the blue suit is utterly and totally broken.

S.04—S.05 The End of Time, Parts One and Two

Written by Russell T Davies **Directed by** Euros Lyn

Supporting cast Bernard Cribbins (Wilfred Mott), John Simm (The Master), Timothy Dalton (The Narrator/Lord President), Catherine Tate (Donna Noble), Jacqueline King (Sylvia Noble), Billie Piper (Rose Tyler), Camille Coduri (Jackie Tyler), Freema Agyeman (Martha Smith-Jones), Noel Clarke (Mickey Smith), John Barrowman (Captain Jack Harkness), Elisabeth Sladen (Sarah Jane Smith), Jessica Hynes (Verity Newman), Russell Tovey (Midshipman Alonso Frame), Thomas Knight (Luke Smith), June Whitfield (Minnie Hooper), Claire Bloom (The Woman), David Harewood (Joshua Naismith), Tracy Ifeachor (Abigail Naismith), Lawry Lewin (Rossiter), Sinead Keenan (Addams), Alexandra Moen (Lucy Saxon), Karl Collins (Shaun Temple), Teresa Banham (Governor), Barry Howard (Oliver Barnes), Allister Bain (Winston Katusi), Sylvia Seymour (Miss Trefusis), Simon Thomas (Mr. Danes), Pete Lee-Wilson (Tommo), Dwayne Scantlebury (Ginger), Joe Dixon (The Chancellor), Julie Legrand (The Partisan), Brid Brennan (The Visionary), Krystal Archer (Nerys), Lacey Bond (serving woman), Lachele Carl (Trinity Wells), Paul Kasey (Ood Sigma), Ruari Mears (Elder Ood), Max Benjamin (teenager), Silas Carson (voice of Ood Sigma), Brian Cox (voice of Elder Ood), Nicholas Briggs (voice of Judoon), Dan Starkey (Sontaran), Jimmy Vee (Graske)

Introducing Matt Smith (the Doctor)

Original airdates December 25, 2009 and January 1, 2010

The Big Idea The Doctor is still trying to avoid the portents of his impending death and discovers it may be too late; the Master is back, but a greater threat looms. The end of time itself is near, and so is the one who knocks four times.

Roots and References *Life on Mars* (talking to someone through the TV); *Silence of the Lambs* (the Master's Hannibal Lecter turn); *Heroes* (the Master's leaping, power-blasting antics); *Prisoner: Cell Block H* (the setting of a grim, yet oddly camp, women's prison); *Star Wars* (the Vinvocci gun turret and the alien cantina where Captain Jack is drinking); *Watchmen* (Wilf being trapped in the chamber echoes the origin of Dr. Manhattan). The eleventh Doctor's first scene is heavily influenced by the suddenly sentient sperm whale in *The Hitchhiker's Guide to the Galaxy*.

Adventures in Time and Space The Time Lords return, having circumvented the

Time Lock that prevents anyone from entering the Time War (as mentioned in "Journey's End"). The opening scenes of Part Two take place in the Gallifreyan Citadel seen in "The Sound of Drums," alongside the hulks of destroyed Dalek saucers ("The Parting of the Ways" and others).

The Doctor returns to the Ood Sphere to meet Ood Sigma ("Planet of the Ood"), where the Doctor mentions in his list of recent activities that he married Queen Elizabeth I, explaining why the Queen was less than pleased to see the Doctor in "The Shakespeare Code." The Doctor remarks that the Vinvocci look similar to the Zocci, the race of Bannakaffalata in "Voyage of the Damned."

Donna remembers the Vespiform, Davros, the Empress of the Racnoss, the petrified Sybilline High Priestess and the Emperor Dalek. It turns out the Doctor has built in a defence mechanism that causes Donna to expunge the energy that would destroy her mind and make her sleep rather than burn up (as established in "Journey's End").

The Lord President is called "Rassilon" by the Doctor. According to Time Lord history, Rassilon was the architect of Time Lord society, helping to create the Eye of Harmony that was the source of the Time Lords' power and ability to travel through time (as established in 1976's "The Deadly Assassin"). The Lord President caused the sound of drums the Master has heard in his head ever since looking through the Untempered Schism as a child ("The Sound of Drums"). The Lord President's gauntlet is very probably one of the Resurrection gloves from *Torchwood*. The Visionary resembles the Seeker from 1978's "The Ribos Operation": both are psychic women who have very similar facial tattoos.

The Doctor's "reward" sees him checking in on his past companions, including Martha, who is no longer marrying Thomas Milligan but is instead married to Mickey! He also finds Captain Jack, at a bar alongside Graske (from the interactive game "Attack of the Graske" and *The Sarah Jane Adventures*), Slitheen ("Aliens of London"), Adipose ("Partners in Crime"), Hath ("The Doctor's Daughter"), Judoon ("Smith and Jones"), Sycorax ("The Christmas Invasion") and Midshipman Alonso Frame ("Voyage of the Damned"). The Doctor gives Wilf and Sylvia a wedding present for Donna, bought using a pound borrowed from Donna's deceased father Geoff ("The Runaway Bride"). The Doctor also checks in on Sarah Jane Smith and, finally, Rose Tyler (before she met him in "Rose"). In the 2010 episode of *The Sarah Jane Adventures*, "Death of the Doctor," the eleventh Doctor states that he also looked in on every one of his companions, not just those of the tenth Doctor.

The Doctor also visits Verity Newman, a descendent of Joan Redfern, who has just written a book titled *The Journal of Impossible Things* that tells story of her great-grandmother during the events of "Human Nature"/"The Family of

Blood." The name of Joan's great-granddaughter (also played by Jessica Hynes), Verity, was the name of John Smith's "mother."

Following his regeneration, the new Doctor notes that he's had worse noses, an in-joke about Jon Pertwee's nose that extends as far back as 1970's "Spearhead from Space" and 1974's "Robot." He also grouses, "Still not ginger!" referring to his desire to have red hair, as noted in "The Christmas Invasion."

The Song Is Ending Effect The Ood have gained the ability to see through time because, in their words, "Time is bleeding." They tell the Doctor that the lines of convergence are now being drawn: "Events from years ago threaten to destroy this future and the present and the past . . . the end of time itself."

Carmen's warning in "Planet of the Dead" — "it is returning in the dark" — is a warning about the Time Lords (or, more specifically, Gallifrey), who have found a way out of the Time Lock that bars the escape from their doom. The Doctor stops them but Wilf, still in the gateway's reactor isolation chamber, knocks four times. (To be precise, four rounds of four knocks.)

Who is the Doctor? The final adventure of the tenth Doctor concludes an era of what is, in many ways, the most human incarnation of the Doctor. Faced with his imminent death, he's passionate, full of emotion and very emotionally fragile. He's a man who is desperate to avoid his end, and rages against it when he realizes his time has come, but he eventually accepts it, says goodbye to those he loved and finally, alone, gives way, saying, "I don't want to go."

The Doctor and Wilf The Doctor, while vastly older than Wilf, treats him almost as a father figure, confiding in him about his iminent death and his recent sins. Wilf still regards the Doctor with awe, even arming himself to protect the Doctor. The Doctor feels similarly, telling Wilf, "I'd be proud if you were my dad."

The Doctor ponders the coincidences that have brought them together, but he never thinks that this could be because Wilf is, unwittingly, the instrument of his eventual death. When stuck in the chamber as it is about to overload, Wilf begs the Doctor not to sacrifice himself. And while the Doctor is initially resentful, he tells Wilf it's an honour to do this for him.

Monster of the Week The Master's resurrection process was interfered with at a critical juncture by Lucy Saxon. This results in his increased agility as well as the ability to use his life force to create energy bolts. It also leaves him constantly hungry, burning up innocent victims to satisfy his appetite.

Stand Up and Cheer The scene in the café is one of the best scenes in David Tennant's tenure in *Doctor Who*. The Doctor talks about regeneration in stark, scary terms, and we see an emotionally naked, vulnerable Doctor, whose time is up and who has many sins on his conscience. David Tennant's performance is never better; the same is true of Bernard Cribbins as Wilf, who is so perfect here: he's excited to see the Doctor but his heart is also breaking watching Donna settle into mediocrity.

Roll Your Eyes The Master suddenly acting as though he wandered in off the set of *Heroes* is a bridge too far. The explanation that his life force is burning out is just about credible and even the energy emanating from him makes some sense. But all the comic book poses and flying and stuff throw it all in the "too much" column.

You're Not Making Any Sense The Time Lords' plan seems to have been written on the back of an envelope (presumably using that clockface language). Just how can anyone triangulate the location of a noise in someone's head?

Interesting Trivia Is regeneration death? This is the great debate. In the past it's been implied that regeneration is a renewal or a rejuvenation, such as "The Parting of the Ways" where it's described as "a way of cheating death." Other stories, like the 1996 TV Movie, state that a physical death has occurred. Here, it's definitively treated as death for that particular persona. The Doctor tells Wilf, "Even if I change, it feels like dying. Everything I am dies. Some new man goes sauntering away and I'm dead."

Why have the Ood accelerated their development? One answer might be that the Ood have three brains, allowing them to see temporal effects in a way that lesser-brain species can't. If so, this might also explain their ability to project themselves into the past, as seen at the end of the previous episode.

Is the Lord President actually Rassilon, the creator of Time Lord society? The simplest answer is "probably," as the war took to resurrecting powerful Time Lords (such as the Master) as times became more desperate. And yet, it does seems odd that more isn't made of Rassilon's identity in this story aside from a single name-drop by the Doctor. It's possible that the Lord President is named after Rassilon, rather like how popes in the Catholic Church take on the names of predecessors.

How does the multiplicity of Masters work? They're not exactly telepathic, because they have to verbally report to each other and the Master isn't automatically aware if one of them gets taken out. Yet they're all on the same page when it comes to carrying out their goals. So it seems as though they're copies who happen to share the same goals and who don't bicker about the details. Coming from a psychopath like the Master, this is actually quite an achievement.

Who was the woman who spoke to Wilf and appeared to the Doctor as one of the two dissenters to the Time Lord's plan? Davies said that he left it deliberately ambiguous, though he and fellow executive producer, Julie Gardner, have stated in a podcast commentary to the story on the BBC website that she was supposed to be the Doctor's mother. However, this is never explicitly stated onscreen. Nor is the identity of the second (apparently male) dissenter ever revealed.

The eleventh Doctor's first scene was written by incoming executive producer Steven Moffat. While this is the last *Doctor Who* story to feature the tenth Doctor, David Tennant's last performance in the role was in *The Sarah Jane Adventures* episode "The Wedding of Sarah Jane Smith." The very last scene where Tennant portrayed the Doctor was running up the stairs in the hotel with Luke and Rani in episode two of that story.

The TARDIS Chronometer Present-day London, between Christmas Eve and Boxing Day. (There's no indication we are still present day plus one year, so it could be 2009 or 2010.) The Doctor visits the Ood Sphere 100 years after the events of "Planet of the Ood," around 4226. The Doctor's reward involves visits mostly to the present day, though his final visit with Rose brings him back to the Powell Estate on New Year's Day, 2005.

Brilliant? (GB) "The End of Time" is about death and dying. It's about grieving and letting go. It may be wrapped in a cockeyed tale of insane villainy and epic struggle, but that's veneer. Take all that away and it's a story about a man facing his demise, as we all must eventually. He deals with it the way we all do: he avoids it, he rails against it, he tries to defy it (in the worst way possible), but, in the end, it comes anyway, in the way least expected. And at that point all he can do is accept it; he can go and visit his friends one last time and see how their lives were changed by him. Then he must greet the end, saying what anyone facing oblivion would say: "I don't want to go."

The scene in Part One where the Doctor sits in a café and talks to Wilf may be, perhaps, the best scene in the tenth Doctor's final year. In it, he talks in stark, scary terms about regeneration. It is a death: the obliteration of a personality, a particular soul inhabiting a man. "The End of Time" is about the process of coming to terms with that.

Of course, to get to that there's a whole episode and a half of buildup to get through. "The End of Time" is a hot mess. It's a great, hulking mass of disjointed set pieces that lumber to an epic climax. Fortunately, most of the set pieces range from great fun (the hungry Master) to painstakingly beautiful (the Doctor and Wilf talking in the café; the Master and the Doctor in the wasteland talking about what drives both of them) to really exciting (the Doctor facing down Rassilon).

However, as with so many stories over the past four seasons, there are a lot of scenes that are there to look cool, as opposed to make dramatic sense (the Doctor surviving a 100-foot drop, the Master's super powers, the involvement of President Obama . . . I could go on and on). I know there's the danger of telegraphing the ending by making those booths look like they're potentially dangerous but, really, Vinvocci glass? (Actually, between that and the Vinvocci escape plan, the Vinvocci ship, and the Vinvocci re-enactment of the *Millennium Falcon* battle from *Star Wars*, pretty much everything lame in Part Two had those cacti involved in it in some way or another.)

My biggest frustration with "The End of Time," though, is Part One. While every scene with the Doctor and Wilf is lovely, the return of Donna awesome and the scenes on the Ood Sphere brilliant, the Vinvocci and its gateway are just there to speed the plot up, as are the Ood's mega-evolution into time visionaries. Naismith and his daughter are creepy but totally underdeveloped. Only the Master's resurrection defies expectations — it's nice to see Alexandra Moen get one last great scene as Lucy Saxon — but it also seems perfunctory.

What's wonderful about "The End of Time" taken as a whole is how it keeps changing the game. It starts out like a bonkers John Simm Master story, and the ending of the first episode may be one of the maddest gambits Russell T Davies has ever perpetrated (and he's responsible for quite a few) as the Master becomes everyone. Then the Time Lords show up . . . only they're villains and, it turns out, they've been manipulating the Master all along in order to bring themselves back. And after the Doctor defeats the Master and the Time Lords and stops the destruction of the time itself . . . then there's the knocking four times. The Doctor has to die not because of the cosmic *sturm und drang* but to save someone he cares about who accidentally locked himself in a cupboard about to be flooded with deadly radiation.

But isn't that just like death? It's random. The person who knocks four times isn't the (literal) James Bond villain or the Master, but someone trapped in a fluky, unlucky accident. The Doctor's raging against his inevitable fate seems a bit too much on the nose, a bit too human and unheroic, but there's something profoundly honest and touching about it too.

It's an unusual final story for an era of *Doctor Who* in that it emphasizes the finality and death of the departing Doctor to the point that the arrival of the new incarnation only serves to confirm the bitter end. This is only fitting, as it's the finale for David Tennant's Doctor, who not only took us on new adventures in time and space but took us to unseen places in the Doctor's soul. In "The End of Time," he takes us even further than we thought he could, as we witness a Time Lord having to face the death of his personality. It's only fitting that his Doctor should not want to go. *We* don't want him to go.

The reveal of the Time Lords as villains is not only a great evolution of the characters and the mythology of the New Series, it serves as a lovely thematic counterpoint: a race who has used their powers to resurrect anyone, cheating death to the point where they've lost sight of everything else, to the point that their ultimate goal is to extinguish living in bodies at all. They've gone beyond what the Daleks set out to do with the reality bomb in "Journey's End." The ending of "The Waters of Mars" becomes all that creepier: the Doctor as "Time Lord victorious" is everything the Doctor wanted to stop in the Time War. Is it any wonder that, when the Doctor accepts the inevitable, he realizes the truth of what he said earlier? Even a Time Lord can live too long.

Who is more appropriate to accompany Tennant's Doctor on his final journey than Wilfred Mott? Bernard Cribbins is great as a comic foil to Tennant, cutting down the Doctor's gravitas by just being so achingly, funnily human. It provides a welcome counterpoint to a Doctor who is full of grim purpose. The scenes in both episodes where Wilf and the Doctor are alone talking to each other are stunning both in how they're written — as the Doctor and Wilf attempt to parent each other — but also in terms of the places the actors go with them. Wilf and the Doctor have a bond forged through tragedy, friends in common and by just being old. It makes the sucker punch that Wilf is unwittingly instrumental in the tenth Doctor's death all that more powerful. Bernard Cribbins is wonderful in his every scene. I'm so glad he got to be a proper, TARDIS-travelling companion at the end of the Tennant era. If only it had happened sooner!

The Doctor's "reward" may cause the story to have more endings than *Lord of the Rings* (or even "The Family of Blood"), but it's absolutely beautiful, as the Doctor says goodbye to all of his friends and learns that his reward is seeing so many people whose lives he changed. While I could have done without Mickey and Martha as the ultimate rebound relationship, the others were quite affecting, particularly the Doctor's goodbye wave to Sarah Jane that says everything with a single gesture, and the Doctor's conversation with Joan Redfern's great-granddaughter. It's nice to see Donna find some small measure of happiness (Catherine Tate is marvellous playing what is essentially a bit part), and the Doctor's present is a lovely hopeful gesture that if her circumstances become better, Donna just might become remarkable again.

And how wonderful is it that, as his last goodbye, he gets to say farewell to Rose in his own way? It seems so beautifully appropriate that this Doctor's last moments before his regeneration were in the council estate where New *Who* started.

For all its bloat, for all the problems in the two episodes leading up to it, "The End of Time" still has the most moving regeneration scene ever. The tenth Doctor, having held back death for so long, cannot do it any longer and takes the TARDIS with him. And as the tenth Doctor changes and dies, everything predicted happens: the new man emerges and life goes on. Steven Moffat, who wrote Matt Smith's first scene, understands that. As funny as the eleventh Doctor's first monologue is, it's also a little tragic, as all the angst of holding back death is gone as a stranger in the Doctor's suit marvels he has legs, arms and is not a girl. (Matt Smith is going to be wonderful as the Doctor.) That's the miracle, blessing and curse of being the Doctor.

I'm still frankly amazed a family show airing on Christmas and New Year's Day would air what is a secular, pop-culture fable about coming to terms with one's own death. Or that Russell T Davies would make such subject matter so entertaining. It's bold, gutsy and, at the end of the day, it demonstrates the incredible genius of Davies. Steven Moffat's stories will be plotted with the precision of a laser, feature the wittiest dialogue, the scariest monsters and the smartest, sexiest women. I don't think he will come up with such a hot mess as this, but by the same token I do wonder if he will come up with a story so emotionally affecting, so satisfying in terms of spectacle, so big and epic and meaningful and ultimately thoughtful.

"The End of Time" is the end of an era for *Doctor Who*. An era that took a long-cancelled television series, unknown by almost two generations of children and forgotten by many, brought it back and made it bigger, better and more brilliant than we could have imagined. Thank you Russell T Davies for doing that. And thank you David Tennant for making the Doctor so wonderful.

As Ood Sigma says, this song is over but the story continues. Or, to use an old Earth saying, a phrase of great power and wisdom and consolation to the soul in times of need: Geronimo!

Second Opinion (RS?) Finally, the biggest mystery of the last two years is revealed! The woman who picked up the Master's ring was . . . Miss Trefusis, prison warden. That was my 15th guess!

She and her previously-unheard-of cult of the former prime minister (okay, Tony Blair probably does have one of these) bring the Master back to life using some lipstick, but it all goes horribly wrong because of a magic potion. Consequently, the Master ends up blond, eats people and shoots energy bolts from his hands.

Meanwhile, the Doctor is sexually assaulted by a pensioner, and Wilf reminisces with him about the good times they had, like "The Sontaran Stratagem." Donna, we are reminded, will die if she ever remembers the Doctor. Except for that one time, about 20 minutes later, when she does remember and, instead of dying, shoots energy from her face and then goes to sleep.

In the big confrontation, the Master does kung fu with electric hands, and he and the Doctor grimace at each other a lot, before sitting down for a bit of a chat. Over at the mansion, the Naismiths display barely concealed incest, little realizing they've been infiltrated by the most inept spies in the history of cactus-kind.

Timothy Dalton makes a pretty good speech and ensures that we won't forget it by spraying masses of spittle with every word. On Gallifrey, he and the other Time Lords stride along a walkway without a railing, because that's how hard they are.

The Master's first act after taking over the Earth is to put the Doctor in bondage, which is really a setup for the comedy rescue of the Doctor. Who — wait for it — doesn't get untied and has to be wheeled down a few steps! H.I. Larious! Then Wilf somehow produces the gun that the Master took off him earlier, and the Doctor makes a big speech about how he'd never take it, never, before grabbing it and jumping out of a spaceship. After falling from a height more spectacular than the one that killed his fourth self and crashing through a glass dome, he suffers some minor cuts and bruises.

The entire threat is resolved by two superbeings who can shoot bolts of magic from their hands. Then, in a fulfilment of the prophecy that says "he will knock four times," Wilf proceeds to knock 16 times and somehow the Doctor knows that this must have been what that not-actually-very-good psychic was talking about.

It turns out that absorbing an enormous amount of radiation won't kill you and make you regenerate immediately, but instead you'll heal just enough to run some lengthy errands. And, like all good comedies, the whole thing ends with a marriage . . . of two companions who never spent any time together onscreen and who will now enjoy the married name of Smith-Jones, but hey, they're the only two black companions, so why not?

There are people out there who like "The End of Time." Then again, there are people out there who drink from the toilet, so I'm not really sure what that proves.

The Psychic Papers: The Time Lords

In 1969, the pre-publicity in the *Sun* newspaper about Patrick Troughton's final story, "The War Games," suggested that the Time Lords were the Doctor's enemies, just like the Daleks and Cybermen. In the event, in their first appearance onscreen, the Time Lords weren't villains, but they achieved something no actual villain had yet done in *Doctor Who*: they defeated the Doctor.

As seen in episode ten of "The War Games," the Doctor's own people, the Time

Lords, were a race of godlike beings. In their first appearance, their powers were considerable. As the Doctor explained, "We can control our own environment; we can live forever, barring accidents; and we have the secret of space-time travel." The only trouble was that they only (ostensibly) used their powers to observe, never to interfere. The Doctor, bored by this, stole a TARDIS and went to explore. In this story, having recaptured the Doctor, the Time Lords sent his companions back to their own time and exiled the Doctor to Earth. It was as bleak as *Doctor Who* ever became.

Eventually, the Doctor's exile was lifted (after the Doctor saved the Time Lords in 1972's "The Three Doctors"), and the more we saw the Time Lords, the more demystified they were. The first story to be set on the Time Lords' homeworld (named Gallifrey in 1974's "The Time Warrior") was 1976's "The Deadly Assassin." Here, the Time Lords weren't so much a collection of gods as a collection of dusty academics and cynical politicians. The Time Lords were scheming, avaricious, cynical and bombastic.

Furthermore, it turned out that, far from simply observing other planets and their history, they had a Celestial Intervention Agency (the initials of which were quite deliberately chosen for satirical effect by writer Robert Holmes). They even gave the Time Lords a pseudo-religious figure, Rassilon, who founded Time Lord society and created the Eye of Harmony, the source of the Time Lords' power and ability to travel through time. Subsequent run-ins with the Doctor's people were paler versions of all this. The more they were seen, the less god-like they were.

When Russell T Davies brought *Doctor Who* back in 2005, one thing he was determined to do was make the Time Lords less a figure of continuity and more figures of mythology. To do that, the Time Lords were destroyed in a great Time War with the Daleks.

The roots of such a war existed in the Classic Series. In 1975's "Genesis of the Daleks," the Time Lords despatch the Doctor and his companions to the time when Davros created the Daleks in the hope they could avert their creation; in the end, he only succeeds in delaying them slightly. In 1984's "Resurrection of the Daleks," the Daleks intend to clone the Doctor and have that clone assassinate the members of the Time Lord high council. Finally, in 1988's "Remembrance of the Daleks," the Doctor tricks the Daleks into using a Gallifreyan weapon, the Hand of Omega, to destroy the Daleks' home planet of Skaro. These events may be seen as the initial skirmishes in what we now know as the Time War.

In "The End of Time," the Time Lords finally become villains. The tenth Doctor's final adventure finds him confronting not just his own act of double genocide but the results of the war that drove his people to become monsters. Perhaps by the act of sacrificing himself to save the life of an old man, he reminded himself what he was fighting for.

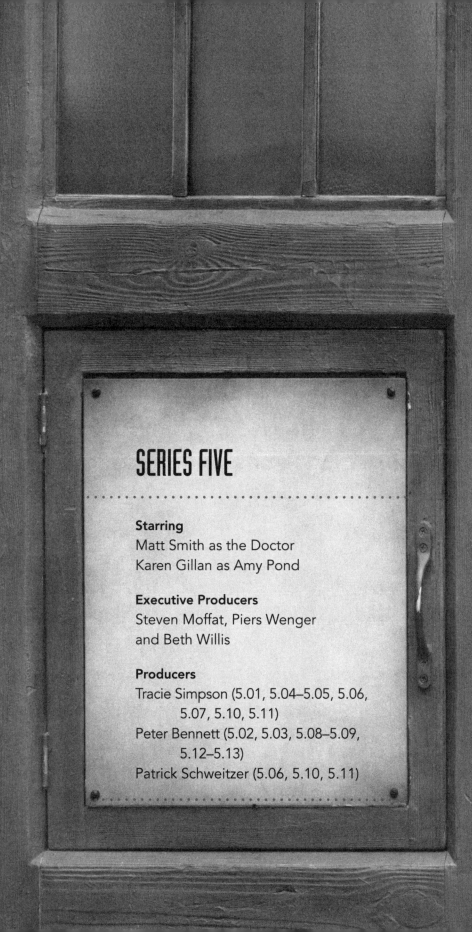

SERIES FIVE

Starring
Matt Smith as the Doctor
Karen Gillan as Amy Pond

Executive Producers
Steven Moffat, Piers Wenger
and Beth Willis

Producers
Tracie Simpson (5.01, 5.04–5.05, 5.06,
5.07, 5.10, 5.11)
Peter Bennett (5.02, 5.03, 5.08–5.09,
5.12–5.13)
Patrick Schweitzer (5.06, 5.10, 5.11)

5.01 The Eleventh Hour

Written by Steven Moffat **Directed by** Adam Smith

Supporting cast Arthur Darvill (Rory Williams); Caitlin Blackwood (Amelia); Nina Wadia (Dr. Ramsden); Marcello Magni (Barney Collins); Annette Crosbie (Mrs. Angelo); Tom Hopper (Jeff); Arthur Cox (Mr. Henderson); Olivia Colman (mother); Eden Monteath, Merin Monteath (children); David de Keyser (Atraxi voice); William Wilde (Prisoner Zero voice); Patrick Moore (himself)

Original airdate April 3, 2010

The Big Idea Prisoner Zero has escaped through a crack in a little girl's bedroom, giving the Doctor 20 minutes to save the world.

Roots and References There are echoes of several children's literary classics, including Tigger's episode with the haycorns in *The House at Pooh Corner* (the Doctor's rejection of any food); *The Cat in the Hat* (his trashing of Amelia's house); Hagrid's first appearance in *Harry Potter and the Philosopher's Stone* (a strange man turning a child's world upside-down) and the ending of *Peter Pan* (the Doctor returning to Amelia only to find her all grown up).

Adventures in Time and Space The opening crash-zoom from outer space to Earth echoes the one used at the beginning of "Rose." The Doctor exhales golden energy in his post-regenerative state, just like his tenth incarnation did in "The Christmas Invasion." He similarly experiences spasms adjusting to his new body (though less severely than his predecessor).

The Doctor repeats some lines from earlier stories, such as "wibbly-wobbly, timey-wimey" ("Blink") and "You've had some cowboys in here" ("The Girl in the Fireplace"). The redesigned TARDIS, with the paint job and St. John's ambulance badge, harkens back to 1963's "An Unearthly Child" and the 1965 movie *Dr. Who and the Daleks*. The TARDIS key glows, just as it did in "Aliens of London" and "Father's Day."

The Atraxi do a scan of previous monsters who've invaded Earth, which shows images of Cybermen ("Rise of the Cybermen," although that took place in a parallel world), Daleks (from "Doomsday"), a Pyrovile ("The Fires of Pompeii"), the Racnoss ("The Runaway Bride"), the Ood (whom we haven't seen invade Earth; they first appeared in "The Impossible Planet"), the Hath ("The Doctor's Daughter"; we haven't seen them invade Earth either), old-style Sontarans (1973's "The Time Warrior"), Sea Devils (1972's "The Sea Devils"), the Sycorax ("The Christmas Invasion"), Reapers ("Father's Day," although that occurred in an alternate timeline) and a Vashta Nerada's victim ("Silence in the

Library"/"Forest of the Dead," which happened in the far future). They also show all ten previous Doctors, in order.

The Doctor refers to the swimming pool in the TARDIS, which was seen in 1978's "The Invasion of Time." The Cloister Bell rings (1981's "Logopolis" et al.). The psychic paper takes a message, just as it did in "New Earth." Article 57 of the Shadow Proclamation ("Rose" et al.) forbids threats against fully established, Level Five planets (1979's "City of Death").

The Doctor mentions he's been knocking around on his own for a while ("The Next Doctor" through "The End of Time"). At the end, he snaps his fingers and the TARDIS door opens, just like River said he would do in "The Forest of the Dead."

The Crack in the Universe Effect The season arc begins with the discovery of a crack in Amelia's wall. The crack is comprised of two parts of space and time pressed together that should never have touched. It's the only thing that young Amelia fears. Prisoner Zero escapes through it.

The crack still concerns the Doctor even after Prisoner Zero is dispatched. It's on the readout of the TARDIS monitor at the end, while the Doctor is telling Amy he just wants someone to travel with. The fact that he turns it off while telling her there's no other reason indicates the Doctor is aware that the crack isn't just contained to one room, that Amy is tied in to it and that he's probably lying to her.

Prisoner Zero says, "The universe is cracked. The Pandorica will open. Silence will fall." We'll see these elements play out down the line . . .

Who is the Doctor? Similar to his behaviour in "The Christmas Invasion," the new Doctor is initially manic (craving all manner of food that he ultimately hates) but eventually settles down. This incarnation seems to have increased powers of observation (which were superhuman to begin with), as he picks up dozens of details from a single glance at the village green. He ensures the Atraxi don't invade Earth almost entirely by Socratic monologue, indicating a quieter, gentler nature. His reputation has clearly grown to the point where he drives away the Atraxi simply by having them realize who he is (this is a point that will be revisited in different ways over the coming seasons).

At the end he describes himself thusly: "Amy Pond, there's something you'd better understand about me 'cause it's important and one day your life may depend on it. I am definitely a madman with a box."

The Doctor and Amy The Doctor's brief adventure with seven-year-old Amelia Pond (and unintended abandonment of her) has had an extraordinary effect on the grown-up Amy. The Doctor is her childhood hero, her imaginary friend and a figure of fannish obsession (as seen by all the arts and crafts she's done about her "Raggedy Doctor"). Being confronted with the Doctor again frightens her, and when he proves he's the same man she met, she's excited by him again and attracted to him. Even after being abandoned again for another two years, she willingly goes off with him into time and space, though she doesn't tell the Doctor it's the night before her wedding.

Monster of the Week Prisoner Zero is an interdimensional multiform from outer space. It can disguise itself as multiple creatures, but it sometimes gets the mouth wrong, speaking as a dog and growling as a human. In its natural state, it resembles a giant snake with sharp teeth. To maintain its disguises, it needs a psychic link, a live feed with a dormant mind. It uses coma patients and can also use Amy Pond, as it's had years to absorb her thoughts. It can dissociate into particles.

Stand Up and Cheer Having saved the world from both Prisoner Zero and the Atraxi, the Doctor calls back the Atraxi and asks if the Earth is protected. When asked what happened to previous aliens that tried to invade Earth, the Atraxi then show images of all ten previous Doctors, culminating with the eleventh Doctor stepping through the image of the tenth, fully dressed in his jacket and bow tie. He then utters the killer line: "Hello, I'm the Doctor. Basically . . . run." Ladies and gentlemen, Matt Smith *is* the Doctor.

Roll Your Eyes After initially disbelieving that coma patients can talk, Dr. Ramsden witnesses it for herself. However, when Rory says he's seen them walking around the village, she flat-out refuses to believe him and tells him he needs to take time off. He even has photos on his camera phone, which she refuses to see! If she's just witnessed one thing she thought impossible, wouldn't she at least consider a second?

You're Not Making Any Sense Propagating a computer virus from a phone that resets every counter to zero (including analogue ones!) in 10 minutes is the sort of idea that your computer-illiterate dad might suggest, using "the Facebook."

Interesting Trivia This is the first TARDIS redesign of the New Series. Interestingly, the exterior is also redesigned, in a style very reminiscent of the original TARDIS, back in 1963 (with a few touches from the Peter Cushing movies). It has white edges around the windows and a St. John's ambulance badge on the door, which hasn't been seen for about 45 years. Inside, the console is raised on a dais with steps leading up to it and glass inside the rotor, a huge central light overhead and an old-style TV screen hanging on a chain. Although the console is smaller, it's less rounded than it was during the Davies era. The room feels less organic than the coral one, but it retains the feel of being cobbled together by whatever spare parts could be found, as evidenced by the bath taps, typewriter and pinball machine parts on the console.

Doctor Who usually illustrates its ability to travel in time to a new companion (and a new audience) by taking her to either the past or the future quite soon after she joins. Here, however, we have a new demonstration of the Doctor's relationship with time: his multiple leaps forward while Amy waits. The adventure happens on two scales: over a period of hours for the Doctor and years for Amy. This not only illustrates a new facet of time travel (and its damaging effects on her psyche), it gives the character room to grow and develop, and her attachment to the Doctor doesn't feel forced. It also lets the audience identify with not one but two brand-new lead characters, thus re-establishing the series under its new management in a quietly efficient way.

If you think there's a strong resemblance between Amy and her younger self, it's because there is. Caitlin Blackwood is, in fact, Karen Gillan's cousin. Gillan suggested Blackwood for the role because family members had commented that Blackwood looked like Gillan did when she was younger!

Alien expert groups include NASA, Jodrell Bank, Toyko Space Centre, the European Space Agency and Australia's CSIRO. Among the experts is astronomer Patrick Moore (mentioned in "Aliens of London") whose monthly program *The Sky at Night* has run continuously since 1962, longer than *Doctor Who*!

In what is the most dramatic branding facelift since the New Series started, there are new opening titles, a new arrangement for the theme music and a new logo.

The TARDIS Chronometer It initially flies over London, billowing smoke, then crashes into Amelia's shed at Easter, 1996. It rematerializes 12 years later in Amy's backyard. Offscreen, the Doctor takes a quick hop to the moon and back to run in the new TARDIS. Two years later, it rematerializes in Amy's backyard again. "Flesh and Stone" will establish this as the evening of June 25, 2010.

Cool? (RS?) With a new Doctor, a new companion and a new production team, this was easily the most important episode of the New Series since "Rose." Matt Smith needed to introduce himself to an audience used to David Tennant, who was incredibly popular and who had just completed the second-longest tenure as the Doctor.

By the end of "The Eleventh Hour," you've probably forgotten who David Tennant was.

Matt Smith is spectacular. He's immediately likeable, eccentric and relatable. He has actual conversations with people, and yet he's not always on their wavelength. He's awkward and ungainly, but it just makes him loveable. He's not flirting with Amy in the slightest, and yet she falls for him anyway.

It's the little touches that make him so fascinating. He measures his height against the much taller Jeff, scolds the latter like a stern parent and makes faces at Jeff's gran. The way he moans as he says, "The Doctor will see you now" is unusual, and yet it doesn't feel at all forced. It's utterly stupendous when he inspires Jeff, and that would probably be the standout speech of any lesser episode — and yet here it's just a throwaway moment.

The entire episode is a vehicle designed to showcase Matt Smith as the new Doctor. What's brilliant is that it makes this look effortless, even though you know intellectually that it's pulling out all the stops, from the spectacular TARDIS flight across London to the sheer spookiness of the open door in Amelia's house. The scene of the Doctor going through everything like a giant 3D photo gives us an unusual take on the character, emphasizing his observational skills and ability to think through a problem, rather than him being a know-it-all. And the detail that leads him to realizing he can save the world in 20 minutes? Rory looking the wrong way. What's more, the Doctor's instincts are spot on: this is indeed the critical clue to the episode's resolution. He defeats Prisoner Zero quite cleverly (using Amy's unconscious thoughts of him), giving him an intelligent and emotional centre; bringing the Atraxi back gives him a hugely assertive authority. By this point, you're ready to follow him to the ends of space and time.

The story also introduces a new companion without overshadowing the new Doctor. Cleverly, it does this by starting with Amelia as a little girl. And she's awesome! In some ways, it's a pity they didn't go with her as the companion. You can see why they didn't, but it's also a shame they couldn't exploit this situation a bit more. The story is going for a fairytale feel — the Doctor even mentions that "Amelia Pond" is like a name in a fairytale — and having a young girl for an ongoing companion would have fit into that rather nicely.

The fish fingers and custard scene is good, but it becomes magnificent when the Doctor stops being wacky and suddenly assesses Amelia: a box falls out of the sky, a man falls out of the box and she's not frightened . . . so that must be one hell of a scary crack in her wall. This is a brilliant segue into the episode proper.

Then we have the jump forward, which repeats one of the cleverer parts of the first series, the opening of "Aliens of London," but this time it happens to the companion instead of to her family. The sucker punch of the police-woman outfit (though Amy's short skirt is a dead giveaway that something isn't quite right), spiced with a few hints of the mysterious disappearance of Amelia, leads into the "Why did you say five minutes?" exchange. This allows enormous character growth to have taken place retroactively, as we see that Amy's been obsessed with the Doctor for most of her life. It gives the episode — and the characters — enormous depth in an incredibly short time.

The village of Leadworth is clearly set up for the ongoing series. We have a bunch of regular characters, a potential mystery in the empty duck pond and exactly the kind of sleepy nonurban setting that Classic *Doctor Who* used to use all the time, but we haven't seen it at all in the New Series. (It's also amusing that it's Rory who scores the hot girl, while the more attractive Jeff is reduced to internet porn.) Bizarrely, however, this is the last we'll see of Leadworth proper or any of the secondary characters except Rory. This is a bit strange, but I suspect the original plan got changed when they realized just how good the three regulars were.

Moffat repeats a number of his earlier tricks: the Atraxi broadcast through everything with a speaker grille ("The Empty Child"), the Doctor sends a remote message saying "Duck" ("Blink") and there's a repeated catchphrase — "The human residence/residents will be incinerated!" — based on wordplay ("The Empty Child," "Silence in the Library"). There's also the Doctor appearing throughout someone's life, starting when she was a little girl, and the adult version of her falling for him ("The Girl in the Fireplace"). And the Doctor defeats the villains by telling them to look him up in their database ("Forest of the Dead"). However, none of these callbacks to Moffat's past work feel derivative but rather like variations on themes that Moffat is interested in. At least one of them (the ending) is vastly superior to its predecessor and the effect of the Doctor on Amy's life has more room to breathe here.

The Doctor as an imaginary friend is a really nice idea. The Doctor as an imaginary friend who comes back is brilliant. The realization that everyone in the town knows of Amy's obsessions is quite amusing, especially Rory admitting that he had to dress up as the Doctor.

There's some edgy stuff here with Amy. She's functional, but she's also traumatized by her involvement with the Doctor, a man she knew as a little girl and whom she's attracted to as an adult. Perhaps not coincidentally, older Amy is — in the broad and accepted definition of the term — a sex worker: she kisses people for money, which is quite shocking in some ways, although the episode also takes just the right tone with it. What's clear is that she and Rory have some sort of arrangement; she might be his girlfriend, but they're clearly not totally monogamous. This is fascinating stuff with a lot of implications for down the line.

"The Eleventh Hour" is an excellent introductory story for newbies, because it doesn't have anything of the past to rely on and so it has to make its own story, its own characters and its own tone. Plus, it's incredibly likeable, moves like lightning and has an immensely satisfying denouement. If you're looking to introduce *Doctor Who* to someone, then start right here. Trust me, they'll thank you for it.

Second Opinion (GB) Let's go through the list of new things here. New Doctor:

stunning. New companion: good (though Caitlin Blackwood was excellent as Amelia; I agree with my co-author that maybe the Doctor should have travelled with her). New TARDIS: okay (I miss the cavernous, alien space of the old one; this is more like a big room). New sonic screwdriver: fneh. New logo: very good. New producers and head writer: based on this, I'd say excellent. New theme music arrangement: oh dear . . .

It's natural in this moment of new everything to notice what's different about *Doctor Who*. We're in a more middle-class, English-village vision of Britain. There's the stately way things unfold, the lovely banter between the Doctor and Amy, the emphasis on fairytale, and 70% more timey-wiminess. But so much of *Doctor Who* as we've known it is there too: the continuity nods to "The Christmas Invasion" and other stories, Murray Gold's rather nice score, the emphasis on the Doctor/companion relationship.

Like "The Christmas Invasion," "The Eleventh Hour" faces the challenge of getting the audience to care about the new central character. This is even trickier for writer Steven Moffat. Traditionally, the new Doctor has to live up to his companions' (and the audience's) expectations based on the previous incarnation. With the Doctor regenerating alone, he has no relationship with anyone. The smart thing Moffat does is have the Doctor meet Amy at eight and again 12 years later. Now the new Doctor has something to live up to: Amy's expectations of the wonderful man she knew long ago and who, in many ways, ruined her life as a result. With a stroke, Moffat enables the Doctor to prove himself to all of us.

"The Eleventh Hour" is owned by Matt Smith. From the moment he climbs out of the TARDIS, he *is* the Doctor. The mini-adventure with Amelia, which starts with him playing Cat in the Hat via Tigger and ends with him taking on the crack in the wall, is a stunning run through the gamut of states of mind that make the Doctor the Doctor. (His treatment of a plate of bread and butter is comedy gold.) The genius is in the temperament Smith brings to it: he plays the Doctor as the mad uncle who takes little kids seriously. When he's finally ready to claim who he is at the end and warns the Atraxi, it's wonderful to watch because he speaks with a quiet authority that's unbelievably disarming.

"The Eleventh Hour" may be the best debut story a Doctor has ever had. No other story has so resolutely established the central character or given him such a showcase to demonstrate what he is capable of. The eleventh Doctor is here. Long may he reign.

Matt Smith

Only 26 years old when he was cast as the eleventh Doctor in late 2008, Matt Smith is the youngest actor ever to play the role. Among the first candidates who auditioned for the role, Smith blew away executive producers Steven Moffat and Piers Wegner with his refreshingly different performance. Moffat had been planning to cast someone in their 40s, and he was completely taken by surprise by the young actor.

As a teenager, Smith trained to become a professional footballer but an injury caused him to put aside football and take up acting. By his early 20s, Smith was performing in West End plays such as *Swimming With Sharks* with Christian Slater and his future *Doctor Who* co-star Arthur Darvill. In 2008, his performance in the BBC series *Party Animals* received acclaim. He also appeared in *Moses Jones* (2009) and opposite Billie Piper in *The Ruby in the Smoke* (2006) and a 2008 episode of *The Secret Diary of a Call Girl*.

While *Doctor Who* keeps him busy, Matt Smith has found time for other roles, including Christopher Isherwood in the 2011 BBC drama *Christopher and His Kind* and Olympic rower Bert Bushnell in 2012's *Bert and Dickie*.

5.02 The Beast Below

Written by Steven Moffat **Directed by** Andrew Gunn

Supporting cast Sophie Okonedo (Liz 10), Terrence Hardiman (Hawthorne), Hannah Sharp (Mandy), Alfie Field (Timmy), Christopher Good (Morgan), David Ajala (Peter), Catrin Richards (Poem Girl), Jonathan Battersby (Winder), Chris Porter (voice of Smilers/ Winder), Ian McNeice (Churchill)

Original airdate April 10, 2010

The Big Idea In the future, all of Britain (except Scotland) is travelling the stars in a giant spaceship. Only there's an ugly secret its citizens keep voting to forget.

Roots and References *Peter Pan* (Amy flying in space, wearing only her nightie); the Biblical book of Jonah (being inside a whale and then vomited back up); the British comic strip *Dan Dare* (mostly for its 1950s design aesthetic); *Judge Dredd* (the twisted reflection of British society); the videoscreen with the Poem Girl is made to look like the BBC test cards used when there was a fault in a program. And a space whale has been a part of *Doctor Who* lore thanks to a frequently announced but ultimately rejected TV script "Song of the Space Whale" by *Judge Dredd* creators Pat Mills and John Wagner.

Adventures in Time and Space *Starship UK* escaped Earth as it was being ravaged by solar flares in the 29th century, events that formed the backstory of 1975's "The Ark in Space." Part of the retro 1950s design of *Starship UK* includes a

Magpie Electricals sign ("The Idiot's Lantern"). Liz 10 recalls the Doctor's encounters with her ancestors, particularly Queen Victoria's knighting and banishing of him on the same day in "Tooth and Claw." She elaborates on the Doctor's offscreen marriage to Queen Elizabeth I in "The End of Time," saying, "So much for the Virgin Queen." We can also see the shadow of a Dalek during Winston Churchill's phone call to the Doctor; more about that next episode.

The Crack in the Universe Effect At the end of an episode, a crack, the same shape as the one in Amy's room, is shown on the hull of *Starship UK*.

Who is the Doctor? The new Doctor demonstrates his enhanced powers of deduction by determining *Starship UK* is a police state just by the behaviour of people in the London Market. More significantly, following the events of "The End of Time" and his regeneration, this new Doctor seems to have found some measure of peace (or at least distance) with what happened to the Time Lords at the end of the Time War. He tells Amy, "There were [Time Lords] but there aren't. Just me now. Long story. It was a bad day, bad stuff happened. And, you know what, I'd love to forget it, every last bit of it. But I don't. Not ever."

The Doctor and Amy The Doctor has taken to calling Amy by her last name, Pond, as a sort of school-chum name. She has already begun to emulate the Doctor in many ways (perhaps unsurprising since, in a way, she's known this Doctor longer than he's known himself): like the Doctor, she unilaterally decides to free the Star Whale after observing and making her own deductions. Moreover, Amy understands what the Star Whale is doing thanks to her own understanding of the Doctor and how being the last of one's kind means never ignoring the cries of a child. She's about to tell the Doctor of her engagement when they're interrupted by a phone call from Winston Churchill.

Monster of the Week The Smilers are robots that sit in booths placed throughout *Starship UK*. They look like the mechanical figures often seen in fairgrounds. Their heads rotate to reveal three faces: one smiling, one frowning and one angry. They seem to monitor activities on the ship and act accordingly, often feeding people to the Star Whale. The Smilers are capable of independent movement away from the booths; the Winders, the humans who maintain law and order, are cybernetically enhanced to become Smilers when necessary.

Stand Up and Cheer The Doctor's outburst when he realizes that the only thing he can do is lobotomize the Star Whale — "Don't talk to me! Nobody human has anything to say to me!" — is astonishing. While shouting was practically a lifestyle choice for David Tennant's Doctor, for a Doctor so quiet and restrained as Matt Smith's, such an outburst of anger is truly surprising and quite moving. You believe him when he tells Liz 10 he may have to come up with another name for himself after doing what he feels he must do.

Roll Your Eyes Just when did the Doctor and Amy clean themselves up after being covered in Star Whale sick?

You're Not Making Any Sense Liz 10 says at the end that "there will be no secrets." But will that be enough to dismantle a decades old, possibly *centuries* old, police state? People living in fear, shadows, secrets, people crying silently because no one wants to talk, children being sent to the dungeon for doing poorly in school . . . It seems absurd to think that's all tied to the fact that the ship was built around a gigantic space fish.

Interesting Trivia After a brief glimpse last story, this is our first real look at the new sonic screwdriver. It's bigger and bulkier than the last, it opens up at the top and appears to have readouts on the shaft. It's also quite similar to the future sonic screwdriver we saw in "Silence in the Library."

One way the Doctor's growth can be charted through the course of the New Series is in how he reveals he's the last of his kind. With Rose in "The End of the World," he's so stricken with survivor's guilt that even naming his race and their demise is a major moment. In "Gridlock," Martha confronts the Doctor with having to remember his people. By the time of "The Fires of Pompeii," he's forced to relive the decision of killing his people with Donna's demands to save Caecilius's family. But in "The End of Time," the return of the Time Lords makes him admit to Wilf that he's been selective in his remembrance and has to confront his people's darker side. And now, he acknowledges it with little angst as a "bad day." The days of the tortured, lonely god are over . . .

Whatever happened to the Welsh? *Starship UK* is comprised of the citizens of England and Northern Ireland but not Scotland (which impresses Amy). But the episode never addresses what happened to Wales. Without the Welsh, there's not much of the "United" in the "United Kingdom" starship. Given that the series is made in Cardiff, it's not as though the production team could have simply forgotten them. Clearly, there's a vast conspiracy at work to either erase the Welsh from future history or else the Welsh are secretly plotting to overthrow the queen and this is the first ominous clue. We demand answers, boyo!

The TARDIS Chronometer Starship UK. The poll registry indicates Amy's age is 1306, which would mean the story is set in 3295.

Cool? (GB) Comparisons between "The Beast Below" and "The End of the World" are inevitable. Both are the second stories in the era of a new Doctor and a new writer/executive producer. Both are frothy little thrill rides set on a futuristic spaceship. Both are more about developing the relationship between the Doctor and the new companion than anything else, and both are the first real opportunity to see what the new Doctor is made of. Both even have moments where the companion suddenly realizes what she's left behind.

It's where they diverge that we see perhaps the biggest differences between Russell T Davies and Steven Moffat's reigns on *Doctor Who*. First there's the Doctor. In "The End of the World," Christopher Eccleston's Doctor is a dark figure with a sweet side. He dances to "Tainted Love," but get him alone and he's living with some serious pain that it takes monumental effort to even admit. He's loud and ferocious. And at the end, he's prepared to let Cassandra literally tear herself apart, concluding, "All things must die."

Matt Smith's Doctor is almost the complete opposite. He's a sweet figure with a dark side. He leaps out of the TARDIS the moment he sees a child crying and straightens his bowtie before being vomited out of a giant creature. He brushes aside his horrible past as a bad day that he'll never forget. But, most tellingly, his one moment of righteous anger and ferocity in the midst of serene enthusiasm is because he's now been forced to effectively kill another creature.

Then there's the relationship between the Doctor and the companion. With Rose, it was all about the romance, and "The End of the World" was the "first date," even though she spent all of the story trapped in a room avoiding death by unfiltered sunlight. Here, with Amy, it's about something much more nuanced. First of all, Amy solves the problem by imitating the Doctor: she observes everything, puts it together and makes a giant intuitive leap. Amy also makes the huge mistake of trying to protect the Doctor, which the Doctor resents intensely and which threatens to destroy their relationship on their first outing. There's an element of romance there — Amy did skulk off with another man the night before her wedding, after all — but Rose's love of the Doctor is forged out of seeing the grand sweep of who the Doctor is and where he can take her. With Amy, her big intuitive leap comes out of intensely empathizing with the Doctor.

But there are three ways "The Beast Below" could benefit from the experience gained by "The End of the World": the first is the need for vivid characters. "The End of the World" has Cassandra, Jabe, the Steward and the lovely plumber Raffalo. "The Beast Below" has Liz 10 (Sophie Okenodo is sublime, loving the opportunity to play a gun-toting monarch) and . . . no one else, really. The characters are all dull types: shadowy authority figure, kid number one, kid number two.

The second thing is that the budget challenges really show. (I know this is an unfair comparison as there are more effects shots in "The End of the World" than any episode of *Doctor Who* made before or since.) The Star Whale is only fully revealed in the final shot because, presumably, that's all they could afford from their special effects house, The Mill, that week. This is disappointing as it should have been revealed as part of the story and not the denouement. This is a story screaming out to show us the money, and for the most part we don't see it.

The last thing missing is the kick to the teeth. It's sweet that the Doctor wants to preserve life and it's great that Amy gets to save the day through cleverness, but there isn't any shock like Jabe's death or Ruffalo's and the Steward's grisly ends. The only person who we see sentenced to death by the Beast is Timmy, but it turns out he wasn't killed after all. It also doesn't help that the episode completely drops the police state element of its first half. The result is a story that's rollicking fun and immensely clever but oddly antiseptic at points too.

There's a lot that's great about "The Beast Below." The Frank Bellamy–esque, retro '50s design, with *Starship UK* looking like a giant Festival of Britain project, is superb. Matt Smith is on top of his game already, and Karen Gillan is great playing Amy as the best babysitter we've never had. And the character dynamic between the Doctor and Amy continues to be fascinating. By virtue of "birth placement," it can't avoid comparison to "The End of the World," but it can also stand on its own as an enjoyable, engaging 45 minutes of *Doctor Who*.

Second Opinion (RS?) This could have been excellent as a two-part story, with a shocking cliffhanger that they're actually floating in space. Instead, too much is revealed too quickly: the spaceship is established in the opening moments, while the reveal that the engines are faked is a throwaway moment that should have been a big revelation.

Nevertheless, what we do get is really fascinating. The design alone is superb: little touches like "Mind the Doors" and "Vator" in the style of a London tube stop are excellent, as is the *Starship UK* logo in the style of the old BBC logo. And the urban decay is very well illustrated with one of the Rs in "SURREY" burnt out in the establishing shot. It's fantastic how the Doctor deduces the existence of a police state simply by observing a girl crying silently and no one asking about it. You can tell that this was written by a parent.

What's most intriguing is the way the entire ship has adapted to its terrible secret. Something that everyone knows is callous but nevertheless chooses to ignore. This has parallels with animal rights and third world labour in our own world: our willful blindness when it comes to the suffering of others. It's a society built on cruelty, just like ours, and — just like ours — 99% of people agree not to discuss it.

Because it's a civilization that desperately wants to not think of itself as evil, every citizen has the right to know and is free to choose to protest. Nevertheless, the state is so expert at convincing its citizens to be complicit in the violence that this right to know actually neuters the problem, in a way that enforced secrecy probably wouldn't. We see this with Liz 10's investigation: she senses injustice and gets to the bottom of it ... only to willingly reset everything whenever this happens. Forgetting has enormous rewards: you can enjoy the safety and amenities of society.

This is fascinating stuff. It also illustrates the falseness of a binary choice, because of course there are more options than either forgetting or protesting. Cleverly, the episode takes this a step further with the Doctor, by giving him three choices, but even this isn't enough, because all three still involve cruelty. It's only when Amy realizes that there's a fourth way — a way that gives the beast as much choice as everyone else — that the situation is resolved.

What's utterly brilliant about this is that she does so partly because she observes everything carefully and partly because she's had 14 years to think, deeply and fundamentally, about what it means to be the Doctor: that to be old and kind and alone means you can't stand by and watch children cry, even when those children aren't the same species as you.

One of the most interesting stories in years.

. . . .

Steven Moffat

Before the New Series was even announced in 2003, there were two avowed fans of *Doctor Who* considered to have enough clout in the modern-day British television industry to revive *Doctor Who*: Russell T Davies and Steven Moffat. Like Davies, Moffat began his television career with children's series, writing ITV's *Press Gang* (1989–1993). After *Press Gang*, Moffat began writing comedy for adults, beginning with *Joking Apart* (1993–1995) and *Chalk* (1997).

In 2000, Moffat created his best-known comedy series, *Coupling*. Moffat wrote all four seasons of the popular series, which was based on his relationship with his wife (and often his producer too), Sue Vertue. Moffat has been a fan of *Doctor Who* since childhood, and his short story "Continuity Errors" was included in Virgin Publishing's *Doctor Who* anthology *Decalog 3*. In 1999, he wrote a Comic Relief *Doctor Who* episode, "The Curse of Fatal Death," which starred Rowan Atkinson as the Doctor. When the series was revived in 2005, he enthusiastically agreed to contribute to it, writing one story in each season: "The Empty Child"/"The Doctor Dances," "The Girl in the Fireplace," "Blink" and "Silence in the Library"/"Forest of the Dead." All but the latter story won the Hugo Award for best short-form drama in science fiction. Moffat also wrote the Children in Need scene "Time Crash."

Coincident with *Doctor Who* was Moffat's move from comedy into drama. He wrote the 2007 series *Jekyll*, which updated the Robert Louis Stevenson novella *The Curious Case of Dr. Jekyll and Mr. Hyde* for modern audiences. With fellow *Doctor Who* writer Mark Gatiss, Moffat created *Sherlock*, a modern-day version of Sherlock

Holmes, which debuted to critical acclaim and high ratings in 2010. He also wrote several drafts of Steven Spielberg's 2011 adaptation of *The Adventures of Tintin* before he was asked to take over *Doctor Who*.

Moffat was Russell T Davies' only choice as his successor, and Moffat became executive producer and head writer in 2010. He has written 11 episodes since beginning his new role, and he describes his role as being in charge of the "fiction of the show," while his fellow executive producers (on Series Five and Six) Piers Wegner and Beth Willis take care of logistical and financial decisions.

. . . .

Karen Gillan

Born in 1987 in Inverness, Karen Gillan dropped out of drama school to work as a model before she landed a role in the ensemble sketch comedy series *The Kevin Bishop Show*. Occasional roles followed, including the Soothsayer in "The Fires of Pompeii." Playing Amy Pond in *Doctor Who* is undoubtedly her breakout role. She has already translated her success into film roles, most notably as Jean Shrimpton in *We'll Take Manhattan* (2012).

. . . .

5.03 Victory of the Daleks

Written by Mark Gatiss **Directed by** Andrew Gunn

Supporting cast Ian McNeice (Churchill), Bill Paterson (Bracewell), Nina de Cosimo (Blanche), Tim Wallers (Childers), Nicholas Pegg (Dalek 1), Barnaby Edwards (Dalek 2), Nicholas Briggs (Dalek voice), Susannah Fielding (Lilian), James Albrecht (Todd), Colin Prockter (air raid warden)

Original airdate April 17, 2010

The Big Idea At the height of the Battle of Britain, Prime Minister Winston Churchill unveils his secret weapon to stop the Nazi menace: the Ironsides; or, as the Doctor knows them, the Daleks.

Roots and References Wartime dramas such as the 1969 film *The Battle of Britain*; 1970s BBC wartime sitcom *Dad's Army* (the walrus-mustached air raid warden); *Where Eagles Dare* (Danny Boy and Broadsword callsigns); Lieutenant Commander Data in *Star Trek: The Next Generation* (Bracewell's positronic brain). The story takes its initial premise from 1966 *Doctor Who* story "Power of the Daleks."

Adventures in Time and Space The Daleks use Time Corridor technology, which was established as their method of time-travelling in 1971's "Day of the Daleks"

WHO IS THE DOCTOR

290

and 1984's "Resurrection of the Daleks." The Doctor tells Winston the TARDIS is a Type 40, something established in 1976's "The Deadly Assassin" (this is the first time it's been mentioned in the New Series). The Daleks' facility for creating robotic humanoids was first seen in 1965's "The Chase."

The Dalek design first seen in "Dalek" makes its final appearance. The "Ironside" Daleks barely survived the events of "Journey's End" and fell back through time. (As the New Paradigm Daleks are derived from "pure" Dalek DNA, the "Ironside" Daleks were presumably impure as they were created from Davros's own cells.)

The Crack in the Universe Effect Much to the Doctor's consternation, Amy doesn't remember either the Daleks or the events of "The Stolen Earth"/"Journey's End." After the Doctor and Amy leave, a crack appears in the storage room where the TARDIS was.

The Doctor and Amy When trying to stop Amy from talking to a Dalek, the Doctor briefly calls her Amelia (we'll find out why in "Curse of the Black Spot"). She gets Bracewell to connect with his human memories by asking him, "Ever fancy someone you know you shouldn't? Hurts, doesn't it? But it's a kind of good hurt," which might speak to her own frame of mind.

Monster of the Week The remaining Daleks have used the progenitor device to create a New Paradigm of Daleks. These Daleks are larger than the old models and use colours to designate rank: the white one is the Supreme Dalek, while the other ranks are scientist (orange), strategist (blue), drone (red) and eternal (yellow). (It should be noted that the only colour ranking designated onscreen in this story is the Supreme Dalek; the rest we picked up from the toys!)

Stand Up and Cheer The Doctor and Amy getting Bracewell to defuse by having him reconnect to his human memories really shouldn't work as a scene because it employs the overused trope of an alien saving the day by discovering his humanity. And yet it does work, spectacularly so, partially by undercutting the Doctor's speech about that trope, but mostly by having Amy connect it with secret, sensual, private yearnings instead. (Contrasting nicely with the Doctor asking him to remember old hurts and people who have died.) Plus, robotic or not, who can resist Karen Gillan huskily whispering, "Hey, Paisley"?

Roll Your Eyes The Dalek saucer interior is, without a doubt, the laziest, most half-assed set decoration in the history of the New Series. It's a warehouse covered over with reflective material, with very 20th-century-looking pillars and vents. Did they sell the entire Dalek saucer set decoration from past stories to various exhibitions? Honestly, a fan video would come up with a more interesting set.

You're Not Making Any Sense The scene where the Spitfires attack the Dalek saucer in space is not only downright embarrassing, it's on a completely different dimensional plane to credibity itself. Bracewell has "ideas" for hypersonic flight and gravity bubbles. Even if those "ideas" were actual constructed devices, having them ready to go on planes (that would have been scrambled outside of London; it's not like there was an airbase next door to Whitehall) in mere minutes — and training the pilots to use them to achieve escape velocity and fly in space — is utterly ludicrous.

Interesting Trivia The Daleks build a robot Bracewell who (somehow) contains a wormhole that they can use as a bomb. But, um, why? Back in "Dalek," we saw that a single Dalek was capable of destroying the entire planet. Here we have several, even before the progenitors, and the humans are handily killing each other anyway, so it wouldn't even be especially taxing. So why bother building a robot who only ends up outsmarting them anyway?

Can the Daleks time travel? In the Classic Series they travelled through time in many stories. They fought a war with the Time Lords, which would have ended (or rather, never started) had they not had the ability to time travel. And we've seen individual Daleks in the Cult of Skaro initiate an emergency temporal shift and end up in the past ("Doomsday"/"Evolution of the Daleks"). But, cult members aside, individual Daleks don't seem to have the ability, presumably relying on their ship, rather like the Doctor. Clearly, they're about as variably skilled as the Doctor is too, because they overshot and then had to lie in wait for him to turn up, which isn't the most efficient of plans.

It's bad news for Churchill on the historical accuracy front: Stukas were short-range fighters used to destroy RAF bases on the English coastline during the Battle of Britain. They never had the range to fly inland to take part in bombing missions on London. The Cabinet War Rooms were considerably smaller than portrayed on screen, though that's mere poetic licence. In fairness, several great lines of Winston Churchill's are borrowed for the script, including "If Hitler invaded Hell, I would give a favourable reference to the Devil."

The TARDIS Chronometer The Cabinet War Rooms and a Dalek saucer, presumably sometime in 1940 during the Battle of Britain. For Churchill, the TARDIS has arrived a month after he initially contacted the Doctor in "The Beast Below."

Cool? (GB) In 1966, David Whitaker wrote a six-part *Doctor Who* serial entitled "The Power of the Daleks," which featured Patrick Troughton's debut as the Doctor. In that story, a scientist in an Earth colony has discovered a disabled Dalek ship. The Daleks manipulate him into believing they will be his servant. The Doctor tries, in vain, to convince the colonists that the Daleks are an actual threat and ultimately is too late, as it turns out the Daleks were simply biding time to rebuild their forces.

It's one of the greatest *Doctor Who* stories of all time. You can therefore forgive hardcore fans for hoping that "Victory of the Daleks" was a remake of "Power of the Daleks," only set in the milieu of Churchill and the Blitz, rather than a futuristic Earth colony. Even if it's a little derivative, it's a perfect idea for a historical drama with the Daleks: the Doctor has to convince a desperate Churchill that his perfect soldiers are ultimately going to destroy the planet while solving the mystery of why they're really pretending to be robots in the first place.

What a shame, then, that this idea is dropped after 12 minutes. What an even bigger shame is what happened instead. The Daleks' plan here makes "Evolution of the Daleks" seem coherent: show up in a historical period and hope the Doctor turns up and identifies himself. Ludicrous doesn't even cover it. Why don't they just become contestants on *The Apprentice*? "You're fired." "Exterminate!"

I don't believe it's writer Mark Gatiss's fault. When Gatiss gets to remake "Power of the Daleks," he's producing some great material and borrowing some of Churchill's best *bon mots* for the occasion. The problem is the stuff in the middle, the stuff that feels like it's being generated to serve marketing needs rather than to serve storytelling needs.

The thing is, I actually like the new Dalek design. It's taken the old VW Beetle design of the Daleks and applied the new VW Beetle aesthetic. It's not a radical rethinking, just a tweak to modern design sensibilities. (They're not perfect; they don't look so great from the back but that can be fixed.) I like the different varieties of colours and the ranking and their bigger size. I would have been fine with their introduction and the return of the Daleks as a regular villainous force as opposed to whatever's left that managed to escape from last time . . . had their reintroduction served any purpose to the episode or the arc of the season.

In the event, it doesn't. The new Daleks are just a glorified piece of marketing for the videogame *City of the Daleks*, the New Paradigm Dalek toys and the graphic novel *The Last Good Dalek*. And that leaves a bitter aftertaste for me, as I think the primary objective of *Doctor Who* is to produce good television, not to sell videogames, toys and merchandise. The fact that the Doctor, who apparently is concerned that he's had to let the Daleks go in order to save the Earth, doesn't immediately say to Amy, "Right, we need to go to the TARDIS and start searching time and space to stop these new Daleks from growing in numbers" is damning, as is the fact that nowhere does the Doctor mention that the Daleks are partially responsible for the destruction of his own people. This tells us it isn't about the story or the long-running characters, it's about making sure remote controlled red Dalek drones are bought at Toys "R" Us.

And yet, even market forces can't justify how terrible the Spitfires versus

Dalek saucer sequence is. It's not just the giant black hole where logic and suspension of disbelief should be that's the problem. It's that the whole sequence is undramatic, with the Doctor stuck in the TARDIS talking on the radio with "Danny Boy." Who the hell is "Danny Boy" and why should we care? If he was an actual character, a pilot we had met at the start of the episode, a face put to the callsign, maybe that would work. But we don't get that. It's just some random voice talking over a CGI sequence that was reverse engineered from a silly and unlikely visual, proving that the same ridiculous flaws that have dogged the series since 2005 will dog it under its new proprietors.

The whole tone of this feels wrong, right down to Matt Smith's embarrassingly bad shouting while clobbering the Dalek, which undermines the brilliant, righteous anger from the previous episode. And yet, frustratingly, there are some really great things in this story as well. The ending with the Doctor and Amy trying to defuse Bracewell by getting him to remember a forbidden love is genuinely touching and frankly feels like it belongs in a much better episode. Ian McNeice is terrific as Churchill, and I love the Doctor fending off the Daleks with a Jammie Dodger. But these elements are lost in the tide of the stupidity that is the Dalek plan and Spitfires in space.

The retconning of "The Stolen Earth" and "Journey's End" is also disappointing. On the one hand, I can respect the view that "The Stolen Earth" renders any subsequent alien invasion commonplace. On the other hand, I think "The Waters of Mars" and *Torchwood: Children of Earth* show how it could be used to the further the series' mythology. I'm disappointed that it has to not only go away but be taken away in such a dreadful story as this.

Second Opinion (RS?) This is an awesome episode . . . for 12 minutes. The Daleks as wartime soldiers is a brilliant move; their camouflage paint-job, hessian tool belt and blackout covers over their lights when outside are all utterly brilliant. The Doctor, full of fury, attacking a seemingly helpless Dalek with a wrench is excellent.

Even the "Power of the Daleks" homage, while derivative, is not unwelcome. Too bad they didn't stick with that the whole way through and have the story be a paranoid tale of three Daleks infiltrating the war rooms so that they could use the war machine to remake themselves — and the episode could have something profound to say about the nature of war, too. That would have been infinitely superior to the story we got.

I disagree with my co-author about the rebooting of past continuity. It's actually quite clever, as it pays homage to the past through the Doctor's acknowledgement of it and also furthers the season arc. So it doesn't feel like a cheat. It's also necessary, because the show has become way too bogged down with everyone knowing about aliens. In order to make a fresh start — which the show absolutely needs to do — there has to be some element of wiping the past away. This is about as courteous a method as possible.

The same isn't true of the new Daleks, which are utterly horrendous. Sorry, Graeme, but they are. They're in bathtub-friendly colours, lining up in product-placement order and have "marketing" written all over them. Worse, they don't even work as a menace. They're awkward, bulky and hunched. And why? There's no reason at all. The Dalek design is timeless and a thing of beauty. There's a reason it's been largely unchanged for almost 50 years. This is a cheap knockoff.

Had they appeared in a story with a cast-iron justification, that might have been somewhat palatable. Unlike Graeme, I blame Mark Gatiss entirely. The plot is incredibly poor, the Daleks' plan makes no sense and the story logic doesn't hold together. (Spitfires in space! Ten minutes after being a theoretical concept!) Gatiss consistently produces some of the worst scripts, and yet he's one of the few to keep being commissioned. Does he have incriminating photos of the producers in bed with Cybermen or something?

This is an extremely poor effort. The redesigned Daleks are enough to make you very, very angry, and they're wrapped around a terrible tale. In a story featuring both the Daleks and Nazis, it's almost criminal that no attempt is made to link the two. This is easily the worst story of the season. On the bright side, it's also the worst story of the season, so it's uphill from here.

5.04–5.05 The Time of Angels / Flesh and Stone

Written by Steven Moffat **Directed by** Adam Smith

Supporting cast Alex Kingston (River Song), Iain Glen (Father Octavian), Mark Springer (Christian), Troy Glasgow (Angelo), David Atkins (Bob), Darren Morfitt (Marco), Mark Monero (Pedro), George Russo (Phillip), Simon Dulton (Alistair), Mark Skinner (security guard)

Original airdates April 24 and May 1, 2010

The Big Idea A ship carrying River Song and a Weeping Angel crashes on a planet, restoring hundreds of Angels. But the crack in the universe is there too . . .

Roots and References *Aliens* (a sequel which sees a military team trying to stop a massive infestation of what had previously been an isolated menace); the Bible's Book of Revelation ("Come and See"); *Poltergeist* and *The Ring* movies (the Angel coming out of the video screen); Steven Moffat's short story "Continuity Errors" in the 1996 *Doctor Who* anthology *Decalog 3* (the Doctor as a complicated space-time event).

Adventures in Time and Space We get a flashback to the Doctor investigating the crack in "The Eleventh Hour." The Doctor mentions having encountered the Angels before on Earth ("Blink"), although those were apparently just scavengers, barely surviving. He also says, "Don't blink, Amy, don't even blink," a reference to that story's catchphrase. The Doctor flicks through a book and absorbs its contents, just as he did in 1979's "City of Death" and in "Rose." Gravity globes were previously seen in "The Impossible Planet."

River Song previously appeared in "Silence in the Library"/"Forest of the Dead" (where she asked the Doctor, "The crash of the *Byzantium*, have we done that yet?"). She says she'll see the Doctor when the Pandorica opens. He says that's a fairytale, but she responds, "Aren't we all?" We'll see this play out in "The Pandorica Opens"/"The Big Bang." The Delirium Archive is the final resting place of the headless monks; we'll see them in "A Good Man Goes to War."

The Crack in the Universe Effect The crack appears on the wall of the *Byzantium* and opens. It's pure time energy, the fire at the end of the universe, and when someone looks at it, they feel kind of sick. If it swallows you, every moment of your existence will be erased. The Doctor realizes that no one recalling the CyberKing stomping around Victorian London ("The Next Doctor") was a clue to the crack's effects, as was Amy not recognizing the Daleks in "Victory of the Daleks." Amy sees the effect of the crack — with clerics swallowed up by it no longer remembered by their colleagues — but it doesn't affect her because she's a time traveller.

One day there will be a very big bang, so big that everything — past and future — will crack, ending the universe. The explosion begins June 26, 2010, which is Amy's wedding day. Feeding it a big, complicated space-time event (like the Doctor or the Angels) will satisfy the crack for a while.

The Doctor who comes back to comfort Amy, asking her to remember what he told her as a child, is not the same Doctor who left her moments ago. (Even though he's seen in closeup, you can see that he's wearing his jacket, though with the sleeves rolled up.)

Who is the Doctor? This story offers an interesting glimpse into what an overachieving time-travelling hero does when he wants to narcissistically reflect on what he's done: he goes to a museum and keeps score on how his actions have been recorded!

The Doctor and Amy Amy finally admits to the Doctor that she's getting married and deliberately left her engagement ring behind when she ran off with the Doctor. Nearly being turned to stone and killed made her think about who she wanted: it's the Doctor, but he doesn't get that, so Amy kisses him to make it clearer. The Doctor rejects her advances (he claims it would never work in the long term; she seems happy with a one-night stand) and then realizes the explosion that creates the crack is centred on her wedding day, which changes his priorities even further.

Monster of the Week The Weeping Angels are different from their first appearance in "Blink." They thrive on radiation and now kill their victims by snapping their necks instead of displacing them in time. Their quantum-locked nature — where they literally cease to exist if anyone is looking at them — now extends to images of the Angels as well; they can attack through still photographs or video footage of themselves. Looking into the eyes of a Weeping Angel places the Angel inside your mind. They can convince you that certain things are happening (like an arm turning to stone), get you to say things (like numbers counting down) and will eventually take over you entirely.

Stand Up and Cheer The opening scene is amazing: we cut back and forth between surreal images like a soldier in a field with lipstick on his cheek to the spaceship he's really on to a museum 12,000 years later with the Doctor reading River's message. Her giving coordinates on the security footage and then blowing the doors open segues into the TARDIS materializing just in time to save her, before we crash into the credits. It's a spectacular entrance for River and a manifesto of what Steven Moffat is capable of, ably aided by Adam Smith's gorgeous direction.

Roll Your Eyes The Angels turning their heads on camera is a scary moment, but it ruins one of the neater aspects of their existence, which is the idea that we too are participating in the Angels' inability to move when watched. In fact, without that, much of the Angels' behaviour both here and in "Blink" makes no sense.

You're Not Making Any Sense River's entire rescue plan is predicated upon the home box, which is activated and flies home whenever the ship is in trouble. She tells the crew that the ship will never reach its destination, before leaping out into space. However, she's then surprised to discover that the ship has subsequently crashed. But if it hadn't, the home box would never have been sent, the Doctor would never have received her message and she would have died a cold, lonely death in space. So what exactly was her plan, then?

Interesting Trivia It's time for a report on what we know of River's timeline thus far. Are you sitting comfortably? Good. Then we'll begin. According to clues dropped in this episode and what we know from "Silence in the Library"/"The Forest of the Dead," she's known the Doctor for some time, she has a doctorate herself and she's serving time for killing someone (described in a way that hints she may kill the Doctor himself). She knows Old High Gallifreyan, can pilot the TARDIS and perhaps married the Doctor. In the future, she's going to become a professor of archaeology and learn the Doctor's true name. Most significantly of all, she meets the Doctor out of order, perhaps uniquely among people he encounters. Pay attention, because we'll revisit a lot of these clues as time goes on (but won't say where, because of — you guessed it — spoilers).

"The church has moved on," says the Doctor, explaining why it now has its own military, with a troop of clerics led by a bishop, soldiers with sacred names and a verger who handles explosives. However, it's not clear whether the church has entirely become a military organization or whether it simply has its own army, but they do have a really cool transmat effect.

This story was, in production order, the first story in which Matt Smith played the Doctor. The first scenes Smith and Karen Gillan filmed were the ones on the beach amid the wreckage of the *Byzantium*.

The TARDIS Chronometer In the Delirium Archive, a museum on an asteroid, 12,000 years after the *Byzantium* crash. The TARDIS then materializes in space to collect River, then lands on Alfava Metraxis. It's the 51st century, according to the Doctor. At the end, it lands in Amy's bedroom, June 25, 2010.

Cool? (RS?) Somebody talks smack to the Doctor (River), something fundamental about the show is undermined (the TARDIS materialisation sound), people boast about how clever they are (Amy after switching off the scanner), impressive scenarios have their impressiveness explicitly highlighted (a forest in a bottle in a spaceship in a maze), there's a clever resolution (turning the ship 90 degrees) and the Doctor gives a punch-the-air speech. ("If you're smart, if you value your continued existence, if you have any plans about seeing tomorrow, there's one thing you never, ever put in a trap . . . me.") Yes, it's a Steven Moffat story, all right.

Like "Blink," the pacing is designed to be so fast that you don't stop and think. Because if you did, you might notice that the Angels look at each other an awful lot and yet can still move. Or the idea that they have "instincts" that cause them to freeze if you have your eyes shut is a completely bogus concept. And if looking into the eyes of an Angel makes you an Angel, why isn't everyone from this story and "Blink" turning into one? It's not just the writing either; we're told that Amy can only open her eyes for a second, but then she has them open for five seconds. Two black characters get sent on a mission of doom, continuing the grand tradition of lazy tropes in television casting.

But these things don't matter, not really, because there's so much here that works well. The dialogue sparkles ("I can run away from anything I like; time is not the boss of me"), the direction is astonishing (little touches like the image of an Angel reflected in Amy's eye are marvellous) and there are some genuinely scary moments, such as the Angel moving inside the recording. That's the best kind of horror because a) it happens only when you're not looking, and b) it plays on the childhood fear that there's something in the TV coming to get you.

Though Amy's solution is very good, she's immediately snarky about it, boasting about how brilliant she is, which makes her instantly unlikeable. Which is a shame, because she's a character you want to like, but every time you get close there's something repellent about her. Her independence is good, but her personality is just too spiky to elicit empathy.

However, that doesn't apply to River, who is fantastic here. I wasn't convinced during "Silence in the Library"/"Forest of the Dead," but Alex Kingston's chemistry with Matt Smith is fabulous. Amy and River also have an instant rapport, which is interesting in light of later developments. River starts off being smug about the TARDIS, but then, during the caves, it's clear that she and the Doctor really are equals: they come to key realizations at the same time, before anyone else; she's the one he turns to for confirmation; and her future-mystery balances his abilities. Her delivery of "I absolutely trust him" when Father Octavian asks if she trusts him is spot-on. He then asks, "He's not some kind of madman?" and she repeats, deadpan, "I absolutely trust him." This is an excellent punchline.

What's awesome is that, as clever as the story is in places, it's not trying to show off; it genuinely wants you to come along for the ride. You figure out the statues should have two heads at precisely the same time as the Doctor and River, because the dialogue has seeded the clues perfectly. The Doctor makes a "clock" motion (which is itself charmingly offbeat) as he figures out the crack's effects. He isn't all-knowing and smug like the tenth Doctor was, but is someone who figures stuff out. That's enormously appealing.

This is also the first Moffat-era story to feature a cliffhanger — and it's amazing! We're used to imminent-danger cliffhangers or ones where key information is revealed. This is a cliffhanger unlike anything we've seen before. It should be the Doctor and friends surrounded by Angels. Cue credits and wonder how they'll get out of this one. Instead, what's happened here is that they've moved the resolution into the cliffhanger itself, which is a fascinating way to play with the structure. Then, brilliantly, the resolution — which you'd think would have almost nowhere to go — is a stunning visual: the camera rotating 180 degrees. It's odd, but extremely effective.

This is really the theme of the story: how you look at things matters. Down becomes up, then sideways becomes down inside the ship. Our attitude to River is very different, depending how much information we have about her; she might be friend, wife or murderer, depending. On the one hand, looking at an Angel stops it; on the other, it's the most dangerous thing you can do.

The scene in the forest where the Doctor takes Amy's hands and tells her to remember what he told her when she was seven is a key scene in the entire season, for reasons we'll come back to. Viewing it first time around or later on changes things entirely.

Amy's countdown is subtle, creepy and effective. Especially since her initial numbers correspond to the Doctor saying a different number, which throws you off. Father Octavian's death scene is also excellent, but for entirely different reasons. Where so much of the story's spectacle relies on its cleverness, this relies entirely on character. Father Octavian has thus far been exactly the kind of stock military man who appears regularly throughout *Doctor Who*. Someone for the Doctor to bounce off. However, in his last moments, we see a man of honour, one who ends his life "at his best," with the Doctor unable to save him. This is heartbreaking.

The Doctor accidentally pulling off a piece of the ship is cute (this moment came from Smith's own clumsiness on set). Biting Amy's hand to prove it's not stone is adorably childlike, and the "I made him say comfy chairs" line is nicely delivered. His turning off the torch to test the statues works so well because of the Doctor's insecurity about whether it's a good idea or not. And the Doctor gets a fabulous line: "Humans, you're everywhere. You're like rabbits. I'll never get done saving you." Given that these were Smith's first scenes as the Doctor, it's remarkable how much he already owns the role.

This is a rich story that rewards multiple viewings. It's also the perfect followup to "The Eleventh Hour" for newbies, if you want to shock and awe them with the power of what *Doctor Who* can be. (Note: do not show them the previous story if you want to achieve this.) Almost everything about this story is firing on all cylinders.

Second Opinion (GB) Back in the previous four seasons of *Doctor Who*, the special moment was when they broadcast "The Moffat Story." It may not be the best story of the season (though it often was), but you could count on Steven Moffat's one contribution to be astonishingly funny and clever and utterly compelling. And it almost always won the Hugo Award.

You would think that Steven Moffat becoming showrunner for *Doctor Who* would mean that every story would be the Moffat Story, but it doesn't. "The Time of Angels"/"Flesh and Stone" didn't win the Hugo, but it's still this season's Moffat Story. And it's everything we want one to be.

The pre-credits sequence of "The Time of Angels" alone is the kick to the backside this season needed. It's intelligent, funny, exciting, gorgeously designed and directed, and has a wonderful payoff. And the whole story follows on from that gambit.

The Weeping Angels are even scarier as a force in numbers, and the desperate escape of the Doctor, River, Amy and Father Octavian's party is delightfully tense. There are some naff innovations (giving the Angels Sacred Bob's voice, which is just recycling the Vashta Nerada using Anita's voice in "Forest of the Dead"), but there are some excellent ones as well, such as the idea that the image of an Angel is just as dangerous as a real one, which allows for a great set piece with Amy.

It only stumbles in bringing the season arc to the forefront. On the one hand, it signals an interesting way arcs are going to be handled by the show's new proprietors: not as a repeated meme or story element, but as a discrete bit of ongoing plot that will influence the course of episodes themselves.

I like this in principle, but in practice it took a story that was already tense and thrilling, interrupted it to dump in a lot of portents (and undo a lot of past *Doctor Who*: alas, poor "The Next Doctor," I knew ye well) and then used it as a convenient *deus ex machina* to get rid of the Weeping Angels. The good news is that it's so well written that the mixing of the crack and the action dealing with the Angels is more seamless than it deserved to be. The not-so-great thing is that the story was going so well it didn't need the crack at all.

That aside, there's a lot to admire. Adam Smith's direction is confident. Matt Smith and Alex Kingston are beautiful as a double act, you can totally believe that these two could one day be (or, in River's case, are already) married. And Father Octavian's sacrifice is beautifully played by Iain Glen opposite Smith. "The Time of Angels" and "Flesh and Stone" are a bright spot to a season that was becoming mired in mundanity. But, as it's the Moffat Story, was there ever any doubt?

The Psychic Papers: Retconning

Retroactive continuity, or retcon, is a term used to describe changes to established history in a work of fiction. For example, Sherlock Holmes died battling Professor Moriarty in Reichenbach Falls in the 1893 short story "The Final Problem." In 1902, the story "The Mystery of the Empty House" establishes that this did not happen, and Holmes instead lived incognito for several years. Nicholas Meyer's 1974 novel *The Seven-Per-Cent Solution* states that Holmes didn't battle Moriarty at all, but he spent several years overcoming his cocaine addiction with Sigmund Freud. Both "The Mystery of the Empty House" and *The Seven-Per-Cent Solution* are retcons of the established history of Holmes.

The only serious example of retroactive continuity ever performed in the Classic Series was in 1988's "Remembrance of the Daleks," which suggested the reason for the first Doctor's visit to Earth in the first *Doctor Who* story in 1963, "An Unearthly

Child," was to bury a Gallifreyan weapon. Otherwise in Classic *Doctor Who*, retroactive continuity tended to be "soft," where the changes are cosmetic or assumed to have always been there. For example, the Time Lords change from godlike beings in 1969's "The War Games" to mendacious politicians in 1976's "The Deadly Assassin." The backstory of the Daleks' own creation changes from what was stated as history in 1963's "The Daleks" to what we actually see on screen in 1975's "Genesis of the Daleks." And the UNIT stories went from being set in the 1980s to being set in the 1970s.

The New Series has tended towards "soft" retcons more often than not, such as the Doctor's age being reset to 900 in "Aliens of London." It's only with "The Sound of Drums"/"Last of the Time Lords" that we begin to see more overt retroactive continuity, with the Master's backstory changed to include him being driven mad by the constant sound of drumming in his head. On the one hand, this retcon doesn't substantially change the events of past stories featuring the Master; on the other hand, it does fundamentally change the viewer's understanding of the Master's frame of mind.

In the run-up to Series Five, *Doctor Who Magazine* published an article about the number of stories set on contemporary Earth over the first four seasons and how a surfeit of cataclysmic events in the "real" world — ranging from the giant Cyberman in Victorian times in "The Next Doctor" to the Daleks transporting Earth to another galaxy and then invading it in "The Stolen Earth" — has broken all credibility. If the contemporary world in *Doctor Who* is supposed to stand in for the real world of the viewer, how can future alien invasions be surprising (or work according to the real-world assumption that aliens don't exist) if Earth has already been the site of several major invasions? The article concluded that the only options available to the production team would be to ignore such events or write them out entirely.

Given that *Doctor Who Magazine* is an official publication, the incoming production team may have tipped off the magazine to prepare the ground for Series Five. The crack in the universe has retconned out both the Cybermen invasion of 1851 and the Dalek invasion of 2008.

Even so, the mechanics of cause and effect aren't examined in depth in Series Five. Were the invading Cybermen in "The Next Doctor" simply written out of existence before they could arrive? Did Miss Hartigan simply live out an unnoticed, unremembered existence as a result, and did Jackson Lake move to London town with his wife and son and never meet Rosita? Or was everyone involved eaten by the crack?

The Dalek invasion is even trickier, given how it touches on events in "The Waters of Mars," which is, according to the New Series' cosmology, a fixed point in time. In that story, Adelaide Brooke, whose father was exterminated by the Daleks in "The Stolen Earth," was inspired to travel the stars after encountering a Dalek. If the Dalek invasion didn't happen, then was Adelaide's father still killed, and how was she inspired to travel the stars? Certainly, "Vincent and the Doctor" and "The Pandorica Opens" imply that, even after history has been changed by the crack, memories of what's been erased, even physical objects, can still remain, so perhaps Adelaide is still inspired by a half-remembered event that no longer happened.

The danger with retcons is that everything can seem meaningless in their wake. When events can simply be wiped away, it's the sci-fi equivalent of waking up and discovering it was all a dream. Without the characters' ability to learn from their experiences, the drama is profoundly weakened. The good thing about retcons is that they let writers do whatever they want, no longer held hostage by whatever came before. If huge, Earth-shattering events changed your characters' lives forever, then a simple retcon can return you to a sleepy English village where no one believes in aliens. Without *Doctor Who*'s ability to periodically reinvent itself, the story would have gone stale and ended decades ago.

The retcon device of the crack in the universe embraces the pros while avoiding the cons, partly by leaving behind enough consequences so that it doesn't feel like a cheap trick, and partly because it's clear that, in the world of *Doctor Who*, wiping out the past is most definitely a bad thing.

Retconning? What retconning? There's no retconning here. And there never was.

5.06 The Vampires of Venice

Written by Toby Whithouse **Directed by** Jonny Campbell

Supporting cast Arthur Darvill (Rory Williams); Helen McCrory (Rosanna); Lucian Msamati (Guido); Alisha Bailey (Isabella); Alex Price (Francesco); Gabriella Wilde, Hannah Steele, Elizabeth Croft, Sonila Vieshta, Gabriela Montaraz (vampire girls); Michael Percival (Inspector); Simon Gregor (steward)

Original airdate May 8, 2010

The Big Idea The Doctor tries to reignite the spark between Amy and Rory by taking them on a romantic getaway. Pity about the vampires.

Roots and References Alan Moore, Steve Bissette and John Totleben's 1980s comic book series *Saga of the Swamp Thing* (the fish vampires); Francis Ford Coppola's 1992 adaptation of Bram Stoker's *Dracula* (the sumptuous visuals). The Doctor mentions owing Casanova a chicken (presumably a nod to the Russell T Davies' version of *Casanova* which was partially shot in Venice and featured David Tennant).

Adventures in Time and Space In what must be the nerdiest sight gag in the history of the show, the Doctor whips out his psychic paper only to discover he's accidentally using his library card. The card is from the Shoreditch Library, complete with picture of the Doctor's first incarnation. You can pause your DVD to see the details: Dr. J. Smith of 76 Totters Lane, Shoreditch, London, and it expires in November. Full marks to whomever was watching 1963's "An Unearthly Child" and 1988's "Remembrance of the Daleks."

The Crack in the Universe Effect Rosanna tells the Doctor, "There are cracks . . . some are tiny, some are as big as the sky. Through some we saw worlds and people, and through others we saw Silence and the end of things." The Saturnyne escaped the Silence through cracks in the universe that took them to Earth. The cracks snapped shut, claiming the Saturnyne homeworld in the process. At the end of the story, the Doctor notes that everything is perfectly silent.

The Doctor and Amy The Doctor goes to extraordinary lengths to get Rory and Amy back together, indicating he does not want to reciprocate her feelings. The Doctor blames Amy's crush on the dazzling life of travelling in time and space, and he tries to make it up to Rory and Amy by taking them to a romantic locale. Once there, the Doctor and Amy act as though they're completely sympatico with each other, leaving Rory to stifle his considerable (and understandable) jealousy. The Doctor heeds Rory's request to not put Amy in danger by ordering her to the TARDIS when the Saturnyne's plan begins (but then Amy and Rory collectively decide to disobey him). Amy calls the Doctor and Rory "my boys," and neither the Doctor or Rory protest this much.

Monster of the Week The Saturnyne are a bipedal form of marine life with a fish-like head and massive teeth. They escaped the Silence to Earth, but only male offspring survived, along with their mother. They use a perception filter to disguise themselves as human, though their large teeth can break the filter, giving the impression they're vampires.

Stand Up and Cheer The Doctor's first encounter with the vampire girls is delightfully goofy. It starts with the Doctor's routine at a mirror, which is like watching the class nerd attempt to be suave before the school dance. It then moves into a brilliant gag with the library card, followed by the Doctor demanding, "Tell me the whole plan!" Pause. "Maybe that will work some day." Just when you think it can't be sillier, the Doctor starts enthusing about how they're vampires as though he's encountered the Rolling Stones talking with Paul McCartney at the back of a pub. And while all this is happening, the girls creepily talk in unison. This really is Christmas.

Roll Your Eyes What the hell kind of climax was that? The Doctor climbs to the top of a tower and turns off a switch. Admittedly, he did so in the middle of a hurricane, but it doesn't look particularly difficult. Plus, it's *Doctor Who*: the jeopardy quotient should be much higher.

You're Not Making Any Sense Why doesn't the Doctor offer to help Rosanna and her offspring relocate to another world devoid of humans? And why does the Doctor blithely leave Venice with 10,000 sharp-toothed offspring still swimming around? True, they won't reproduce, but they're certainly a deadly hazard to any gondolier who falls into the canal.

Interesting Trivia This is the third explicit use of a perception filter this season and is far from the last. That's partly because the season is riffing on the theme of how what we see isn't trustworthy and that events (and people) change depending on how you look at them. Which is an awesome theme and works really well when it's integrated into the plot. What's less awesome is the reliance on the sci-fi MacGuffin of a perception filter to cover a multitude of sins. It's a cheat to begin with and becomes untenable with overuse.

Given this story is pure fantasy in a historical setting, about the only real challenge to historical accuracy is that one doesn't see much of Venice's famous canals except in CGI shots. But then, this story ended up being shot in Trogir, Croatia (along with "Vincent and the Doctor," there doubling for France), so perhaps that's not so surprising.

The TARDIS Chronometer After picking up Rory from his stag party, the Doctor takes Amy and Rory to Venice, 1580.

Cool? (GB) One thing that must be said about writer Toby Whithouse: the man comes up with some of the best dialogue on television. The comedic lines are also great ("funny how you can say something in your head and it sounds fine . . ."; "fish people from space have never been so . . . buxom") but it's not just the funny stuff. I love the opening scene where Guido says of Isabella, "She's my world," and Rosanna replies, "Then I will take your world." It's utterly delicious.

Whithouse also writes witty, nuanced scenes that give the actors an opportunity to have fun with the material. I love the scene where Rory, awkwardly, attempts to recite to Rosanna and the Steward an elaborate backstory for himself and his "sister" Amy. However, it's the question-for-a-question scene between the Doctor and Rosanna that really lights up the screen. In "School Reunion," Whithouse wrote a brilliant confrontation scene between the Doctor and Finch, but here he moves it up a level with a flirtatious game between protagonist and antagonist. Matt Smith shows that, when this new Doctor wants to, he can flirt with the best of them, and at the same time the Doctor shows a steely resolve amidst the witty repartee. (What's great is that Helen McRory matches him barb for barb and quip for quip.) Matt Smith just gets better and better, playing the Doctor like a mad old uncle, totally unselfconscious that he looks so young and dorky.

Whithouse also helps with Rory's reintroduction. Like Mickey in "School Reunion," Rory provides a lot of comic relief (attempting to fend off Francesco by making an impromptu cross; comparing his penlight with the gigantic UV light that the Doctor pulls out of his pocket . . .), but Rory is so thoroughly decent and heartfelt that you laugh at the things he does, not at who he is. He also gets the best moments with the Doctor: Rory's criticism that the Doctor makes people take risks because they want to impress him is absolutely spot on, and the Doctor knows it. And try as Amy might to deflect the question, Rory is right to ask if Amy ever thought of him during her adventures. To play broad comedy while making a character authentic is quite difficult, but Arthur Darvill is superb at doing just that. As an added bonus, Darvill and Matt Smith make a superb double act.

Rory's decency, though, leads to one lingering concern: he seems remarkably okay for someone whose fiancée has attempted to cheat on him. In fact, his attitude is one of resignation rather than betrayal: as though he knows he can't compete with the Doctor and so never bothers. Amy, by contrast, selfishly chooses to have everything and never addresses questions about her behaviour or her seeming lack of interest in Rory. She doesn't even apologize to Rory for hurting his feelings. The more this season progresses, the more problems I have with Amy: she seems self-centred and smug, like someone who knows she can get away with just about anything because she's smart and pretty. And she does.

This episode excels at the character pieces. The plot is slight but very clever. (The way the Saturnyne manage to duplicate vampiric traits without being vampires is really quite good, and it's an unexpected twist in a story by the creator of *Being Human*.) The adventure rolls along at a great pace. However, it's let down a bit by the location work. While it tries to be a sumptuous, high-quality period piece, the Croatian filming location — coupled with too few CGI shots of canals — fails to bring Venice alive. (The episode could have just been called "The House of Calvierri" and set it anywhere in 16th-century Europe.) And if you're going to use sunlight as a weapon, the scene needs to be lit as though it's actually sunny outside.

It only really falls apart towards the end. It's disappointing that Guido is dispatched through such an overused method. (I'm sure it was Anton Chekov who said if you have a room full of gunpowder in the first act, you must have someone sacrifice themselves and blow it up by the end.) Even worse, there's no drama or jeopardy to the climax: the Doctor flips a switch to turn off the earthquakes and, frankly, just lets Rosanna kill herself because he can't be bothered to provide her with any alternatives or find a way to stop her. This is even more frustrating because it undercuts all the good will Matt Smith and Helen McRory built up in their previous confrontation. Still, Whithouse gives Rosanna a great parting line: "Tell me, Doctor, can your conscience carry the weight of another dead race?"

While the last 10 minutes or so of "The Vampires of Venice" are a letdown, the rest of the story is exciting, engaging fun. Any story with the exchange "You kissed her back?"/"No, I kissed her mouth" has entertainment value on its side.

Second Opinion (RS?) It's the sixth episode of a new series and, quite unexpectedly, the new production team decides to add a new companion. He's a romantic interest for the lead companion, comic relief and someone the Doctor can make fun of. But Adam didn't work out too well, so what about Rory?

What's brilliant about Rory is . . . well . . . pretty much everything! Arthur Darvill is extremely good at the comedy: his natural timing makes you simultaneously laugh and wince a little because you'd probably be doing the same thing in that situation. Just the way he nervously sidles sideways when he realizes he's sitting in front of gunpowder is amusing enough, but then he bumps into a hanging chicken for good measure. Best of all, this isn't overplayed, allowing the viewer to empathize with his situation, rather than point and laugh.

And then, just when you've written him off as the comic relief, he goes and accuses — accuses! — the Doctor of making people want to impress him. When they're trying to figure out how to defeat the vampires, Amy volunteers to infiltrate the school, the Doctor protests and Rory observes. Amy is completely passionate about helping out the Doctor, and there's nothing anyone — not even the Doctor — can do to dissuade her. Rory's right: this is precisely what makes the Doctor dangerous.

The relationship between Amy and Rory is also quite believable for anyone who's managed a complex living arrangement. Amy's a kissogram, remember, so she and Rory have to have some sort of understanding to begin with. Indeed, having strippers at Rory's stag night is fundamentally no different than Amy kissing the Doctor in the previous episode. Both are exploring other people before committing.

Rory knows that he's scored significantly above his level with Amy, so he needs to take her on her own terms. He isn't someone who rails against perceived injustices (as the Doctor would) but is instead flexible, accepting and accommodating (when the Doctor comments that he and Rory are Amy's boys, Rory doesn't argue, he meekly accepts the truth of it). These are enormously appealing qualities in a life partner. He's attracted to her liveliness, while she's attracted to his stability.

I can't quite believe the production team brought Rory on board the TARDIS and, unlike Adam, that they kept him on! That's a game-changing move and one that's going to pay off magnificently down the line. But I suspect that the main reason Rory was kept on is because Arthur Darvill nails it, every single time.

5.07 Amy's Choice

Written by Simon Nye **Directed by** Catherine Morshead

Supporting cast Arthur Darvill (Rory Williams), Toby Jones (Dream Lord), Nick Hobbs (Mr. Nainby), Joan Linder (Mrs. Hamill), Audrey Ardington (Mrs. Poggit)

Original airdate May 15, 2010

The Big Idea The Dream Lord presents Doctor, Amy and Rory with two realities: one in a doomed TARDIS, the other in Upper Leadworth facing deadly pensioners. But which is real and which is the dream?

Roots and References Neil Gaiman's comic *The Sandman* (the Dream Lord); *Last of the Summer Wine* (the town full of elderly people); Monty Python's old ladies (Mrs. Poggett); *Star Trek: The Next Generation*'s Q (a demigod controlling reality and changing his look to suit the occasion). The title is a play on William Styron's 1979 novel (and the 1982 film adaptation), *Sophie's Choice*.

Adventures in Time and Space The Dream Lord calls the Doctor the Oncoming Storm ("The Parting of the Ways") and mentions his relationship with Queen Elizabeth I ("The End of Time, Part One").

The Doctor mentions the TARDIS jumping a time track (1965's "The Space Museum"; "The Empty Child"). The Doctor claims to have thrown the TARDIS manual (first seen in 1978's "The Pirate Planet") into a supernova because he disagreed with it. If you pause, you can see that the locker under the console bears a plaque reading, "TARDIS — Time And Relative Dimension In Space. Build Site: Gallifrey Black Hole Ship Yard. Type 40. Build Date: 1963. Authorised for use by qualified Time Lords only by the Shadow Proclamation, Misuse or Theft of any TARDIS will result in extreme penalties and possible exile."

Who is the Doctor? The Doctor figures out the identity of the Dream Lord quickly because "there's only one person in the universe who hates me as much as you do." Which, once you realize the Doctor's talking about *himself*, makes a lot of sense and gives new insight into the Doctor's frame of mind.

The Doctor and Amy Many things the Dream Lord tells Amy become more complicated with the revelation that the Dream Lord is the Doctor's dark side, notably, "Always leaves you alone and in the dark. He'll never apologize." When Amy protests that the Doctor trusts her, the Dream Lord points out that she doesn't know his real name. The Dream Lord similarly taunts the Doctor that he prefers to travel with the young who grow up eventually.

Monster of the Week In the Upper Leadworth reality, the village's senior citizens are taken over by the Eknodine, an alien race displaced from another world. Their eyestalk can protrude from their human hosts' mouths, and they exhale a poisonous gas that turns people into dust. In both realities, the Dream Lord, a manifestation of the Doctor's dark side, terrorizes the TARDIS crew.

Stand Up and Cheer Trapped in their house, surrounded by deadly aliens, Rory . . . cuts off his own ponytail. It's utterly out of place, but it's also the sweetest gesture Rory could ever make.

Roll Your Eyes It's bad enough that we have to tolerate the Dream Lord popping up in different costumes like some cut-rate version of Q from *Star Trek*, but did we really have to see Toby Jones in an open-necked 1970s lounge outfit, complete with gold medallion? It's going to take an eternity to get that image out of our heads.

You're Not Making Any Sense It's obvious that the Upper Leadworth reality comes complete with shared memories (with their own perspectives) for Rory and Amy. What's really odd is that the Doctor, who is supposed to be looking for obvious signs that this is a dream, never questions them about the extent of their memories of their lives after he left them.

Interesting Trivia Who did you think the Dream Lord was going to be? If you're a newbie, move along to the TARDIS Chronometer (unless you're feeling particularly brave). But if you're a Classic Series fan, you probably had a list of the usual suspects lined up. Particularly since the episode hints that we're supposed to know his identity. Possibilities include the Master (a fellow Time Lord who hates the Doctor with all his being), the Celestial Toymaker (a powerful being from another dimension who enjoys playing deadly games with people) from 1966's "The Celestial Toymaker" or, most likely, the Valeyard (an evil future version of the Doctor, who previously put the Doctor on trial and wanted to steal his remaining regenerations) from 1986's "Trial of a Time Lord." That it's not an obvious choice is a credit to the script, especially with its dramatically satisfying answer. However, as bona fide Classic Series fans, we're disappointed that it didn't turn out to be Yartek, leader of the alien Voord . . .

The TARDIS Chronometer Hi newbies, welcome back. You're probably wondering where the TARDIS actually landed. Well . . . it didn't: it's floating somewhere in space at an unknown point in time.

Cool? (GB) If *Doctor Who* episodes could be used as texts in a high school English class, a composition assignment might be "Write an essay about 'Amy's Choice,' explaining what Amy's choice actually is."

It's a very good question. The title is a play on *Sophie's Choice* where a woman has to make an unbearable, agonizing decision. Amy's choice isn't all that hard. She doesn't seem to like the Upper Leadworth reality very much; she goes along with it only because Rory likes it. As soon as Rory is killed, she realizes how much she loves him and commits suicide in the hope that she can be with him.

On that level, Amy's choice — and indeed "Amy's Choice" — is frustrating. The Doctor seems to be more or less okay with helping a pregnant woman commit suicide. Worse, there's the sheer selfishness of the act that borders on unreasonableness. Would a pregnant woman so cavalierly take her own life just because her man died?

The whole thing takes on a different spin when you consider that the Doctor figured out the identity of the Dream Lord very early on. He immediately destroys the TARDIS in the cold star reality once the Upper Leadworth reality is destroyed because he knows that both realities are false.

Suddenly, a lot of what seem like frustrating character flaws are, in fact, the plot poking through. That Amy doesn't feel any connection to her unborn child, aside from the occasional nuisance contraction, is a sign that the reality is bogus, not that Amy is horrendously selfish. The Doctor is happy to go along for the ride, as it were, into the wall of Amy's house, because he knows it's not real.

Perhaps "Amy's Choice" could have been a sharper story, with a more poignant dramatic conflict, had Amy felt some kind of connection to the baby she was carrying; that she had to give up something by killing herself, that the choice became impossible. Perhaps that was simply too adult, too controversial a conflict for a family show. I'm more inclined to say it was a missed opportunity.

And yet, it still raises the question: what was Amy's choice? Was it simply, as the Dream Lord puts it, which man she wants to be with — and she chooses Rory when he's taken away? Perhaps. But, equally, perhaps not.

My frustration with Amy in "The Vampires of Venice" — that she essentially gets off scot free from the emotional blowback of her actions at the end of "Flesh and Stone" and chooses to ambiguously stick around with Rory while travelling in the TARDIS — is addressed in this story. Rory finally questions why she ran away the night before their wedding. The dark side of the Doctor, in the form of the Dream Lord, also confronts her about this and with the harsh reality that she's not unique as a companion.

What's interesting are the two realities, the two dreams Amy lives in. The Upper Leadworth dream, as the Doctor points out, is Rory's dream: living in the posher end of the idyllic village they've grown up in, finally in a good job, Amy pregnant and the Doctor gone. The cold star dream is, in many ways, the Doctor's dream: deadly danger with a ticking clock. (The fact that the Doctor does nothing to prevent this disaster, beyond observing it, is another tell that this isn't real.) Amy's choice, perhaps, isn't that she has to choose between two men but between two dreams.

In the end, Amy's choice is for both — and neither — options. She opts out of Rory's dream, out of a boring existence in a picturesque village to be in the TARDIS with the Doctor, but she also chooses to be with Rory in that reality.

Amy doesn't choose the status quo, to live in the same ambiguity as before. Her acknowledgement that she never told Rory she loved him — that her engagement to Rory happened out of inertia almost — indicates Amy's new desire for intentionality in her relationship with him. Amy knows what she wants. It's not Leadworth or Upper Leadworth, and it's not knocking about the galaxy with her fantasy figure.

Rory too has a choice to make. He protects Amy from danger and, faced with his imminent death, he cuts off the symbol of his settled ordinariness, which he loves so dearly. Rory chooses to go beyond his own dream.

But what does all this say about the Doctor, whose dark side engineers a reality where Amy is forced to choose what she wants?

What's great about "Amy's Choice" is that it's full of nuances like this, revealing new sides to the regular characters. What I haven't said here in all this pondering is what a great hoot this story is. It's delightfully entertaining with the world's most infirm alien invasion and a punchy script by Simon Nye. Toby Jones adds buckets of mischievous gravitas to his portrayal of the Dream Lord. The Occam's Razor explanation of the Dream Lord's identity is superb, giving us a glimpse of the self-loathing that still lurks under the more serene surface of this new Doctor.

Amy's choice in "Amy's Choice" isn't that difficult, and it misses a trick or too, but there's a lot going on that makes it well worth your time.

Second Opinion (RS?) Exactly what's going on with Amy? Why does she run off with another man the night before her wedding? Why does she later try to jump him, despite being in a relationship? How can she have her fiancé on board the TARDIS and yet still be attracted to the Doctor?

The answer, fundamentally, is very simple. It's because human nature is complex and because Steven Moffat is the writer of *Coupling*.

What if your fantasy person walked into your life? Would you go with them, no matter what? How about if it was consequence-free? Because of time travel, Amy gets to explore her wild side, with the assurance that she can still make it to the wedding in the morning.

The thing about Amy killing herself while pregnant needs to be addressed head-on. It might be a clue that this is a fake reality . . . or it might just be her choice to do so. Which she is perfectly entitled to make, because it's her body to do with as she pleases. The idea that anyone — Rory, the Doctor, fans at home — can judge her morality based on what she does with her own body, even at full-term pregnancy, is abhorrent.

And this is just one aspect of the choice Amy faces. The main one is, of course, between two men she's in love with. The entire season has been examining the idea of a choice and whether it's possible to love two people equally and simultaneously. And clearly it is, only the tradeoff is exponentially more complex than a monogamous relationship.

Amy's no Captain Jack (not that there would be anything wrong with her if she was). She's genuinely torn between two men, each of whom offer vastly different things. And instead of picking one or the other, this episode shows that the idea of a simple choice between two competing options is a false binary. Instead, there's another option: she can have a life with the Doctor but also with Rory. It's a love triangle without the need for resolution.

The Amy-Rory-Doctor dynamic represents a very fundamental issue of human relationship-forming. Is it possible to find your one true love? It's unrealistic to expect that they'll be able to fulfill everything you need, so isn't monogamy actually unfair pressure on a couple? And for *Doctor Who*, the three-way dynamic provides an endless source of dramatic tension. Is Amy more drawn to the Doctor even as she's engaged to Rory? It depends on her mood — and that's profoundly interesting.

What's going on with Amy? That's easy: she's human.

5.08—5.09 The Hungry Earth / Cold Blood

Written by Chris Chibnall **Directed by** Ashley Way

Supporting cast Arthur Darvill (Rory Williams), Meera Syal (Nasreen Chaudhry), Robert Pugh (Tony Mack), Nia Roberts (Ambrose), Alun Raglan (Mo), Samuel Davies (Elliot), Neve McIntosh (Alaya/Restac), Richard Hope (Malohkeh), Stephen Moore (Eldane)

Original airdate May 22, 2010

The Big Idea A drilling project awakens a race of monsters living below the Earth, leading to planet-sharing negotiations.

Roots and References Jules Verne's *A Journey to the Center of the Earth* (the journey down the tunnel in the TARDIS with a Victorian-looking machine, an eccentric at its controls and the dirt flying by the portal). Mo reads *The Gruffalo* to Elliot, who also quotes Sherlock Holmes.

Adventures in Time and Space This is a virtual retelling of many of the key issues from 1970's "Doctor Who and the Silurians." A number of Classic Series stories are also echoed: 1970's "Inferno" (the drill to the centre of the Earth), 1984's "Frontios" (the ground swallowing people), 1971's "The Dæmons" (an invisible barrier around a village that prevents anyone getting in or out), 1973's

"The Green Death" (an infected man who starts glowing green) and 1989's "Battlefield" ("There'll be no battle here today"). The continuity-obsessed may wish to point out that Project Inferno actually went further down into the Earth's surface than Tony and Nasreen's team; however, it's doubtful that the details were made public.

The Doctor asks for celery after decontamination is turned off, which has profound restorative qualities for Gallifreyans, as established in 1984's "The Caves of Androzani." The Doctor talked about fixed points in time in "The Fires of Pompeii" and notes that human and Silurian negotiations are not one of them.

The Crack in the Universe Effect There's a crack in the Silurian cave, and it's significantly wider than we've seen previously. The Doctor identifies it as a space-time cataclysm, a rip in the continuum. Where there's an explosion, he says, there's shrapnel, and he pulls out a piece of the TARDIS from it.

Who is the Doctor? We have a never-before-seen insight into the Doctor's physiology when the Silurians' decontamination process just about kills him. The Silurians assume he's a human, but it turns out removing human germs would destroy other things keeping him alive.

Monster of the Week The Silurians, a.k.a. *Homo reptilia*, the previous occupants of Earth. They're cold-blooded reptiles, with a venomous sting in an extendible tongue that takes 24 hours to recharge. The sting is supposed to kill, but instead it mutates the victim.

Stand Up and Cheer The appearance of the crack at the end of the story. After two episodes of formulaic runaround, the crack's appearance is shocking. Then, in quick succession, Rory is killed, wiped from existence, and we discover that the explosion that causes the crack's existence will also destroy the TARDIS. This is a triple whammy of an ending that profoundly changes the direction of the season and one that you couldn't possibly have seen coming.

Roll Your Eyes It's supposedly a big important drilling project in the middle of nowhere — and there's so few staff and no security?

You're Not Making Any Sense What holds the dirt in place in the subsidence holes? Underneath, there's no support (we see people's hands poking right through) so why doesn't the dirt just fall down the tunnel?

Interesting Trivia In previous seasons, the arc element played in the background, only coming to the fore in the season finale (think of the Bad Wolf or the Master's ascendence). Here, we have a different take, as the crack is responsible for a major mid-season shakeup, as Rory is killed and his entire existence erased. Amy's personal history is changed: she forgets him and only his engagement ring remains behind, as it was in the TARDIS. This is a huge shock ending to an episode that was otherwise unrelated to the season arc brought close to home by affecting a character we've grown to love. The crack becomes more than a curious mystery, it's dangerous — and that danger has just become personal.

Earlier drafts of the script for "Cold Blood" have a much more dramatic opening, starting with a scene in the TARDIS where the Doctor is begging Amy to remember (though not revealing that it's about Rory) that smash cuts to the remainder of the story. This was changed to the more elegiac opening narration by Eldane.

The TARDIS Chronometer The TARDIS lands in a church graveyard, in Cwmtaff, South Wales, 2020. It then travels through the Earth and ends up in a cave near the Silurian city. At the end, it materializes back on the surface.

Cool? (RS?) Once upon a time, there was a tense and gripping story that pitted humans against Silurians, each side committing terrible acts out of fear rather than malice, with the situation only resolved by a shocking genocidal act on behalf of people we thought were the good guys. That version was made in 1970 and featured wobbly Silurian monster suits, a rubber dinosaur and badly rendered effects. This two-parter is essentially a pared-down version of the same story, but with today's makeup and CGI.

Sadly, while the moral debate at its core still has legs, this story doesn't bring a single new idea to it. So the whole thing is just a cover version of a much more successful earlier hit. Possibly great if this is your first exposure to it, but not very exciting if you've had the original playing in your head. It does have a boppy beat added to it, in the form of the Silurian makeup (which might look like it's come straight from an episode of *Deep Space Nine*, but at least there's no wobbling involved), but that can't disguise the fact that there's only 40% new material here.

Of the original stuff, there's a really shocking aspect to this story, and it's to do with Rory. I'm not talking about his dying and being wiped from existence; I'm talking about his character arc. First, he impersonates a police officer in order to investigate the missing bodies. Then he reassures Ambrose, the picture of calmness. When Restac asks who speaks for the apes, Rory has unquestioned authority. And when Alaya is tasered, he rushes to her and says, "You're not dying. I'm not going to let you. Not today." Remind you of any time-travelling heroes you might be familiar with? What's interesting is that he doesn't succeed at any of these things; Rory doesn't solve the mystery of the graves, he can't calm Ambrose, he can't reason with Restac and he can't save Alaya. But that's not really the point. The point is that he tries.

Even when the Doctor gives his speech to Ambrose, Tony and Rory about being the best they can be, the only one who really takes it in is Rory; Ambrose kills the hostage and Tony starts the drill, but Rory is the one nodding along.

Tellingly, while the other two confront Alaya, Rory doesn't even interact with her, except to try and save her life.

And then, at the end, he commits the ultimate selfless act, saving the Doctor from being shot. For this, he pays a heavy price: not just dying but being wiped from existence. It's an incredible shock because Rory's character arc has been so strong. It's a twist ending, it demonstrates the power of the crack in a way that hits close to home and it gives the Doctor and the viewer more knowledge about what's happening than Amy, creating dramatic tension.

It's a shame that the rest of the story is so banal, then. It's not actively bad, but it so desperately wants to be a 1970s Pertwee-era story that it's not funny. You've got the negotiating table, as two flawed species try to hammer out a peace deal despite their manifest difference; a tiny cast trapped in a village in Nowheresville by artificial means; an infection that causes people to glow bright green; and, most tellingly of all, an enormous mine.

And yet, in contrast, you have Matt Smith as the Doctor. He saves what should be a boring runaround, simply by being so damn loveable. He's a big kid, who has a great rapport with Elliot, which has nicely played consequences when Elliot runs off and the Doctor isn't able to be a grownup. His eating grass and then spitting it out is hilarious and, when asked if he misses his home, answers, "So much," with an enormous depth of feeling.

The moment when he sees through Alaya's claim that she's the last of her species is gripping, as he brings a level of emotion just slightly to the surface, saying, "So don't insult me," but then calms down when he realizes that peace is much more important than yet one more person feeling slighted. This is a nicely understated illustration of the story's stance.

His deferral of negotiations to the two humans present is an excellent moment, giving the Doctor a natural authority without dominating the situation.

Speaking of which, Nasreen is awesome, perhaps my favourite guest star in a long, long time. Her clapping after the Doctor makes a big speech, even when no one else does, is excellent. She's ballsy, demanding to be taken in the TARDIS, refusing to let her romance get in her way and even flicking the Doctor's suspender, for good measure. I love how spiky she is at the beginning ("Did you just say 'jungle planets'?"), but she comes on board with the Doctor's ideas once she has more evidence — and then her decision to stay underground is a natural outgrowth of this strong characterization. It could have gone very badly, if she'd decided to stay for Tony, but instead she decides to stay for herself. The fact that she'll have company is nice, but incidental. This is where the story excels.

On the other hand, there are some shockingly poor or lazy bits. When Amy and Mo enter the chamber with the Silurian army, why do the lights turn on one by one? Ambrose is upset that the Silurians took her son and hurt her dad, but she seems to have entirely forgotten her husband. Alaya looking at the humans and telling them that one of them will kill her and that she knows who it will be is very effective indeed (especially as the list includes Rory, and you wonder if he just might be capable of it); conversely, in the second part, when one of them does actually kill her she says, "I knew it would be you," like a gloating 14-year-old who has something to prove, which undercuts her original menace. And the Doctor tells Malohkeh — someone who's just tortured and dissected his friends — that he rather loves him. I'm sorry, what?

Oh, and whichever Silurian is operating the camera that feeds into the human's computer has a fine sense of drama, framing shots for maximum tension, zooming in for a closeup of Restac at key moments and cutting at just the right second. Did they teach that at the Silurian School for the Performing Arts?

"The Hungry Earth"/"Cold Blood" isn't actively terrible, and it has some nice moments. It threatens to be a bit boring on occasions, but it's saved by the Doctor, Rory and Nasreen, all of whom are excellent. (Amy vanishes almost entirely from the first part, although in truth you don't much miss her.) It's an understated touch that the Silurian males are peaceful while the females are warlike. And the crack gives the story a shocking sting in the tail, which is very welcome. But in the end, all these great elements are dragged down by the bulk of the two-parter itself, which is a formulaic runaround and twee moral debate that was done better and more convincingly 40 years ago, even with poor rubber suits and bad special effects. Perhaps getting the boy band to cover a Led Zeppelin song wasn't the best idea in the history of everything.

Second Opinion (GB) My co-author is wrong when he says that it's a cover version of "Doctor Who and the Silurians." What "The Hungry Earth" and "Cold Blood" are attempting to adapt is Malcolm Hulke's 1974 novelization of that story, "Doctor Who and the Cave Monsters," which had almost all the innovations this story seemed to make: a greater sense of scale and Silurians who seemed scarier.

However, it's when I read "by Chris Chibnall" that my heart sank.

Chibnall's a good writer on a lot of other programs, but with the *Doctor Who* universe he seems to think everything should be grim and nasty. His *Torchwood* stories always have unhealthy helpings of both, and he can't help himself here. (Indeed, I'm convinced "42" was spared from total bleakness by Russell T Davies.) There's an imprisoned Silurian, and she says she knows she will get killed and who will kill her — and, guess what, she does get killed by the person she predicted.

It's not actually grim or edgy at all. It's lazy, lazy writing. It would have been far harder to write a story where, in spite of the anger, the fear and Ambrose's anguish, the humans somehow manage to keep Alaya alive. That would create real, palpable drama among the human characters we care about, and it would require a more dramatically satisfying reason for Silurian and human negotiations to break down. But no, it's grimmer for Ambrose to inexpertly torture Alaya to death so that we can have Neve McIntosh show up as her character's sister and let everything fall apart in the most predictable fashion imaginable.

It's a massive dumbing down of the original story (or its novelization), which had subtlety and nuance. It's made worse by the clear signs of budgetary constraints. We experience a lot of things by computer readout in New *Who* but drilling through Earth shouldn't have been one of them. There's no sense of scale. (The CGI money clearly went into the Silurian city, which is impressive.) And whatever people say about the original 1970 story's rubber-suited monsters, they could at least be bothered to populate their scientific base with actual extras.

The Doctor is next to useless here. This season's innovation with the character has been to demonstrate how much the Doctor observes and how he subsequently reacts. Here, he lets Elliot wander off without a second glance and contributes nothing to the story. Amy is left to negotiate for the planet, but she looks as though she's in some inescapable staff meeting at work. Rory is about the only one who really acquits himself out of the regular characters, and he gets killed in a manner that would have seemed clichéd in 1970. The only bright spot is all this mess is Meera Syal as Nasreen, who injects levity, excitement and optimism into her part. Which is everything that's missing from the rest of this story.

The Psychic Papers: The Silurians

In 1970, *Doctor Who* radically changed its format. The TARDIS was grounded and the third Doctor (now played by Jon Pertwee) was exiled to Earth where he became scientific advisor to UNIT. Writer Malcolm Hulke remarked that this meant the show was left with only two types of story: mad scientist and alien invasion.

Hulke knew what he was talking about. He had been commissioned to write a story under the new "exiled to Earth" format. But Malcolm Hulke was not only a clever script writer with dozens of credits (including *The Avengers* and *Danger Man*), he had strong political convictions as well. Hulke was a member of the British Communist Party and even wrote for East German television in the days of the Berlin Wall when such a thing was considered taboo.

Saddled with this new format, Hulke and script editor Terrance Dicks came up with a cunning idea: they inverted the alien invasion story. Hulke's 1970 story, "Doctor Who and the Silurians," was about a race of bipedal reptile people, once the dominant species on Earth, who were discovered in suspended animation in caves. These reptiles had gone into hibernation for millions of years to avoid a potential disaster (the Earth's moon coming into orbit), during which time the human race evolved from the apes the reptile people used to hunt.

The alien invasion came from beneath the Earth as opposed to from outer space; this innovation put humanity in the position of being the perceived invaders, as the Doctor attempted to broker peace between humans and reptiles. Hulke's tale was a masterpiece of subtlety, with both sides committing bigoted injustices and demonstrating an equally legitimate claim to Earth. "Doctor Who and the Silurians" ended tragically, with a faction of the reptile people releasing a plague that nearly wiped out the humans. (Curiously, when the Doctor recounts this history in "Cold Blood," he leaves out this fact.) Though the Doctor manages to reach a settlement, the humans blow up the reptile people's base after they go back into hibernation, sealing them in their caves.

It was an excellent, complex story, full of interesting commentary on human conflict and the sense of entitlement that nation states possess. There was one problem, though: what the reptile people were called.

In "Doctor Who and the Silurians," the reptile people are called Silurians by the humans (though it is not a term the reptile people use for each other) because the Doctor deduces that they came from the Silurian period, roughly 450 million years ago. Unfortunately, such life could not have existed during the Silurian period.

In 1972, Malcolm Hulke revisited these ideas for his story "The Sea Devils." Here, the Doctor faced off against another race of reptile men, who were called Sea Devils by humans. The "Sea Devils," while a different species from the "Silurians" also went into hibernation at the same time as their "Silurian" brethren. In this story, they were being drawn out of hibernation as part of a plot by the Master.

The Doctor foiled their plans, but not before he declared that whoever called these reptile people Silurians originally (that would be the Doctor) got it wrong and that they were, in fact, more properly called Eocenes, since they came from the Eocene period (around 50 million years ago). Only the Doctor got it wrong again. The Eocene period is also the incorrect geological era.

Confusing things further is the fact that when these two species of reptile people next reappear, in 1984's "Warriors of the Deep," they freely accept and call each other "Silurians" and "Sea Devils," even though both terms are misnomers.

The two types of reptile people are vastly different: while the "Silurians" have distinctive scales and a third eye that can generate some form of psychokinesis, the "Sea Devils" have fish-like heads, no third eye and are amphibious.

In the *Doctor Who* novels of the 1990s, the most common term used for these creatures was Earth Reptiles (or, to be more politically correct, Indigenous Terrans). Sadly, these terms didn't make it to the New Series. In "The Hungry Earth," the Doctor encounters a third type of reptile people. These are land-based, like the "Silurians," but do not possess the third eye and have humanoid facial features; they also have an extendable tongue with a venom sting. By this point, the Doctor has started calling them "*Homo reptilia*," which *still* is not accurate, as it is a not a proper taxonomical name!

Silurians, Sea Devils, Eocenes, *Homo reptilia*, Earth Reptiles or Indigenous Terrans, these monsters are still widely known to *Doctor Who* fans as Silurians, so we call them that throughout this book. Clearly, though, the Doctor should have asked them what they called themselves!

5.10 Vincent and the Doctor

Written by Richard Curtis **Directed by** Jonny Campbell

Supporting cast Tony Curran (Vincent); Bill Nighy (Dr. Black, uncredited); Nik Howden (Maurice); Chrissie Cotterill (mother); Sarah Counsell (waitress); Morgan Overton, Andrew Byrne (school children)

Original airdate June 5, 2010

The Big Idea After finding a monster in a painting, the Doctor and Amy discover the tortured, beautiful genius that is Vincent van Gogh.

Roots and References The film *Vincent*; the scenes depicted in van Gogh's paintings *Starry Night*, *Wheatfield with Crows* and *Cafe Terrace at Night* are recreated, while the Krafayis is found in *The Church at Auvers*. *Sunflowers* also plays a key role. The song "Chances" by Athlete accompanies the scene where the Doctor and Amy take Vincent to the Musée d'Orsay.

Adventures in Time and Space The Doctor's alien-identification kit displays images of his first two incarnations when it "reads" his face in the mirror. (It's the third appearance of William Hartnell's Doctor this season so far, after "The Eleventh Hour" and "The Vampires of Venice" if anyone's keeping score.) The Doctor has taken Amy to Arcadia, which fell during the Time War according to "Doomsday." (The fact that it's there to be visited may be a hint of the crack's effects.) The Doctor inadvertently calls Vincent "Rory."

The Crack in the Universe Effect Amy has forgotten Rory, but Vincent still senses her loss ("I hear the song of your sadness") and so does Amy on some level: she's found to be crying.

Who is the Doctor? The Doctor is outside his comfort zone when it comes to dealing with Vincent's depression, but he becomes quite close with the painter and decides to offer him the boon of going to the future to see how his work will be regarded. While Amy believes this will change history, the Doctor knows better. It shows the Doctor's ultimately optimistic outlook (he believes that there is hope in the universe), as he admits he did it just so that he could add to the number of good things in Vincent's life.

The Doctor and Amy In spite of the crack erasing Rory from existence, Amy appears to have no interest in the Doctor any more; she doesn't even flirt with him (or Vincent, despite him being single). In many ways, Amy has moved on from her initial feelings for the Doctor. The Doctor, for his part, has been indulging Amy out of guilt about Rory.

Monster of the Week The Krafayis are invisible, vicious scavengers. They can be seen by certain people like Vincent and by the Doctor's scanning device, which shows it as a four-legged reptile with a parrot-like head. They tend to travel in packs, but this one has been abandoned by its kind, as it is blind.

Stand Up and Cheer The scene where the Doctor brings Vincent to the future to see the painter's works now revered is incredibly moving. It's all down to Tony Curran's stunning performance as we see in his eyes a man who can scarcely take it all in. Bill Nighy is lovely, adding hues of sympathy and gravitas to Dr. Black's assessment of van Gogh. Nighy's response when he briefly twigs to who just kissed him is sweet. As anyone who has seen his films knows, Richard Curtis has a canny sense of what a pop song can add to a scene; "Chances" is a great choice here. The result is a near-perfect scene that's tear-jerking and comes by it honestly.

Roll Your Eyes It's a common failing of historical stories that everything reverts to hyperbole. The Doctor keeps referring to van Gogh as "the greatest painter" of all, in the same way Shakespeare was the greatest writer, Agatha Christie was the greatest mystery writer and Dickens was the greatest novelist . . . Why can't the Doctor meet anyone who is, you know, just very good?

You're Not Making Any Sense So what happened to the massive, invisible, dead Krafayis lying in the church?

Interesting Trivia Unsurprisingly, writer Richard Curtis admits he fudged several historic details on the grounds of poetic licence. Van Gogh painted *Still Life: Vase with Twelve Sunflowers* in 1888, about two years before this story was set. (Also the real painting doesn't have "For Amy" written on it!) While characters talk about the June 1890 setting as being within van Gogh's "final year" or "months" before his death, the story is set a mere seven weeks from Vincent's suicide on July 29, 1890. The story also studiously avoids mention of van Gogh's self-mutilation (he cut off his own earlobe in 1888). It's also implied that Vincent van Gogh suffered from a bipolar disorder and was, to some extent, synaesthetic, though this is largely speculation. The setting isn't given onscreen, but the church is in Auvers-sur-Oise, a village just north of Paris where van Gogh spent his final months.

The Doctor's frustrated remark about van Gogh not being a "proper" painter like Gainsborough is, in many ways, a joke based on contemporary assessment of Vincent's work and the Impressionists in general.

Tony Curran's native Scottish accent leads to the charming in-joke that, thanks to the way the TARDIS translates things, Amy's Scottish accent sounds like a Dutch accent to Vincent and vice versa!

The original British broadcast of this story featured an advisory with a phone number for viewers to call if they had been affected by the issues raised in this program. While commonly used with contemporary dramas in Britain that touch on a sensitive theme, this is the first time it was ever included for *Doctor Who*.

The TARDIS Chronometer Outside Paris's Musée d'Orsay in 2010, then in an alley in Auvers-sur-Oise, sometime between June 1 and 3, 1890.

Cool? (GB) Historical stories in *Doctor Who* generally mean travelling in time to journey through Cathay with Marco Polo, or fight the Gelth with Charles Dickens. "Vincent and the Doctor" does something very different. It's a historical story by way of character study; it's not about events but about a specific person. There's a great little science-fiction monster MacGuffin stuck in the middle of it, to keep the kids from fidgeting, but this story is about the Doctor and Amy getting to know Vincent van Gogh.

It's an astonishing gambit; the plot is pretty much done away with in the first half hour, leaving the rest for what must be the longest but sweetest coda this season. It asks the question: what would the Doctor do if he's faced with a remarkable but wounded man? He would become his friend, spend time with him, try to understand him and make his world a little better. This episode takes the *Doctor Who* format and stretches it in new ways, creating something very special and deeply affecting.

Writer Richard Curtis and the production team rise to the challenge of presenting a story about the most famous sufferer of bipolar disorder to a family audience; the result is a sensitive, thoughtful treatment of Vincent van Gogh and his life. While Curtis's script avoids some of the harsher realities of van Gogh's life, it doesn't shy away from the fact that van Gogh is also doomed to end his own life and the fact that the root causes of an ugly mental illness are not going to be waved away by a fictional Time Lord. It's quietly, achingly honest.

The Krafayis is a great idea for a monster; it's somewhat surprising no one has ever thought of an invisible beast before and the Doctor being chased by it through the streets is an exciting, funny sequence. It also works thematically as a way of talking about Vincent's own demons: he sees things no one else can and it drives him to the edge. This could have been disastrously on the nose, but it actually works because the story has enough restraint to not overdo the parallels. The moment when Vincent has empathy for the blind Krafayis, rejected by its kind and now mortally wounded, is really powerful.

Tony Curran not only looks like van Gogh, he seems to embody him. It would have been easy to have an actor show off a few dramatic tics and be done with it, but Curran plays Vincent with all his contradictions: world weary, romantic, despondent, passionate and barely holding it all together. It's a stunning performance. The astounded look on Vincent's face when he enters the gallery devoted to his work is as breathtaking as it is heartbreaking.

Curran is delightful working with Matt Smith, who just keeps getting better. Smith is great with the monsters and the Doctory stuff, but his scenes with Vincent are remarkable: he genuinely seems alien here and, faced with something as incomprehensible as depression, he's even more out of his depth than the humans who deal with Vincent. The Doctor's scenes with Vincent after the Krafayis' death, lying in the grass and in the Musée d'Orsay, have a real tenderness. The Doctor's sudden decision to show Vincent the future feels genuine as a result.

Appropriately for the man behind *Four Weddings and a Funeral*, it's an unapologetically populist story, with a climax delivered to the rousing strains of a pop song. But Richard Curtis's script is by turns funny, melancholy, exciting and heartbreaking. The dialogue is the wittiest this season. ("Is this how time normally passes? Really slowly and in the right order?") But there are also some lovely thoughtful moments too, such as Vincent's explanation of sunflowers: "Always somewhere between living and dying. Human as they tilt to the sun but also a little disgusting."

The ending is heartbreaking: Vincent learns his work will have lasting value — and Amy learns that this knowledge won't matter to him. "Vincent and the Doctor" is ultimately about encountering someone not even the Doctor can save. All the Doctor can do, all any of us can do, in the face of such tragedy is to simply add to the pile of good things. It's one of those moments when art really reflects the truth of life. And one of the reasons why "Vincent and the Doctor" is not only the best episode this season, but it's also some of the best television of the past five years.

Second Opinion (RS?) Appropriately for a story about an artist, this episode is all about its visuals. Many of Vincent's more famous paintings are recreated, from the café to his bedroom, while Vincent himself is introduced while holding his own self-portrait. Sequences such as his exploration of the TARDIS and the museum are almost entirely dialogue-free, using the image to tell the story.

There's also the contrast between Vincent and the Krafayis: one sees too much, the other too little. The Krafayis is both invisible and blind; it can neither see nor be seen. Vincent, on the other hand, sees beyond what the average eye can see (which drives him mad) and is far too visible in the town: everyone knows him, but no one appreciates him.

The appearance of the sunflowers on the coffin of the slain girl is fabulous. They're a stark reminder of Vincent's earlier point about them being halfway between living and dying, they contrast neatly with Amy's earlier use of them to brighten up Vincent's surroundings and they're just so damn yellow that you can't help but be transfixed by them.

But my favourite image of all — indeed, perhaps my favourite in the entirety of *Doctor Who* — is the transformation of the night sky into *Starry Night*. It starts with Vincent inviting the Doctor and Amy to see through his eyes and the invitation then extends to us. Instead of a simple transition between the real image and the painting (as happens earlier in the story with *Wheatfield with Crows*), this effect really does invite us into Vincent's view of the world. We see the stars first as actively burning balls, then the entire sky transforms into a still painting, but it does so by suggesting movement, with rolling waves across the sky. Rather than just telling you, it shows you exactly why van Gogh is so amazing.

Even the non-art visuals are great. The cat in the alley when the TARDIS materializes is a nice image; the light through the lattice criss-crossing Amy's face when they hide in the confessional is quite striking; and the scenery, thanks to the location filming in Croatia, is gorgeous. When the Doctor looks around a corner after the departing Krafayis, he's next to a poster of a clown, which is a nice visual joke.

"Vincent and the Doctor" has a lovely script. However, what makes it truly shine is the way it looks: lush, gorgeous and rich, just like van Gogh's paintings. And the secret to understanding the universe and perceiving more than the average eye is capable of? Simply looking hard enough.

5.11 The Lodger

Written by Gareth Roberts **Directed by** Catherine Morshead

Supporting cast James Corden (Craig), Daisy Haggard (Sophie), Owen Donovan (Steven), Babatunde Aleshe (Sean), Jem Wall (Michael), Karen Seacombe (Sandra), Kamara Bacchus (clubber)

Original airdate June 12, 2010

The Big Idea In order to find out what's keeping the TARDIS from landing, the Doctor has to pretend to be an ordinary bloke. How hard can that be?

Roots and References The basic idea was taken from a *Doctor Who Magazine* comic strip (with the same title); *The Odd Couple* and *Spaced* (flatshare sitcoms); *The Amityville Horror* (haunted house); Gerry Anderson's Supermarionation series like *Thunderbirds* (the Doctor calls himself "Captain Troy Handsome of International Rescue").

Adventures in Time and Space The Doctor mindlinks with Craig (as in "The Girl in the Fireplace") albeit this time by headbutt. The first headbutt gives Craig basic biographical information including glimpses of the Doctor's past ten incarnations. (This brings William Hartnell's appearances in this season up to four, the most since 1966!) The Doctor refers to himself as the Oncoming Storm ("The Parting of the Ways" and subsequently). The Doctor's non-technological means of analyzing the time disturbances is reminiscent of the time flow analogue the Doctor constructed out of everyday objects in 1972's "The Time Monster."

The Crack in the Universe Effect At the end of the story, a crack forms in the wall of Craig's kitchen. Meanwhile, Amy discovers her engagement ring in the Doctor's coat. There is a damaged time engine — someone's attempt to build a TARDIS — on the top floor of Craig's home.

Who is the Doctor? While the Doctor's tenth incarnation was quite sociable with humans, the eleventh seems to be stymied by several basic human interactions. The Doctor doesn't seem to know what football is (though he's good at it) and continues to be vague about money (hoping £3,000 in cash is enough for rent), so probably many things elude him about his favourite species.

Monster of the Week The crash program of the time engine, which is trying to find a suitable operator from the human populace, a process that inevitably kills the human. It can create realistic holographic images of people in distress, including a helpless old man, a desperate father and a frightened little girl in order to lure people inside.

Stand Up and Cheer Anyone who ever wondered what the Doctor would be like in a mundane office environment will love the Doctor's star turn in Craig's job. He charms management, topples business obstacles like they were monsters, calls the bluff of problem clients and becomes the centre of office life. All in a six-hour period.

Roll Your Eyes The camouflage of the time engine is wonderfully done, and it sets up elements for future stories. Even so, we're seriously perception-filtered out this season. It's quite possibly the most overused piece of technobabble in *Doctor Who* that's not "timey-wimey."

You're Not Making Any Sense You would think that, with the rising number of missing persons cases in Colchester, the police would use the vast network of

CCTV cameras that are all over British cities to track the missing people to Craig's flat, or at least to the neighbourhood.

Interesting Trivia In a story that showcases the eleventh Doctor, he gets to wear a football jersey with the number 11 on it, he wakes Craig at 7:11, it's the eleventh episode of the season and the upstairs door has two vertical lines that look like an 11, especially when the light from the alien process glows behind them. After headbutting Craig to pass on key information about himself, the Doctor gasps and points to his own face, saying "eleventh," thus formally identifying himself as the eleventh Doctor for the first time.

One of the more interesting details revealed in this episode about the TARDIS is that its controls respond in relation to where the operator stands. Which, in many ways, makes a lot of sense, as flying through space and time is quite complex, and there are a limited number of controls.

This story is a loose adaptation of Gareth Roberts' own 2006 comic strip in *Doctor Who Magazine*, which found the tenth Doctor and Mickey sharing Mickey's flat for a week while waiting for the TARDIS to arrive with Rose and Jackie. The football sequence is pulled from the comic strip, but the confusion between the sonic screwdriver and the electric toothbrush worked the other way, with disastrous results for Mickey's teeth!

Early drafts of Gareth Robert's script had the antagonist turn out to be Meglos, the villainous cactus from the 1980 story "Meglos." Part of the joke of his appearance would have been that the Doctor didn't remember him, leading Meglos to try and prompt him with details from the original story! The change was made because of Meglos's similarity to the Vinvoccis in "The End of Time" and because it was decided that the menace needed to be much more frightening.

The Doctor comes by his football skills naturally: Matt Smith was well on his way to becoming a professional footballer when an injury caused him to take up acting instead.

The TARDIS Chronometer The TARDIS briefly lands in Colchester, Essex, in the present day. Otherwise, it's stuck in the time vortex.

Cool? (GB) It must be the silliest image of the season (and that's saying something): the Doctor, soaking wet, with a towel barely concealing his modesty, ponders what's in the flat upstairs when he is surprised by Craig's would-be girlfriend Sophie. What does the Doctor do? He immediately covers his bare nipples with his hands. It's the most absurd gesture, but at the same time it illustrates how utterly out of his depth the Doctor is. That he does it all so unselfconsciously makes me conclude that Matt Smith must be as much an alien as the Doctor.

All season, the Doctor's character has been gloriously restated as someone more alien than we've known him in the past five seasons: more unknowable and much odder. Taking his cues from past Doctors like Patrick Troughton and the delightful tradition of somewhat potty scientists in British culture like Magnus Pyke and Patrick Moore, Matt Smith has played the Doctor as a full-on eccentric. He's ungainly, awkward, enthusiastic and completely clueless as to how dorky he seems. He walks to the beat of a different orchestra on another planet, never mind one different drum.

From the moment the Doctor air-kisses Craig, you know this episode is going to be is a showpiece for Smith's delightful brand of wackiness. The first 15 minutes, where the Doctor desperately tries to ingratiate himself with Craig, all the while seeming odder and odder, is a brilliant piece of writing and acting. The whole episode is full of similar moments where we witness the Doctor at his most alien, a Time Lord who really has no clue about how to be mundanely human but has great fun trying.

Had this been Eccleston's or Tennant's Doctor, many of the beats of this story would have been the same. The difference is that those Doctors might have more easily passed for human: Eccleston's Doctor might have been more bipolar and Tennant's a bit of a know-it-all, but the characters they played had more recognizably human emotional colouring. Matt Smith's genius is that he's more opaque. You don't quite get what he's about. Watch the Doctor's one-two punch of insulting and then inspiring Sophie to look at her life and what she's doing. All three of the actors who played the Doctor in the New Series would perform that scene with their own particular genius, but Smith does it in a way that is unexpected.

The thing is, the Doctor is only half of the equation here. For the comedy of the Doctor posing as a human to work, you need someone totally and comfortably human to provide a baseline. Hello, James Corden. I'm not the biggest fan of Corden's work on *Gavin and Stacey*, but he's great here, playing an ordinary bloke who likes his life and now has the strangest flatmate ever — and that man destroys his life, piece by piece, taking away his popularity on the football pitch, his aspirations at work and his girl. Corden milks the absurdity of Craig's situation for all it's worth, and he and Matt Smith have great onscreen chemistry. Corden also has great chemistry with Daisy Haggard's Sophie (who is charmingly awkward throughout). Even though the rom-com elements of this story are well travelled, they get a lovely *Who*-ish spin at the climax, with the inevitable declaration of true love preventing the solar system from blowing up.

All the problems with "The Lodger" take place outside the bubble of the Doctor, Craig and Sophie. Nothing is done to establish the other victims — a cell phone conversation, or a vignette before they pass by the flat — to indicate what's motivating them to leave. As a result, the revelation that the crash program is looking for people interested in escape comes out of nowhere. (Not to mention the basic flaw that they can't detect the Doctor, who is even more desperate to leave, given the TARDIS is lost.) On the other hand, the mounting horror of the situation is quite effective, and the payoff of what's on the second floor works well, even if the time engine could have just as easily been occupying the floor without perception filters being dragged out for the umpteenth time.

Really, though, where "The Lodger" ultimately succeeds is in the little moments of genius on Matt Smith's part. Like staring off in the middle distance while deciding what century sounds more normal or joking about Craig's similarity to the sofa in a manner where you can't decide if he's being affectionate or cutting. And that's without considering the Doctor's dominance of the call centre or the hilarious desperation of the Doctor to keep Craig from evicting him. The Doctor has rarely been weirder, stranger, funnier or more alien.

It's the eleventh episode of the season, but "The Lodger" is really Matt Smith's housewarming party as the Doctor. Aren't you glad you were invited?

Second Opinion (RS?) This is a small-scale story, but it's the small-scale things that really make it something special.

The Doctor's wonderful alienness has some lovely subtle touches. He showers with his phone earpiece in and keeps his sonic screwdriver in a bathroom cup. When Craig winks at the Doctor and says that if he ever needs space to just shout and he'll get out of his hair, the Doctor winks back and shouts, "I wasn't expecting this!," although you get the sense that he's more likely imagining an invasion by tiny goblins than a romantic rendezvous.

There's also a poster for a van Gogh exhibition on Craig's fridge, complete with a print of the self-portrait we saw last episode. And when Craig goes to put his hand on the panel — something that has killed everyone else who's done this — he says, "Geronimo!" having already absorbed some of the Doctor's catchphrases.

Plus, the Doctorish aspects of the Doctor are all confined to small things. He gets to make a heroic speech about how there will be no annihilation while he's around, only it turns out to be about a football game. He deals with a bully by . . . hanging up on him. When Craig tells the Doctor all about his prospects and then wonders why he's telling him all this, the Doctor says that he has that kind of a face: people never stop blurting out their plans when he's around. And his method of saving the day involves nothing larger than a simple "Kiss the girl!"

There's a catflap in the door, which is thematically appropriate for something unwanted having infested Craig's building. And the final moment of the story is a tiny clue: the engagement ring from Rory, which Amy finds in the Doctor's pocket while searching for a pen.

"The Lodger" is a story that should never have worked. However, thanks to a combination of winsome appeal on the part of Matt Smith and James Corden, a script that knows how to mine the fish-out-of-water comedy to perfection, and a whole host of small but lovely touches, this is one of the standouts of the season. Sometimes good things really do come in small packages.

5.12–5.13 The Pandorica Opens / The Big Bang

Written by Steven Moffat **Directed by** Toby Haynes

Supporting cast Arthur Darvill (Rory Williams), Alex Kingston (River Song), Tony Curran (Vincent), Bill Paterson (Bracewell), Ian McNeice (Winston Churchill), Sophie Okonedo (Liz 10), Christopher Ryan (Commander Stark), Ruari Mears (Cyberleader), Paul Kasey (Judoon), Barnaby Edwards (Dalek), Marcus O'Donovan (Claudio), Howard Lee (Dr. Gachet), Simon Fisher-Becker (Dorium), Chrissie Cotterill (Madame Vernet), David Fynn (Marcellus), Susan Vidler (Aunt Sharon), Frances Ashman (Christine), William Pretsell (Dave), Halcro Johnston (Augustus Pond), Karen Westwood (Tabetha Pond), Caitlin Blackwood (Amelia), Joe Jacobs (guard), Clive Wood (Commander), Nicholas Briggs (Dalek, Cybermen and Judoon voices)

Original airdates June 19 and 26, 2010

The Big Idea The TARDIS explodes, taking the universe with it, save for a few people at the eye of the storm — and a Dalek.

Roots and References The myth of Pandora's box; Cleopatra (River's disguise); *The Mummy* (entombed in the Pandorica; the fez); *Robin of Sherwood* ("Nothing's ever forgotten"); gatherings of supervillains ranging from the Legion of Doom in *Super Friends* to the Sinister Six in *Spider-Man*. The Doctor rocks out to Queen's "Crazy Little Thing Called Love" at the wedding.

Adventures in Time and Space We return to the scene of the Doctor taking Amy's hands from "Flesh and Stone." It's almost exactly as it was last time, except that when the Doctor says, "I don't know yet but I'm working it out," and glances, we see that he glances at his younger self. We see Liz 10 in 5145, still reigning 1,100 years after we last saw her ("The Beast Below"). River bargains for a Time Agent's vortex manipulator ("The Sound of Drums" and elsewhere). When the Doctor first wakes up after the explosion, he exclaims, "Legs!" just as he did in "The End of Time, Part Two."

The Doctor determines that the two sonic screwdrivers come from different timestreams through an energy discharge that, while unnamed, is probably the Blinovitch Limitation Effect (1983's "Mawdryn Undead"; presumably it didn't lead to a bigger explosion, and it didn't lead to a similar discharge of energy when the two Doctors or Amys met, because of the universe-being-destroyed thing). There's a sarcophagus of an Egyptian mummy in the National Museum, echoing 1975's "Pyramids of Mars."

The Crack in the Universe Effect We learn that the TARDIS exploding causes every sun to supernova at every moment in history. This retroactively creates the crack and causes the universe to never have existed. Although the crack erases someone's existence, it doesn't erase every trace of them, leaving behind little things like faces in photographs and luggage that can't be accounted for. Furthermore, by having lived next to a crack for over a decade, Amy's memory has become very powerful. It allows her to (unconsciously) restore Rory and allows the Doctor to return by sowing the seeds of memory in her mind.

A crack appears on the TARDIS monitor and a voice says, "Silence will fall." This crack later closes, as does the one in Amy's room. When the Doctor is rewinding, the crack appears in the street outside Craig's house.

There are still loose ends: the identity of the Silence and why they wanted to destroy the TARDIS and the universe. We'll return to at least some of these questions next season.

Who is the Doctor? The Doctor is prepared to sacrifice himself, mostly because it will restore the universe to its original condition, but also because it will give Amy her mum and dad back. Which is, really, the Doctor all over. Typically, the Doctor plants clues so that he can escape this fate (that said, they're quite risky clues that could have never been picked up on by Amy).

The Doctor and Amy It turns out that the Doctor did indeed lie to Amy in "The Eleventh Hour" about having no reason for taking her; he did it because he knew she was tied to the crack. In spite of this, the pair are as close as ever: he only wants to see Amy before he sacrifices himself. However, this story also marks the point where things transition from the relationship between Doctor and Amy to Amy and Rory, as Rory lives through 2,000 years protecting Amy, and Amy finally marries Rory. Nonetheless, the newlyweds abandon Leadworth to travel with the Doctor. The love triangle continues . . .

Monster of the Week The Alliance includes Daleks, Cybermen ("Rise of the Cybermen" et al.), Sontarans ("The Sontaran Stratagem"/"The Poison Sky"), Terileptils (1982's "The Visitation"), the Slitheen ("Aliens of London"/"World War Three"), Chelonians (the 1993 New Adventure novel *The Highest Science*), Nestenes and Autons ("Rose"), Drahvins (1965's "Galaxy Four"), Sycorax ("The Christmas Invasion"), Haemogoths, Zygons (1975's "Terror of the Zygons"), Atraxi ("The Eleventh Hour"), Draconians (1973's "Frontier in Space"), Silurians ("The Hungry Earth"/"Cold Blood"), Hoix ("Love & Monsters"), Roboforms ("The Christmas Invasion," "The Runaway Bride") and Judoon

("Smith and Jones"). There are also very quick flashes of Blowfish, Weevils (both from *Torchwood*) and Uvodni (from *The Sarah Jane Adventures*).

Stand Up and Cheer Amy restores the Doctor by remembering the TARDIS, thanks to the links the Doctor seeded in her dreams using the old wedding saying: something old, something new, something borrowed, something blue. It allows Amy to be heroic, walking over the table in her wedding dress and bringing her "imaginary" friend back to life.

Roll Your Eyes The Doctor, River and Amy spend hours at Stonehenge, searching for something odd — and they miss a Cyberhead lying out in the open?

You're Not Making Any Sense If the Doctor drops off the note to Amelia after meeting her in the museum, how does the Doctor originally know when to arrive at the museum in the first place? This one keeps making our heads hurt . . .

Interesting Trivia The most evil creatures in the universe form an unholy alliance in order to build the Pandorica. Which turns out to be technology so advanced that it can protect the inhabitant not only from time itself, but from the destruction of the entire universe. Wouldn't this kind of technology have been rather useful in the dastardly plans of, um, pretty much everyone involved in its creation? Even the Daleks never exhibit this level of technological sophistication. (The closest is the Genesis Ark, but that was Time Lord technology.)

The alliance features the Daleks, who have time-travelling abilities, but it also consists of all number of alien races (and their spaceships) who aren't time active. So how did races from the distant future all end up in 102 AD? Did the Daleks operate a time-taxi service and then kindly return them to their own eras when it was all over?

Auton Rory spends centuries watching over the Pandorica, becoming part of its history in the process. For the most part, his role is static, simply waiting nearby, but his presence proves to be useful when he definitively saves the Pandorica (and hence Amy) from the Blitz, pulling it through war-torn London before finally deciding to change his clothes, several thousand years after the Roman empire fell. Although, given that the Pandorica can protect the Doctor from the collapse of the universe itself, it probably wasn't in too much danger from a few bombs.

When the alliance is revealed, Steven Moffat's script simply states that the Doctor is confronted by every enemy he's ever faced. Budgetary practicalities intervened, however, which limited it to creatures the New Series already had costumes and prostethics for. This meant that CGI creatures (such as the Pyrovile from "The Fires of Pompeii") were left out and a number of Classic Series monsters (such as the Draconians) are only namechecked. It also led to borrowing some of the spinoff series' monsters, such as the Uvodni and the Weevils.

The TARDIS Chronometer Planet One, the oldest planet in the universe. The TARDIS then lands on Earth in 102 AD, a little way from Stonehenge. River takes the TARDIS to Amy's house, June 26, 2010, and then it lands in a cave. It explodes in space, forming a new sun in the alternate history. When the Doctor is restored, it materializes at Amy's wedding. The Doctor then moves it outside.

Cool? (RS?) The final two-part story of the 2010 season is, like its titular Pandorica, one big puzzle box. The first episode is all about getting into the box, the second is all about getting out. And, as the Doctor points out, it's far easier to break into a prison than it is to break out. Or, at least, it's more straightforward.

"The Pandorica Opens" is a stupendous sucker punch of an episode. Moffat pulls off an awesome trick: you know, right from the beginning, that the only thing the Pandorica can possibly hold is the Doctor himself. The clues are subtle but not too subtle: a being of immense power, someone who's feared by everyone, locked away in an inescapable prison yet seemingly able to escape anyway. What's brilliant is the wholly unexpected twist that the Pandorica is indeed meant for the Doctor . . . only not yet, because it's all an extremely clever trap.

That cliffhanger is awesome and almost everything in the two-parter is structured around it. The entirety of the first episode is leading there — something we've seen many times before — but all the pre-wedding stuff of "The Big Bang" is leading away from it as well. This isn't just a moment where the action reaches a temporary crescendo, as so many cliffhangers are, but a genuine hinge around which everything pivots.

The lead up is excellent as well, with characters from several stories this season, culminating in River summoning the Doctor through unconventional means. It gets us off to a rollicking start, even if it borrows similar beats from "The Time of Angels." The 102 AD setting seems odd at first, but is worth it for the "greatest military machine ever assembled" line. And the reintroduction of Rory is pitch perfect.

Matt Smith is stupendous once again, particularly his scene on top of Stonehenge. In retrospect, you know intellectually that the real reason the ships don't attack is because they had something else in mind all along, but the speech is delivered so powerfully that you suspect it gave them cold feet anyway. Matt Smith delivers it like a man who's had too much to drink — and it works! By all sanity it shouldn't, but it does. He slurs his words, he staggers around like he's lost his balance and he basically shouts out to the assembled armies of the universe, "Come and have a go if you think you're hard enough!" — and my little fanboy heart was pounding like a demon.

Indeed, the only downside to "The Pandorica Opens" is Amy, who has nothing to do other than die. There's her reunion with Rory, yes, but it pales in comparison with the Doctor's much cleverer version. Instead, Karen Gillan gets to snap at people inappropriately and otherwise do nothing other than stand around looking pouty.

That cliffhanger is a whammy of an ending: the Doctor trapped for good, the universe about to be destroyed, Amy killed — at the hand of Rory no less — and River trapped in a dying TARDIS. This is Davies-esque in its scope, and if you watched it first time around, you had a delicious week to wait, wondering how any of them were going to get out of that one. And then you most definitely wouldn't have guessed the answer, which may be full of time-travel malarkey, but it's both fun and dramatically satisfying.

This is really a three-part story. Part one consists of "The Pandorica Opens," but "The Big Bang" is cleaved neatly down the middle. Returning to Amelia was so fabulous it seems a shame we couldn't have seen her throughout the episode. The time-travel hijinks are mind-meltingly delectable, but they're carefully seeded to appear plausible. They even get away with replaying whole scenes we've seen only minutes earlier, but it's necessary, given how complicated everything is. Even the Dalek works, largely because it's calcified and not the day-glo version. And Rory's arc is heartbreaking: the boy who waited.

The Doctor backtracking through the season was a clever way to celebrate the stories we've been watching thus far. Between this and the painting at the beginning of "The Pandorica Opens," almost every story of the season gets a visit. And the replay of the scene in "Flesh and Stone" with the backtracking Doctor asking Amy to remember something he hasn't yet told her is amazing. It's almost exactly as we saw it back then, complete with the Doctor in his jacket (and rolled-up sleeves) for the continuity buffs among us who thought we'd spotted a mistake. This is a stupendous payoff to the season, tying it together magnificently.

Then there's the wedding, which had a lot of people confused.

It's a startling change in tone, almost a completely different story. And yet, the clues to the Doctor's return have been there all along: in "Cold Blood," the Doctor tries to get Amy to remember Rory, showing that memory can overpower the effects of the crack. As it does in Roman Britain, when she breaks through her amnesia. Then there's the moment in "The Pandorica Opens," when the Doctor tells Amy just how powerful memory is, when he talks about luggage and rings left behind. Importantly, the Doctor isn't dead, he's just stuck on the wrong side of the crack — and Amy's had a lifetime of living next to the crack, filtering it through her thoughts. So it makes sense that she can overcome its effects by the power of memory, because those are the ground rules already established.

The return of the TARDIS using the "something blue" phrase is astonishingly powerful. The whole sequence redeems Amy's character from its season-long slump, because she stops being the I'm-not-bovvered cool girl and has to interact with the emotion of the story. Here, Amy is genuinely happy, not caring what anyone thinks as she walks over the bridal table and talks about her raggedy Doctor and laughs along with the Doctor's "uncool" dancing instead of at it. We finally get a likeable Amy, but it's still a mystery why we couldn't have had one all season long.

Matt Smith's fez antics are hilarious, and his physical acting continues to inspire. Look at the way his legs instantly splay sideways when the TARDIS is jolted. He's not going for the usual choices and simply jerking against the console, but he's instead doing some sort of Bee Gees move. His "radish" dance with the kids at the wedding is infectious. And the way he says, "It's a fez, I wear a fez now" in a tone full of gravitas is laugh-out-loud funny. Nothing he does should work and yet everything does. He's spent the entire season making the uncool cool, which is really a gift to all of us at home. I love this man.

"The Pandorica Opens"/"The Big Bang" is an excellent conclusion to the season. It's one that celebrates the episodes that came before it in both obvious and subtle ways, it's telling three intricate and interconnected stories, and it even manages the big emotion of a Davies-era finale. It swings around its cliffhanger as though it were a dancing pole, but it also takes us in unexpected directions. Ultimately, it fulfills the season's mandate to reimagine *Doctor Who* as a fairytale with a childlike quality to the story that's both gentle and sweet. It doesn't get much better than this.

Second Opinion (GB) "The Pandorica Opens"/"The Big Bang" works by repeatedly fooling the viewer. First it shows us an object, the Pandorica, whose contents contain: "A goblin. Or a trickster, or a warrior. A nameless, terrible thing, soaked in the blood of a billion galaxies." Is it a new menace? Or is it the Doctor?

It turns out that the Pandorica is completely empty. It's a trap. All the monsters in the *Doctor Who* universe wanting it? Just play acting to get the Doctor in position. The result is an incredible, devastating blow: by the time the viewer and the Doctor realize that the Pandorica is an elaborate con put on by every enemy the Doctor has had, it's too late for everyone. And if all that isn't distressing enough, Rory's sudden resurrection is also a deception; he's an Auton who kills Amy.

Then, when all looks bleak, the Doctor shows up. In a fez.

In the same way that the fez is a way of distinguishing past, present or future Doctors disguised as a character eccentricity, "The Big Bang" is similarly deceptive. You don't initially notice that most of the episode has the four main characters and a (stone) Dalek running through an empty museum because it's all breathlessly paced, brilliantly characterized, and moves back and forth through the fourth dimension as though the script were written on a Snakes and Ladders game board. The result is something that feels incredibly epic though it's actually quite small-scale.

But then, paradoxes abound in "The Big Bang" as Amy is saved by her 10-year-old self, Rory the Auton turns out to be Rory the human and the Doctor conspires with his own past to save the future. And it's all done with such complete and total panache that you love every second of it. With only five actors running the show for most of the 60 minutes here, it's just as well that they're this good. Matt Smith in particular is brilliant at playing the self-deluded nerd, the cleverest man in the room and an impossibly sad old man.

It still suffers from the chronic *Doctor Who* finale complaint of painting itself into a corner with the high-stakes jeopardy and then employing a solution that comes, no matter how well seeded, from left field. Amy remembering the Doctor into existence is no different than Rose the time goddess wiping out the Daleks in "The Parting of the Ways." But the neat thing is how the viewer is misdirected from noticing, thanks to the *deus ex machina* solution appearing in the denouement rather than the climax. It has the exact opposite effect: for once the problem is resolved without any cost or sacrifice; in fact, Amy gets everything she ever hoped for.

"The Pandorica Opens"/"The Big Bang" might be the greatest magic trick *Doctor Who* has ever pulled. Like all good magic tricks, it requires a series of complex deceptions to pull it off. And, in the end, it fools the viewer into leaving this season with a smile on their faces. That's the best kind of magic.

. . . .

Arthur Darvill

Prior to *Doctor Who*, Arthur Darvill was mostly known for his theatre work, not just as an actor, but as a musician and composer who had scored two musical plays by the time he was 27. He appeared on stage with Matt Smith and Christian Slater in a West End production of *Swimming With Sharks* and had a small role in the 2008 BBC adaptation of *Little Dorritt*. He continues to work in the theatre; in 2011, he played Mephistopheles in *Doctor Faustus*.

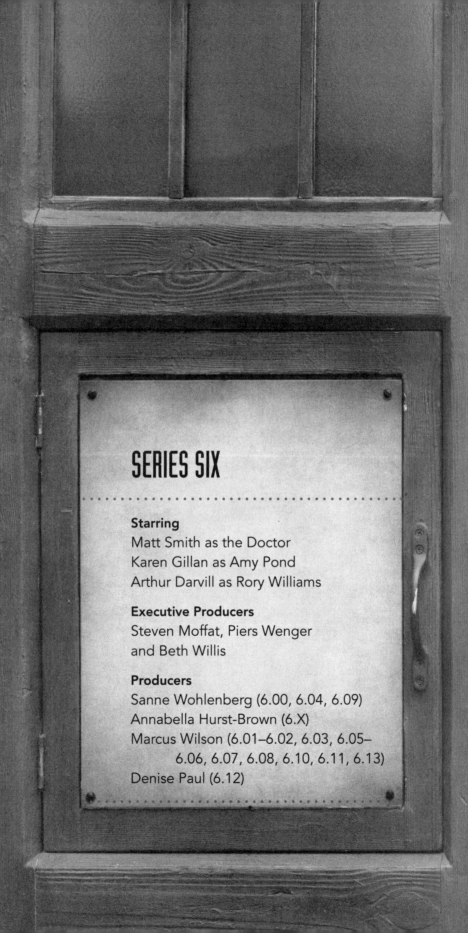

SERIES SIX

Starring
Matt Smith as the Doctor
Karen Gillan as Amy Pond
Arthur Darvill as Rory Williams

Executive Producers
Steven Moffat, Piers Wenger
and Beth Willis

Producers
Sanne Wohlenberg (6.00, 6.04, 6.09)
Annabella Hurst-Brown (6.X)
Marcus Wilson (6.01–6.02, 6.03, 6.05–
    6.06, 6.07, 6.08, 6.10, 6.11, 6.13)
Denise Paul (6.12)

6.00 A Christmas Carol

Written by Steven Moffat **Directed by** Toby Haynes

Supporting cast Michael Gambon (Kazran/Elliot Sardick), Katherine Jenkins (Abigail), Laurence Belcher (Young Kazran), Danny Horn (Adult Kazran), Leo Bill (pilot), Pooky Quesnel (Captain), Micah Balfour (co-pilot), Steve North (Old Benjamin), Bailey Pepper (Boy/Benjamin), Tim Plester (servant), Laura Rogers (Isabella), Meg Wynn-Owen (Old Isabella), Nick Malinowski (Eric)

Original airdate December 25, 2010

The Big Idea The Doctor needs the help of old miser Kazran Sardick to save a doomed spaceship with Amy and Rory on board, and so he arranges for Sardick to meet the ghosts of Christmas past, present and future.

Roots and References Obviously, Charles Dickens' *A Christmas Carol*; *Star Trek* (the bridge of the galaxy class ship resembles the ship's bridge in the 2009 film version, right down to the ubiquitous lens flares); *Jaws* (the shark); *Peter Pan* (the sonic screwdriver in the shark is cribbed from the clock in Captain Hook's crocodile). Certain elements were lifted from writer Steven Moffat's short story "Continuity Errors" from the 1996 *Doctor Who* fiction anthology *Decalog 3: Consequences.*

Adventures in Time and Space Whatever it is Amy and Rory are getting up to on their honeymoon, it involves Amy dressing in her policewoman kissogram outfit ("The Eleventh Hour") and Rory dressing in his Roman centurion gear ("The Pandorica Opens"/"The Big Bang"). Sardick's controls for the clouds are isomorphic, a beloved piece of technobabble from the 1975 story "Pyramids of Mars." During the montage of Christmas Eves with Abigail, the Young Kazran and the Doctor wear fezzes ("The Big Bang") and long scarves like the fourth Doctor.

Who is the Doctor? In what must be the funniest, truest gag in the whole story, the Doctor shorts out the psychic paper with a lie too big for it: namely that he's universally recognized as a responsible and mature adult.

Monster of the Week The crystalline ice clouds surrounding the planet are filled with flying fish, including a shark that resembles the Earth-born version . . . except it can, you know, fly.

Stand Up and Cheer A musical number in *Doctor Who* would normally be anathema, but Abigail's song is gorgeous: Murray Gold's music and lyrics are stunning and Katherine Jenkins sings it beautifully. It works in terms of the plot, and director Toby Haynes draws out every ounce of romance. It's snowing.

Kazran is a changed man who gets to be with his love one last time. Amy and Rory are saved. It's Christmas, and it's beautiful.

Roll Your Eyes Steven Moffat is clearly recycling from his other series, *Sherlock*, with the demonstration of the Doctor's instant deductions of Kazran and his character through rapid-fire editing and swooshing camera moves.

You're Not Making Any Sense The climactic paradox, where Young Kazran sees his older self as a cruel man like his father, which then changes the older self, doesn't hold up to close scrutiny. Why would it only change Kazran's outlook in the present? Why wouldn't it change his physical circumstances, his other decisions in life, even his being there in the present? How does changing Kazran's personal timeline only achieve one desired outcome?

Interesting Trivia In Steven Moffat's short story, "Continuity Errors," the Doctor needs to obtain a special book in order to stop an alien invasion, but he meets resistance from a difficult librarian. The Doctor makes repeated trips back in time to change the librarian's past so that she's a nicer and kinder person, and he eventually changes her timeline enough that she relinquishes the book. The librarian in "Continuity Errors" became Kazran Sardick in this episode.

One of the nicer visual touches is seeing how, as Kazran's personal history and memories change due to the Doctor's intervention, different objects appear in his home. He suddenly gains pictures of his Christmas Eve journeys with the Doctor, which took him mostly to Earth in the past: to Egypt, New York, the Grand Canyon and eventually Hollywood in the 1950s. He even, briefly, has a portrait of Abigail on his wall instead of the portrait of his father (it changes back after Kazran, in the past, learns that Abigail's terminal illness leaves her with only one day left).

This story marks a return to the tradition begun in 2005 where every Christmas special features a song written by *Doctor Who* composer Murray Gold. In "The Christmas Invasion," Gold's "Song for Ten" played as the Doctor, Mickey and the Tylers shared Christmas dinner. Gary Williams performed the song on the broadcast episode (which was a great pastiche of Holland-Dozier-Holland's pop songs from the 1960s), though Neil Hannon from The Divine Comedy performed it for the official soundtrack album. Hannon also performed the song "Love Don't Roam" in "The Runaway Bride" (which played during the dance at the reception). "Voyage of the Damned" featured the first onscreen performance of a song: Yamit Mamo sang "The Stowaway" on the *Titanic* dance floor. In "A Christmas Carol," "Abigail's Song" is performed by actress (and popular singer) Katherine Jenkins. Jenkins is actually the second featured guest star to perform a song onscreen; Miranda Raison performed "My Angel Put the Devil in Me" in "Daleks in Manhattan" (though Yamit Mamo sang it on the soundtrack album).

The TARDIS Chronometer An unnamed planet, originally a colony of Earth, sometime in the future.

Cool? (GB) There was a time when the Christmas special meant a grand, undemanding, but thoroughly exciting and totally accessible adventure. Then "A Christmas Carol" happened.

Let me be clear here. There is a large part of me that wants to love this story. It's beautiful to look at; it's easily the best-directed episode of *Doctor Who* under the new regime. Matt Smith is absolutely stellar, knowing when to be manic and knowing when to be calmer for deeper emotional resonance. The use of *A Christmas Carol* is brilliant, avoiding a trite and clichéd retelling of Dickens' novella and instead using the text in thematic ways appropriate to *Doctor Who*: the "Ghost of Christmas Present" sequence on the ship is haunting, and is without a doubt one of the smartest things Steven Moffat has written.

So why, then, does "A Christmas Carol" leave me so frustrated? In many ways, it's the same problem I had with "Continuity Errors," on which this story is based: if the Doctor can simply travel back into the timeline of the people he's interacting with and change a few details here and there, it renders *Doctor Who* into nonsense. Why doesn't he, say, pop back in time to make van Statten a nicer person in "Dalek" so that he won't collect alien specimens in the first place? Or avert the accident that created Davros in "Genesis of the Daleks"? Or invest heavily in Max Capricorn so he doesn't want to drop the *Titanic* on Earth in "Voyage of the Damned"?

There's a reason why, at every opportunity in the Russell T Davies era until now, the Doctor has explicitly stated (in "Parting of the Ways," "The Runaway Bride" and others) that once the TARDIS lands in a timeline, it can't go back on itself. And the reason isn't just that *Doctor Who* continuity rubbish (I couldn't care less about tropes like the Blinovitch Limitation Effect); it's that it's boring and not dramatic at all. Case in point: we have an actor of Michael Gambon's stature and he spends two-thirds of the story essentially watching television.

The other thing that bothers me is that, at great story expense, ideas have become king on *Doctor Who*. The operative word has become *clever*. How clever the adaptation of *A Christmas Carol* is, how clever the Doctor bouncing back and forth in Kazran's timeline is (oh look, he pops forward in time to get the security code from the old Kazran!), how clever the dilemma Kazran faces is, how clever the paradox at the end is. Well, clever is great. But clever is no substitute for making exciting, accessible television the whole family can watch, especially on Christmas Day. That the climax of this story hinges on a paradox, and one pitched at such a cerebral level, should tell you something's fundamentally out of whack here. While watching it with very smart people, I had to pause to explain what happened. When did *Doctor Who* become something only those highly versed in science fiction could watch?

Admittedly, "A Christmas Carol" has sops for the general public: there are sharks and Katherine Jenkins sings. All that is very cool indeed, but it only serves to distract. There is some great drama generated by the cleverness: the unexpected consequences of the Doctor's intervention — Abigail breaks Kazran's heart and confirms his decision to become like his father — are heartfelt and lovely. But it feels like, after four years of a story's emotional content directing its plot, the show has swung to the other extreme, where everything, including the characterization and the drama, is dictated by the ideas.

The other thing is, in spite of the fish and some great individual gags (the Doctor breaking the psychic paper), it all seems so serious. The *Doctor Who* Christmas special was traditionally a wonderful time to be inconsequential and silly, and I loved it for that. "Voyage of the Damned" and "The Runaway Bride" are two of the finest romps ever concocted. But the word "romp" would never occur to anyone here. Nothing is left to chance. It's plotted with the precision of a clockwork device and with such serious intent that it pretends to have fun rather than actually being fun.

And yet, I can't simply dismiss "A Christmas Carol" for being cerebral fare so obsessed with timey-wimeyness that it's forgotten the silly side of things. I love the ending (once the paradox nonsense is done with). I love that it leaves us with Kazran only having one more night with Abigail and that the concluding sentiment is Christmas is a time to celebrate being "halfway out of the dark." There is, frankly, so much to love about "A Christmas Carol," but there is so much that worries me as well.

Second Opinion (RS?) Bah, humbug! It's my turn to apologize for my co-author having lost his soul. Usually I'm the persnickety one while Graeme's happy if he's being entertained. For some reason, we've swapped places this time around, because "A Christmas Carol" is great fun! It's awesome, and it gets better on subsequent viewings.

It has it all: time-travel malarkey with the Doctor being outrageous, a sweet romance, a ticking clock, Amy and Rory being sexy, cool monsters and a heartbreaking character study. Yes, Michael Gambon spends the episode watching television — and it's great! Graeme has it backwards: if you're going to have an actor watching television, then you need a really good one to make it emotionally engaging, and Gambon nails it.

I don't even find the plot offensively "clever." The Doctor has to avert disaster by messing around with Scrooge's history until Scrooge becomes nice. That's not nerdish cleverness; that's poetry. Who cares if the Doctor could do this in every episode? The fact that it doesn't actually work is a big clue as to why he might not and the episode is just having so much fun with it that you don't really care (or shouldn't, anyway).

"A Christmas Carol" is also the most Christmassy Christmas special yet. Rather than a few nods to snow, this immerses itself in the yuletide season. I watched this on Christmas Day, just before bedtime, having overeaten massively, my house awash in presents — and it was the perfect end to a perfect day. Don't listen to the Scrooges. This is the perfect Christmas present.

6.X Space / Time

Written by Steven Moffat **Directed by** Richard Senior
Original airdate March 18, 2011

The Big Idea The TARDIS accidentally lands inside itself, causing our heroes to meet themselves.

Roots and References The *Red Dwarf* episodes "Future Echoes" and "Out of Time" (a comedic time loop plot featuring only the regular cast).

Adventures in Time and Space The idea of the TARDIS materializing inside itself was seen in 1972's "The Time Monster" and 1981's "Logopolis," although each time it was actually the Master's TARDIS. Amy repeats her line from "The Big Bang": "Okay kids, this is where it gets complicated."

Stand Up and Cheer Amy flirting with herself. We'd describe our reactions in more detail, but ECW's lawyers assure us that anything we could possibly have to say would be excised from the book anyway.

You're Not Making Sense When Rory asks the Doctor if he's ever seen Amy drive, he says no, but he has — albeit in an alternate reality — in "Amy's Choice."

Interesting Trivia "Space"/"Time" was part of the 2011 Comic Relief fundraiser on BBC1. In a similar vein to the BBC's Children in Need, Comic Relief is a comedy-themed fundraising effort for international development work. The brainchild of comedian Lenny Henry and writer Richard Curtis ("Vincent and the Doctor"), this biennial campaign culminates in Red Nose Day, which features original comedy programming and special one-off episodes of popular series. *Doctor Who* has been occasionally involved with Comic Relief, starting with a comedy version of *Doctor Who* in 1999, "The Curse of Fatal Death," which starred Rowan Atkinson, Richard E. Grant, Jim Broadbent, Hugh Grant and Joanna Lumley all as the Doctor; it was written by future executive producer Steven Moffat. In 2009, the *Doctor Who* spinoff *The Sarah Jane Adventures* produced a mini-episode for Comic Relief, "From Raxacoricofallapatorius with

Love," guest-starring British comedy legend Ronnie Corbett as a pint-sized Slitheen.

The TARDIS Chronometer In deep space and also inside itself.

Cool? (RS?) The end of the previous season saw the series take a startling new direction: a married couple on board the TARDIS. We'd never seen this before, but possibly for good reason. One of the truisms of genre television is that whenever a couple gets together, the drama is instantly sucked from the program. So this was potentially dangerous territory for the show.

"Space"/"Time" shows how to hold our interest. Wrapped around a gorgeous vignette of timey-wimeyness is Amy and Rory doing what they do best: being sexy. The entire problem occurs because Rory gets transfixed by Amy's, um, skirt. And in amongst overlapping Doctors, TARDISes and explanations, we have Amy flirting with herself, not once but twice.

This is exactly how to use Amy: she's confident, sexy and self-deprecating (at least, she is to her other self, saying several things that the viewer at home has probably complained about). There's no trace left of the unlikeable Amy, and, well, she's flirting with herself. In that skirt. Skirts.

Um, sorry, where was I?

Oh yeah, and there's the lovely Moffat plot. This continues to prove my assertion that Moffat is at his best when he's working with a short script, a few key actors and a single set. The figure eight of a story is cute, plotted to perfection and ends precisely when it should, before it has the chance to outstay its welcome.

Second Opinion (GB) I loved this episode . . . when it aired in 1988 as an episode of *Red Dwarf*, called "Future Echoes." All Steven Moffat really does here is steal from the beats of that and half a dozen other episodes of *Red Dwarf*, mixing mind-bending time-travel gags with blokey humour. The thing is, I preferred watching it with Lister, Rimmer and Cat.

I also don't think it's very funny. The spacey-wacey, timey-wimey gags, once again, substitute cleverness for substance. What's on display is a cute moment in an episode, but stretched out it becomes something sci-fi nerds will appreciate, not anything with broad appeal. And the blokey humour is completely misplaced. I concede that the two Amys flirting is quite funny (and everything else that's been said), but otherwise what we have are women-driver jokes, an upskirt gag and lesbian jokes. So nice to see that Moffat is raising the bar. And if my co-author weren't so busy thinking about both Amys (hmmm, excuse me one moment . . .), I think he'd be the first person to complain how utterly sexist the punchline, "Pond, put on some trousers," actually is.

The thing is, Steven Moffat is capable of better. This was the man who, given two characters, the TARDIS control room and five minutes, created the exceedingly funny "Time Crash." "Space"/"Time" is derivative and lazy. A real wasted opportunity.

6.01–6.02 The Impossible Astronaut / Day of the Moon

Written by Steven Moffat **Directed by** Toby Haynes

Supporting cast Alex Kingston (River Song), Mark Sheppard (Canton Delaware III), William Morgan Sheppard (Old Canton), Stuart Milligan (Richard Nixon), Chuk Iwuji (Carl), Mark Griffin (Phil), Marnix van den Broeke (The Silent), Sydney Wade (Little Girl), Nancy Baldwin (Joy), Adam Napier (Captain Simmons), Henrietta Clemett (Matilda), Paul Critoph (Charles), Kerry Shale (Dr. Renfrew), Glenn Wrage (Gardner), Jeff Mash (Grant), Peter Banks (Dr. Shepherd), Frances Barber (Eye Patch Lady), Kieran O'Connor (prison guard), Emilio Aquino (busboy)

Original airdates April 23 and 30, 2011

The Big Idea The Doctor, Amy, Rory and River encounter the Silents, just as the moon landing is occurring.

Roots and References *The Graduate* (the Doctor calls River "Mrs. Robinson"); the *Apollo 11* moon landing; Edvard Munch's painting *The Scream* (the Silents); *Memento* (working from fractured memory, writing clues on one's body). The Doctor appears in the Laurel and Hardy movie *The Flying Deuces*. Joy is a fan of *Star Trek* (which aired its final episode in June 1969 while the rest of America was watching *The Mod Squad*; Joy is quite the geek).

Adventures in Time and Space The Doctor says, "I thought I'd never get done saving you," a reflection of what he said in "The Time of Angels." He also requests jammie dodgers ("Victory of the Daleks") and a fez ("The Big Bang"), and he opens the TARDIS door with the snap of his fingers ("Forest of the Dead"). Rory pokes the Doctor to check if he's real in exactly the same way the Doctor poked Auton Rory in "The Pandorica Opens." Amy and Rory reference the universe blowing up in "The Big Bang." There are flashbacks to "The Eleventh Hour" and "Vampires of Venice." The Silents are using a time engine similar to the one found abandoned on Aickman Road in "The Lodger." Rory confirms that he can remember the 2,000 years he waited ("The Big Bang"), but doesn't think about it all the time. River's scanner is marked Magpie Electricals ("The Idiot's Lantern"). River says the day is coming when the Doctor won't recognize her and it will kill her, foreshadowing what will happen to her in "Forest of the Dead."

The TARDIS becomes invisible, for the first time since 1968's "The Invasion." The Doctor says, "Brave heart, Canton," echoing the fifth Doctor's catchphrase.

The bricks in the Doctor's cell are made from zero balance dwarf star alloy (1981's "Warriors' Gate").

The Doctor Is Dead Effect The season starts off with a bang as a much older Doctor (still in his eleventh incarnation) is apparently killed by a figure in a NASA spacesuit that he recognizes (but whose face we don't see). The Doctor is shot twice: the second time while regenerating, which kills him. The foreknowledge of this event drives this season. Also involved is a mysterious woman with an eye patch who is seen in the orphanage opening a panel that doesn't exist and saying, "No, I think she's just dreaming." Further, Amy reveals that she's pregnant, although later says it's a false alarm. However, the TARDIS scanner can't decide, flipping between results. All these things somehow tie in with a young girl who was in the astronaut suit in 1969. The girl came from an orphanage; in her room, Amy's picture is among the girl's own baby pictures. The girl is seen regenerating at the end, though we don't see her subsequent form.

The Silents/Silence also continue their involvement after trying to destroy the universe and the TARDIS last season.

The Doctor and Amy To prove she isn't lying, the Doctor asks Amy to swear on something that matters. She chooses fish fingers and custard, the symbol of their first meeting. She loves Rory even though she knows Rory assumes she's talking about the Doctor. Even so, she tells the Doctor that she might be pregnant but doesn't tell Rory.

Monster of the Week The Silents are tall with elongated faces and hands; they wear suits and ties. They can fire lightning from their hands, albeit slowly. Once you look away, you forget they were even there, and your mind edits information about them. Their tunnels run under the entire planet and have for centuries. Although they're everywhere in the world, they're concentrated in America. They're parasites, getting others to do things for them via posthypnotic control.

Stand Up and Cheer The Doctor fighting the Silents with a video of the moon landing. Holy crap. No, seriously, go and watch this scene again. The Doctor fights — and destroys — the Silents with a freaking video. This is astonishing.

Roll Your Eyes When he realizes the others are hiding something from him, the Doctor says, "Don't ever play games with me, you're not clever enough." While this may technically be true, it's a ridiculously arrogant thing to say and undercuts the power of the character.

You're Not Making Any Sense It's a really clever way of getting the humans to rise up against the Silents by giving them a subliminal command to kill any Silent they see, but wouldn't people then notice a lot of dead aliens lying around, bullet holes in the Oval Office — and wouldn't the Silents react defensively?

Interesting Trivia The Doctor's companions burn his body because there are alien races who would tear the Earth apart for a single cell of Time Lord DNA. Except that burning something doesn't destroy every cell. So we should all sit back and wait for the Earth to be torn apart, then.

The Doctor says that the TARDIS loves Saturdays, which is a nice reference to the show's timeslot. Saturday was the traditional timeslot for the Classic Series (which was originally conceived as a way to fill a Saturday afternoon slot).

The Silents have tunnels under the whole of Earth, presumably with time engines all over the place (such as the one from "The Lodger"). This suggests that their empire is both old and incredibly vast. Yet we have to ask what they were doing when previous alien races invaded Earth or tried to shape its development (just as they do). Did a host of malevolent aliens encounter the Silents while trying to encourage humanity to build the pyramids and then promptly forget about them?

The Doctor tells Nixon to tape everything that happens in his office, so that he'll know if he's under the Silents' influence. This is a reference to Nixon's famous secret tapes, which were ultimately used as evidence against him during the Watergate investigations. Previous presidents had taped some White House conversations and phone calls, but Nixon taped everything. (Though, in our world, Nixon didn't start this practice until around 1971.) However, very few people were initially aware of this fact, so it probably wasn't done via a big tape recorder on his desk, as seen here.

The older Canton is played by William Morgan Sheppard, the father of Mark Sheppard, who plays younger Canton, a move suggested by the latter. Both are quite well known on American genre television, including several appearances in various incarnations of *Star Trek*.

This is the first *Doctor Who* filmed on location in the United States. (The closest the series had been before was photographing background plates for "Daleks in Manhattan"/"Evolution of the Daleks"). Filming took place in Utah, mostly around Monument Valley, and the production team threw in as many iconic American elements as possible, including the station wagon, the yellow school bus (a suggestion of Arthur Darvill) and the Stetson. The scenes set in Florida, Nevada and New York, however, were shot in Cardiff.

According to audience measurement service Kantar Media, an estimated 4.11 million people recorded and viewed the program within a week of broadcast, making "The Impossible Astronaut" the most recorded television event of all time.

With Series Six, versions of *Doctor Who* that aired outside the U.K. had a new opening sequence that appeared after the teaser, but before the credits.

It's narrated by Karen Gillan as Amy saying, "When I was a little girl, I had an imaginary friend. And when I grew up, he came back. He's called the Doctor; he comes from someplace else. He's got a box called the TARDIS, which is bigger on the inside and can travel anywhere in time and space. I ran away with him and we've been running ever since." The introduction was written by Steven Moffat and is included to help the series appeal to a broader audience, particularly in the United States.

These two episodes were co-produced by BBC America (which is acknowledged in the end credits). BBC America presumably kicked in extra money to the production to allow them to film in Utah. With *Doctor Who*'s growing popularity in the U.S., it's easy to imagine why BBC America went for the opportunity to help finance *Doctor Who*'s first production shot in America. And it paid off: the ratings for "The Impossible Astronaut" were the highest ever for BBC America. However, this is not the first time North Americans have co-produced *Doctor Who*: the first three series were officially a co-production with Canada's public broadcaster, the Canadian Broadcasting Corporation (CBC) (a credit to CBC was included in the latter part of Series One, and all of Series Two and Three). Unlike most co-productions, CBC didn't have any say in scripts and casting; they simply provided money upfront for *Doctor Who* before it was made.

"The Impossible Astronaut" was dedicated to Elisabeth Sladen, who played Sarah Jane Smith in both the Classic and New Series and starred in *The Sarah Jane Adventures*. Sladen passed away from cancer three days before the episode aired.

The TARDIS Chronometer Utah, the present day. The TARDIS then travels to the Oval Office in Washington, D.C., in 1969 and then to Florida. Three months later, we visit the Valley of the Gods in Utah, Area 51 in Nevada, New York City, the Glen Canyon Dam in Arizona and the launch site of *Apollo 11* at Cape Canaveral. Six months after that, we visit New York again.

Cool? (RS?) —good. Even the resolution is in the teaser, with the Doctor announcing, "It's Neil Armstrong's foot" just before the credits, which is an awesome trick. If you're looking at it in the right way, this tells you everything you need to know, but you'll never guess where this is going when you watch it the first time.

- c) made magnificent by juxtaposing it with the story's theme: in among all the remembering and the forgetting, the Doctor and River's out-of-order romance is a tragedy, because the one thing they don't have is shared memories.

The introduction of the Silents is mesmerizing. After years of cribbing from the Classic Series, the New Series finally delivers its own heavyweight monster. Best of all, they're scary. Downright terrifying (except, ironically, when they're killing people with lightning, which is just goofy). And, looking back, you can clearly deduce at least two occasions (perhaps three) in the previous season when they were present. That's awesome.

- There's also River and the Doctor kissing, which is a) saved from sappiness by what Matt Smith does with his arms, which is hilarious; b) a sweet moment, all the better for having had such a long and unusual buildup; and -

Matt Smith continues to impress. Surrounded by armed security guards, the Doctor talks his way into being accepted simply by charming Canton. And he plays the older version of himself with a weariness that isn't forced but has just the right shading, especially if you know what's about to come. The way he holds the wine bottle, clinging to it like an alcoholic, is subtle but brilliant.

- reverse order, which doesn't quite jibe with what we've seen elsewhere. True, she first met him at the end of her life, but if it was a strict time reordering, then she wouldn't need the diary. Fortunately, later events will demonstrate that this isn't -

Even the resolution to the cliffhanger is hidden inside monochrome flashbacks that whizz by in seconds. Plotwise, everything actually makes sense — Canton recovers, Amy misses, they escape — but what's missing is the emotional content. How does the Doctor deal with the emotional aftermath of his best friend attempting to murder a child? We have no idea, because the next scene is set three months later in an entirely different state.

- happened. She says her worst day ever will be the one where she meets him but he doesn't know her. And if you look back at "Silence in the Library," you can see the stricken look on River's face, indicating that the moment the Doctor doesn't know her is the moment of her doom . . . It's strongly implied that the Doctor and River meet in strict -

Welcome to the sophomore Moffat season spectacular, which mixes up the format by kicking off with the two-part season opener that cuts –

- true. Out of order sequencing is not only possible, it's happening all the time. -

Where the Silents work so well is not just in their sheer scariness (although that's extremely effective), but in their *raison d'être*: you forget them the instant you look away, which is just delicious. It makes them an incredibly difficult enemy to fight and immediately gives them a strong foundation.

- ("[We do] what we're told") and then she's genuinely shaken. Her delivery of "spoilers" is heartbreaking, because it's whispered in a painful tone, entirely free of her usual smugness. There's no better way to illustrate the gravity of what's just -

– across history in a series of vignettes that come straight from the Moffat playbook. However, this opening salvo accomplishes absolutely nothing. The

Doctor spends an enormous amount of effort trying to attract Amy and Rory's attention, when he could simply materialize at their front door. It's silly, and it's only saved by Matt Smith's charm. (I love his waving at the camera in the Laurel –

Alex Kingston has never been better as River. Faced with something truly shocking (the Doctor's death) first she goes on the rampage, then she's bitter -

– and Hardy movie.) The one for "Day of the Moon" is infinitely better, because it has the requisite surprises but it also advances the –

In fact, "Day of the Moon" is rather spectacular. In every sense of the word. Where "The Impossible Astronaut" tells a fairly straightforward story, "Day of the Moon" breaks all the rules of narrative. The first time around, it's like watching the opening five minutes of any Steven Moffat story over and over again: stunning set piece follows stunning set piece (like the Doctor in the *Apollo 11* cockpit, which happens about halfway through the episode, rather than in the opening teaser where it belongs). Individual scenes may be great, but without an anchor, it's easy to feel as though the script is being too clever for its own—

– plot: everyone is rescued from certain death; an invisible TARDIS appears in an impenetrable cell; River jumps off the top of a building and lands in the pool with the TARDIS sideways. This would be the highlight of the episode were there not an even better scene to come.

Then there's a narrative jump to a haunted house, for what seems like no good reason. There is one, but by the time you actually put the dots together, you'll likely be frustrated rather than impressed;–

Part of the issue is that the story cuts randomly around for no story-related reason. Previously, we've had the easter eggs of "Blink" or the time windows of "The Girl in the Fireplace" to justify the temporal wackiness, but here it's fundamentally just a trick.

– after all, anyone can do something random, in order to try and surprise you–

- slaughter is mostly implied except in River's case, where it's simultaneously shocking and beautiful. It shouldn't be, but it is. This entire sequence may well be the single most stand up and cheer moment in the entirety of *Doctor Who*. That's breathtaking.

It also helps to have watched the rest of the season in order to appreciate what's going on here. Not just for the answers to the big mysteries like the Eye Patch Lady, but for all the subtleties of character that are in play here. It's actually quite brilliant the way it eventually fits together, but you'll have to wait a long time — several months, on first viewing, thanks to the mid-season break — to be emotionally satisfied and I'm just not convinced that's such a great idea.

– and if there was a master plan all along, well and good, but you need to give some payoff in the short term.

Fortunately, there's a payoff in the short term, and that's the climax of the second episode. The Doctor fights forgetfulness with an unforgettable image. And it's magnificent. In one fell swoop, you can see just how effective this is, as the Doctor turns the entire human race into unwitting killers. The subsequent mass -

And then we finally see the theme, as Nixon asks if he'll be remembered. The answer is yes, but not in the way he imagines. This is what the entire story is all about: the power of memory –

"The Impossible Astronaut" is a decent setup with a tacked-on opening, kicking off the season arc and introducing a new monster, but it mostly proceeds in a straightforward fashion, doing what it should. "Day of the Moon" is a totally different beast, ruining its own effectiveness by trying to be too clever –

– to edit.

– and then ending up being ridiculously effective anyway. It shouldn't work, but in the end it's actually quite incredible. You might need a whiteboard, some marker pens and a Byzantine brain to understand it, but once you get it, it all pays off. Honest.

Second Opinion (GB) Okay. Kill the Doctor, then have him regenerate and *really* kill him. That's one way of getting our attention.

This is a hugely dense story, particularly when the plot with the Silents gets underway. That's a little worrisome to me. Part of what has made *Doctor Who* work is that it's a game everyone can play. Bringing in a story that's an assemblage of so many dangling plot threads threatens to make it something only the cool kids get, like *Lost* or *Battlestar Galactica*. Great programs both, but not mass-audience friendly.

Steven Moffat forestalls this somewhat by simply turning up the cool factor. The whole opening sequence of "Day of the Moon" basically shoves the resolution of the last episode into a 15-second flashback that amounts to "stuff happens." And yet it's also brilliantly cool as we see Canton pursue Amy, Rory and River while the Doctor is in Area 51 in a straightjacket. And all this turns out to be a massive con for the benefit of the Silents. It's great.

The rest of the episode makes up for dangling plot threads with more coolness. Amy's "Schrödinger pregnancy" is offset by the incredibly eerie sequence in the children's home (kudos to Kerry Shale, for what may be the creepiest performance in New Series history) and the really sweet way it brings together Amy and Rory. All the elements that make my head hurt just thinking about them — the Silence's whole plan, the identity of the Astronaut and the last moment's impact on the Doctor's death in "The Impossible Astronaut" — are balanced out by the white-hot moments between the Doctor and River, the comedy of Nixon showing up at key junctures, and the payoff of Neil Armstrong's speech ridding the world of the Silents.

In a story with an amped-up cool factor, Mark Sheppard as Canton Delaware III is the King of Cool. Canton's a cunning inversion of the lone outsider figure, who succeeds not because he plays by his own rules but because he's more progressive in his thinking than everyone else (in every respect). It could have been a hollow American parody were it not for Sheppard's incandescent charm. I love how he flirts with the Doctor in the Oval Office.

And, finally, Alex Kingston and Matt Smith are let loose, and you can see why their characters would hook up: it's the darkness in River that attracts her so to the Doctor. But the absolute revelation in this story is Karen Gillan, who manages to bring so much to Amy in both episodes, plumbing the depths of despair and fear, and engaging the audience in new and exciting ways. It's as though Gillan realized she needed to bring her game up to match Smith, Kingston and Darvill's work last season and decided to better them all. If so, job done.

So much of this story is, frustratingly, left unanswered and unresolved. But that's okay, for now, so long as we have as so many cool moments to make it worthwhile as we do here.

. . . .

The Doctor's Age

Just how old is the Doctor? In 1967's "The Tomb of the Cybermen," the second Doctor states definitively that he is 450 years old in "human terms." The third Doctor, in a conversation in 1970's "Doctor Who and the Silurians," implied that he had been a scientist for several thousand years (although he never actually says the word "years"). The fourth Doctor was 749 in 1976's "The Brain of Morbius" and bounced over and under the 750 year mark throughout stories broadcast in the late 1970s. The sixth Doctor was around 900 according to 1985's "Revelation of the Daleks" and the seventh Doctor was 953 in 1987's "Time and the Rani."

However, the Doctor is 900 years old in "Aliens of London," 903 in "Voyage of the Damned" and 906 in "The End of Time, Parts One and Two." In "The Impossible Astronaut," the Doctor is 1,103. So how do these reconcile? One possibility is that he's simply forgotten by now, which is what Steven Moffat has occasionally advocated, though it seems odd for the Doctor to claim he's hundreds of years younger than he actually is. He could also be lying about his age but, again, why increase the number sequentially at different times with people he's never met before?

However, since the changeover between the Classic Series and the New Series, it's possible that some big event occurred. Something with the power to change one's personal history. Something like a Time War.

What works especially well about this theory is that it gives the Doctor more autonomy, not less. So rather than being a woolly explanation — "Oh, he's really 1,286 in 'Voyage of the Damned,' he just forgot after all this time, so he's picking an arbitrary number" — it gives a concrete answer: the Doctor really is 903 in that story.

So there we have it. Thanks to Time War shenanigans, the Doctor was in his late 900s by the end of the Classic Series and is in his early 900s in the New Series. Sorted.

6.03 The Curse of the Black Spot

Written by Stephen Thompson **Directed by** Jeremy Webb

Supporting cast Hugh Bonneville (Henry Avery), Oscar Lloyd (Toby Avery), Lee Ross (boatswain), Michael Begley (Mulligan), Tony Lucken (DeFlorres), Chris Jarman (dancer), Carl McCrystal (McGrath), Lily Cole (the Siren), Frances Barber (Eye Patch Lady)

Original airdate May 7, 2011

The Big Idea Aboard a pirate ship, anyone with even the slightest injury is cursed with a black spot, caused by a mysterious being that rises from the waves.

Roots and References *Treasure Island* (the black spot); *Pirates of the Caribbean*; *Star Trek* (an apparently malevolent alien turns out to be a benign computer program, and the Siren resembles an evil version of the Emergency Medical Hologram from *Star Trek: Voyager*); Greek mythology (the Siren); *War of the Worlds* (Earth diseases killing aliens).

Adventures in Time and Space A spaceship in another dimension coexisting invisibly with ours also occurred in 1978's "The Stones of Blood." Captain Avery was mentioned in 1966's "The Smugglers," whose plot revolved around a search for Avery's treasure involving his former shipmates.

The Doctor Is Dead Effect The Eye Patch Lady appears in a gap in the hull of the pirate ship and says to Amy, "It's fine, you're doing fine, just stay calm." Immediately afterwards, the gap disappears. The Doctor rechecks Amy's pregnancy scan, which continues to offer both positive and negative results.

The Doctor and Amy Amy points out that the Doctor only calls her Amelia when he's concerned about her — a paternal trait that continues on from "Victory of the Daleks." She's right; the Doctor is worried about her (specifically about her indeterminate pregnancy) and Amy, for her part, is still troubled about the Doctor's impending death, only she doesn't know the Doctor's full name to call him by it.

Monster of the Week A virtual doctor from an alien ship, who appears in the form of a woman bathed in light. When you receive even the slightest injury, a black spot appears on your hand. She can pass through the gap between worlds using any reflective surface and charms her victims with a song, which is actually an anaesthetic.

Stand Up and Cheer Amy in pirate regalia is just glorious. She's feisty and looks fantastic. This is easily the most fun moment of the story.

Roll Your Eyes "We're shark bait, every single one of us, waiting until the wind changes," says one of the crew to another at the episode's outset, thus telling him something he already knows. Thanks for that, me hearty.

You're Not Making Any Sense This must be, without a doubt, the absolute worst example of CPR on television, ever. First of all, it's not a miraculous technique that cures all ills, it's a way to keep someone alive until more sophisticated help arrives. Secondly, Amy does a bare minimum amount of it. But worse than all that . . . they're *inside the TARDIS*. They don't have a defibrillator or some super-scientific device (like maybe a *sonic screwdriver*) that would resuscitate Rory?

Interesting Trivia Henry Avery is a historical figure. He was one of the most notorious pirates, one of the few who managed to retire with his loot and not get killed or arrested. Avery's capture of the *Ganj-i-Sawai*, a Muhgal ship where he found his biggest fortune (almost $200 million worth of goods, and that's not adjusted for inflation) was, from all accounts, blood-chilling, and it involved rape, torture and all manner of brutality — the sorts of things that depictions of pirates on film and television studiously avoid. "The Curse of the Black Spot" tries to provide motivation for Avery's departure from the navy and his turn to piracy as well as offer an explanation as to how Avery escaped being captured.

How can a 17th-century pirate fly a spaceship? This would be ridiculous if he were trying to operate 21st-century technology (give him a computer-driven passenger ferry and see how far he gets), but it's downright ludicrous when he learns to fly a futuristic spaceship after a few minutes of observing the Doctor in a wholly different sort of ship, one which he'd have no hope of understanding either.

The TARDIS Chronometer The TARDIS lands in the hold of the pirate ship *Fancy*, in the 17th century. It's then transported to the sick bay of an alien spaceship.

Cool? (RS?) Shiver me timbers, it's a pirate story. Hoist the mainsail, slap the scrubbers and move yer wooden legs, me hearties, because this is yer chance for buccaneerin' and adventure on the high seas, full of decadence, danger and debauchery! Arr.

Or not.

An important ingredient in any pirate story is fun. Big beards, pirate hats, planks and a wooden ship are the perfect recipe for nonstop entertainment.

Not on the ingredient list: darkness. If you're writing a tragic tale of a father betraying the trust of his dying son, don't set it aboard a pirate ship. Just don't.

What's more, following the heavy season opener, this was perfectly placed to be a light and frothy standalone episode. That it's not is a big mistake and one that's going to be a recurring problem this season. Done well, a dramatic tale can be very powerful, but this is anything but done well.

There are some nice moments, but they're few and far between. The Doctor blowing on the metal is pretty funny, while Amy rocks a pirate costume in a scene that should have been the template for the whole episode, rather than an aberration. A few of the pirate observations at the beginning have the potential to go somewhere, but they don't. And any lighting director worth his salt should have put his foot down and turned the lights up.

Instead, what we have is a schizoid story that's split between hiding on a pirate ship and bio-babble on an alien spacecraft. Neither is, in any way, compelling nor does it make much sense. If putting a lid on a barrel of water keeps the Siren out, then why not put the treasure in a box? Why does the Doctor (and other crew members) make only cursory attempts to stop anyone other than Rory from being taken? If it's that easy, why didn't the pirates hold back their comrades much earlier? Why do the earlier crewmembers end up in stasis beds when the Doctor, Amy and Avery are free to wander round?

The Doctor keeps being wrong about everything, which is supposed to be amusing but ends up just being annoying. And we get a message from Fred (where the script starts commenting on its own awfulness), when Amy says, "We stopped paying attention a while back." Indeed. Rory is quickly earning the title of *Doctor Who*'s Kenny, as he dies more and more frequently, with less and less payoff each time.

Worst of all is the resolution. Rory asks Amy to save him, on the basis that she'll never give up. After a clichéd CPR scene that could have come from any action thriller made in the '80s, Amy does indeed give up. This might be a subtle clue that something's different about Amy, feeding into the season arc. Or it might be poor writing. Then Rory comes back to life on his own for no discernable reason other than plot contrivance. This is bad, bad television.

The only interesting parts are those related to the arc. So we have a random moment of the Eye Patch Lady, which helps to make this story seem more important than it is. And, at the end, we realize that while Amy and Rory are keeping the Utah death a secret from the Doctor, he's keeping the secret about the pregnancy from them. It's a lovely parallel that serves to subtly push the TARDIS crew apart. No doubt this part was written by Steven Moffat, because it's heads and shoulders above anything else in the story.

"The Curse of the Black Spot" could so easily have been a fun, rollicking pirate story of hijinks on the high seas. Instead, it struggles to make a pirate story work and ends up turning into *Star Trek*. Neither of these things should ever happen on *Doctor Who*. Someone should have stepped in and put this out of its misery at the planning stage. Not fun.

Second Opinion (GB) Twenty questions about "The Curse of the Black Spot":

1) Does writer Steve Thompson, executive producer Steven Moffat and the entirety of BBC Wales really think the viewers are that stupid?

2) Did anyone involved in the making of this episode actually research what CPR is, much less watch it being done? (I would even accept watching an episode of *ER* as research.)

3) Which has the most rubbish, half-assed design for a spaceship set: this or "Victory of the Daleks"?

4) Does Amy actually hate Rory? She's pretty much ready to give up doing CPR after a couple of half-hearted set of compressions — even though every CPR procedure in the world states that you keep performing it until you're at the point of exhaustion.

5) For that matter, does the Doctor hate Rory? He can't even be bothered to help, even though every CPR procedure in the world states that if a second person is there they can trade off to ensure that neither party becomes exhausted too quickly.

6) Why did Steve Thompson allow his inner six-year-old to write the whole bit about alien bogeys? Because it's so gross I just fast-forward through it now.

7) Is the alien tech creating the Siren really so stupid as to not understand the concept of a minor cut?

8) Does the Doctor actually contribute in any way to this episode? As near as I can tell, he's wrong about nearly everything and off-loads Rory's care onto Amy.

9) Did the producers just simply think, "Who cares that Avery doesn't have much of a character? We have that sexy bloke from *Downton Abbey* playing him, with a sexy beard. No one will notice."?

10) Why not do more with Amy, in pirate gear, in charge?

11) Why a son? For the love of all that is holy. *Why a son?*

12) TARDIS. Time machine with super-science. Why does the Doctor leave it to CPR?

13) You have a wicked cool location for a pirate ship. Why set half the story on an alien spacecraft?

14) Is health care on other worlds so bad that its practitioners don't even use speech?

15) Is Avery's son so stupid that he stows away on a pirate ship without knowing it's a pirate ship?

16) How many times in this episode are we supposed to chalk things up to dramatic convenience?

17) Does Rory recover from drowning just to spite the Doctor and Amy?

18) Did Steve Thompson just write the happy ending and say, "They fly off into space even though they can't fly a ship and will probably continue to be pirates. Let's not think about it any more."?

19) Why do a story with the most credulity-stretching cuddly band of pirates ever? If they used even a tenth of the historical record, they could have had a story that was genuinely exciting.

20) I repeat: do they really think the viewers are that stupid?

6.04 The Doctor's Wife

Written by Neil Gaiman **Directed by** Richard Clark

Supporting cast Suranne Jones (Idris), Michael Sheen (voice of House), Paul Kasey (Nephew), Adrian Schiller (Uncle), Elizabeth Berrington (Auntie)

Original airdate May 14, 2011

The Big Idea In search of another Time Lord, the Doctor takes the TARDIS outside the universe, where a sentient asteroid puts the soul of the time machine into a woman.

Roots and References *Frankenstein* (the patchwork people); the Nicene Creed and other religious texts (the notion of a god from outside space and time becoming human); *Peter Pan* ("Did you wish *really* hard?"); *The World's Most Dangerous Game* (hunting Amy and Rory for the sport of it). The title is derived from a joke title the 1980s *Doctor Who* production office put on the schedule in order to root out leaks to the press.

Adventures in Time and Space The Doctor himself created a psychic cube in order to send out a distress signal to the Time Lords in 1969's "The War Games." The idea that TARDIS rooms could be deleted in order to create thrust was thoroughly demonstrated in 1982's "Castrovalva" (which featured the Doctor's companions struggling with the dilemma that they might delete the room they're in; the Doctor possibly added the hardwired failsafe that protected life forms as a result). House is full of rift energy ("Boom Town" onward). The

Cloister Bell (1981's "Logopolis" onward) rings when House first breaches the TARDIS. House feeds on Artron energy, the energy that drives the TARDIS (from 1976's "The Deadly Assassin").

Idris glows with regenerative energy ("The Christmas Invasion"). She calls the Doctor "thief," re-establishing the backstory that the Doctor stole the TARDIS ("The War Games" again). The Doctor states for the first time in over a season that he killed all the Time Lords ("Dalek" onward) and he's the last of their kind. The illusion Amy sees of an aged Rory points out that he was once again forced to wait thousands of years for her ("The Big Bang"). Amy's recollection of "delight" is her wedding day ("The Big Bang"). The Doctor attempts to open the TARDIS doors with a snap ("Forest of the Dead"); curiously though, he doesn't try the TARDIS key!

The Doctor points out to Idris he's changed the desktop theme of the control room ("Time Crash") a dozen times so far (various TARDIS remodellings since the 1970s) and has rebuilt the TARDIS console before (1983's "The Five Doctors"). Idris leads Amy and Rory to the archived control room that was destroyed in "The End of Time, Part Two." Upon discovering Nephew has been "redistributed" by the junk TARDIS's arrival, the Doctor remarks, "Another Ood I've failed to save" ("The Satan Pit"). The Doctor suggests taking Amy and Rory to the Eye of Orion, which is the most tranquil place in the universe, last seen in "The Five Doctors."

The Doctor Is Dead Effect Amy is still distracted by the Doctor's impending death. A dying Idris tells Rory, "The only water in the forest is the river." She says they'll need to know this one day . . .

Who is the Doctor? This story highlights the relationship of the Doctor with his TARDIS: he calls her "Sexy" (but only when no one is around). Finally able to talk with the TARDIS, the Doctor and Idris argue like an old married couple. He breaks down and cries for the first time in this incarnation at the prospect that he won't be able to talk with her anymore. Rory asks if the Doctor has his own room, but the answer is evident: he doesn't need one — he has the TARDIS.

The Doctor and Amy The Doctor knows Amy well enough that he's told her all about him being the last of the Time Lords at some point off screen. (The only time they spoke about it onscreen was when the Doctor dismissed it as "a bad day" in "The Beast Below.") Amy knows the Doctor well enough to tell him, "Don't get emotional. That's when you make mistakes." Amy and the Doctor both send Rory to take care of the other.

Monster of the Week House is a sentient asteroid. The Doctor suggests it's more like a sea urchin: the asteroid is a crust and a disembodied intelligence is inside.

It feeds off the rift energy from TARDISes. It sustains and controls the other inhabitants of the asteroid, using body parts from dead Time Lords to keep them alive, and it can transfer its intelligence inside the TARDIS.

Stand Up and Cheer Idris's final scene with the Doctor is beautiful. The Doctor's in tears, like a lost little boy, and Idris is struggling to find "a big, complicated word but so sad." And that word turns out to be *alive*.

Roll Your Eyes Rory is killed. Again. For the third time in three stories, and the fourth time overall. All we need is for Amy to turn to camera and say, "Oh my god, you killed Rory . . . you bastards!"

You're Not Making Any Sense Nothing about Idris makes sense. Why is she completely undamaged while Auntie and Uncle have almost none of their original body parts? And how can she contain a complex space-time entity like the TARDIS for so long, especially since removing it outright can blow a hole in the universe?

Interesting Trivia This story was written by a little known author named Neil Gaiman. We kid. Gaiman is an award-winning novelist, screenwriter and graphic novel writer whose works include *The Sandman*, *American Gods*, *Neverwhere*, *Coraline*, *Good Omens* and a whole lot more. Gaiman began blogging enthusiastically about the New Series shortly after its premiere and eventually met Steven Moffat just as Moffat was about to take over as executive producer, which led to an awkward conversation where Moffat asked, hypothetically, if he were to become producer if Gaiman would, hypothetically, be interested in contributing.

Idris chides the Doctor for pushing the TARDIS doors in instead of pulling them open, as the sign on the door instructs. And yet, to be utterly pedantic, the "pull to open" sign on the door is referring to the panel containing the telephone, not the door. Writer Neil Gaiman has subsequently acknowledged this but also pointed out that most metropolitan police boxes nonetheless opened their doors outward back in the day. Which may be true, but that's not what Idris said. In any event, the TARDIS doors opening inward was purely a production convenience: opening it inward meant it was easier to avoid showing the inside of the police box prop.

Petrichor is actually a relatively recent word, coined by Australian chemists Isobel Joy Bear and Robert G. Thomas in 1964 in an article in the scholarly journal *Nature* to describe a smell for what they term the "apparently unique odour which can be regarded as an 'ichor' or 'tenuous essence' derived from rock or stone."

The TARDIS constructed from junk was another winner from a *Blue Peter* contest. The contest asked viewers to design a TARDIS console using household items. The winning design by Susannah Leah, who was 12 at the time, includes skipping ropes, a miniature piano, a SatNav (that "sometimes gets things wrong") and implements for the Doctor to brew a cup of tea, including tea and milk contained in old telephone cables!

The TARDIS Chronometer Outside the universe (the Doctor metaphorically compares it to a little soap bubble on top of a soap bubble, only it's not) on the asteroid that contains House. Also within the universe, somewhere in deep space.

Cool? (GB) Welcome to the Neil Gaiman Episode (capital N, capital G, capital E) of *Doctor Who*. Richard Curtis was big, but Neil Gaiman is the first time a writer has the status of a special guest star. I say this because my one disappointment with "The Doctor's Wife" is that it feels too often like the Neil Gaiman Episode. Certainly the central conceit of this story is the sort of thing that only a writer of Gaiman's stature would be permitted to attempt. If Gaiman has only one shot at this, I would much rather see what he would do with an ordinary *Doctor Who* story with a monster, horror, comedy and all the usual trappings, instead of the all-important *Doctor Who* story that definitively addresses the mythos around the Doctor's relationship with the TARDIS.

That aside, it's magnificent. Indeed, the best moments of "The Doctor's Wife" are precisely those that involve a Gaimanesque take on the traditional *Doctor Who* format. Amy and Rory being hunted by House through the TARDIS is genuinely creepy (especially the scene where Amy reaches out through the dark to find the tentacles protruding from Nephew's head). The Doctor and Idris attempting to chase the TARDIS in a mini-TARDIS made of junk is quite exciting and funny (I love how Rory is considered "the pretty one" by Idris!). The Doctor's confrontation with Auntie and Uncle (itself a distorted, angry version of the Doctor's confrontation with the Atraxi in "The Eleventh Hour," right down to "Basically . . . run!") is powerful stuff.

I love Gaiman's innovation of having Idris experiencing everything out of sequence, as she reflects on actions that won't take place until much later and how that pays off brilliantly with her touching death scene that ends in her greeting the Doctor for the first time. Watching the Doctor and Idris bicker like an old married couple and then marvel at what they can do together plays exactly as you'd imagine, only you never thought such a scene could happen, much less work. That's good writing. It helps that Matt Smith and Suranne Jones have such delightful chemistry, and that the Doctor and Idris's relationship is multi-faceted: they're old lovers, they're a married couple, they're new friends, they're reckless adventurers, all at once. We know by now that's well within Matt Smith's range, and it's great to see Suranne Jones matching him quirk for quirk.

"The Doctor's Wife" is a love letter to *Doctor Who*. Not just '60s *Who*, which Gaiman grew up with (Gaiman has written about his love of "The War Games" before, and the psychic cubes were a nice shout-out to that) but to '80s *Who*, with references to deleting rooms (he even had the Zero Room in an earlier draft), and especially to the Russell T Davies era, with the Doctor telling House to fear him because he killed all the Time Lords. It's a potent reminder of the lonely God figure that has been largely abandoned by the new landlords, and its restatement is surprisingly powerful as a result.

"The Doctor's Wife" is the sort of script Matt Smith must love, as we get to see the Doctor in every possible emotional state, and Smith doesn't falter once. It's also great to see Karen Gillan and Arthur Darvill working together for a change; usually Amy and Rory are separated or thrown in with a lot of characters; we rarely see them alone together, and they make a lovely pairing.

About the only performance I disliked is Michael Sheen's House, but my problem isn't with the actor. If you're going to get someone of Michael Sheen's stature to voice a character for *Doctor Who*, don't put so much reverb and treatment on the voice that the actor is unrecognizable. I think Sheen would have been just fine unadorned, frankly.

If there has to be a story where the TARDIS incarnated into a real person and talked to the Doctor, I couldn't imagine a better-executed example of it anywhere. And the ending is stunning. I hope there's another Neil Gaiman episode (capital N, capital G, small e) down the road.

Second Opinion (RS?) "The Doctor's Wife" has garnered plaudits from all over fandom, not least of which comes courtesy of my co-author above. But I didn't like it and here's why.

The ideas on display here are brilliant . . . but they're a lot more brilliant when they're left in the background, as they have been for almost 50 years. The Doctor and the TARDIS have a special bond? Okay, sure, but I think that works better when it's just there. The TARDIS has been deciding the Doctor's journeys all these years? Again, a good idea, but so much more effective when left to the imagination. Having the TARDIS actually operate levers to indicate how sentient it is really demonstrates what didn't work for me: the story takes everything subtle about *Doctor Who* and puts it up on the screen.

The main plot wants to be a big, heartbreaking tragedy where the Doctor loses somebody incredibly important to him. That's a great idea. But it's lost under the weight of so many sci-fi MacGuffins that I found myself struggling to care. And so many things happen for plot convenience: Auntie and Uncle drop dead once the story's finished with them, the Doctor lets Idris out of the cage, and House both wants to leave (despite no hint of that beforehand) and turns moustache-twirlingly evil just for the sake of it. There's probably a great two-parter buried in here somewhere.

Even the production isn't immune. The climax involves a disembodied voice saying things like "No, no, that's hurting, no, stop," as though this were an amateur video production. The failsafe would have worked better for me as the climax's hinge if it had appeared (or even been mentioned) before and I found the Doctor crying to be strangely unaffecting. Even the title felt off: an in-joke that's too much "in" and not enough "joke."

"The Doctor's Wife" has things that I like — Auntie and Uncle's dialogue is hilarious, we finally get to see more of the TARDIS interior, there's a genuine sense of claustrophobia — but the parts never gelled. A shame, as I wanted to like it a lot more, but I just couldn't connect to it.

The Psychic Papers: The TARDIS

Fourteen minutes and 23 seconds into the first *Doctor Who* story, "An Unearthly Child," events take an unexpected turn. Up until then, two schoolteachers, Ian Chesterton and Barbara Wright, are trying to figure out their puzzling new student, Susan Foreman. They follow her to a junkyard at 76 Totters Lane where, inside, there's a police telephone box and a defensive old man. The teachers become convinced Susan is being locked in the police box, Barbara runs in to it . . . and ends up inside a futuristic spaceship.

With that, *Doctor Who* went from being ordinary, though odd, to something that was, literally, fantastic.

In the Classic Series, the TARDIS is bigger on the inside because it's dimensionally transcendental, which more or less means that the interior exists in a different dimensional space from the exterior. It's hard to say who came up with the idea; it was probably BBC head of drama Sydney Newman, who is often regarded as *Doctor Who*'s creator. Newman was also keen that, outwardly, the time machine used by the Doctor should look like a commonplace object. BBC documentation shows Newman rejecting the more high-concept idea of making the spaceship invisible, because he felt it needed to be a "tangible symbol" that was recognizable to people.

Anthony Coburn, who wrote "An Unearthly Child," is generally credited with the idea of using a police box. Designed in 1930 by Metropolitan Police engineer G. Mackenzie Trench, the police box was a common piece of "street furniture" in Britain in the days before two-way radios, and they were plentiful in 1963 as a means for officers to keep in touch with their headquarters. (Though not for long: they would be all but extinct by the end of the 1960s.) The TARDIS has the ability to blend in with its surroundings (using a system later named the chameleon circuit). However, in "An Unearthly Child," a fault in the Doctor's machine has caused it to be permanently stuck in the police box shape. That said, no version of the TARDIS has ever looked like an authentic police box; they tended to be taller and thinner than the TV version.

According to Susan, she came up with the nickname "TARDIS" from the initials of its full name: Time And Relative Dimension In Space. However, by the time the Doctor starts meeting other Time Lords in 1966's "The Time Meddler" and 1969's "The War Games," it's clear that other Time Lords call it the same; perhaps the acronym subsequently took off on Gallifrey? (Around 1965, the D started standing for "Dimensions." The original phrasing only returned because Christopher Eccleston insisted on it while making "Rose.") Technically, the Doctor's vessel was classified on Gallifrey as a TT Type 40, Mark 3 capsule. In "The War Games," "The Pirate Planet" and other stories, it's established that this particular capsule was antiquated and due to be retired when the Doctor stole it.

Time Lords use TARDISes to travel to other worlds and other times in order to observe them. They're research vessels, much like the bathyspheres used in Earth's oceans. As explained in 1978's "The Pirate Planet," TARDISes work by dematerializing from one place, navigating through the time vortex, and then rematerializing elsewhere. The ship doesn't technically fly, though it can do when the occasion is needed (such as in "The Runaway Bride"). According to "Journey's End," six Time Lords are needed to properly operate it; the reason the Doctor often has difficulty flying the ship is that he's doing the work of six people! Originally, the Doctor was unable to pilot the ship to any particular destination; over the succeeding centuries and incarnations, he has become better at controlling the TARDIS, though accuracy is still a challenge.

During the 26-year history of the Classic Series, the TARDIS interior more or less stuck to the original sets that BBC designer Peter Brachacki used in "An Unearthly Child": a bright, white control room with walls adorned by large circles ("roundels") and a six-sided console with a centre column (later called the "time rotor") that moved up and down when the TARDIS was in flight. During the Classic Series' 14th season (1976–1977), the Doctor briefly travelled in a secondary control room that was smaller and wood panelled. Brachacki's basic design was modified radically with the steampunk-influenced design of the 1996 TV Movie, and again with the coral and copper versions in the New Series. However, even those designs still use a six-sided console and roundels. The differences in control rooms were explained in "Time Crash" to be "desktop themes" that the Doctor can change when the mood strikes him, or following a catastrophic situation like the Doctor's regeneration blowing up the control room in "The End of Time, Part Two." In the New Series, the TARDIS console has made use of ordinary objects in its controls. Production personnel have suggested that this is because, following the Time War, the Doctor has no access to spare parts, so he has to jury-rig solutions using available junk.

The TARDIS interior was originally limited to a control room, a console and some "space age" sleeping quarters. The 1970s saw an expansion to reveal vast corridors; the TARDIS interior is, in fact, infinite. Over the years, many different rooms were introduced including the Cloister Room (which, in 1981's "Logopolis," contained, predictably, a cloister like those seen in colleges or universities; in the 1996 TV Movie, this was changed to a cavernous space that contained the TARDIS's link to the Gallifreyan Eye of Harmony), the Zero Room (used to heal the Doctor during acute regenerative crises, as seen in 1982's "Castrovalva"), as well as a TARDIS library, art gallery, swimming pool and separate personal rooms for the companions, which were introduced in the 1980s mostly to combat the optics of a younger-looking Doctor travelling with nubile females.

Originally, the TARDIS was simply a vehicle to take people to the setting of the next adventure and only seen at the start and finish of a story. During the 1960s, particularly, it was rare to see inside the TARDIS during a story. However, by the 1980s, more time was spent inside the TARDIS; its interior rooms became as much a setting as the places the Doctor travelled. When it began, the New Series primarily used the TARDIS as a vehicle; over the ensuing seasons, more action has taken place inside the ship. Surprisingly, little has been seen outside the control room, though it's been stated there are rooms for the companions, as well as mentions of a squash court, multiple bathrooms, the swimming pool and the library (in "The Eleventh Hour," the library was *in* the swimming pool). To date, the only other rooms seen in the New Series are a wardrobe ("The Christmas Invasion") and various corridors ("The Doctor's Wife").

The TARDIS is indestructible (or at least is supposed to be), and it has some unique features including the ability to turn invisible (1968's "The Invasion" and "The Impossible Astronaut"/"Day of the Moon") and to displace itself when faced with a threat (1968's "The Krotons"). It used to be powered by the Eye of Harmony, a black hole held in stasis by the Time Lords (a link to it is seen in the 1996 TV Movie), but in the New Series, it tends to use space-time rift energy as a fuel source. The TARDIS is powered through something called Artron energy.

Probably the best-known feature of the TARDIS is its distinctive sound for materializing. According to River Song in "The Time of Angels," this sound is made because the Doctor doesn't brake properly! In real life, the sound was created by BBC Radiophonic Workshop engineer Brian Hodgson, by running his house key up and down a set of piano strings. The recorded sound was slowed down, played backwards and further treated, creating the grating, engine-like noise still used decades later.

In both the Classic and New Series, the Doctor has always treated the TARDIS as though it were alive (the Doctor tends to call it "she" or "old girl") and certainly the ship has demonstrated at least semi-sentience on occasion. One conundrum of "The

Doctor's Wife" is whether Idris is the actual ship demonstrating its own sentience or simply the TARDIS using Idris's personality as a means of communicating. Either way, it's a reminder that the TARDIS is the true silent partner in the Doctor's adventures.

The TARDIS is an essential part of the *Doctor Who* mythos. It has become a part of the *Oxford English Dictionary* ("a building or container that is larger inside than it appears to be from outside") and its police box exterior has outlasted its real-life counterpart by several decades. But, at its heart, it is the wardrobe from Narnia, or the ordinary-looking magic door that takes us to see marvellous, miraculous sights. It's the ultimate product of the imagination, which is always bigger on the inside.

6.05—6.06 The Rebel Flesh / The Almost People

Written by Matthew Graham **Directed by** Julian Simpson

Supporting cast Mark Bonnar (Jimmy), Marshall Lancaster (Buzzer), Sarah Smart (Jennifer), Raquel Cassidy (Cleaves), Leon Vickers (Dicken), Edmond Moulton (Adam), Frances Barber (Eye Patch Lady)

Original airdates May 21 and 28, 2011

The Big Idea The Doctor goes on a mysterious mission to a remote acid factory in the future to find out more about the Flesh, fully programmable matter that creates "almost people" doppelgangers.

Roots and References *Blade Runner* (the Gangers have the same concerns about identity as the Replicants); *Moon* (clones doing expendable work in the future); *The Thing* (monsters posing as people); *The Name of the Rose* (the monastery setting); *Avatar* (the initial way the Gangers are used). Jimmy (and his Ganger) play "You Don't Have to Say You Love Me" by Dusty Springfield and Muse's "Supermassive Black Hole" plays in the TARDIS control room as Rory loses at darts.

Adventures in Time and Space While adjusting to his new body, the Ganger-Doctor experiences past regenerations, misquoting his first incarnation in 1963's "An Unearthly Child," citing the third Doctor's popular phrase ("reverse the polarity of the neutron flow") and speaking with the voices of the fourth Doctor ("Would you like a jelly baby?") and the tenth Doctor ("Hello, I'm the Doctor!"). The Doctor quizzes his Ganger about Cybermats (from 1967's "The Moonbase" and elsewhere). The Ganger-Doctor later insists on being called by his usual alias of John Smith.

The Doctor Is Dead Effect Thinking she's speaking to the Ganger-Doctor, Amy tells the real Doctor about his impending death. Amy twice sees the Eye Patch Lady in the monastery. The Doctor's real reason for visiting the monastery is to see the Flesh at an early stage of development, so he can figure out how to humanely sever the link between a Ganger and its human controller. It turns out that Amy is actually a Ganger; the real Amy is pregnant and her delivery is being supervised by the Eye Patch Lady.

The Doctor and Amy Amy is mistrustful of who she thinks to be the Ganger-Doctor, though when she's told the truth, she is gracious enough to tell the proper Ganger he's twice the man she thought he was. When the Doctor has to sever the connection to Amy's Ganger, the Doctor promises Amy he will find her.

Monster of the Week The Flesh is a liquid substance that is fully programmable matter. It replicates the form and mind of a human host, creating a Ganger (short for doppelganger). They're used as disposable substitutes for humans in dangerous jobs. In actuality, the Gangers are independent life forms that are having human personalities implanted on them. An accident keeps them alive, and one of them is capable of changing its physical form.

Stand Up and Cheer All the elements independently come together in the climax. The Doctor (who is disguised as his Ganger to infiltrate their camp) uses a phone call he placed earlier to Jimmy's son, because he believes it will restore Jimmy's sense of decency. And it does.

Roll Your Eyes At the point where Jennifer said she was too weak to open the valve and needed big strong Rory to help, Amy should have magically appeared in a good fairy costume and said, "You stupid idiot! She's obviously lying!"

You're Not Making Any Sense Just how does the Doctor experience the psychic pain of the Gangers more than his actual Ganger double? It's just for dramatic convenience: Amy needs to mistrust the man she considers to be the Doctor's duplicate.

Interesting Trivia One of the more subtle threads in the story is the backstory of Jennifer and her Ganger. Listen to her tell the story of being lost on the moors as a child and imagining a stronger version of herself who helped her get home: it's setting up the fact that Jennifer isn't altogether mentally stable and probably experienced a dissociative episode. Discovering she's a Ganger has probably led Jennifer to a full-on psychotic break. Which may explain why Ganger-Jennifer is capable of so much more than the other Gangers: physically (while Ganger-Cleaves twists her head around at one point, none of the other Gangers demonstrate the extreme shapeshifting that Ganger-Jennifer does), psychically (Ganger-Jennifer claims to be able to remember all the times her previous Ganger forms were killed) and psychologically (going so far as to create another Ganger of herself and then have it killed to gain Rory's trust — extremely sociopathic behaviour for someone who wants to liberate all Flesh life). Ganger-Jennifer becomes the "strong" Jennifer, whereas the original

Jennifer dies of exposure — what should have been the fate of the "weak" Jennifer on the moors all those years ago.

Just how does a solar tsunami work? It's supposed to be this intensive wave of solar radiation (that the TARDIS barely gets out of) and yet nothing gets burned and it doesn't seem to do anything else very deadly aside from frying the monastery's electronics. So why not call it a "solar flare" and be done with it?

Rory remarking on his mum loving Dusty Springfield is a sign of how things have shifted with the change from Russell T Davies to Steven Moffat: families were sacrosanct under the Davies regime; every companion had a family that featured frequently. We've never seen Amy's restored family beyond their cameo in the coda of "The Big Bang" and this is the first time Rory's family has been mentioned at all.

The TARDIS Chronometer A monastery on an isolated island sometime in the 22nd century. At the end of the story, the TARDIS visits Jimmy's home and the corporate headquarters of Morpeth Jetsan.

Cool? (GB) No *Doctor Who* story in the New Series has frustrated me more than "The Rebel Flesh" and "The Almost People." It honestly had the potential to be the best story of the season, if not one of the all-time greats. But the potential gets squandered in all sorts of preventable ways.

The main problem is it lets so much rest on its high concept: disposable clones have to face down their human masters and determine for themselves what makes them human. Questions of identity and memory and what makes an individual life unique work in art-house science-fiction films like *Moon*, *Blade Runner* and *Never Let Me Go*; in a fast-paced adventure television series, the high concept sort of gets lost in translation.

It's not for want of trying: one Doctor played by Matt Smith is a lot of fun, but who knew how much better it would be with two? The rapid-fire banter between the pair is great, as they finish each other's sentences and admire the other (it's even better when you consider Matt Smith effectively had to play the same scene twice). But, while entertaining, this actually exacerbates the problem: the twist that the Doctor was his Ganger all along may show how Gangers can be wonderful, but it should have also raised the question of what makes someone unique.

There's a similar distancing with the Ganger-Jennifer. All the clues are there: this sweet woman is actually mentally unbalanced, and the experience of being a Ganger has made her psychotic. More could have been done to convey this: more shown from her point of view, the extent of her rising madness revealed, other characters reflecting on it or discovering the real Jennifer was on medication. As it is, no one even wonders why Jennifer alone can change her form in such extreme ways, and Rory doesn't experience any real sense of betrayal from the woman he's been protecting. It's a wasted opportunity; we could have had a compelling antagonist instead of this merely curious dissonance that the nicest human is the meanest Ganger.

All these facets conspire to make the war between the humans and the Gangers seem perfunctory. Cleaves just sort of grouchily comes in the room and kills Ganger-Buzzer, and everyone agrees it's kind of, sort of us versus them now. With everything emotional kept at a distance, the ramp up needed to make this a war between equals fizzles. It's all oddly antiseptic.

Plus there are all these random details that go nowhere, such as the eyes in the walls and Dicken's cough. I suspect there were more connections lost in the edit room. That's a pity if it's true.

Because — argh! — so much of it is right. The cast is perfect. Raquel Cassidy's sarcastic charm (which made her relationship with Matt Smith so winning in *Party Animals*) is perfect for Cleaves. Marc Bonner is lovely in the scene where, dying, he bequeaths his life to his Ganger. Even if all Marshall Lancaster does is reprise his role from *Life on Mars*, he does it well. Julian Simpson's direction is among the best this season. Best of all, Matthew Graham writes beautifully for the Doctor. I love how the Doctor detects the tsunami using a snowglobe and casually determines Cleaves is a Ganger by using a microwaved meal. And Graham's dialogue for both Doctors just sparkles.

The final cliffhanger, which reveals the Doctor's agenda, is incredible, and Matt Smith is astounding as he summons up the courage to kill Amy's Ganger. In many ways, the cliffhanger is another big problem, eclipsing everything that came before it.

If more had been done to make connections and bring the audience into the drama as opposed to just showing it at a remove, "The Rebel Flesh"/"The Almost People" would be the standout of the season. As it is, it's close but not quite near enough.

Second Opinion (RS?) First things first: who the hell would mine for acid? Are there chemistry labs the world over in desperate need?

This is a workmanlike story written around two fabulous cliffhangers. The first is an excellent twist that genuinely forces the story to the next level. A fairly generic tale of copies wanting to be human becomes more personal and layered when the Doctor is duplicated, leading to such twists as the two Doctors swapping roles.

However, it's with the second cliffhanger that the story really ascends. Unlike last year's twist at the end of "Cold Blood," this isn't just a tacked-on shock of an ending but the culmination of so much that came before. By the time it hits, we know the full implications of Amy being a Ganger, and it also wraps up the various glimpses of the Eye Patch Lady and Amy's Schrödinger pregnancy. It also explains why the first half of the season has done almost nothing with Amy and Rory, despite a married couple on board the TARDIS being a new direction for the show.

What's cleverest of all is the Doctor's foreknowledge. Looking back, you see that the entire story has been about the Doctor investigating the early Gangers to find an effective and humane way to kill Ganger-Amy. It's a shocking scene: he encouraged all other Gangers to work out their differences with their counterparts and to embrace life; with Ganger-Amy, he's cold-hearted and ruthless. We know that the Gangers have every right to live, yet the Doctor denies Ganger-Amy that existence. In among the various shocks that the last few minutes throw at us, this may be the most shocking of all.

The remainder of the story feels far too generic to be worthy of a two-parter. The characters are fairly dull, so much is left unaddressed and the resolution is entirely too pat, both in the cliché of Jimmy's son and the fact that no character has both the original human and the Ganger surviving, because that would make things too challenging. However, it's almost worth sitting through the clichés for the middle cliffhanger and then entirely worth it for the final one. The major beats of the story are well plotted, for maximum impact. It's just a shame about the minor ones.

6.07 A Good Man Goes to War

Written by Steven Moffat **Directed by** Peter Hoar

Supporting cast Alex Kingston (River Song), Frances Barber (Madame Kovarian), Charlie Baker (Fat One), Dan Johnston (Thin One), Christina Chong (Lorna Bucket), Joshua Hayes (Lucas), Damian Kell (Dominucus), Neve McIntosh (Madame Vastra), Catrin Stewart (Jenny), Richard Trinder (Captain Harcourt), Annabel Cleare (Eleanor), Henry Wood (Arthur), Dan Starkey (Commander Strax), Simon Fisher-Becker (Dorium Maldovar), Danny Sapani (Colonel Manton), Hugh Bonneville (Henry Avery), Oscar Lloyd (Toby Avery), Nicholas Briggs (Cybermen voice), Harrison and Madison Mortimer (Baby Melody Pond)

Original airdate June 4, 2011

The Big Idea The Doctor raises an army to retrieve Amy and her baby.

Roots and References *Lord of the Rings* (raising an army of different races); *Ocean's Eleven* (a mastermind brings together a gang to pull off a heist); Sun Tzu's *The Art of War* (controlled planning for a decisive victory); *Thunderbirds* (Madam Vastra's driver is named Parker).

Adventures in Time and Space This episode features the parallel Earth Cybermen

("Rise of the Cybermen" et al.), now controlling a vast space fleet; a Silurian ("The Hungry Earth"/"Cold Blood"); a Sontaran ("The Sontaran Stratagem"/ "The Poison Sky"); River's prison ship ("The Time of Angels" et al.); Dorium and the Maldovarium ("The Pandorica Opens"); Judoon ("Smith and Jones" et al.); and Danny Boy and his space planes ("Victory of the Daleks"). The clerics of Demon's Run are the same order we saw in "The Time of Angels"/"Flesh and Stone."

There are references to the Untempered Schism ("The Sound of Drums"), the Doctor calling the Atraxi back to Earth ("The Eleventh Hour"), sexy fish vampires ("The Vampires of Venice"), Rory being dead and not existing ("Cold Blood"), Rory being plastic ("The Pandorica Opens") and the Doctor rebooting the universe ("The Big Bang").

The Doctor Is Dead Effect Amy has been on Demon's Run since before Utah, but she was mentally experiencing what her Ganger experienced. Her visions of the Eye Patch Lady, now known to be the human leader of the enemy forces, Madame Kovarian, were reality bleeding through.

River Song is revealed to be Melody Pond, Amy's daughter. As a baby, she was kidnapped by Madame Kovarian's forces; she grows up to become the girl in the astronaut suit.

Who is the Doctor? He's angry about what happened to Amy and notes that this is a new feeling (perhaps just for his eleventh incarnation). When Madame Kovarian says that good men need rules, he corrects her, pointing out that good men don't need rules, which is why he has so many. He also faces the realization that his reputation has preceded him in both dangerous and disturbing ways.

The Doctor and Amy He raises an army to find her and tells Colonel Runaway that she's one of the people he loves. Although Amy knows he wasn't directly responsible for the baby being kidnapped a second time, she nevertheless still blames him.

Monster of the Week The Headless Monks wear hoods to cover the fact that their heads have been removed, leaving only a tied-off stump at the neck (although the hoods still maintain the shape of a head). Without a head, they cannot be persuaded of anything.

Stand Up and Cheer Rory, in his centurion outfit, boards a Cybership and faces down a group of armed Cybermen, saying he has a question and a message from the Doctor. After Rory asks where Amy is, while standing in front of a window looking onto a vast Cyberlegion, the Cybermen want to know what the message is. Immediately, we see most of their ships explode, whereupon Rory asks, "Would you like me to repeat the question?" In an episode full of breathtaking moments, this one would be fantastic if it were the Doctor confronting the Cybermen. That it's Rory is just sublime.

Roll Your Eyes Many fans at *Doctor Who* conventions are involved with cosplay (where people dress up like characters from the show). One look at the lesbian Silurian and her Victorian housemaid and you can't help but wonder if they were created for convention cosplay first, with plot mechanics to be worked out later.

You're Not Making Any Sense There's a surprise reveal of Captain Avery and his son Toby, from "The Curse of the Black Spot." However, at the end of that story, Toby was attached to a breathing tube and would die if he ever left the medical ship. So how is he alive — and tubeless — on Demon's Run?

Interesting Trivia When exactly were the Amys swapped? The Doctor states that it occurred "before America," and indeed there was a long period of time when Amy and Rory were at home, as we saw at the beginning of "The Impossible Astronaut." It would make sense that the swap occurred then. But see "Closing Time" for some potential implications of this.

Gangers are controlled by the original via telepathic remote control. So how does a Ganger baby work, exactly? We can speculate that in the intervening centuries — this adventure takes place several thousand years after the early Gangers we saw in the previous episode — the technology improves. Certainly, the Amy and Melody Gangers had no trouble maintaining their human appearance, as the earlier Gangers did. This would also explain why neither the original Amy nor baby Melody needed to be wired into a harness.

We're told that the written word takes longer to translate than the spoken word when run through the TARDIS translation matrix. This doesn't quite jibe with what we've seen before, such as the Doctor reading River's graffiti in "The Pandorica Opens" as soon as the TARDIS materializes. It makes some sense that the TARDIS wouldn't translate Gallifreyan (Time Lords wouldn't need their own language translated for them and probably wanted to keep their written language secret from outsiders), but it's a bit of a mystery why the ship has so many problems with the (very simple) language of the Gamma Forest. What's even more surprising is just how it managed to translate at all, given that the TARDIS has dematerialised before the words resolve themselves.

In January 1995, Steven Moffat posted the following to the *Doctor Who* Usenet newsgroup rec.arts.drwho (at the time the equivalent of an online forum like Gallifrey Base today): "Here's a particularly stupid theory. If we take 'The Doctor' to be the Doctor's name — even if it is in the form of a title no doubt meaning something deep and Gallifreyan — perhaps our earthly use of the word 'doctor' meaning healer or wise man is direct result of the Doctor's multiple interventions in our history as a healer and wise man. In other words, we got it from him. This is a very silly idea and I'm consequently rather proud of it." It only took 16 years for this theory to find its way into the show.

This episode formed a cliffhanger, of sorts, before a mid-season break. Although not the first part of a two-parter, it nevertheless left several plot threads (mainly around what happens to Melody/River) hanging. Viewers had a break of almost three months, which was unprecedented in *Doctor Who*'s history, to wonder about River's revelation. Although we can't help but think the cliffhanger from the previous episode would have had an even stronger impact.

The TARDIS Chronometer Demon's Run; aboard a Cybership 20,000 light years away; London, 1888; the Battle of Zarathustra, 4037 A.D.; the Maldovarium (said to be 5145 in "The Pandorica Opens"). Since Dorium sold parts to the Headless Monks, it's likely that the Demon's Run segment is contemporaneous, making it the 52nd century.

Cool? (RS?) "A Good Man Goes to War" is another Moffat spectacular, full of sensational set pieces, big action and witty dialogue. It also has the puzzle box nature of its fellows, but this time it contains the solution, not the mystery. And the wonderful thing about Moffat is that he's thought through his solutions, making them just as satisfying as his mysteries are intriguing.

It's also a story that, fundamentally, is about the Doctor. Yes, it's a big game-changing mid-season finale, but it's also interested in asking questions about what makes the Doctor tick. So when the Doctor rises so high, it is ostensibly via organizing an enormous army to go to war, but what makes this special is the fact that the war is almost entirely bloodless. In any other sci-fi or action series, the climactic battle with two enormous armies would feature explosions, deaths of important characters and perhaps a musing on the tragedy and inevitability of war. But *Doctor Who*'s hero is, at the end of the day, a man of peace. When he takes down an enormous army — whose sole purpose is to kill him — using words and trickery, it's a moment to realize that compassion is better than strength, that intelligence beats violence and that *Doctor Who* is a very special show indeed.

"The Doctor will rise higher than ever before and then fall so much further." This is the central line of the episode, and it had a lot of people very confused. The Doctor rising so high isn't so mysterious, although people did wonder if a few Silurians getting shot really qualified as the promised war of the title. But when did the Doctor fall? In losing a baby that he quickly learns will be just fine? In the next episode to air, 12 weeks later, assuming what we just saw was actually a cliffhanger?

The Doctor's fall comes not from the plot mechanics but from character.

It's important to remember who delivers that fateful line: River Song, someone who deliberately stays away from the main action and who cares deeply about the Doctor. She obviously knows the baby will be fine (she's even the one who tells him that), and the only part of the war she witnesses is the mopping up.

Everything about the fall centres on Lorna Bucket (from the Gamma Forest) and her limited language. It's her mistranslation that gives River her name, and Lorna believes that "doctor" means "great warrior," thanks to the Doctor's interventions on her planet. This leads to the Doctor's fall; it's not losing something in a fight, it's gaining a reputation as a man of war. The Doctor fights in the name of good, but he fights nevertheless. He's not a pacifist who allows himself to be overrun, but rather he's a very contradictory makeup of someone decent and moral, who abhors violence and never carries a gun, but still manages to best his enemies in every battle. After a while, this sort of thing tends to tarnish your reputation.

Tying that in with the Doctor's forthcoming death — which he now knows about — and you can see where it all collapses for him. His impact on the universe hasn't always been positive and that disturbs him deeply. Truly, he's never risen so high, nor fallen so far.

The entire buildup to the battle, while spectacular, really is just the Doctor giving the word and everybody leaping in behind him. His fame has spread so far and wide that people are desperate just to catch a glimpse of him and will gladly go to their deaths at the mention of his name. It's also what motivated Amy's kidnapping in the first place. The clerics want a Time Lord as a weapon and they go to enormous lengths to create River Song, thus hurting the Doctor where he's most vulnerable. His reputation brings unforeseen consequences for him and for those he cares about.

This thread is an outgrowth of the Russell T Davies era, where the Doctor's impact on events became more noticeable. Alien invasions were foiled, but the world learned of them. The Doctor started claiming authority in a way he never had before. The early Moffat stories continued this theme, with multiple stories resolved with the Doctor simply saying, "Don't you know who I am?" (which gets an explicit shout-out here, when the married soldiers mention the Atraxi). In the best Moffat style, the seeds were sown a very long time ago.

The revelation about who River is comes at the perfect time. It makes sense to tie this off before it stopped being mysterious and started being infuriating. That the resolution feels inevitable once revealed is a testament to the strength of the writing, which gradually led us to this place where the pieces all slot together. What's amazing is that when you rewatch previous River stories with this knowledge, they not only make perfect sense but extra layers are visible.

Credit has to go to Alex Kingston, who clearly knew who her character was from the beginning, because she shades those earlier performances with just the right emotion that it pays off magnificently upon rewatching.

"A Good Man Goes to War" is the culmination of a number of long-term plot and character arcs. It's filled with spectacle, which makes it appealing to the casual viewer (and will have many diehard fans punching the air on several occasions), but it's also a hugely important story, both in terms of what we've already seen and what's to come. Pivotal, in every sense of the word.

Second Opinion (GB) What complete and utter tommy-rot. My co-author may well be right that the Doctor's rise and fall is about his bloodless coup and tattered reputation, but who cares? The hype fails to connect to the experience. It's all about the *idea* of how far you can rise and the *idea* of how far you can fall. Ideas are now more important than visceral, exciting, emotional experiences, and, to me, that is what's so wrong with *Doctor Who* right now.

There's no real cost or consequence for the Doctor's "fall." He looks a bit put out, has a bit of a bust up with River and then picks up and leaves as though everything is okay just because Melody turns out fine several decades later. Worse, Amy is upset at losing her baby, pushes the Doctor away and then when told by Jenny that it's not the Doctor's fault, *she agrees*. It's a moment that defies rationality, dramatic sense, emotional reality *and the actual plot of the story*. And it means the Doctor skates away scot-free from even more consequences.

It's as though *Doctor Who* has become *Seinfeld* with its no-hugging, no-learning outlook on life. (Only it keeps the hugging.) I don't mind the Doctor discovering the disastrous results of his reputation; I just want it to matter to him in some way, shape or form. As it is, he looks vaguely saddened by Lorna's death, I guess. Maybe that will have to do.

The crazy thing is, I liked a lot about "A Good Man Goes to War." The opening 15 minutes are like those homemade trailers you see on YouTube where a montage of crucial scenes allow you to infer everything else that is supposed to happen in the movie. It's a fascinating, almost pointillist form of television that works remarkably well: we never see the full story of Madame Vastra or Strax or the Doctor's hunt for Amy with the Cybermen, but we know it all the same.

The other wonderful thing is how this story single-handedly redeems Neve McIntosh and Dan Starkey's reputations after "The Hungry Earth"/"Cold Blood" and "The Sontaran Stratagem"/"The Poison Sky," respectively. McIntosh's Vastra is so great I'd be happy for a spinoff with her any day. Starkey's Strax is my favourite portrayal of a Sontaran in the New Series, possibly because it's so brilliantly removed from a typical Sontaran, and Starkey makes the idea of a

Sontaran forced to perform a penance as a nurse just work. To top it off, Matt Smith gets a really great moment as the Doctor's anger briefly gets the better of him, and Arthur Darvill rocks every scene he's in.

But ultimately "A Good Man Goes to War" is a hollow confection. The cliffhanger should be an "*OH!*" moment, but it's just an "oh" moment. And with no one to actually condemn the Doctor, he is left with the revelation that his reputation is not the one he wants. Ho, as they say, hum.

6.08 Let's Kill Hitler

Written by Steven Moffat **Directed by** Richard Senior

Supporting cast Nina Toussaint-White (Mels), Caitlin Blackwood (Amelia Pond), Maya Glace-Green (Young Mels), Ezekiel Wigglesworth (Young Rory), Philip Rham (Zimmerman), Richard Dillane (Carter), Amy Cudden (Anita), Davood Ghadami (Jim), Ella Kenion (Harriet), Albert Welling (Adolf Hitler), Mark Killeen (German officer), Paul Bentley (Professor Candy), Eva Alexander (nurse), Tor Clark (female teacher)

Original airdate August 27, 2011

The Big Idea The TARDIS crashes in Hitler's Berlin office, which makes it a lucky day for the robot seeking to kill the universe's greatest war criminal.

Roots and References *InnerSpace* (the crew of the Teselecta); the British comic strip *The Numskulls* (a bunch of little people controlling a bigger one); *Inglourious Basterds* (River's rampage across Nazi Berlin); *The Princess Bride* (the Doctor pretending his legs work) and *Back to the Future* (Mels bringing together her own parents). For the second time this season, *The Graduate* gets quoted ("Hello, Benjamin"; River even parodies Anne Bancroft's famous pose).

Adventures in Time and Space Young Amelia Pond ("The Eleventh Hour" and elsewhere) is seen in flashback and also as the TARDIS interactive voice interface. Other options for the interface include Rose, Martha and Donna, all rejected by the Doctor because of the guilt they invoke in him. Mels regenerates in the same manner we've seen since "The Parting of the Ways." The Doctor mentions "The Vampires of Venice" ("That's a belter") to the dying Mels.

River's body is capable of surviving a hail of bullets as she's within the first 15 hours of her regeneration, as established in "The Christmas Invasion." The TARDIS shows River how to fly it, which tallies with her quip in "The Time of Angels" that the Doctor wasn't there when she learned how to operate it. The Doctor wears his tux from Amy and Rory's wedding ("The Big Bang") and starts telling River a series of rules about him, chiefly, "Rule 1: The Doctor lies" (as River herself notes in "The Big Bang" and elsewhere). He gives River the diary she uses to note her encounters with the Doctor ("Silence in the Library"/"Forest of the Dead" onward).

The Doctor lies about the TARDIS control room operating in a state of temporal grace where guns can't be fired (1976's "The Hand of Fear" and elsewhere, though back then the lie worked). The deadly smoke coming from the damaged console is probably mercury vapour (1968's "The Wheel in Space"). The Teselecta crew use a compression field to miniaturize themselves; the Slitheen use similar technology to fit into their skinsuits ("Aliens of London"/"World War Three"). Rory is still driving his Mini Cooper ("The Eleventh Hour").

The Doctor Is Dead Effect As the girl in the astronaut suit, Melody Pond regenerated into a toddler at the end of "Day of the Moon." She called herself Mels and grew up with Amy and Rory in Leadworth (thus causing the paradox that Melody is actually named after herself). Mels regenerates again into the woman the Doctor and his companions know as River Song. Melody/River was programmed by the Silence to kill the Doctor; it's confirmed by the crew of the Teselecta that River is the person in the astronaut suit who kills him in Utah.

The Doctor's death at Lake Silencio in Utah is a fixed point in time ("The Fires of Pompeii" and others), which means it's an event that cannot be altered. According to the Teselecta's databank, the Silence is a religious order, which believes that "silence will fall when the question is asked." The question itself, however, is unknown: it is the first and oldest question, and it's hidden in plain sight.

The Doctor and Amy Poisoned, the Doctor imagines young Amelia saying "fish fingers and custard," and he finds the strength to save Amy, Rory and River. Amy calls the Doctor her best friend, and as a child she described the Doctor to Mels as "funny" as opposed to "hot," which says a lot about how she sees him.

Monster of the Week The Teselecta is a robot that is operated by 423 miniaturized humans. It can change its shape to look like anyone. Inside the Teselecta are robotic antibodies that kill anyone who doesn't have permission to be on board.

Stand Up and Cheer The montage showing Amelia growing up with Mels and Rory is an amazing sequence that shows, in an astonishingly short time, everything you need to know about Amy and Mels' relationship, and Mels' character. As an added bonus, we see the moment Amy finally realized Rory was in love with her. The sequence is even better (if not mind-blowing) knowing that Mels is actually Melody/River.

Roll Your Eyes We find out giant swathes of information about the Silence, what they're up to and how it all relates to the ongoing story arc . . . not in a story with the Silence, but in a five-minute conversation where the Teselecta info-dumps everything the viewer needs to know. It's inelegant, to put it politely; utterly rubbish, if we're brutally honest.

You're Not Making Any Sense The Doctor points out the silliness of the Teselecta's premise — they travel back in time to kill dead people — but Carter's explanation that they simply arrive near the end of criminals' timelines to torture them doesn't hold much water, either. Especially when you consider they killed Zimmerman without so much as checking his death-date and similarly attempted to dispatch River without any analysis when in her timeline she was . . . though apparently this matters enough to not kill Hitler in 1938.

Interesting Trivia Mels' regeneration reveals some new facts about the process. First of all, we have the first onscreen confirmation that skin colour is among the physiological traits that can change. The Doctor had already indicated in *The Sarah Jane Adventures* story "Death of the Doctor" that he could regenerate as "anything I like," but this is the first time we've seen it. Perhaps a black Doctor isn't far off . . .

Melody/River also notes in passing that she can knock a few years off her age ("just to freak people out," which is probably a nod to fans who complain that River looks younger when she dies in "Forest of the Dead" than she does currently), which must have come in handy since she regenerated into a toddler in early 1970 at the end of "Day of the Moon" but still looked like a kid with Amy and Rory in the 1990s.

Just who runs the Teselecta, anyway? Carter claims they're agents of a "Justice Department" with a mission to travel through time, find criminals near the end of their timelines and "give them hell." To what end? Up until this point in the New Series, the only people who can travel through time are the Time Lords (who are all but gone), the Daleks (who are busy exterminating everyone), the mysterious Time Agency (that Captain Jack was at one point a member of back in "The Empty Child") and, judging from the Time Engine used in "The Lodger" and "The Impossible Astronaut," the Silence. Is the Justice Department part of the Time Agency? Or is it a new player on the scene with the means of time travel? Time (and Steven Moffat no doubt) will tell . . .

The TARDIS Chronometer The Doctor meets Rory, Amy and Mels in a field near Leadworth in the present day, and they travel back to Berlin, 1938. The Doctor takes River to recuperate in 5128 where she decides to study archaeology at the Luna University.

Cool? (GB) Finally. Just when we've had enough relentlessly grim stories in succession, we have some *fun*. Series Six starts with the Doctor being killed and winds its way through enough angst, death and misery to make the David Tennant era positively cheery by comparison. (And let's not forget, my co-author's ridiculous opinion aside, that even the Christmas special was a joyless machination.)

Enough of that. "Let's Kill Hitler" is almost insanely goofy. From the awesome title to the setting in the Nazi *Wehrmacht* where Hitler is immediately locked in a cupboard to the outlandish idea of the Teselecta (where "I have eyeball" has a totally different meaning), this is the story which rediscovers that *Doctor Who* can be scary and horrific but it's also supposed to be bright, colourful and wildly giddy. It is something I didn't think possible any more: it's a romp.

If this episode had been in the Russell T Davies era, it would have been the loose, frothy season opener. In the new regime, its position has been flipped with the darker, more adult two-part story in the second half of the season. Which may be why "Let's Kill Hitler" is so welcome. In the past, seasons built towards a more mature, ambitious story. Here, we've been living in its shadow. That's not necessarily a bad thing, but it might explain why this episode works so well. It's an exciting, funny kick-off to the second half of the season.

Steven Moffat once told me in an interview, "*Doctor Who* is not a comedy, but it has the grace of one." With this story, he remembers that axiom. Moffat recycles a gag from his 1999 *Doctor Who* Comic Relief sketch with the Doctor upstaging all of River's murder attempts, but it's still bloody hilarious. The Teselecta is a licence to print jokes. The very idea of a *Star Trek* bridge that actually controls a walking, talking, shape-shifting robot is great, and it's topped by all these brilliant throwaway gags, like Harriet needing to check Zimmerman's skintone because they accidentally made Rasputin green, and "Time can be rewritten. Remember Kennedy?"

And the dialogue. Oh my word. The "gay Gypsy bat mitzvah" line would be the funniest of the season were it not for Rory's line 20 minutes later: "Okay, I'm trapped inside a robot replica of my wife. I'm really trying to not see this as a metaphor." Rory definitely gets all the best gags in this episode.

The unfolding antics contain all the heavy lifting this story does with the season arc. Some of the necessary exposition is poorly done — Teselecta-Amy might as well have provided a PowerPoint presentation on the Silence, complete with bullet points; at least that would have been more televisual — but overall it hits emotionally resonant moments. In particular, when the Doctor does everything in his power to see that recently regenerated psychotic killer Melody Pond becomes River Song, it's really quite touching. Like everything that works in this episode, the success of the storyline begins with comedy — the Doctor shows off for the Teselecta that he's actually okay — before moving into pathos: by almost dying, the Doctor shows River how to be a better person.

If there's a problem with "Let's Kill Hitler," it's that, for such an arc-heavy, continuity-heavy episode, there is an appalling lack of consequences following from "A Good Man Goes to War." Amy seems more annoyed that the Doctor hasn't checked in, rather than out of her mind with worry that her daughter is lost. The case could be made that Amy didn't know she was pregnant and didn't bond with her daughter, so perhaps, for that reason, she's perfectly okay that she won't raise her and will only know Melody as her childhood friend (even though Melody befriended them in a plot to kill the Doctor).

But that analysis is awfully hard to swallow. The truth is, Amy and Rory have lost their child, and, regardless of them knowing who she grows up to be, there should be some kind of consequence, some kind of development in Amy and Rory's relationship with the Doctor. But Amy is unchanged. Rory is unchanged. The Doctor is unchanged. The only person who matures is River, and that's out of plot necessity, so the character can go from point A in the "The Impossible Astronaut"/"Day of the Moon" to point B as the River Song we know and love. Either that's dreadful drama more interested in the timey-wimey gimmick than real emotional resonance, or Amy, Rory and the Doctor are sociopaths who live without any sense of affect. It's honestly hard to decide which it is sometimes.

The fact that "Let's Kill Hitler" can hide this gaping problem is a sign of how funny and delightful it is. I wish there were more of these purely entertaining stories in this season, but I'm still waiting for one that's both entertaining and honest.

Second Opinion (RS?) At last. After a half-season of almost unrelenting bleakness, we finally have a story that's not just fun, it's utterly gonzo. You have to sit back and enjoy the ride on this one, because there's really no other way to experience it. From Rory's strange day to River choosing a new outfit, this is an episode that does the unexpected and makes it hilarious, over and over again. Hell, it's an episode set in the Nazi regime with "Hitler" in the title — and yet it's an out-and-out comedy. Why does the Doctor change into a top hat and tails when he only has minutes to live? I have no idea, but who cares, it's that kind of episode.

There are so many things I love about "Let's Kill Hitler," from the crop circle summoning of the Doctor and the hilarious Leadworth flashbacks to the Doctor disarming the guns and Nina Toussaint-White's performance as Mels. The conceit of having an episode where they go back in time to meet Hitler and then lock him in a cupboard for the duration is just bonkers. And then there's the Teselecta, just about the most brilliantly nuts idea in the history of everything.

In fact, the only odd thing about it is the attempt to weave a serious story through the middle. The Doctor is saved because he demonstrates compassion to and love for River, which inspires her to make an enormous sacrifice for him.

That's a lovely story . . . but wouldn't it have been so much better if we'd stuck with the psychopathic River for at least another episode and delivered that resolution next time? The way it plays here, her turnaround barely feels earned; consequently, the enormity of her sacrifice doesn't resonate. Essentially, she's a bit loopy for a few minutes, before becoming the River we know.

Oh, and when River kisses the Doctor a second time, why doesn't it kill him all over again? Are we supposed to presume that River took the time to wipe off her poisonous lipstick in the middle of one of the most dangerous eras in human history, when a stealth weapon might come in handy? It's telling, I think, that it's the serious bits in this episode are the most illogical. Or perhaps it's just that their flaws aren't covered by comedy.

"Let's Kill Hitler" is an unbelievably welcome breath of fresh air. If Series Six had been a whole season of madcap wackiness like this, I'd be a happy camper. Once upon a time, *Doctor Who* was the most fun show on TV. With "Let's Kill Hitler," it is once again, even if briefly. Don't try to puzzle it out or overanalyze it, just relax and enjoy.

The Psychic Papers: Sex and the Single Time Lord

For a Time Lord who has lived over 900 years, the Doctor is remarkably discreet when it comes to his love life. He may have travelled with many, many attractive female (and male) companions, but do you know how many women he's kissed on the lips on screen? Nine. Eight of those have been in the New Series; the other one was in the 1996 TV Movie.

That's right. In the Classic Series, the Doctor racked up *zero* snogs. The closest the Doctor came to a romantic dalliance was in 1964's "The Aztecs," when he met an Aztec widow named Cameca. The Doctor and Cameca had a mildly flirtatious relationship (for an older couple), and the Doctor became engaged to her by unwittingly participating in a ritual for betrothal involving pouring cocoa. Such are the hazards of time travel.

That was it for the Doctor getting some in the Classic Series.

As time progressed, the Doctor became more and more aloof about such things. In 1979's "City of Death," the fourth Doctor famously tells Countess Scarlioni, "You're a beautiful woman, probably." The implication is that the Doctor is above such interests as sex and love. That said, judging from body language, the Doctor does seem to enjoy the company of his companion Romana (played by Lalla Ward) a great deal in this story; indeed, actors Tom Baker and Ward married the following year!

The Doctor's lack of sexuality was further refined with the fifth Doctor, who never noticed when his companions changed into prettier clothes, and the seventh Doctor, who seems completely uncomfortable having to deal with a broken-hearted girl in 1987's "Delta and the Bannermen." This eventually led to a longstanding belief among *Doctor Who* fans that the Doctor was asexual. The presumed asexuality of the character was, in some ways, a unique selling feature of the series: unlike *Star Trek*, which saw Captain Kirk teaching all manner of aliens that thing Earth people call "kissing," or just about every American adventure series, which sees the heterosexual action hero bed the female guest star of the week, the Doctor was simply not interested. It was a quality that made him beloved of queer fans, who appreciated a hero who was outside the heterosexist norms of television.

The first time we had any indication that the Time Lord had anything less than chaste desires was the 1996 TV Movie. In a scene where the amnesiac, newly regenerated eighth Doctor regains his memory, he proclaims to the woman he's with, Grace Holloway, "I am the Doctor!" and then kisses Grace full on the lips. There are some who have suggested the Doctor was actually just very happy to be alive and have his memories, but, as Russell T Davies pointed out in a *Doctor Who Confidential* interview, judging from the duration of his kiss (and the fact he kisses Grace again a moment later), he must have been *really* happy.

Many long-time fans were outraged at the assault on the Doctor's asexuality. Others were perfectly happy with it (especially given that it was Paul McGann doing the kissing). But the floodgates were open. Steven Moffat's 1999 Comic Relief *Doctor Who* parody, "The Curse of Fatal Death," had Rowan Atkinson intending to marry his companion Emma (played by Julia Sawalha). Even during the 1990s, Moffat argued in online forums (and at the monthly gathering of *Doctor Who* fans at the Fitzroy Tavern in London) that the idea of the Doctor having a romance wasn't a betrayal of the character. In 2005, he put down his banner, so to speak, with "The Empty Child"/"The Doctor Dances."

And yet, it's all remarkably covert. The Doctor speaks metaphorically about Rose's assumption he's not sexual, describing it as his ability to "dance." It could simply mean what's said explicitly in the text (the Doctor dances) or its subtext (the Doctor is capable of sexual attraction).

The template was set for the Doctor and romance. He might be romantically inclined or he might not. There's enough plausible deniability to support either view. Rose and the Doctor's relationship demonstrates this: the kiss in "The Parting of the Ways" is either a long-awaited snog or an absorption of chronal energies. Rose proclaims her love for the Doctor in "Doomsday," but the Doctor never expresses his feelings. A veil is drawn over what happens between the Doctor and Reinette in "The Girl in the Fireplace." Astrid and Lady Cristina both initiate their kisses with the Doctor in "Voyage of the Damned" and "Planet of the Dead," respectively.

In spite of being a creation of Steven Moffat, the eleventh Doctor is a throwback to the asexual Doctors of the past. He shows no interest in Amy in "Flesh and Stone."

(He compares himself to "Space Gandalf" in a "Meanwhile in the TARDIS" scene on the Complete Fifth Series boxset.) He's unworldly enough to think bunk beds are a good idea for Amy and Rory's room in "The Doctor's Wife" and really doesn't want to know the specifics of the pair's sexual relationship in "A Good Man Goes to War."

But then there's River Song.

River Song is the first real indication that the Doctor is capable of honest-to-goodness, for-real romance. River kisses him in "Day of the Moon" as though she's kissed him many times. And the Doctor seems okay with it in "A Good Man Goes to War" and "The Wedding of River Song." The revelation that River has Time Lord traits may also indicate why this is so: perhaps he's simply only interested in those of his own kind. (This might even explain why he looks so enamoured with Time Lady Romana in "City of Death.")

And yet . . . we don't really know River's true motivations or the actual nature of the Doctor's relationship with her, because of the out-of-order sequence in which they meet. There is still plausible deniability.

It must be noted that it's somewhat odd that, in spite of the first five years of the revival being helmed by British television's most famous gay man, Russell T Davies, the Doctor has only kissed a man onscreen once: Captain Jack in "The Parting of the Ways." The Doctor's seeming preference for women might be seen by those who championed the Doctor's asexuality as a retrogressive step: the Doctor's lack of interest in women set him apart from the Captain Kirks and James Bonds of the world. However, the Doctor apparently danced with all the women *and* the men at Amy's wedding, and he certainly flirted outrageously with Captain Jack in "Utopia." Perhaps the Doctor uses both hearts, so to speak. Or maybe he's just as aloof when it comes to relations with men as he is with women.

Nonetheless, the question still remains: is the Doctor a time-travelling jack-the-lad or a celibate, unworldly asexual? Who knows? It's still up to you to decide . . .

6.09 Night Terrors

Written by Mark Gatiss **Directed by** Richard Clark

Supporting cast Daniel Mays (Alex), Jamie Oram (George), Emma Cunniffe (Claire), Andrew Tiernan (Purcell), Leila Hoffman (Mrs. Rossiter), Sophie Cosson (Julie)

Original airdate September 3, 2011

The Big Idea The Doctor receives a distress call from a little boy who is afraid of monsters.

Roots and References *The Twilight Zone* episodes "It's a Good Life" (George controlling his surroundings) and "Miniature" (living inside a doll's house); *Time*

Bandits (the cupboard); *EastEnders* and *The Bill* (the ongoing soap opera in the council estate); *The Indian in the Cupboard* (toys coming to life); peg dolls from Germany and the Netherlands (the dolls); *A.I.* (an artificial boy wanting the love of his parent).

Adventures in Time and Space The Doctor name-checks the Sontarans and the Emperor Dalek in his list of bedtime stories he liked as a kid. He also liked *Snow White and the Seven Keys to Doomsday*, which is a play on the 1974 *Doctor Who* stage play, *Doctor Who and the Daleks in the Seven Keys to Doomsday*. The Doctor still loves Jammie Dodgers, following from "Victory of the Daleks."

The Doctor Is Dead Effect We're reminded of the Doctor's impending death with a message on the TARDIS scanner at the episode's end.

Who is the Doctor? There's another oblique reference to the Doctor's past as a parent as he mentions he's a bit rusty relating to kids.

Monster of the Week The Tenza are a cuckoo-like race whose young find foster parents to live with. They create a psychic perception filter to make foster parents think the child was born to them. They have powerful psychic abilities, which is dangerous when a Tenza grows up to become an eight-year-old boy with pantaphobia: the fear of everything.

Stand Up and Cheer It's probably the best pre-credits teaser of the season: a little boy experiences all manner of common terrors as his bedroom at night becomes the scariest place in the universe. He starts wishing, "Please save me from the monsters," and in the TARDIS, thousands of light years away, the Doctor gets the message. Didn't we all wish that rescue was a cry away when we were young and scared of the dark?

Roll Your Eyes Aside from the giant props, just about everything inside the doll's house looks like a real location. The scale is completely wrong. Which brings up an interesting point . . .

You're Not Making Any Sense Just how does it work inside the doll's house? Are all the victims miniaturized inside it? Or is it an other-dimensional psychic space? Is one side completely open? The giant props would indicate it's the actual doll's house, but the size of the physical space indicates it's some other dimension. And then there's the ability of the dolls to turn humans into things like them . . .

Interesting Trivia This story was more-or-less flipped in broadcast order with "The Curse of the Black Spot": it was originally episode three (and for a long time bore the title "What Are Little Boys Made Of?"). Episodes are occasionally swapped in close proximity, but moving an episode from one half of the season to another is rare. Little has been said as to why the switch was made, presumably to improve the mix of stories in the first half of the season, particularly with the big mid-season break. In its original form, there was a sequence with

Madame Kovarian looking through the hatchway. Moving "The Curse of the Black Spot" forward meant adding such a sequence in that story, as well as the conversation in the TARDIS about the Doctor's death and Amy's pregnancy.

The TARDIS Chronometer A tower block on a council estate somewhere in England. Judging from George's age and his "date of birth," it's early 2011.

Cool? (GB) The opening sequence is stunning, not just as wish fulfilment of a terrified child actually contacting the Doctor, but because of the gorgeous direction by Richard Clark. The way Clark starts with an almost elegiac series of images of a tower block and then shows how an ordinary child's bedroom can be a place full of terror is incredible. (As an added bonus, the shot of the TARDIS materialization reflected in a puddle is an almost exact duplication of the opening shot from 1969's "The War Games.")

The problem with "Night Terrors" is what happens after that opening.

This should have been the story that Mark Gatiss knocked out of the park: horrific goings-on in a contemporary council estate isn't a million miles away from the Grand Guignol in modern drag Gatiss pulled off in *The League of Gentlemen*. And for the first little while it looks like we're getting that story. The scenes where the Doctor, Amy and Rory pretend to conduct a survey as they search for George are quite funny. The Doctor's initial scenes with Alex and George are lovely, and quickly become brilliant once the Doctor realizes that there are monsters in the cupboard. (I love Daniel Mays and Matt Smith's double act throughout.) Purcell and Mrs. Rossiter are perfectly rendered grotesques, and the horror of what happens to both of them is brilliantly realized.

But here's the problem: this should be a fusion of kitchen sink drama and the fantastic, but there's not enough of either, because everyone winds up in the doll's house, where there is neither.

It's a cruel bait and switch. We expect terror in a council estate and instead get "Fear Her" nicking the best bits from "The Empty Child." The living peg dolls are mildly unsettling but mostly for the anticipation of how many will turn up at *Doctor Who* conventions in years to come. Converting Mrs. Rossiter off-screen and immediately showing Purcell's grisly fate erases the tension they could have provided inside the doll's house, leaving us stuck with Amy and Rory in an aimless runaround. The revelation that it's actually the doll's house in the cupboard is muted because, in the first place, for the scale to work it would have to be one of those elaborate 18th-century German monstrosities and, in the second place, they never do the obvious thing and have the Doctor looking in on Amy, Rory and the dolls. (It wouldn't even necessarily blow the CGI budget. Amy and Rory could just break the fourth wall to reveal the cupboard door in front of them.)

So much could have been done with being stuck in a doll's house in a kid's cupboard: toys from other games could have mingled in, which might have made *The Indian in the Cupboard* reference even sharper, and more could have been done with the physics and geometry of such a place. But the episode avoids any such creative dalliances and instead goes for a Steven Spielberg ending, where it's all about father and child finally coming together.

But that ending isn't even remotely earned. Daniel Mays plays Alex with this perpetually bewildered expression on his face, which comically undercuts any sense of horror the character must be experiencing, knowing that his son is not really his son. It's unclear as to why George goes into the doll's house or why he would be in any danger since he created the environment. It's all about what *Family Guy* creator Seth McFarlane calls "the bullshit moment": the inexplicable, sentimental climax that happens because it neatly restores everything.

If "Night Terrors" had kept up the strength of the first 20 or so minutes, it could have been one of the best things Mark Gatiss has ever written for *Doctor Who*. Richard Clark was more than up to the task of directing it. But "Night Terrors" loses its way the second Amy and Rory's lift crashes into the doll's house, and it only gets worse from there. It promises so much and delivers so little.

Second Opinion (RS?) "Night Terrors" has one aim in mind: to be scary. It doesn't care about anything else, be it plot logic (as my co-author ably illustrates), characterization (Alex is a stock cliché of a bumbling dad) or resolution (Alex's inability to pay the rent is never dealt with). Instead, it's all about the scare value.

And, with that in mind, it works. It's bloody terrifying! The peg dolls are incredibly disturbing, but so is the landlord, for entirely different reasons. The atmosphere is freaky, with the block of flats oozing urban decay and claustrophobia. Even Mrs. Rossitor manages to be disturbing when she really shouldn't be.

I still maintain that Mark Gatiss has pictures of Steven Moffat in a compromising position with an Ood; why else would they keep commissioning him? At least he's playing to the season's prime motivation (to be dark) with an episode he knows a talented director will light well and shoot moodily. This episode would probably have had a lot more impact if every other story in the season weren't aiming for the same thing, but you can't have everything.

The main reason this works better than "Fear Her," for example, is that the story uses the child's fears as its basis, not the child himself. The kid playing George can't really do much other than blink a lot, but even that is creepy. It's an episode with a lot of flaws, but it skirts the most obvious one.

This was moved in its placement from early in the season to much later, but you can barely tell . . . which highlights a huge failing of Series Six. The second half of the season should be vastly different from the first because of character development, particularly following from what Amy and Rory have now been through. They've gone nowhere and that's a huge problem. They're stuck being the comic relief, rather than three-dimensional companions.

"Night Terrors" might be stupid, it might make no sense and it might lead nowhere, but it does succeed in being utterly terrifying. It's a successful one-trick pony; it's just a shame that it's performing the same trick as every other pony in the circus.

. . . .

New Media

Ever since *Doctor Who*'s return in 2005, the New Series has been a cross-platform experience. The show has been bolstered by content on the official BBC website that included behind the scenes material, games, mini-websites set within the fictional *Doctor Who* universe and more.

Starting with Series Two, this increased content included dramatic presentations. "The Christmas Invasion" was supplemented by "Attack of the Graske," an interactive game on the BBC's red button service (and later added to the BBC website). The game featured a live-action component written by Gareth Roberts, directed by Ashley Way and starring David Tennant (in his first full appearance in his new costume!). Following this came webisodes, called "TARDISodes," that were shown in advance of every episode of Series Two. Also written by Gareth Roberts and directed by Ashley Way, the TARDISodes were prequels to the TV episodes, showing, for example, what happened to the crew of the S.S. *Madame de Pompadour* before "The Girl in the Fireplace" or supplementary material, such as an emergency broadcast during the Cybermen invasion in "Doomsday." Aside from an appearance by Noel Clarke in the TARDISodes for "School Reunion" and "Rise of the Cybermen," no regular cast members were featured and only very rarely actors from the actual broadcast stories.

With Series Five, supplemental content appeared on the DVD releases. The Complete Fifth Series DVD boxset included two short scenes under the umbrella title "Meanwhile in the TARDIS." These scenes bridged the gap between "The Eleventh Hour" and "The Beast Below" (explaining how Amy wound up floating in space at the start of the latter story), and "Flesh and Stone" and "The Vampires of Venice," which follows from Amy's attempted seduction of the Doctor. These scenes were written by Steven Moffat and directed by Euros Lyn.

The Complete Sixth Series DVD set was supplemented by additional scenes under the umbrella title "Night and the Doctor," which were written by Steven Moffat and directed by Richard Senior. Unlike "Meanwhile in the TARDIS," these four scenes don't bridge gaps between episodes but feature Matt Smith, Karen Gillan, Arthur

Darvill and Alex Kingston in a variety of comic scenarios featuring the Doctor, Amy, Rory and River. (A further scene is effectively a prequel to "Closing Time" featuring James Corden and Daisy Haggard as Craig and Sophie.)

Also new to Series Six were prequels to several episodes including "The Impossible Astronaut," "The Curse of the Black Spot," "A Good Man Goes to War," "Let's Kill Hitler" and "The Wedding of River Song." These appeared on the BBC website and the Complete Sixth Series DVD set. Unlike the TARDISodes, these featured the regular cast and actors from individual episodes.

. . . .

6.10 The Girl Who Waited

Written by Tom McRae **Directed by** Nick Hurran

Supporting cast Josie Taylor (check-in girl), Imelda Staunton (voice of the interface), Stephen Bracken-Keogh (voice of the handbots, uncredited)

Original airdate September 10, 2011

The Big Idea On a planet with two timestreams, Amy waits 36 years for the Doctor to save her. And then things really become complicated.

Roots and References C.S. Lewis's *Narnia* series (time passing much faster in a fantastical place); *2001: A Space Odyssey* (the white room); *A.I.* (the handbots); Tim Burton's *Alice in Wonderland* (the topiaries).

Adventures in Time and Space The title is taken from the repeated description of Amy as the girl who waited for the Doctor, seen in "The Eleventh Hour"; she also refers to him as "Raggedy Man" from the same story. There's a reference to an amusement park on Clom ("Love & Monsters") and the Doctor wearing a fez ("The Big Bang").

Jettisoning TARDIS rooms (including a karaoke bar!) to provide more thrust was seen in 1982's "Castrovalva" (and more recently in "The Doctor's Wife"). The *Mona Lisa* previously featured in 1979's "City of Death."

Who is the Doctor? Chen-7, the one-day plague (so-named because you only live for one day), affects two-hearted races like Time Lords. If the Doctor stepped into the red waterfall area, he'd be dead in a day. When Rory suggests he research his destinations before landing, the Doctor protests that he doesn't work that way.

The Doctor and Amy Older Amy hates the Doctor for not rescuing her, probably tying into their long history of him making her wait, starting when she was a little girl. He seems prepared to allow either Amy to survive, giving Rory the choice, but outright lies about the possibility that both could.

Monster of the Week Handbots are robots who see with their hands. The hands have organic skin and can deliver an anaesthetic, while their faces are blank. There's a secondary delivery system of needles inside the head. They can transmat.

Stand Up and Cheer Amy dancing the Macarena should be comedy gold, but it's played for heartache — and, astonishingly, it works. Older Amy changes her mind because of her connection to Rory, and this pivotal moment is done in slow motion with tears welling up in her eyes (and very likely the viewer's too).

Roll Your Eyes Rory yells at the Doctor for travelling without planning and says he no longer wants to travel with him, then has to make the most difficult choice of his life, solely because the Doctor flat-out lied. However, at the story's end, Rory is remarkably quick to accept the Doctor's assurances that everything seems to have worked out. This implausible behaviour massively undercuts the drama of what preceded it.

You're Not Making Any Sense Amy doesn't need to eat for 36 years (or presumably use the bathroom) because of the time-field compression. That is, she doesn't feel hungry when a week passes, because only 30 seconds have really passed. This suggests that her body responds to the "slow" time field, not the "fast" one. So why does she age, then?

Interesting Trivia Does the time differential actually make sense? Fortunately, one of us has a Ph.D. in mathematics, so we decided to follow the money. We're told that residents in the fast time zone get to live their entire lives in a single day, and we briefly glimpse children, so some of those lives may be rather long. Between the red waterfall door closing and Amy appearing on the scanner saying she's been in the room for a week, 23 seconds pass. If 23 seconds in slow time corresponds to a week in fast time, then 24 hours in slow time corresponds to 3,756 weeks, or 72 years, in fast time. So yes, quite impressively, the two synch up very nicely indeed! This means that the Doctor landed the TARDIS 12 hours (in slow time) after Amy walked through the red waterfall door, which might have been a bit of an oversight on his part, but we can probably put that down to the trouble he has reconciling the TARDIS with the time differential.

This episode features the smallest-ever cast list in the New Series with only three non-regular speaking parts, two of whom are voice parts and the third an image on a screen. Furthermore, it's this year's Doctor-lite story: after the initial sequence, all of Matt Smith's scenes are in the TARDIS and they're minimal. The only Classic Series episode that featured fewer cast members was 1964's "The Edge of Destruction," a "bottle" story set wholly on board the TARDIS. Since that story featured four regular cast members, rather than two and a half, "The Girl Who Waited" is arguably the most minimalist cast in *Doctor Who*'s entire history.

A different actress was initially going to be cast for older Amy, but Karen

Gillan insisted on playing the part herself, wearing a prosthesis. She underwent extensive training for the part, altering her vocal inflection, posture and body language with the help of a voice coach and a movement coach.

The TARDIS Chronometer Apalapuchia in the far future (Earth's treasures have been raided).

Cool? (RS?) Once upon a time, there was a *Doctor Who* episode that featured only the regular cast plus a couple of voice actors, with the main characters separated after one of them pressed the wrong button. Thousands of people were kept in featureless white rooms to avert disaster, but the security system went awry, making the environment hostile to the TARDIS crew. The episode had meaningful things to say about the nature of humanity and its ability to survive. That episode was the first part of 1975's "The Ark in Space" and is widely regarded as one of the standout classics of all of *Doctor Who*.

"The Girl Who Waited" could have been a basic retread of the rest of that story, with aliens to fight, horrific possession and pitched battles. Instead, it chooses to stay with the premise and think through the effects of the environment. The result is a minimalist story that's low on action but high on thoughtfulness. And it's fantastic.

This is something *Doctor Who* doesn't normally attempt: a hard-science-fiction story. *Doctor Who* usually uses the trappings of sci-fi as a setting, with the occasional element (such as time travel) to mix it up, but it doesn't really engage with the rules of an alien world in a fundamental way. "The Girl Who Waited" is, at its core, all about its setting. The one-day plague sets everything in motion: the planet has developed a fast timezone so that people can live out their lives in the 24 hours they have left; there's a way of interacting between the two timezones, because that's the kind thing to do; and the Doctor can't enter the red waterfall zone, thus removing him from the action.

The episode also addresses a central moral dilemma: if you erase someone's timeline, is it murder? Tellingly, this question can only arise in the context of a science-fiction story, but it's given emotional resonance, thanks to the setting and its established rules, and also because it happens to Amy, rather than the guest star of the week. Karen Gillan was absolutely right to insist on playing the older Amy. Gillan has mostly been a featherweight actress, with "pouty" and "pissed off" her only two settings. Here, however, she shows what she's capable of, and it couldn't come at a better time. It's her acting that sells the entire story: she makes the moral dilemma feel real. Yes, the last 36 years of Amy's life have been crappy. But does that give the Doctor the right to erase them?

"The Girl Who Waited" takes us to some edgy places, with the Doctor not only lying about the possibility of saving both Amys but locking the older one out of the TARDIS, which is incredibly shocking. It works especially well because the scene is set up so that you think older Amy is going to die nobly, saving Rory and her younger self from the handbots. But the truth is so much worse: not only does the Doctor lock her out, but he then shunts the final decision to Rory. Rory's dead right when he says it's unfair, because it really is: it's not just an unfair situation, it's unfair of the Doctor to force Rory to make the choice. By doing so, the Doctor intends to absolve both of them of full responsibility, but the end result isn't pleasant for anyone. The scene with Amy pleading with Rory to both let her in and keep her locked out is heartwrenching.

Steven Moffat once said that the power of *Doctor Who* is that every week you have no idea what type of story you're about to experience. It's an acknowledgement of the wonder that *Doctor Who* promises. This is never demonstrated more vividly than in the scene where Amy emerges into the garden of topiary bushes and Grecian statues. Following only white rooms, her new surroundings are astonishingly beautiful. It's an effective bait and switch, as we're suddenly shown the beauty and wonder of Apalapuchia. In a great many episodes the Doctor tells his companions (and us) about the beauty of the universe, only for the TARDIS to end up in a dank corridor somewhere, but this moment vividly illustrates the wonders of the *Doctor Who* universe.

Indeed, almost every aspect of this story does its damnedest not to be contrived: the setup is intricately thought through, the CGI setting looks like a real garden, the moral dilemma has legs and the resolution comes at a cost. The story is fundamentally about character, which is exactly what we turn to drama for.

The only way in which this episode doesn't work is, alas, in the context of the bigger picture. Amy is incredibly pissed off that she's had to wait 36 years for Rory (and the Doctor) to show up. She initially takes a lot of this out on Rory . . . who's remarkably acquiescent for a guy who waited for her for almost two millennia. Have you ever tried blaming your significant other when they already suffered the same thing, only much more intensely? I guarantee that they'd bring this fact up. Especially — and I can't stress this enough — if they suffered for 55 times as long as you did.

The resolution also just sort of happens. Younger Amy is saved, at the cost of older Amy, and Rory questions the Doctor for a second, then just goes along with it. Earlier in the story, Rory angrily told the Doctor he didn't want to travel with him any more, but now — after something much worse has happened — Rory meekly accepts it. It would have been so easy to have Rory mad at the Doctor and ask to be returned home the next time they landed on present-day Earth. Given what happens in the next episode, this would have worked really nicely as a segue.

Instead, we get throwback television. The Doctor, Amy and Rory never suffer any ongoing emotional trauma, never face lasting consequences and never develop as characters. It means they're fundamentally the same from episode to episode . . . but that's Old TeeVee. That's the kind of preventative measure used in the past when episodes might be screened out of order or only part of a season shown. Nowadays, in the DVD age and with greater emphasis placed on in-season continuity, it's not only possible to have character development, it's expected. That *Doctor Who* doesn't is not just bizarre, it actually hurts the stories.

Larger issues aside, "The Girl Who Waited" is sensational. That so much is achieved in a Doctor-lite episode, relying so heavily on the performance of the previously lightweight Karen Gillan, makes it even more astonishing. Oh, and the title is fantastic. More like this, please.

Second Opinion (GB) I'm sure by now, dear reader, you've come to realize that I have certain . . . concerns about this season. Namely, things have taken a turn for the cerebral. The excitement in *Doctor Who* now is in seeing big, grand, well-developed ideas play out. And my complaint has been, largely, there's nothing wrong with clever ideas but where's the emotion? Where's the heart?

"The Girl Who Waited" shows how this kind of *Doctor Who* should be done. It has something for the head and something for the heart.

On paper, this is the episode I'd most want to avoid this season. It's hard science fiction involving time travel and parallel lives and being forced to choose one alternative timeline over another and the ethics behind such a decision. But Tom MacRae's genius is that he makes those big ideas come alive by connecting them to the characters.

Older Amy doesn't want to give up her life, and that feels utterly right. Amy is the sort of person who, if I were to put it generously, lives in the moment. Less generously, I'd say she's utterly self absorbed and often quite selfish. There's a certain pragmatism to Amy and her not wanting to have four decades of lived experience erased feels honest. Where Donna wanted to be rid of the world that was destroying her mother and her life as she knew it in "Turn Left," Amy only has her miserable, eked-out existence to fall back on. It's heartbreaking in its truth. Everything my co-author has said about Karen Gillan's performance is spot-on. (I love the scene where older Amy briefly considers putting on lipstick for Rory.) Gillan takes every small emotion and revels in it.

The result of all this is ideas that don't just dazzle the mind, they come to life. They connect to the viewer in a meaningful way.

And then there's the unexpected ending. I honestly did not know how this would end. I assumed some timey-wimey MacGuffin would allow Rory to get to be with Amy and also give older Amy what she wanted but leave us only partially satisfied. But, no. The Doctor slamming the door in older Amy's face is Occam's razor–like in the simplicity with which it settles the debate. The Doctor has lied. There is no way to save both Amys. It resolves the plot neatly but it also does something *Doctor Who* has been avoiding a lot lately: it gives us a kick to the gut. We feel older Amy's loss poignantly. Giving Rory the decision is needless. He's too cowardly to give in. All older Amy can do is tell Rory to not open the door, not so she can sacrifice herself but to hold on to whatever dignity she has left.

That's what I want from *Doctor Who*. Give me the biggest ideas possible. Do clever timey-wimey things. Just make it real to the characters. Give it shocking consequences and big thrills. Make it grab me by the brain, the heart and anything else.

6.11 The God Complex

Written by Toby Whithouse **Directed by** Nick Hurran

Supporting cast Sarah Quintrell (Lucy Hayward), Amara Karan (Rita), Dimitri Leonidas (Howie Spragg), Daniel Pirrie (Joe Buchanan), David Walliams (Gibbis), Dafydd Emyr (P.E. teacher), Spencer Wilding (the Creature), Rashid Karapiet (Rita's father), Caitlin Blackwood (Amelia), Roger Ennals (gorilla)

Original airdate September 17, 2011

The Big Idea Hell appears to be just like a 1980s hotel. There's a room with your greatest fear, and a Minotaur is stalking everyone.

Roots and References *The Shining* (the creepy hotel); The Eagles' song "Hotel California"; the *Star Trek: The Next Generation* episode "The Royale" (a simulation of a hotel that you can never leave); *Nineteen Eighty-Four* (a room with each person's greatest fear); *The X-Files* (Howie the conspiracy freak); the Greek myth of Theseus and the Minotaur (the Minotaur at the centre of a labyrinth). Joe quotes from the nursery rhyme "Oranges and Lemons" ("Here comes a candle . . .") while the Doctor uses Lord Sugar's catchphrase, "With regret, you're fired," from the British version of *The Apprentice*.

Adventures in Time and Space The Minotaur is a "distant cousin" of the Nimon, a (literally) bull-headed race of aliens from 1980's "The Horns of Nimon." (The Nimon similarly ran a complex that constantly changed its architectural configuration.) One of the rooms contains a simulacrum of the Weeping Angels ("Blink," "The Time of Angels"/"Flesh and Stone"). Among the photos of the conquered on the Employee Wall are a cat nun ("New Earth"), a Sontaran ("The

Sontaran Strategem"/"The Poison Sky") and a Judoon ("Smith and Jones"). The Cloister Bell (1981's "Logopolis" onward) can be heard in the Doctor's room. Young Amelia Pond ("The Eleventh Hour") is in Amy's room.

The Doctor Is Dead Effect The Minotaur's final words and the Doctor leaving behind Amy and Rory indicate he's getting ready to face his final fate.

Who is the Doctor? The dying Minotaur tells the Doctor, "An ancient creature drenched in the blood of the innocent, drifting in space through an endless shifting maze. For such a creature, death would be a gift." And then with its dying breath adds, "I wasn't talking about myself."

The Doctor and Amy Throughout the episode, the Doctor muses about whether it's a good idea to take Amy and Rory through time and space, telling Rita it was their choice but "offer a child a suitcase full of sweets and they'll take it." Rita's death and the Minotaur almost claiming Amy galvanizes the Doctor: he breaks Amy's absolute faith in him, and he then takes her and Rory back to Earth (even giving them a house and car as a farewell present) and then leaves. When Amy asks why now, he tells her, "Because you're still breathing."

Monster of the Week The Minotaur is an alien that looks like the legendary creature. It feeds off the psychic energy created by a person's faith and has been imprisoned for centuries on a spaceship that abducts people with faith in order to feed the Minotaur.

Stand Up and Cheer Rita's death is as incredible as it is heartbreaking. She finally understands, better than the Doctor, what is happening and refuses to put him in harm's way. Her humble request, that the Doctor not watch her die so he doesn't see her lose her faith and her dignity, is at once beautiful and devastating.

Roll Your Eyes Did Rita's greatest fear really need to be the stereotypical disapproving Anglo-Indian parent? In a story bristling with original ideas, why borrow from *Bend It Like Beckham*'s playbook?

You're Not Making Any Sense How is it that Joe merits not just a room but a ballroom filled with his greatest fear? It's an impressive visual, we'll give it that, but it doesn't quite work given the rules established in the story.

Interesting Trivia What was in the Doctor's room? And what does he have faith in? (Or, as Amy puts it, "What do Time Lords pray to?") "The God Complex" shies away from giving a definitive answer but here are some ideas, and, perhaps, some clues. In 1989's "The Curse of Fenric," the Doctor repels vampire-like creatures using his faith in his companions (he actually mutters the names of past companions onscreen). Is that the case here? Possibly. But let's look at the evidence. The contents of the Doctor's room are never seen but we do hear the Cloister Bell, indicating imminent disaster for the TARDIS. (The Doctor simply says, "Of course. Who else?") Both Amy and Rita articulate their respective faiths throughout. What if the Doctor is too? The Doctor keeps insisting that he will save everyone from the Minotaur. What if the Doctor's faith is in his own ability to save people? If so, what greater fear to make the Doctor dig into his faith than seeing the imminent destruction of Amy and the TARDIS?

The types of fears are fascinating: Lucy fears a "brutal gorilla" from a childhood story; Joe fears ventriloquist dummies; Howie fears a room full of girls that mock his stammer; Rita fears her disapproving father; and Amy fears abandonment, which she experienced as a child with the Doctor. Other rooms show fears like P.E. teachers, clowns and photographers. It makes one wonder what fears other aliens experienced? What would a Sontaran face? (Losing to a Rutan? Becoming a nurse, perhaps?) Or a Judoon? (We can't possibly speculate, but we're amused by the potential conversion experience: "Blo ko slo ko praise him . . .")

Gibbis comes from the planet of the doormats. Not literally (though that would be interesting). The planet Tivoli lays claim to the dubious distinction of being the only planet to welcome any invading force. Their planetary anthem is "Glory to (Insert Name Here)." It's a great comic conceit, but it does stretch credulity a little. Either they're very good at manipulating the situation to their own ends (as the Doctor accuses Gibbis), or they've just been very fortunate to only encounter invading forces that want to oppress or enslave them as opposed to, say, exterminate them.

The TARDIS Chronometer The Minotaur's prison ship, and outside Amy and Rory's new flat (it's unidentified where but it's definitely somewhere urban in Britain).

Cool? (GB) There is something really sinister about hotels. They're a sort of liminal space — between one state of being and another — that is totally artificial. They promise the comforts of home but, beyond a bed, a TV and wifi, deliver them in no way, shape or form. In short, a hotel is the perfect setting for a *Doctor Who* story. And, straight off, I have to give "The God Complex" credit for making hotels scary for the first time since *The Shining*.

While I consider that accolade significant, it is by no means the greatest of this episode's achievements. It's a thoughtful, mature, moving story, rooted in character. Its sole gimmick — everyone has their own room with their own fear in it — is designed to enhance the character and theme. And it has what is easily the best-realized monster this season.

Visually, it's a treat. The pre-credits sequence is unsettling and fascinating (the use of "praise him" in type and in ransom-note style lettering is an inspired touch), and the first time the Minotaur is seen, claiming Joe in the hallway while the Doctor watches through the door, is stunning. Nick Hurran knows his stuff as a director. Toby Whithouse has a brilliantly comic creation with Gibbis (hooray for *Little Britain*'s David Walliams for portraying him so wonderfully) and once more Whithouse riddles his script with funny dialogue. ("You are a medical doctor, aren't you? You haven't just got a degree in cheese-making, or something?" "No. Well, yes. Both, actually.") But Whithouse's real achievement this time is in creating a story where a group of disparate characters are forced to confront what truly motivates them.

"The God Complex" is a story about faith, but it's only a religious faith for one of the characters. It's the deep desires, compulsions, passions, beliefs and perspectives that drive people. The "hunger in himself to be more serious" as the poet Philip Larkin put it. It's a thoroughly secular way of looking at faith, and yet it also poses the question, does faith in anything ultimately help us? On the surface, the answer appears to be no: Howie's conspiracy theories, Rita's Muslim beliefs and Amy's devotion to the Doctor don't save any of them. And yet, Howie has managed to overcome his stammer, Rita is thoroughly decent and Amy's trust has saved her from many scrapes. Maybe the answer presented is more complex.

Perhaps the most fascinating aspect of this is the subtle way it assails the subject of where the Doctor places his own faith. More than in any episode since the Tennant era, the Doctor repeatedly declares he will save everyone, including the people who want to sacrifice themselves, like Joe and Howie. The Doctor even insists on saving the fish in the hairdressing salon. He keeps professing that no more will die in spite of the evidence that he's incapable of saving anyone. (Or anything. Gibbis eats the fish!) If the Doctor's own faith is in his ability to save people (or simple optimism that people can be saved), it adds an extra dimension to Rita's death: she knows the Minotaur steals faith, and she points out the Doctor's own hubris. She wants to save him, or slow down his destruction, by isolating herself from him. Even more than that, it adds a punch to the climax: the Doctor is not only breaking Amy's faith in him, he's breaking his own faith in himself.

But here is where "The God Complex" fails. The Doctor breaking Amy's (and his own) faith is too subtle. I can see what is being attempted: Amy's greatest fear is of being abandoned by the Doctor. The Doctor says that young Amelia's fear was absolutely right: he only came for her on a whim because he wanted to be adored. But this moment isn't loud or brutal enough. I first thought the Doctor needed to be cruel — to tell Amy hurtful truths about herself — like he was to his companion Ace in a similar scene in 1989's "The Curse of Fenric." However, on further reflection, I don't think it lacks cruelty; it lacks honesty. It needs the Doctor to say, "I couldn't save your daughter. I couldn't save Rory. The only reason you still have them, in some way, is a fluke. I haven't made you a better person. You will die if you travel with me." It's frustrating this isn't articulated. The whole episode is building to this moment, where Amy and the Doctor are forced to confront the harsh reality of their travels and it's done so gently as to not have any impact (though, in fairness, the Doctor calling her "Amy Williams" was shocking).

A big reason this scene isn't so discordant is that Matt Smith is so bloody incredible. One of the nice things about Smith is that he has a great internal barometer for how he should pitch his performance. In an episode where not much else is going on, like "The Curse of the Black Spot," he's loud and in your face with his quirkiness. But here, in a more mature, subtle script, he's beautifully restrained. He still cuts loose with the eccentricity where it suits (I love how he conspiratorially tells Rita to call him sometime) but he's very much at home being introspective, capturing the Time Lord as he's forced to examine if he's helped Amy and Rory in the long term. Smith is also great opposite Amara Karan as Rita. The viewer has to feel that the Doctor and Rita work as a couple, and that Rita is "companionable" material. Karan and Smith excel at this, and Rita's death scene — beautifully underplayed by Karan, who doesn't dilute the power of Rita's request for privacy with histrionics — is one of the great moments of *Doctor Who*. I really wish Karan had stayed on.

But the very casting of Karan brings up a thornier problem I've had with the production team over the past two series. Throughout this book, my co-author has raised the fact that people of colour are often cast in a limited range of roles (often less than exemplary) and argued there should be a wider spectrum of parts available. I've always differed somewhat with Robert in that I felt one of the best things about the first four seasons was that characters were cast colour-blind, regardless of the role or its qualities. Over the past two seasons, however, we have the exact opposite situation. Amy and Rory apparently come from a middle-class English village straight out of *Midsomer Murders*, with few minorities. Meera Syal and Sophie Okenodo are the only nods whatsoever to diverse casting of major roles in Series Five. Until now, Series Six's biggest minority speaking parts were the ahistorical black secret service agent in "The Impossible Astronaut," Colonel Runaway in "A Good Man Goes to War" and Mels in "Let's Kill Hitler," all of which were minor roles. Now we have Amara Karan as Rita. She's a stunning actress but I can't help but feel the only reason we're seeing her in *Doctor Who* under its current management is because the script called for a Muslim. There's something very wrong about that, and the surfeit of white people onscreen; the production team urgently needs to address this.

When the Doctor leaves Amy, it feels like real closure between them. (There is also that sense with Rory earlier in the episode when he says of Howie overcoming his speech impediment, "Not all victories are about saving the universe.") Whether or not that actually sticks remains to be seen, but I kind of hope it does. If it doesn't, then it would render what the Doctor has learned from this story meaningless.

This aside, "The God Complex" is a powerful, thoughtful episode. I honestly wish there were more like them.

Second Opinion (RS?) Imagine setting your story in a hideous '80s hotel. Then picture a labyrinthine structure so that the whole thing is essentially nothing but corridors with bad carpet and the occasional room with bad wallpaper. As icing on the cake, include a Minotaur-like monster that no CGI wizard could hope to render realistically. And if you've ever watched *Doctor Who* before, you must surely know this.

Now stop imagining. Congratulations, you're Toby Whithouse.

This episode had the potential to go very badly indeed. Even the core idea — each room is filled with someone's worst nightmare and the faith that fear evokes is what the beast feeds on — isn't much more than a cliché, slightly inverted. And it continues the unrelenting bleakness of the season.

Fortunately, the story is saved almost entirely by its direction. The quick cuts as someone converts, complete with shocking laughter, printed text and semi-opaque images, are astonishing. The policewoman's notepad, with voiceover and sped-up writing, conveys the menace very effectively. The shots of the corridors expanding work really well, particularly seeing the Doctor from above, standing at a corridor crossroad. And although the beast looks like it came straight from a 1980s Classic *Who* design team (who probably stayed in that very hotel), the momentary flashes at the beginning are so effective that I didn't even mind how much screen time it gets later on. This is how to make a poor costume work.

Credit is, however, due to Whithouse for the one area in which he excels: characterization. Rita is incredibly memorable, and even smaller parts like Joe and Howie shine. But it's with Gibbis the coward that we really see the power of character. Virtually everything Gibbis says is hilarious, from describing his job as town planner and his planet's anthem to asking to be dropped in a nearby galaxy at the end. If he were just the comic relief, I'd be hugely satisfied. But Whithouse takes this character further and shows us the nastiness behind the humour. Gibbis consistently takes the coward's way out — which is probably what you or I would do in these situations — but he isn't given a reprieve, despite surviving the adventure. There's not only the Doctor's admonition of his people, but the way he's seen eating the fish on camera, a moment that's masterfully conveyed as shameful, despite the fact the character doesn't realize he's being observed. And his attempt to explain away his actions is pitiable. This is deeply unsettling, because you have no idea whether to laugh at him, sympathize with him or recoil in horror at his true nature.

The ending comes out of left field. Returning Amy and Rory to Earth is an odd and sudden development, that doesn't really have any thematic buildup. It seems bleak, rather than joyous or epic.

"The God Complex" has a lot going on, both in itself and as part of the season. It should have been terrible, but Nick Hurran's direction not only saves a lacklustre idea, it turns it into one of the more impressive episodes this season. A success, if precariously so.

6.12 Closing Time

Written by Gareth Roberts **Directed by** Steve Hughes

Supporting cast James Corden (Craig Owens), Daisy Haggard (Sophie), Alex Kingston (River Song), Frances Barber (Madame Kovarian), Seroca Davis (Shona), Holli Dempsey (Kelly), Chris Obi (George), Lynda Baron (Val), Paul Kasey (Cybermen), Nicholas Briggs (voice of the Cybermen)

Original airdate September 24, 2011

The Big Idea The Cybermen are draining power from a shop in Colchester, where the Doctor decides to spend his last day before facing his death.

Roots and References *Dawn of the Dead* (being converted to a soulless creature in a shopping centre); *Mr. Mom* and *Three Men and a Baby* (Craig's parenting); *Are You Being Served?* (the shop). The Doctor says, "Up diddly up, down diddly down," which is from the theme to *Those Magnificent Men in Their Flying Machines.* He sarcastically puts down a news story about a *Britain's Got Talent* contestant (a bit of an in-joke since *Britain's Got Talent* tends to be the top-rated show on Saturday nights every spring in Britain, frequently beating out *Doctor Who*!) while Kelly mentions *Britain's Next Top Model.*

Adventures in Time and Space Cybermats first appeared in 1967's "The Tomb of the Cybermen," the third Cyberman story. The Doctor says, "You've redecorated; I don't like it," which is taken from 1972's "The Three Doctors" and 1983's "The Five Doctors." He also references K9. The Doctor reprograms the Cybermat to use as a weapon, just as he did in 1975's "Revenge of the Cybermen." The Doctor speaks baby again ("A Good Man Goes to War"). Amy's perfume, Petrichor, is the smell of rain on dust (from "The Doctor's Wife") and it bears the slogan "For the girl who's tired of waiting" (from "The Eleventh Hour" onwards). Craig and Sophie previously appeared in "The Lodger."

The Doctor Is Dead Effect The Stetson and the blue envelopes that Amy, River and the Doctor received in "The Impossible Astronaut" are actually from Craig's house. The Doctor ponders his death and recalls that "silence will fall when the question is asked." In the final scene, we learn that River Song is still under control of Madame Kovarian, who uses the Silents and the clerics to place her into the astronaut suit, so that she can kill the Doctor.

Who is the Doctor? He's feeling old and near the end of his life, so he's been on a "farewell tour," making social calls and seeing the universe before facing death. He feels selfish because he's put people in danger, but he also acknowledges that he lived his dream.

Monster of the Week Cybermats resemble rats but are silver and have a blank snout that folds back to reveal teeth. They're small infiltrators that collect power from the local area to transmit to the Cybership. They're shielded from metastatic energy.

Stand Up and Cheer The final scene with the Doctor, as he prepares to leave on his final journey — with the slow motion, the children in the street staring, their voices as adults many years later — is a brilliant segue into the final scene with River, which is itself quite powerful. But it's the slow movement and out-of-left-field voiceovers that really bring home the message of this episode: the Doctor is facing his imminent death and he knows it.

Roll Your Eyes If Amy's now a supermodel, so famous that people stop her to sign autographs, then what on Earth is she doing in a shop in Colchester in *Essex*? It's like Heidi Klum showing up in a shopping mall in Scranton, Pennsylvania.

You're Not Making Any Sense The first step in Cyber-conversion, as clearly established in "Rise of the Cybermen," is to cut out the brain. But with Craig, the Cybermen not only put his entire body in a Cybersuit, we actually hear the chainsaw sound and a Cyberman says that the conversion is complete. And yet it's so clearly not, because he hasn't had his limbs removed, his brain cut out or, indeed, suffered any damage whatsoever.

Interesting Trivia It's time to finally address a burning issue of the New Series: just where did these Cybermen come from? Originally, they were the Cybus Corporation Cybermen from a parallel world ("Rise of the Cybermen"/"The Age of Steel"), who were sealed into the void ("Doomsday"). In "The Next Doctor," their ship fell through the void and into the past, so we know at least some of them escaped. But there's a big difference between a ragtag group of survivors and an entire Cyberlegion, as seen in "A Good Man Goes to War." Along the way, they've dropped the Cybus branding, suggesting that they're either not the same Cybermen or else they've reinvented themselves. One possibility is that they merged with this universe's Cybermen, whom we haven't seen at all since the New Series started, although they seem to have retained their own look. Another possibility — given that all the spacefaring Cybermen postdate the Davies era — is that the Cybermen escaped the void through the crack in the universe. This could account for their numbers, although it also suggests there should be Davies-era Daleks roaming the universe too. The most likely explanation is that there were other survivors from the void that we don't know about, who went on to build their Cyberarmy in this universe, although it's slightly odd that we're never told this. As it sits, it looks as though someone on the production team forgot that these Cybermen were from a parallel universe and hoped we'd forget too.

The older Doctor in "The Impossible Astronaut" was said to be 1,103 years old, almost 200 years older than the younger Doctor in that story. Events since then have been roughly continuous for the Doctor (as he travelled with Amy and Rory), meaning that the only gap in which he could age 200 years is between "The God Complex" and "Closing Time." Writer Gareth Roberts has confirmed that the gap does indeed occur here and that the Doctor spent the intervening centuries popping in and out of history to wave at Amy and Rory (as seen in the opening scene of "The Impossible Astronaut"). This seems like an . . . odd way to spend 200 years.

How did Amy become a supermodel so quickly and one mega-famous enough to have a cosmetics company sign off on a multimillion-dollar advertising campaign for a perfume that a) is named after dirt, and b) has her own vanity slogan? Perhaps the Doctor not only gave Amy and Rory a house and a car but the means to corner the scent market.

When do this episode's events take place for Amy and Rory? It seems unlikely that Amy was a supermodel in the gap between "A Christmas Carol" and "The Impossible Astronaut" — and Rory wouldn't have needed to ask what petrichor was in "The Doctor's Wife" — so that suggests that it takes place after "The God Complex." Except that, according to Craig's newspaper, it's April 19, 2011, which is three days before Utah. So either Ganger-Amy was a supermodel and Rory apparently paid no attention to his wife's perfume, or the Doctor dropped Amy and Rory several months in their own past and, instead of lying low so that the timestreams didn't cross, Amy became so famous that her face is plastered in department stores? Neither option makes much sense.

The TARDIS Chronometer On a street corner near Craig's house in Colchester, April 2011. The TARDIS also travels back several hours so that the Doctor can clean Craig's house.

Cool? (RS?) You know you're going to die. You've spent 200 years gadding about, but finally, the day is almost here and it's unavoidable. What do you do in your last 24 hours? Visit the most amazing scenery you can possibly find? Or drop in on a mate and hang out in suburbia?

The A-plot of "Closing Time" is a fun little story involving Cybermats threatening a shop, with popular guest star James Corden — this time with a baby in tow — playing straight man to Matt Smith's wackiness and as much ensuing comedy as the script can possibly milk. The recurring gag where the Doctor and Craig are mistaken for lovers is pitch perfect, as are the lovely little touches like the Doctor grinding pepper over Craig or giving him a massage, or Craig sulking because he doesn't know the monster names.

The major problem with this plot is that, yet again, everybody who matters is white and everybody who isn't has a minor role (such as a stereotypical security guard) with minimal lines and is killed off. Why is Shona killed in the pre-credits teaser, while Val survives the episode? Answers on the back of a postcard, please. The two actresses could have easily been cast in the other's role, but it's telling that they weren't.

Rather than being a remake of "The Lodger," "Closing Time" is an attempt to have a normal *Doctor Who* adventure that's drowning in foreboding. The Doctor's death is imminent and he knows it. Which means the episode is much darker than it seems at first, but a) this feels earned for a change, and b) it's offset by the comedy. The Doctor is drawn into the adventure reluctantly and small scenes, like him demonstrating toys for kids or cleaning Craig's house, feel bittersweet rather than fluffy.

Craig also gets to counter the Doctor's assertion that all he does is put people in danger. He does, but they also have a say in the matter. And, as Craig points out, those closest to the Doctor tend to survive anyway. Or become super-models, as the case may be. Speaking of which, why, oh why, wasn't Amy's face on the ad in the opening shot? It would have been brilliantly disconcerting to have had the Petrichor ad sitting in plain sight. Somebody missed a trick there.

The only real downside is that, for the second time running, Craig defeats the villain with the strength of his love. There's some technobabble from the Doctor to explain that this isn't really the case before he admits that it is, which helps, but — and I want to stress this, so pay attention — Craig blows up the villain with love! Again! What is this, a bad Hollywood script?

The Doctor isn't just aware he's going to die; he's actually feeling his age. So he's maudlin and reflective, glad that he lived his dreams but fearful of death at the same time. Contrasting this state of mind with a baby was an inspired move, as it really adds a sense of lost potential to the Doctor's musings.

The ending, where the A-plot suddenly gives way to the arc scene with River Song, really took me by surprise and had my jaw on the floor. After not seeing the Silents since the season opener, they return, Madame Kovarian reveals she's still in control of River and we end on the astronaut suit floating underwater, as the jigsaw pieces of the season finally begin to slot together. This is shockingly unexpected. Madame Kovarian's "they made you a doctor today" suggests that River's entire existence may be a sham, although it might also refer to the fact that she received her doctorate that day. It's an astonishingly effective scene, but it does show up one of the season's limitations.

That is, where were the Silents? Okay, maybe they were there all along and we never noticed, but honestly. Here's the perfect recurring monster for the New Series, and next to nothing was done with them. Even the major revelation about what they are occurred in an episode they didn't appear in ("Let's Kill Hitler"). What we really needed was a major mid-season battle with the Silents where we learned crucial information about them and were reminded that they were out there. Even just having them make random appearances (that characters could then forget about) would have been both effective and easy to achieve. Instead, they were simply forgotten about, and not in a good way. Who thought this was a good idea?

"Closing Time" is a fun little episode made weightier by being seeped in foreboding and by doing the heavy lifting before the season finale. It has what is probably the single most important arc scene of the season and an amazing segue into it. And it definitively answers its central question: seeing amazing scenery on your own is way less fun than dropping in on your mate and having a few laughs. That's not a bad take-home message at all.

Second Opinion (GB?) Things I liked about "Closing Time," in no particular order:

- The fact that the Craig's baby thinks his name is Stormageddon, Dark Lord of All. That's so awesome. And if you've ever taken care of a baby, you know it's probably true.
- Lynda Baron as Val. I suspect writer Gareth Roberts would have had Mollie Sudgen (Mrs. Slocombe from *Are You Being Served?*) play Val had he a working time machine. But Baron is the next best thing. She's charming, and the running gag where she mistakes the Doctor and Craig as a gay couple is a nice 21st-century spin on the comedy of double entendre and misunderstanding.
- The wonderful scene where the Doctor talks to Alfie, er, Stormageddon, about the wonders of the universe. Zapping a child's nightlight into a planetarium show stretches believability even by the standards of the sonic screwdriver, but the scene is so lovely and Matt Smith is never better than when he plays the Doctor as so old and weary. And the baby is adorable.
- The brief snatch of the Cybermen theme from Series Two that's thrown

WHO IS THE DOCTOR

400

onto the soundtrack when the Doctor arrives on the Cybership. It made me all nostalgic.

- The running gag of the Doctor shushing everyone, baby and adult, into silence.
- Following on from "The Lodger," the way the Doctor becomes best friends with everyone in the shop. The scene where the Doctor extricates Craig from trouble with George and Kelly is delightful.
- The scene where the Doctor tries to prevent Craig from looking behind him and seeing that they're on a ship full of Cybermen by telling him he's really in love with him. Matt Smith and James Corden deserve some kind of comedy medal for that.
- The "power of love" ending, which is precisely the same kind of "bullshit moment" used in "Night Terrors," but here it actually works because the whole episode has been about Craig and Alfie coming to terms with each other. And the way the Doctor subtly aids that along, translating Alfie's needs, getting Craig to wear a papoose and generally asking Alfie to cut his dad some slack, is really quite sweet. I do concede that it must be the most rubbish Cyber-conversion ever for the ending to work. But, in fairness, it's actually set up in the script to be the most rubbish conditions for Cyber-conversion.
- The Cybermat attack in Craig's house is the gazillionth repeat of the trope where an alien terror lurks in an ordinary domestic setting. And, no, I'll never get tired of it, especially when it's done as well as this.

Things I didn't like about "Closing Time," in no particular order:

- Not enough Daisy Haggard as Sophie. Boo.
- The sonic screwdriver shooting green laser bolts. Who the hell on the production team let that through? *It's not a weapon*. It works by soundwaves.
- I might have preferred another alien threat rather than the universe's most decrepit force of Cybermen. But I have to admit, they work well precisely because viewers know what they are; with that established, we can get on with an exciting, funny story based in character and horror.

God, I love this story.

6.13 The Wedding of River Song

Written by Steven Moffat **Directed by** Jeremy Webb

Supporting cast Alex Kingston (River Song), Frances Barber (Madame Kovarian), Simon Fisher-Becker (Dorium Maldovar), Ian McNeice (Emperor Winston Churchill), Richard Hope (Dr. Malohkeh), Marnix van den Broeke (the Silent), Nicholas Briggs (voice of the

Dalek), Simon Callow (Charles Dickens), Sian Williams (herself), Bill Turnbull (himself), Meredith Vieira (newsreader), Niall Greig Fulton (Gideon Vandaleur), Sean Buckley (barman), Rondo Haxton (Gantok), Emma Campbell-Jones (Dr. Kent), Katharine Burford (nurse), Richard Dillane (Carter), William Morgan Sheppard (Canton Delaware)

Original airdate October 1, 2011

The Big Idea The Doctor goes to face his death in Utah, but thanks to River Song things don't go according to plan, and time just stops.

Roots and References The Vogues' song "Five O'Clock World" (the 5:02 world); *Max Headroom* and *Mad Max* (the Live Chess arena); DC Comics' *Crisis on Infinite Earths* (a world where time does not exist and history is combined together); the Indiana Jones movies (the cave full of skulls, and the Doctor's "I hate rats!" is a parody of Indy's "I hate snakes!"); *Hustle* (the reveal that everything has been a con).

Adventures in Time and Space The Doctor becomes convinced it's his time to die when he discovers his oldest friend, Brigadier Lethbridge-Stewart (from 1968's "The Web of Fear" onward), has died. In the 5:02 world, Charles Dickens ("The Unquiet Dead") is being interviewed about his upcoming Christmas special, and Winston Churchill ("Victory of the Daleks") is the Holy Roman Emperor. Churchill's attending physician is the Silurian scientist Malohkeh ("The Hungry Earth"/"Cold Blood"). Dorium's head still has life even though he was beheaded in "A Good Man Goes to War." Time goes wrong because River tries to rewrite a fixed point in time ("The Fires of Pompeii" and "The Waters of Mars"). The Doctor says, "Don't you dare," when River threatens to change history, echoing what she will later tell the Doctor when he offers to avert her death in "Forest of the Dead."

The Doctor rips the data core from a dying Dalek. Amy still remembers her experiences with the Doctor because of the crack in her bedroom (as established in "The Big Bang"). Her office has the model she made of the TARDIS ("The Eleventh Hour") and drawings of Daleks, Weeping Angels ("Blink" et al.), Silurians (and scenes from "The Hungry Earth"), Cybermen (in a scene from "The Pandorica Opens"), Smilers and the inside of the Star Whale (both from "The Beast Below"), and the vampire girls ("The Vampires of Venice"). The Doctor toys with the idea of going to all of Captain Jack's stag parties and visiting Rose as a child. The Silence mentions Rory's trait for dying multiple times (too many episodes to name). In Area 52, Madame Kovarian is kept within a perimeter marked with signs warning people not to interact with the prisoner, just as the Doctor was in Area 51 in "Day of the Moon." River comes to visit Amy and Rory after the events on the *Byzantium* in "The Time of

Angels"/"Flesh and Stone." We also receive the final piece in the mystery of why Queen Elizabeth I hates the Doctor ("The Shakespeare Code"): she was waiting to elope with him!

The Doctor Is Dead Effect After some convincing (and time itself nearly collapsing), River kills the Doctor. Only it turns out the Doctor is actually hiding out in the Teselecta (a Doctor in a Doctor suit) to fulfill the fixed point in time.

The Silence consider themselves the "sentinels of history," and they believe that silence must fall when a specific question older than the universe is asked. The question, and the answer, will be made known in the Doctor's future, so the Silence are dedicated to eliminating the Doctor in order to eliminate when the question must be asked.

Who is the Doctor? Why, that's an excellent question . . .

The Doctor and Amy The Doctor asks Amy and Rory to be with him when he dies because he wants to remember what he's leaving: "My friends have always been the best of me." Amy, for her part, acknowledges the Doctor is her best friend, though she has a little trouble getting used to the fact she is now the Doctor's mother-in-law!

Monster of the Week We learn more about the Silents, particularly that they are the leaders of the Silence (the religious order/army sworn to destroy the Doctor). The reason their human servants, such as Madame Kovarian, wear eye patches is that the patches are "eye drives," external storage devices that retain the memory of seeing the Silents.

Stand Up and Cheer It was inevitable the Doctor was going to somehow cheat his death, but the idea that he would do it in the Teselecta is really novel, as is the reveal of how the Doctor managed to pull an elaborate con on River, Amy, Rory and history itself. It's all about the misdirection: the Doctor looks as though he's bravely facing his inevitable fate, the wedding looks like an elaborate ritual involving his name, but then it's revealed later he popped back in to ask Carter for help, and the ritual naming was a way to get River to realize he's not going to actually die.

Roll Your Eyes The Doctor seems unimpressed with River's grand gesture that the whole universe still loves and cares about him. Honestly, so were we. It seems like just a giant excuse to get everyone to a nice vista for the wedding ceremony.

You're Not Making Any Sense How does the 5:02 world work? Presumably it doesn't have all 100 billion or so people who have lived since *Homo sapiens* first came into being (there wouldn't be enough of those Mini Coopers hooked up to hot-air balloons for one thing), so there must be only a representative sampling of the populace. There is still causality and an apparent progression of events: there are still days and nights (though we only ever see day), the War of the Roses is in its "second year," Christmas is still coming soon and the Doctor has managed to grow a beard. So in what way has time stopped? Other than the notion that the clocks state it is always 5:02 on April 22 . . . which isn't the same thing as time stopping at all.

Interesting Trivia The climax of the episode plays on the assumption that the viewer has had since "Forest of the Dead" when the Doctor said, "There's only one reason I would ever tell anyone my name." Namely, that River's somehow intimate with the Doctor. Which is why during the wedding ceremony it only seemed natural that he would tell her his name. But it turns out this was a ruse on the viewer as well as Amy and Rory: the Doctor hasn't revealed his name after all. Which means that River must have found out his name at some other point, perhaps another wedding ceremony. Or perhaps an incident like the one the Silence are trying to prevent. Or perhaps she was *already* told the Doctor's name. (What did the Doctor whisper to Melody to tell River Song in "Let's Kill Hitler"? Melody, who doesn't know she will become River yet, says, "I'm sure she already knows.") Time will, hopefully, tell. Unless the Doctor's name actually *is* "Lookintomyeye," in which case, all bets are off. (Indeed, this could explain why he never tells anyone his name!)

Which brings us to the all-important question: are the Doctor and River actually married or is it a sham? The Doctor claims to be following the "short form" of a ritual that includes handfasting, parental consent and the Doctor revealing his name. However, if he didn't actually reveal his name then all of it could simply be a con to finally get River to realize he has a plan to escape his death and to let time start again. Afterward, Amy still seems to treat the union as though it were a real one, and River doesn't disabuse her of that notion; though, by River's own admission, River may be lying.

And then there's the matter of the Doctor being inside the Teselecta. In "Let's Kill Hitler," the Teselecta seemed barely able to walk convincingly and its reactions were somewhat slow; now the Doctor is not only able to convince Amy, Rory and River he's the real thing in Utah, he's able to fake regeneration and, once in the 5:02 world, he's able to convincingly grow a beard. The Doctor must have been tuning up the Teselecta quite a bit.

This story featured two bits of interesting casting: the first was NBC *Today* show anchor Meredith Viera who reads a news item. As part of *Today*'s "Anchors Abroad" segment, Viera visited the *Doctor Who* set, met members of the cast and recorded her cameo against a green screen. (Her director was Richard Senior, which would indicate Viera's part was shot during the making of "Let's

Kill Hitler.") Meanwhile, Mark Gatiss, who has written several *Doctor Who* episodes (most recently "Night Terrors") and who previously appeared onscreen as Professor Lazarus in "The Lazarus Experiment," played Gantok under the pseudonym "Rondo Haxton."

Nicholas Courtney, who had played Brigadier Lethbridge-Stewart opposite six incarnations of the Doctor across three decades of the Classic Series (and most recently reprised the role in the 2008 episode of *The Sarah Jane Adventures* "Enemy of the Bane"), died in February 2011. The Brigadier's death, and its pivotal effect on the Doctor, was a way of honouring Courtney and his important role in the Classic Series. Steven Moffat acknowledged on Twitter that the eye drives were also a tribute to Courtney, who in 1970's "Inferno" played an alternate version of his character who wore an eye patch. (The cast played a practical joke on him by all wearing eye patches at one point — an anecdote that became a part of *Doctor Who* convention lore for decades!)

The TARDIS Chronometer The Doctor travels to a crashed Dalek ship, then to various locations in the 52nd century in search of the Silence, ending at the Seventh Transcept of the Headless Monks. He travels to Utah, but when River refuses to kill him, time becomes stuck, creating the abortive 5:02 world timeline.

Cool? (GB and RS?) Has it really been six and a half seasons since the Doctor first took Rose Tyler's hand and told her to run? Despite some bumps along the way, it has been six and a half seasons of incredible television.

Comparing "Rose" with "The Wedding of River Song" reveals the profound way the program has evolved since it began in 2005. *Doctor Who* began as rollicking high adventure mixed with melodrama and comedy. All those elements remain, but it's also become a series with a highly developed mythos, with complex story and character arcs that stretch across seasons.

In "Rose," the only sign of a larger-reaching arc was the Doctor's oblique remarks about a war, hinting at something bigger than the romp with the Nestene. The entirety of "The Wedding of River Song" is the Doctor wading through the season's arc and past continuity (including Charles Dickens in a nice little shout-out to the bygone days of New *Who*).

It's incredible that the Doctor is spurred on by the death of the Brigadier, a character who never appeared in the New Series proper (just a guest appearance in *The Sarah Jane Adventures*, another unthinkable development when "Rose" was first broadcast), and it's accepted without an onscreen explanation of his significance. In 2005, the idea was to avoid the Doctor's past adventures and make the series as friendly as possible to newbies. Now, it not so much embraces past adventures from the Classic and New Series as it kisses them full on the lips. In many ways, this state of affairs shows how popular the program has become. You don't need to constantly bring viewers up to speed when so many people are watching.

One thing this episode does well is resolve the season-long arc. There's a magnificent and thoroughly satisfying resolution to the Doctor-is-dead story-line: he cheats death via the Teselecta. It's a brilliantly concise answer that was impossible to predict but makes perfect sense. It's the best kind of payoff to a genuinely intriguing problem.

Unfortunately, that payoff is crammed in the last few minutes, so the rest of the episode is one big pause button with funky visuals. Everything else just rolls on: the final question is just the start of the next arc, Amy and Rory are in the same holding pattern they've been in all season, and the Silents do their thing without any variation. Fourteen episodes later, we're still no closer to understanding why the Silence wanted to blow up the TARDIS and destroy the universe last season.

And while the Doctor's solution is clever, it's also frustrating from a character standpoint. The Doctor is moved by the Brigadier's passing to . . . cheat death, yet again. His survival was, in many respects, unavoidable because the Doctor must live, but this resolution seems so sudden. Indeed, when the Doctor leaves the room with the Teselecta and then pops back in a few seconds later saying, "Thinking about it . . . ," you wonder if he didn't walk down the corridor, get in the TARDIS, do a bunch of stuff for several hours — and then travel back in time to the corridor a few seconds after he left it, with his plan all hatched out. That would have been more fun and more thoughtful. But mostly more fun.

"The Wedding of River Song" shows off what Steven Moffat does so well with his stories. There's a charming riddle at its centre, and lots of big and colourful ideas. The opening sequence of the 5:02 world in its eye-popping glory — complete with steam trains travelling above Central London amid Mini Coopers on hot air balloons and pterodactyls — is stunning. The 5:02 world as a mash-up of human history works well. But, surprisingly for Moffat, it isn't really all that well thought through. If time is frozen, how can there still be causality and the passage of time? Calendars and clocks aid people to understand time, so how is it they're the only things actually affected by time being stuck, as opposed to people being frozen in the same moment or stuck in a loop? We almost suspect that the whole thing was reverse-engineered to make the cool visuals work, another common facet of *Doctor Who* since 2005.

On television, parallel universes serve only two functions: to allow old guest stars to visit and the regular cast to dress up. So we have Churchill, Malohkeh and company, as well as the Doctor with a beard, Amy and River with eyedrives, and Rory in an army uniform. There's an attempt to give Amy some edge by killing Madame Kovarian in the parallel world, but this is precisely what's wrong with parallel stories. Anything can happen, consequence-free. Amy remembers murdering Kovarian, which is an attempt to link the two universes, but River absolves her of it. The episode wants to have its cake and eat it too, but that leaves us very unsatisfied. It's still no learning (with some hugging).

The other amazing thing that has happened since the New Series debuted is the steady increase in North American interest in the series. If anyone told us even during Series Five that Series Six would be promoted on a U.S. network late night show with Matt Smith interviewed, we wouldn't have believed you. Now people sport T-shirts bearing Craig Ferguson's slogan that *Doctor Who* represents "the triumph of intellect and romance over brute force and cynicism." But the show's popularity stateside makes a lot of sense: *Doctor Who* connects to the *zeitgeist* of American television, as an ongoing dramatic saga fascinated with good-looking young leads trading quips. All the same, it's time for Karen Gillan and Arthur Darvill to go. The past two seasons have taken Amy and Rory as far as they can. It's time to destabilize things and have the eleventh Doctor make other friends.

River's story is now complete, so the sensible thing to do is probably to let her go, but we don't imagine for a second that they'll take that option. But that's okay, because we love River.

"The Wedding of River Song" isn't an unlikeable episode, by any means. It has a heady mix of cool visuals, intellectual puzzles, an adorable leading man and a delicious resolution to the season as a whole. It doesn't go where you'd expect the big death-of-the-Doctor finale to go, which is good, but where it does go isn't nearly as strong as it could be.

What will *Doctor Who* do next? Judging by the looks of things, Steven Moffat has planned out everything through to *Doctor Who*'s 50th anniversary and possibly to the departure of Matt Smith. For the time being, the Silence will continue to bedevil the Doctor.

In spite of our reservations and frustrations with this season, we look forward to what comes next. Because, after all we've seen in this New Series of *Doctor Who* that is no longer new and yet always new, we're confident about one thing: it will constantly surprise us. Here's to the future.

Who is the Doctor? In the end, the Doctor remains an enigma. His motivations are only ever partially understood. His origins are only partially known. His lives are only partially explained. Dorium states that Silence must fall when the question — the oldest question, hidden in plain sight — is answered. And on the fields of Trenzalore, at the fall of the eleventh, "when no living creature can speak falsely or fail to answer," the question will finally be asked and answered; a question the Doctor has been running away from all these years:

"Doctor Who?"

The adventures in time and space continue . . .

APPENDIX

The Animated Episodes

The Infinite Quest

Written by Alan Barnes **Directed by** Gary Russell **Animation by** Firestep

Produced by James Goss and Ros Attille **Executive Producers** Mark Cossey, Russell T Davies and Julie Gardner

Cast David Tennant (The Doctor), Freema Agyeman (Martha Jones), Anthony Head (Baltazar), Toby Longworth (Caw/Squawk), Liza Tarbuck (Captain Kaliko), Tom Farrelly (Swabb), Lizzie Hopley (The Mantasphid Queen), Paul Clayton (Meregrass), Steven Meo (Pilot Kelvin), Barney Harwood (Control voice), Stephen Greif (Gurney), Dan Morgan (Lok/Warden)

Original airdates April 2–June 30, 2007

The Big Idea The Doctor and Martha must find the Infinite, which will give anyone their heart's desire, before the despot Baltazar and his parrot can get to it.

Adventures in Time and Space The Doctor mentions that creatures like the Racnoss ("The Runaway Bride"), the Nestene ("Rose") and the Great Vampires (from 1981's "State of Decay") rampaged through the void in the dark times.

The Doctor and Martha Martha's heart's desire, predictably, turns out to be the Doctor. Though, to her credit, she realizes he's illusory right away.

Monster of the Week According to the Doctor, the masked Baltazar is the "Scourge of the galaxy, Corsair King of Triton, the greatest despot who ever lived."

Stand Up and Cheer The pre-credits sequence, where the Doctor arrives just in time to stop Baltazar from destroying Earth, casually talking about him as though he's a quaint museum exhibit and ultimately destroying his ship using a spoon, is pretty cool.

You're Not Making Any Sense The Doctor seems to buy the story that Baltazar has a copy of the datachip, ancient technology, a little too easily. Connect this with his casual dismissal of Kaliko's and Mergrass's deaths, and he just seems especially thick.

Interesting Trivia "The Infinite Quest" was originally shown as 13 three-minute episodes during the BBC Children's series *Totally Doctor Who*.

The TARDIS Chronometer Earth, Boukan, Myarr, Volag Nok and an asteroid. All taking place during Baltazar's era, the 40th century.

Brilliant? (GB) The artwork is beautifully designed — the oilrigs on Boukan and Baltazar, in particular, are gorgeous — and the animation, though limited, is well done for what it is. The opening sequence is really great.

The rest of it is just sort of there.

Part of the problem is that it's written for broadcast in three-minute segments and doesn't flow properly when stitched together. But if the whole idea is to deliver a bunch of high stakes scenarios in a row, they need better payoff. The pirate sequence is just leaden: the Doctor is supposed to be standing on the plank about to be executed, but you wouldn't know it. This happens repeatedly. It's like the Doctor's adventures have been put on Ritalin.

The voice acting isn't particularly great either. David Tennant and Freema Agyeman sound like they're in a recording booth disconnected from the action. Anthony Head might as well be reading the phone book for all the interest he seems to have summoned up. The only stellar performance is Toby Longworth's Caw and Squawk.

"The Infinite Quest" offers 45 minutes of innocuous entertainment for children. Taken as such, it's probably less annoying to watch than a Disney direct-to-DVD release, though heaven knows it tries.

Second Opinion (RS?) Children's television can go one of two ways. The good way, as seen in *The Sarah Jane Adventures*, is to treat the audience with respect and realize that, ultimately, children are far more discerning than adults when it comes to what really counts.

"The Infinite Quest" goes the other route. The lazy route. The route that says that TV made for children can be poorly thought-out, superficial and condescending. The route that is interested in caricatures, not characters. The route that talks down to its audience.

This is very bad indeed. There's nothing of interest here and it's frankly a waste of Tennant's and Agyeman's talents. If you've never seen it, don't even bother. It's infinitely dull.

Dreamland

Written by Phil Ford **Directed by** Gary Russell **Animation by** Littleloud

Produced by Ed Cross and Mat Fidell **Executive Producers** Anwen Aspden, Sarah Muller, Russell T Davies and Julie Gardner

Cast David Tennant (The Doctor), Georgia Moffett (Cassie Rice), Tim Howar (Jimmy Stalkingwolf), Lisa Bowerman (Saruba Velak), David Warner (Lord Azlok), Stuart Milligan (Colonel Stark), Clarke Peters (Night Eagle), Nicholas Rowe (Rivesh Mantilax), Peter Guinness (Mister Dread), Ryan McCluskey (soldiers)

Original airdate November 21–26, 2009

The Big Idea The Doctor decides to get some good old-fashioned chili from an American diner . . . in Roswell, New Mexico.

Roots and References The Roswell crash and UFO lore (the Roswell setting);

Men in Black (the Men, er, in Black). The Everly Brothers' "All I Have To Do Is Dream" plays in the diner.

Monster of the Week The Viperox are large, nasty, insectoid aliens. Their battle drones have weapons in their exo-skeletons. They don't arrive with an invasion force; they instead come to a planet and hatch one.

Stand Up and Cheer You're the Doctor and you're stuck deep in the bowels of Area 51? What do you do? Pilot an alien ship out of there. The Doctor is old school.

You're Not Making Any Sense The Men in Black are ultra-sophisticated androids who can be defeated using bows and arrows. They should have been decommissioned in 1872, never mind 1972.

Interesting Trivia "Dreamland" was shown on BBC's red button service in six parts (a 12-minute episode, followed by five 6-minute episodes). It then debuted in its entirety on BBC2 and was released on DVD.

The Men in Black — who are robots dispatched by the interplanetary Alliance of Shades to clean up any evidence of aliens on Earth — later appear in live action form in *The Sarah Jane Adventures* story "The Vault of Secrets," using the exact same backstory and weapons, thoroughly enshrining them in the *Doctor Who* universe.

The TARDIS Chronometer Roswell, New Mexico, June 1958.

Brilliant? (GB) Let's get this out of the way right now: the animation is just downright ugly, even by the low standards of modern kids' TV animation. The characters are not so much in the uncanny valley as the hideously unlikely one. Cassie's teeth are bad even by the standards of the English. And don't get me started on how everyone walks . . .

All I can say in response to that criticism is: deal with it. Because "Dreamland" is the forgotten gem of the David Tennant era. Why this wasn't made in live action instead of "Planet of the Dead" defies all understanding.

It's as though everyone learned from the mistakes of "The Infinite Quest." The story is less obviously episodic, and it has better character development and dialogue. But probably more than that it actually sounds like a proper *Doctor Who* episode. The actors no longer seem to be trapped in a voiceover booth. Everyone, especially David Tennant, is more engaged in the action, and the sound design is better integrated. You can close your eyes and almost fool yourself into thinking you're listening to a live-action episode.

Phil Ford's script is exciting and full of brilliant concepts, from the Viperox hatching its invasion force to the true purpose of the grey aliens in Area 51 to a brilliant spin on the Men in Black concept that makes utter sense in the *Doctor Who* universe. It's let down a little by the usual stereotypical tropes involving Native Americans, but thankfully it's not as cringe inducing as it could be.

All in all, it not only sounds like *Doctor Who*, it feels like it too. If only it looked like it . . .

Second Opinion (RS?) Unlike "The Infinite Quest," "Dreamland" is perfect children's TV. I watched this with my eight-year-old nephew (who loves *Doctor Who*) and my seven-year-old niece (who doesn't), and they were both enthralled from beginning to end. And so was I.

What's great about this is the way it has an actual story to tell, rather than just being bits and bobs slotted between cliffhangers. In a way, it reminds me of exactly the kind of story you'd expect from *The Sarah Jane Adventures* if it were animated and had time travel. It's thrilling and dramatic, and it uses its conventions perfectly. This is very likely because it's written by Phil Ford, one of the breakout stars of *The Sarah Jane Adventures'* writing team, who knows how to structure a dramatically satisfying narrative.

My co-author is wrong on the animation, by the way. It's vastly superior to "The Infinite Quest." And so is everything else about this story. If you've never seen it, go find a copy. It's dreamy.

Recommended Resources

"Sounds a rum sort of library to me."
— The Doctor, "The Trial of a Time Lord" (1986)

If you want to learn more about the exciting world of *Doctor Who* and how it was created, there are all sorts of places you can go for information. *Doctor Who* is probably the most documented television show in history, with a wealth of material written or produced about the making of the past five decades of *Who*.

The Worlds of Doctor Who

For the fictional universe within the program, we recommend BBC Books' *Doctor Who: The Encyclopedia* by Gary Russell, which documents all the people, places and things in the *Who* universe. It keeps being revised and updated, most recently released in a version for that whizzy new iPad.

A more kid-friendly series of books are by author Justin Richards: *Monsters and Villains* (BBC Books, 2005), *Aliens and Enemies* (BBC Books, 2006), *Creatures and Demons* (BBC Books, 2007) and *Starships and Spacestations* (BBC Books, 2008). Most of these were reworked into a bumper volume, *The Ultimate Monster Guide* (BBC Books, 2009).

The Making of the Classic Series

Probably the best resources on the Classic Series are three books by David Howe, Mark Stammers and Stephen James Walker, *Doctor Who: The Sixties* (Virgin Publishing, 1992), *Doctor Who: The Seventies* (Virgin Publishing, 1994) and *Doctor Who: The Eighties* (Virgin Publishing, 1996). These books were among the first to demonstrate a high quality of research; the authors scoured BBC records and interviewed anyone closely associated with the making of the series. Sadly, these books are out of print but are still available on eBay.

The *Doctor Who* Classic Series range of DVDs all have excellent, well-researched special features with thorough interviews, which document the making of every *Doctor Who* story from 1963 to 1989. The most important is "Origins," on how *Doctor Who* was created in 1963; it features original BBC documentation and a rare, otherwise-sealed archival interview with *Doctor Who* creator Sydney Newman. It can be found on the "An Unearthly Child" DVD.

The BBC Archives website has available a fascinating series of documents about the creation of *Doctor Who* including original production memos, audience reports and more. These can be found at bbc.co.uk/archive/doctorwho/.

The Making of the New Series

For the first six seasons of the New Series, *Doctor Who Confidential* reveals some interesting details, although these documentary shorts can often be little more than a bulked-up version of an electronic press kit.

Since 2005, *Doctor Who Magazine* has published a companion to each series, which includes behind-the-scenes information thoroughly researched by *Doctor Who* historian Andrew Pixley. The earlier companion volumes included material from Russell T Davies such as his original pitch document for the New Series and annotated outlines for the first couple of seasons.

The most candid volumes are from executive producer Russell T Davies and *Doctor Who Magazine* contributor Benjamin Cook. *Doctor Who: The Writer's Tale* (BBC Books, 2008) chronicles the making of Series Four from its earliest concepts and tracks the intricacies of production that changed its shape along the way. The end result is one of the most comprehensive documents on the writing process for television ever published. Included are scripts-in-progress of "Voyage of the Damned," "Partners in Crime," "The Stolen Earth" and "Journey's End." The 2010 follow-up to this book, *Doctor Who: The Writer's Tale — The Final Chapter*, is a memoir of creating the final specials before David Tennant's departure (and *Torchwood: Children of Earth* for good measure).

General Resources

First published as *Doctor Who Weekly* in 1979, *Doctor Who Magazine* is the longest-running magazine related to a television program in the world. As the official magazine, it regularly goes behind the scenes of the New Series and still maintains a regular connection to the Classic Series. *DWM*'s articles are always detailed and well researched, and its interviews often surprise. Since 2004, *DWM* has included a monthly production feature written by Russell T Davies (and latterly by Steven Moffat) that almost never says anything completely truthful about the current production but always does so in the most entertaining way possible.

Shannon Patrick Sullivan's site *A Brief History of Time (Travel)* (shannonsullivan.com/drwho) is the best online repository of information on the making of the more than 200 episodes of the Classic and New Series.

Analysis

For in-depth analysis, there's Gary Gillat's *From A to Z* (BBC Books, 1998), a stunning series of essays that cover all 26 seasons of the Classic Series. For diverse insights, we recommend the *Time Unincorporated* series (Mad Norwegian Press, 2009–2011). Well, we should, given that we edited two of the three volumes. You might want to check out *Chicks Dig Time Lords* (Mad Norwegian Press, 2010), a celebration of the show by the women who love it (plus some guy with a question mark in his name).

Fandom

If you loved the debates touched on in this book and want to become involved in them, there are lots of ways with *Doctor Who* fandom. There are online forums (we recommend gallifreybase.com), review sites (The *Doctor Who* Ratings Guide at pagefillers.com/dwrg, edited by that question-mark guy) and conventions. We love Gallifrey One in Los Angeles in February (gallifreyone .com) and Chicago TARDIS in November (chicagotardis.com).

But if you want a great fan community, both of us heartily recommend the Doctor Who Information Network (dwin.org). Based in Canada, DWIN is North America's oldest and largest *Doctor Who* fan club. They publish a bimonthly fanzine, *Enlightenment,* which is full of lively commentary on the world of *Doctor Who.* We would recommend it even if we hadn't been involved with the organization for over a decade!

Acknowledgements

If it takes a village to raise a child, then it takes much more to write a book, particularly one on a television show that invokes as much devotion as *Doctor Who*.

First and foremost, we'd like to thank Shannon Patrick Sullivan and Jon Arnold for their work — above and beyond the call of duty — in going through our manuscript and keeping us on the straight and narrow in so many respects. Often with very little notice. This book would be much, much poorer without their feedback. We would also like to thank Scott Clarke, Deborah Stanish and Anthony Wilson for their thoughtful comments during the book's development, which helped us considerably.

This book also would not be what it is today without the passion and good humour of our editor at ECW Press, Jen Hale. We deeply appreciate Jen's dedication to making this project something that can be appreciated by all walks of *Doctor Who* fan, from newbie to expert, and her championing this project. It would seem an unsung part of the book editor's job is putting up with passionate authors who are precious about their words, and we're impressed with her ability to work with us so diplomatically. The same goes for our copy editor, Crissy Boylan. Thanks to Natalie Racz for the awesome cover.

As with any guide to *Doctor Who*, what we have written is a distillation of many lively conversations we've had all over the place during the past six years. We'd like to thank many of the people who have engaged with us in these debates, some of which involved alcohol: Dennis and Christine Turner, Cadence Gillard, Gian-Luca DiRocco, Mike and Nina Doran, Rod Mammitzsch, Jim Sangster, Shaun Lyon, Cameron Dixon, Sean Twist, John Anderson, Laura Riccomi, Arnold T. Blumberg, Michael Thomas, Lynne Thomas, Lars Pearson, Christa Dickson, Daniel Changer, Jaymie Maley, Matt Bailey, Alison Kealey, Andrew Cartmel, Steven Schapansky, Christopher Burgess, Warren Frey, Steve Traylen, Jason A. Miller, Felicity Kuzinitz, Greg McElhatton, Rob Jones, Andrew Flint, Kenyon Wallace, Robert Shearman, Heather Murray, Ryan Piekenbrock and pretty much the entirety of the Toronto *Doctor Who* Tavern (first Thursday of the month at Pauper's at Bloor and Bathurst!). Thanks also to the Doctor Who Information Network for providing us with the space, through *Enlightenment* and their blog, to try out some of our ideas.

Special thanks must go to Julie Hopkins and Shoshana Magnet for their indulgence, handholding, advice and for being ever so patient with our hobby (or lifestyle choice, as we like to call it). Thanks also to our employers, who must be wondering where we got to for several months. We're also grateful to Michael Watts, Jennifer Plank, Hindy Bradley, Gareth Roberts and Mark Askwith.

This book was written in Brazil, the Dominican Republic, Mexico, Australia, Poland, France, Britain, Portugal, South Africa, Zambia, Zimbabwe and, in Canada and the United States, in Ottawa, Toronto, Oakville, Hamilton, Montreal, Vancouver, Sudbury, Chicago, Miami, Los Angeles, Atlanta, Syracuse, Santa Fe, Detroit and a cottage on Christie Lake. You can imagine just how grateful we are to the people who invented laptops and wifi, without whom this book might never have existed.

And thanks to you, the reader, for reading this! If you have any questions or comments, we'd love to hear them. You can email us at whoisthedoctor@gemgeekorrarebug.com.

We said at the outset of this book that we're here because we believe *Doctor Who* is the greatest television series on Earth. After reading this, we hope you can see why.

Allons-y!

GRAEME BURK is a writer and *Doctor Who* fan. He was the co-editor (with Robert Smith?) of two anthologies of fan writing on the Classic and New Series, *Time, Unincorporated* (Mad Norwegian Press, 2010 and 2011). He has had his work published by magazines, websites and small presses throughout North America; three of his stories were included in the *Doctor Who* short fiction anthology series *Short Trips*. For ten years he was the editor of *Enlightenment*, the fanzine of Doctor Who Information Network, North America's oldest and largest *Doctor Who* fan club. A finalist for a Writers Guild of Canada screenwriting prize, he currently has a screenplay in development. He loves Toronto but lives in Ottawa. His website can be found at gemgeekorrarebug.com; follow him on Twitter @graemeburk.

ROBERT SMITH? is, scientifically speaking, the world's foremost expert on mathematical modelling of zombies. Pretty much by default. Professor of biomathematics by day and slayer of the undead by night, he also has a question mark in his name, in case you hadn't noticed. Oh, and he's spent 12 years editing *The Doctor Who Ratings Guide*, the foremost *Doctor Who* review website (pagefillers.com/dwrg). His books include *Modelling Disease Ecology with Mathematics* (American Institute of Mathematical Science, 2008), the two volumes of *Time Unincorporated* that Graeme mentions above (Mad Norwegian Press, 2010–2011) and *Braaaiiinnnsss!: From Academics to Zombies* (University of Ottawa Press, 2011). He's hoping to collect some sort of award for the most diverse bookshelf in existence.

At ECW Press, we want you to enjoy this book in whatever format you like, whenever you like. Leave your print book at home and take the eBook to go! Purchase the print edition and receive the eBook free. Just send an email to ebook@ecwpress.com and include:

Get the
eBook free!*

*proof of purchase
required

- the book title
- the name of the store where you purchased it
- your receipt number
- your preference of file type: PDF or ePub?

A real person will respond to your email with your eBook attached. And thanks for supporting an independently owned Canadian publisher with your purchase!